A.J. FOYT LEGACY

A.J. FOYT LEGACY

THE EPIC STORY OF AN AMERICAN SPORTS LEGEND

VOLUME TWO

ART GARNER

Foreword by **Tony Stewart**

OCTANE PRESS

Octane Press, Edition 1.0, May 2026

On the cover: A.J. Foyt in 1986. *Dan Boyd*
On the front endpapers: Foyt gets a push after running out of fuel on the last lap of the 1978 Indianapolis 500. *John Mahoney*
On the rear endpapers: A.J. Foyt. *Grindstone Media Group*

Hardcover ISBN: 978-1-64234-195-9
ePub ISBN: 978-1-64234-198-0

LCCN: 2026933329

Project Edited by Faith Garcia
Designed by Tom Heffron
Copyedited by Katie Carter
Proofread by Dana Henricks

OCTANE PRESS

octanepress.com

Octane Press is based in Austin, Texas

Printed in China

For EJ

CONTENTS

"He is, by all odds, the most remarkable athlete of his time."
—Jim Murray, *Los Angeles Times*, May 23, 1990

"I'm glad I've been among some of the great race drivers. There are so many great, great drivers, I'd just like people to say I was one of the best ever. I don't feel like I've been better than anyone else. I'm just A.J. being A.J."
—Anthony Joseph "A.J." Foyt Jr., *Detroit Free Press*, June 3, 2012

FOREWORD

CHECK THE RECORD BOOK

By Tony Stewart

A.J. has a phrase that he's always used to put me in my place. Anytime I brought up something I'd accomplished that I thought was important, he'd say, "Check the record book"—meaning, of course, that he'd already been there and done that.

More than any other driver, he could play that trump card: "Check the record book."

But in November of 2002, I had him. I clinched my first NASCAR Cup championship at Homestead-Miami Speedway. I'd finally won something that A.J. hadn't. No, he'd never actually *run* for a NASCAR title, but that didn't matter. I had one, and he didn't.

Late that evening, pretty deep into our infield celebration, I called A.J.

When he answered, I said, "Check the record book, big boy."

He laughed and said, "You did good, cowboy."

I could tell that he was genuinely happy for me.

It's hard to believe, but I've known A.J. for thirty years. That goes back to 1995, when I had a race-day job with his pit crew at the Indianapolis 500. I'm not sure how that happened, but someone—probably George Snider—must have talked with A.J. and told him that I was all right.

He had already been my hero for years. In May of 1982, I had just turned eleven, and I was watching the 500 on television. A.J. started outside the front row, but Kevin Cogan ran into him before they even got the green flag. That started a chain-reaction wreck, and the race was stopped.

During the delay, A.J. and his crew repaired the car on pit road. It had a bent steering arm and maybe some other suspension issues. Even back then, Indy car teams might spend half a day setting up the chassis on a perfectly level surface plate. Chris Economaki was a pit reporter on the telecast, and he asked

A.J. how precise these quick fixes could be. A.J. admitted that he and the crew were "just guessing."

Chris said that Foyt would have no way to know if the car was right until the race restarted. Everyone looked tense.

When the green flag finally waved again, A.J. jumped out and led the first twenty-two laps.

I knew I'd seen something special. No other driver in that race was going to climb out of a damaged car, work on it himself, then rifle it off into Turn One like nothing had happened. You couldn't miss A.J.'s determination and confidence.

By the 1995 race, A.J. had retired from Indy cars, so Eddie Cheever was driving. No offense to Eddie, but I didn't care *who* was in the seat. Being around A.J.—that was the whole deal for me. My job was to operate the "dead man" valve on the fuel tank, which stops the flow of methanol to the car. As it turned out, I never had to do a damn thing. Just after the green flag, Cheever and Stan Fox crashed in Turn One. We never made a lap, much less a pit stop.

That was a big year for me because I won USAC's Silver Crown, sprint car, and midget championships. No one had ever done all that in the same season, so it got a lot of attention. I'm sure it led to me getting a chance that fall to drive A.J.'s Indy car in a four-day test at Phoenix. He was evaluating drivers for 1996, the first season for the new Indy Racing League. He also brought a NASCAR Cup car, which he planned to run in a race or two.

What I remember most about that week is A.J. busting my chops almost non-stop. It began at the hotel every morning when the team met for breakfast. I was a short-track racer, and because short-track racers work late, most like to sleep late, too. I'd be the last guy to breakfast, still wiping the sleep from my eyes, and A.J. would start in on me. Then a funny thing would happen: I'd ride with him to the track, just the two of us, and he'd be nice and polite. But as soon as we got to the track and he had his audience back, he'd get on my case again.

A.J.'s nephew, Tommy LaMance, was the team manager. I quietly told Tommy, "I don't know how much longer I can let him bust my balls before I start giving it back to him."

Tommy said, "If you want to go to the airport early, that's the way to do it. Give A.J. a hard time, and you'll beat us all home."

Finally, I had enough. A.J. was picking on me, but then he broke away to climb into his Cup car.

Now, A.J. was sixty years old, and he had put on a few pounds. As he was crawling through the window, his belly was touching the top of the opening.

I said loudly, "Hey, wait a minute!"

Everyone stopped what they were doing. A.J., still only half in the car, turned toward me.

I said, "Let me get some wheel-bearing grease to help you slide in."

The mechanics all stopped and stared. This smartass kid had mouthed off to the boss, and *no one* did that. You could have heard a pin drop.

Then A.J. started laughing hard. That was the cue that it was all right for everyone else to laugh, too.

For the rest of our time in Phoenix, A.J. rode me twice as hard. I think he wanted to see what I might say next.

A month later, A.J.'s team was taking part in the filming of a TV commercial at Texas World Speedway. They needed someone to drive the No. 14 car, and I was glad to help out. Then I spent a day or two with A.J. at one of his ranches in western Texas. That was the first extended one-on-one time we had together. I tagged along on a four-wheeler as he drove a tractor, clearing acres of brush. He'd stop and point to different areas, telling me how he'd knocked down a tree that used to be there or moved a bunch of dirt to fill in a hole. I could see the pride he had in that ranch and how he'd helped shape it. That land and everything on it was his because of what he had done in race cars.

That period was the start of me getting to know A.J. as a human being rather than just as a racing legend. I don't think many people have had that opportunity, aside from some of the older buddies he's had forever. He has a way of putting up a shield when he's in public, but, for whatever reason, he drops that shield when we're together. It's a relationship I cherish.

People talk about me being a lot like A.J., and he's even mentioned that himself. As I've gotten older, I can see that, unintentionally, my path became a modern version of his path. Each of us would drive anything, anywhere, and we were versatile enough that we could jump into different types of cars and be competitive. And neither of us showed up just to get a participation ribbon. We came to *race*.

I was too busy steering my own career to try to pattern it after someone else's. But if people are going to compare you to another driver, hell—you couldn't do much better than A.J. Foyt.

We did a lot of the same things, but I have to be honest: Even if I had matched or surpassed every record he held, in my mind, he'd still be up on a pedestal all alone.

And why wouldn't he be? Right now, we're in an age when racing is relatively safe, which is a good thing. When A.J. was on top, there'd be another driver killed or at least badly injured every week. Nothing was safe: not Indy cars, not stock cars, not sports cars, not sprints and midgets, *nothing*. Yet A.J. went to France and won Le Mans, came to NASCAR and won the Daytona 500, won the Turkey Night Grand Prix for midgets, won the Hoosier Hundred, and won the Indianapolis 500 four times when that seemed impossible. He'd get hurt, sometimes badly hurt, but he'd heal up and get right back after it.

Anytime a driver steps out of the series he knows best, he opens himself up to judgment. It's easy to look bad, and—I guarantee you—that's why most guys won't even try. But I doubt there was ever a time when A.J. Foyt climbed into a race car and worried how it would look if he didn't run well. He was too busy thinking of how he could win that race.

And, you know, he did that a lot—just check the record book.

INTRODUCTION

ONE TOUGH DUDE

Monday, September 25, 1990

Milwaukee Medical Center

The two young doctors paused for a moment outside the intensive care hospital room of their most recent patient. James Stiehl and Jeffrey Johnson had worked well into the night saving the shattered legs and feet of race car driver A.J. Foyt. Plans were already underway to move Foyt to Methodist Hospital in Indianapolis, and while it was unusual to move a trauma patient so soon after surgery, it wasn't out of the question. But both doctors wanted to check their work before agreeing to Foyt's release.

Foyt was waiting for them. He was sitting up the best he could, his left leg hanging from a sling, his right leg in a cast from the ankle to just below the knee. His chin had been stitched up where it had been cut by his helmet strap as it tried to rip off his head. There were no pleasantries.

"Sir, you've got some pretty bad injuries here," Stiehl said. He was the med center's orthopedic trauma surgeon. He'd gone to work using a combination of plates, pins, and screws to piece together the driver's legs. "I think we've done a pretty good job, but I can't tell if you'll be able to race a car anymore."[1]

Stiehl recalled, "He just gave me a real hard look and said, 'We'll see.' I'd never seen anything like it. He was different. He was not like a normal human being. You could see it in his eyes. This was not going to do him in."

Johnson, the hospital's foot specialist, had been called in as Foyt's feet swelled grotesquely and concern grew about compartment syndrome, where swelling muscles restrict blood flow, causing severe tissue and nerve damage. If that happened, Foyt could lose a foot, or even part of his leg.

Johnson had spent several hours painstakingly making numerous small incisions to relieve the pressure. Now he wanted to check for the possibility of infection. Removing the dressings, some of which had dried on the wounds, was a painful process. Foyt didn't flinch.

"He was really tough and able to take a lot of discomfort," Johnson recalled. "I remember thinking, *This dude is tough*. Nothing bothered him. This was going to be a nuisance for a while, but it wasn't going to slow him down. You could tell that in the short time I interacted with him."[2]

The wounds were cleaned, and both doctors, who would rise to the top of their fields in the years ahead, approved the transfer. There wasn't a lot of chitchat as Johnson applied new dressings.

"He was like, 'Let's go, I gotta catch a plane.'"

Thursday, October 10, 2024
Foyt Wine Vault, Speedway, Indiana

I don't know who was more surprised to see the main room of the Foyt Wine Vault jammed with people—A.J. Foyt or me. He'd made a late decision to come to Indianapolis to attend an IndyCar test at the Speedway and had agreed to do a book signing the evening before. With pre-event promotions limited to social media, we weren't sure how many people would show. We even worried no one would show up.

Shortly before the doors were opened, a representative of the publisher came in and said he'd counted six hundred people in a line that went around the corner and down the street. That was going to be a problem. We had two hundred and fifty copies of *A.J. Foyt: Survivor, Champion, Legend.*

A Disneyland-like maze had been set up in the room, and there was an excited buzz as people filed in. A cheer went up, and there were chants of "A.J., A.J." when Foyt entered the room and sat at the signing table next to me. He had an incredulous look on his face.

"Are all these people here for your book?"

I laughed then realized he was serious.

"No, A.J.," I said. "They're here for you."

At first he didn't seem to understand. Then he dropped his head, and when he looked up a moment later, his eyes were misty. He realized the people were there to see him, although I still don't think he understood why.

A production line had been set up to make the signings go as quickly as possible. I would address and sign each book and pass it on to A.J. for his signature. If someone wanted their picture with A.J.—and everybody did—we were ready to use their cell phone to take a quick shot.

As each person or couple posed with Foyt for a photo, they would tell him about a race they'd seen him win, or how many Indy 500s they'd been to. The room was loud, and after being around race car engines his entire life, A.J.'s hearing isn't the best. I was pretty sure he didn't understand what most were saying, but he'd smile and nod his thanks.

I started to listen in on the stories and realized they were talking about much more than races they'd attended. Many times, they wanted to tell A.J. about a kindness he had extended to them or someone they knew. Others—many in tears—told how he had impacted them in the face of personal tragedy or challenge. The same determination that had surprised two trauma surgeons had inspired them to keep going during the darkest moments of their lives.

At one point, there was a break in the flow of books, and for a moment we were alone. I tried to reinforce with A.J. what some of them had been saying. "You've had an incredible impact on so many people," I said.

He looked straight ahead, and I thought maybe he didn't hear me. Then his eyes watered again.

"Well," he said. "I always tried my hardest."

When we ran out of books and there were still at least a hundred people in line, A.J. agreed to sign additional copies when he got back to Texas and mail them to buyers. He also posed for photos with anybody who wanted one. I was exhausted afterward and have no idea how A.J. made it through the evening. He didn't need to do that, and I will be forever grateful.

Volume two of A.J. Foyt's biography is filled with more stories about race victories, championships, and the setting of records—many of which still stand today.

I've also tried to better capture the desire, drive, and determination that separated Foyt from other drivers and made him so much more than a race car driver to so many people. To start, it's worth repeating the words of the late Parnelli Jones, a driver many thought had more pure talent behind the wheel.

"He has such great desire," Jones said of Foyt when they were going head-to-head, week-after-week, in every kind of race car on every type of race track.

"More determination than anybody in racing. Even me."

14

CHAPTER 1

CROSSROADS

1978

February 15

Muhammad Ali, the heavyweight boxing champion of the world, was in trouble.

With only one round to go in his title fight against Leon Spinks, most in the crowd at the Las Vegas Hilton Hotel thought Ali needed a knockout to win. The overwhelming favorite in the nationally televised fight had spent the early rounds dancing and clowning. Spinks had never gone more than ten rounds, and the champ expected the younger fighter to tire. It hadn't happened, and despite a furious comeback attempt to the chants of "Ali, Ali, Ali," it was the defending champion who looked exhausted.

Ali had retired at the end of 1976 only to return to the ring the following year in need of money. In September 1977, he'd successfully defended his title against Earnie Shavers, a slugger who staggered the champ early in the fight with a blow to the head. In what *Sports Illustrated* called "Ali's Desperate Hour," the champ somehow fought back to score a controversial win, despite being "on very wobbly legs."[1]

Afterward, many of those closest to Ali, including his father, begged him to retire permanently before being badly hurt. Dr. Ferdie Pacheco, who served as Ali's personal physician and cornerman during much of the fighter's career and was known as the "fight doctor," quit at the end of the year when Ali refused to retire.

Yet Ali wanted another fight—needed another fight. "His financial affairs were in chaos," noted Jonathan Eig in the fighter's definitive biography, *Ali: A Life.*

◀ A.J. was back in his 1977 Indy 500–winning Coyote for the '78 race.
John Mahoney

Ali had failed to invest wisely, squandered much of his fortune, and saw the rest siphoned off by a massive entourage. "I spent a lot of it foolishly," Ali admitted. "They may not let me quit until I can't fight no more."[2]

Spinks had seemed to be a safe opponent. Although the twenty-four-year-old 1976 Olympic heavyweight gold medalist was twelve years younger than Ali, this would be only his eighth professional bout. The fight was labeled "a farce" by some in the media when it was announced, and Ali quit talking to reporters as a result.

It had been anything but a farce. While Ali rocked Spinks several times with punches in the dramatic final round, the champ was staggered himself by counterblows. In the end, it was too little too late as Spinks was "too young and too strong." Spinks was awarded a split decision, although most thought the challenger a clear winner.

The drumbeat for Ali's retirement started immediately. Pacheco, who was part of the CBS Sports broadcast team and had openly pulled for Ali during the fight, said, "If this means Ali will quit fighting, then I must go on record as saying I'm glad Ali lost."

The first reporter to talk with Ali in the ring was CBS's Bob Halloran. Ali's face was already badly swollen, he had tears in his eyes, and his voice was barely audible, but his message was clear: "I would like to do something which has never been done before, to be the third man to regain the title."

CBS commentator Jack Whitaker closed out the broadcast noting, "One would hope Ali would not come back. Age will always beat an athlete. And age now has a firm hold on Mohammad Ali."

Watching the fight that Wednesday night from the bar in his Daytona Beach hotel was Anthony Joseph "A.J." Foyt Jr. He was set to compete the next day in a qualifying race for the Daytona 500 and had joined a group of NASCAR drivers, crew members, and officials to watch the fight.

Foyt had watched Ali fight several times in the past, dating back to a few days before the 1965 Indianapolis 500 when the then Cassius Clay knocked out Sonny Liston one minute into the first round of their championship rematch. Foyt had watched the closed-circuit broadcast at Victory Field, the home of the Indianapolis Indians minor league baseball team located just a few miles down 16th Street from the Speedway.

"We barely got into our seats when that mystery punch decked Liston in the first round," he recalled. Dan Gurney, Junior Johnson, and a few other drivers began calling A.J. "Cassius" soon afterward, a reference to the fighter's cocky and outspoken nature. Rather than irritate Foyt, he embraced the moniker.[3]

The comments on Ali's retirement hit home with Foyt. The only four-time winner of the world's most prestigious auto race—the Indianapolis 500—A.J. had spent the past couple of months trying to decide if he wanted to try for a fifth. The man America's leading sports columnist called "the greatest in the world at what he does," wasn't sure he wanted to keep doing it.[4]

The euphoria of his dramatic come-from-behind victory in the 1977 Indy 500 had been replaced in the second half of the year by defeat and disappointment.

The crowd's cheers and chants of, "A.J., A.J., A.J.," at Indianapolis had turned to boos and catcalls by the end of the season. The man Foyt said was like a second father to him, Speedway owner Tony Hulman, had died suddenly. The health of parents Emma Evelyn Foyt and Anthony Joseph "Tony" Foyt ("The only man I can trust," according to A.J.), continued to deteriorate. Meanwhile, his oldest boy, Anthony Joseph "Tony" Foyt III, had taken over as lead trainer of his thoroughbreds. His daughter, Terry, had made him a grandfather, and his youngest son, Jerry, was entering high school.[5]

Those were just the emotional issues. There were also practical challenges to consider. The Coyote race cars and Foyt engines that he had spent the last seven years building and developing were nearing the end of the line. The sport was rapidly changing, with new cars and engines developed by computers and college-educated engineers replacing the ranks of backyard mechanics, of whom Foyt proudly considered himself a member.

Against this backdrop at the end of 1977, Foyt had retreated to his ranch in Hockley, Texas, about forty miles northwest of Houston, to contemplate his future. While his wife, Lucy, was an admitted "city girl" and preferred their sprawling home in a tony part of Houston, A.J. used the ranch as his safe place, away from the demands of his businesses, sponsors, and race team.

He had continued to add to the original property, known in the area simply as "A.J. Foyt's ranch," since purchasing it in the mid-1960s, buying up adjoining land as it became available, and other farms and ranches in the area. His idea of escape or a vacation was working from sunup to sundown, often with his father at his side. A perfect day would find him on a bulldozer, knocking down trees and moving dirt.

He could simply retire from racing, of course. Unlike Ali, he had invested wisely and was financially secure. There was enough going on with his Houston car dealership, his growing stable of racehorses, and his other business interests to keep him more than busy when he wasn't at the ranch. He also planned to continue as a race team owner when he retired as a driver. None of that, however, would scratch the competitive itch—the overwhelming desire to be the very best—that had driven him since his first exhibition race as a five-year-old.

After the fight, Foyt was approached by Gary Kale, the motorsports reporter for United Press International. Kale asked if he thought Ali should retire. A.J. typically responded quickly to questions, often answering before a reporter finished. This time he paused, giving his response added thought. He slowly shook his head no.

"I admire the guy," Foyt said of Ali. "He has guts and quality. I wouldn't be surprised to see him try and regain the title." Then he took the discussion in a different direction, and it was clear Foyt was talking as much about himself as he was Ali. "Sometimes you just want to be taken for a regular guy," he said. "You just want to be A.J. and lose yourself in a crowd. But then you're disappointed if nobody recognizes you. Ali may feel the same way. He wants to be before the public. It's nice being looked upon when you're on top.[6]

"It's like me and racing. If I think I can continue to do the job, I'll do it. He's like me with certain goals. People said I stayed in racing to win Indy for the fourth time, something nobody else had ever done. Ali said after the fight he'd like to regain the heavyweight championship for a third time, something nobody else has done.

"If he decides to come back, he'll get into shape. Spinks was hungry, the younger guys usually are. They have nothing on their mind except the sport. I ate, slept, and worked racing when I first got started. The older you get, the more things you have on your mind, especially if you're successful. You have so many things going for you that you don't have time to train properly."

Seven months later, Ali would return to the ring, defeating Spinks to regain the title and retiring soon after. He staged yet another comeback in 1979, retiring for good after losing two bouts.

Foyt, at age forty-three, had already decided to race again in 1978 before the Ali vs. Spinks fight, and his year was off to a good start. He turned in the third-fastest qualifying time for the Daytona 500 in his new Buick stock car, and in typical Cassius style, talked about winning the Daytona and Indianapolis 500s in the same year.

The reason for Foyt's confidence was on display in his 125-mile qualifying race. He led the most laps and benefited from a late caution flag to hold off David Pearson, Donnie Allison, and pole sitter Cale Yarborough to score Buick's first win since 1955. Although it was just a qualifying race and didn't count toward the NASCAR championship, that didn't matter to Foyt, who wasn't a series regular. It was still a victory—his first in NASCAR since leaving the Wood Brothers in 1972.

"When you drive a lil' ol' Buick like you could drive to church to a win, you got to be happy," a jovial Foyt said afterward, obviously enjoying being back on top.[7]

Foyt's mood marked a 180-degree change in attitude from the end of 1977. One columnist wrote that A.J. was so pleasant, "he could charm a cobra."[8]

The Daytona 500 changed that. In a wreck-filled event, Foyt fell behind early and was chasing the leaders, Yarborough and Benny Parsons, trying to get a lap back when Parsons blew a tire at about 190 miles per hour, spinning into the infield. Debris littered the track, and Foyt slowed as he arrived on the scene a moment later.

"A.J. tried to back off," said Lennie Pond, who was behind Foyt. "I saw his hand go up, but I was [too close]. I didn't tap him hard, but it doesn't take much when you are going that fast."[9]

Foyt said Pond wasn't "looking any farther ahead than the end of his nose.[10]

"I looked in my rear-view mirror, and the nearest car was three lengths [back]. I was still running about 185 and said, 'Well, he's still got all the room in the world,' so I kinda pulled to the inside of the track. The next time I looked back, somebody was giving me a big boot in the (butt)."

The Buick went into a broad slide before the tires suddenly gripped the track, launching the car into a series of barrel rolls.

"I was about fifteen to twenty feet in the air, running 180 mph, upside down," Foyt said. "I knew it was going to be rough from then on."

The car finally came to a rest right side up, but with its roof crushed. There were a few anxious moments with no movement in the car as Foyt hung by his safety belts, slumped over the steering wheel. The first medics to arrive signaled Foyt was unconscious and worked to stabilize his head and neck, finally extracting him from the car with his helmet still on. Waiting in the infield care center was Jack Starne, his Indy car crew chief who had been with Foyt since midyear 1967.

"They brought him into the hospital and they had his arms on his chest and one of them fell on the side of the stretcher and was dangling down," Starne recalled years later. "I thought, *Oh no, school's out.* That was the first thing that went through my brain."[11]

Shortly thereafter, however, Foyt began to regain consciousness and complained about shoulder pain. Gordon Johncock, who'd been in the International Race of Champions two days earlier and stayed to watch the 500, ran to the care center. A doctor told him Foyt was "talking but confused." His face was cut and scratched and beginning to swell, and he looked as bad as Ali a few nights earlier. Johncock said he thought A.J.'s head and shoulder may have hit the track during the barrel rolls. When Foyt continued to complain about the shoulder, he was bandaged and given an IV for the short trip to Halifax Hospital.

Jackie Stewart, providing commentary on the *ABC Sports* broadcast, called it "an incredible accident" and wondered aloud, "How he wasn't more seriously hurt, I will never know."[12]

X-rays at the hospital indicated Foyt had a separated shoulder, and despite complaining of a headache, he tried to leave. Richard Petty had been held overnight at the hospital just two days earlier after losing consciousness in a crash, and now doctors insisted it was protocol. Foyt finally relented but chased everyone out of his room. Early the next morning with his arm in a sling, he left the hospital and boarded a private jet for the trip to Houston.

"I shouldn't have come out of that wreck," he'd say later, his flare for the dramatic when describing one of his crashes on full display. Although the ABC cameras missed the accident, he'd been able to piece it together with still photography. "My shoulder came out of the window at 180 mph and the car hit every time on my side. It slammed me outside the window and it slammed me back in. Theoretically my arm should have been torn off and my head with it, because it busted the whole side of my helmet off."[13]

He was sufficiently recovered three weeks later to enter the 250-mile USAC stock car race at Texas World Speedway, and qualified on the pole in a field that included Daytona 500 winner Bobby Allison. Although A.J. said beforehand he wasn't sure how far he could go in the race, he led throughout and edged Allison, who was the only car on the same lap at the finish. Allison filed a protest, saying Foyt passed him illegally under a caution flag, although USAC saw otherwise.

Over the next month, Foyt proved there was still life in his Coyote Indy car as he finished third at Phoenix, fourth at Ontario, and second at Trenton, while winning the Ontario stock car race. As practice started for the Indianapolis 500, he found himself leading the USAC stock car standings and running second to Danny Ongais in the Indy car ranks.

Tragedy had struck after the Trenton race when a chartered flight carrying USAC officials back to Indianapolis crashed in a thunderstorm. All nine aboard died, including Ray Marquette, the former *Indianapolis Star* reporter who'd become vice president of public affairs, and Frank DelRoy, chair of the technical committee. It was a devastating blow for an organization already stretched thin and reeling from the death of Tony Hulman and would add to the growing unrest among car owners and drivers.

While Foyt's Daytona injuries hadn't impacted his driving skills, it did cut into his testing and development schedule leading up to Indianapolis. He scrapped plans to build two new cars for the Speedway and instead entered an updated Coyote he designated as a 1978 model, and the 1977 winning car, now four years old. He also announced George Snider would be his teammate.

The updated car was still in pieces when it arrived at the Speedway and was finished in the tight confines of the team's Gasoline Alley garage. Parts were becoming scarce for the Foyt engine, and he bought back several blocks from other teams, saying he had enough parts for "three or four engines." Engine guru Howard Gilbert wasn't so sure they'd made the right decision.

"We stuck with the engine because we knew what it would do, we knew what the reliability factor was that we built into it," Gilbert said. He warned that it, "had gone about as far as it can go, we've gotten just about all out of it there is to get. I think this season probably will see its demise."[14]

None of that seemed to bother Foyt as he skipped opening weekend at the Speedway and instead shuttled between Louisville to watch his racehorses run and Talladega, where he qualified second for the May 7 NASCAR race.

His stable of thoroughbreds had grown to twenty, and three of his horses had been among a record 319 nominees for the Kentucky Derby. That simply meant Foyt was willing to put up the one-hundred-dollar nomination fee for each. While Poker Joker, Foyt's Ack, and Short Chute would all have successful careers, only Poker Joker scored enough points in preliminary events to qualify for Derby consideration. A.J. decided against entering the horse, later saying, "None of them were good enough."[15]

When the Talladega race was washed out, he flew to Churchill Downs and watched as What Reason, his four-year-old filly, splashed to victory in the rain. It was the seventh win of the meet for his stable and moved A.J.'s son Tony to the top of the trainer rankings.[16]

"I'm not disappointed he's not into auto racing," Foyt said of his son. "I feel I'm doing what I really want to do and I'm successful. I want him to be the same way. If not auto racing, then something he really wanted to do.[17]

"Kids these days have too much free time, so I gave my boy something to do. He was interested in horses as a kid, so I got interested."

It didn't take long for A.J. to discover racehorses could be just as frustrating as race cars. "They are just as temperamental. A car can't tell you what's wrong and horses can't tell you either. It's a guessing game."[18]

It wasn't until Wednesday, May 10, that Foyt took to the track in the "new" Coyote, running only a couple of laps. He hadn't run many more by the end of the week, but one of those was at more than 200 mph, putting him in the pole position discussion.

After Saturday's qualifying at the Speedway was rained out, Foyt said he would stay in Indianapolis rather than go to Talladega as originally planned for the rescheduled NASCAR race. However, when he woke Sunday morning and discovered it was still raining in Indianapolis and the weather service said it was expected to continue all day, he decided to roll the dice and headed for the airport.

Arriving minutes before the green flag, he pitted from his second-place starting position on the pace lap after discovering his radio wasn't connected. Sent to the back of the field as a result, it took him seven laps to move into the top five, and he was second to Yarborough when his engine began to stumble. He lost a lap before it cleared, and although he ran with the leaders thereafter, he was never able to make it up and finished third.

The week delay in qualifying appeared to benefit Foyt as he had more practice time. But with a record ninety-two entries, he warned, "With only one weekend left, you've got to be careful. You can't take as many chances. If you break your car trying to put it on the pole and have to go to the end of the (qualifying) line, you ain't gonna be in the race. It's as simple as that."[19]

On pole day, he turned an early morning practice lap at 203.666 mph, the fastest unofficial lap clocked by the electronic eye at the Speedway. He'd just started his qualifying run when he slowed in the first turn, pulled to the inside of the track, and drove back to the pits. He complained to USAC officials that just as had happened in 1977, he'd been given a faulty pop-off valve that regulated turbocharger boost pressure. Officials checked and assured Foyt the valve was operating properly, pointing out it was set to allow nineteen pounds of pressure versus the legal limit of twenty-five. It was up to the teams to set the boost pressure, and Foyt's had misset the valve.

Once the valve was reset, Foyt's car was pushed to the end of the qualifying queue, although it soon became apparent the line was too long to allow for a Saturday run. With rain in Sunday's forecast, he briefly considered qualifying Snider's car, before deciding against it. The team then made another mistake, waving off Snider's run that would have been fast enough to put him in the field, when a crew member misread the stopwatch. Foyt confronted crew chief Starne on pit road, and frustrations boiled over, with the two friends going toe-to-toe in perhaps the biggest public blowup they would have. Some fans began to boo.

Foyt finally stepped away and eventually seemed to take the blame. He indicated someone else set the valve, but he'd failed to check it as he normally did. He admitted the bigger mistake was taking the green flag to start an official qualifying run when he knew something wasn't right.

"It was just my screw-up, as usual. I'm not complaining. I had my chance and I blew it, it's as simple as that. I'm no newcomer here. I took the green flag. It was my decision. It was wrong. You win some and you lose some. I lost this one."[20]

He said he realized complaining about the pop-off valve looked bad to the fans:

> I couldn't see two years in a row something like that happening. And I felt bad because I know the fans probably said, 'What's he trying to pull?' I've never tried to pull nothing in my life in racing. I guess when you've won as much as I have, people say, well, you know, A.J. gets everything the way he wants it. When I make mistakes, I admit 'em. But when I don't make mistakes, I'm not going to let somebody else tell me I made mistakes and this is the way I've been all my life. I'm not going to change at this stage. If you write what I say, fine. But if you write a lie about me, I get upset. It's very simple.[21]

He nearly compounded the problems the next day, forgetting to raise his hand to signal the start of a qualifying run. He recovered the next time by and ran four laps at just over 200 mph, his speed matching Ongais, the second-fastest qualifier. As a second-day qualifier, however, Foyt would start nineteenth with Snider right behind him. It was still better than Mario Andretti, who missed qualifying entirely while away in Europe, where he led every lap of the Belgium Grand Prix and took the lead in the World Driver's Championship. Andretti would start last in the 500, driving a car qualified by Mike Hiss.

Foyt said he would

> play it real conservative at the start. You probably won't see me charge up through there the first few laps. We'll let the cars kind of string out a bit and then go from there. There's a couple of people up there I'll be watching. I will make sure I have plenty of room where I can get myself out of trouble. I hope I'm wrong, but I think you'll see a lot of breakage. We might be the first to break, but that's the way we're going to set up our race strategy. We're not gonna try to set any speed records or nothing like that.[22]

He "made a mockery" of the final practice session on Carb Day, turning a lap at more than 199 mph, five mph faster than anyone else. On the next lap, he was in the pits, saying he'd damaged the engine. As he had in the past, he decided to return to Houston to rebuild it. Some thought it was just a ploy by Foyt to get out of town so he was able to skip a function presenting him with the Jim Clark Memorial Award (car owner Jim Gilmore picked it up instead) and the race parade, which he had often tried to avoid in the past. He also had Ron Hutcherson qualify his stock car at Charlotte, saying he'd race in the 600 miler if Indianapolis was rained out.

It was hot and humid on race day, and it was the chassis, not his engine, that gave Foyt problems on the slick track. Although it took less than ten laps for him to break into the top ten, he never challenged for the lead as he ran out of fuel twice and made long pit stops, putting him hopelessly behind. He finished seventh, nine laps behind Al Unser, winner of his third 500, with Snider eighth. Foyt ran out of fuel on the backstraight after taking the checkered flag, and fans broke down the track's fencing for the second year in a row, surrounded Foyt's car, and pushed it back to pit road.[23]

Unser created a stir afterward when he said Janet Guthrie, who had made her second Indy 500 start and finished ninth, had been "out for a Sunday drive."

"I think she done a fine job—for her ability," Foyt said, adding, "but put her against us and we're all running the same equipment and running good, well I don't think we have to worry about her ever beating us. I don't believe car racing's cut out for ladies. Not that they don't have the ability, but I think it's a man's job."[24]

He did have nice things to say about a trio of young male drivers.

"With Danny Ongais, Rick Mears, and Tom Sneva, you've got a threesome coming along now much like Mario and me and Parnelli Jones came along. I think you'll hear a lot from those three names. Right now you need some other boys to come along 'cause Mario (38), myself (43) and Al (39) and Bobby (44) and Johnny Rutherford (40), we're all about the same age and you'd hate to see all the top names leave at once."

Rick Mears

It had been a rapid rise for Mears, who'd been an off-road racer less than two years earlier. Now he was running a partial schedule for Roger Penske, filling in for Andretti when Mario was racing on the grand prix circuit. He'd already earned co-rookie-of-the-year honors at Indianapolis and perhaps even more importantly, Foyt's respect.

Mears recalled the following experience with Foyt years later:

> It was at Milwaukee or Phoenix, and I was having what at that time was my best race. Near the end of the race, I see A.J. coming around to put a lap on me. I thought, *Okay, I'll just run my pattern*, knowing he'll be watching me because that's what I would do—watch somebody and figure out how I'm going to go around him before I get there. He's getting closer and closer, and pretty soon he's right behind me. He follows me for a couple of corners, picks his place, and goes by. I finished fifth and was tickled to death. The team was all happy, and we're jumping up and down.[25]
>
> I went in the truck to change clothes, and when I came out all my guys were saying, "What the hell did you do to Foyt?" I said, "I didn't do anything." I didn't know what they were talking about. They said Foyt had just come by and said, "You tell that damn Mears if he ever pulls that crap on me again, I'm gonna stick him in the fence." I thought, *Holy shit, I didn't do anything.*
>
> So now I'm a nervous wreck. I'm just a snot-nosed kid, and I've got *the man* mad at me. The next time I saw him was at Ontario. He was signing

> some autographs, and I had to walk by him to get out to pit lane. I thought, *Uh-oh, here we go. I might as well get this over with.*
>
> So I walked by him, and he was facing off to the right, and I patted him as I walked by and kept going out to pit lane. Then I heard, "Hey, Mears," and I thought, *Oh shit.* I stopped and turned around and walked back to him. As I got close, he put his arm around me and said, "Oh man, we had a helluva race didn't we." I thought he was gonna be mad, but he was all smiles.
>
> He'd been watching me on the track, so I think I earned a little bit of respect by not doing something stupid. I learned his bark was worse than his bite. He's just a big teddy bear, although he might not like me saying that.

Two weeks after the 500 at Milwaukee, Mears won his first Indy car race:

> It was getting toward the end, and I caught Al [Unser] and was just starting to work on him. I felt like I had enough to get him. But before I did, he ran out of fuel.
>
> When I ran into Foyt later, I was telling him I didn't feel good about the race because I didn't get to *win* it. I'd wanted to pass Al and win the race. He just started laughing at me and said, "Are you kidding me? Believe me, you'll lose more that way than you'll win." And boy was he right. I ended up losing a lot more than I did winning. Those were some of his first words of wisdom.
>
> We became good friends, and we'd chat a lot. For quite a few years at Indy, I was on the upper floor in the [Speedway] motel, right on the corner by the staircase where you come up. His room was down at the far end. If I had the door open getting some fresh air, he'd stop, and we'd shoot the shit for a little bit.
>
> He's a competitor, and there was always a method to his madness. He didn't win all he's won by not being smart about it. He was always trying to pick my brain, as if I didn't know it. We'd be chatting, and he'd say something like, "Those 800-pound springs—those are terrible, aren't they," looking for an answer one way or another, trying to figure out what we were running. I'd try not to say too much.

After the 500, Foyt decided to focus on the USAC schedule, selling his Buick to Petty. Foyt ran every weekend through the summer months, often alternating between his Coyote and a new Camaro for the stock car series. He won the stock car race June 10 at Mosport, a road course in Canada, but was involved in an accident the next day in his Indy car. The following week, the Coyote fell off the loading ramp before Milwaukee, damaging the wing and suspension.

"It was terrible seeing it broken up, but like anything else that breaks, you pick up the pieces, mend it and start over," Foyt said of the damage. He realized the Coyote design, now five years old, was showing its age but wasn't sure he wanted to start over with an all-new car.[26]

"I don't know if I want to go through the development program again. I've been so far behind schedule because of my injuries, that I've been playing catch-up. I'll try to get through this season and then make up my mind."

Ever since the problems at Indianapolis, he'd become increasingly upset with his crew members, openly complaining there were "too many engineers and not enough people who want to work, and I'm getting damn tired of it."[27]

It wasn't just his pit crew attracting Foyt's ire as the Indy car teams arrived at Texas World Speedway for the August 6 200-mile race. A dispute between the four-cylinder powered teams and those with V8 engines had reached a tipping point. The teams using the smaller engines developed a list of rule changes they wanted to see instituted by USAC going forward. Presented by George Bignotti, the list included full-time use of pop-off valves, four-cylinder engines to be allowed eighty inches of boost compared to seventy-two for the V8s, and a lowering of the fuel economy standard from 1.8 mpg to 1.4 mpg.

At about the same time, Roger Penske announced the formation of Championship Auto Racing Teams, or CART. The outgrowth of a "white paper" written by Dan Gurney, CART was made up primarily of the Cosworth V8 powered car owners and patterned after the Formula One Constructors' Association (FOCA). It was designed to give car owners greater control over the sport and its rules while diminishing USAC's role. Ironically, the only car owner to join CART whose team was still using four-cylinder engines was Bignotti's boss, Pat Patrick, who'd already ordered six new Cosworth V8 powerplants at $32,500 each. The white paper also demanded bigger purses from the tracks.

"It appears that a 'showdown' with the Indianapolis Motor Speedway is, or should be, the first target," Gurney wrote in the white paper. "They are the ones who can afford it. We should renegotiate the TV contract (our rights—not theirs) and we should double the purse," to about $2 million.

Caught in the middle was Foyt. While his loyalty to the Speedway was unquestioned, his allegiance to USAC was less so. He'd never hesitated to criticize the organization in the past and often clashed with officials at the track. Most of those he knew and respected had been killed in the plane crash. He was reluctant to join CART, however, concerned about the direction it might take and the impact on the sport.

To call attention to their demands, the four-cylinder teams said they would boycott qualifying on the high-speed Texas track, where the rules gave them little chance of starting up front. When told they wouldn't be allowed to start if they didn't post a qualifying speed, the four-cylinder cars cruised around the track, averaging about 100 mph. Cognizant of where the race was being held, the protesters put Texan, independent team owner, and Foyt buddy Jim McElreath out front to state their case.

"We need to change the rules a little, but I don't know how we should go about it," said McElreath, uneasy in his spokesman role. "There is no need in making something obsolete just because we won't change the rules. The V8s are going to out-qualify us anyway."[28]

Foyt took the protest personally and saw it as an attempt to embarrass the series and what he considered to be his home track.

"Good race people don't realize that they're hurting themselves and they're also hurting the sport," Foyt said in deference to his friend McElreath. Then he went after the ringleaders, Patrick and Bignotti. "I broke eight V8 engines at Indianapolis trying to qualify in 1973 and the four-cylinder was the kingpin. The development of the V8 has now caught up with them. A bunch of them bought four-cylinders this season and they're not happy. Now they want to penalize the others. They made a lot of mistakes and they don't want to go before their owners and sponsors and admit it."

As usual Rutherford, who called nearby Fort Worth home, was more tactful in his response:

> I have mixed emotions. It's a situation that has been building ever since the V8s came into existence. We've worked very hard to get the V8 running properly and obviously it's a superior engine and the fours just can't keep up. Even if the guys wanted to shell out all the money in the world, none of the V8s will be available until next April. That's the corner we've painted ourselves into. It's a bad situation right now. They could have handled it in a more diplomatic manner. Instead, they pushed it off on the race fans. I just don't know if anything was solved.

As a result, tensions were higher than normal as the start of the race approached and pegged for the Foyt team when they spotted a broken radiator support on his car as they were rolling it out to the grid.

"I thought, *Here we go again, we'll run five laps and be through*," Foyt admitted after the race. However, "the crew was finally on the ball," and hustled the car back to the garage, replaced the support, and returned it to the grid with minutes to spare.[29]

Foyt, who'd qualified second to Sneva, took the lead at the start and stretched it out before being slowed in lapped traffic. He then made a lengthy pit stop to make a wing adjustment, with Sneva, Mears, and Rutherford moving to the front.

A caution flag allowed Foyt to catch up, and when the leaders pitted, he stayed on the track, assuming the lead. All the cars needed to make one more pit stop for fuel, most just a quick splash and go, although Foyt would require a longer stop for a full load. As the caution flag stretched on, however, Foyt decided to take a chance. With the field finally coming to an expected green flag, he pulled alongside the pace car and blocked it from pulling off the track. As the pace car started another lap, Foyt peeled off at the last moment and raced down pit road to make his refueling stop, rejoining at the back of the now eight-car field. When the race restarted, he began turning laps at full speed and took the lead. The question was, did he have enough fuel to finish?

"No," said Gurney, handling the commentary on *ABC Sports*. Then he laughed. "But don't underestimate Super Tex."[30]

When all the other cars were forced to make their late stops, Foyt kept going and moved to the front, winning by nearly a lap over Rutherford, with Steve Krisiloff third.

"If you're gonna win, I wanna win in front of my hometown people," Foyt said in Victory Circle. His voice rose and cracked as he tried to go on. "I won this race for my mother, who's in the hospital, and Di Gilmore." He turned away for a moment, struggling to regain his composure. His mother's heart was acting up again, and Diane Gilmore had been diagnosed with an aggressive cancer. "Di's having an operation on Tuesday," he said. "As much as both of them love racing, neither one of them's here, so this win meant a lot to me—for them."

On the television broadcast, Ken Squier added, "Some people call him rough and gruff. But when he wants to be, he can be the most sensitive and quiet and introspective person you could hope to meet."

A few minutes later, the rough and gruff Foyt was back as Krisiloff walked into the victory celebration and started yelling. He was upset over the pace car maneuver, saying it was unsafe. It took everyone by surprise, and no one seemed sure what he was yelling about. When Krisiloff repeated the charge, Foyt lunged for him and landed a glancing blow. Both drivers swung wildly before Foyt crew member John Fisher, "a grizzly bear of a man," according to Squier, grabbed Krisiloff around the waist and carried him away from the celebration.

"He's a typical Yankee, he's always running his jaws," Foyt said of Krisiloff later in the press box. "He said I cheated him on the pace car, but I don't know what he was talking about.[31]

"He was giving me some smart mouth. I'm not listening to that from anybody. I just reached out and popped him one. I would have done more than that if I could. Four-cylinder crybaby."[32]

He also delivered a backhanded compliment to his team. "My crew worked like it was supposed to. They finally forgot what heroes they were.

"When we won Indy for the fourth time, it was hard not to let down. A lot of times I wasn't there to give the crew some direction. We had to change the wing and a lot of things today. We had that teamwork in the pits."[33]

In an effort to placate the "crybabies," USAC soon proposed several possible rule changes to its competition committee made up of car owners. The fuel mileage target would be lowered from 1.8 mpg to 1.5 mpg, and full-time use of the pop-off valve would be reinstated with the manifold pressure set at seventy-four inches for all engines. The proposals required full USAC board approval and were turned down in a vote along party lines, with the V8 teams against the changes and the four-cylinder teams in favor. Foyt, one of the committee members who voted no, was the most outspoken of the opposition. "Either get equipment that is competitive or get out of racing," he snapped.[34]

In the midst of it all, an Indianapolis television station reported Foyt had bought the Speedway for $99 million, not including the golf course or motel, a story he laughed at.

"That's a bunch of bull, somebody trying to start a rumor. There's always somebody trying to start a rumor about me.

"It's not for sale. I'm quite sure nobody has a chance to buy the Speedway. I'd hate to put a price on what the Speedway is worth, at least $200 million. So I'm not going to buy it, not for the kind of money it would take."[35]

After winning at Milwaukee in the Camaro and finishing fourth at the same track in the Coyote, Foyt arrived for the Labor Day Indy car race at Ontario unsure of his prospects. Both the Coyote chassis and Foyt engine were clearly near the end of the line. In early practice, he turned laps well off the pace of the front-runners, who were running at over 200 mph. So it didn't surprise anyone when he tested another car, although the car surprised almost everyone as it belonged to the team of Parnelli Jones and Vel Miletich.

Jones and Miletich were in the second year of a loose relationship with Ongais and his financial backer, Ted Field. It had started unraveling after Indianapolis when the team was hit by a series of engine failures. Field decided to buy the equipment Ongais had been using and hire away the pit crew, which left the Vel's Parnelli Jones team with a car and engine but not much else.

"It's just one of those things that happen," Miletich said. "We knew A.J. was looking around for something else to drive and A.J. knew we were looking around for someone to drive our car.[36]

"I don't see any problems at all," he said when asked how Jones and Foyt would get along. "They're like a couple of brothers. They fight and roll in the dirt with each other, but let anybody else say anything about them and they'll have a fight on their hands. They have a lot of respect for each other."

Jones seemed to agree.

"I think it will be mutually beneficial," he said. "Sure, we had differences on the track. That's common knowledge, but I think that old stinker and I can get along together. We can handle the chassis and A.J. can handle the engine. I think A.J. is the best I've ever seen working with an engine. I'm not taking anything away from Al [Unser], but he just doesn't have A.J.'s technical knowledge. Al is more of a racer. A.J. is both a racer and engine builder and designer. He can take a car out and tell you exactly what's wrong with the engine. Al can't and I can't."

Jones also cautioned, "I don't know if it'll be a one-race, two-race or a 10-year association. That's something that will have to be worked out. But I'm looking forward to the prospects."

On Wednesday, Foyt ran a few laps in the car Al Unser had driven at Indianapolis in 1977 and Ongais had practiced at 202 mph earlier in the year at the Speedway. Foyt decided to try it in the race, marking the first time since 1966 that he would drive an Indy car for another team.

"There's no use trying to fool myself," Foyt said. "I think we wrung as much out of the Coyote as we could. There's no doubt it's come to the end of the line. When that happens, you're just lying to yourself if you think you can stay competitive.

"The old Foyt engine has become a dinosaur. It's 200 pounds heavier than the Cosworth and that's too much of a handicap these days. The pieces are becoming harder to find and I'm getting too old to go through building my own cars and engines. It's easier to buy some from Vel and Parnelli, or go racing with them."

By Thursday morning, the No. 21 blue-and-white Parnelli was in Foyt's garage, sporting both his Gilmore Racing signage and American Racing Wheels decals of Jones/Miletich. Car problems delayed his qualifying attempt by a day and cost him the pole position, as he ran a lap 1.5 mph faster than Sneva did on day one.

It was a short race as he broke the transmission on the first lap. Afterward, he indicated he wanted to run the Parnelli again, and the rumor mill started up. Robin Miller wrote in his weekly column that Bignotti would split with Patrick and become chief mechanic for the Jones/Foyt team in 1979, although Big George dismissed the story.

"It sounds like somebody had a few too many drinks in the bar," he said, "though I wouldn't hesitate a minute if I was asked. A.J. and I always got along with the race car. It was a few things away from the track that drove a wedge between us."[37]

It was not to be, however, as Foyt decided to purchase the Parnelli and run it himself, seeming to admit he'd probably become too set in his ways to drive for someone else.

"A lot of the press comes to me and say I would win a lot more if I wasn't my own boss. I do run out [of fuel] every now and then. I don't really have a coach to blame except myself. They are my own cars."[38]

Two weeks later at Michigan, Foyt's No. 14 was on the Parnelli along with a new paint job, combining traditional poppy red—or "Foyt Orange," as almost everyone called it—with the blue from the Jones/Miletich car. It was a good-looking machine, and Foyt qualified third, led nine laps, and was running second to Ongais late in the race when engine problems slowed his pace, dropping him to fifth at the finish.

The real news at Michigan came when Foyt lined up for the year's first International Race of Champions. He'd skipped the series the previous year, complaining about money and saying he was "tired of racing the same guys all the time." In a slightly different format—a qualifying race for the Indy car regulars—he took a half-car-length victory over Al Unser. Afterward, Foyt was asked what brought him back to IROC.

"I got $50,000 appearance money," he gloated, looking directly at series President Les Richter, whom he often clashed with over money. "Plus a year's interest."[39]

A week later at Trenton, Foyt put the Parnelli on the pole and led the first thirteen laps before a burned piston knocked him out, with Andretti—the recently crowned World Champion—going on to victory.

From Trenton, the USAC teams flew to England for the country's first Indy car races. Foyt elected to ship his Coyote overseas, and it paid off as he won the opening event at Silverstone, dodging the raindrops to come from tenth starting position to edge Mears. He also became the most popular American since Franklin Delano Roosevelt.

"It was a popular victory for European fans to whom Foyt is something of a legend, the Texan from across the ocean, whose image grew larger than life," wrote one reporter. "Foyt delighted them by going the Gary Cooper route, doing everything with a blushing smile and muttering, 'Ah shucks.'"[40]

According to *AutoSport*, a leading European racing publication, "A.J. Foyt captivated Silverstone on the track and off. For four long days he patiently signed autographs, posed for pictures and answered questions. What's more, he did it with a smile on his face. When he scribbled his name on somebody's program, he chatted with them, looked them in the eye. Certain of our hallowed Grand Prix superstars could study this advantage. Bless his heart, he has been, as the song goes, 'Oozing charms from every pore.'"[41]

Foyt recalled something else from the trip. After winning at Silverstone, he wanted to take his crew out for a steak dinner.

"The best part of the trip was after we won, about eight of us went into this fancy restaurant," A.J. recalled forty years later. "They said they wouldn't give us a table because we ain't got no ties, you can't come in here. I said fine and handed him a hundred-dollar bill. He said, 'Come on in, let me see if I can't get you a table.' Money talks wherever you go."[42]

Mears bounced back to win the next race at Brands Hatch, with Foyt fourth. Years later, Mears said in good-natured recollection he should have swept the British series,

> USAC gave him the win at Silverstone, or I would have won that one too. We didn't run in the wet back then. He and I were going back and forth depending on pit stops. I think I was leading when it started to sprinkle, and they red-flagged it. We waited and waited for the track to dry out. Finally, we started running again and I came in to pit, and it gave Foyt the lead and it started sprinkling again. They waited about five minutes and called the race. I thought, *Why didn't we try and dry it out like we did the first time when I had the lead?* I just took it as A.J. had the pull there.[43]

Back in the states a week later on October 15, the other A.J. Foyt soon appeared. He dropped out of the second IROC race at Riverside, saying again that he was through with the series, as Andretti went on to victory.

"I'm not driving in this damn thing anymore," Foyt said after parking his Camaro on lap eighteen of the thirty-lap race. This time a reporter noted Foyt avoided autograph seekers by "putting his shoulder down and bulldozing his way through. Foyt jumped the wall leading to the garage area, ripped off his helmet and threw it to the ground, kicking it once for good measure before going into hiding. Foyt could have been a little less theatric about this departure, but that's not his nature."[44]

Two weeks later at the season finale for Indy cars, Andretti was in Foyt's sights. He was involved in a late-race battle with Rutherford when the two came up on Andretti, who was already two laps down. Andretti let Rutherford by but momentarily held up Foyt, costing him an outside chance at victory.

"What was Mario trying to do out there?" Foyt asked. "I nearly hit him, especially in all that traffic. I couldn't figure that out at all. It didn't look like he knew what was going on. Mario was all over the place."[45]

With the USAC stock car championship at stake in the last race of the year at Texas, Foyt set a new track record in qualifying and battled Bobby Allison throughout before emerging with both the race win and the title. Afterward, he sounded like anything but a newly crowned champion.

"I'm just tired of racing this year," he said. He'd made thirty-four starts and one transatlantic trip. "I've run myself into the ground. I got hurt at Daytona and I just haven't felt as good as I should have. I'm going to concentrate on Indianapolis next year and I'm certainly not going to have this kind of schedule."[46]

Instead of going to his ranch to start a couple months of recuperation, however, he headed to Indianapolis, where negotiations between CART and USAC were coming to a head. Talks had continued during the season and despite his reluctance, Foyt had been dragged into the discussions. Both organizations knew he was the linchpin, and whichever group he sided with would have an advantage. He refused to pledge allegiance to either side, hoping against hope that a compromise could be reached. More meetings were scheduled, and they were sometimes contentious.

"At one meeting in Phoenix, A.J. took a gun out of his briefcase and calmly put it on the table," recalled McLaren boss Tyler Alexander, although Foyt said he doesn't remember the incident. "We told him he could put the gun away, we wanted him with us and we'd come to talk, not to shoot one another!"[47]

The two organizations had the same goal—to make racing more affordable—but different strategies. USAC wanted to lower the cost of racing, while CART wanted to increase the amount of money the teams earned through higher purses and a bigger cut from the television contract.

USAC's first attempt at rewriting the 1979 rules once again set fuel mileage at 1.5 mpg, called for the pop-off valve to be used at all times, and with all engines having eighty inches of manifold boost available. In an unexpected move, rear-wing area was reduced from forty-three inches to thirty-six. The changes made few happy and pushed Foyt further toward joining the other car owners.

"I think it is the most asinine thing grown men making rules have done in my whole career," he said. "Midget and sprint car people are telling us what to do and we're all fed up with it. We are spending the money and not the board, which doesn't know what racing is. I've got ten million dollars invested and they've got nothing. We're the ones who have got the money in these cars and we're the ones who should say what we want."[48]

The CART members and Foyt gathered in mid-November for a series of meetings at the Speedway Motel to review its counterproposal. The rules package, over which the whole thing had supposedly begun back in Texas, offered a starting point for negotiations. It called for seventy inches of boost for the eight-cylinder cars, seventy-four for four-cylinder engines, while making no changes to the 1.8 mpg target or forty-three-inch rear wing. It called for a maximum of fourteen races, with a minimum of thirteen days between events.

The real changes and major stumbling blocks continued to be power and money. While USAC would sanction all Indy car races, the proposal in effect neutered the group, establishing a new board of six CART members and five from USAC. It put the board in charge of all television negotiations and set purse guarantees above and beyond television and accessories of $75,000 for 150-mile races, $100,000 for 200-mile races, $125,000 for road races, and a 20 percent increase in the purse of each of the three 500-mile events. The increases were minor for some races, but for Ontario and Texas, it would require significant increases. Indianapolis had been offering a million dollars for nearly ten years, but the amount had increased by only 15 percent over that period. A 20 percent increase would be significant.

"That's the kind of money I think people should pay to get A.J. Foyts," Patrick said of the purse demands.[49]

Foyt allowed his name to be used in support of the CART proposal and helped to work out one seemingly vital compromise: changing the board structure to include six CART and six USAC members, with USAC President Dick King as the non-voting chairman.

Despite the offer, USAC refused to budge, and its board—meeting in emergency session at its headquarters just down the street from the Speedway Motel—unanimously rejected the proposal in a twenty-to-zero vote. Afterward, CART said it would run its own series of races in 1979.

"Effective today we are going to control our destiny," Patrick announced. "There's no longer a USAC championship division as far as we're concerned."

In the midst of the back-and-forth came word that Di Gilmore had died. The surgery Foyt had talked about after the Texas race had failed to slow her cancer's spread. Her funeral on December 12 created a temporary truce as leaders from both USAC and CART gathered in Kalamazoo, Michigan. The entire Foyt team attended, dressed in the red-and-white checked shirts she had designed, and for the second time in little more than a year, A.J. was called on to serve as a pallbearer for one of those closest to him.

The next night in a CART meeting back at the Speedway Motel, Foyt asked for more time to try and broker a deal with USAC. He was still talking with King. However, there was little other support for continued discussions, and in the end, he "more or less reluctantly" agreed to make the vote unanimous. He also defended CART's leadership.[50]

"It was harder for me to make the vote than anyone else in the room. But I don't feel like we're doing the wrong thing. I feel this is definitely in the best interest of auto racing. Everyone seems to think this is a Patrick/Penske powerplay, but it's not at all. Everyone in here today had an equal voice in what we were going to do and I think it's going to be a good organization."[51]

The Speedway was the wild card. IMS President and USAC board member, Joe Cloutier, voted against the CART proposal and said USAC would continue to sanction the 500. At the same time, he said CART drivers would be permitted to race if they had an FIA license. In its own attempt to lower racing costs, Cloutier said the Speedway would change its rules to make the much-cheaper stock block engines more competitive.

CART said it would join with the Sports Car Club of America (SCCA) to secure the necessary FIA licenses for its drivers. Through it all, both sides were careful not to criticize IMS, with Foyt stressing, "We have no problems with the Speedway."

That was about to change.

GILMORE
14

CHAPTER 2

A.J. AND THE SEVEN DWARFS

1979

A.J. Foyt's dalliance with CART lasted a little more than two months, and when they broke up, they did so in spectacular fashion.

Roger Penske, Pat Patrick, Dan Gurney, and the other CART leaders knew from the start that Foyt's support was tenuous at best, his tendency to flip-flop positions well established. They catered to him whenever possible, holding the first meeting of the new year on January 4 in Houston—which Foyt hosted—and scheduling the next one around the January 20 USAC awards banquet in Indianapolis, where A.J. would be honored as stock car champion.

Foyt had continued to talk with USAC and Indianapolis Motor Speedway management and was probably the only one who thought a compromise was still possible in early January. He wanted additional discussions to be held and planned to ask for more time at the Indianapolis meeting. He made it no further than Memphis, however, where weather grounded his flight. Another board member, Chaparral team owner Jim Hall, found himself stuck in Tulsa.

"I called Patrick and asked if we could have another meeting in three or four days so Jim and I could be present," Foyt said later. "Patrick started saying, 'We gotta go forward' and that we couldn't have another that soon. I said we'd agreed to have 100 percent representation and that if I wasn't going to get mine, then maybe I'd see you cats later. Patrick said, 'If you want to stay, fine, and if you want to leave, fine.'" Patrick later confirmed the conversation.[1]

Both sides announced schedules for the coming year, USAC with traditional races planned for Milwaukee, Trenton and Texas, along with 500-milers at Ontario, Pocono, and Indianapolis. CART set two races at the Penske-owned

◀ The Parnelli race car and Cosworth engine were Foyt's choices for the 1979 Indy 500. *John Mahoney*

Michigan track and two at Phoenix, run by another CART member. Other races were in the planning stage. Penske, who'd been tagged "The Captain" by *Sports Illustrated* after Captain Bligh of *Mutiny on the Bounty* fame, showed he was willing to play hardball. Dipping into CART's $15 million war chest, he bought a two-year lease at Trenton, switching the races there to CART from USAC. CART also scheduled the events to go up against USAC's Milwaukee dates and announced NBC would televise the Trenton races.

"I'm only a conscientious guy who, when I get involved, I want to do whatever I can to make it go," said Penske, who was emerging as a driving force behind CART. "I'm doing whatever I can on a professional basis and in good faith with the car owners."[2]

It was all too much for Foyt. On January 31, he submitted a letter of resignation to Patrick.

"The original goals of CART were to improve the benefits for the car owners and to form a more workable relationship with the USAC board of directors on things like rules and specifications," the letter read. "I think now those goals have changed considerably. I don't think CART should be sanctioning races and promoting its own races. The USAC board has been responsive to the requirements of the car owners and other participants and is going to put more control into the hands of the participants and people who are involved on a day-to-day basis."[3]

Foyt told Dick Mittman of the *Indianapolis News*, "I thought the deal with CART was not to go out and buy racetracks and conquer the world. I just feel I've been with USAC for many years (since 1957) and I wasn't going to throw it down the drain. There were too many quick decisions."[4]

He doubted the two groups would reconcile, especially after he left. "I'm doing what I think is best for my business and racing. I don't need racing anymore, but I love it. I have no quarrels with anybody. Parnelli and I talked about it. I talked to most everybody by phone. I imagine I'll get bad-mouthed, but I'm sorry."

The bad mouthing started almost immediately. Robin Miller wrote an article in the *Indianapolis Star* quoting an anonymous CART member saying Foyt had "bailed out" because he had failed to perform his assignment, which was to "take care of the Speedway." Another speculated Foyt may have been an "undercover agent" for USAC. A.J. immediately shot back.[5]

"I asked two or three questions that I already knew the answers to and received flat-assed lies," he said. "They used me to get CART formed and now there are only one or two guys doing all the talking. They're on an ego trip and they want to conquer the racing world, but I have no desire to do that."

The cloud hanging over the USAC/CART civil war followed Foyt to Daytona. Most of the NASCAR crowd were amused by the battle between the two open-wheel groups.

"I got snowed by CART," Foyt said during a prerace press conference. "I originally split from USAC because they were giving drivers a bad time, but I probably made a mistake by joining the opposition. And when I found out I wasn't in agreement with what CART stands for, I withdrew my directorship and went back to USAC."[6]

He called Penske "a heck of a salesman" but also a "flim-flam" man who "is on an ego trip—he's for one person, himself. He's made a mistake and should be man enough to admit it. I made a mistake by jumping and I'm telling everybody that I was wrong.

"If things don't straighten out," he warned, "this could set back championship racing by ten years."[7]

On the racetrack he turned in the eighth-fastest qualifying time in a new Hutcherson-Pagan-built Oldsmobile. He found himself drafting and pushing leader Darrell Waltrip late in the second of two qualifying races when a caution flag slowed the field.

"He pulled up beside me," Waltrip said of Foyt. "Gave me one of those 'I promise I won't pass you' looks. Let's draft to the finish.' I didn't fall for that. I know how crafty ol' A.J. is."[8]

"I've had to race against him before. He's a sly old devil."[9]

On the last lap, Foyt went high going into the third turn in an attempt to pass Waltrip. He was expecting the third-place car, driven by a rookie named Dale Earnhardt, to follow and help push him past Waltrip. Earnhardt went low instead, making his own run for the lead. Ultimately, both cars dropped back, Foyt finishing second and Earnhardt fading to fourth.

An upset Foyt refused to talk with reporters afterward, while Earnhardt admitted making a mistake. "I should have had second," he said. "It was just a miscalculation on my part."[10]

In the Daytona 500, being televised live for the first time, Foyt led a few laps early but was running about thirty seconds behind race leaders Donnie Allison and Cale Yarborough near the end. He was having his own little battle with Richard Petty and Waltrip, the threesome swapping positions nearly every lap, while Allison and Yarborough ran nose to tail.

Going down the backstraight on the final lap, Yarborough made his move for the lead, and Allison tried to block him. The two leaders banged together several times and slammed into the third turn wall before sliding down to the inside of the track.

Petty, Waltrip, and Foyt didn't see the leaders crash, and when the yellow lights flashed on, Foyt hesitated momentarily, forgetting that at the time, stock cars—unlike Indy cars—raced back to the start/finish line when a caution was displayed. The hesitation allowed Petty and Waltrip to pull away, and without drafting help, Waltrip was unable to get past Petty at the finish line. A lap later, Foyt and the rest of the world were treated to the sight of Yarborough fighting with the Allison brothers.

"*Oh, crap! I just blew this,*" Foyt would later recall thinking. "That's one I really screwed up. I was used to the yellow coming out in USAC. Normally when you see the yellow, you'd better back off or you could be killed pretty easily."[11]

The 1979 USAC season started with a March 11 stock car race at Texas. Foyt was dominant, qualifying on the pole and leading ninety-five of 125 laps on his way to victory. The same day, twenty-one drivers turned out for the first CART race at Phoenix. Gordon Johncock emerged as a controversial winner when there was confusion about how many laps had been run. Even Johncock said he thought Al Unser was the winner.

True to his word, Foyt skipped the IROC finale the following weekend at Atlanta, Mario Andretti taking the title. He also decided not to run in the NASCAR race, not wanting to deal with the media about the off-track happenings.

In an effort to slow the cars and provide a "NASCAR finish" for fans, USAC decided to greatly reduce boost levels for its first Indy car race of the year, which was held March 22 at Ontario and run as part of an Indy car/stock car double-header. V8-powered cars would be allowed fifty inches of boost, while four-cylinder machines were given fifty-eight inches. Twenty-six Indy cars turned out, but few of the drivers had ever won a major event. One reporter dubbed the entries, "A.J. and the Seven Dwarfs."[12]

Despite expectations that defending race champion Danny Ongais, defending USAC champion Tom Sneva, and a few other CART drivers would race at Ontario, none showed up—amid rumors they'd been pressured to skip the event. After taking the pole position for both races, Foyt slammed the missing owners and teams and, for the first time, suggested the dissidents be blocked from racing at Indianapolis.

"By not running here they hoped they would bring Ontario to its knees," Foyt said of CART's leadership. "Their attitude is detrimental to racing and that's our livelihood. They are not showing any support for our sport. As far as I'm concerned, I would like to see Indy turn down their entries. How do you think their sponsors would like that?[13]

"The ones I feel sorry for are Danny, Rick Mears and Tom Sneva. I know Danny and Rick would rather be racing here, it's in their own backyard. And you know Tom has been talking about reduced speeds for a long time. They're not here because someone is putting a lot of pressure on them."

Foyt was just getting warmed up:

> I can hear them saying, "Yeah, A.J. would like us to miss Indy 'cause it would give it to him." Well that's a lot of bull. A.J. doesn't duck anyone. I've beat the whole lot of them more than they've beat me. I've beat 'em on their own tracks, at their own game, in midgets, sprints, stocks, Indy, Europe too.
>
> They'll probably say "A.J.'s on an ego trip," too, but that's a lot of bull, too. My days are numbered. I'm forty-four and there can't be too many years left. The truth is I'd rather stay out of the limelight. Life was a heck of a lot simpler when I was running midgets, drinking beer and getting in fights at Ascot. In those days I didn't have to explain to the press everything I did.
>
> But I don't mind talking about what CART is trying to do to USAC and racing in general. They're hurting people like Ray Smartis (Ontario general manager). He has the most beautiful racing facility anywhere and has struggled for years to keep it going to give racing a showplace and now

> these CART guys are trying to put him out of business. Why not give them some of their own medicine and keep them out of Indy?

Despite claiming he had to "work [his] butt off," Foyt became the first driver to sweep both ends of a doubleheader on the same day and did so in dominating fashion in front of twenty thousand fans. Those who thought he might let others lead or even win one of the races didn't know him. Afterward, he was about as subdued as anyone could remember following a victory.

"They should have been here," he said of the other teams. "I think it's a farce. This doesn't do anybody any good. If anything will drive me out of racing, it's hassles like this. In the long run, everybody is going to lose."[14]

Miller tried to lighten the mood, writing an April 1 column saying Foyt had bought the Speedway for $20,000 and among other changes, was replacing track president Joe Cloutier with race queen Linda Vaughn. Despite several references to it being April Fool's Day, the nuance was missed by many and led to clarification articles over the next few days.[15]

It was more of the same two weeks later at Texas, although Foyt changed cars, pulling a Coyote out of storage for the race. He led eighty-three of one hundred laps, giving up the front spot only during pit stops. A late caution period made it close at the end, with Foyt winning by only a car length over Gary Bettenhausen in what would be the last victory for a Coyote race car and the Foyt powerplant. Afterward, A.J. again urged the Speedway to bar the CART teams. "I think that will bring them to their knees when Indy turns them down," he said. "I don't lose any sleep over them."[16]

While he wasn't losing any sleep, he certainly was attracting their rage. Johncock, once a good friend who had credited Foyt with helping him win his first 500 in 1973, was particularly outspoken:

> I don't think very much of what he did. He was one of the founders of CART, a ringleader. Then he defects. Why? Now there is no question that he can get away with whatever he wants to in USAC. Without him, there would be no USAC and that's a weapon he holds over their head. Foyt has always gotten away with a lot in USAC. Now he can get away with everything and maybe he figured he would go back to them and be king again, win his fifth Indianapolis 500 and then retire.[17]
>
> Foyt never won a race in NASCAR when he was driving his own car. Sure, he has won with his own car in USAC, but that's because he always intimidated everybody. Now he is really happy. He has a situation in USAC where if his car doesn't break, he has a 100 percent chance of winning every race.

Initially, Speedway management said they weren't considering barring CART teams from competing in the 500. It seemed a moot point, however, when Patrick said, "As of now we do not intend to enter the Indianapolis 500." CART was demanding boost pressure be returned to seventy pounds for V8 engines and that the race have joint USAC/CART inspection officials. None of the CART teams had filed an entry as the April 15 deadline approached, and Patrick threatened to hold a million-dollar race on the same day as the 500, most likely at Penske's Michigan International Speedway.[18]

"They've already got a hell of a lot of power, there's no doubt about that," an anonymous USAC spokesperson said of the CART leadership. "And they love the feeling of power. To them, the sky's the limit now. If they try to force a showdown with the Speedway, it would be sickening."

With the possibility of CART teams skipping the Indy 500, Foyt filed four entries to help fill the field if necessary, including a pair of Parnelli-Cosworth machines, backed by two Coyotes with Foyt engines.

CART blinked first, with forty-four cars entering as a group on April 12, bringing the total entries to a record 102. Patrick said he would continue to press the organization's demands and that it was no guarantee its drivers would compete in the race. Johncock, for one, wasn't backing down.

"I don't see how they (USAC) can survive," he said. "It's just a matter of time before they're out and gone. The sooner the better as far as I'm concerned.[19]

"My biggest concern is with officiating. They gave A.J. two races last year. They let him cheat. In both, he was supposed to be one lap down but they gave the laps back to him. They're going to go on doing that at the Speedway. If he had sixty gallons of fuel in his tank, they'd let him do it. I think he's laughing about it now, but the shoe's gonna be on the other foot before too long."

Al Unser joined in: "What I worry most about is that I'll be leading the race with five laps to go and out will come the black flag. There's no way USAC is going to let one of us win that race if they can help it."[20]

It didn't take Foyt long to fire back: "Those CART guys are just a bunch of people trying to take over racing. They're hot at me because if I think something's wrong, I say it and go my own way. I don't run with the pack."[21]

Behind the scenes negotiations continued, and on April 17, Penske, Patrick, USAC President Dick King, and the Speedway's Chief Steward Tom Binford met privately in Detroit. They reached tentative agreement on the formation of a new entity to be known as the Indy Car Series. The board would be made up of four CART car owners and four others selected by USAC who could not be drivers, mechanics, or race organizers. USAC would sanction all races beginning in 1980. The board would manage all aspects of the series, including rules, purses, scheduling, and television negotiations.

Patrick, who would be the first chair of the new board, was so confident a deal had been worked out he told a previously planned press luncheon the next day in New York City the CART teams would definitely race at Indianapolis and there should be no more talk of a boycott or a competing race.[22]

Those reassurances had little impact on the USAC Board of Directors when they met in an emergency session to discuss the proposal April 19 at the organization's headquarters down the street from the Speedway. Only fifteen of the twenty-one board members were present, and USAC Chairman Reynold MacDonald took the unusual step of inviting Foyt to attend the meeting, even though he had no standing with the board, saying it was in the "best interest" of USAC.[23]

The Indy Car Series agreement was discussed, but with Binford oddly one of those missing, there was no one to champion the proposal, and there was no motion for approval. Instead, the representatives expressed concern that CART would boycott the 500, or perhaps qualify then demand rule changes, painting USAC into a corner. Board member and car owner Rolla Vollstedt motioned that the entries of six CART ringleaders—Penske, Patrick, Hall, Gurney, Bob Fletcher, and Team McLaren—be rejected. Foyt then spoke to the group, telling them, "Now is the time to act. USAC must take a stand. I'm in favor of rejecting the entries."[24]

MacDonald, a business owner who worked with many in the auto industry, resigned his position, stating possible conflicts of interest. Cloutier recused himself and left the room. The remaining board members voted 13–0 to reject the six entries.

The CART teams were gathering in Atlanta on Friday, April 20, to start practice for their second race of the year when word started to spread about the rejection, stating the teams were not "in good standing with USAC." NASCAR also weighed in, indicating the CART drivers wouldn't be welcome at the Charlotte stock car race being held the same day as the Indy 500.

The banned CART teams filed suit in Indianapolis, claiming the action violated the Sherman Antitrust Act and saying, "It's just like when A.J. Foyt jumped ship and went back to USAC, it's making us stronger." Foyt was named to the list of defendants along with USAC, IMS, and several other USAC car owners and drivers. The CART teams were later joined in the suit by its drivers, Johnny Rutherford, Johncock, Wally Dallenbach, Mears, Mike Mosley, Steve Krisiloff, and Al and Bobby Unser.

USAC argued the drivers had not been banned from the race and should not be included, but U.S. District Court Judge James E. Noland ruled otherwise, implying they needed the teams in order to make a living. The inclusion of the drivers proved to be a key addition to the suit.

Al Unser, Rutherford and Dallenbach all testified in court, and Noland ruled the drivers "had the right to work" and that USAC could not arbitrarily "keep these men from making a living. Because of the irreparable harm that could be suffered by these drivers—the keystones of these teams—there is no way the driver plaintiffs can sit out the Indianapolis 500." Noland ordered the entries of the six CART teams reinstated.[25]

"I felt like I was on death row," Rutherford said when the ruling came in. He added he had no hard feelings toward Foyt. "I've never considered A.J. anything but a friend."[26]

Although Foyt's deposition was entered into evidence, he wasn't called to testify. Instead, he was in Louisville for the Kentucky Derby and to watch three of his horses run in support events. Gallant Reward and Barbizon's Flower both placed in their races, although the third, Grand Entry, finished out of the money. Foyt ignored reporter attempts to reach him for comments on the Indianapolis ruling while at the Derby, but when he returned to the Speedway, it was clear A.J.'s feelings toward Rutherford weren't mutual.

"I don't consider that S.O.B a friend," he said when told of Rutherford's comment. "Him and Gordy, either one. I'll run across them later.[27]

"Indianapolis and USAC made those drivers what they are today and they turned against them. They were telling lies on themselves. You're not going to fool the racing public. They know what goes on. My baby child could beat most of them. It's awful for someone who didn't care about Indianapolis. They went to court and cried like babies. It's got where it's a pain in the ass to go racing. It's bitch, bitch, bitch."

When asked about Johncock's implication that Foyt opposed the CART teams and drivers because it would make it easier to win his fifth 500, he laughed. "Yeah, that's why I've beaten them so much more than they've beaten me, because I'm so scared of them.[28]

"They didn't want to run here in the first place. They can't back up any of their statements. They all blame this thing on me, but I didn't have a vote."

Foyt was only slightly less controversial on the track when, on his first day of practice, he turned a lap of more than 194 miles per hour, easily the fastest of the month and faster than anyone thought possible with the fifty-pound boost limit.

He refused to say what level his pop-off valve had been set at and called continued complaints about limits "hogwash. It makes no difference if you're satisfied with it or not, you've gotta try new things to find out. When the boost was seventy-five inches, they said raise it to eighty inches. Then they don't want any limit. One day it's this and one day it's that. Most of them don't even know what a piston is."

Only Mears, who'd been the fastest all month, didn't seem upset by Foyt's lap. "If I'm going to get beat out by anyone, it's an honor to get beat by A.J. That's just going to make us work harder."[29]

No one was going to beat Mears when official qualifications opened, as he turned in a four-lap average of 193.736 mph, six mph slower than the year before. Foyt was sixth fastest. He complained about engine problems but had nice things to say about Mears.

"He didn't look like a rookie today. He's one of those guys who will be the Foyts and Unsers of the 1980s."[30]

Turns out the teams of Foyt, Mears, and pretty much everyone else had found a way to override the pop-off valve during qualifying—not exactly illegal, but not in the spirit of the rules either. USAC tried to tighten the regulations and inspection process for the second weekend of qualifications and several teams were disqualified. When it was over, those teams filed a protest, saying they hadn't done anything different than what was done the first weekend.

When at first the protests were denied, the teams threatened to file suit seeking reinstatement for the cars. A compromise of sorts was worked out, allowing the cars one more qualifying attempt. If they matched or bettered the speed of the thirty-third starter, they'd be added to the field. One appeal, filed by rookie car owner Wayne Woodward, arrived after the deadline, and when it was denied, he filed suit in Marion County Superior Court, asking that the race be stopped unless his car was allowed another qualifying attempt.

While the final Carb Day practice was going on at the Speedway, Judge Michael T. Dugan agreed to hear the case, then granted the Speedway's request to add the qualified drivers and car owners to the suit. Summons were issued for all thirty-three drivers to appear in court Friday morning, and officers of the court were dispatched to the Speedway to serve the drivers.

Major Ronald L. Chappell of the Marion County Sheriff Department headed up the operation and took on the challenge of serving Foyt. It didn't go well, according to an *Indianapolis Star* reporter: "Chappell, armed with the summons, approached Foyt, held out the summons and said, 'A.J., this is . . .' and before he could finish Foyt slapped the summons from Chappell's hand and told him where he should place the document."[31]

Chappell said later if the race wasn't scheduled for Sunday, he probably would have arrested Foyt for disorderly conduct. "I really restrained myself because this is the '500' and I can understand their strain." Ongais escaped on his bicycle to avoid a summons, nearly running down a server in the process.

"It used to be fun," Foyt told a reporter while hiding in his garage. "You'd just go out there and settle your differences right on the track. Now forty lawyers would come running up to you like a bunch of jerks. Lawyers and judges ruin this country."[32]

When neither Foyt nor Ongais were on hand for the start of proceedings Friday morning, Dugan issued contempt of court citations and ordered bench warrants for their arrest. Ongais turned himself in by noon, and the contempt charge was dismissed. Ironically, Dugan also dismissed Woodward's original lawsuit for which the summons had been issued.

Foyt was on the lam, having driven to Louisville Friday morning to watch his horses run. One of his crew members heard about the arrest warrant on the radio and contacted Donald Bringgold, a high-profile Beverly Hills defense lawyer who was in Indianapolis to attend his thirty-first 500. He was also a friend of Foyt's, having drafted contracts for him in the past. It wasn't easy, but Bringgold convinced A.J. the warrant was serious and he could find himself in jail at race time if he didn't return immediately. Foyt headed to the airport and chartered a plane for a quick flight back.

Foyt arrived at about 2:20 p.m. As Bringgold began apologizing to the court on the driver's behalf, the judge cut him off. He wanted to hear personally from Foyt, who wasn't exactly contrite when asked why he shouldn't be held in contempt for slapping the summons away.

"All this nonsense and harassment that has been going on, you get a lot of people walking up and saying I'm so and so and this and that," Foyt said under oath. "So I've learned to ignore a lot of it. You know, because I was trying to get to the garage. I was mobbed with a whole bunch of people.

Dugan asked, "As far as you're concerned, Mr. Foyt, you didn't do anything wrong yesterday, is that right?"

"Well, in my opinion, no," Foyt responded. "I didn't really feel that I did."

After a little more back-and-forth, Dugan seemed to give up, saying, "Under the circumstances, I'm not going to make any finding of contempt."

Told later about Foyt's comment that lawyers and judges were ruining the country, Dugan thought for a moment and said, "You know, he's probably right."

By race morning, Foyt expressed the feelings of many when he said, "In all my years, I have never seen anything so screwed up. All this has set racing back ten years. Who cares? The public doesn't give a damn. My crew doesn't give a damn. And I don't give a damn. I don't care if I run two laps or 200."[33]

When the race finally took the green flag, Al Unser, driving Jim Hall's new ground-effect Chaparral, dominated early. Foyt was running comfortably in the top five when on lap ninety-four he stalled the car on a pit stop and was nearly lapped by Unser.

"That was my mistake," he'd say later. "I killed the engine in the pits, lost the time and then I had to start running as hard as I could."[34]

He caught a break when Unser dropped out with a busted transmission a few laps later. Penske teammates Mears and Bobby Unser moved to the front and started to swap the lead. When Bobby was slowed with a transmission problem of his own fifteen laps from the finish, Mears took over with Foyt second, still nearly a lap behind. A late yellow flag and a new rule allowing cars to bunch up under caution put Foyt within striking distance, although there were seventeen cars between him and the leader. Still, he was the legendary Super Tex.

"I knew Foyt was back there somewhere," Mears would say. "I wasn't going to forget about him." He needn't worry as Foyt was experiencing his own problems.[35]

"There was no way I could get him," said Foyt, who was the only USAC driver in the top five. "I lost a cylinder or something on my last pit stop and the engine went sour from there. I was just glad to finish second. On the last lap that S.O.B quit. I was just so damn happy to get across that finish line."[36]

As he coasted past the checkered flag to the loudest cheers of the day, Foyt clasped both hands above his helmet and wiped his "brow," rolling to a stop before the first turn.

He had high praise for Mears, saying, "He's one of the fine, upcoming drivers. He drove a great race today and stayed out of trouble and I'm just real glad for Rick."[37]

He'd also say later, "If the engine don't stall on me I could have won easily."[38]

With the 500 over, the question was, what happens now? Much depended on what Foyt decided to do. Both series planned races for June 10. USAC had its traditional date at Milwaukee and CART at Trenton. Not only was the Trenton race in direct opposition to Milwaukee, it was in the same geographic market as Pocono, which was scheduled to hold its annual 500-mile race at the end of the month. ABC would televise Milwaukee, while CART had failed to land a network for Trenton.

Only six entries for the Milwaukee race had been received a few days after the 500, and the race was in doubt until Foyt said he'd be in the field. Entries began to flow in, and ticket sales jumped.

Nineteen cars started the race, but there was little competition for Foyt. Despite complaining about the flu, he qualified on the pole and led 123 of the 150 laps on his way to victory. It was a better race at Trenton, where Bobby Unser edged brother Al. Milwaukee counted more than 18,000 spectators, while the Trenton crowd was put at about 15,000.

It was clear afterward that as long as USAC had Foyt in an event, it could attract a crowd and stage a race. Despite having a sparse and uncompetitive field and 12,000 fewer fans than the year before, most felt USAC had won the weekend battle.

Smartis, the Ontario track general manager Foyt had gone to bat for earlier in the year, then reached out to CART in an attempt to broker a deal. Penske, who considered holding the Trenton 500 (kilometers) the same day as Pocono and honoring tickets originally sold for the Pennsylvania track, backed off and said no competing race would be held "as a good faith move." Pocono's Dr. Joseph "Doc" Mattioli wasn't impressed.[39]

"If that's an olive branch, it's the thorniest branch I've ever seen," he said. "I could care less if they ran or not. They've caused more confusion and commotion and everything and have hurt the sport of auto racing. If they don't stop their public relations nonsense, well, they're not the kind of people I want to do business with."

Penske's move also saved CART the embarrassment of having one of its key members, Ongais and backer Ted Field, skipping a race to run in the Music 500 at Pocono. Sponsor Panasonic wanted its car in the race that featured three nights of music concerts, and Ongais just wanted to race.

Ongais—Foyt's quasi Parnelli teammate—was fast becoming a fan favorite. Notoriously reclusive, the Hawaiian born Ongais had come from the drag racing ranks, where he'd been a Funny Car champion. He'd connected with Field—a would-be driver, budding media mogul, and heir to the Marshall Field fortune—and went road racing in 1977. With backing from Field's company, Interscope, he graduated to sports cars and then Indy cars. Danny "On-the-Gas" always drove on the edge, and if he didn't win or break, his race often ended in a massive crash.

At first it appeared some of the other CART teams and drivers would race at Pocono. Mattioli tried to broker a deal for Andretti, who lived within commuting distance of the track, to drive Foyt's second entry. Andretti had a rare off weekend from defending his Formula One World Championship or driving for Penske in CART.

"I was hoping Mario would be here," Foyt said after arriving at the track. "I brought a brand new car for him." Andretti, however, said he wanted to stay neutral.[40]

"If I was to run for Foyt it would add sparks to the fire," Andretti said.[41]

In another article he added,

> It would only strengthen USAC, at least for one race. I don't want to be in that position. I hate it I'm not going to be racing at Pocono. I mean, I really hate it. Some of the things I've seen make me sick. Some of this

> crap is done for petty reasons, by people who never contribute anything constructive, but run to the press to air our dirty laundry and get their faces on TV. I refuse to get involved. I've told all of them, Roger, Patrick, King, that there has got to be a compromise. It's not realistic to continue to go along against each other. The further apart they get as the season progresses, the worse it becomes.[42]

When a last-minute effort to put Tom Sneva in A.J.'s second car failed, Foyt captured the pole, although Ongais was able to make it close. Janet Guthrie made the most news with her fourth-place qualifying run. With Ongais refusing to answer anything more than cursory media questions and skipping the front-row picture, it was left to Foyt to hold court. He seemed more than happy to oblige.

"All those veteran drivers at CART better come to their senses," he said. "They're a bunch of old men like me, and will be gone from the racing scene in five years." He was especially hard on Johncock, his new favorite target. "Gordie made some derogatory statements about USAC after they saved his hide when he was broke and they let him run. He's been out of line with his statements. In fact, he's so dumb he can't even sign his name."[43]

Bored of the USAC/CART discussion, Foyt—who always stayed up on the news of the day—led reporters in a different direction, sharing his views on everything from the latest oil crisis, inflation, recession, President Jimmy Carter, and the war in Nicaragua where reporter Bill Stewart had just been killed.

"That television correspondent had no business being in Nicaragua. If Roone Arledge [ABC news chief who had been an early supporter of televising auto racing] wanted the civil war covered down there he should have gone himself."

On Carter, Foyt commented, "I don't think he could teach Lassie to sit." Foyt said the rise in oil prices was a rip-off and that he'd sold his oil wells because he couldn't make a profit. He wondered if toothpaste was the cause of the rise in cancer. But he saved his biggest attacks for the legal system.

"A guy walked in my dealership and said, 'I was feelin' fine, a guy honked a horn, I jumped and hurt my back.' He took me to court and beat me for $10,000. And they showed that the man never laid off from work for two days, never really went to the doctors and yet the goddamn judge awarded it. I appealed it three times, and I lost every time. That's what tees me off about the law."[44]

When the on-track action finally started, Ongais led early and was still hounding Foyt when he dropped out about one hundred miles from the finish. When his only remaining challenger, Larry Dickson, ran out of fuel three laps from the end, Foyt cruised to a two-lap victory over Jim McElreath in a five-year-old Eagle-Offy.

Instead of seeing Penske's offer not to challenge the Pocono race as an olive branch, USAC took it as a sign of weakness and offered a new proposal. The technical issues were not the hangup. The issue was power, and USAC proposed a board made up of five of its members plus five from CART and track management from Indianapolis, Ontario, and Pocono—clearly tilting control in USAC's favor. In another move, the Speedway announced that invitations to its 1980 race would include a commitment to compete in the other 500-mile events at Ontario and Pocono and that it would be run according to USAC regulations. It was clear the war would continue.

As a result, and despite more than 50,000 spectators turning out at Pocono, Smartis announced a few days later that the Labor Day Ontario 500 would be sanctioned by CART rather than USAC, although USAC drivers and teams would be invited to compete. Foyt, who was in Daytona where he finished eighth in the Firecracker 400, wasn't interested:

> I felt all along that Ontario would go CART because Penske and those other guys had to run a 500-mile race. They flat had to. Penske is really running CART. Patrick isn't that smart about racing.[45]
>
> I race because I like it and for the betterment of the sport. When you have to buy people to get races, I'm not interested. They had to make a deal with Smartis to get that race. They offered him a seat on their board. He sold out the other two tracks (Indianapolis and Pocono). They all three had agreed to stay together. There's no doubt in my mind that Roger Penske and Pat Patrick told Ontario it wouldn't have to put up the money for the race until they get the people in.

Even though Smartis denied the accusations and would never be placed on the CART board, Foyt wouldn't budge. Instead, he looked into leasing the Indianapolis Motor Speedway for a Labor Day weekend race. Both the Speedway and USAC gave the proposal serious consideration. The plan called for a pair of 250-mile races—one for Indy cars and one for stock cars—with ticket prices set at five to ten dollars. The idea lasted only a few days when Foyt pulled out, saying it would only make things worse. He refused to go to Ontario, although several USAC drivers did compete. He also warned if the two groups didn't get together soon, "our sport is going to fall apart."[46]

He returned at Texas, where he dominated again over a USAC field of just sixteen Indy cars on July 29. Two weeks later at Milwaukee, on what would turn out to be the last USAC Indy car event of the year, he led the first half of the 200-lap race before dropping out with a fuel pump problem. No matter—he'd already wrapped up his seventh Indy car championship.

He turned his attention to the USAC stock car circuit, and for a while it was like old times, running four races in ten days with a handful of crewmen. He won back-to-back races at Milwaukee and another on the dirt at the Illinois State Fairgrounds in Springfield. The race at Springfield was stopped at one point for excessive dust, and the track watered it down. When it was restarted, Foyt was the lone driver willing to run the high groove, and although he fell back at first, he was soon running rings around everyone else on his way to perhaps his most satisfying victory of the year.

Repeating as stock car champion was proving more of a challenge than Foyt expected. He was facing a strong crop of rookie drivers led by a cocky Rusty Wallace and Kenny Schrader. Needing points, Foyt entered the next race on the schedule at Du Quoin. He'd won his first race on a mile dirt track there in 1960 and seven more since, although he hadn't raced at the track in four years. Both Wallace and Schrader were making their first starts at the "Magic Mile."

"I was here ten years ago to watch and Foyt won it," Wallace said at the time. He'd met Foyt the previous year and tried to spend as much time with him as he could during practice. "Last year he didn't seem like too nice a guy, he seemed kind of mean. But this year I get along with him real well. I tried to pick up as many pointers as I could without butting in the way."[47]

Foyt qualified on the pole, with Wallace back in eighth. Schrader, who'd been too nervous to approach Foyt, started third.

"Going down the back straightaway at the start, I ever, ever, *ever* so gently bumped his car," Schrader recalled, "just so if I never got to really talk to him or race with him again, I had a story I could tell. I bumped A.J. at Du Quoin!"[48]

Foyt faded to fourth at the finish and Wallace came on to win—his first on the USAC circuit. Asked if he felt guilty about beating the man who helped him learn the track, Wallace said, "I don't feel guilty about nothin'. All I can think about is winning the big 250-mile USAC race in Milwaukee."

Wallace did win at Milwaukee and picked up a bunch of points after Foyt dropped out with engine problems. When Foyt skipped the next two short-track events and Wallace did well, it set up a finale between the drivers on November 11 at Texas with the championship at stake. The race was also open to NASCAR drivers.

Wallace had a chance to do something Foyt had never accomplished—win a championship and rookie-of-the-year honors in the same season. Reporters fawned over the brash twenty-three-year-old who'd come to dethrone the king, and Wallace was happy to oblige, saying Foyt was the best stock car driver in the world. But he didn't stop there:

"We used to talk friendly, but after I beat him at Du Quoin, he wouldn't talk to me," Wallace said. "Then I beat him again at Milwaukee and he talked even less. I was beating him bad, gaining a good fifty feet on each lap. There was no doubt that we had the fastest car that day."[49]

"I just want to win. I think I can beat A.J. this time because I've done it before. I *had* the drive to beat A.J., but it's gone now since I've done it. The way I figure it, the pressure is all on him. He always tries harder to win at home. I'll beat him and [Bobby] Allison and all of them. I'm coming to Texas to win the national championship."[50]

Foyt qualified on the pole with Wallace second. He led from the start with Wallace not far behind but never leading, engine problems soon knocking the rookie out. Foyt then turned back challenges from NASCAR's Bobby Allison and Richard Childress and was in command a few laps from the finish when he suddenly veered into the pits, Allison going on to win. Foyt immediately headed for his passenger car, but one reporter overheard him tell a crew member, "I could have won it easy, but I didn't want to have to go up there (the media center) and put up with all the crap from the press."[51]

Told of Foyt's comment, Allison, who still believed he beat Foyt in a previous race at the track, said he'd take the win any way he could get it.

"A.J. had his Irish up over the way the press was handling my involvement and that of Rusty Wallace," Allison said. "Rusty's a young man with a lot to say."[52]

Years later, Foyt admitted to stopping even though the car was running well.

"The crew asked me what happened, and I said it got hot. I got out and got ready to leave. Hutch (crew chief Dick Hutcherson) was mad at me. He said, 'You son of a bitch—you could have run another lap.' They wanted to know what to tell the press, and I said, 'You all explain it,' and then I got in my car and drove off. The press had bad-mouthed me, saying the younger drivers was going to do this and do that, so I just said, 'The hell with you.'"[53]

The season over, Foyt again retreated to his ranch. He'd won USAC titles in both Indy cars and stock cars, more than $345,000, five of seven Indy car races, and four more stock car events. Yet everything paled compared to the civil war ripping apart Indy car racing.

If Foyt had refused to join with CART in the beginning, it's unlikely the organization would have been strong enough to break with USAC and stage its own series. If he had stayed with CART and not returned to USAC, the organization would have emerged—for better or worse—in control of Indy car racing. Flip-flopping between the two, however, had allowed the war to continue causing long-term harm to the sport he loved.

Larry Foyt

While Foyt's comment at Indianapolis that "my baby child could beat most of them" in regard to other drivers was overlooked as hyperbole, there was an element of truth to the statement. A.J and Lucy—with the consent of their daughter, Terry—had adopted their two-year-old grandson, Larry. Terry had divorced Larry's father, country-western singer Larry Roberds.

Terry recalled the arrangement more than forty years later:

> Our son, Larry, was their first grandson, and they were very close. I was living out in the pool house behind my parents' house, and we were in there all the time. One day they said they'd like to legally give him our name for insurance and inheritance reasons. It's not like I wanted to give up my son, or anything like that. I had already gone back to the Foyt name, and I agreed to it because I thought it would benefit my son.[54]
>
> That's something I don't like to talk about too much. Everything turned out good for Larry—he's blessed. But there's a lot of stuff I feel like I missed, and it hurt a lot at times. But he's done remarkable, and I'm close to my son. Everything is good.

Larry also said he was "blessed" to have two sets of parents:

> I still have a relationship with my birth father, and I'm still close with my birth mother. But at that point Lucy and A.J. were my parents, and I grew up with them. A.J. laughs and says I was a mamma's boy, and I was just

super close with my mom Lucy. They really raised me, and I've been happy to call them mom and dad ever since.[55]

It was a pretty normal childhood. I do remember being young and being very proud of A.J.'s accomplishments. Whether it was the trophies or whatever. I would be wearing an AJ Foyt Racing shirt to school and just very proud of everything. A.J. was still traveling a lot, but when he was home, he was still very intense. He ruled very sternly—you didn't want to be in trouble. I think that kept me being a good kid for the most part.

14

CHAPTER 3

DEATH AT DAYTONA

1980

As the two Indy car organizations continued their war into the new year, it paled compared to the challenges the country and most Americans were facing. Iranian students and revolutionary guards had seized the American Embassy in Tehran and taken fifty-three people hostage. President Jimmy Carter struggled with how to respond, finally imposing an embargo on Iranian oil. Gas prices rose as a result, and several states started rationing gasoline. The stock market was in shambles, interest rates were skyrocketing, and unemployment was on the rise.

Yet the war between the two American open-wheel racing groups went on despite those and other warning signs. Perhaps most alarming, attendance at Indy car races had fallen by nearly a third the previous year while NASCAR's rose, and Formula One set a new record.

CART announced a thirteen-race schedule for 1980 called the "Indy Car World Series," with at least four of the races to be televised by NBC. The series landed a major sponsor when PPG, a supplier of paint for the domestic auto industry, signed a three-year contract and established a $500,000 driver point fund. CART leadership also made it clear there would be no race opposing the Indianapolis 500 and that its members expected to race at the Speedway on Memorial Day weekend. USAC countered with a ten-race schedule, although with few details.

A.J. Foyt's sponsor, Jim Gilmore, offered a ray of hope, saying the driver was playing an "instrumental" role in getting the two groups talking again. "The climate is good for reconciliation at this time," Gilmore said. "I feel confident that a workable agreement will be ready. The economy and other factors dictate it."[1]

◀ Foyt was forty-five years old and still running sprint cars on dirt in 1980.
John Mahoney

Gilmore spent several weeks with Foyt on the Texas ranch during the offseason. The sponsor had been hit hard by his wife's death, and when his drinking increased, Gilmore's children appealed for help, with Beth Gilmore asking A.J., "Can you do something for Dad?" Foyt put him to work on the ranch, and while it helped, Gilmore would continue to struggle in the years ahead.[2]

Despite Gilmore's hopeful words, Foyt was more cautious. "I would like everybody to come race with us in '80. Like I say, I've won just as much with 'em as I have without 'em. It makes no difference either way. I've raced with the best all over the world and haven't had to back up too much to the pay window."[3]

A meeting between Foyt and Pat Patrick, with Goodyear racing head Leo Mehl serving as a mediator, helped jumpstart the talks. Foyt thought an agreement had been reached and expected an announcement on January 30. The two sides would reunite under yet another new organization, the Championship Car Council, made up of three car owners from each group to oversee the sport. The CART schedule and $800,000 point fund would become part of the new organization. Foyt was stunned when USAC rejected the proposal, and—as he often did—took it personally. Furious he wasn't consulted before any decision was announced, he turned in his resignation, nearly a year to the day after he'd resigned from CART.

"It hurt me that USAC didn't consult me in the peace meetings and it hurt me that USAC didn't buy the proposal," he said. "There has to be a reason I was ignored, and it makes me wonder if maybe USAC didn't want to get back together.[4]

"I'm making no commitments to either group, but I've resigned from USAC. I'm going to run wherever I feel like and pick my races. I'll probably just run the important ones, like Indy, Pocono and Ontario."

USAC President Dick King took the brunt of Foyt's barrage. Their on-again, off-again relationship hit a new low.

"He feels bad we didn't ask him, but it's a fact that A.J. doesn't like to attend meetings," King said after their blistering hour-long phone call. "He even admitted that when we were talking. And it wasn't like he was being left out of anything because we've kept in touch the past month about what was happening. There's been a lot of water under the dam between A.J. and I and I'm just hoping he'll settle down and start thinking right.[5]

"But I'd never try to outguess that man."

Fed up with Indy car racing, Foyt headed for Daytona. "I might wanna run one NASCAR race, I might run ten," he said after arriving. He was asked if he would be accepted by the new breed of stock car drivers coming into the series. "I really don't know and I really don't give a shit," he said. "If you're a winner, you're accepted everywhere you go. If you're not a winner, you're just another race car driver."[6]

He'd brought the full team to Daytona. His father Tony was there, along with Jack Starne, Billy Woodruff, John Fisher, engine man Ron Puryear, and Tim Delrose. Car builder Dick Hutcherson had his own crew on hand and served as crew chief.

Despite the array of talent, things didn't go well. The No. 51 Oldsmobile was fast enough, but the engines just didn't last very long. Any hope of a pole position expired along with an engine. The next day Foyt ran a lap faster than pole winner Buddy Baker's speed, but then that engine stumbled too. In past years those kinds of problems might have caused an even greater explosion in Foyt, but he was surprisingly docile as he prepared for the qualifying race. He even defended his engine shop—sort of.

"We've really only blown that one engine," he pointed out, "but we've had trouble with three or four others." When asked about the engine used in qualifying, he shrugged. "That was just a qualifier. You expect to lose that engine."

At other times, he sounded ready to hang up his helmet:

> Hell, my days are over with—I've had my flings, set my records. I'm getting old. I've worked hard all my life to get where I am. I don't want to be, or have to be, tied up at some racetrack every weekend anymore. I'm tired of a lot of the hassles involved in racing. I'll race where the money's at. I'll race if I'm invited and if I'm not, I've got my horses and my businesses. I've got plenty to do without racing every weekend.[7]

He finished sixth in his qualifying race, earning him an eleventh starting position in the 500. Foyt was debriefing with his crew when the second qualifying race started. It wasn't long before an explosion reverberated through the garage area.

A Good Boy Gone

Although Ricky Knotts, twenty-eight and from Paw Paw, Michigan, was unknown to many in racing, he'd had his share of success. Like so many other drivers with a dream, he'd dominated the local dirt tracks near his home before moving on to the highly competitive ASA circuit, where he held his own against drivers like Rusty Wallace. He performed best on the high-speed short tracks, including Winchester, Indiana, where he bested Darrell Waltrip for a victory, and Toledo, Ohio, where he won over a field including Mark Martin.

Although he'd failed to qualify for NASCAR races at Michigan and Charlotte in the past, Knotts and his father Richard, a dealership salesman, had worked through the winter preparing their car. They hoped to make their first series start and Ricky's first start on a superspeedway in the Daytona 500—an incredible jump from Toledo.

Operating on the smallest of shoestring budgets, it was just the two of them and a friend who towed the orange-and-black No. 31 Oldsmobile on an open trailer to Daytona, where they hoped to pick up a volunteer pit crew if they were lucky enough to make the 500.

Despite failing to crack the top sixty in qualifying and being more than twenty miles per hour slower than pole sitter Donnie Allison, he was still guaranteed a spot in one of the two 125-mile qualifying events, which featured some of the hardest and most desperate racing of the year. The Knotts figured at the very least it would be good experience for Ricky, and an opportunity to compete against the best in the sport. Out of tires, his dad borrowed a used set from Foyt's team, which was parked nearby in the garage area.

It was quickly apparent that Knotts wouldn't be racing in the 500 as the leaders closed in to lap him and several other cars shortly after the start. Knotts was following Slick Johnson, who had four previous NASCAR starts, and was just ahead of Blackie Wangerin, who'd been competing at Daytona in various series for ten years. All three wanted to stay ahead of the fast-closing front-runners.

As they jockeyed for position, the Johnson and Knotts cars touched, and when the rookie driver backed off, he was hit by Wangerin, sending both cars spinning. Knotts's car glanced off the outside wall, then shot down the thirty-one-degree banking and across the grassy infield, picking up speed as it went. It slammed into the concrete barrier on the inside of the track, the impact lifting the car into the air and causing the explosion heard by Foyt and others.

Wangerin and Johnson had different views on what happened.

"We were drafting the slower car (Johnson)," Wangerin said. "We were going to go by on the outside, but he cut off the groove and put (Knotts) into the wall. There was no way I could miss hitting him."[8]

Johnson said Knotts, "nudged me on the right rear. You can see the yellow paint on my car. I looked up in the mirror and saw the cars spinning. He just ran out of racetrack."

Wangerin would say later the hood on Knotts's car may have popped up just before the accident, blinding the young driver and possibly causing the wreck.

The listless body of Knotts was pulled from the car and taken to the infield care center, where he was soon pronounced dead of "massive head injuries."

While the second impact had been out of view for everyone in the garage and pit area and most in the stands, it was caught by television cameras and shown repeatedly in the press box. A film of the second impact from a different angle was considered so vicious that the footage was destroyed.

Race winner Donnie Allison was shaken when told Knotts was dead.

"I didn't know," he said. "I knew he had been in a pretty bad wreck because I saw the car. But I didn't know he was dead."[9]

"When you buckle up in these things, you have to accept that. All of us. That's part of it. Give my regards to the family."[10]

He was asked about Knotts's lack of experience, especially on a superspeedway.

"I've come to accept there are a lot of inexperienced drivers in these qualifying races," he said, choosing his words carefully so he didn't upset officials. "With the scheduling here, I don't think rookies have enough time to practice. They're nervous and when [they're] nervous it makes me nervous. It's a shame because sometimes a lot of it can be prevented.

"I guess it was just his day to go."

Nearby, a distraught Richard Knotts stood beside his son's destroyed race car, now covered by a black tarp.

"My son is dead," he said quietly to a group of reporters, not trying to hold back the tears. "I cannot believe my son is dead. I didn't think it was that bad.[11]

"He was a good boy. All he wanted was to be a Grand National Driver. He won't now. But he was never afraid. Never scared." They'd spent everything except return gas money to get to Daytona, and the father wondered aloud how he would get his son's body back to Paw Paw for burial, where Ricky, twenty-eight, had left a wife and daughter.

Knotts's death was the first in eight years at Daytona and a stark reminder of the dangers of the sport. The vicious nature of the crash and the fact that so little was known about Knotts left many reporters trying to answer one important question. Why?

"The image of his stock car striking an infield concrete wall haunts me to this day," wrote Godwin Kelly, the motorsports writer for the *Daytona Beach News-Journal* nearly forty years after the race.[12]

One of the journalists struggling to tell Knotts's story was Dave Kindred, influential sports columnist for the *Washington Post.* He'd go on to earn sports journalism's highest honor, the Red Smith Award for lifetime achievement, and be inducted into the National Sports Media Hall of Fame. In 1980, he was just one of many writers searching for a way to explain the death of a young driver. For help, he turned to Foyt. Kindred had been covering A.J. since 1969, when as a reporter for the Louisville *Courier-Journal* he started going to races at Daytona and Indianapolis, where they mostly talked horseracing.

"When I was getting started, he was kind of a scary guy," Kindred said of Foyt years later. "You knew that if you didn't approach him right or said something stupid, he'd let you know it. You kind of circled him before you got too close. But if your questions were good, he was a good interview.[13]

"I wasn't a race guy. I didn't know anything about race cars. I was fascinated about the people who did it. He didn't avoid us, and he answered all the questions. I remember his general tone was fatalistic. If it was going to happen, it was going to happen."

Foyt answered the questions directly. The answers didn't surprise regular racing fans who'd heard him address the issue before. But the story, under the banner headline "They're Alive While Baiting Death" across the top of the front page of the *Post*'s sports section, shocked many regular readers of Kindred's column who had only a passing awareness of auto racing.

"Why does a man race cars?" Kindred wrote. "Death awaits. A man knows it. Why then?" He asked A.J. if he was a fatalist.[14]

"That's exactly right," Foyt responded. "The Man put us here—and He'll take us. That's a square deal if I ever heard of one. When your time's up, it's up—not before, not after."

Asked if a death had ever made Foyt think of quitting, he talked about his first Indy 500 in 1958 and the story of Pat O'Connor.

"I had a good friend—I won't tell you his name—killed. And he just laid on the track while we went by. The thought went through my mind whether I wanted to go on. I had to know in my mind if I wanted to do it. You just have to accept life the way it is—and I went on."

Kindred asked if the possibility of Foyt's own death bothered him.

"Not me. It does a lot of people. But I've damn near went out a couple times myself. It's something you learn to live with."

As a final question, Kindred asked Foyt how he kept going following the death of a driver. The question seemed to surprise A.J., who shrugged.

"It's fun."

Unlike Jim Murray of the *Los Angeles Times* and other sports columnists who often condemned auto racing, Kindred tried to explain why drivers raced. He was more successful than most.

"People who pay to watch car races do not pay to see death," he wrote. "They come to cheer men on a wire . . . Drivers work on 'the ragged edge,' their machines teetering on a delicate balance . . . that once lost can mean death . . . Man does it all because it is his nature, his majestic nature, to reach beyond himself . . . so does a race driver take life to its limits."

Kindred and most other journalists at Daytona weren't aware of another part of the story. Unknown to those outside of Foyt's inner circle—and they knew better than to tell anyone—A.J. reached into his briefcase and pulled out enough cash to help Knotts get his son's body home and cover the cost of the funeral. Future stories would put the amount anywhere from $1,000 to $5,000. Foyt asked Hutcherson to see that the money got to the father but not to tell him where it came from. "Tell him good luck."[15]

Despite Foyt's admonitions, news of the help leaked out and a reporter eventually asked him about it.

"Who told you that?" an upset Foyt demanded. "Don't believe everything they tell you and don't get that story going around. I didn't do anything. I just sent word I was willing to help if they needed anything."

Hutcherson refused to elaborate but tried to shed some light on Foyt.

"He wants to act like a bad ass. He'll yell and bark, but he's really soft-hearted. You might see him chewing out his crew members here at the track, but if you see them at a bar at night and say something cross about A.J., they'll fight you over him."

Years later, Foyt acknowledged,

> I never cared to blow my horn when I did things like that. I did that a lot of times but I did not want people to know who did it. I knew they [the Knotts] didn't have much and I told them just to find his daddy and do whatever they had to do and let me know and I will pay for it. I was always known to be the bad guy and really deep down, I was not as bad as it looked like on the surface.[16]

The race itself was a disaster for Foyt. In danger of going a lap down early in the event, he simply parked his car and left. "Quit" was listed as the official reason for dropping out. Baker went on to win, shattering Foyt's eight-year-old race record.

Disgusted by the car's performance and unsure of his future plans, Foyt sold it to a group fronted by Don Whittington before the next speedway race at Atlanta. Whittington and his brother Bill had burst onto the IMSA sports car circuit, where they'd won the endurance races at Riverside and Watkins Glen, the 24 Hours of Le Mans, and the 1979 World Endurance Driver Championship. Don had earned a spot in the IROC series and set his sights on both NASCAR and Indianapolis, having also bought a couple of Indy cars from Parnelli Jones.

The Whittingtons' cars were devoid of sponsorship, and most thought they were rich kids playing at racing. What Foyt and others didn't know at that point—and wouldn't know for another five years—was that they were among the biggest marijuana smugglers in the country and used their racing activities to help launder their take.

Don Whittington had bought his way into a car at Daytona as Waltrip's teammate, but crashed in the race. When Waltrip balked at being part of a two-car team, Whittington said he'd start his own and Foyt was only too willing to help by selling him the troublesome Oldsmobile. A.J. sealed the deal by agreeing to oversee the crew for Whittington's first race at Atlanta, the car still carrying No. 51 and its poppy-red paint job.[17]

Making his first NASCAR Cup start at Atlanta was Rusty Wallace, only slightly less outspoken than the last time he crossed paths with Foyt. Wallace was driving for Roger Penske, who was taking the first tentative steps of returning to NASCAR after a two-year absence.

The two new teams were slotted together in the garage area. Wallace qualified seventh and Whittington tenth. The engine in the Wallace car was overheating, however, and wouldn't last long in the race. The backup engine was identical and also suspect. Tex Powell, who was serving as crew chief for the Penske effort, approached Puryear, who was handling the engines for the Foyt/Whittington car and asked about borrowing an engine. Puryear said he'd ask the boss, but given Foyt's history with Penske and Wallace, wasn't hopeful.

"You wouldn't have thought at the time that he would have loaned Roger Penske a motor," Powell would say. "But he did. He comes across pretty strong, pretty harsh sometimes, but underneath he's a fair guy. Really first class."[18]

Wallace finished a remarkable second at Atlanta to Dale Earnhardt, who won his first superspeedway race. Whittington wrecked in Atlanta's IROC race and then crashed out early in the main event. Six weeks later at Talladega, Whittington wrecked the now refrigerator-white Olds again, ramming another car going just ten miles an hour after it had blown an engine.

After Atlanta, Foyt attended a CART board meeting as an "invitee." Once again, the organization was on the brink of reuniting with USAC, this time around a proposal made by new Indianapolis Motor Speedway President John Cooper. When the talks seemed ready to collapse at the last minute yet again, Foyt said he was in full agreement with the proposal and that it was time for USAC to "fish or cut bait." If USAC backed out again, CART should "go racing anyway."[19]

Foyt's comments seemed to have an impact as USAC's leadership eventually came around, agreeing to the formation of the Championship Racing League (CRL). The six-man board of governors included Foyt, King, and Rolla Vollstedt from the USAC ranks and Penske, Patrick, and Jim Hall from CART. The Indy 500 would be run under existing USAC rules, while the CRL would work to consolidate the rulebook for events later in the year.

Foyt helped answer one of the first questions facing the reunited series: who would carry the No. 1. Both he and Rick Mears had won their respective series titles. When Foyt said he would stay with the No. 14, No. 1 was passed on to Mears.

The first races to be run under the CRL banner were the doubleheader at Ontario April 13. Foyt arrived late after spending time with his ill mother and qualified slower than the year before, in tenth place. When a thirty-minute practice session was scrubbed race morning, he left the track without saying anything and didn't return for the race. Foyt's absence did not go unnoticed.

"A.J. Foyt's sudden disappearing act left a bad taste in the paying customer's mouth," wrote Robin Miller in the *Indianapolis Star*. "It was another example of why Indy car racing has so much trouble gaining any national respect."[20]

It was apparent at Ontario that during his year dominating the USAC Indy car ranks, Foyt had failed to keep pace with the technology advancements being made by his CART counterparts. There was one glaring problem—his cars were old.

The recession had forced Parnelli Jones to shut down his engine and fabricating operation, and while Foyt bought out the remaining inventory, he was still left with a pair of Parnelli chassis at least two years old. The two Coyotes he also entered at Indianapolis were even older. He'd spent a lot of time in the offseason working on the old Foyt engine and seemed determined to give it one more try, wedging it into a Parnelli.

Not that Foyt didn't have other opportunities. Hall reportedly offered him the Chaparral when Al Unser left, but the car was sponsored by Pennzoil, and Foyt was loyal to Valvoline. The ride eventually went to Johnny Rutherford, who posted a dominating win at Ontario in the car. Miller also reported a rumor that Foyt turned down a million-dollar offer from the flamboyant owner of Essex Petroleum, sponsor of Team Lotus in Formula One, to drive a new Colin Chapman–designed ground effects car at the Speedway. The sponsorship, but not the car, ended up with Andretti and Penske Racing.

It was apparent from the first practice session at Indianapolis that Rutherford and the Chaparral were the class of the field. While other teams had built ground effects cars—most notably Penske and Gurney—they required further development, and no one could run with Rutherford.

Foyt spent much of his practice time complaining about the pop-off valves, saying they wouldn't work properly on the updated Foyt engine. He eventually gave up trying to resurrect the engine, switching back to the Cosworth-powered Parnelli, in which he quickly turned the fourth-fastest time of the month.

Nothing went right for Foyt on pole day, however. Rutherford and Bobby

Unser had already posted formidable times when Foyt's first qualifying run was interrupted by engine problems. With rain on the horizon, he hustled back to the garage and tossed everyone out—even his father and Gilmore—while he worked with Starne and Howard Gilbert to replace a magneto. His second run was interrupted by lightning, rain, and hail. With only a few minutes remaining for a pole attempt, he convinced officials to let him on the damp track. He recorded the twelfth-fastest time, considered a remarkable achievement by many.

"It beats nothing," Foyt said. "That's about the slowest we've run since we've been here, but it just seemed like everything was against us today. I've had days like this before. Hell, I just give up."[21]

The troubles continued on Carb Day when he pulled in after one lap, climbed out of the car, tossed his helmet on the ground, and started berating his crew. "Damn it, how many people do I have working for me?" he asked before taking a wrench to the rear wing. Afterward, he started in again on the boost levels, ground effects, and an old target—wings:[22]

> I think this is the greatest racetrack in the world. It is what made championship racing. It is the granddaddy of all sports events. But it has lost its luster with [the boost] restrictions they have put on it. I'd say I don't have the enthusiasm I used to.[23]
>
> They should take away the wings and ground effects and get back to racing. Then we would see the guys who have the finesse. Wings are a crutch. Anybody can set up a car with a wing. In those days you had to be awfully brave, run hard and make the race.
>
> The driver skill is gone. I don't know half these people. I'm not saying you don't have to have some skill. But you take those cars out of the museum and go down the back stretch with the drivers we've got today and 90 percent of them would crash. They'd never make one lap.

He pointed to the thirteen practice crashes as evidence the combination of slower top speeds resulting from boost limits and ground effects was making the sport more treacherous.

"It's more dangerous now than when we raced over 200. What's happening now is that we're running the same speeds on the straight and the turns. Now you have to flatfoot it, trying to make up in the turns what we lose on the straightaways." The speed difference "is where you used to separate the men from the boys, who had the talent and who didn't. Now with the restrictions, just about anybody is a race driver. Driving one of these cars is like sitting on the freeway, taking your family to dinner. I hope they throw all these rules away next year and let us just go racing like we used to."[24]

His prerace gloom and doom turned into a prophecy as Foyt failed to make his classic charge to the front, never challenged the leaders, and didn't crack the top five, eventually dropping out twenty-five laps from the finish with an engine problem. It was a dominating victory by Rutherford, who finished nearly thirty seconds ahead of Bobby Unser.

Partly because of the thirteen caution flags—that saw nearly a third of the race run at reduced speeds—and partly because of the pace of cars when they were racing, it was the slowest 500 since 1962. Foyt reminded everyone what he thought of the regulations.

"Anytime you call this crap a race it's ridiculous," he told the trackside reporter. "Anytime a bunch of junkers beat my car, it's bull. Whoever cheats the best wins. I'm not going to race at Indy until they change the rules. My grandson could've won it today."[25]

He didn't cool off later in his garage. "A good hot rod race is better than this. We looked like a herd of turtles."[26]

Rutherford agreed to a point, saying, "I think some of the crashes were caused by the lower speeds. Guys were taking chances out there because we couldn't pass when we wanted to."

However, when told of Foyt's comments, Sneva, who drove from thirty-third to second, said, "That's ridiculous. This is the best show we've had in a long time. We ran wheel-to-wheel. It was more entertaining for fans." Bobby Unser said of Foyt, "He just has an out-of-date car."

Another who disagreed was the *Star*'s Miller, who wrote in his post-race column, "Foyt, who in his twilight years is becoming senselessly bitter, claims he won't be back until everyone decides to go racing again. But there was quite a bit of racing going on—A.J. was just too far back to see it."[27]

Following through on his threats, Foyt skipped the next Indy car race at Milwaukee rather than run at the reduced boost levels. When he filed an entry for the June 22 race at Pocono—to be run under the same limitations—the retirement articles started again. When he turned in the fastest lap in practice, the stories were replaced by those wondering how he was cheating.

"They can think or say what they want but I'm not cheating," he said. "I had some problems at Indy so I stayed home and did my homework while everyone else ran Milwaukee. I had my homework done at Indy too, but a lot of stuff just backfired on us. I never come up that short. But I made a major discovery and I'll be a contender Sunday—you can bet on that."[28]

He scoffed at questions about his retirement and enjoyed taking reporters to task:

> The day I retire I'll make the announcement, not the newspapers. They pissed me off at Indy this year, so you don't have to look for me retiring until maybe after next Indy. I've read so many bad stories you all have wrote about me. I've learned to consider the source. People will mail me the bad stories, or call me. That's normally the way I hear about them. Some fan will call me long distance and say, "A.J. did you see what this guy wrote about you?" I say, Well, hell, they've got to write about something.[29]

On race day, Foyt took the lead from the start and dominated in the early going, leading sixty-seven of the first eighty-five laps. He had just lapped Andretti when he slowed. He admitted running a low gear ratio that put added stress on the engine and seemed not to mind when an engine problem knocked him out.

"We were turning excessive rpms," Foyt said. "We had to stay up with the ground effect cars. I knew it was marginal if we lived all day. We really turned it tight. We knew it was taking a chance, but we had to take a shot. I like to win and I'd just as soon break it while I'm out front leading than run around at the back like we did at Indy."[30]

Andretti dropped out a few laps later and implied Foyt had to have been cheating: "There's no way, at forty-eight inches [of boost] he could pull out and pass us the way he did. It's not in the cards my friend. You're damn right he was playing games. I guess it all depends on how serious you are about winning. But it's all gonna catch up with him. He doesn't have to do this. He's too good a race driver to pull this shit."

Foyt was already gone when Andretti made his comments, so reporters asked Howard Gilbert about the cheating allegations. He called charges that the team was using nitrous oxide "crazy. It would take a bottle as big as a semi to carry him 100 laps.[31]

"I think he proved today he is serious. When he gets serious it shows up. He told me before the race he was going to jump up and take the lead. They [Unser, Sneva, and others] were putting him down and he wasn't about to let 'em put him down. Mad adds two miles per hour for him."

Foyt admitted struggling with how to vote on the pending CRL regulations. In 1979 he'd been in favor of trying the forty-eight-inch boost limit, then strongly opposed to it. After Pocono, he sounded as if he was for it again. CRL required four of six votes to pass a rule, so some compromise would be required from the group:

> I'll be honest with you. I've talked to Hall and Penske and Gurney—all of them—and I still can't say which way I'll go. What do the people want? What do *we* really want? None of us can tell you what we want or what's good for racing. I've been racing all my life and I feel I'm as smart as any man about automobile racin', but as far as coming down and telling you, I can't.[32]
>
> I'm pretty much in favor of leaving the engine situation the way it is now. Do away with skirts completely. The fans just pay to see a damn good race. They don't care about wings, skirts, ground effects, nothing. I would like to see the rules froze for three to five years so everybody will know what direction to go in.

In the end, Foyt got much of what he wanted, including the forty-eight-inch boost limit and freezing the regulations for three years. In a compromise, non-movable ground effects skirts would be allowed in 1981, but not the articulating skirts currently being used on some cars. In a surprise, Penske joined with Foyt, King, and Vollstedt in voting for the regulations while Hall and Patrick were in favor of higher boost levels.

Peace in the Indy car world lasted less than three days. That's when Cooper, whose original proposal had jump-started negotiations in the first place, said the Speedway would look beyond USAC for someone to sanction the 500. "There is growing evidence to the effect that USAC has become an organization governed by selected car owners," Cooper said. "That, of course, would not meet our criteria of having an independent authority sanction the 500."[33]

While the regulations were similar to the original proposal, the makeup of the board was what bothered Cooper. He had wanted a board of seven with only three car owners, a driver, a track operator, the USAC president, and a seventh member unanimously selected by the group. He was also upset his personal proposal to establish the "Hulman Cup," a million-dollar points fund for the Indy car champion, was ignored.

"I listened to competitors complain all week at Pocono about a certain team getting away with breaking the rules," Cooper said. "Well I don't know whether the rules were broken or not, but I do know that it's impossible to have officials who are working for the participants. It's like having (quarterback) Roger Staubach hire the referees."[34]

Faced with Cooper's threat, USAC severed all ties with the CRL.

Cooper's announcement and USAC's move put Foyt over the edge. He returned to Houston and refused to take calls from reporters, leaving it up to Gilmore to field questions.

"This year he'll wait and see," his sponsor said. "If things stay the way they are, he'd just as soon not get involved as he did last year in the USAC-CART disagreement. Without using the word definite, I'd say the brakes are on. He's looking to '81. He's starting now to build two brand new cars for Indy and two brand new stock cars."[35]

One reporter managed to get Tony Foyt on the phone and asked him when A.J. would get back on the track. "Whenever he gets ready." *Click.*

When not working on his new cars, Foyt spent most of his time after Pocono watching his racehorses and campaigning for Gilmore, who was making an unsuccessful run for Congress. His mother's health continued to go downhill, and he spent time with her. It wasn't until early September that he submitted a surprise entry for the Hoosier Hundred dirt track race, an event he'd won a record six times and finished second in five times. He'd failed to qualify the last time he entered in 1977, however, and hadn't driven in an Indy car dirt track race in four years.

He entered the race as a favor to friend Tim Delrose, who in late 1979 purchased a pair of new dirt track cars, planning to run for the 1980 championship. Foyt had convinced him then to hire Gary Bettenhausen to drive the car.

"A.J. asked me who I was trying to hire to drive," Delrose said, recalling a late 1979 conversation. "I mentioned a couple of names and he kept saying, 'Nah, keep going.' Then I mentioned Gary, and he said, 'That's the guy you want. He ain't afraid of nothin'.'"[36]

Gary was the son of the late Tony Bettenhausen, who had helped Foyt early in his career before being killed at Indianapolis in 1961. After winning sprint car championships in 1969 and 1971, the younger Bettenhausen seemed on the verge of stardom in 1974, driving for Penske in both Indy cars and NASCAR. Then he severely injured his left arm in a sprint car race and was out of racing for eight months. When he returned, he discovered he was also out of the Penske rides. Many gave up on the driver as he struggled to rebuild adequate strength for the dirt tracks. He still needed help putting on his helmet, but Foyt told Delrose Bettenhausen could handle the ride.

Delrose, who'd hired Rutherford in the mid-1960s after he shattered both arms in a crash and nobody else would touch him, said he was open to hiring Bettenhausen but that Gary was playing hard to get.

"Here's how you do it," Foyt said. "Offer him five hundred bucks to come to the next race and qualify your car. That's all. Just practice and qualify. He'll do it."

Foyt was right. Bettenhausen took the bait and was now locked in a title battle for the dirt track championship, trailing Pancho Carter. Looking to steal points from Carter, Delrose asked Foyt to drive the second car, which carried No. 14, in the Hoosier Hundred. Already planning to be in nearby Lexington, Kentucky, the day before for the annual thoroughbred auction, he agreed. The only person happier than Delrose to hear Foyt say yes was promoter Bruce Walkup who said ticket sales immediately jumped.

Showing no signs of rust, Foyt qualified fourth alongside Carter and four places better than Bettenhausen. He moved into second and was closing on the leader when he was bumped from behind by another car, knocking his oil cooler loose and—soon after—his car out of the race. Foyt bristled when a reporter expressed surprise he'd run so well.

"If I didn't feel like I could run up front I wouldn't be here," he said. "I got tired of all the hassle and decided to go back to racing like it used to be."[37]

Bettenhausen finished strong and took the win, closing in on Carter for the national championship. Both Bettenhausen and Walkup credited Foyt with making the race a success.

"If he hadn't been here, it would not have been the Hoosier Hundred," Bettenhausen said. For Walkup, it had been even more important. "We were about $14,000 behind in advance sales over last year when we announced Foyt," he said. "We came within $700. Most of those late sales were to women over forty."

Foyt agreed to drive the second car again at Terre Haute, but a conflict arose when the race was rescheduled. Delrose turned to Kenny Schrader, who was looking to make his first USAC championship dirt car race.

"So, I'm climbing in this car for the first time to go out to qualify, and I see it's got A.J. Foyt's name on it," Schrader recalled. "I'd never made a lap in it. Never sat in it. And it's got A.J.'s name on it. Talk about shitting razor blades."[38]

Bettenhausen held fast time until Schrader went out and broke the track record, earning the pole position and upsetting Bettenhausen.

"Bettenhausen is having a heart attack," Delrose said. "He says, 'What the hell are you doing? We're trying to win the national championship.' I said don't worry, I'll talk to the boy.[39]

"I took Kenny down to the first turn and said: 'I put you in the car today so you're gonna run it. You're gonna start where you qualified. But try and stay away from Gary. I'm trying to win the national championship. It'd be great if I could do it.' He said, 'I know exactly what to do.'"

Schrader grabbed the lead in the first turn before backing off, allowing Bettenhausen past. Schrader finished third, ahead of Carter. Delrose and Bettenhausen went on to win the title, and Schrader also came away a winner.

"That one day was the most important day for advancing my racing career," Schrader would say, "and that was because of Timmy Delrose. And through him I also got to know A.J. better."

CHAPTER 4

MILLERGATE

1981

It wasn't until the annual USAC banquet in Indianapolis at the end of January that A.J. Foyt emerged from his Texas exile. He presented the national championship ring to Johnny Rutherford and watched as Gary Bettenhausen and Tim Delrose picked up trophies for their national dirt track title. Rumors about Foyt dropping thirty pounds during the offseason proved to be just that, with one writer referring to A.J. as "rotund."[1]

Foyt was recognized for "his outstanding contributions to motorsports," an honor typically awarded to someone already retired. If he was getting ready to step down, he was going about it in an odd way. Two new race cars—one Indy car and one stock car—were nearing completion at a cost of well over a million dollars.

The first on the track was an Oldsmobile Cutlass Supreme, an example of the new "downsized" models Detroit was building in response to government regulations requiring improved fuel economy and lower emissions. The regulations put an emphasis on smaller cars, and NASCAR was reluctantly making the move too, reflecting changes in the marketplace.

The new machines were proving to be a handful on the high banks of Daytona. One rolled six times, and another did a spectacular reverse summersault. While both drivers walked away, there was widespread concern about the stability of the cars. Foyt built himself a special rear spoiler and—when it slowed him too much—started drilling holes in it. NASCAR said the spoiler modifications were against the rules and ordered him to change it back. So, he was not in the best of moods when a reporter asked him what he thought of the new production cars.

"They're the biggest pile of junk in history," said Foyt—who was one of the largest car dealers in the country, selling about 5,000 new vehicles and grossing $60 million a year. "I just can't see how Americans can look at 1981 cars and buy

◀ A.J. and George Bignotti. *John Mahoney*

them. To me they're very dangerous. If the EPA keeps messing around with the automobile manufacturers, they're gonna kill us all."[2]

He finally had the Olds to his liking by the qualifying race. Despite admitting to being "a little rusty," he led laps and ran up front before taking fifth in a wild finish, less than a car length behind winner Darrell Waltrip.[3]

In the 500, he drafted with the lead group of cars in the early going but was never able to move to the front. "I changed a gear, and it turned out to be a big mistake," he admitted. "I was just trying to keep it together."[4]

He got himself in trouble after a slow pit stop when he tried to beat the pace car back on the track and avoid going a lap down. He ignored an official's stop sign in the process, was black-flagged, and lost another lap, eventually parking the car just past the halfway point when the engine started smoking.

Foyt's other new car, the latest Coyote, was a stunner. He'd reunited with Bob Riley, whose 1973 Coyote design was the basis for the 1977 race winner and one of the most successful rear-engine Indy car designs at that point. It featured a new paint scheme: Foyt Orange accented with a wide white stripe below the cockpit and above the side pod. Valvoline stepped up its sponsorship in a big way, and its logo was now emblazoned across the side of the car.

Riley and Foyt had split following the 1973 Indianapolis 500, the designer upset by the violence of the tragic race and the lack of recognition he'd received for his work. He only stayed away from the sport for a short time before going to work for Pat Patrick and George Bignotti, where he designed a series of successful race cars called Wildcats. That relationship had become tenuous when the team tried several other cars during 1980, and it ended completely at the conclusion of the season. Patrick hired Gordon Kimball, who'd played a key role in the design of Jim Hall's dominant Chapparal, making Riley a free agent.

"Downforce was really becoming a big deal, and I got a call from Foyt about doing a car for '81," Riley recalled. Time had helped heal his hurt feelings, and he was anxious to work on a new design. "I thought it would be great to do another car for Foyt.[5]

"Then I got a nasty letter from Patrick's lawyers [saying] I couldn't use anything that I had done during the years I worked for him. I showed that to Foyt and we had a big laugh. I just completely ignored him.

"It was a really pretty car. I finally got the engine enclosed, and the wing was up and back. We had some good sidepods for downforce."

While the car turned in good aerodynamic numbers, what the wind tunnel didn't tell them was that the carbon fiber body "was about fifty pounds overweight," according to Riley.

The car wasn't completed in time to do any on-track testing and in what had become the new norm, Foyt spent the first Saturday in May at Churchill Downs for the Kentucky Derby. His mother was in the hospital again, and when her health continued to worsen, he returned to Houston immediately after the Derby. He flew to Indianapolis Sunday evening after realizing "there was nothing more I could do."[6]

It was an incredible year at the Speedway, with 105 entries. The Coyote wasn't even the most radical car. That honor went to the jet black "Batmobile" of Danny Ongais, originally designed for a Porsche engine. The "Yellow Submarine" Chaparral of Rutherford and Hall remained the benchmark, while Patrick's new Wildcat VIII, Dan Gurney's new Eagle, and the updated Penske chassis all turned competitive laps as speeds once again crept near 200 mph.

Foyt ran a few shakedown laps on Monday, and Tuesday was rained out. It wasn't until Wednesday that the car got on the track at speed. Qualifying was only three days away, and Foyt and Riley were in uncharted territory, struggling to come to grips with the new design.

"We didn't know how to handle that much downforce," Riley admitted years later. "We didn't know how to support the car with the springs and shocks. We ended up taking some panels out of the side pods and cutting holes underneath to reduce the downforce. It was pretty drivable after that. Had we been able to test more, that car would have been really, *really* fast. Jack Starne told me later that if we had just known how to handle the downforce, nobody would have been able to touch us."[7]

All week long there'd been speculation about the turbocharger boost levels the different teams were using to attain their speeds. Boost levels were unregulated during practice, and many exceeded the forty-eight-inch qualifying and race limit as they worked to understand ground effects and downforce. Foyt didn't post a top ten lap time until Thursday, with radar guns clocking the Coyote at more than 214 miles per hour on the backstraight—seven mph faster than anyone else. Reporters wanted to know how he was so much quicker than the other cars. Forty years later, A.J. said he didn't remember what boost level he'd been using, but at the time he tried to brush the reporters off, telling them he was too busy to answer questions.

"I'm tired of hearing how I'm cheating," he said at one point. "Is there some crime for going fast down the straightaways? I've been working with my engine all winter and it's a strong one."[8]

In his Friday pre-qualifying story, *Indianapolis Star* reporter Robin Miller noted, "Many in the pit population were skeptical about Super Tex's boost." While hinting Foyt was exceeding the forty-eight-inch level, it was an innocuous, throwaway line near the end of a long story. Foyt was incensed, however, when told the story implied he was cheating.[9]

Foyt was notoriously secretive during practice, always returning to the garage before discussing car setup and changing radio frequencies daily so other teams couldn't listen in. After running a few laps during Friday's Happy Hour practice session, he climbed on his motorcycle and rode out to the entry of Turn Three, where he'd spotted someone using a radar gun.

"You point that son of a bitch at me again, and I'll shove it up your ass," he warned.[10]

Then he went looking for Miller. He found him among a group on the grassy area between pit road and the track, where the teams signaled their drivers and people often congregated during practice.

According to a non-bylined article in Saturday's *Star*, "Foyt came up behind Miller and slapped him in the back of the head then jerked the sports writer by the hair on top of his head and pulled him behind the scoring tower.[11]

"What the fuck are you writing this shit for?" Miller said Foyt screamed. "Is it a crime to go fast?"[12]

Years later Miller added, "He threatened to cut my balls off in front of 30,000 witnesses."[13]

At first Miller brushed off the incident, turning down several lawyers who urged him to take legal action. "He just blew up," he said of Foyt. "Then he cooled down. It's nothing unusual. He's done it for years. He's just a baby. I wasn't going to fight him. I just wanted to talk to him. Once he cooled down, we talked. But he didn't have to do what he did."[14]

Foyt proved just how strong his car was the next day during qualifying. With rain delaying the start by four hours and more in the forecast, there was a premium on posting a qualifying speed. The urgency increased with the news Evelyn Foyt had suffered another stroke overnight and, given her ongoing heart problems, doctors were pessimistic about her recovery. He was the second car on the track once qualifying started.

"Right before qualifying, they said, 'A.J. is going for the pole,'" Riley remembers. "I thought, *He goes for the pole all the time.* I wondered what was different."[15]

His attempt was cut short when the track announcer said, "There's a squirrel on the track," bringing a laugh from the crowd. Foyt declined an offer to let his car cool before trying again—he wanted to go as soon as possible.

His first official lap was a stunning 198.369 mph, his fastest of the month. His second was over 197 mph, but his third dropped again to 195.6 mph. "I guess I can't hold my breath long enough anymore," he said. "I was trying a little too hard. I tried to make it up by cutting across the apron [in Turn One on lap four], but I like to went through the fence. I was in deep trouble."[16]

His car skidded up the track and into the wall between turns one and two. "I didn't know whether to shut it down or keep going down the backstretch," Foyt said. He kept going, finishing with a four-lap average of 196.078 mph.

"He bounced right off the wall," Riley said. "He white-walled the tires. I thought for sure he would crash. But he was still on it coming down the back-straight. I guess that's what they meant by going for the pole."[17]

Anxious to return home to Houston and surrounded by reporters, he answered questions as he walked to Gasoline Alley. He paused several times to talk about his run, admitting he probably should have stopped after hitting the wall, but balanced it with his desire to post a time and leave.

"I went into [Turn] Three a little easy," he said of the final lap. "I said it's going to be a little silly when you pop a tire or something breaks. I've spent enough of that sheet time. But I was kinda caught in circumstances. You couldn't really afford to pull in and you really couldn't afford to go. I said if the tire blows I'm the ignorant idiot. I turned the steering wheel left and I'll tell you, my heart," he said, making a fluttering motion. "I've gambled all my life, so why quit now."[18]

Only nine drivers posted times before the rains came, and when Foyt left, he was on the temporary pole. Many of the fastest cars had yet to run, however, and he knew he was a longshot to retain the top spot.

Arriving in Houston, he went straight to St. Luke's hospital. Although extremely weak, his mother had watched qualifying and saw A.J. brush the wall. "I thought you were going to be up here with me," A.J. recalled her saying. He told her he was looking forward to celebrating Mother's Day in the morning.[19]

When Evelyn drifted to sleep, Foyt went home but was only there for a couple of hours before the hospital called. His mother had suffered another stroke, and there was no indication of brain activity. His father and sister were already at the hospital when he arrived, and they were arguing about putting her on life support. A.J. made it clear where he stood.

"Daddy," he said, "Momma don't want to live like that." Tony added he didn't want to see his wife suffer anymore. Eventually, they agreed to forgo life support.

At 5:48 a.m. on Mother's Day, Evelyn Foyt, sixty-five, passed away. The cause was listed as heart failure, although A.J. would blame "a blood clot to the brain" for her death.[20]

About the same time as St. Luke's was confirming Evelyn's death, the 183-page Sunday edition of *The Indianapolis Star* was hitting the streets. Foyt was about to discover why public relations executives constantly warn their clients, "Never pick a fight with anyone who buys ink by the barrel and paper by the ton."

The front page of the sports section featured a lead story headlined, "Foyt Brushes Wall, Still Grabs Early Pole," in which it said the driver "handled the crisis like the champion he is." A large photo of Foyt, labeled "The King," anchored the center of the page.

Underneath the photo was a personal column from Miller, headlined, "A.J.'s Nasty Side Hidden by Legend." Miller wrote, "Taking on a legend is never easy, but there are some things about Anthony Joseph Foyt Jr. that have been kept in the closet for too long and it's time to let them out."[21]

After reciting Foyt's accomplishments on the track, Miller went on:

> As his legend began to expand in the early 1960s, so did his ego. His successes brought him recognition, money and, worst of all, hero status.
>
> He became known as "Super Tex" and later, "The King." After daily doses of positive reinforcement from his racetrack disciples, he began believing it.
>
> This wasn't a rare disease. It happens to many famous people who are constantly coddled by others.
>
> With this kind of liberty, Foyt has been allowed to throw temper tantrums for any and all reasons. Some people play golf for relaxation. A.J. got his entertainment from berating his crew, the press, tire engineers and officials.
>
> The sad side of this story is that thirty minutes after one of his outbursts, Foyt would be cracking jokes with the same guy he had abused as

> if nothing happened. And what's worse, usually the person would be so thrilled "The King" was giving him an audience, it was forgotten.
>
> This type of immaturity was accepted by these people because a lot of them were directly involved in racing and would rather get along than hold grudges.
>
> Occasionally, shoving someone up against a wall and threatening a right hook was part of Foyt's repertoire, but whether it was verbal or physical it all had the same intent—intimidation.
>
> The press abides by Foyt's moodiness every time. He can slam the door in their faces or push them out of the way, but when he decides to open up, everybody is always there listening to his every word. However, that's not the media's fault—it's their job because people want to know what A.J. says.

Miller recapped a number of Foyt's run-ins and listed several instances where Foyt's ethics were questioned:

> 1967: Changing the body configuration immediately following his third victory before the car was officially inspected by the USAC tech crew.
> 1973: Using an oversized engine at Indy.
> 1974: Using an oversized sprint engine to win at the Indiana State Fairgrounds and the World Series of Auto Racing at Pocono.
> 1977: Being the only driver allowed to use left side tires (a softer compound) on all four wheels of his winning Coyote.
> 1978: Forcing the pace car to stay on the track in the Texas 200 during a yellow light—aborting a re-start—so he could dive in the pits and take on fuel . . . Foyt had enough fuel to finish without stopping again and won the race. Steve Krisiloff, who went from second to third because of the maneuver, tried to voice his objections afterward but was bodily removed from the scoring stand by a couple of Foyt crewmen.
> 1979: Pulling his car, which finished second, out of the USAC inspection line (against the rules) and into his garage for 10 minutes behind closed doors before allowing it to go through inspection.
> 1980: Carrying a nitrous oxide bottle providing for more engine power, in his driver's suit at Pocono.

Miller didn't quote a single source for the accusations, and at the end of the story included a disclaimer of sorts:

> Now all of these alleged infractions have never been proven or even protested, but still have been subjects of discussion among members of the immediate racing family.
>
> But of course, few people would ever talk or write about any of these matters officially because, well, it was A.J. Foyt. In the eyes of many people he could do whatever he wanted to do because he was sacred.

> The point is this—Foyt will go down in history as one of the fastest and greatest race drivers. Some people dismiss Foyt's actions with the excuse that "he is an intense, fierce competitor, and a winner."
>
> That may be true, and he may have everything anyone in racing could ever want—except of course, maturity.

Miller wasn't the first to describe Foyt in that light. Jim Murray, the *Los Angeles Times* columnist, wrote in 1974, "You might call him the terrible-tempered Mr. Foyt, but first his disposition would have to improve 100 percent before his temper could merely be called terrible. A.J. runs on rage . . . plays no favorites. He bullies the car, the track, his own pit crew, mechanic, the stewards, starters, press and public with equal fervor."[22]

Murray, however, was well-known for his anti-racing columns. Miller was the lead racing reporter for the nation's leading newspaper when it came to motorsports coverage. He once worked on Jim Hurtubise's pit crew and tried driving himself. For him to criticize Foyt was considered sacrosanct by many and the "nasty side" diatribe unacceptable. Although others in racing's tight inner circle agreed with him, few were willing to make the stand publicly.

The timing of the column coinciding with Evelyn Foyt's death couldn't have been worse, although it probably saved Miller from another confrontation with the driver. While A.J. remained in Houston to help with the funeral arrangements, he continued to be the center of attention in Indianapolis as Millergate swirled.

Another *Star* motorsports reporter, Dave Overpeck, got involved in his role as president of the American Auto Racing Writers and Broadcasters Association. On Monday he presented a letter protesting Foyt's actions to USAC President Dick King. The letter urged the organization to take "significant punitive action" against Foyt for the "unprovoked physical attack" on Miller and called it "an affront to all members of the media who cover auto racing."[23]

Overpeck then held a press conference, taking questions from his colleagues. He said USAC needed to publicly condemn Foyt's actions and called for him to apologize to Miller.

"We can't have any driver taking physical liberties with writers," Overpeck said. "If this is the way he is going to act, then certain disciplinary action is in order. We cannot tolerate assault. He slapped Robin this time. It could be you or me next time." He said USAC's failure to act would provide "an open license for this type of conduct in the future by A.J. or anybody else who cares to do it.

"This protest comes from the writers and broadcasters association," Overpeck stressed. "What the paper plans to do, I don't know. Whether Miller plans to take criminal action against Foyt, that's a personal decision."

Not all members were in agreement with Overpeck. "On the one hand, as a journalist, I would take great offense at being touched," said Paul Page, anchor for the race's radio broadcast. "But knowing Foyt, I'm not surprised he was mad about being called a liar or a cheater. You have to remember there are no rules for practice. And I don't think Miller should have written the story without attributing his sources." Asked if he expected A.J. to apologize, Page said, "It's hard to say because A.J. is an extremely complex man. There have been times when there was no one in the world I was madder at, but there have been times when he has been one of my best friends."

J.D. Lewis, sports editor of the *Columbus Republic* (Indiana) wrote, "The fact is that racing is full of cheaters and always will be. Most of the successful teams in auto racing that haven't stretched the rules simply don't know how. Race drivers and crews have always argued and fought among themselves, but rarely have they aired their dirty linen in public as Miller did for them on Sunday. Miller may find that the number of friends he has along pit row will shrink once they read how their gossip ended up in print."

If Miller, Overpeck, *The Star*, or anyone else thought an apology from Foyt was forthcoming, they were mistaken. Instead he filed a $3-million libel suit, saying Miller's column falsely accused him of racing misconduct, was defamatory, false, and malicious.[24]

The newspaper responded with a statement: "*The Star* stands behind the column. We have no reason to retract it." Miller acknowledged the timing could have been better, saying, "It's unfortunate it happened this May. But he started it. I didn't. If he wants to pursue it, I guess we'll go to court. I'm not worried."[25]

He should have been. The lawsuit was filed in Houston's U.S. District Court, the same one that had ruled against *Sports Illustrated* in 1972 in the "Hillbillies and Fags" case. Some of the language in the suit, filed once again by attorney Larry Bass, was very similar to the *SI* case, saying Miller's column was "published solely to create animosity between the plaintiff and the other race car drivers, to ridicule the plaintiff and amuse the subscribers and readers."

The *Star* and Foyt eventually reached an agreement, with the paper running a story on November 1 recounting what had led up to the suit and what passed for the newspaper's apology.

"The *Indianapolis Star* acknowledges, as Robin Miller's article had pointed out, that the alleged unprofessional conduct mentioned in the article had never been proven nor protested. To this newspaper's knowledge, they remain unproven and unprotested allegations."[26]

A month later, the judge in the case accepted the agreement, noting, "Everyone is satisfied." Foyt's attorney said, "There was a monetary settlement but by agreement of the parties there will be no disclosure of the terms." The settlement was believed to cover Foyt's legal fees, estimated at about $10,000 and well below the $3 million he sought.[27]

Foyt refused to speak to Miller for more than a year, but at the July 4 race in Cleveland the following summer, he approached the reporter.

"At that point, I was convinced he was gonna drag my body into Lake Erie and drown me," Miller recalled.[28]

"Hey asshole," Miller remembered Foyt saying, "I don't think you and I should hate each other anymore."

"A.J., I don't hate you," Miller said.

While they weren't exactly friends—that would come many years later after Foyt retired as a driver—they'd be civil with each other, even during the split that would divide the Indy car racing world and find the two on different sides of the battle.

Miller continued writing for the *Star* until 2001 when he was fired for violating the paper's ethics policy, a charge he disputed so vehemently he was escorted out of the newsroom by security guards. Rather than end his career, Miller became a media celebrity, working at ESPN, Speed Channel, and *NBC Sports* on television and at *RACER* magazine. He openly worshipped his racing heroes, including Gurney, Bobby Unser, Mario Andretti, and Foyt.

"Robin used to stir up lots of shit," Foyt said years after the incident. "He would make things up for people to read. He was running around with some of the younger drivers, and a lot of them were putting shit in his head. But a lot of the things he said was pretty true too.[29]

"Most writers are too scared. So, while most of them are bullshitting, Robin's telling the truth. He doesn't care if you're A.J. Foyt or Mario Andretti or Roger Penske. He calls a spade a spade. A lot of people used to not like Robin. Hell, I used to not like Robin, but I got to liking him. People would bad-mouth him, but 99 percent of the stuff he wrote was true."

Miller looked back on the experience years later and wrote, tongue firmly in cheek, that they'd had "a 'small' disagreement over a technical fact. Lawyers told me to sue for assault, but I retaliated with a column suggesting A.J. was the king of cheaters."[30]

"Neither one of us handled it very well."[31]

Evelyn Foyt was buried on Wednesday, May 13, in a Houston ceremony attended by most of Foyt's team and many in the racing community, including Mari Hulman George and Tony George. Most of the team was back in Gasoline Alley on Thursday, but it was difficult for any of them to focus on their work.

"It was a very stressful time," remembered Starne years later, his voice dropping into a whisper. He thought of Evelyn as a second mother. "We tried to carry on, but it was very difficult. I don't like to think about it even now, to be honest with you. Even today it bothers A.J., and I know it bothers me. She loved A.J. to death and was just a wonderful, wonderful lady. He misses her even today. All of us do."[32]

Foyt said in his autobiography, printed two years after Evelyn's death, "I'll admit, I miss my mother. When she died, a big part of me died with her.[33]

"I dream about my mother all the time. I dreamed the other night that she was dying again. I could see all those tubes in her and Daddy was there and Marlene and Lucy, and I woke up about three in the morning just scared to death."

He was also bothered by the picture the media sometimes painted of him and the way it impacted his mother.

"I used to worry a lot about what the newspapers said about me, there were always rumors about me being wild and having all these broads and everything, and even though they didn't bother Lucy, they bothered me and it worried me mostly because I didn't feel that Mother would understand like Lucy did. Now that she's gone, I don't give a shit what they say."

As expected, Foyt's qualifying time didn't hold up for the pole position, and it was bettered by Bobby Unser in a Penske and Mike Mosley in the new Eagle, both qualifying at more than 200 mph. He'd start the 500 on the outside of the front row.

He returned to the track in time to keep his promise to Mari Hulman George, honorary chairman of the Indiana Special Olympics, to participate in a day of activities at the Speedway. He took a tumble doing the broad jump and laughed with everyone else. He came back to win the fifty-yard dash, although second-place finisher Gordon Smiley, ten years younger, claimed Foyt jumped the start.

The Parnelli Foyt drove in 1980 had been sitting in Gasoline Alley all month with a "For Sale" sign on it but attracting little interest. Foyt ran a few half-hearted laps in the car, failing to get it above 186 mph, and then parked it. It wasn't until the final day of qualifying that he realized George Snider, who'd been working on the No. 14 car, was in danger of not qualifying for the 500 for the first time in seventeen years. He also hadn't driven an Indy car in a year.

"I felt like I owed him a shot," Foyt said. He asked Snider if he could run laps at 188 mph, the speed most thought would be needed to make the field.[34]

"Oh, I don't know," Snider responded. "Time's a little short."

Foyt helped Snider change the springs and the rear wing, then sent him out for a couple of practice laps. Three laps later, Foyt called him in. Snider was fast enough.

They pushed the car into the qualifying line, and Foyt told him, "Just hang on." Four laps later with an average speed of 189.255 mph, Snider was solidly in the field.

Or was he?

One of the hottest and most popular young drivers in auto racing was the twenty-five-year-old Tim Richmond. He captured the 1980 Indianapolis rookie of the year award, but after a couple of big crashes had shifted his focus to NASCAR. He'd returned to run the 500 but had crashed again and struggled after that to find speed, finally being bumped from the field Sunday afternoon.

Now Richmond's sponsors, UNO and Valvoline, were looking for a qualified car they could either buy or rent. They had talked with Foyt in January about Richmond being his teammate, but A.J. wasn't interested at the time. Now they went back to him again about Snider's car, and this time he was more receptive. By Wednesday they'd worked out a deal for Richmond to replace Snider in the No. 84 Parnelli. The move was immediately criticized by some.

"It should be against the rules," said Bobby Unser, expressing a common viewpoint. "I've always thought so. I think it cheats the fans when you start buying rides. It goes against the entire sport."[35]

One driver who didn't mind was Snider.

"He brought the car to the racetrack wantin' to sell it. At the last minute we decided to go ahead and get it qualified and maybe that would be a better chance to get rid of the race car. It was an agreement I had with A.J. A deal's a deal.[36]

"There are two reasons I race," he added. "I like racing and for the money. Money overruled racing this time. I'd say I'm not going home with empty pockets."

Richmond's backers spent about $100,000 to rent the ride, with $25,000 going to Snider. Richmond also said Snider assured him he was okay with the deal.

"If he had the least little inkling of wanting to be in the car I wouldn't be in it, period," Richmond said. "I don't operate like that."[37]

He called it "a chance of a lifetime. I couldn't think of a better tutor to have than A.J. Foyt. Whoever drives for him is going to have a lot of good done for himself."

Richmond arrived back at the Speedway from Charlotte, where he'd been practicing for the NASCAR race, on Wednesday about 7:00 p.m. to be fitted to the car. He admitted to being intimidated by Foyt, who was on the cover of the *Sports Illustrated* prerace issue with the headline "The Story of the World's Greatest Race Driver."[38]

"I didn't say a word," Richmond said. "I just walked in and he said get in the car and I got in it. When you talk about the best race car driver, my choice is always A.J. Foyt because he has won with everything. That's the sign of greatness, to be able to drive them all. That's what I want to do, drive them all."[39]

Foyt ran in the top five early in the race, but his radio never worked properly, which made pit stops an adventure. On one stop, the crew changed the tires when he wanted only fuel. On the next, they put on the wrong tires, and he began to fall back, losing several laps before it was corrected. When on the track and running properly, he was one of the fastest cars, passing second place Andretti at one point. Shortly thereafter, he ran out of fuel, however, and by the time he made his way back to the pits, refueled, and restarted, he was in thirteenth—nine laps behind the leaders, where he would finish. Afterward, the "nasty side" of Foyt that Miller had written about was on full display.

"I have a bunch of dumbasses working for me," he said. "I've never been amateurish in my life, but we were. The radios didn't work. They cost us the race. I tried to tell them I was running out of fuel. See you next year."[40]

Foyt's troubles were overshadowed by several accidents and a controversial finish. A fire in the pits sent Rick Mears and six crewmen to the hospital, and Ongais destroyed the Batmobile in one of the most spectacular one-car accidents seen at the Speedway. Jim McKay wondered on the *ABC Sports* broadcast, "if it's all worth it."

Bobby Unser had the best car throughout and took command in the second half of the race. He took an unnecessary chance when returning to the track after a pit stop, however, accelerating past between six and eight cars—depending on who was counting—before merging into the line behind the pace car. Andretti, who'd been in second and behind Unser coming out of the pits, pulled in behind Foyt and watched as Unser "disappeared."

Foyt signed a complaint along with Andretti, Johncock, and others, charging that Unser had failed to properly rejoin the line of cars. Always a gray area, officials viewed the ABC footage, which showed Unser bypassing several gaps where he could have joined the line. The morning after the race, Unser was penalized a lap and Andretti named the winner. Even Andretti was unhappy with the ruling, saying it should have been done immediately while Unser still had a chance to regain the lead.

Now it was Unser and Penske's turn to file a protest. They pointed out that Andretti had jumped around Foyt before the restart and should also be penalized. In a hearing, Andretti stated Foyt had waved him around because A.J.'s car was "lame." When the arguments continued, Foyt was asked to testify and reluctantly returned to Indianapolis. He appeared as Andretti's final witness and said his car was "loading up" while running slow laps and "wasn't going anywhere.[41]

"I tried to get his (Andretti's) attention on Turn Four," Foyt said in the sometimes-raucous hearing. "I slowed down and with my left hand waved him up beside me. He stayed beside me until he realized what I wanted him to do. I hit the brakes (on the main straight). I wanted him to get by me. I might have moved out of the groove three or four feet. I waved him by. I knew he expected a fast start and no way was I going to make a fast start."[42]

Although he'd been slow on restarts most of the race, Rutherford, Al Unser, and others testified they hadn't noticed Foyt's car "loading up." Bobby Unser made it clear what he thought was happening:

> If [the testimonies of Rutherford and Al Unser don't] overcome the concoction that Foyt and Andretti whipped up among themselves, I don't know what does. It's clear in my own mind why Foyt testified for Mario. That was to prevent me from winning a third time and being eligible to be another four-time winner. It's just like Foyt to do something like that. I think that alone substantiates Foyt lying about his engine loading up. He should have thought of something a little more believable. Foyt and I have always disagreed on things in general. We haven't been enemies, but he does anything to remain the center of attention. That's why he did it, to help prevent me from being a four-time winner and to be the center of attention.[43]

Unser told another reporter, "He saw a chance to get me and he took it. That didn't surprise me. The man just has no feeling. He's always been like that. He doesn't care about other people. As far as what's right or wrong, you won't find a more flighty guy. He absolutely, totally, lied in that hearing."[44]

Foyt countered, saying, "It's cut and dried. You can see what happened. Bobby stretched the rule too far. It's a terrible thing that happened and he's too smart. He deserved to win."[45]

The hearings dragged on until October when, in something of a surprise, Unser was fined $40,000 but declared the winner. Despite the victory, Unser remained bitter, saying the process had been part of a conspiracy to drive a wedge between the top CART teams, and he announced his retirement.

With the Indianapolis 500 over and hearings underway to decide the winner, the uneasy truce between USAC and CART crumbled. Pocono turned down a three-year offer from CART to sanction races at the track, and the organization responded by saying any of its teams participating in the June 21 Pocono 500 could be suspended for sixty days. Facing a shortage of cars, USAC then opened the race to entries from its dirt track series in order to try and fill the field.

"Bobby Unser talked to me and attempted to have me withdraw my entry blank for the race, but I said no way," Foyt said. "I told Bobby I didn't agree with him or CART and that I was going to run. Auto racing, I always thought, was very professional. But lately, with the bickering between CART and USAC, I rather think we rank with amateurs. It's sad."[46]

A handful of CART drivers, including Tom Sneva, entered anyway. Anxious to try a new March chassis, Foyt bought one from George Bignotti for himself and entered Snider in the Coyote. Sneva was fastest in practice, but when rain canceled qualifying, Starne drew the number one starting position for Foyt in a lottery.

Seven dirt track cars completed the field, and only a handful of the rear engine machines were truly competitive. The race still set a Pocono record for lead changes as Sneva dominated early before dropping out. Foyt caught a break when he was out front and the rains came again, ending the event after 305 miles. It would be his last Indy car victory. Snider finished fourth, one lap back. A.J. said afterward that he'd been "embarrassed" by the team's performance at Indianapolis.

"You know, I lost my mother at Indy and I guess everybody was thinking about something else besides racing, me included. Maybe that's why we embarrassed ourselves there. So I want to say I won today for my father on Father's Day."[47]

"We worked day and night on the car for about a week," he said of the new March. "But we've been racing a long time and we know what you've got to do and what you can't do."[48]

Foyt skipped the CART race at Atlanta and instead went to Daytona for NASCAR's Firecracker 400, where he dropped out early. After saying he would stick with stock cars for the rest of the year, he reversed course, surprising everyone by joining CART and filing an entry form five days before the $500,000 Michigan 500 on July 19.

"They told me in order to run here, I'd have to join CART," Foyt said. "If you want to play their ball game, you've got to play by their rules. It's a 500-mile race. There's a lot of prestige to it. I just want to race, that's the biggest thing. Everything Roger Penske does, he does first-class. I don't always agree with him, but I have to admit he does things first-class."[49]

Unmentioned was the $10,000 appearance fee reportedly paid to Foyt and an understanding that he could race where and when he wanted in the future, unrestricted by CART regulations.

"I'm here because I want to race," he said. "It had nothing to do with money. No amount of money could have brought me here if I didn't want to race. My bankers and some of my friends have been trying to talk me into retiring from racing for about ten years, so it's not the money."[50]

Despite making his first appearance at the track in three years and having only a few laps of practice, Foyt qualified sixth at more than 198 mph. He was driving the new Riley-designed Coyote, the cockpit of the March having been so tight it gave him cramps at Pocono. His car was also running without the fixed side skirts allowed in CART, but thanks to the downforce generated by the Coyote design, it didn't seem to matter. He did express concern about the speeds on the track's high banks.

"It's about like [driving] a five-ton truck, loaded, with no power steering," he said. "This is the type of track where you can run yourself out fast. You'll probably see the pace slow down after 250 miles. You're going to need strategy. That's where it's going to be dangerous, especially if there's a lot of heat."[51]

Penske disagreed and seemed to take a shot at Foyt. "For drivers that are in condition, it won't be a problem."

When rain postponed the race until the following Saturday, Foyt left the track and didn't return until late Friday, missing the practice session. Hoping to help mend fences, he invited Mari Hulman George and her son, Tony, to attend the race as his guests.

The race got off to a rough start when a refueling fire in the pits forced action on the track to be stopped for ninety minutes while it was extinguished. Once the race restarted, Foyt kept pace with the leaders, although he never led. Stopping for tires and fuel on lap seventy-nine, he was still getting up to speed when he suddenly shot up the track between Turn One and Turn Two and into the Armco fence. He slid along the steel guardrail until grinding to a halt at the start of the backstraight. Both right-side tires were gone and the mammoth right-side pod of the Coyote was sheered away. Foyt's motionless head was tilted backward.

While NBC's television broadcast missed the start of the accident, Riley, sitting in the grandstands so he could see the whole track and keep his eyes on Foyt, saw it all. His first fear was that something broke on the car, and he said he was sick to his stomach.

"He was coming out of Turn Two and *bang*! He hit the outside wall real hard. He didn't lose it. It just jumped out there. You could see it was a really bad accident."[52]

Initial speculation was that Foyt hit an oil slick and skidded up the track. He'd later tell a distraught Riley a tire blew.

"He said a tire went down," Riley would say forty years later. "I know they were trying lower and lower air pressure. But I don't know for sure what happened. He may have just said that because I felt so bad. That was the way he was. For all I know, he said a tire went down just to make me feel good."

Although at times Foyt would say "something broke," years later he repeated the tire story. "It wasn't his fault. They'd [Goodyear] been up there testing and wanted to run real low air pressure. It was on the restart of the race, and they said, 'If you run a lap or two, the air pressure will build up.' 'Cept nobody told me. So, I went in the turn, and the right-front tire come off the wheel. Wasn't his fault."[53]

The first rescue crew to reach the car immediately signaled for the Jaws of Life to help cut Foyt out of the machine. His uniform was ripped away on his right side where his arm had hit the wall at one point, and his helmet was cracked.

It took several minutes to cut away the car, and he started to come around as they removed him via a backboard, transferred him to a gurney, and then placed him in an ambulance for the quick trip to the infield care center. There was plenty of blood and an obvious compound fracture of his right arm and puncture injury to his left leg. CART medical director Dr. Stephen Olvey, concerned about other injuries, including a concussion and broken leg, started an IV. He wrapped the still-groggy Foyt's upper body as best he could and called for a helicopter to transport the driver to the University of Michigan hospital in Ann Arbor, the prearranged trauma center for the race.

Helicopters weren't yet part of the standard safety equipment at a racetrack, and the only chopper on the grounds was Penske's, who quickly made it available. It wasn't configured for medical use, however, and more than a dozen people tried to jockey the stretcher into the cockpit behind the pilot, Foyt eventually ending up kitty-corner from the back across the front passenger seat. They banged his broken arm against the doorway several times in the process, and as a result, Foyt was soon fully awake and letting everyone know he was in a great deal of pain.

"When he came to, A.J. said, 'I'm really hurting,'" said sponsor and friend Jim Gilmore after Foyt had departed. "He was pretty badly shaken up. He hit hard. He's a fine, tough guy, though. He's going to be OK."[54]

At U of M, doctors upgraded him to fair condition, noting "a rather serious compound fracture of the right forearm" but "no evidence of head or spine injury." Crew Chief Starne was one of the first to reach the hospital. He had called Lucy to alert her to the accident, and she was already on her way to Ann Arbor.[55]

"I went in to see him just before he went in for surgery," Starne recalled. "They had his arm hanging up on a hook—kind of like in the meat market—and blood was just pouring out. An aide was mopping it up. I couldn't believe it."[56]

A two-hour surgery set the arm and reconstructed his elbow. Doctors said he should regain full use of both, although there could be some muscle loss. Afterward, Foyt jokingly complained to the doctors about the long and jagged scar that ran from his forearm to the back of his elbow.

"With all the staff and equipment y'all got here, why can't you cut a nice straight incision?" he asked. In the years to come, he often delighted in telling the story and showing off his scar.[57]

A hospital spokesperson said Foyt was alert and talking and was expected to remain at U of M for at least a week but acknowledged the driver already wanted to go home.

Sunday morning, Mike Harris, the Associated Press motorsports reporter, stopped by the hospital in Ann Arbor to check on Foyt's condition. He thought he'd seen the end of the driver's career. He spotted Lucy Foyt and tentatively approached her. He introduced himself, asked how A.J. was doing, and was surprised by the response.

"He'll be fine," Lucy said, indicating he'd drive again. "He's hurting right now, but he'll be fine."[58]

"Most people would have just given up after a crash that bad—just said, *Enough of this. I'm never going back racing again,*" Harris recalled thinking. "But it never even occurred to him. That's just what he did. He was just an amazingly tough man."

On Monday, Foyt took his private jet home from Ann Arbor, and after spending a couple more days at Memorial City General Hospital in Houston, he headed for his ranch. He had his own ideas about rehab for the arm, and it included painting the miles of white fencing surrounding his properties. He left no doubt about retirement, saying he already had two new cars on order for the coming year.

"Nah, I'm not quitting," he said on the way to his ranch. "The only thing that scares me in a thing like this is thinking how close I was to losing an arm or hitting your head hard. If something like that happens, I hope it goes all the way."[59]

Although a concussion wasn't part of the original diagnosis, it soon became apparent he'd sustained a significant head injury with all the classic symptoms, including nausea and continued headaches that felt "like fingers being punched through my eyes."[60]

"That's never happened before," he said. "The doctors said that was from the inner brain being jammed against the outer brain. It's getting harder to come back from each crash. I'm tired of hurting."[61]

Despite the lingering problems, he was more determined than ever to stage a comeback. Even though doctors urged extended rest for the head injury, he was back on the road within two months, attending the Hoosier 100 and a horse auction in Lexington, Kentucky, where he bought four more thoroughbreds.

Foyt would never again drive a Coyote. The 1981 car was rebuilt and sold to Bob Harkey, whose career came to an end following a practice crash in the car at Indianapolis in 1983. It would be rebuilt again and displayed at the Speedway Museum.

A shaken Riley quit Indy car racing a second time following the Michigan crash, shifting his focus to sports and stock cars. Although Riley would eventually return to help Foyt again in 1991, he said A.J. was never the same driver after Michigan.

"I don't believe he was ever a great driver again after that accident," Riley said. "He was a very good race car driver, but he was no longer the phenomenal talent I had witnessed for so many years—the guy who was able to bounce a car off of Turn One at Indy in qualifying."[62]

abc
BELL

CHAPTER 5

COOGIN!

1982

The calls for A.J. Foyt to retire started soon after his Michigan crash and continued through the offseason.

"He has nothing to prove, no more worlds to conquer, and each time he climbs into the cockpit of a race car he is risking death or injury for money and fame that he does not need," wrote Bob Barnet in the Muncie, Indiana, *Star Press*. "Come on Tex—hang 'em up and give us a chance to remember you as a great champion who knew when to quit."[1]

An executive from Chevrolet called during the winter with an offer for Foyt to drive the Camaro pace car for the upcoming Indianapolis 500. A.J. was, after all, a Chevrolet dealer. "Wasn't that nice of them," Foyt said. He didn't hang up on the suit but let him know in so many words that he intended to be "following the pace car at the start of the race, not driving it."[2]

The 1970s had been good to Foyt in more ways than one. In addition to winning his fourth Indy 500, numerous races and championships, he'd gone through the decade without suffering a major accident, and it had been more than fifteen years since his crash at Riverside. Now, at forty-seven, he discovered it was taking him longer to bounce back.

"There's no sense kidding yourself," he acknowledged. "I don't care who you are, the older you get the harder it is. I've aged more than a year in the last six months. That's why I'm having to think about retirement. I don't have a whole lot of time left. I'm not looking forward to just being a car owner, but it's coming.[3]

"I guess what got me motivated again was when the docs started putting pressure on me not to race. That made me want to get back all the more."

◀ Chris Economaki interviews Foyt following crash at start of 1982 Indy 500. *IMS Photo Archive*

When Foyt turned down the pace car offer, Chevrolet approached another of its dealers, Jim Rathmann, who had retired three years after winning the 1960 Indy 500. Rathmann said he knew what Foyt was going through. "A.J. has the disease. It's like gambling or drinking, you get hooked."[4]

Foyt's rehab for his rebuilt arm had gone well. He'd painted the miles of fencing around his properties and just about everything else that didn't move. He used a spray gun instead of a brush because it required ten pounds of pressure to pull the trigger. He went through "about a thousand gallons of paint" in a little more than a month, and when he was done, he pronounced himself ready to go.[5]

"The elbow feels real good where the screw is. They wanted to operate and take it out, but I wouldn't let them. I said maybe after May, but it's not bothering me."

He went to Daytona in mid-January to test his arm and a new Oldsmobile stock car. He walked around subconsciously holding his arm as if it was still in a sling and showed off his jagged, half-inch-wide and dark purple scar to anyone who asked. He bragged about moving his two little fingers on his right hand, saying doctors told him he'd never be able to do it again.

"I've only raced in about ten races in the last two years, so I've got to get back in shape," Foyt said. "I'm as green as the race car. Mainly I came here to get comfortable in a car and see if I want to race or get back in a rocking chair. If you can run here, you can run anywhere in the world. In a champ car, you don't wrestle the wheel like you do in a stock car."[6]

He ran his first laps in the latest machine from Dick Hutcherson and Eddie Pagan at more than 190 miles per hour and attracted a crowd of journalists afterward. Foyt was happy to be back in the limelight. When reporters pointed out it had been ten years since he'd won the Daytona 500 or any NASCAR race, he reminded them he won a Daytona qualifier in 1978. He regaled them with tales of the Michigan crash, embellishing an accident that needed no embellishment.

"I bounced off the wall twelve or thirteen times," he told the NASCAR scribes, and most were hanging on every word. "I was on two wheels upside down, slammed my body—with my arm hanging out of the car—into the wall. It sort of scraped all the flesh from my arm and I knew it was broke because it hurt like hell. But I wasn't going to be held back by a slight little injury. Doesn't hurt any more than an old toothache."[7]

Those who listened carefully also heard a new message from Foyt. No longer did he expect to win. He hoped to "run well" and called racing "a hobby."

"I enjoy racing, I enjoy the racing people, and I think they're glad to see me come back. Everybody has to have a hobby. This is mine. If I come back decent, I'll be pleased. Of course I'd like to win it, but first I've got to prove to myself I can run with these guys again."[8]

At one point, he even agreed with a reporter who said he seemed to be more laid back.

"I guess I have mellowed," he said. "But when I'm workin' I'm still probably a miserable bastard. I just don't have time to B.S."

Foyt continued to help Rick Wilson, a twenty-nine-year-old driver in his second season running the NASCAR circuit. After dominating the local Daytona short tracks, Wilson was trying to make it in the Cup series with his own team and bought an Oldsmobile like Foyt's from Hutcherson-Pagan.

The relationship had started at Daytona the year before at the Firecracker 400. After qualifying eighth—faster than Foyt—Wilson couldn't find anyone willing to draft with him in practice and for a good reason: He was making just his ninth Cup start, hadn't finished a race, and showed a tendency for crashing.

"Nobody wanted to risk getting their cars chewed up by a rookie driver and I couldn't blame them," Wilson said. He complained loudly enough that Foyt finally said, "Let's go. Get your butt out there."[9]

"We drafted each other and tried a lot of things," Wilson said. "He's got his own ways and when he says something, you listen and you do it. He'll help you as long as you listen to him, and as long as you don't think he's too dang high a God or whatever, to listen to. He'd be watching me out running and I'd come in and he'd be cussin' and raisin' hell and say why'd you do this and why'd you do that. I'd say, 'Well, I'm just learnin'.'"

No one was sure why Foyt had decided to help Wilson, least of all Wilson. "For some reason he likes me," he said. "A lot of people have said to me they don't understand why he likes me—because he don't like nobody.

"One thing about A.J.," Hutcherson added, "he either likes you or he don't."

Wilson also became a checkpoint for reporters looking to interview Foyt.

"A lot of people in the media have come up to me and asked, 'What kind of mood's A.J. in today?' They'll stand around a little while, see if he's hollerin' and cussin' and then edge in a little by little. If he's rantin' and raisin' hell, they won't get within ten yards of him."[10]

Not happy with the ninth-fastest time in practice, Foyt bought the sister car to Buddy Baker's Buick from his old car owner, Hoss Ellington. The Buicks dominated qualifying and were the hot ticket. They featured a new "front steer" chassis design, and Foyt wanted to see what all the buzz was about. He elected to stick with his Oldsmobile and ran with the leaders in his qualifying race, fading to fifth at the finish. He blamed himself, saying he "just screwed up" and was too timid in the last lap scramble. He also had a scare when the car of Gary Balough blew an engine while they were running side-by-side.

"Whooee, didja see that time with Balough?" he asked as he climbed from the car, his voice jumping an octave or two as it often did when he was excited. He enjoyed recounting the event, sound effects and all. "Balough blew an engine or somethin' and got sideways. I could see him coming up at me and I couldn't do anything but back off and I said, 'Gawdammit, here he comes,' aagghhh, and I went whoawooohhh, and I said, 'This is it.' Don't know how I missed him.[11]

"I feel real happy, like a kid with an ice cream cone."

He didn't even seem to mind when he blew the engine in his car during the final practice session. He bought a new one from Junior Johnson and spent the evening before the 500 at the track helping his crew swap powerplants.[12]

The race itself was another story. He never led, and after making several attempts to fix the car's handling, parked it after 145 laps. "It was just too bad to drive. Otherwise I'm not talking."[13]

He headed for the Daytona airport next to the track and was winging his way west before the race was over. Some speculated he'd been physically unable to complete the race, and he'd admit to as much later, saying, "I felt like a whipped puppy."[14.]

He tried again a month later at the NASCAR race in Atlanta but completed only seventeen laps before parking his car. He finished last in a thirty-nine-car field, and no one could remember the last time Foyt finished last in anything. If he knew, he wasn't saying, and he refused to talk to reporters as he left.

The retirement questions eased when Foyt took delivery of two new Marches for the Indy car season, then started anew when he skipped the first two races at Phoenix and Atlanta. The decision to order the Marches rather than build a new Coyote was a major concession by Foyt. At $150,000 each and $100,000 per Cosworth engine with spares, it was also a major investment. But there simply wasn't the time—nor the desire—to start over again with a new Coyote.

"I couldn't test no more," A.J. said, looking back on the aftermath of his Michigan crash. "So we decided to start buying cars."[15]

In addition to his own experience driving one to victory at Pocono, the March in the hands of George Bignotti and Tom Sneva had proven itself to be the fastest car on the ovals, and teams had ordered a baker's dozen of the new 82C from the English company. Tony Foyt and Jack Starne were dispatched to London to work with the company and make changes to the car's nose, cowling, and windshield to reflect what they'd learned with the Coyote—changes Foyt complained were then made to all the new cars. One change he wanted that wasn't made to the other cars was a bigger cockpit. He had ballooned to about 250 pounds during his recovery, and while he was losing weight, one reporter at Daytona wrote, "His stomach looks like the Goodyear blimp at low altitude."[16]

Although Tony Foyt made the trip to England, he'd never really reclaimed the position of crew chief after leaving the team to help care for his wife during her illness. Starne now filled the role. Although in reality, little had changed—A.J. was in charge. Tony made it clear several times he wished his son would retire but said he wouldn't "even try to guess" at when A.J. might step back.[17]

"He's got his own mind," the elder Foyt said. "I knew the accident would not make him stop. He'll stop only when he wants to. I'd like to have seen him quit years ago. I just give up on it. When he wants to quit, he'll quit. I just don't say anything anymore."

The team arrived at the Speedway on Friday, May 7, the day before practice started. Valvoline held a press conference marking Foyt's twenty-fifth year at the track, and a light rain failed to dampen his mood as he captivated the assembled media. He looked sharp as always, with a gray suede sport coat, sports shirt, and slacks over his cowboy boots. Introduced as the "tough Texan," and the "world's greatest race driver," he seemed melancholy at times.[18]

"Yeah, I guess I'm kind of a bastard sometimes. But I'm a pretty serious man at the racetrack. A lot of times I've got things on my mind you people don't know about. I'm moody, but maybe I have mellowed a little bit. I'm kind of like the weather around here."

While Foyt was making his first tentative laps in an Indy car since the Michigan crash, Rick Mears was flying. He'd put in a reported 3,000 miles testing the new Penske PC-10 chassis, and it took him only eleven laps to set a new unofficial record of 203.7 mph, breaking Foyt's four-year-old mark.

Mears's speed was soon topped by his new teammate, Kevin Cogan. With only a limited amount of experience, Cogan had burst on the scene the previous year with a fourth place as a rookie at Indianapolis and was then scooped up by Roger Penske for the 1982 season. As pole day approached, ten drivers were over 200 mph, including Foyt—despite running just twelve hot laps all week, saying he was "still tuning myself up."[19]

Cogan, described by Robin Miller as "a super smooth Indy sophomore," was the first of the Penske stablemates to take the track in qualifying. After blowing an engine in his primary car in practice, he moved to his backup and set a new track record. It didn't last long as Mears turned in a stunning four-lap average of 207.004 mph to capture the pole.[20]

Having drawn a late qualifying spot, Foyt watched the early runs from his second turn suite, mixing with family, friends, and sponsors. His hopes of qualifying early so he could go to Churchill Downs where one of his horses, Amazing Love, was running in a major stakes race had been ruined by the late draw. He took it as a good omen when the horse finished first. Then he watched as Sneva crashed during his qualifying attempt, in nearly the same spot where Foyt had glanced off the wall the year before.

Next up was Gordon Smiley. Attempting to make his third straight 500, Smiley had told bystanders he would win the pole or crash trying. He was on his warmup lap when he lost control in the third turn and made a hard right, straight into the concrete wall. In one of the most horrendous crashes ever seen at the Speedway, there was a flash fire, and the March broke apart—the engine compartment going in one direction, the driver cockpit in another, and Smiley's helmet bounding down the track. Debris was scattered over several hundred feet, and gouges six inches deep were cut into the track surface. First responders weren't sure where to look for the driver. Smiley died instantly—the first fatality at the Speedway in nine years.

When it became apparent the cleanup and repairs from Smiley's crash would take some time, Foyt moved away from the now-somber group in the suite. He said he thought of Pat O'Connor, who was killed in a third-turn crash in 1958 on Foyt's first race at the Speedway. He said he was "trying to be by myself. Something like that takes the race out of me."[21]

While waiting, he watched replays of Sneva's crash and saw that the March was "pushing," the front end losing traction. No. 14 was already in the qualifying line when he returned to the pits, and Foyt asked Starne to "crank some more wing in the front end." The move would increase downforce on the front wheels and improve the handling, but he worried whether they had done "too much," as it could also slow the car.

His first lap was more than 204 mph, faster than Cogan's average. A bobble between Turn One and Turn Two slowed his second and third laps before he topped 204 again on his last circuit. The speed was third fastest overall and good for a front-row starting spot, but he didn't feel like celebrating, calling Smiley's death "a terrible tragedy."[22]

"You're never ready for something like that, at least I never am," he said. "These cars are safe, until you hit wrong. I don't care if you're in a Sherman tank, if you hit wrong, it's all over."

The team's original plan for George Snider to qualify the second March went awry when the car wasn't completed by midweek before the final qualifying weekend. Instead, Foyt opened his checkbook and secured Smiley's backup car for Snider to drive, which he easily put into the field.

With the race approaching, Foyt sounded like the A.J. of old. There was no talk of racing being a "hobby."

"I'm not here to run second, let's put it that way," he said. "I don't care if it's a heat race or a helmet dash, I want to win whatever I'm in. If it's a go-kart race, I still want to win."[23]

Jim Gilmore, who was back for his tenth year as a Foyt sponsor and friend, saw the change. "A.J. is a very highly motivated man. I just don't think the guy is ever going to quit. A lot of people say A.J. has changed. Well, he hasn't changed a darned bit."[24]

Something else had changed. Throughout the month, Foyt was greeted by cheers and applause whenever he ventured out of his garage. He stopped often to sign autographs. Many fans wore the "Foyt plus 25 equals 5" buttons being sold at concession stands in recognition of his twenty-five years of racing at the Speedway and his pursuit of a fifth 500. The boos of the last couple of years were nowhere to be heard.

"I'm glad of that," he said. "They must still like me. Maybe I've been around so long I've grown on them."[25]

Seventeen of the cars in the starting lineup were Marches, and Foyt warned that so many drivers in the same basic car would make the racing not only closer but also more dangerous. He said ground effects "give you a false feeling of security," when actually, "you have to concentrate more. You can't afford to lose that concentration for a second, 'cause if you do, you're liable to be in the wall."[26]

He also expressed concern about the relative inexperience of the field, with nine rookie drivers and two more starting their second 500. Cogan, the driver lining up next to Foyt on the front row, was only two-years-old when A.J. started his first Indy 500 in 1958. The fastest rookie qualifier, Chip Ganassi, hadn't even been born yet. Foyt took the unusual step of asking officials to mark the cars of rookies with three black stripes on the rear wing to help identify the first-time drivers, a move USAC and the Speedway agreed to make.

Nothing seemed to bother Cogan as he turned in the fastest laps on Carb Day, edging out teammate Mears. Cogan insisted he planned to take it easy at the start and "keep out of trouble."[27]

The field was tightly bunched when Mears led it down to the start. Some would say later the start was too slow—"Way way, waaaaay too slow," according to Bobby Unser—but Mears said he did nothing different from previous races he'd started from the pole.[28]

As the front row slowly accelerated toward the start/finish line, Cogan's car suddenly veered to the right "as if he turned the wheel intentionally," Sam Posey said on the television broadcast. Cogan's right-front tire hit Foyt's left front and sent the No. 14 car into a slide. Then the rear tires hit, with the second impact straightening Foyt's car and sending him snaking down the track.

"I was going sideways back and forth and I caught it," Foyt said. "It was just strictly luck."[29]

Not as lucky was Andretti. Cogan ricocheted off Foyt and shot back across the track into Andretti's path. Andretti slammed into the middle of the Penske, knocking it up and over the front of his car. Both cars hit the wall. They were out of the race.

After regaining control, Foyt drove slowly around the track with the remainder of the field, the red flag having been displayed to stop the race before it started. While the other cars pulled into the pits, A.J. drove by the accident scene, shaking his fist at Cogan, then pulled over and stopped. He got out of the car and surveyed the damage, the main problem being a bent left steering arm that helps set and maintain the tire position. It could be repaired during the red flag period, and he sent crew men running back to Gasoline Alley for parts and tools. Then he went looking for Cogan.

The young driver had immediately run to Andretti and tried to explain what happened, but Andretti didn't want to hear it, pushing him away before turning to talk with a group of reporters, including Bill Flemming of *ABC Sports*.

"This is what happens when you have children doing a man's job up front," said Andretti, who had been replaced by Cogan at Penske Racing. "Cogan, I guess, just messed up and cut right in front of me. I had no choice but to T-bone him." Later Andretti said Cogan initially claimed Foyt had caused the crash.[30]

Another ABC reporter, Chris Economaki, chased down A.J. and asked what had happened. "Well I don't know, he ran into my goddam left front," said an upset Foyt.

"Who you talking about?" Economaki asked.

"Coogin!" Foyt yelled, mispronouncing the other driver's name in a response that would become part of Foyt lore.

When Economaki asked Cogan if he was to blame, he said, "I don't think so. I didn't do anything wrong. I didn't do anything out of the ordinary. It just veered to the right."

While this was going on, Foyt's crew was able to repair the steering arm, although there wasn't time to reset the geometry they'd spent much of the month fine-tuning. He was calm and hopeful as the restart approached, and Economaki asked about the car's handling.

"I think we can get it pretty close," A.J. said before admitting, "We're just guessing. If it's too bad I'll just have to park it."

He didn't waste any time finding out. Side-by-side with Mears when the green flag was finally displayed, Foyt never lifted, taking the lead in the first turn and stretching it to ten car lengths by the end of the first lap. It was the first time he'd ever led the opening lap of the 500, and he did it at record speed. He set another record for the second lap and would go on to set new marks for ten miles, twenty-five miles, and fifty miles before pitting. Watching from the television booth, Posey was in awe.

"Amazing courage to be able to do that," he said. "Almost anybody else, you would think, would have given it a turn or two to feel it out. Not A.J. Foyt. He is one of the most remarkable race car drivers ever to get in the cockpit of a car and this is proof positive."

Added Jackie Stewart, another member of the broadcast team, "A.J. Foyt is a man possessed. Certainly he's driving like a young A.J. Foyt. I've never seen him drive so hard. He was so angry after the start of the race that he seemed to get in there, put his race face on, and drive with a sort of gritted determination perhaps we haven't seen for ten years."

Foyt led through the first round of pit stops and was still running with the leaders as he made his second stop. This time, however, the fuel nozzle stuck open momentarily as it was pulled away from the car, dousing Foyt with methanol.

Realizing what happened, he ignored a crewman trying to stop him and took off, hoping the wind would put out a possible fire or at least keep the flames behind him while helping to evaporate the methanol.

"Fuel just poured into the cockpit when he pulled out," Starne said. "It was like he was sitting in a bomb. He couldn't slow down on that lap because he didn't want flames to come shooting out of a turbocharger and set the thing off."[31]

"I've never seen so much fuel without a fire in my life," Gilmore added.[32]

Foyt was wearing a new five-layer Racestar driver's uniform. Not only was it more fire resistant with three separate Nomex layers, it included a layer of Kevlar and one of GORE-TEX, a relatively new material designed to repel fluids. It was expensive at $45 a square yard, but worth it.[33]

"I was probably silly for what I did," he said of returning to the track. "I was trying to make a lap. I knew we still had a good chance to win the race. Right before that happened the car started handling beautiful. I was sitting back there riding where we wanted to. I couldn't ask the car to perform any better, it was just fabulous."[34]

He unlatched his belts and was prepared to jump from the car as he returned to the pits, but the crew quickly ascertained there was no fire and poured water over him for good measure. "If that (fire) would have happened, I would have looked like a Buddhist monk," he'd say.[35]

It took some time to refasten the belts, however, and by the time he returned to the track, he was a lap down in eighth place. "The car was never the same," Starne said.[36]

The next stop was more methodical, the crew concerned about the fuel nozzle, and Foyt pulled away without incident. Only not for long. Accelerating hard out of the pits, he was unable to shift out of third gear and was back after one lap.

Foyt sat in the car, becoming increasingly frustrated as crew members tried to pop the transmission out of gear. After several minutes, he unlatched his belts again and climbed out, this time for good. He ripped off his gloves and tossed them into the cockpit. "No sense fucking with it now," he shouted before pulling off his helmet and dropping it into the car. He walked around to the right rear and flipped off a body panel covering the transmission linkage, demanding a ball-peen hammer and a long screw driver. Then he started pounding away at the balky linkage, the crowd loving every moment.[37]

"I would say Foyt is a bit unhappy," track announcer Tom Carnegie said in the understatement of the race.

Billy Woodruff was one of the crew who'd been trying to unjam the transmission: "When he's coming back down pit road, he's yelling on the radio to get a screwdriver and to knock that thing out of gear," Woodruff recalled years later. "I ran out there with a screwdriver and a hammer, and I beat on that son of a bitch. You couldn't beat on it no harder than I was beating on it.[38]

"Then I started seeing the belts flying. The crowd's hollering, and here he comes. I got me a double handful of that screwdriver, and he beat on that thing. I was praying to God, 'Please don't let this thing come out of gear. He'll kill me.' But he couldn't get it out either."

After a few minutes, Foyt gave up and headed back to Gasoline Alley, chased by a horde of journalists who wanted to know about the prerace accident. He finally stopped at the entrance to his garage.

"It was a stupid deal," he said before slamming the door. "The guy had his head up his ass."[39]

After about twenty minutes he invited the Houston reporters inside. Another twenty minutes passed and he emerged in street clothes, saying he had only a few minutes to answer questions, most of which were posed by Economaki. Then, as he'd done several times before in past years, he climbed on his motorcycle and roared away.

The pace-lap accident overshadowed an exciting finish as Gordon Johncock turned back Mears's challenge to win by 16/100ths of a second, the closest finish in history at that point. Mears pulled alongside Johncock several times in the final laps, including going into Turn One after taking the white flag, but backed off each time when Johncock came down the track.

"If it had been me in Mears's place, the third-place car would have won the race," Foyt said later. "But that's the difference between me and Mears. He took second, which might be fine for him. But not for me."[40]

Mears laughed nearly forty years later when reminded of Foyt's comments.

"That was just typical A.J. I knew that was bullshit. He's smarter than that. He wouldn't have four Indy wins and all these other races and championships by making decisions like that. It was just A.J. being A.J."[41]

It was never confirmed whether driver error or a broken part caused Cogan to lose control at the start. Some thought Cogan was in too low a gear and too hard on the gas pedal when the field began to accelerate, the incredible torque produced by the 800 horsepower Cosworth engine yanking the car to the right. It was a mistake made by drivers in the past and would be made by others in the future. A broken driveshaft or CV (constant velocity) joint could cause a similar reaction and would later in the race when Tony Bettenhausen suddenly turned into the wall in nearly the same manner and location.

Both explanations were plausible, although many fans had already made up their minds. Cogan was seen as a rich kid playing with race cars, and they began to boo him wherever he went. He later implied that Penske and team manager Derrick Walker had hidden the fact something broke on the car. Years later, Andretti acknowledged a broken part probably did cause the crash, and at times Foyt would agree—although not always.

Cogan would be released by Roger Penske at the end of the season, and while his career continued for another sixteen years, he would forever be known as "Coogin!"

Foyt announced he would race at Milwaukee in two weeks, his first trip to the track since posting a dominating victory in 1979. It was good news for the promoters who, after several lean years during the USAC/CART war noted, "A.J. usually means a sellout." It would be Foyt's first time to drive a ground effects car for 150 miles on a tight, one-mile short track, and some voiced their concern about his stamina.[42]

His first stop, however, was Churchill Downs, and it marked a welcome change of scenery as Amazing Love won a second-straight stakes race.

"This is very relaxing for me," he said in Victory Lane, holding his son Tony's two children. "I really enjoy horse racing. It's a whole different game than with the cars."[43]

"My friends in car racing look at me funny, but I figure at this late stage, as old as I'm getting, I'm going to start enjoying what A.J. enjoys instead of doing what somebody else thinks I should do."[44]

He arrived too late at the Milwaukee track for practice, although it didn't seem to matter as he qualified seventh. In the race he finished second to Johncock and ahead of Mears in third, although Foyt complained he'd won, noting he'd made one pit stop compared to Johncock's two.

"We didn't stop but once," he said, and headed for the official scorers. "I don't think he beat me."[45]

"Foyt finished second?" Johncock shot back. "I thought he dropped out. I hadn't heard about him or seen him." Eventually, the scorers convinced Foyt the finish was correct, and no protest was filed.

Gordon Johncock

Johncock's snarky remarks surprised some, but his relationship with Foyt had deteriorated in recent years and would continue to go downhill. They'd once been good friends—as good a friend as A.J. had among the other Indy car drivers.

Johncock had driven Foyt's cars on occasion, and it was Foyt who stopped Johncock from going to the site of Swede Savage's crash during the 1973 Indy 500, a move Johncock credited with helping him win the race. It was Johncock who suggested Foyt call Gilmore about sponsorship, and it was Johncock who ran to check on Foyt after his crash at Daytona. Foyt had also said Gordy "could match any driver in the world in the way he rides the curves at Indianapolis."[46]

While he was always available to the media and responsive, Johncock's answers were often straightforward and to the point, seldom effusive or entertaining. He was shy, even introverted, compared to many of his contemporaries and seldom the first choice of journalists looking for a quote.

"He keeps things inside and doesn't make any waves," his wife Lynda said after the second Indy 500 win. "If he had an outgoing personality like A.J. Foyt, Mario Andretti or Bobby Unser, people wouldn't be wondering why Gordy has suddenly become a winner. They'd know that he's been a winner all along."[47]

The Foyt/Johncock relationship had started going downhill when they ended up on opposite sides of the USAC/CART civil war. And while Mears was able to laugh off Foyt's comments about the 1982 finish, Johncock never could. And the more Johncock won, the greater the divide between him and Foyt grew.

"Johncock is like most guys who win Indy: They change overnight," Foyt is quoted as saying in his autobiography that was published shortly after the 1982 race. "He's become one of the biggest crybabies in racing. Just because he won the 500 he thinks he's super big now and everybody should do things his way."[48]

While Johncock declined requests for interviews regarding Foyt, he did open up to *AutoWeek* on the occasion of the fiftieth anniversary of his 1973 race win.

"We had a pretty good relationship when I first started," Johncock said of Foyt, "but it got to where I realized how bad he was able to cheat at racing, and it really kind of got to me. There'd be times he'd qualify and come back to the garage area, and USAC inspectors wanted to go in the garage and he wouldn't let them in, so I guess that had to tell you something. Then guys would clock him on the backstretch and see how much faster he was going than other cars."[49]

Johncock told *AutoWeek* that at times he wished he had lost the 1982 500 because then Mears would have five Indy wins, "and I wouldn't have to hear about Foyt winning number four all the time. I gave Foyt his number four and he took my own number three away (in 1977). That one most definitely still eats at me. I'd have to say my biggest disappointment in life was when that engine blew and gave him his fourth win."

When Foyt announced he would race in the July 18 Michigan 500, he said Johncock told him, "You're just here for the money. You'll make a big deal out of it and probably quit after ten laps."[50]

"Listen buddy boy," Foyt says he responded, "you ain't never seen the day you can run with me."

A.J. missed the opening practice session at MIS while attending the funeral of his sponsor's father, Jim Gilmore Sr. The first thing he noticed when he arrived at the track was the cement wall replacing the Armco railing that had nearly torn his arm off the year before. "I hit that guardrail so hard it isn't even there anymore," he joked.[51]

"You feel safer and run a little higher on the track (with a cement wall)," Foyt said. "The wall is higher, so you get less effect from the wind. I know I'm lucky to have my arm, but an accident like that isn't going to keep me out of racing."

He qualified eighth and took it easy in the early going, keeping the leaders in sight but not challenging. It was a long race. That changed when he was judged to have passed the pace car following a pit stop and was black-flagged, losing a lap on the stop-and-go penalty. Forced to run hard, he eventually got back on the same lap as the leaders, passing Johncock and Andretti in the process. "The car was really flying," he'd say. "It looked like things were just falling in place. The car was very capable of winning."[52]

He was fourth behind Andretti, Mears, and Johncock with about 200 miles remaining and coming to the green flag after a caution period. Running high on the track, he was passing a line of slower cars in the bottom groove, including Héctor Rebaque, who'd spent much of the race in the pits and was eighty laps behind the leaders. Rebaque was a veteran of forty-three Formula One races over five years but was a rookie on the Indy car circuit and making just this third oval track start.

His mechanical problems solved, Rebaque was running hard and came up on Spike Gehlhausen, who was twenty laps behind and having transmission problems. When Gehlhausen's car suddenly stuck in second gear and slowed, Rebaque swerved to the right and lost control, his car shooting up the track and spearing Foyt.

There was a magnesium flash fire as both machines pushed into the wall. The impacts sent one of Foyt's wheels flapping against the cockpit and knocked the others askew as the two machines slid down into the infield. Rebaque jumped out of his car unhurt. Foyt tried to wiggle out, but his feet were caught in the pedals. First responders covered the car with firefighting foam to be safe.

"For a minute," said Gilmore, who'd been watching on television, "I thought we were in terrible trouble."

Trapped in his car, Foyt raised his arms to indicate he was okay, and it took five burly rescue workers to lift him from the cockpit and carry him to a stretcher. He had a puncture wound on his left leg, a badly bruised right ankle and a sore tailbone. Doctors in the infield care center wanted to transfer him to a local hospital for X-rays, but he refused, saying he'd return to Houston for any further treatment.

Starne drove Gilmore's car into the compound, and Foyt left the care center barefooted and got in for the ride to the local airport and his plane. He emerged a moment later to talk with the NBC crew and a few print journalists who'd been waiting for him.

"I was a victim of circumstances," he said. "I just happened to be there and there was nothing I could do about it. Some of these guys should take tests. They're in over their heads. Only seven or eight know how to drive."[53]

Johncock went on to win over teammate Andretti, his third victory in four races.

Foyt missed the next race at Milwaukee while his backup March was prepared. He was unhappy with the car from the start at Pocono, qualifying twelfth. He pitted on lap four to have a wheel tightened and was never competitive, stopping for good on lap seventy. He refused to talk to reporters, although the track's press notes provided a comment supplied by an unnamed crewman who reported Foyt as saying, "I'm bleeping tired of driving that ill-handling bleep."[54]

He skipped the next two road course events while Rebaque showed off his road racing skills with a win at Road America. It was also Rebaque's last race in an Indy car as he was injured the following week in a testing crash at Michigan. He'd run one more F1 event in early 1983 then retire at age twenty-eight.

Foyt was back for the September 26, 150-miler at Michigan. In a repeat of Indianapolis, he qualified third behind the Penske cars of Mears and Cogan.

Cogan took the lead on the start as Mears dropped back. Foyt then moved up to challenge for the front spot, diving under Cogan as the pair went into the first turn to start lap nine.

According to Dick Mittman in the *Indianapolis News*, "As they got into the center of the turn, Cogan powered slightly in front, but also came right down across the path of Foyt. There was no way Foyt could avoid T-boning the blond Californian's car.[55]

"I was past him," Foyt said. "I couldn't believe it when he came down on me like that."

Both cars shot up the track and into the outside wall. Cogan's rolled down to the bottom while Foyt's came to a rest at nearly the same point where he'd hit the fence the year before. He struggled out of the cockpit and walked around to the front of the car, where he sat down to await the safety crew. When they arrived, he put his arm around one of the crew members and steered him, limping, toward Cogan. Foyt asked Cogan repeatedly what he was trying to prove and why he hadn't just backed off.

"I saw Mr. Foyt having a strong conversation with Mr. Cogan," said driver Bill Alsup. "Cogan had his helmet on. The smartest thing Mr. Cogan did was keep his helmet on."[56]

Cogan said, "I was driving in my usual groove and we got together and spun out. I was driving my normal groove on the racetrack."

The *Indianapolis Star* was more reluctant to blame the young driver. "Whether Cogan came down into Foyt or the four-time Indy winner drove into the Speedway sophomore was a tough call," wrote Robin Miller. "It looked a lot like one of those things that happen whenever open wheeled cars run side-by-side."[57]

Cogan would later say more about the incident:

> I made a mistake in not speaking up [at the time of the Michigan crash] but anything I say goes against me because the press takes what Foyt says as gospel. He says I ran into him but the film shows just the opposite. He obviously didn't have the lead going into the corner. All he had to do was lift. When he was yelling at me after the crash, he kept saying why didn't I back off. Why should I be the one to back off? I was leading. If he thought what he did was intimidating, he made a mistake. I'm comfortable leading a race, it wasn't my first time.[58]

Foyt agreed to a hospital trip, where X-rays of his left foot proved negative. His sense of humor wasn't injured, and he was able to joke about the crash afterward. "This is run over A.J. Foyt year." After returning to Houston, he complained of a sore wrist and X-rays confirmed he'd broken it in the crash. Combined with two destroyed Indy cars, his season was over.

Penske fired Cogan at the end of the year, and there was speculation Foyt would replace him. He was eventually asked what it would take for him to team with Penske.

"Big numbers," A.J. said. "I would have driven for Penske if he would have come up with the money." Instead, he ordered a new March and started piecing together another car from the two machines he'd wrecked at Michigan. Penske hired Al Unser to take Cogan's place.

Thanks to his good start to the season, Mears would hold on to win the CART championship. He was also being increasingly compared to Foyt. During A.J.'s first seven years, he'd won seventeen USAC races, three national titles, and one Indy 500. Mears's record was identical, with seventeen race wins, three national titles, and one Indy 500. Mears was typically humble and gracious when asked about the Foyt comparisons.

"It's just a great honor that we're anywhere close to what A.J. Foyt has done. If we continue it throughout the years and run as long as Foyt has and continue with our good fortune, and if I stay with the right people, maybe we can even better it a little bit."[59]

At the end of the year, Bobby Unser announced he was retiring.

"For the first time I realized that I had been thinking only of Bobby Unser and perhaps it was time to think about my family," he said. He was the first to retire from the group of drivers who'd dominated Indy-car racing for the past twenty years—Foyt, Andretti, Al Unser, Johncock, and Johnny Rutherford—and the calls for others to retire soon followed.[60]

"I wish all drivers could reach a point in their careers where the voices in the background, the voices that say, 'quit, before it's too late,' drown out the roar of the engines," was one typical column. "Frankly, I'd like to see some other guys follow Unser's lead, and the sooner the better. A.J. Foyt for one. The only thing that has kept Foyt alive this long is a superhuman sort of toughness, and a lot of luck. He may still be a tough old bird, but I can't avoid the feeling he has used up his supply of luck."[61]

With his son sidelined for the season, Tony Foyt finally agreed to see a doctor. His persistent cough was worse, and he tired easily. The news was not good—late-stage lung cancer. Father and son took the news stoically, and there was no talk of second opinions. These were the finest doctors in the country. Tony wanted to know how long. The doctors sensed there was no need to sugarcoat their response.

Two to six months.

AL UNSER
2

CHAPTER 6

ONE MORE FOR TONY

1983

A.J. Foyt gave no indication he'd heard the advice of Bobby Unser and others urging him to retire. Instead, he ordered a pair of new cars from March for the 1983 Indy car season to replace the two destroyed the year before. He visited the Hutcherson-Pagan shops in North Carolina to oversee construction of a new Chevrolet Monte Carlo stock car and retained Dick Hutcherson as his crew chief. And for the first time in three years, A.J. went back to work in his engine room alongside Howard Gilbert.[1]

Anxious to get back in a race car and see if his broken hand was fully healed, Foyt joined Cale Yarborough in early January for a few days of practice at Daytona International Speedway. The new Monte Carlo was a big aerodynamic improvement over the previous model, and the pair spent much of their time drafting with each other, swapping cars and running laps at well over 190 miles per hour.

While in Florida, Foyt saw Bill France, who asked him to drive in the upcoming 24 Hours of Daytona sports car race. Although Foyt hadn't driven a sports car since the 1967 win at Le Mans, he promised to consider it. He was upbeat after the practice with Yarborough and excited about the coming season.

"I'm rarin' to go," he said. "I know what it takes, and I know what it feels like to win the Daytona 500, with all the prestige that comes with it. I'd give anything to be back here in Victory Lane."[2]

He returned to Houston as his father began an aggressive regimen of trial radiation treatments. Foyt family doctor Gary Friedman wasn't hopeful, warning that Tony might have as little as six weeks to live. A.J. began a vigil at Memorial Hospital, at the same time throwing himself into planning for the upcoming racing season as a distraction.[3]

◀ With Roger Penske. *John Mahoney*

He continued to receive calls from France about driving in the sports car race. Working behind the scenes was Jack Arute, who handled public relations for Pepsi, NASCAR team owner Junior Johnson, and driver Darrell Waltrip. With the cola wars in full swing, Pepsi was sponsoring Waltrip's stock car in 1983 and was also the title sponsor of the Daytona 24.

Waltrip had yet to drive in a sports car race and was anxious to compete in the endurance classic. When Pepsi indicated it was agreeable to sponsoring a car in the race, Arute connected them with the Aston Martin entered by the British Nimrod team.

Arute, who got along well with A.J., sold Pepsi partly on the idea Foyt would be one of the team's drivers. He pitched the idea to A.J. as a chance to win one last trophy for his father. At first Foyt turned him down, saying he wanted to stay with Tony. Besides, the Aston Martin had little to no chance of finishing, let alone winning. The all-conquering Porsche 935 was on a six-year winning streak. Then Waltrip tried.

"Pepsi asked me who I wanted, and I said A.J. Foyt," is how Waltrip remembers it coming together. "I figure he's run this race before, and he's the right guy to get. So, I called him and told him about Pepsi and the Aston Martin. A.J. said, 'I ain't got no time for that, blah, blah, blah. I ain't messing with an old car like that.'"[4]

When Tony caught wind of the calls, however, he urged A.J. to go to Daytona.

"I really did not want to go because I felt like I needed to be [with my father]," Foyt recalled. "He was the one that kind of pushed me into going. He said, 'There is not a damn thing you can do sitting here. Get the hell out of here and go out and have some fun.' I thought, if I never win another race, it would be great if I could win this one."[5]

Foyt was still reluctant to make a commitment. Then about a week before the event, Waltrip called again.

"I asked him what it would take to get him down here," Waltrip remembered. "He said, 'It would take money. You got any money?' I called up the Pepsi people and said, 'A.J. says he needs $10,000.' And they said, 'We'll pay it. Get him down there.' I called him back and said, 'I got the money.' He said, 'I'll see you tomorrow.'"[6]

Some reports put Foyt's stipend from Pepsi at closer to $30,000—a hefty sum when the entire first-place team would split only $36,000. According to Arute, however, money wasn't the driving force.

"Money was a motivator," Arute acknowledged, "but I'll swear until I go to the grave, it was not about the money. He wanted another trophy for his daddy. But try to get A.J. Foyt to admit that vulnerability—that ain't gonna happen."[7]

Whatever he was being paid, it seemed to be worth it to Pepsi and Daytona, and ticket sales surged when it was announced that Foyt would team with Waltrip.

Shortly after agreeing to the Pepsi ride—but before it was announced—Foyt received another call, this one from Preston Henn, a flamboyant sports car owner and occasional driver. The eccentric Henn, who often wore a battered cowboy hat, owned several Florida drive-in movie theaters and had made millions by turning them into swap meets and flea markets during the day. A master marketer, he used racing to promote his "T-Bird Swap Shops" and sometimes drove his own car.

Arute says he initially approached Henn about the possibility of Foyt joining the team if the Aston Martin dropped out. Henn's Porsche 935 was one of the prerace favorites, and he had two top French sports car drivers, Bob Wollek and Claude Ballot-Léna. But Henn needed a third driver to replace Keke Rosberg, the reigning Formula One World Champion who'd withdrawn at the last minute. Henn didn't want to wait for the Aston Martin to break down, offering Foyt more money—a reported $50,000—to drive for his team. A.J. told him it was too late. He'd already agreed to the Pepsi deal. Henn told Foyt to be sure and keep him in mind if the Aston Martin broke and he still wanted to race.[8]

The Nimrod team struggled in practice, and Foyt could do no better than thirteenth in qualifying behind a fleet of Porsches. Setting a new track record and earning the pole was Wollek. Henn's car was the best money could buy, built by Porsche specialists Andial and referred to as the "L" or "Moby Dick" version of the 935. It featured an elongated and aerodynamic "whale tale" designed for the high speeds of Le Mans and being used at Daytona for the first time. Its twin-turbo engine pumped out tons of horsepower but also made it difficult to drive under the best of circumstances.

Henn and his lead driver, Wollek, were an unusual pair. The French driver had won the German sports car championship for Porsche in 1982, earning the Porsche Cup, which signified the brand's top driver. Extremely confident, he was sometimes derisively known as "Brilliant Bob." In later years, he would become known as "Monsieur Porsche."

After qualifying, Henn, who'd never met Foyt, asked Don Whittington to make an introduction. Henn was serving as his team's third driver but knew he was the weak link and reminded Foyt of the offer to drive his car should something happen to the Aston Martin.

Despite the qualifying problems, there were moments of levity within the Nimrod team.

"We had a prim and proper British team manager, a hillbilly like Darrell Waltrip, and Foyt," Arute says. "It was when only drivers could work on a car if it broke down on the track. In the prerace meeting, the manager said that if our car breaks down, A.J., as the most mechanically inclined of the drivers, would be dispatched to make the repairs. 'Fuck that,' Foyt said."[9]

When told there would be a torch in the car, it was Waltrip's turn to object.

"I don't mind driving this stupid car with the stupid steering wheel on the wrong side, but I'm not driving no goddamn car with a torch in it," Arute recalled Waltrip saying. Foyt, familiar with the English term for a flashlight, egged Waltrip on.

"You're right, Darrell, that's dangerous," he said, barely able to contain his laughter.

"In typical fashion, Darrell started filibustering," Arute remembered. "When he finally takes a breath, the British guy goes, 'Ah, Mr. Waltrip, a torch is a flashlight.'

"Waltrip just glared at A.J. That's just another example of A.J.'s personality."

When the race started, Wollek jumped into an early lead, but it was short-lived as he was in the pits after just two circuits to replace a turbocharger, losing six laps in the process. The car was forced to the pits again to change the other turbo, dropping further back and falling to thirty-eighth place, more than a dozen laps behind the leaders.

The Nimrod wasn't faring any better. Unable to make up much ground during his stint in the car, Foyt ordered a steak from his favorite Daytona restaurant. It was barely six hours into the race, and A.J. was just finishing his dinner when the car pulled into the pits, the Aston Martin engine smoking badly. Its race was over.

With his car out, Foyt went looking for Henn. Even though the Porsche was back on the track, it was still many laps behind the leaders. A.J. said he was willing to drive the car—but not at night—and when Henn agreed, Foyt went back to his hotel for a few hours' sleep, saying he'd return in the morning.

"I know my limitations," said Henn on adding Foyt. "You have A.J. who can drive anything with wheels on it. It looked to me like the only decision to make. I wanted somebody who could sprint at the end if need be. I don't have that much experience in a situation like that. Even though he hadn't driven one of these cars in a while, he's still A.J. Foyt."[10]

There was only one concern. "I asked A.J. if he could fit in the seat. He tapped me on the stomach and said if *I* could, he could."

Consistently fast laps by Wollek and Ballot-Léna and an abnormally high attrition rate among the leaders during a rainy night had Henn's car in second place by the time Foyt returned. Having never sat in a Porsche 935 before, he practiced the shift pattern in one of the cars in the garage area before going to the pits to start his first shift.

Wollek had just moved the 935 into the lead when he was called in for a scheduled driver change. It was starting to rain again, but A.J. said he was ready to go. There was only one problem: Wollek wasn't aware of the plan to put Foyt in the car. He would later say he'd never been told, while Henn claimed the information was lost in translation.

"It was a confusion in our languages," Henn said. "Wollek did not understand Foyt was replacing *me.* Bobby thought we were replacing *him* with A.J. He did not realize how good—no make that great—a driver A.J. is."

As Wollek started to exit the car, he spotted Foyt, whom he'd never met. A.J. had his helmet on and was moving toward the car. Wollek put two and two together, and despite being exhausted from running flat out through the night, he dropped back into the seat and tried to close the door. A crewmember stopped him, and others pulled the Frenchman from the car.

As Foyt drove away and before he could talk to Henn, Wollek was approached by David Hobbs, an English driver serving as a pit reporter for the televised coverage of the race. Egged on by Hobbs, who asked, "How do you feel about a complete stranger, to you, getting in that car in this rain?" Wollek didn't hold back.[11]

"Well, I'm upset about it because he doesn't know the car, he doesn't know the rain, he doesn't know anything. We have been working very hard because we had two turbos broke and you know, early on, and we were about twelve laps behind. Now we are one lap leading and *Mr. A.J. Foyt* is driving for the PR. I'm fucking upset about it."

Wollek was partly right about the reason Foyt was in the car. After all, promoting his swap meets was why Henn entered the car in the first place.

"I knew I couldn't lose with A.J. at the wheel," Henn said. "He hadn't been in a sports car race in 17 years, so I knew even if he splattered the car against the wall, we were going to get tremendous publicity."[12]

Watching the drama unfold from further down pit road was Hurley Haywood, who was driving another Porsche 935 that had been running with the leaders before suffering mechanical problems. He'd met Foyt once when he raced at Indianapolis in 1980 and was introduced by his car owner, Lindsey Hopkins, who was a friend of Foyt's. "A.J. told me to watch my mirrors and, when I saw him coming, to move the hell over," he recalled. "I said, 'Yes sir.'" Haywood decided to focus on sports car racing and already had multiple wins at Daytona and Le Mans and sports car championships to show for his efforts.[13]

"Bob Wollek was a good friend of mine and he was really, really pissed that A.J. was brought in with no practice in the car," Haywood said. "It was not a pleasant race. The weather was bad and the driving conditions were pretty horrible. The 935 was a very powerful car, so you really had to be careful. Bob was really mad and afraid A.J. would crash the car and do something really stupid."

Fortunately for Henn and Foyt, the race was soon placed under a full course caution because of the increasing rains. For the next two hours, he drove around slowly behind the pace car, becoming familiar with the shifting pattern and the rest of the car. When the green flag finally came out, he showed Wollek and everyone else he did know a little bit about the car and the track, turning the race's fastest lap—with the rain still falling.[14]

Wollek and Foyt traded two more driving periods, and when Wollek turned the car over to Foyt for his final stint, there were no histrionics. Wollek had opened a five-lap lead, and A.J. added three more to the margin. Foyt was in the Henn car for five hours, more than half the time remaining on the clock when he reported for duty. In Victory Lane, all the drivers played nice. Although not exactly apologetic, Wollek's opinion of Foyt had changed.

"A.J. and I did not have words," Brilliant Bob said. "I was nervous because he didn't know the car, he didn't know if it had four or five gears, where were the buttons and lights.[15]

"This car is not easy to drive. I didn't think it was a good idea, but A.J. is not just any driver. He got away with it, and I'm happy he was with us."[16]

Haywood was also impressed:

> A.J. adapted to the car and weather conditions really quickly. That was one of the traits A.J. had. He could take any car and evaluate its performance potential and adapt to it.[17]

> I'm often asked, "What are the things that make for a really good racing driver?" One, you've got to be patient, wait for your opportunity. And you have to be able to adapt to any condition. You're given a car at the start of the race, and it's perfect, and it goes downhill from that point on. A lot of drivers can drive it early, but when the performance goes off, they're kind of lost. Guys who really do well in the long-distance races are guys who can adapt to an ever-changing canvas. You have no idea who's driving the car in front of you. So you have to approach each car with the utmost caution. That's sorta not A.J.'s style, but he adapted to that mentality very quickly.

For his part, Foyt reveled in his performance, the celebration, and the controversy about Wollek's earlier comments. Although he didn't address the remarks directly, there was no doubt he was aware of them:

"That was the first time in about fifteen years I've run in the rain," he said. "There was rain and fog at Le Mans, but it didn't rain this hard. You had to be careful. I was probably more nervous than these boys about the whole thing. I had a lot of pressure on me. If I go out and spin, they could say A.J. went out and lost the race for them. But I felt I could help the team, and I think I did."[18]

"I knew nothing about the car. All I did was get in it and go. I just didn't take any chances. Except for all the funny gears, it just drove like a race car, and a race car is a race car. It wasn't that tricky. I ain't met one yet I couldn't drive."[19]

In Victory Lane, Foyt says he asked Wollek, "How many times have you been to Le Mans?"[20]

"At least a dozen times," A.J. says Wollek responded.

"How many times you won?" Foyt asked, already knowing the answer was none. "Hmm, I've only been to Le Mans once," Foyt concluded, "and won."

Late to the celebration was Jim Gilmore, who'd come to Daytona with Pepsi for the race. Like the rest of the Foyt entourage, he'd been at the airport waiting for a flight home when they got word their driver was back at the track.

"He fooled us when his car broke down last night," Gilmore said. "We figured that was it. We went home and went to bed. We were flying out this morning, but A.J. didn't show and he didn't show. Then we heard he was out here racing again. So we skipped our flight and lost our luggage. Sure enough, A.J. was at the track, leading the race."[21]

When asked afterward how much of the prize money he expected, Foyt supposedly said none. All he wanted was the trophy to take home to his daddy. Of course, he'd already had checks coming from Pepsi and Henn and later admitted he did pretty well for his weekend in Daytona.

"I got about as much for driving the Aston Martin as I did for winning with the other one," he said, which put his overall take as high as $60,000.[22]

"I had been covering A.J. since the early 1970s, but I didn't see his prime in the 1960s," recalled Associated Press reporter Mike Harris, who was at the race. "He wasn't *the guy* anymore. He was the *most famous* guy, but he wasn't the best driver anymore. But Daytona was by far the best drive I ever saw him make. It was pretty amazing."[23]

Watching it all in disbelief was Waltrip. "I brought him down there and paid him ten grand. He blew up my car then drove somebody else's car and won the race. That was A.J. Foyt."[24]

Back in Houston, A.J. went straight to the hospital to present Tony with the trophy. He wasn't surprised to hear his daddy say, "Golly, it's a little ole thing.[25]

"He never would brag on me," Foyt said. "I gave him a couple of trophies on Father's Day over the years and I won those four Indys, but he never would get carried away on me. But I knew he was proud. Whenever anybody came to visit him in the hospital, he'd show 'em that trophy and say, 'Look what my boy brought me.' That made him happy."

Foyt was back in Daytona by midweek to get ready for the 500-mile stock car race. Yarborough turned in a qualifying lap of more than 200 mph and then lost control the next time around, flipping and destroying his car. Foyt then stepped forward to loan Yarborough his Monte Carlo for the Busch Clash, a race for NASCAR regulars A.J. wasn't eligible for.

"That was mighty generous of him, I'll tell you that," Yarborough would say. "I don't know many—I don't know *anybody* else—who would have done that. I appreciated that very much."[26]

Instead, Foyt and Richard Petty provided awkward color commentary on the television broadcast. At one point, Petty joked the only reason Foyt loaned Yarborough his car was to make sure it was set up properly for the 500. A.J. didn't seem amused.

Yarborough was one of the few aware Tony Foyt was very ill and not expected to live much longer. He'd met the older man on his first trip to Indianapolis in 1966 and had always gotten along well with him.

"I thought a lot of Tony," Cale said. "He was a lot like A.J., or maybe A.J. was a lot like him. They were just about the same person."

Foyt led nearly half of his qualifying race for the 500, before being passed by Dale Earnhardt on the last lap. Afterward, the questions were about Foyt's father. Although A.J. hadn't seen it yet, reporter Ed Hinton of the *Atlanta Constitution*, one of the best journalists covering NASCAR, had broken the story of Tony Foyt's illness earlier in the day.

"Old Tony Foyt is dying," Hinton wrote. "It's cancer. He's got maybe four months. If he's lucky, very lucky, one more Indy 500 will roll around in time for the last flicker of his life."[27]

The story was picked up by newspapers across the country and at Memorial Hospital, Lucy rushed around pulling the sports section out of every *Houston Post* she could find. Upset he couldn't read about the Daytona races, Tony called the *Post*, complaining they'd forgotten to put the sports section in the day's newspaper.[28]

On the eve of the Daytona 500, several other reporters asked Foyt how he was doing. There was no mention of his father, just winning and losing.

"The feeling is just as strong as it ever was. I still like to ride that bull. If I win, I will be very happy. If I lose, I'll be miserable—as always."[29]

He seemed more interested in talking about business and politics, and the conversation took a right turn.

"I think Detroit is putting out a lot of garbage," he said. The year before, he blamed the government. Now he blamed the people working in the factories:

> All cars anymore are about halfway junk, and it's the people themselves who are responsible. All the pride is gone. Everybody is looking for a free handout. The people who are building cars are going to have to work a little harder so they can be proud of what they do. That's the biggest thing I see that's wrong with this American generation. They just don't care, regardless of how much you pay them.[30]
>
> Not long ago I tried to hire a guy. I offered him two and a quarter ($225) a week. He said, "Why should I work for [that] when I can go out and draw unemployment at $147 a week?" That's the attitude nowadays. People just laugh at you. I think the older people should be taken care of, but let the younger people go hungry if that's what they want. I was hungry one time. They can get out and work. There are jobs open for anybody who wants to work.

There'd be no trophy for Tony from the 500. Despite radio troubles in the early going, Foyt was still running in the lead draft at the halfway point, only to be slowed by ignition troubles late in the race. He finished eleventh, three laps behind winner Yarborough.

As the team's preparations for the Indy 500 continued in Houston, the radiation treatments were leaving Tony Foyt increasingly weak and in growing pain. He'd lost weight and could only walk a few steps at a time. When it became apparent the trial wasn't going to work for Tony, A.J. went to have a heart-to-heart talk with his father. It was a short discussion.

"Daddy, I don't like the way this stuff is looking," he said.[31]

"It's all over," Tony replied.

Foyt says he thought about skipping Indianapolis but knew his father wouldn't stand for it, and it was never discussed.

"He never wanted me to see him weak. I really don't think he wanted me to see him die."

As the team loaded up the cars for the trip to Indianapolis, A.J. planned another hospital visit. He had the transporters pull into the parking lot at Memorial and unload the cars. Then the crew, decked out in their red-and-white checkerboard race day uniforms, lined up. Up in Tony Foyt's room, A.J.'s sister Marlene helped her father on with his robe and to the window to see the team arrayed in his honor. Somehow, he found the strength to go down to the parking lot in a wheelchair and greet everyone, who quickly surrounded their boss.

"It was a really, *really* great moment," recalled Jack Starne. "It was probably the last time I saw him. I don't remember exactly what was said, but I know it was something about winning. Something like, 'Y'all need to get yourselves up to Indy. The race is gonna start, and you need to be there.' Something like that. That's the only thing we ever really thrived on. Do the best you can, and try to be number one, and if you're not, you got to keep working at it."[32]

George Snider was there, too. He and A.J. had firmed up their plans well in advance of the 500 for a change.

"He wanted to know what I was doing there," Snider said of Tony. "I told him 'I came to see you.' He could be a gruff old guy."[33]

At one point Tony joked, "Y'all gonna take me with you?"[34]

"Shit, if you want to go, we'll roll you up in there," A.J. said, grabbing control of the wheelchair, "Come on."

But both men knew it was a pipe dream.

"Nah," Tony said, "You'd better just take me back up to the room."

It was the last time most of the group saw Tony Foyt alive.

CALUMET FARM RACING
AND
A.J. FOYT ENTERPRISES
GOODYEAR
ILMORE
Foyt
RACING TEA

CHAPTER 7

CALUMET FARM

1983

When A.J. Foyt left his father's bedside, he headed not for Indianapolis but for Lexington, Kentucky, where a press event was planned for the introduction of the team's sponsors for the upcoming 1983 season.

Valvoline was returning and happy to be back on the side of Foyt's car for a third straight year. The other sponsor was new to the sport and a surprise: Calumet Farm. With eight Kentucky Derby wins, two Triple Crown winners and more than 500 stakes victories, Calumet Farm was the most famous and prestigious name in horse racing—as legendary as the Foyt name in auto racing.

Since his first trip to the Keeneland thoroughbred auctions in 1974, Foyt and his son Tony had become increasingly involved and successful in horse racing. When Tony earned his trainer's license at twenty-two in 1978, he'd taken over several of A.J.'s horses. They'd established A.J. Foyt Racing Stables, the jockey silks consisting of a Coyote-orange vest with black-and-white checkered flag arm sleeves. All three Anthony Joseph Foyts had worked together to build a large barn at the ranch in Hockley with thirty-three stalls, the same number as there are cars in the starting lineup of the Indianapolis 500. The ranch was home to about fifty mares and twenty-five active racehorses, with additional horses stabled in Kentucky and Arkansas.

Young Tony was coming off his most successful season to date, having posted twenty-six winners during meets at Oaklawn, Keeneland, and Churchill Downs. The biggest winner was a filly named Amazing Love, a horse they'd bought for $40,000 in 1980 at Keeneland. She'd earned more than $80,000 during the year with victories in several stakes races at Churchill Downs. A.J. was obviously proud of his son.[1]

◀ A.J.'s new sponsor, Calumet Farm. *Dan Boyd*

"When he went out training on his own, it was like throwing him to the wolves," he said. "Just like I was thrown to the wolves when I was his age and started racing at Indy. He makes the decisions because he knows the horses best."[2]

Having seen firsthand his father's temper around race cars, Tony found him easier to work with when it came to horses.

"You can explain stuff to him, sometimes easier than you can to other people," Tony said. "He knows you're trying for him and that's all he expects.[3]

"It's competition. In a way it's a lot like racing cars. You put in a lot of work getting a horse ready for a race, and sometimes no matter how hard you try or what you do, you can't win."[4]

Tony's career was about to take another turn along with the sponsorship announcement. Both were the result of J.T. Lundy, who'd been president of Calumet Farm for less than a year. The son of a tenant farmer, Lundy had worked his own small piece of land near Calumet before meeting Lucille "Cindy" Wright, one of the heirs to the farm. It was a classic case of good girl meets bad boy, and they married when she turned sixteen and he was twenty-one.

J.T. and Cindy worked hard to build their own small farm and horse breeding operation into a million-dollar business, but it was still small-time compared to the likes of Calumet and the area's other horse farms. That changed in late 1982 with the death of Lucille Wright Markey, Cindy's grandmother and namesake who had been running Calumet for years. The direct heirs—Cindy and her three siblings—had no experience or interest in running the farm, and they handed the job to Lundy, who took it on with relish.

A high school graduate, Lundy was crude and rude by Kentucky's blue-blood horseracing standards. "'Fuck it,' or 'fuck 'em' were favored phrases." He was overweight, with the face of a boxer who'd had his nose broken several times, and he continued to wear the work clothes of the farmhand even after taking control at Calumet. While the local aristocracy wore coat, tie, and top hat to the Derby, Lundy "dressed up" with an open sport shirt and corduroy pants.[5]

No matter how others saw him, Lundy considered himself to be the savior of Calumet. Despite its reputation, the farm had fallen on hard times during the 1960s and 1970s, at one point posting four consecutive years of losses. The recovery had actually started in 1978, however, thanks to a horse named Alydar. That year, "Aly" finished second in each of the Triple Crown races to Affirmed but won the country's fancy with his heart. Even more important from a financial standpoint, Alydar proved to be a superior stallion, and as demand for stud rights soared, the farm's profitability returned.

Still, Calumet had fallen behind in many areas, from basic maintenance to keeping up with advancements in thoroughbred training other top stables were making. Lundy launched a multimillion-dollar renovation project, covering everything from painting the Farm's twenty-three miles of iconic white fencing and its red-and-white barns to building a state-of-the-art veterinary clinic. He also signed a lease on a private jet for $30,000 a month so he could travel to races and other industry events.

To help pay for it all, Lundy doubled Alydar's stud fee to $250,000, began offering more stud opportunities, and started selling lifetime breeding rights to the stallion—an industry first. Alydar became known as "Lundy's ATM." The moves upset many in the horseracing world, and Lundy began freezing out longtime customers while allowing new ones to purchase rights. One of those who benefited was Foyt and his horse Amazing Love, who was soon in foal to Alydar.[6]

Lundy's real love was auto racing, and Foyt was his idol. The pair had met at the Keeneland auctions in the 1970s, and while Lundy may not have fit in with the Kentucky landed gentry, he was right at home with Foyt.

They were both "country crazy," said Lyle Robey, Calumet's attorney, who enjoyed listening to the pair swap stories. "You know, they're the kind of guys who would drive a car through a fence and see how many times and at what rpms they'd have to ram the post before it came down."[7]

The pair also saw each other at NASCAR races, Lundy having become part owner of a successful team with West Virginia coal mine operator Harry Ranier. The team's drivers, including Yarborough and Buddy Baker, were winners of multiple races, among them three Daytona 500s. It was a Lundy/Ranier car Yarborough flipped and destroyed during qualifying at Daytona in February.

The Indy car sponsorship deal was yet another way for Lundy to move closer to his idol. Although little money changed hands, the deal was worth millions to Foyt. In addition to stud rights with Alydar, other thoroughbred stallions were made available to mares from the Foyt racing stables, and some of their horses were moved to Calumet. Tony also was making the move to the farm and would be responsible for training about ten horses for his father, ten for Calumet, and several others for individual owners, including one for Yarborough.

Lundy agreed to purchase a fleet of vehicles from Foyt's Houston Chevrolet dealership, although the Coyote-orange color clashed with the traditional devil-red and blue colors of Calumet. "He must have gotten a real good buy on some real bad paint," J.T. said of poppy red, although not to Foyt.

Lundy staged an extravagant outdoor luncheon at the farm to announce the Indy sponsorship, complete with mint juleps, crab claws, beef tenderloin, and oysters on the half-shell. Even Alydar made an appearance, one of the few times A.J. found himself upstaged. The press reception drew praise from Valvoline, one executive calling it "the most successful press party the company had ever seen."

Lundy also announced the farm's latest prized thoroughbred, which had been renamed "Foyt," would run in the Peter Pan Stakes at Belmont Park in New York on the same day A.J. was driving in the 500. While renaming a racehorse was generally considered unlucky, the colt—a younger brother of Alydar—was undefeated since the change. Although he would miss the Kentucky Derby while recovering from a few minor but nagging injuries, if Foyt performed well in the Peter Pan, he would be entered in the Belmont Stakes, the final leg of the Triple Crown.

"We have been friends and admirers of A.J. and A.J. and I have been the best of friends for years," Lundy said. "We've been talking about sponsoring one of his cars at Indy for a long time. This year we did it. A.J. is as interested in horses now as cars and I think his secret ambition, since he has won everything in motor racing, is to win a Kentucky Derby."[8]

Foyt said, "The deal that was set up was more out of friendship than money." He announced he would drive the No. 14 Valvoline-sponsored car, while George Snider, winner of the USAC Gold Crown series in 1982, would drive the No.1 Calumet Farm March. One of the auto racing writers in attendance wondered if Foyt had considered allowing Rick Mears, the CART Indy car champion, to use the No. 1 as A.J. had in the past.[9]

"(Roger) Penske tried to buy No. 1 from us, and we might have given it to him if he would have offered a considerable amount of money," Foyt said. "But all he offered was chicken feed. Besides, George earned No. 1, he ought to be able to wear it."

Asked about his father's health, Foyt noted it would be the first time he'd driven in the 500 without his father in his pit. "It's kind of a sad feeling. He's been with me my whole career. He's been more than just a father. He's been a friend, someone there 24 hours a day. If I had a problem, he was there."[10]

Inevitably there were questions about whether his father's illness was causing him to think about his own retirement. While he didn't mention Bobby Unser by name, it was clear who he was talking about in his reply:

"When I decide, I'm not going to be like a lot of drivers and use the 'family' excuse; that I'm quitting to spend more time with my wife and kids. If I was ever going to use family as an excuse, now would be the time. But when I quit, it will be because A.J. Foyt wants to quit."[11]

At the same time, he acknowledged he was slowing down:

"I've lost a lot of hair and got fatter," he laughed. "Some say I've mellowed. If that's true, maybe it's for the better. I think I've slowed down some. I realize I'm probably the biggest fool to get back in a race car. But other people like to play golf or swim. I like to race."[12]

"The biggest thing is your eyes, because seeing is the start of everything in sports. When your eyesight goes, then your legs and arms go. If you look at athletes who are prominent in any sport, you'll find they probably have good eyesight and don't wear glasses. I've been fortunate not to have to wear them. But I can feel my eyes slowing down. I can feel it when I'm reading late at night and I'm tired. If they slow down much more, I'll retire."[13]

He had harsh comments for Kevin Cogan and the influx of younger drivers at Indy. He also took on the growing influence of lawyers, not only in the sport, but America in general.

> [Cogan's] excuses were a bunch of hogwash. The real problem at Indy today is that too many owners are selling the rides to young drivers who can get sponsors, and some of those drivers aren't ready for Indy. I'm probably a better driver today than I was twenty years ago, but I'm not as brave. I took some chances then I wouldn't take now. When I think of the things I did, well, I shouldn't even be here talking to you.
>
> There used to be restrictions against it [inexperienced drivers], but now you've got a lot of lawyers who'll take you to court over it. I think that's

> one thing wrong with our whole country. A judge sentences a man to die, and then a lawyer gets another judge to grant a stay of execution. I believe in an eye for an eye, a tooth for a tooth, no matter what a lawyer and judge 300 miles away does.

Foyt went from Lexington to Louisville, where he attended the Kentucky Derby. He left for Indianapolis in a good mood as one of his horses, Steel Robbing, won a preliminary event on the Derby card.

It wouldn't last for long.

The Passing of Tony Foyt

It wasn't until Monday, May 9—two days after the Derby—that Foyt and Snider turned their first slow laps of the month, shaking down their cars. The cars remained slow until Foyt decided to switch to a smaller rear wing, allowing for more speed down the straights but less downforce in the corners. Something was missing, and that something was Tony Foyt, who was not by his son's side for the first time in twenty-six years.

"Away from the racetrack the fires don't burn as brightly as they once did," Snider said of his friend. "It's getting to the point where it's old now and he's got a lot of other interests. Once he gets in a race car, he's just as competitive as ever. I think he wants to win that fifth one here really, really bad. When he does that, he'll be down the road."[14]

The first weekend of qualifying was rained out, ramping up the pressure on Foyt off and on the track. Rather than stay in Indianapolis, he went back to Houston to be with his father. Returning to the Speedway Friday afternoon, he ran a few practice laps, one at more than 201 miles per hour, one of the top speeds of the month.

His plan to qualify early Saturday morning and then fly home was disrupted when his car, along with twelve others, was ordered out of line because the side skirts were too long. Not surprisingly, Foyt exploded.

"The officials are complete idiots," he said. "We're talking about 1/16th of an inch. It's not right. My father is about to die and I should be back in Houston. This is what broke USAC to begin with, chicken shit like this. They should say you've got five minutes to have the car running. They've done it in the past when the wings were too high or something like that. You lowered them real quick and went on. You don't lose your place in line. I think today was a very bad day for the United States Auto Club."[15]

At one point, Foyt called his sister and told her he wouldn't be back until Sunday.

"He was in terrible pain," Marlene Foyt-LaMance said of her father. "I told daddy A.J. wasn't going to qualify, and we should turn off the TV, but he said no. He was determined to see his son qualify."[16]

Officials eventually agreed to allow the teams to adjust the skirt length on the cars, although they'd be considered "second day" qualifiers and positioned behind those who qualified earlier. Foyt's four-lap average was among the best at just under 200 mph, but his twenty-fourth starting position would be his worst yet in the 500. Snider, whose car passed initial inspection, qualified thirteenth in the Calumet Farm machine.

"I haven't had the time to practice like I should," Foyt said. "I have some problems in Houston and I'm on my way back there now. There was no great need to run fast. They've got to change their ways here. This is a lot of bullshit. The cars have been checked every day. The whole day's screwed up. All I can tell you people is we'll run the hell out of them on race day."[17]

Dr. Gary Friedman was waiting at Tony's bedside when A.J. arrived at Memorial Hospital Saturday evening, having come straight from the airport. Tony, who'd watched his son qualify, had been dropping in and out of consciousness ever since. Friedman said it wouldn't be long now, and A.J. asked if anything more could be done for his daddy.

"Gary said, 'We can keep him alive for two or three days, but he's just gonna lay here,'" Foyt recalled. "I said, 'Leave him be. He's suffered enough.'"[18]

Any hope of Tony hanging on for one more 500, one more possible win, were gone. One of the final conversations between father and son would later be recounted by William Nack, an award-winning writer who mostly covered horse racing but to whom A.J. opened up for a *Sports Illustrated* article entitled "Twilight of a Titan":

> Not long before the old man died, in a hospital room in Houston, Tony's doctor, Gary Friedman, gave two generations of Foyts his final notice at bedside: "If you have anything to say to each other, or you're holding back, I think maybe you ought to say it. I'll wait outside."[19]
>
> Friedman left, and A.J. began to bite his lip.
>
> "I've assigned the accounts over to you," Tony said. "You know everything. You know what I want you to do. What do you think?"
>
> A.J. could hardly speak. "Well, Daddy, things aren't working like we hoped."
>
> "I know it," said Tony.
>
> "You have anything you want to talk about?"
>
> "No, not really," Tony said.
>
> "Well, I don't really have much to say. If anything ever happens, I'll do what I can to try to carry on."
>
> "I know that," Tony said. "But don't worry about things."
>
> "Are you sure you ain't got something to tell me?"
>
> "No," the old man said. "I've told you everything."

Tony Foyt, age sixty-nine, drifted into a coma about 8:00 p.m. on Saturday, May 21, and died about 10:00 p.m. A.J. often noted that his mother and father died two years apart, both on the day he qualified for the Indianapolis 500. In both cases he'd been able to reach their bedside in time to say a final goodbye.

"That had to be their will, to hold on until I got back. A lot of times I get tears in my eyes. I know it's silly. But it's like I lost something that I never really had. You know, it's kind of like a dream. Am I in a dream? Am I going to wake up or what? I guess I lost it all so quick. We all worked our butts off, and when my parents can finally turn around and have life easy, everything was just swept out from under 'em."[20]

The funeral was held on Tuesday, May 24, and parts of the I-10 freeway through Houston were shut down to accommodate the procession on its way to Memorial Cemetery, where Tony was laid to rest alongside his wife, Evelyn. Starne was one of those who returned from Indianapolis for the funeral.

"I loved both of those people very, very much," Starne said years later of Foyt's parents, who had hosted his wedding reception. "My wife and myself both did. We still visit the cemetery at least twice a year."[21]

Although he'd been preparing for his father's passing for months, it still hit Foyt hard. Since the death of Pat O'Connor at Indianapolis in his rookie year, he'd spent his entire career avoiding close relationships with anyone in racing to escape the feeling of a debilitating loss in a profession where death was always around the next corner. Now the person he was closest to at the track was gone.

"I remember my father saying many times, 'I didn't only lose my father, I lost my best friend,'" A.J.'s son Tony said. "As long as his dad was alive, he knew the race car was going to be as good as it could be. After they raced together for all them years, and came up like they had, when he passed away it wasn't the same."[22]

Tim Delrose, the close friend of both Tony and A.J., immediately noticed a difference.

"When his dad died, he was in a bad state mentally," Delrose recalled. "He kept thinking about his dad and mom. He missed his dad so much. He'd talk to him every day. They'd talk about what they were doing, what they were going to try, what they were going to do different. Always trying something to go faster and safer. Now that was missing.[23]

"That really got to him. It changed his personality and the way he did things. I worried about him. I was worried he might make a mistake at a racetrack. You can't afford to make mistakes at 200 mph. You can't afford to make a bad move. You have to know what to do and when to do it. It has to be instinct. You can't think about it—you might get killed."

Much of what father and son had done together for the past twenty-six years had centered around the Indianapolis Motor Speedway, and the return to the track so soon after Tony's death wasn't easy. Everything about the Speedway, from the garage in Gasoline Alley to the track cafeteria to their favorite restaurants, reminded A.J. of Tony. The rest of the month was a blur, a string of condolences dredging up memories and emotions.

"I don't know if I'm up to winning this year," he admitted at one point. "My parents were the two people I wanted to win for. They're all I've ever had in my life. I've got a lot of thinking to do. But the way I feel now, to hell with it. To be honest, I could take that helmet, close up (the garage) and walk away. It doesn't even seem like the month of May."[24]

Even the media seemed to pause in its ongoing back-and-forth with Foyt, offering a series of tributes to the driver and his father. None was better than Bob Barnet's of the *Star Press*, who'd been covering Foyt for years:

> This strange, somber man is one whose trade has burned him and scaled him and broken his bones. It also lifted him to peaks of exaltation known only to the handful of mortals chosen by Lady Luck as her own. He is back to face an old adversary and likely will come again no matter who prevails in this renewal of a battle in which man challenges force and fate, not because of money or prestige, but because the challenge is there.[25]
>
> He is a fighter whose intelligence requires that he do all in his power to even the odds and whose bravery demands that he accept the battle. The white-hot pride of the born competitor sends him on and on and he has lived because his skill is as great as that of any man who has driven a race car onto any racetrack. A.J. Foyt is a better race driver in this 1983 race because of the load of sorrow he carries and his unquestioned desire to please the man he knows will be watching as the race is run.

With Foyt secluded in his garage, Jim Gilmore tried to explain what Tony meant to the team and the relationship between father and son:

> [Tony] gave the crew stability. When he and A.J. wanted something done, it was done. We still look around the garage and think he is there telling us what to do. I know A.J. would like nothing better than to win this year.[26]
>
> A.J., because of his family tragedy, hasn't had many hot laps, but the machine is excellent. I have visions of the young guys going out fast and trying to make a big show, then after about 200 miles—if we're not bumped or blow a pit stop—A.J., with his genius and patience, taking control. We feel our chances are excellent.

Despite Gilmore's optimism, the race was the low point of Foyt's Indianapolis career. Coming in for an early stop and wing adjustment on lap twenty-four, the transmission broke when Foyt accelerated hard out of the pits. Except for the first-lap accident in 1966, it was the earliest Foyt ever exited the 500, and the thirty-first place finish his worst ever. Snider was already out, finishing in the thirty-second spot. Ironically, the transmission had always been one of Tony Foyt's responsibilities, often building it himself.

"Everything frowned down on us this month," Foyt said. "My daddy has always been such an important man in overseeing this team, and he's gone. And I was bouncing back and forth so much that we didn't get to practice as many miles. The crew just got rusty. Then that part broke. I'm pretty disgusted and that's not how I want to leave this place. I'd be pretty surprised if I'm not back. I won't be racing for my father anymore, but I still want to win another one for myself."[27]

The news from Belmont Park wasn't any better. On a wet track, Slew O' Gold—son of Triple Crown winner Seattle Slew—dominated a five-horse field on his way to a twelve-length victory in the Peter Pan Handicap. Foyt ran last most of the way before closing late to finish third. The horse would never win a major stakes race but would stand at stud for more than fifteen years.

A.J. was long gone from the Speedway when Tom Sneva took the checkered flag, and he was the only driver to miss the victory dinner the following night. Joining Sneva in the celebration was crew chief George Bignotti, who received the mechanic of the race award, renamed in honor of Tony Foyt.

After the 500, Foyt retreated to Houston and sought solace with friends and family, and seclusion working on his ranch. ABC's Jack Arute was one of the few visitors, and A.J. spent the day showing him the ranch and what he and Tony had built.

"It was an eerie show and tell," Arute recalled. "In the garage was a toolbox that his father had used from when he started as a midget owner back in the 1940s. A.J. spent an hour showing me each and every tool in that box. Each was hand-engraved with Tony Foyt's name or initials, and each had a story attached. As A.J. went through the toolbox, you saw both the sadness and the pride A.J. possessed."[28]

It wasn't until shortly before the Fourth of July that Foyt told his team to get his stock car ready for the Firecracker 400 in Daytona. It meant missing the Indy car race in Cleveland on Sunday, July 3, but he hadn't planned to run the race on the airport road course.

The car was strong right off the truck, and Foyt qualified sixth, with Yarborough on the pole. Foyt was happy to be back at the track, joking with other drivers in the garage area. Safely in the field, he elected to participate in a final practice session to test the car in the draft. He was running in tight formation when the Monte Carlo shuddered, then shot up the track, slamming into the first turn wall. An engine connecting rod had broken, putting a hole in the oil pan and spraying fluid over the tires. It was an extremely hard hit, and as he crawled from the car, he noticed his driver's seat was split down the middle.

"I hit a ton," Foyt said after being released from the infield care center. "If it had been anywhere else on the track, I might have been able to save it. I'm just sick. We were really looking forward to the race. The way my luck has been, I ought to go home and sleep it off."[29]

While the crew thought the car could be repaired in time for the race, Foyt ordered them to load it up and take it home. He was already feeling stiff and sore and didn't think he could drive it for 400 miles.

On his way out of the track, however, he was stopped by Preston Henn, who was scheduled to co-drive that night with Hurley Haywood in the annual Paul Revere 250-mile IMSA sports car race. For safety reasons, NASCAR didn't allow its drivers to compete in both the IMSA race and the Firecracker the next morning, but since there was no longer a conflict, Henn asked Foyt to take his place. Foyt tried to decline, saying he was too sore, but Henn, who disliked driving at night even more than Foyt, persisted. Haywood had put the car on the pole, and there was a good chance of winning the race, but not if Henn was the second driver. Finally, Foyt relented, saying he would go to the hotel and rest, then return in time for the 10:00 p.m. start. He barely made it.

"I whiplashed my neck and I really became sore," Foyt said. "And my thighs and all through my groin area is all bruised where the seat belts pulled in the crash. I hurt so much I couldn't get out of bed before nine tonight."[30]

Unlike Bob Wollek earlier in the year, Haywood—who would tie Yarborough for most victories at the Daytona track with a win—wasn't concerned about Foyt taking over his car without the benefit of a practice session.

"Preston came up and asked, 'Do you want to drive with A.J.?' and I said, 'Are you kidding? I'd love to,'" Haywood recalled more than forty years later. "A.J. Foyt was a hero of mine from day one. Before I really got started in racing, I knew who A.J. was and about all his accomplishments. He was so versatile in any car he got into. I don't care if it was a sports car, Indy car, stock car—he was good at everything. When I started racing, I kinda said, 'I want to pattern myself after what he's done.'"[31]

Haywood jumped into the lead at the start and pulled away, pitting with twenty-five laps, or about one hundred miles, remaining before he turned the car over to Foyt.

"There was a lot of size difference between A.J. and myself," Haywood said. "So, when he got into the car, he was basically sitting on the rails of the seat. I helped get him tucked into the car with the seat belts and all that stuff, and then I said, 'Okay, don't blow it.' He just looked at me like, 'Watch out—do you know who you're talking to?'"

It wasn't long before the engine started misfiring and the alternator gauge began flickering, the car having thrown its alternator belt. Over the radio, Foyt discussed a stop to replace the belt, but the team determined that despite their lead, it would take too long and cost them any chance at victory.

Instead, Foyt began shutting down anything drawing power from the battery that wasn't vital. The biggest drain came from the headlights, and for a while he turned them off and on, depending on where he was on the track. Eventually, he turned them off entirely even though there were few lighted areas in the infield and backstraight portions of the course at the time.

"A.J. was doing a really great job," Haywood said. "He was driving in a really uncomfortable seat for him. When the lights started to come off and on, we were certain the IMSA guys were going to call us in to fix it. But they were a little bit afraid of A.J.'s reaction. We were working with them, and as long as we passed the finish line with the lights on, they said we were okay."

Despite the slower pace, Foyt was still more than ninety seconds ahead of the second-place car when he took the checkered flag just past midnight:

> Hurley built a good lead, and I was just trying to protect it. With nine laps to go the battery went, and with two laps left it got real bad. I couldn't even flip on the lights in the turns anymore. I was scared as hell. I couldn't see a thing in some places, so I just aimed for the darkest hole. It was like driving

> in Houston on the freeway. It wouldn't be until I'd come out of [the oval's] turn three and started to head back around toward the pits that I felt like I was back in the world again. That's when I could see a few lights. If the race had been two laps longer, we never would have finished.[32]

A beaming Henn said, "The old man did it for us again."

For a moment the pain was gone, both emotional and physical, as Foyt basked in the glow of the floodlights in the winner's circle.

"I said to myself, 'what else can go wrong?'" He recounted his father's death, the troubles at Indianapolis, the crash the previous day and the alternator problem. "Things were going so bad, I figured I'd just go until the car stopped, or I drove off into the darkness for good. And then when you least expect it, something gets rosy again. Winning has a way of cheering you up and making the pain go away."[33]

Haywood remembered the night as "the start of a really nice friendship. He's an amazing person. If you got sideways with him, he was brutal. But as long as he trusted you, and you were a good friend, he would do anything for you. He had a wild sense of humor. Most people don't realize that. He'd make me laugh a lot."[34]

The next morning, the pain was back stronger than ever, forcing Foyt to visit the hospital for X-rays. Doctors were surprised to find several cracked vertebrae and a ruptured disc, apparently aggravating the injury he'd suffered at Riverside nearly twenty years earlier. They were even more surprised to learn he'd driven the winning race car the night before. It wasn't until he returned to Houston and complained about a sore wrist that doctors discovered he'd broken it as well. At one point he had an allergic reaction to one of the drugs "and damn near died. There was a point where I thought I was going to die and I didn't care. When I broke my back it didn't hurt this bad."[35]

Doctors prescribed the one thing he didn't want to hear—rest. He wanted to keep his mind and body busy, and if he wasn't racing, he wanted to be working on one of his ranches. He felt well enough three months later to enter the Charlotte 500 in October, but before leaving for the track, he reinjured his back doing some heavy lifting at the ranch. That's when the doctors laid down the law. No more racing for the foreseeable future.

"The minute A.J. would start feeling better, he'd be right back to work, and the problems would start all over again," said his orthopedic surgeon, Dr. John Perkins. "A.J. now has two slipped discs in his back as the result of moving heavy objects at his ranch. I've treated A.J. for a number of years and seen him do things when he shouldn't. He's an extremely competitive individual, but this time I've absolutely forbidden him to drive anything."

Somewhat sheepishly, Foyt admitted, "The doctor is right. If I rush this thing I could screw up our entire program, and that would be stupid. I haven't earned what I have in racing by being stupid."

Banished by his doctors from the racetrack, Foyt took the opportunity to attend a launch event hosted by Jim Gilmore at the Indianapolis Motor Speedway Museum for his autobiography, *A.J.: My Life as America's Greatest Race Car Driver*. It was a gala affair, attended by Bill France and other racing dignitaries.

For the most part, the book received poor—sometimes blistering—reviews. And with good reason. It was written with William Neely, a former manager of Goodyear public relations who'd also cowritten *Stand On It: A Novel by Stroker Ace*, which was an entertaining book turned into a successful movie starring Burt Reynolds. The autobiography, however, was filled with braggadocio and worse—numerous timeline and factual errors.

"A.J.'s wife, Lucy, says he is insecure," wrote Shav Glick in a *Los Angeles Times* review. "A.J. denies it . . . but the autobiography tends to substantiate her viewpoint. No one secure would spend so many words telling how great they were. The sad part is that he doesn't need to prove it. Everybody knows it."[36]

A.J. would later say neither he, nor anyone else in his entourage, proofread the book, and he was supposedly embarrassed by it. The book still sold well, and the subtitle was changed for future printings to the slightly more subtle, *The Life of America's Greatest Race Car Driver*.

Foyt was quoted as having something to say—usually not good—about almost everyone in the sport. Some of the highlights/lowlights included,

"Winning the [Indy 500] alone doesn't make you that important. Johncock's name—or Mears or Bobby Unser's or anybody's for that matter—doesn't seem to have the power that mine does. They all backed into about as many wins as they've gotten by actually outrunning somebody."

On the team owners Foyt had clashed with over the formation of CART: "I'll bet Roger Penske and Pat Patrick . . . have yet to put a damn dime of their own money into racing, at least for the sake of improving the sport. You'll never see the day when they do put any money back."

About European drivers: "Not only don't they charge hard; they get upset if anybody else does."

And concerning Lotus guru Colin Chapman: "The man everybody gave credit to for the rear-engine revolution, never cared a damn thing for his driver's safety."

The harshest criticism was saved for young drivers, especially Cogan:

> There was that Cogan thing, where he was flat to blame. Most of the new guys aren't even man enough to fight . . . They wait until your back is turned and then they run to the press and let them do their talking for them. Hell, if I'm right, I stand up for my rights. I don't sit there and whine like the Cogans of racing. I guess he thought he could buffalo me. Well, I got news for his young ass: I've been hurt before, and there was no way I was going to let him get by with it . . . I hate to put the mouth on him, but the kid's nothing but a big fake.

GILMORE
Foyt
Copenhagen
GILMORE
GILMORE
SIMPSON
Copenhagen
IT SATISFIES
SIMPSON

CHAPTER 8

A LITTLE HELP FOR HIS FRIENDS

1984

For the start of the 1984 season, A.J. Foyt returned to the site of his only wins the previous year: the road course at Daytona International Speedway. He said his plans for the year included only the three 500-mile Indy car races at Indianapolis, Michigan, and Pocono; about ten NASCAR events; and a handful of sports car races.

He'd been lured back to the Daytona 24 by car owner Preston Henn with the promise of a new Porsche 962, the latest evolution of the car dominating sports car racing in Europe. When Foyt arrived in Daytona, however, he discovered the world's first and only 962 was still in the hands of the Porsche factory team and would be driven by Mario Andretti and his twenty-one-year-old son, Michael. Despite the change in plans, Foyt seemed not to care.

"Plain and simple, I just like racing," A.J. said. "This isn't like Indy. That race probably drains you more than this one. [Indy] wears you down mentally because for three hours, it's nothing but intense pressure. Here it just becomes a gradual ache."[1]

He was teamed again with Bob Wollek and joined by Derek Bell, another top sports car driver who'd already won the 24 Hours of Le Mans three times. Some were surprised to see Foyt and "Brilliant Bob" in the same car again, but not Henn.

"A.J. is happy to be driving with Wollek because he knows he's good. Foyt's a smart old codger and didn't get where he is by being stupid. And it's a good deal for Wollek, too. Nobody in the United States knew who Wollek was until he said those things about A.J. That controversy put Wollek on the map!"[2]

Mario, returning to Daytona for the first time in twelve years, put the 962 on the pole, with Wollek qualifying fourth in the same car Henn's team drove

◀ Working on a teammate's car. *Dan Boyd*

to victory the year before. The Andrettis dominated the early going, leading one hundred laps before dropping out with transmission and engine troubles.

Foyt ran the first shift and held his position while complaining about the traffic in a race that started eighty-two cars with wide speed discrepancies. For the first time, a chicane was added in the middle of the backstraight, and while it served its purpose of slowing the prototypes, it created another tight corner where the fastest cars were overtaking the slower ones at a high rate of speed.

The team was fighting for the lead near the halfway point when it was slowed by a manifold leak, limiting turbocharger boost pressure to about 70 percent. They lost ground as a result but were still able to finish second, nine laps behind the winners—an unlikely trio of South African drivers. Afterward, all they wanted to talk about was racing against Foyt.

"I don't know many people in this country, but everybody's heard of A.J. Foyt," said Tony Martin, who was on his first trip to America. He'd been sitting near Foyt but unable to work up the nerve to introduce himself. "He's just what he's cracked up to be. An excellent driver—an absolute magician in a motorcar."[3]

"To drive against guys like A.J. Foyt is something I've always wanted to do," he added. "To beat him, I can't believe."[4]

Ten days later, Foyt and Wollek teamed together for the Miami Grand Prix, and Henn painted his Porsche Foyt Orange, with sponsorship from Valvoline and Jim Gilmore—who'd recently purchased the biggest Chevrolet dealership in Florida—splashed across the front. Foyt had never been to the street course and studied a map of the layout before practice. When the team decided to change the car's engine after just two laps, Foyt's session was relegated to taking a van around for a few laps during the lunch break.

Once the state of the art in prototype racing, Henn's 935 was being increasingly surpassed by newer cars. The best Wollek could do was tenth in qualifying. Foyt wasn't feeling well on race day, driving only about forty-five minutes of the three-hour event. Wollek brought the car home fourth.

Bell rejoined the team for the 12 Hours of Sebring, Foyt's first time back at the track since finishing second in 1967, having said then it was too dangerous. Henn and changes to the track convinced him to return.

They qualified sixth, and Foyt took the lead at the three-hour mark. They led for one hundred consecutive laps at one point, with Foyt pushing the margin to more than three laps before car problems slowed their pace. When an exhaust header cracked with about ninety minutes remaining, draining power from the engine and eliminating any chance of winning, Foyt decided it was time to leave.

"The car's sick and I ain't gonna win," he said. "I'm going home. I'll be in Houston before the race is over."[5]

Despite the disappointment, he'd finished the three major events with a share of second, third, and fourth place in Henn's dated 935. Foyt even hinted he might add another sports car race to his schedule if the right machine was available.

"We may go back to Le Mans," he said, "if we get a new Porsche."[6]

While his sports car efforts were going well, the same couldn't be said of his stock car operation. Chevrolet was GM's dominant NASCAR brand, but Foyt took a chance and switched to Oldsmobile, hoping it would give him an edge over the rest. The first results were miserable, with a thirty-ninth at Daytona and thirty-fifth at Atlanta. At Daytona he complained, "It was so loose, I just couldn't hold it. I thought I'd better park it before I wrecked somebody."[7]

It was a relief when May finally rolled around and he shifted his focus to Indianapolis, although his first stop was in Kentucky for the run-up to the Derby. A.J.'s son Tony had blossomed at Calumet Farm, posting four winners at Churchill Downs from Foyt's stables, and two more from Calumet. Ten more had finished in the money.

"Tony is gaining quite a good reputation for someone so young," said Edgar Allen, an official at Churchill Downs. "The Foyts have a solid organization and have built an excellent racing operation. A.J. is here almost every day when he's not riding at Indianapolis."[8]

When Foyt finally arrived at the Speedway, he was up to his old tricks, never running a full lap flat out. In addition to new March Cosworths for himself and George Snider, he had a third March powered by an experimental Chevrolet V6 he'd been playing with. Foyt had all three just over 200 miles per hour in practice and one lap at over 205 in his own car. But he was only eighteenth on the speed chart as qualifying approached, with Andretti running an unofficial lap at more than 212 mph.

With a record 117 cars entered and an influx of new drivers on the track, Foyt didn't hold back when asked what he thought of the new generation of competitors. Some had heard the rant before:

> None of them have had to come up through the school of hard knocks. Ninety percent of them don't know what it's like to sleep in the back seat of a car between races or have to run hard in order to make enough money to pay the rent.[9]
>
> These momma's boys today aren't hungry because they've all got rich daddies or million-dollar sponsors. These kids today just don't have any idea of what tough is, even though they think they do. Don't get me wrong, there's some really talented kids, like Al Unser's boy. But all it takes anymore is money. Any clown with $200,000 can become a big brave race driver. The cars have become so easy to drive, all it takes is balls. And that's the trouble.

Mario seemed to have the pole position in hand when the ignition failed coming out of the fourth turn on his last qualifying lap and the car coasted across the finish line. Tom Sneva stepped up and ran four laps at just over 210 mph, taking the pole and setting the stage for Foyt's attempt.

Using a "rich" fuel blend, Foyt ran his first lap at better than 209 mph and said after, "I'm quite certain I could have beaten Sneva's time." He never completed the second lap, however, because a burned piston ended his run. The crew went to work changing the engine, but when it became apparent they wouldn't make the 6:00 p.m. deadline, Foyt took out Snider's No. 4 car.[10]

The two drivers seldom agreed on car setup, and Foyt complained later, "I was an accident waiting to happen . . . I was just very loose. We didn't have time to change the springs around like I had on the other car. I [nearly] spun the first lap. I was in trouble all four laps."

He hung on to post a speed just over 203 mph, good for twelfth on the starting grid.

Also having trouble was Johnny Rutherford. After breaking both feet in a practice crash at Indianapolis in 1983, he'd missed the race and a good portion of the season, and there'd been few rides available as the new year approached. When he seemed in danger of missing the tenth anniversary of his first win at the Speedway, Foyt offered him a car for the race.

Rutherford opted to join the team of Doug Shierson instead, who promised to enter him in all three 500-mile races. Shierson also wanted Rutherford to mentor the team's new rookie driver, Danny Sullivan—who was moving to Indy cars after a season in Formula One—and to help develop the team's new DSR-1 race car.

The DSR-1 proved to be a major disappointment. With limited practice time, neither Rutherford nor Sullivan was able to get the car above 200 mph. When Shierson lined up a Lola for Sullivan and told Rutherford he was free to find another ride, Johnny went straight to Foyt and asked if the offer was still good. A.J. confirmed the March with the Chevrolet V6 was available, but it wasn't going to be easy.

The V6 was still in a developmental stage, and Rutherford's first two qualifying attempts ended with engine problems. The team worked on the Chevy in the days before the second qualifying weekend, but it was all for naught, as a despondent Rutherford saw his third and final attempt in the car end in a cloud of smoke.

Not ready to give up yet, Foyt huddled with Gilmore and got the okay to purchase Al Unser Jr.'s backup March for about $150,000. "If you can play with the big boys," Foyt said, "you pay with the big boys."[11]

The March was delivered at 2:00 p.m., and with thirty-three cars already in the field and rain forecast for Sunday, Foyt wanted Rutherford to make a qualifying run. After Johnny ran a few practice laps under 200 mph, Foyt changed the rear wing to the one from the No. 84 car Rutherford had been using and taped up the nose for better aerodynamics.

"I asked him to pick us up a couple more [mph]," Foyt said. "And he gave us 203. He's a helluva driver."[12]

A relieved Rutherford was finally in the field.

"Thank God for Jim Gilmore and A.J. Foyt. When the Chevy expired, I figured that was probably it. I had a couple of other offers, but they really weren't what I wanted.

"It was something to watch Jim and A.J. go into action. They went to bat for me. It is still not quite right, but A.J. said we had one shot today, so let's go for it.

Some expressed surprise that Foyt would go to such lengths for Rutherford, one of only two drivers with a chance to match his mark of four Indy 500 wins.

"As long as he just ties it, that's fine," Foyt laughed. "Through the years I've had my good days and bad days. It seems like Johnny has had a couple two or three accidents lately and they weren't his fault. Everybody was kind of getting down on him.[13]

"He's a very capable race driver. I just want to prove a point to people that Johnny's not washed up. He's as good as anybody out here and probably better than 90 percent of them."

Also making the field with considerably less drama was Snider, Foyt's regular Indy sidekick, in the No. 14 car. He'd watched from the sidelines most of the month, running less than twenty hot laps before qualifying alongside Rutherford.

With three cars in the race, Foyt was surprisingly relaxed the week before the 500, even playing in the Speedway's annual golf tournament—something he'd avoided in recent years. As allowed under the rules, the identities of two of his cars were switched, putting him back in the No. 14 Valvoline car for the race and Snider in the Calumet-sponsored No. 4 machine. Foyt liked the look of the black March he'd bought for Rutherford and left it that way for the race.

There was also a surprise visitor to the Foyt garage as Henn stopped by to let A.J. know that both a Porsche 956 and a new 962 had been lined up for Le Mans. The 956 was the 1983 race winner, and the 962 was all-new. Although Wollek was now driving for the new Lancia team, Hurley Haywood, one of the 1983 Le Mans winning co-drivers and A.J.'s winning Daytona Paul Revere partner from the year before, was set to team with Foyt.

Henn offered Foyt his choice of the two cars and the opportunity to move from one to the other if his original pick broke down or fell too far behind. It seemed like an offer too good to refuse, but while Foyt had been receptive to the idea at Sebring and had nothing scheduled for June, he was noncommittal. Henn seldom took no for an answer and entered Foyt as one of the team's drivers.

In the 500, A.J. failed to make his typical quick start and instead dropped back. He'd guessed wrong on the chassis setup, and was several laps behind by the time he got the car handling properly. He finished sixth, officially three laps back of winner Rick Mears, although he argued without success that he was only two laps down. Snider finished eleventh while Rutherford dropped out just past the halfway point with engine troubles.

"The first 150 miles or so we pushed the front end and that got me down," a dejected Foyt said. "I softened the springs too much because we had thought the weather was going to be hotter than it turned out. The last 200 miles we ran as quickly as we could and I think we were going as fast as anybody out there. It's just a shame we had to get so far down at the beginning."[14]

Although he said he would "probably go to Le Mans," he didn't sound like someone looking forward to his next race and refused to say whether he would drive at Indianapolis again.

"I don't know," he said back in his suite. "I ain't gonna lie about it. I really don't know. I hoped we'd have finished better this year, but I really don't know."

Mears's second 500 victory was hailed as a changing of the guard. Along with Michael Andretti, Al Unser Jr., and others, a new generation was taking over at the Speedway. Mears took exception with Foyt calling the new drivers "momma's boys."

"When I hear I didn't come up the hard way, I say bull. I never ran midgets, but Foyt never ran Baja. Parnelli Jones was my hero and he always said he never drove anything as demanding as those off-road racers."[15]

Foyt decided to forgo the trip to Le Mans at the last minute, saying his aunt—Tony's little sister Marguerite—was ill, and he needed to stay close to home. A.J. had remained in touch with Marguerite over the years and supportive of her convent's charity activities, including donating vehicles for fundraising. In turn, she would often lead prayer groups for A.J. when he was injured and visit him in the hospital. Marguerite would recover and live to be ninety-one, passing away in 2008.

"I would have loved to do the race with him," Haywood said of the missed opportunity. "He is a God over there. The fans really love him. It would have been really cool to drive with him, but it just didn't work out."[16]

A.J. did add another race to his schedule: the July 1 U.S. Grand Prix. Despite its name, the event was for Indy cars on a course set up in the parking lot at the Meadowlands sports complex in New Jersey, across the Hudson River from New York City. CART pulled out all the stops to make Meadowlands a success, and that included having Foyt in the field. It was the first time the series was holding a race in the shadow of the country's biggest city, and a live television audience was set to join an expected 60,000 spectators. It was a chance for the series and teams to woo the Madison Avenue executives who controlled the marketing and advertising sponsorships and were becoming vital to the success of Indy car racing.[17]

"This is New York," said Chris Pook, who'd been instrumental in establishing the Long Beach Grand Prix near Los Angeles. "You're delivering a race to the sponsors right where they live, lock, stock and barrel.[18]

"It took sixty-eight years for the Indianapolis 500 to become what it is today," Penske added. "This race has the potential to mean just as much to the New York area as the 500 does to Indianapolis and it won't take sixty-eight years either."

While Foyt helped promote the event, doing telephone interviews from his race shop in Houston, nothing went right from the moment he arrived at the track. His car hauler was slowed on the trip by road conditions and stopped twice by police, who cited it for not having some of its permits. "I was madder than hell," Foyt said, "but what can you do?" Foyt made the best of it, sitting in the grandstands to watch the first day of practice and qualifying while signing autographs.[19]

When the car finally arrived, his mood worsened. He ran only a few slow laps and pulled back into the pits, saying the car was undriveable. He was the slowest of thirty-seven entries—fifteen miles an hour slower than pole sitter Mario Andretti—and worse yet, constantly in the way. After failing to qualify, he was offered a "promoter's option" starting position along with three other cars.

After arguing with Jack Starne, he rejected the offer, saying, "If I can't go fast enough, the hell with it." He ordered the car back on the transporter and headed for the airport.[20]

"He complained that the brakes, gears, tires, and just about everything else were not running right, all in terms unprintable here or anywhere else," wrote one reporter. "The feeling was that Foyt probably came to collect an appearance fee, made his appearance and cleared out."[21]

If there was one thing that could cheer Foyt up, it was his horses, and instead of running in the Firecracker 400 at Daytona, he watched as Turn and Cheer won the Firecracker Handicap at Churchill Downs. The win paid $36,000, nearly as much as Richard Petty took home at Daytona while winning his 200th race. It was the third straight win for Turn and Cheer—one of the horses A.J. had gotten from Calumet—and Tony saddled two other winners that day, moving his total to twenty-four for the meet, second among all trainers.

In Houston, A.J. had minor back surgery to remove some scar tissue but decided to go ahead with plans to drive in the July 22 Michigan 500, where his luck had been anything but good in recent years. He went along with Gilmore's desire to add a second car for Rutherford. With Foyt becoming more selective in his races, Gilmore said he hoped Rutherford would take up the slack in the future. While only three years younger than Foyt, Rutherford had fewer distractions and wanted to race more often.

"A.J.'s like a golf ball in a tile bathroom," Rutherford said at the press conference Gilmore called to make the announcement. "He ricochets from here to there."[22]

Gilmore said he wanted to stay in racing when Foyt decided to step away and that Rutherford could play a key role in helping to develop younger drivers.

"Now it's really the Gilmore-Foyt-Johnny Rutherford team," Gilmore said. "If Johnny sticks with us, I think we can build something historic. We just hope we can prove we mean business to Johnny and A.J."[23]

At the track, Rutherford qualified tenth and Foyt a disappointing seventeenth, ten mph slower than the pole sitter Mario Andretti. It got worse during tech inspection when it was discovered the rear wing on his car was a half-inch too long. CART sent a female member of the inspection team to tell Foyt his qualifying run was being disallowed, and that didn't sit well with A.J.

"I told them I wanted to hear it from a man," an upset Foyt said. "One thing led to another and I said to take the car back to the truck. They could throw it out if they wanted to. But when I own that race car, nobody's going to tell me what to do with it. They've tried that at Daytona, they tried at Indy. So what makes 'em think they can get away with it here.[24]

"It's bad enough to qualify as poorly as I did," he said. "Now they want me to start last. I just don't know if this place is worth it. I've already busted up three straight cars here. And I've busted myself up pretty good too. I carry a few scars from this place and I'm not anxious to get any more."

Told he could be added as a "promoter's option"—the same offer he'd turned down at New York, he joked that "Mr. Gilmore said he didn't want to be obligated to (track owner) Mr. Penske." When Foyt said it was up to Gilmore if he started, it was the sponsor's turn to laugh, telling reporters, "You guys know better than that."[25]

The next day Foyt decided to run and started thirty-third and last. When asked what changed his mind, he grinned. "Roger Penske gave me $20,000. Naw, seriously, we came up here to race in Jim Gilmore's backyard and I've got a lot of fans up here. We did a lot of testing and I think we'll be competitive."[26]

Competitive he was, as aided by a series of crashes, caution flags, and strategic pit work, Foyt moved through the field and finally into the lead on lap 118, where he stayed for fifteen laps. During a caution period, the crowd of 70,000 stood, waved, and cheered as Foyt waved back.

Running in second was Al Unser Jr., who said, "It kinda gave me chills up my spine, that this man is really that great. They only do that with A.J. If the fans would ever do that with me, I would be so happy. It would mean that I've achieved something that very few people do."[27]

However, Foyt's time at the front was short-lived as he began to suffer back spasms. For the first time anyone could remember, word spread that A.J. needed a relief driver. Already out was Al Unser, and he stepped forward but was blocked by a sponsor conflict. Then Danny Ongais came to A.J.'s pit, ready to take over.[28]

Foyt pulled in, got out of his car, and walked to the pit wall. As he did, the spasms subsided. He decided to finish the race, but with the leaders running more than 200 mph, he was now many laps behind and eventually dropped out with suspension problems. Rutherford finished seventh, one lap behind winner Mario Andretti, who was in the middle of a six-win season and on his way to a national championship.

Not only had Foyt avoided a trip to the hospital for the first time in three years at Michigan, he seemed to undergo an attitude adjustment. Whether it was the cheers from the crowd or Gilmore seemingly positioning Rutherford as the future of the team, Foyt didn't sound like someone who planned to retire anytime soon.

"I don't like playing catch-up or follow-the-leader," he said. "I'd like to get back the edge we used to have, and we're going to try to do it over the next two or three years. We're going to go do some testing and get things back together the way they were."[29]

On another occasion, he shared more about how his parents' deaths had affected him:

> I don't want to use my mother and father as an excuse, but I've just kind of laid back the last couple of years. I didn't know how much I wanted to race and I'm just now getting my head back on my shoulders. I still have the desire to win or I wouldn't be here.[30]
>
> I'm finally getting through the depression. Some of it comes with time, the rest is just making myself get a grip. There comes a point when you've gotta say, "They're gone and won't be coming back. It's over with. They were here and I was fortunate to have them and now I have to go on."

As if to prove a point, he entered the NASCAR race at Talladega, his first stock car event in four months, where he qualified twentieth.

"I haven't been down here for a while," he said. "It makes it tough, but that's the reason I'm A.J. Foyt. I like a challenge."[31]

The challenge didn't last long as he was one of the first out of the race. Disgusted, he canceled plans to race later in the year at Charlotte, saying his car wasn't competitive.

At Pocono August 18, Rutherford again outqualified his boss in twelfth with Foyt seventeenth. It was Foyt making the biggest move at the start, climbing to sixth as the first round of pit stops approached. One of the challenges the new team faced was a lack of pit crew members, with one team handling both cars.

"Before the race, we had a team meeting," Rutherford recalled. "A.J. says, 'If Rutherford's in for a stop, I'll stay out. If I'm in, Rutherford stays out.' So, we were running not too bad if I recall, and I got the sign to pit. I came in, and they jacked the car up and took all four wheels off and then it got real quiet. I wondered what was going on, and I looked in the mirrors, and A.J. was right behind me in the pits, and the entire crew had gone back to change his tires and get him out. So much for team meetings."[32]

It didn't matter as both Rutherford and Foyt dropped out within two laps of each other before the race's halfway point, finishing twenty-seventh and twenty-eighth.

Pocono also turned out to be the last race for the short-lived Gilmore-Foyt-Rutherford racing team. Three weeks later, Mears suffered a devastating crash at Sanair Speedway in Canada, which left him with a brain bruise and shattered feet. Rutherford took over Mears's car for the race, and after a fifth-place finish, Penske offered Rutherford a chance to drive the car in the three remaining oval track events on the CART schedule, including the September 23 Michigan 200. Under contract and already entered at Michigan, Rutherford went to Gilmore and Foyt and asked for his release, which they granted.

"I'll always be indebted to them," Rutherford would say. "They came through when no one else did. That's a side of A.J. few people know."[33]

After initially planning to skip Michigan, Foyt decided to take Rutherford's place in the team entry. Following practice laps at more than 205 mph and before qualifying, he asked CART to check his car. When officials said the wing was too far back, he got in a shoving match with Billy Kamphausen, CART's assistant technical director and no match size-wise for Foyt.

"A.J. did the pushing and our official did the back-stepping and it's gonna cost him [Foyt] $500," said Wally Dallenbach, CART's competition director. "He's a good friend and I don't like doing this, but nobody wants my job either."[34]

Foyt left immediately, and it was up to Gilmore to once again talk to reporters.

"A.J. and I have seen some things here that are inconsistent," Gilmore said. "We feel a lot of this harassment is overboard. All the '84 Marches have the same tread width. They're all the same. They're all factory built. It's just funny that our car measures different. It's this kind of harassment that's put the car in the trailer."[35]

Driving Mears's March, Rutherford qualified on the pole, shattering the track record at more than 215 mph and setting a new Indy car mark in the process. (Foyt's 217 mph speed recorded at Talladega was now considered to be in the "open" class.) Rutherford led nearly half the race before crashing out near the end as Mario Andretti posted yet another win.

Foyt wasn't ready for his season to end yet, and for the first time in six years, he entered the October 14 race at Phoenix, a track he'd won at five times but not since 1975. He still hadn't paid his $500 fine, and CART said he wouldn't be allowed on the track if he didn't.

"If Dennis Wood (Phoenix track president and general manager) pays it, we'll run," Foyt said. "If he don't, I won't. You just get tired of it. I've been a pretty nice guy the last couple of years, but that stuff is over with. I don't feel I was wrong. For $500 I'll beat the heck out of somebody. It won't be no darn push."[36]

It was an easy choice for Wood, who knew what having Foyt in the field meant for ticket sales.

"He told me the other day on the phone, 'I'm sorry I can't come, but there's no way my pride will let me pay that money when they're in the wrong,'" Wood said. "With what A.J. has given to this sport, I felt there was no reason to keep him from racing for a lousy $500."[37]

His fine paid, Foyt qualified fifteenth and moved up to challenge the leaders before dropping out with a suspension problem, finishing fourteenth.

Two November races remained on his schedule: a NASCAR event at Atlanta and—for the first time in four years—the Caesar's Palace Grand Prix, held in the parking lot of the Las Vegas casino. At Atlanta, he seemed happy with his twenty-second qualifying position but had to withdraw when the race was rained out and the makeup date conflicted with Las Vegas.

The Ceasar's Palace setup was similar to Meadowlands, and he didn't do much better, qualifying twenty-second in a twenty-five car field. He was running near the back when he was bumped from behind and his car caught fire. He pulled into the pits and was doused with buckets of water, extinguishing the fire and leaving him soaking wet.

It was a dismal end to a dismal—and winless—season. It was also in stark contrast to Andretti's, who ran the full Indy car schedule for the first time since 1974 for a new team formed by actor Paul Newman and Lola importer Carl Haas. Mario Andretti was unanimously named driver of the year on the basis of his six wins and fourth Indy car title. He said he had no thoughts of retirement, noting, "A.J. will be 50 in January and he's still at it."[38]

Foyt mused about his troubles on and off the track, saying he planned to hire another driver to run for the series championship in 1985. He said he'd run only a handful of events and, "I'll just sit at home so I don't get in trouble."[39]

Jerry Foyt

The success of racing sons Michael Andretti, Al Unser Jr., Geoff Brabham, the Bettenhausens, and others created an interesting problem for Foyt at home. Jerry Foyt, twenty-two, was working toward a degree in economics at the University of Texas when he told his mom he was going to drop out and try his hand at racing. He said someone needed to carry on the family name, and he owed it to his father to try.

Jerry had spent recent summers working at the dealership in various entry-level positions, and his parents were hoping he would work there after graduation.

The first inkling A.J. had that something was amiss came during a call home.

"Lucy said, 'When you get in, I need to talk to you,'" Foyt recalled. He could tell something was wrong. "I said, 'What about? What's the problem?' Because she doesn't get upset. I knew there was something."[40]

When he arrived home, Lucy began to cry as she told him of her conversation with Jerry. It had always been her dream to have their children graduate from college, a dream supported by her husband. Tony and Terry had followed their own dreams in different directions, and now Jerry wanted to drop out. They decided to fly to Austin and have lunch with their son.

"I told him I'd rather have a Foyt get his master's degree than win twenty more Indys," A.J recalled. "People would push him every race, and they can needle you into getting killed. The Foyts don't have to carry on the name."[41]

"It hasn't been an easy life," he reminded Jerry, who'd "seen [his father] broke up and hurt. Everybody looks at the nice side—the glamour of A.J. Foyt. But it wasn't all that nice."[42]

He told his son he was counting on him to help run the businesses. "I don't want you driving these cars. Why take a chance of crippling yourself up for life? I want you to finish school, because somebody's got to watch after this stuff after I'm gone."

He later told a reporter he wanted to "Let the kids run the businesses. If they want to keep 'em, fine. If they want to sell 'em, we'll get rid of 'em. I'd like to get back to the racing 100 percent."[43]

It would take time, but Jerry eventually understood his mother's abhorrence to his racing.

"I can't imagine the life and times she had to go through. Although she never showed it, I'm sure it was hard on her. It was just part of our lives. I think my father was pretty fortunate and bulletproof tough. There weren't all that many accidents that I can remember, but when they did happen, they were big. You never knew when a call would come in. We all waited for his call on Sundays."[44]

Born August 22, 1962, Jerry says he has vague memories of his father's 1967 Indy 500 win. "I was fortunate to grow up during his real legendary time. You didn't have a day or a month go by that something about him achieving something or doing something wasn't in the news. Being able to grow up and be around his race shop with my grandfather and sitting in all the race cars was a pretty big deal."

Outside of Indianapolis, however, he didn't get to go to many races.

"If it wasn't for the Dick Wallen's racing videos, I'd never get the goose bumps I do watching him run against Parnelli [Jones], Herk [Jim Hurtubise] and [Rodger] Ward. He was amazing, and I love watching those old films."

While his dad was often away at a race, his time at home was mostly spent at the ranch:

> That was our place. He has never been one to sit around, so if he was off, we weren't going to be just sitting around the house in Houston. We were going to the ranch.

> He works like nobody I've ever known. Always has. He would be out working before I got up and worked until close to dark on his bulldozers or whatever other projects he had. I remember standing there while he cleared land and knocked trees over—that was pretty neat. It's his favorite thing to do. He gets more relaxation and satisfaction working with his heavy equipment than anything else besides racing.
>
> Back then, we had a station wagon and pickup trucks. I remember him putting me on his lap and telling me to take the wheel, going seventy-five, eighty. He just told me to stay between the lines.

Like many families, Christmas was a special day for the Foyts with big gatherings including both sets of grandparents.

"The best thing about Christmas was wondering what that minibike or the motorcycle you were graduating to would look like," Jerry recalled. "Or whatever had an engine on it that you could take out on the open land and wear out. I can remember having minibikes, mini dune buggies, and cart buggies before I had a bicycle. When we were out at the ranch, it wasn't much fun riding a bicycle. It was all about the suspension and the motor."

Jerry was close to his grandparents and often spent time with them when his dad was away racing. "I have great memories of spending more time with them than you normally got to spend with your grandparents. I was blessed with great grandparents.

He was especially close to his grandfather Tony.

"He was such a great, great man. He was completely different away from the track. My whole life, he was the only one I knew my dad not to challenge. He might have been tough on the racing side, but at home he was very supportive and a wonderful grandfather. I just did not have the maturity during the time I got to spend with him to realize how great he was and nurture off of that. One of my biggest regrets was not having enough adult time to spend with him."

Tony's death was hard on Jerry, but not as hard as it was on his father.

"It was tougher on him than anything I've seen—ever. I was at college, so I wasn't at home to go through the day-to-day of that. You don't realize what you have until it's gone. Had I been a little more mature, I probably wouldn't have left their side."

Jerry stayed in school, graduated from the University of Texas in 1985, and went to work at A.J. Foyt Chevrolet. He recalled,

> I worked for his management team. They were mentoring me. [Dad] had an office there and would come to the dealership quite a bit when he was in town. He was "one of them," and I think his team loved him for that. It wasn't unusual for a customer to come in for a transaction or service and have an opportunity to meet him.
>
> The most important value I got from him was the hard work ethic. Don't think you're better than anybody else. Get down and do the work

> that you expect other people to do. Try to know your work as good or better than the people that work with you or for you. That's something we've seen him do his entire life. His moral character and ethics are pretty strong. When I was growing up, you'd be way too afraid to lie to him. Might as well just face the music.

Jerry would also get to try his hand at racing, enrolling in the Skip Barber driving school in 1987 as Jerry Zarr, using his mother's maiden name. He paid his own way and got Lucy's approval beforehand, but both decided not to tell A.J. It wasn't until a couple of months after the class that Foyt learned about it and wasn't particularly happy when he did.

"I didn't want it and I haven't encouraged it," A.J. said. "That's what he's wantin' to do. It's his life. I never agreed to it until his mother agreed. I never thought he'd get her to agree to it. Some way he finally convinced her. I never thought I'd see the day.[45]

"He just went out there as Jerry Zarr. He didn't want people knowin' who he was. He wasn't goin' out there and trying to live off his father's shirttail (by saying) I'm A.J. Foyt's son. I was quite proud of him for that."

While proud of his son, A.J. didn't exactly give his blessing—or anything else—to the effort. At the time, Jerry said,

> My dad and I get along real well and we respect each other greatly. But the one thing we don't see eye-to-eye on is racing. Morally, financially and verbally, he's against me driving race cars. He's discouraged my racing to anyone who wants to get involved with me and they usually listen because they don't want to step on his toes.[46]
>
> The only thing holding me back is the same thing that's holding back a lot of other guys—money. I quit begging and pleading a long time ago. I think Dad wants to see me stick to a business life and that's his prerogative. I agree it makes sense. He would like to see me have it easier than he did.

Jerry competed in a number of different cars and series, including Sports 2000, ARCA and ASA stock cars, and the Firehawk series for mostly showroom stock machines, where he shared a car with his father in one event.

"Everything I did was pretty minor league stuff," Jerry says. "But that was a wonderful time for me. I had an opportunity to race at some pretty neat racetracks: Elkhart Lake, Watkins Glen, Phoenix, Sears Point, Laguna Seca, Lime Rock, Sebring."[47]

He also looked back on another accomplishment.

"I hope I had a hand in easing up his resistance to racing for Larry and Anthony. When I tried it, [Dad] was near the end of his competitive time in racing. He had his own reasons why he didn't want to see any of us, including my brother or sister, involved in racing. He and my mother were the only ones who knew what to expect. When I had children, I had a different viewpoint and probably wouldn't have been enthusiastic about seeing them involved. The sport has some harsh consequences sometimes."

Jerry stayed in the automotive business after A.J. eventually sold his stores and rose to the executive ranks of one of the largest dealership chains in the country.

GILMORE
Foyt
Copenhagen
GILMORE
GILMORE
SIMPSON
Copenhagen
IT SATISFIES
SIMPSON

CHAPTER 9

HERO OR AN ASS

1985

With his fiftieth birthday just around the corner, it took only a few weeks at home before A.J. Foyt started working on his plans for the coming season.

"There's still some racing left for us," he said. "We're trying to gear up so we can go racing again instead of just showing up."[1]

"I got lazy," he admitted at a conference of Goodyear distributors. "I didn't race. I didn't test. I got behind. If you don't work, you won't stay number one. You'll lose, like me."[2]

He purchased two new Marches and took them to the wind tunnel, adding his own tweaks. After a disastrous first year driving an Oldsmobile in NASCAR, he created a separate stock car team and the GM division stepped forward to provide additional support.

Jim Gilmore continued to push for a second driver to run the entire Indy car season and perhaps even a third to build the future of the team around. At the top of Foyt's list was Al Unser, who'd been dropped as a full-time driver by Roger Penske at the end of 1984 and replaced by Danny Sulivan, the ex–Formula One driver who'd had an impressive rookie season. Penske offered Unser a car, but for only the three 500-mile races.

"I'd love to have Al," Foyt said. As in the case of Johnny Rutherford, he was offering a ride to one of the two drivers who could tie his mark of four Indianapolis 500 wins. "I personally feel he's the most underrated driver around today. He's smart and he's got a lot of ability. The outside world doesn't know how good he is. I think he's one of the best to come along in my time. Bobby Unser was a hard charger. But I think Al is a smarter race driver."[3]

Unser said he was flattered but was keeping his options open. Foyt's offer had been for the Indy 500 only, and he was holding out for another full season.

◀ A.J. loves his ice cream. *Dan Boyd*

"I'm not sure yet who I'll be driving for next year," Al said, "but hopefully something will come up. I'm not ready to call it quits yet. A.J. said if I ever needed a ride, I'd have one on his team. He and I go back a long way together, and I'm honored he'd want me."[4]

Gilmore continued to push for a young driver to build the team's future around and seemed to favor John Paul Jr., who'd had a meteoric rise through the sports car ranks and occasional Indy car rides, including a win in the 1983 Michigan 500. Foyt preferred Al Unser Jr., who he thought would be a perfect match with his father. Both seemed to slip away in late 1984, however, when "Little Al" signed with Team Lotus, which was planning a return to Indy car racing, and Paul signed to replace Sullivan at Shierson Racing.

Foyt also voiced new discontent with CART, which continued to expand its schedule with no increases in its purses. He didn't like that the schedule was evenly split between oval tracks and road courses. He noted last place in the Indianapolis 500 paid more than second place in the recent Michigan 500, and the winner's share at Michigan had actually decreased.

"I won more money at Milwaukee with my Offys in the '60s than I could today," he said. "If I had to come here and worry about making enough money to get home on, it'd be hard to do. I think they ought to have 10 to 12 races a year with a minimum half-million-dollar purse. The objective when CART was formed was for guys in the back to get some money. It seems CART has gotten drunk on (scheduling) more races."[5]

While Indy car purses remained stagnant as it expanded its schedule, NASCAR was cutting back its schedule as the R.J. Reynolds Tobacco Company and its Winston brand poured more money into the series, committing more than $11 million over the next five years.

"The Indianapolis 500 is supposed to be the greatest race in this country and it pays a measly $400,000 to the winner," Darrell Waltrip pointed out. "We just made it look like a heat race."[6]

As the first race of the year approached, the 24 Hours of Daytona, it appeared Foyt might yet pull off his dream pairing of the two Unsers on his Indy car team. Lotus had belatedly pulled the plug on its Indy car project and released "Little Al," but there were no full-time seats available. Before Foyt and Gilmore could act, however, Paul Jr. was arrested a couple of days later on January 21 on federal racketeering and conspiracy charges. His namesake father had financed the family's racing program by importing marijuana and involved his son in the operation. While the government's real focus was on Paul Sr., his son refused to testify against his father, and federal prosecutors decided to try and up the pressure by charging Paul Jr. with felonies that would eventually send him to prison.

Under pressure from sponsor Domino's, Shierson canceled Paul Jr.'s contract and signed Unser Jr. to be the team's driver. Having missed his chance to pair the Unsers, Foyt then invited "Big Al" to join him for the 24 Hours of Daytona, where he was teaming once again with Wollek in Preston Henn's new Porsche 962. Foyt had nixed Henn's original pick, 1984 Porsche Cup winner Henri

Pescarolo, saying only half-jokingly, "I'd be outnumbered two to one," if a second French driver was added.[7]

Unser agreed but was cautious about any further commitment. He said he'd only talked "slightly" with Foyt and had "no idea" when asked if the Daytona start might lead to more races, saying only, "When he called me the other day, it made me feel good that he asked me.[8]

"I'd like to run in all fifteen (CART events) this year," Unser said. "Maybe after Daytona A.J. and I can sit down and talk about the season. Or maybe something else will come along."[9]

Henn admitted it was costing a pretty penny to get Foyt back in his car. Estimates put Foyt's fee at twice that of any other driver, and Henn admitted he had turned to the race promoters for financial help.

"It's worth it," he said. "It's good publicity for my businesses and the track here will probably get another $20,000 in revenue this weekend just because A.J. has showed up. He's still the biggest name in racing.[10]

"You look at him, you don't realize he's fifty. Anybody that ever wanted to be a race driver had A.J. as an idol. He's still a phenomenon and still drives awful damn hard too. He has tremendous reserves and can rise to the moment at hand."

Foyt needed all the reserves he could muster as he and Wollek both came down with the flu as race weekend approached. Paul Jr., who'd been bailed out of jail in advance of his March trial, turned in the fastest qualifying time while Wollek qualified fourth.

"It (endurance racing) is babysitting a car," Foyt said before the start. "The big thing in a 24-hour race is to stay out of trouble and to keep the car going. It's going to be very competitive this year. Any of the top twenty prototypes could win."[11]

It was Foyt's first time behind the wheel of the new 962, although Wollek had driven it several times in Europe. It seemed not to bother Foyt.

"It just takes a few laps to adjust," A.J. said. "If you're a race driver you adapt. You may not be the fastest right away, but if you're a race driver you'll catch up fast."[12]

Foyt started the race and dropped back as several cars battled for the lead, only to fall by the wayside. Midway through the event, two cars emerged far ahead of the rest—Henn's team chasing the similar Porsche 962 of Al Holbert, Al Unser Jr., and Derek Bell. Once again, Henn picked up another driver from the ranks of those out of the race, adding Thierry Boutsen, an F1 regular and occasional sports car driver for Porsche. With Foyt and Wollek still under the weather and Unser reluctant to drive in the dark, Boutsen kept the team close while driving most of the night hours. They were cutting into the leader's margin by about ten seconds a lap but were still two laps behind entering the final hour.

That's when the front-runners were slowed by an electrical problem. It took thirteen minutes to repair, and by then it was too late. Wollek had taken over Henn's car and brought it home ahead of Holbert's squad.

"These boys knew what they were doing out there," Foyt said, giving the credit to Wollek and Boutsen, who between them drove 499 of the 703 laps. "As it got close to the end and we were still second, we all agreed to go for broke or break the car. We also agreed that Bob could run the fastest of us."

He also credited Henn with putting together the winning team.[13]

"He's the promoter all right, the persuasive one, the guy who'll keep callin' ya, keep buggin' the hell out of ya' till he makes it happen."

It was the biggest win of Boutsen's young career. "A.J. was a legend to me since I was a kid, but I think I only understood about half the things he said to me," he said of the Texan. "But one thing was real clear. At the end he said, 'Boy, we won!'"

It was a tough loss for Holbert, whose team led 2,043 of the 2,503 miles and jokingly labeled Henn's group "a band of gypsies."

His year off to a good start, two weeks later Foyt agreed to compete in the International Race of Champions for the first time in four years. He was also happy with his new Oldsmobile, having turned in the fourth-fastest qualifying time for the Daytona 500 and finishing eighth in the qualifying race.

He moved into the lead on the fifth lap of the forty lap IROC event and led a freight train of the world's best drivers for the next thirty-four laps, with Cale Yarborough pushing from second, just as Foyt had pushed Yarborough in the past. Coming off the fourth turn on the last lap, Yarborough went low to try and pass Foyt and was nearly alongside when he was tapped by Tom Sneva in third, turning Yarborough into Foyt and sending all three cars spinning. Foyt finished third, sliding through the infield grass and across the finish line, Waltrip sneaking through for the victory. While Foyt laughed with Yarborough about the finish, he had nothing good to say about his Indy car counterpart.

"Sneva's a squirrel," he said. "He ran out of brains—as usual—and ran into the back of Cale. There ain't no sense in all that bullshit."[14]

Also laughing was Sneva when told about Foyt's comments:

> He says a lot of things. When I get to be that age, maybe I'll get away with that too. Something is bound to happen at Daytona when three cars head into an area wide enough for two.[15]
>
> As for Foyt, if you're on the same side of any issue with him, you are his buddy. He's hot and cold. If your opinion differs from his, you're an SOB. One minute you can be close the next minute he's got some remarks to say about you. That's just A.J. and you got to accept it about him."

In a race dominated by Bill Elliott, Foyt was able to hang with the leaders in the early going of the Daytona 500, but his hopes of a good finish ended before the halfway point with a blown engine. From there, he headed down the east coast of Florida to Miami, where he'd team again with Wollek in the three-hour sports car race. It was a key event for Henn, whose biggest swap meets were in the greater Miami area.

Foyt qualified the car in second, and Wollek kept it near the front at the start before being penalized for passing the pace car. He said the pace car driver waved him past, but officials didn't see it, and he was sent to the back of the pack. Foyt took over and made an impressive run through the field. He took the lead on lap fifty-three and held it for twenty laps before a blown turbo knocked the car out.

The 962 was repainted Foyt Orange for the 12 Hours of Sebring on March 23. They could do no better than thirteenth in qualifying, fifteen seconds off the pole time. Foyt was already in a foul mood and working on the engine when he was approached by Jonathan Ingram, the IMSA beat reporter for the popular racing magazine *On Track*. In his report on the Miami race, Ingram wrote the team turned up the boost when Foyt took over the car, allowing him to knife through the field, but knowing the engine would not last until the finish.

Henn showed Foyt a photocopy of the article with the comments about the charge to the front highlighted. Egged on by Henn and Wollek, Foyt backed Ingram up toward the car.

"He picked me up with one hand and held me against the car," Ingram recalled. "He screamed, 'You're a dumb cocksucker,' and started winding up with his other arm to hit me. I think he realized he probably would have really hurt me and pulled his punch."[16]

The team had the car straightened out by the start of the race, and even though they fell two laps behind in the early going, they started moving forward near the three-hour mark. Foyt made up one lap and Wollek the other. They moved to the front with four hours remaining and cruised to a two-lap victory when the leaders dropped out.

Near the nine-hour mark, with Foyt behind the wheel, he took evasive action, driving into the grass to avoid another car and running over a broken tailpipe in the process. The tailpipe came up through the floorboard "and hit me right in the ass."[17]

"I was almost over there with the airplanes," Foyt said of the off-track excursion that took him near the Sebring airport runway. "I tried to go by a car and misjudged it and hit the dirt. I didn't want to tell my co-pilot because I didn't want him to get worried."[18]

Wollek, who was scheduled to drive the final two hours, didn't have to be told something was wrong as he took over and discovered the driver's seat had been locked into place by the damage. He couldn't slide it forward from Foyt's driving position and after struggling to reach the steering wheel and pedals for several laps, Wollek returned to the pits, giving the car back to A.J. Wollek would say later he wanted Foyt to have the thrill of driving under the checkered flag at the only major race he hadn't won and complete his hat trick of winning the world's three major endurance races (Le Mans, Daytona, and Sebring). Foyt cruised to a two-lap victory and joked about it later.

"Hell, I didn't want to get back in. If it was going to break, I wanted it to be with him in it. I heard every noise imaginable in that car during the last hour."

With two months remaining until the Indianapolis 500, Foyt entered five cars at about $150,000 each, although he'd yet to add any additional drivers to the team's lineup as Al Unser had decided to accept Penske's offer.

Foyt did, however, land a major sponsor in the form of the U.S. Tobacco Company's Copenhagen brand. Like R.J. Reynolds in NASCAR, the company had marketing dollars to burn due to the government's restrictions on tobacco television advertising. While he continued to receive support from Gilmore and a handful of associate sponsors, including Valvoline, Tony Lama Boots, and Kmart, he tried to limit the number because he didn't want his car "looking like a popsicle . . . It's ridiculous. 'But if Penske does it, A.J. Foyt's gotta do it. If A.J. Foyt has to do it, Joe Blow's gotta do it. If he wants to be a winner."[19]

It was also a nod to racing's new reality.

"The average layman can go out and buy the same stuff I've got, and really not have the ability I've got, and maybe outrun me. Before you had to build a lot of your stuff. You had to put a lot of your time into it and come up with your ideas. Now you've got expert after expert, aerodynamics after aerodynamics. You've got so much more money behind the whole thing. It's just unbelievable. I just never thought we'd be spending money on automobile racing like this."

For the first time in years, he tested at the Speedway, spending three days jumping between a March and a Lola, eventually settling on the March after turning a lap of 207 miles per hour. He also added Henn's Porsche crew chief, Mike Colucci, to his crew and let Tony George, Mari Hulman George's son and Tony Hulman's grandson, run a few slow laps in the March.

He skipped the opening Indy car race of the year on the street course at Long Beach. Mario Andretti, the No. 1 on his Lola as the national champion, dominated the event, turning in the fastest qualifying time and pulling within two of Foyt's pole position record of fifty-three. Then he led seventy of ninety laps for the victory.

After a relatively quiet first week of practice at the Speedway, and with Pole Day looming, Foyt took his March out for a few practice laps during "Happy Hour" late Friday afternoon. He'd run laps at 210 mph during the week, and with others running around 215 mph, he decided to make some changes, still hoping to challenge for the pole. Out early Saturday morning before qualifying, he discovered the March had developed a severe push, the front tires breaking free, and the front of the car "pushing" up toward the wall. He decided to make "a stab in the dark" and try different springs, change the bothersome side panel, and take the unusual step of qualifying on used tires.[20]

His first two qualifying laps were slow, about 207 mph, and it fell off from there, his final laps at 204 and 203 mph—good for only twenty-first in the starting lineup. "It was so damned loose I couldn't drive it," he'd say later. "I was just trying to get a halfway decent average and the last couple of laps I just about knocked down all the fences."

Jim Phillippe, the public address reporter on pit road whose job it was to interview each new qualifier, warily approached Foyt. He'd had his share of interesting interviews with Foyt in the past, but this one set a new mark, including one for brevity.

"It ran like a tub of shit," he said before storming off. Phillippe didn't miss a beat. "Well A.J., I guess the fans have never had it explained quite that way before!" For years to come, *Indianapolis Star* reporter Robin Miller would refer to the car simply as the TOS March.

Facing an initiation under fire was Anne Fornoro, and although no stranger to a racetrack, she was working her first event as the team's U.S. Tobacco (UST) public relations representative. She was the daughter of successful midget racer Russ Klar, married to driver Drew Fornoro, and the daughter-in-law of Nick Fornoro, another former driver and flagman on the CART circuit. She'd been working with Chris Economaki at *National Speed Sport News* when the opportunity at UST came up, and for the last year she'd been involved in the marketing efforts east of the Mississippi including auto racing, fishing, and pro rodeo. "It was a dream job," she said.

She'd worked with Teo Fabi and UST's Skoal Bandit entry at Indianapolis the year before and shifted to the Copenhagen brand when it signed on with Foyt. Their first meeting was over the telephone when she was putting together press materials. "I was surprised at how soft spoken he was," she recalled. "And kind. He was always very kind to me. Tough, but kind."

She'd already learned "he was not the type where you would prepare him ahead of time. You never knew what he was going to do next. He was A.J. Foyt and he got away with a lot of stuff. I learned early to roll with the punches and try and mitigate disasters."

Now she waited while Foyt blew off steam, then persuaded him to open the doors of garage twenty-nine and invite in a group of stunned reporters. It was the start of a relationship spanning more than forty years and counting.

"The man was downright patient, honest and charming in his own sort of way," wrote one surprised reporter in attendance.[21]

"It's a shame a car like that can run 214–215 easy and be all screwed up like that," Foyt said. "I would have to say it was one of my worst disappointments. We just flat screwed up. Or I did. I wouldn't blame the crew. That's why I'm so mad at myself. If it had worked out the way I hoped we might have been sitting on the pole. I guessed wrong. In a deal like this you are either a hero or an ass. I took a shot and lost. Like rolling the dice."[22]

Safely—if not happily—in the field, Foyt sold the Lola to the team of Derek Daly and began filling the seats of his other cars. He leased the 1984 March he'd driven the year before to rookie Mike Nish and agreed to provide "assistance" to the young driver. Nish had been working as a mechanic for Dick Simon with hopes of driving one of his cars. When Simon ran out of engines and money, he arranged a meeting between Foyt and Nish.

"He said he needed quite a bit of money and we were real honest with him, we just didn't have it," Nish said. Then Foyt had a change of heart. "He said, why don't you come over, get the thing through tech inspection and let's get you in it."[23]

Foyt had taken a liking to Nish. "He reminds me a lot of myself. He likes to work on the cars and he don't mind getting dirty."

The twenty-five-year-old Nish was running super modifieds, sprint cars, and midgets with some success but had made only one Indy car start and had yet to complete his rookie test. Nish said,

> We got more than we bargained for. I was supposed to supply my own crew but his guys have been more than willing to help. He's overseeing the whole program. He does the setup on the car, he jumps in there and works on it with everybody. I guess he likes guys who work on the cars. Last night I was working on a motor changeover and he came over and slapped me on the back.
>
> [Foyt is] kind of like my Dad. He's a hard man but he's a gentle man. He just wants me to go out and to get where I feel comfortable. He thinks I can get the job done. I hope I can live up to that for him.[24]

After Nish passed his rookie test, Foyt made an unlikely choice and let Chip Ganassi try the No. 84 car. Ganassi was coming back from a crash at Michigan the year before that saw him go flipping through the infield. He'd emerged with serious head and chest injuries and a broken hand but said he was fully recovered. Before the crash, he'd performed well in parts of two seasons driving for Pat Patrick, with eight top-ten finishes and the series' most improved driver award in 1983. Since the crash, however, he was having a hard time finding a ride. He'd approached A.J. at Daytona, in what turned out to be a short conversation.

"A.J., I heard you're looking for a driver," Ganassi recalled saying.[25]

"I thought you quit," A.J. said.

Foyt said he'd keep Ganassi in mind, and Chip went to the Speedway in April to watch A.J. run a test session.

"You know, we'd been off for the winter and it typically takes a second to get built up to the speed," Ganassi recalled years later. "Not him. He literally went out on his first flying lap and was right there, instantly up to pole speed. Without touching the car. It was just crazy."[26]

When Ganassi didn't hear anything more, he figured he'd better keep looking and was surprised when A.J. approached him.

"It's been hard to convince people I'm ready and able to drive again," Ganassi said at the time. Foyt had given him a nickname, which was always a good sign. He'd started calling Ganassi "Yank" or "Yankee." "I was walking around hat in hand. A.J. said he was still thinking about it. I'd get up every day and think, 'this is the day I'll get a ride.' It finally happened."[27]

"A.J. believes in me and was willing to give me a chance. I came here hoping for a break and I got one thanks to A.J. Now it's up to me to make something of it."[28]

Years later Ganassi would look back and say, "I was trying to get back on my feet after my crash, and Tony George and his mother [Mari Hulman George] helped me out. I didn't really know if I had a ride or not. I stood around watching all the first week. Finally, the second Monday, Foyt said, 'All right, get in the car and do some laps.' I think I did four laps or something, and he said, 'That's enough.' Four laps!"[29]

After several days of practice during which Ganassi estimated he did about fifteen laps, he was running speeds that would easily make the race. As his qualifying attempt approached, however, he admitted to being a little nervous. "A.J. just said, 'Get in the car and do the job.'"[30]

Each of his four laps was faster than the previous lap, and by the time he was finished, Ganassi had turned in a faster time than Foyt the week before.

"A.J. said, 'Yank, if I knew you were going to do that, I would have given you more laps,'" Ganassi recalled.[31]

Foyt then turned to Snider and asked if he wanted to try and qualify the No. 44 turbo Chevy. Snider pitted after one practice lap. The car was running hot from a gasket leak, and water was gushing out of the overflow valve when he stopped. There was no time to change the engine or even fix the leak.

"Hell with it, let's put new tires on it and go," Foyt said.[32]

"He's drove for me many years and knows if I tell him a car's working good we can run with it," Foyt said later. "He's got confidence I'm not going to tell him something where it would be crazy to do something silly. I've never given him a bum steer on something like that."[33]

Snider ran only one warmup lap, afraid each lap might be the engine's last. Then he turned in four laps fast enough to start thirty-second.

"I knew what I had to do," Snider said. "A month and a half ago I wouldn't have given a plug nickel that I'd be in this race. I hadn't talked to A.J. and had no intention of running here. I'm getting too old for this last-minute stuff."[34]

Not as lucky was Nish, who was still looking for more speed in practice when he slid up the track and into the wall. He emerged unhurt, but the car was too badly damaged to fix for a qualifying attempt. Nish would go on to set several international land speed records, but he never qualified for the Indianapolis 500.

Another driver who wasn't in the field was Gordon Johncock, who'd decided to retire. A reporter asked Foyt for his thoughts on Johncock, and he decided to make an announcement of his own, indicating he'd quit after the 1987 Indianapolis 500. It was the first time he'd put an actual date on his retirement.

"I'll retire after the thirtieth one," he said. "We gotta do thirty races if I ain't too old. Then I'll retire."[35]

When the race started, it didn't take long for Foyt to realize something was seriously wrong. "It just kept on pushin', pushin', pushin," he said. "I knew after about ten laps that something was wrong. I just didn't know what. I was using all the track I could, just to keep from hitting the wall."[36]

What he couldn't see and the crew didn't notice on two pit stops was the right-front wing cantered up and acting as a wind dam. It was lap sixty-eight when he finally figured out the root of his problem and headed for the pits. Radio communications had been spotty, and the crew was unprepared for his arrival. Foyt gestured wildly as he tried to tell them to fix the wing while they scrambled to change tires and add fuel—normally the first things done on a pit stop. Even that didn't go well as they had trouble with the right-rear tire.

After fuming in the cockpit for more than a minute and becoming increasingly frustrated by the lack of attention to the wing, Foyt climbed out to take the matter into his own hands. Grabbing some tools, he got on his knees in front of the car alongside Jack Starne. After flipping the wing several times, he gave up and headed for the pit wall. The team was still trying to refuel the car. A.J. decided to show them how to properly vent the process and stuck his arm in the buckeye, splashing methanol on the rear of the hot car, which ignited. Barely breaking stride, Foyt grabbed a bucket of water and dumped it on the car as firemen rushed to extinguish the flames.

Back in the garage, Foyt seemed to slough off the problems and his twenty-eighth-place finish, saying, "We've been coming here long enough to know it's not a bed of roses." Snider had already dropped out and finished thirty-second, and Ganassi—who'd been running well—didn't last much longer, finishing twenty-second.

"The car was really good," Ganassi said. "I mean, it stuck like a slot car. A.J. had a way of setting up the car so it just plain stuck. It was a great car to drive, but we had a mechanical problem in the race."[37]

Fortunately for Foyt, Sullivan's exciting "spin-and-win" victory over Andretti helped lessen the spotlight on his team's miserable performance. At least until the normally mild-mannered Jim Gilmore unloaded. Although Copenhagen had come on board as a sponsor, his name was still the largest name on the side of the No. 14. He'd been against trying to get four cars in the field and said the team missed the presence of Tony Foyt, who'd run a no-nonsense garage.

"I'm disappointed and discouraged," Gilmore said. "We didn't do a very good job. The way we prepared for the race was just dumb. If we are going to remain in racing, it is ridiculous to do it that way.[38]

"We're not running a pleasure resort in those garages. It's a real joke and we handled it in a very dumb way. We looked terrible. It was humiliating for A.J. He apologized to me for his own personal failures. A.J. expressed to me, 'I fell down.'"

Gilmore continued to talk about keeping the team going even after Foyt retired.

"God, I'd do anything for that guy. He's like a brother. We're not going to quit."

Gilmore's remarks hit home, and Foyt later acknowledged the challenges he and the team were facing:

> You know, I'm just trying to get them to operate more on their own, without me saying, "Do this, do that," because they're smart people. I'd put 'em up against anybody. Through the years [I've been] kind of a one-man operation. I call all of my shots. But I'm spread thin. My father, when he was living, he knew what I wanted. I'd tell him and he'd make sure it was done, so it let me spend more time with the other businesses. Now I need to spend more time with racing, but I can't afford to.[39]
>
> I really don't have the in-between man. Jack (Starne) has been with me many years and works hard and heck he was about in tears. He said,

"Maybe it's me." I said, "No, it's just that you're not one of the group any more. You're an outsider now. You gotta say, "This is what I want." And he's still trying to handle it all himself instead of overseeing a lot of it.

I think by the end of the year it'll work out and I look for us to have a good season. I don't mind how many more mistakes we make this year as long as we're learning something. And I think we all learn pretty good. I'm putting more responsibility on Jack to run the team. I really need to get him some more help because since I lost my father I got him doing a lot more at the race shop and going through bills with me and paperwork which he never was involved in before. So what I've done is take him halfway away from the race team and tried to bring up some other people. So, we got caught this year without a full-fledged chief mechanic. And what I mean, he *is* a chief mechanic, but not spending 100 percent of the time like he used to.

It was after the race that Ganassi's real adventure began. He recalled the following:

When the race was over, I said, 'Hey, what about my prize money?' [Foyt] said, 'Come down to Houston in a couple of weeks, and I'll give it to you. Call my secretary, and set it up.' So I did, and when I got there, I saw Jack and he said Foyt never came to the shop anymore.[40]

So, I called Foyt, and he says, "Where are you?" I tell him I'm at the race shop, and he asked why. I told him I came for my prize money, and he says, "There ain't no money at the shop," and then he says, "Goddammit, I'll come and pick you up."

About an hour later, I hear this car screech up, and he says, "Goddammit let's go." We drove for a couple hours, and we end up at his ranch. I spent the next two days digging fence post holes. We're up at five or six in the morning. It's scorching, at least one hundred degrees, and I'm digging fence post holes by hand. I don't have a change of clothing, and I'm in my dress slacks and Gucci loafers. There was no talk about racing at all. He was telling me all about his ranch. You wouldn't even know the guy was in racing. I wanted to talk about it, but he didn't. I was about twenty-five years old at the time. I was afraid to say anything, you know?

Then he says he's flying up to Mid-Ohio in the morning and he'll give me a ride home. He had a Hawker then, a real nice plane, and they served a hot breakfast and everything. So, we get to Mid-Ohio, and I've got a rental car, and I say, "Hey, where's my prize money?" and he says, "I'll mail it to you." Of course, I eventually got it.

But that was A.J. He was in his own world. He never really let down his guard, never let his true feelings show when he was at the racetrack. The fact of the matter is he's a sharp guy, and he's nobody's fool. He was a great guy to be around, and he has a good heart in there.

While Foyt said all the right things after the 500, his team continued to struggle. He ran four more Indy car races during the year but failed to finish any. He didn't qualify at the Meadowlands but this time accepted a promoter's option. He crashed in practice at Michigan when a wheel broke and again at Phoenix. At Pocono, he heard the taunts of some of the series' younger drivers.

"I think seeing Foyt out on the track is sad," said Bobby Rahal, who also called Foyt a "has been" at a press luncheon before the race. "It's like seeing Muhammad Ali at the end of his reign. You just want to tell the guy, 'Hey, give it up. Don't tarnish your image.'

"Racing has changed so much. I think A.J. is probably capable of winning if he was willing to spend the time necessary to do it. The days when you could be involved in something besides the race are gone. It's so competitive, you've got to be there. I think what he's doing to his image is sad."[41]

Sneva, who'd felt the wrath of Foyt earlier in the year after the Daytona IROC race, piled on: "The sport is so much more sophisticated now. You can't come to the racetrack a day before the event and expect everybody to move over for you. They're not going to do it. You can't prepare for a race the way A.J. does and expect to accomplish anything. And yet, every year, we hear how A.J. is back with a new dedication."

Both drivers had a point. Foyt continued to miss valuable practice time while tending to his other business operations. And if nothing else, the comments by Rahal and Sneva indicated the up-and-coming Indy car drivers could no longer be intimidated by Foyt, either on or off the track.

"I have nothing to prove," Foyt said when asked about the comments. "My record speaks for itself. What have either one of them ever accomplished? Who won the biggest race in America this year?" he said, referring to the 24 Hours of Daytona. "Who won at Sebring, drove most of the race, drove through the rain? I haven't run many races, but in the races I've run, I've done well. I can't be faulted if the equipment breaks."[42]

After turning the fastest lap in Pocono practice, Foyt qualified seventeenth. He raced from there to tenth in just five laps and was running seventh when problems again surfaced, his day ending when he returned to the track with a loose wheel after a pit stop.

The NASCAR program showed a glimmer of hope as Foyt qualified sixth at Daytona for the Firecracker 400 and fourth at Talladega. He led laps in both races, and his fifth place at Talladega was his best NASCAR showing in six years. He also checked off one of the few remaining boxes on his bucket list by competing in the Southern 500 at Darlington on Labor Day weekend.

Known as the "Lady in Black" or the "Track Too Tough to Tame," Darlington had been America's first superspeedway when built in 1950. Indy cars had raced at the track during the July 4 holiday through the mid-1950s, the last time in 1956, the year before Foyt joined the series. Only 1.366-miles in length, it was egg-shaped with uneven banking and a rough surface. Dwarfed by other tracks in recent years, including Daytona and Talladega, it was still considered by many to be the country's toughest oval track. Like Indianapolis, Darlington required first-time drivers to pass a rookie test, and while officials offered to wave it for Foyt, he insisted on going through with it.

"I'm going to Darlington as a bona fide rookie. I don't want anything waived. Why should I be different than anyone else? I know a lot of guys would have too much pride and ego to take the rookie test, but I'm not that type of person."[43]

"I'll do everything every other first-year driver does at Darlington, including the rookie test," he said. "I've always worked for everything I have and have gone by the rules to win. I'm not changing now."[44]

He couldn't resist the opportunity to editorialize.

"That's what's wrong with the world today. People set rules and then allow them to be broke. When I was a kid, it was hard to borrow money from the bank. That was the rule, and people knew it. Now people just keep getting more and more credit, and look where we are. Nobody knows the rules anymore, and we're worse off for it."[45]

Cale Yarborough served as his coach, and an embarrassed Ricky Rudd was charged with passing judgment on Foyt's test.

"I came over to give him any help I could," Yarborough said. "But what kind of help do you give someone like A.J. Foyt. I can tell him what not to do, rather than what to do."[46]

Foyt was clearly enjoying the experience, which included putting the first "Darlington Stripe" on his car.

"All I know is the fourth turn [now Turn One] is probably the trickiest. The rear end kept wanting to come around all day. So I just figured I'd leave my foot in it and see what it would do. It started tó spin so I just let it go and rode the wall. But I'm a rookie. I'm allowed to make a few mistakes, aren't I?"

Rudd agreed and gave Foyt a passing mark, overruling Yarborough and Waltrip who joked Foyt needed "more seasoning."

"This is a famous race with a lot of tradition," Foyt said. "It's kind of like the Kentucky Derby. Win or lose, at least I can say I've been here."

In the race, he lost a lap early then settled down before using up his brakes—a classic rookie mistake. He was also overshadowed by Bill Elliott, who won his third of four NASCAR major events during the year and a million dollars from Winston as part of a special promotion. Even "Million Dollar Bill" was asked about Foyt.

"He's a man I've admired for many years," Elliott said. "He's got a mighty big spotlight."

Only now, it wasn't the sort of spotlight anyone wanted to be in. Not even a return to Daytona for the season-ending sports car race helped. He qualified Henn's Porsche back in twenty-fourth spot, but Holbert started the car and drove it into the lead during the first hour. Foyt took over, and while he was able to hang with the leaders, a busted turbocharger soon knocked him out, leaving the team to finish thirty-eighth. It was a stark reminder of just how far he'd fallen since winning the 24 Hours of Daytona just eleven months earlier.

A.J. FOYT
BELL
Copenhagen
GILMORE
VALVOLINE
14

CHAPTER 10

STILL THE MASTER

1986

It was a slimmed down and upbeat A.J. Foyt who showed up to start the racing season at Daytona in 1986, having shed about thirty-five pounds. He said he'd lost the weight "by just workin' hard and changin' from pop to diet pop. It wasn't no special diet. Now I look like a race driver again." Once more the drumbeat started—Foyt was serious about racing. "And I'm more involved in my racing team again. Racing has always been my first love and I'm going back to it."[1]

"People are funny. They expect me to win everything like I used to. It makes it hard. It's even harder when I'm not winning. That's what A.J. Foyt is all about."[2]

He was back with Preston Henn at Daytona on the first day of February for the twenty-four-hour race with two new teammates, Bob Wollek having moved on to another Porsche team. Always looking to provide his team a promotional advantage, Henn paired Foyt with the defending Indianapolis 500 champion, Danny Sullivan, and the top rookie from the race, Arie Luyendyk. Both were solid road racers. Sullivan, who'd been helped by Henn early in his career, was looking forward to the race.

"I loved doing Daytona. It was so competitive, so many good cars. It was a good event to start your season off with. You get to freshen up your skills a little bit, run traffic, and I got a lot of time in the car. They both said they couldn't see at night and wanted me to drive, so I got a lot of wheel time. It was a great way to get back in the groove and get rid of the cobwebs."[3]

More than twenty prototypes were entered, nearly half of them Porsche 962s. Other prototype entries came from Jaguar, Corvette, and several March chassis powered by different engines. Henn's car could do no better than fourteenth in qualifying, the slowest of the Porsches, while Wollek ended up on the pole.

◀ Copenhagen colors. *David Nearpass*

From the start, problems plagued all the prototypes, and there were wild swings among the leaders as first one car and then another had lengthy pit stops. Although leading early, Wollek's 962 didn't make it past the six-hour mark before it was involved in an accident and knocked out. Despite the multiple problems, the race was being run at a record pace as the drivers went flat out when they were on the track.

Sullivan took the lead during the night, and by 7:30 a.m. Sunday morning, the Henn car was in front by fourteen laps. The second-place machine—driven by a group that included Jochen Mass, one of the world's top endurance racers—sat in the pits while an oil leak was repaired. Two hours later, it was the Henn car in the pits to fix an oil leak of its own and a balky turbocharger.

"We probably should have left it alone, it never was right," Foyt said of the turbo. "It worked right for about two laps, but that didn't make up for the eight we lost."[4]

Back on the track, Foyt found himself nine laps behind, but in another crazy turn of events, Mass would soon be in the pits again for another extended stop. By the time he returned, it was Foyt who had built a nine-lap margin.

Easily the fastest car on the track while all this was happening was the 962 of 1985 IMSA champion Al Holbert, who was teamed again with Al Unser Jr. and Derek Bell. In the early morning darkness, the team had fallen thirty-five laps or nearly 125 miles behind the leaders when Unser was forced to repair a broken throttle cable out on the course.

With less than two hours remaining, the Henn car still led by six laps when Sullivan brought it into the pits with a sticking throttle. For ten minutes Foyt worked alongside the mechanics searching for the cause of the problem, while Holbert rapidly cut into the margin.

Finally, Foyt decided to take the car out, sticking throttle or not, lifting the pedal with his toe when braking. Twice more he returned to the pit to increase the turbo boost, and when he finally was running again, he found himself behind both Holbert and Mass. He was able to get by Mass for second and back on the same lap with Holbert, but there was no catching him. It was the first time in race history the two leading cars finished on the same lap as they both traveled a record 2,534 miles.

"We should have gone on and gambled it," Foyt said about the fruitless efforts to fix the sticking throttle. "If we hit somebody, we hit somebody."[5]

He was somewhat philosophical afterward but didn't want to hear about the race being payback for the year before when Holbert had suffered late problems, allowing A.J. and Wollek to win.

"I don't look at it as turnabout being fair play. Today we just got outrun. We had a lot of little problems."[6]

Danny Sullivan

The race was Sullivan's first chance to spend extended time with Foyt, and he took advantage of it. He recalled,

> I was up 40 straight hours. I got to the track at eight o'clock in the morning for practice and stuck around talking with A.J. until the race started at 4 p.m. When I wasn't driving, I was either admiring the way A.J. drove or talking with him. It wasn't the fastest car there by any stretch of the imagination, but thanks to A.J., we came within a hair of winning. He showed me the pace and explained the race strategy. He said, "Just run this pace and let those other guys go."[7]
>
> He turned out to be absolutely right. We took over the lead at 10 p.m., and we led to the last hour when something broke. We still finished second. I'm convinced A.J. has forgotten more than most people will ever know about racing.

Sullivan first crossed paths with Foyt in 1982, when he ran three Indy car races, including the Indianapolis 500. Prior to that, much of Sullivan's career had been spent in Europe competing in various steps on the ladder to Formula One.

"When I did my first couple of Indy car races, I was in awe of just about everyone. From what I had been doing, these were not easy cars to drive. I started off at Atlanta and Big Al [Unser] helped me there tremendously. I had never done an oval. So I was in awe of what they could do and just trying to learn."

Sullivan finished a surprisingly strong third at Atlanta. He then qualified a respectable thirteenth at Indianapolis and ran well before being involved in an accident. At the Milwaukee Mile the following week, however, he was lost:

> That place was one hell of a racetrack. The track was bumpy and rough, and you had to make the car work.[8]
>
> I was out in practice and not doing particularly well. I'm back in the pack. I come out of Turn Two, and I see Foyt closing on me pretty fast. Now he'd won there like eleven times [ten actually, including stock car victories]. He was really good at that place.
>
> So, I rolled out of the throttle to let him pass and followed him as close as I could for a couple of laps. I learned more about how to get around Milwaukee in those two laps than I would have learned in two days of practice. Following and watching his line and where he went, where he picked up the throttle, how he entered a corner, and where he placed the car—it was an unbelievable education. Boy did it help me to get comfortable with that place.

For 1983, Sullivan had landed a ride in F1 in a car sponsored by Benetton. The Italian fashion house was looking to establish the brand in the United States and built a marketing campaign around the good-looking Sullivan. He performed well on the track, including a second at Brands Hatch and a fifth at Monaco after starting twentieth. He excelled off the track as well, Benetton's campaign landing him on television and in everything from *Sports Illustrated* to *People* magazine. Sullivan fell victim to the politics of F1 at the end of the season, and when he returned to Indy cars, he discovered the promotional campaign had not gone unnoticed by Foyt, who started calling him "Pretty Boy" or "Hollywood":

> Foyt just loved that. If he's got something he can dig on you, he's gonna do it and he gave me a ration of shit about that. But that was just part of the banter. That was Foyt. I always found if you stood there and talked to him for a few minutes, he *is* a good guy. He's a tough cookie. He doesn't suffer fools lightly, and you've got to stand your own ground. But I didn't find him hard to have a conversation with.
>
> He can be a pretty intimidating character, especially at Indianapolis where he is the king. But if I had a question, I could go talk to A.J. Like everyone, I don't care if it's A.J. or Mario or Big Al, you had to pick your time. If they were busy or just had a bad practice, that's never a good time to ask a race car driver anything. But if you picked the right time and could put up with the bluster and everything else, he was pretty damn good on helping you out. Even when you were competing against him.

Foyt didn't have much good to say about the new drivers making their mark in Indy car, but Sullivan received his seal of approval.

"Ninety percent of these guys are a different breed of cats," Foyt said. "They wreck a car and they expect another one to be waiting for them the next week. I give a guy like Danny Sullivan credit 'cause he came up through [the ranks] and put more into it than a lot of other ones. Among the other young guys, Al Unser Jr. is good and so is Michael Andretti, but that's about it."[9]

Foyt and Sullivan teamed together again in Henn's Porsche a month later for the Grand Prix of Miami, although it almost didn't happen. At the center of a dispute was Henn and race organizer Ralph Sanchez, longtime South Florida business rivals. Henn claimed he'd been shorted the appearance money to bring Foyt and Sullivan in for the event. Foyt was supposed to receive $10,000. Sullivan, who'd already filmed a guest appearance on the *Miami Vice* television show set to run the Friday night before the race, was reportedly promised $7,500. Henn noted Foyt was paid the year before by the organizer to race at Miami.[10]

"It's standard that promoters pay for people of that caliber to come to their race," Henn argued. "The deal hasn't changed. There's only one A.J. and Danny's the young bull with all the PR right now."

Sanchez thought differently. He saw the 1985 payment as a one-time deal to lure the winner of the 24 Hours of Daytona.

"Last year Preston came to me and said he needed some help to get A.J. here, so I agreed to help him out. But now it's up to him to get his team here. I've got thirty cars coming and two drivers in each one. If I start doing that (paying drivers), I could be creating a monster."[11]

At first Foyt declined to comment, but Henn was only too happy, not letting any facts get in the way. "When A.J. heard that Sanchez is saying he doesn't need him, and he's not going to do anything for him, well, you know A.J."

The back-and-forth continued and it wasn't until Sanchez added a qualifying race the week before to help promote the main event that Foyt broke his silence. "It's about as Mickey Mouse an idea as I've seen," he said. "This is a two-dollar qualifying race and I'm not going to tear up a $400,000 car. I'd rather start dead last."[12]

Then he started talking about money.

"You race all your life to get a name and when you get it, I think the promoter owes you something," he said. "You think Elizabeth Taylor just shows up places? Other movie stars? I'm not here just for my health. That's not how the game is played."

Most of the other drivers seemed to agree about the qualifying race but were more tactful in their comments. Foyt looked like a prophet when all seven Porsches entered in the qualifier were involved in accidents. If nothing else, the bickering and "he said/he said" kept the event in the headlines as race day approached.

Although everything was settled prior to race weekend, Foyt still wasn't happy.

"The appearance money wasn't the whole situation," he said. "If I'm going to race, I'll race for nothing. Preston and him (Sanchez) had the war. It didn't mean nothing to me. I get paid appearance money everywhere I go. You don't have to argue about the whole thing. I guess what made me mad is when he put in the paper that names don't draw people."[13]

Foyt spent much of the day before the race working on the car's setup. Some were surprised it was Foyt, not Sullivan, who was setting up the car for the race. Sullivan wasn't one of them.

"He knew as much—if not more—about those cars as anybody," Sullivan said. "They're race cars. He knew what worked. Maybe he didn't know all the tricks to the Porsche 962, but he knew all the tricks of racing. You've still got to make the car handle. That doesn't change on any car. You have the basic setup, but you still had to make that damn thing work. Foyt had so much knowledge. And he's A.J. Foyt. When he asked Porsche for help, trust me—he got it."[14]

Relegated to eighteenth starting position after skipping the qualifying race, Foyt immediately began picking up positions and moving toward the front when the three-hour event started. His pace was slowed, however, when the team called him into the pits for several unplanned stops. To Foyt, it was a reminder of the stops made late in the 24 Hours of Daytona that he felt cost them the race.

During one stop, the crew didn't seem ready for him, and in another a crew member accidently hit the kill switch used in emergencies to turn off the engine. When the engine wouldn't immediately re-fire, Foyt got out of the car, kicked the pit wall, and stormed off.

"He thought we shouldn't have called him into the pits as much as we did," Henn explained. "He didn't think that the things we called him in for were too critical. He was probably mad because things didn't go smoothly as they should have in the pits. And he was right."[15]

Sullivan jumped in the car, and partly as the result of high attrition and partly the result of a strong drive on his part, he brought it home in second place behind Wollek. Foyt was nowhere to be found afterward, although Henn and Sullivan gave him all the credit.

"I'd like to thank A.J. for all the help he gave me. He talked over the course with me and outlined exactly what I had to do in order for us to do well. There is no doubt in my mind that A.J. is still the master."[16]

Henn agreed.

"When it comes to setting up the car, he's the guy who knows more about that than anybody else in the business. He's our team. And what Big Daddy says, goes."[17]

Despite their success, Foyt's relationship with the flamboyant and unpredictable Henn was beginning to sour. Within a few days, the question of appearance fees and whether A.J. would defend his title at Sebring started anew. At first Henn said Foyt's schedule was too busy, then indicated the driver might boycott the race over appearance fees. That was enough for A.J., who told Henn to "pipe down.[18]

"I'm tired of this. I want it knocked off. I don't like people doing my talking for me. I'm getting a bad name because of all this. I've never had any problem with appearance money before. If I don't get it, I don't get it. Hell, that never has mattered to me."[19]

In the race, Foyt and new teammate Drake Olson had the 962 up to second from their fifth place starting position when the transmission failed, ending the team's chances just past the halfway point.

Foyt would run one more IMSA race with Henn in mid-June at West Palm Beach, Florida. Early in the event on a tight course, Wollek hit Foyt from behind, damaging the nose of Wollek's car and the rear spoiler of the Foyt machine. Both cars pitted for repairs, and when they returned to the track, Foyt was behind Wollek. It didn't take long before they came together again.

"My old friend A.J. showed my car a piece of the wall," Wollek said.

"The second time A.J. punted him on purpose," Henn said, Foyt having already left. "[Foyt] said to me, 'What would you have done?' I said I would have done the same thing."[20]

It would be Foyt's final drive with Henn, and of all things, the paint job might have been the tipping point that ended the relationship. The stark white Porsche was covered in Swap Shop signage—and hearts.

"That's not A.J.'s style," Foyt said. "I like to go first class. To me it got to where it was fun and games for Preston and them. Every time I put myself in a race car, it's serious business."[21]

Sensing their relationship was near an end, Henn encouraged Foyt to start his own IMSA team and said, "I think he'll enjoy the racing a lot more."[22]

Hurley Haywood, for one, wasn't surprised to see Henn and Foyt go their different ways.

"Preston was unique. He was a fantastic team owner—very colorful in his cowboy hat and boots. He came from a very humble background and was a real wheeler-dealer. He was a pawn shop owner after all, and used to negotiations, whether they be good or bad. A.J. was not used to that. It was A.J.'s way or get out of the way. Something happened—I don't know exactly what it was—but it kind of fell apart."[23]

Rare Brick

Foyt went from Sebring to Oaklawn Park in Arkansas, where his dream of having a horse in the Kentucky Derby was gathering speed. At times he even allowed himself to fantasize about winning the Derby and the 500 in the same year.

Rare Brick was performing surprisingly well and appeared headed for Churchill Downs on the first Saturday in May. He was not one of the horses sired by Alydar or the other elite studs at Calumet but was spotted by Tony at a yearling auction, who recommended the colt to his father. The lineage was not unknown to them. A.J. previously owned Rare Brick's half-sister, Top Brick.

The horse was one of those being trained by Tony, whose career had blossomed at Calumet Farm since his father entered into the sponsorship in 1983. Tony had become the farm's lead trainer in 1984 and set a record by posting twenty-seven wins during one meet at Churchill Downs, a mark that stood for nearly thirty years.

"It's the kind of deal you'd love to stay with them as long as they want you," Tony said of his relationship with Calumet. "It's a real pleasure to train for them. It's a big break for me in my career."[24]

"A big part of the reason I'm here is because of my father's encouragement and backing. I think all fathers want their sons to do well, but my father was really supportive. We got some nice colts here. With the studs they stand at Calumet, they're capable of having two or three good—and I mean real good—horses at any time."[25]

Rather than train Rare Brick at Calumet Farm, they took him to the ranch in Texas to break. Tony brought the horse along slowly, running him first in Minnesota before facing gradually stronger competition. They then moved to the annual spring meet at Oaklawn Park in Arkansas, the final step before the Kentucky Derby. A.J. had purposely spent less time with Tony and overseeing the Foyt Stables operation.

"I just don't want him to be as close to his father as I was to mine," A.J. said. "I think sometimes, you can get too close. That's what happened to me. And I almost snapped."[26]

Although Rare Brick was undefeated in six races and had never trailed since his first race, he'd never faced elite competition, never been seriously challenged, or run a race more than a mile. Some wondered aloud if Rare Brick was being promoted as a Derby contender because of the hype around the Foyt name more than the horse's performance on the track. Tony bristled at such talk and, like his dad, had little use for the media.

"I don't want to run in the Derby just to be able to say, 'I ran a horse in the Kentucky Derby,'" Tony said. "I want to go in with a confident feeling. I don't care where the horse finishes, as long as I feel confident going in that I had a shot. I'm not going to run just to run."[27]

Rare Brick opened the meet with an impressive twelve-length win over a horse already nominated for the Derby. His next race was the Rebel Stakes March 29, and D. Wayne Lukas—one of the sport's premier trainers—flew in a horse called Clear Choice from his stable in California specifically to test Rare Brick. Foyt's horse started fast as normal, then turned back several challenges by Clear Choice before winning by a head. It was Tony's first win in a $100,000 stakes race.

"He just made it," Tony said. "That colt made three runs at my horse. It was a courageous effort for him to hold on like that."[28]

In attendance for the race was A.J., and he had a hard time not gloating as he took center stage in the winner's circle, a position Tony gladly ceded to him.

"I don't care how he won, he won," said A.J., sounding like he sometimes did after a car race. "That doesn't bother me. He likes to run with horses. He likes the company.[29]

"He made it clear it doesn't matter if you pay a dollar or a million dollars for a horse—you never know whether they're going to show heart or not. And heart is the most important thing in any type of competition. They've either got it or they don't."[30]

After the win, interest in Rare Brick skyrocketed. Josephine Abercrombie, considered one of the shrewdest horsewomen in the business, bought a half interest in the horse, and Tony was able to hire jockey Pat Day to ride him in the upcoming Arkansas Derby. Day was one of the top riders in the country, having been named jockey of the year in 1984, and was on his way to repeating the feat in 1986. If everything went well, they'd be entered in the Kentucky Derby. Win them both, and A.J. would pocket a million-dollar bonus.

The excitement was all for naught. In a workout a few days before the Arkansas race and a little more than two weeks before the Kentucky Derby, Tony noticed the horse was laboring and hot, both unusual traits for Rare Brick and an indication of a possible injury. X-rays revealed a bone chip in his left-front ankle. Arthroscopic surgery was performed, knocking him out of Derby contention.

"It's a big letdown," Tony said. "As long as I've been training (nine years), he was the first legitimate chance I had to go to the Derby. I believe if he had been 100 percent he could have won. It kind of takes a little of the steam out of you."[31]

"But I learned a long time ago how unpredictable racing is. Any kind of racing. Cars or horses."[32]

Despite saying, "That may be the most disappointing thing that has happened to me in sports," A.J. went ahead with his plans to attend the Derby.[33]

"He looked forward to the Derby every year," Tony later explained. "There's only one Indianapolis 500, and there's only one Kentucky Derby. Only one race with that prestige. He got to know a lot of the owners and the trainers and the jockeys. You always had a few people who would come by and want his autograph, but nothing like at Indianapolis. You got a lot of people at the Derby who were race fans, but they understood he was there to enjoy himself too."[34]

Not every trip to the Derby went without incident, however. In a story A.J. often told, including to *Sports Illustrated*, he'd been approached by someone who probably had too many mint juleps:

> I was just pulling out of the parking lot at Churchill Downs and this stranger came up to the window of my wagon. He sort of bent over and looked in. He indicated to me that he wanted to say something, so I rolled

> down the window and he kind of leaned in and said something to me about how he didn't like my horses, and I sort of shrugged. And then he said to me, 'A.J., yer f---off.' Now, he had some friends with him, and I reckon that he was trying to be a big shot in front of them. Maybe he'd seen me on television or something, and now he had me live. I came boiling out of the car and fwwaaaaap! I hit that sucker. I hadda hit him twice. He was saying, 'Please don't hit me again, Mister Foyt, please don't hit me again.' Nobody says f---off to me, no matter where it is."[35]

Rare Brick would return following surgery before the year was out, and—with A.J. in attendance—win again, his eighth in eight trips to the gate. But when additional bone chips were discovered after the race, more surgery was required, and Tony decided to retire him to stud. The A.J. Foyt Stables would field many winners in the years ahead but never come as close to the Derby as it did with Rare Brick.

Even though Rare Brick's injury had cost him a chance at the Kentucky Derby, Foyt arrived in Indianapolis in good spirits. He'd held a winning ticket as fifty-four-year-old Bill Shoemaker rode Ferdinand Early—a 17–1 longshot—to victory, becoming the oldest Derby-winning jockey in the process. The win followed Jack Nicklaus's April victory in the Masters, making Nicklaus the oldest golfer ever to win the tournament at forty-six. Foyt saw the events as a sign.

"First Nicklaus in the Masters, now the Shoe," said the fifty-one-year-old Foyt. "With them doing it, I guess I have to hold up my end for auto racing."[36]

Despite the concerns expressed by Jim Gilmore the year before, Foyt again entered five cars in the 500, although no drivers were named. As a concession to Gilmore, he'd kept Jack Starne in Houston and focused on the Indy car effort during the first part of the year. In addition, Foyt had moved Sherby Blankenship, a former motorcycle racer and service manager at his dealership, over to help manage the racing program. He'd also brought in Franz Weis, a top engine builder, to help Howard Gilbert.

The cars had arrived too late for preseason testing, but Foyt ran the opening race of the year at Phoenix. The No. 14 featured a new paint scheme with a large black stripe running the length of the car—a nod to the Copenhagen sponsorship. He qualified thirteenth while Mario Andretti captured the pole, his fifty-fourth and breaking a career tie with Foyt—who hadn't won an Indy car pole in twelve years.

In the race, Foyt lost a wheel while driving slowly during a caution, and longtime crew member Cecil Taylor stepped forward to take the blame, saying he'd failed to make sure the wheel nuts were tight.

"I guess I was ready to leave the country when that happened," Taylor recalled. "That's pretty serious, losing a front wheel. Could have been a terrible thing if they were running at speed. I'm sure he would have crashed. Don't think I felt good about it."[37]

Taylor said Foyt was critical as expected, "But it was constructive criticism, like a gentleman. He wasn't cussing and carrying on. It seems like he's taking a new look at things. He's trying to reason things out, trying to take time to weigh things."

For a change, there was plenty of garage space in Gasoline Alley as the Speedway had torn down the wooden "horse stables" used for seventy years and replaced them with a massive concrete complex that resembled a giant storage facility. Foyt, whose cars had long been based around garage twenty-nine, found himself on the front row in garages three through seven.

He still spent most of his time behind the closed roll-up doors of the new garages and ran only a handful of practice laps. When he hadn't cracked the top twenty on the speed charts as qualifying approached, the "has been" comments started again. Only this time Tom Sneva tried to be more diplomatic.

"I don't think [other drivers] take him as seriously as they used to, because he doesn't come around all the time," Sneva said, seemingly trying to soften the criticism. "He hasn't been as competitive lately as he used to be. You get concerned for him. He's done so well over so many years that you're concerned about him not doing his reputation any good. But it's something in your blood. You don't want to quit racing. It's not the money or anything else."

Foyt remained defiant.

"I have nothing to prove," he said. "For people to make that statement—of course Sneva and all of them have denied it—makes no difference to me what people say. Hell, maybe they feel that way. I haven't won nothing real big in a long time. Then again, look at last year. We won Sebring and we won the (Daytona) twenty-four-hour race. The two biggest (endurance) races in the United States and I won them both."[38]

He missed a chance to quiet the skeptics when he failed to qualify on the first day of time trials. After waiting until late in the day to put his car in the queue to qualify, one of the side skirts was judged to be a fraction too long, the delay for repairs costing him any chance of making a run.

He was back the next day and turned in the fifth-fastest overall time, good for the twenty-first starting position. Despite the problems, he seemed happy with the results.

"They say the older you get, the slower you go. Seems I'm getting faster with age."[39]

Which led to the next question: Did he still plan to retire after the 1987 race, his thirtieth 500?

"I don't know. That's getting too close. I'd be lying to you if I told you the truth."[40]

In the days before the 500, Foyt spent time with Chuck Yeager, the former Air Force test pilot driving the pace car for the race. Unlike many pace car drivers who showed up a day or two before the race for a few practice laps, Yeager came in for the second week of qualifications and stayed.

Yeager was someone Foyt could look up to. An enlisted man who rose from private to the rank of Brigadier General, Yeager had been shot down over France, evaded capture, and escaped through Spain back to England. He returned to combat duty and became an ace, shooting down five German planes in one day. After the war, he became a test pilot and was the first to officially break the sound barrier while flying the X-1. He'd led the astronaut training program, although as only a high school graduate, he was ineligible for the program itself. He'd recently become even more famous—if possible—when profiled in the 1983 movie *The Right Stuff*.

Since retiring from the Air Force in 1975, he'd refused to slow down, vowing to fly as long as he was physically able and having just set a number of climbing and cross-country speed records for turbo prop aircraft, including a New York-to-Paris mark. A longtime Corvette driver and rep for the AC Delco parts division of General Motors, he was a natural for the pace car honor.

When not on the track or near the pace car, he could often be found in Foyt's garages. Yeager also sounded a lot like Foyt when the subject turned to death.

"When you do research flying you become a fatalist," he said while at the Speedway. "You don't pay an awful lot of attention to the outcome because if you get killed, you get killed. That's the way we think."[41]

Rain wiped out race day, and the two spent much of the time together, finally leaving the track together "to go get drunk." The two developed a strong bond that would last until Yeager's death.[42]

When the rain continued through Monday and turned the Speedway's infield into a quagmire, the decision was made to postpone the race until the following Saturday, May 31. The fact it would be the first live broadcast of the race also played into the decision. The lengthy delay left scores of reporters with column inches to fill, and many turned to Foyt with questions about his least favorite subject—getting old. While gerascophobia was a common problem, Foyt took it to new level.

"I don't even want to think about old age," he'd said in his autobiography. "You want to know the truth? I don't want to get old—I mean toddling, slobbering, soup-spilling old.

"I'm not the type who will grow old gracefully."

And while he'd been the one to originally bring up the success of Nicklaus and Shoemaker and "the need to hold up my end," he'd grown tired of the comparisons.

"I don't give a $%&# about this old-timers crap," he told one reporter. "I have never had anything to do with them before. I lead A.J. Foyt's life, not Willie Shoemaker's life, not Jack Nicklaus's life. About the only thing Shoemaker and I have in common is I know how to get on a horse. Shoemaker doesn't have as far to run as I do, and Nicklaus gets to rest between tees."[43]

As Foyt often did, he talked about his eyes letting him know when he was old.

"You're just as old as your eyes. My eyes have always been good and that's why, at this point in my life, I feel competitive. I've always felt your reflexes are controlled by your eyes. I don't think age has one iota to do with your reflexes."[44]

"Maybe people think I'm over the hill. Good. I'll surprise them." He told the crew, "We're going to run all damn day, and I don't care if we're dead last. We're going to run until the race is checkered-flagged."[45]

When the race was finally run, he got as high as eleventh by the midway point despite battling brake problems that forced him to be careful in traffic and "mind

[his] P's and Q's"—at least until he saw an opportunity on lap 135 to make up more time following a caution flag and darted down pit road.

"I tried to get away with it all day," he said of the brake problem. "It finally bit me. I had to get on the brakes hard and it locked up." He slammed the inside pit wall, sending crew members leaping for cover and breaking the car's rear wing. His race was over, and Bobby Rahal went on to score a popular victory.

"I was coming in pretty hot," he recalled years later. "The pits were real rough that year and when I hit the brakes that thing jumped up and spun and I felt like an idiot coming up the pits backwards. I was just trying to keep running. I should have parked it earlier but hindsight is 20/20. It's just one of them deals."

He'd run six more Indy car races with mixed results. For the first time in four years, he raced at Milwaukee the week after the 500, refusing to talk about any kind of "farewell tour" culminating at Indianapolis in 1987. At times, however, he sounded like a geezer reminiscing about the "good old days."

"If you had told me we would be running this fast here five years ago I'd have never believed it," he said after qualifying in the top ten. "I can remember my first year here in a roadster and I was backing off at the start-finish line and jumping on the brakes. Now you don't even use the brakes. We drive all the way into the corner before we lift and then you're back on the throttle. It's hard to believe."[46]

A couple weeks later in the Michigan 500, he finished ninth, although it was more the result of a high attrition rate as he dropped out with engine problems forty miles from the finish. Johnny Rutherford was victorious, becoming the oldest driver at forty-eight to win a 500-mile race.

Prior to the event, Charlie Vincent, the motorsports reporter for the *Detroit Free Press*, wrote what sounded like Foyt's retirement tribute column.

"There was a time when he was lean and hungry and the damnedest thing you ever did see on four wheels.

"In his prime there was no one like him.

"His prime, though, was in the last decade."[47]

He finished fourth at Pocono where the forty-four-year-old Andretti won, but after that the season took another nosedive, and Foyt failed to finish at both Phoenix and Tamiami Park near Miami.

He talked about the coming year, but there was no mention of retirement.

"I know if I'm going to win, I've got to put more into it. That's why we're looking for a couple new (crewmen) to work with. What we're doing is gearing up for next year."[48]

Although the results didn't show it, for a change Foyt had been happy with his NASCAR program, driving a new aerodynamic Oldsmobile Delta 88. As promised, the GM division had increased its NASCAR support, and several teams, including those of Buddy Baker, Bobby Labonte, Benny Parsons, and Rick Wilson, were running the redesigned cars.

Foyt's car was slightly more aerodynamic than the others, his Oldsmobile featuring a special "narrow-body" built just for him. While the narrow—and illegal—car was considered too risky for the series regulars to run, Olds felt it could chance that and other experimental features on Foyt's occasional entry. It wasn't the first time a car builder had tampered with car size, Chevrolet and Smokey Yunick having famously built a smaller-scale version of its 1966 Chevelle.

"At the time NASCAR templates fit down the center of the car and looked primarily at the slope of the front and rear windshields and front and rear of the car," explained Ed Welburn, one of the junior designers and engineers working on the car. "So we made the car narrower. Our job was to make everything look right. Everything needed to be done to scale."[49]

Welburn's responsibility was the front headlights, back when NASCAR racers used actual headlight frames rather than the decals on today's car. "The first chrome-plated headlight frames we made melted," said Welburn, who would go on to be lead designer at General Motors. "We heard A.J. was not happy."

After starting twentieth in the Daytona 500, Foyt hooked up with Cale Yarborough and moved toward the front. They were running together near the halfway mark when Yarborough slowed abruptly for the pace car that had darted onto the track following a blown engine. Foyt and two others passed both cars in the smoke and confusion.

Chaos reigned in the pits when Foyt responded to a black flag, a NASCAR official standing in front of the car while crew chief Dick Hutcherson tried to figure out what was happening. After indicating Foyt was on the same lap as the leader, officials reversed themselves, saying he was one behind. He eventually dropped out with engine problems.

"Cale slowed so bad coming off Turn Two that I thought something happened to him," Foyt said. "I wasn't the only one to pass him, three other guys followed me. So I wasn't the only one who thought something happened."[50]

Foyt was fast in subsequent events but failed to finish. His final NASCAR race of the year was planned for November 2 at Atlanta, but this time he didn't even get to start as officials finally discovered the car was "two and a half inches narrower than regulations allowed.[51]

"He was off in specifications of the grills, front fender and front air dam," said NASCAR director Dick Beaty. "He told us, and we concur, he couldn't get the car fixed in time to qualify." Copenhagen's Eddie Thrap protested that, "it was the same car he has been running in all of his 1986 NASCAR starts," which was true of course, but didn't make it any more legal. Terry Labonte offered his backup car, which didn't have an engine, but Foyt figured by the time he put one of his in, it would be too late to practice and qualify.

Aerotech

While the regular racing season was all but over, things were heating up with Oldsmobile. Foyt had been working with designers and engineers for several years to develop what was being called the Aerotech, a rolling test bed and technology showcase.

The program started in late 1984 as an effort by Oldsmobile engineers and marketers to highlight a new engine the division was betting its future on, the

Quad 4. A 2.3-liter, four-cylinder, sixteen-valve powerplant blending fuel economy with high performance, it was scheduled for production in 1988.

With all five GM divisions selling similarly styled cars, the marketing groups for the various car lines searched for something to differentiate it from the other four. In Oldsmobile's case, the theme was advanced technology, with the Quad 4 as its centerpiece.

The effort was led by the division's chief engineer, Ted Louckes, himself a motorsports supporter. He lobbied the corporate higher-ups for approval to develop a "research vehicle," with the idea to go after the world closed-course speed record. Louckes had asked Foyt, the first big name to make the switch to Oldsmobile in NASCAR, to drive the car.

Foyt had set the world closed-course speed record at Talladega in a Coyote in 1974, then lost it to Mark Donohue in Roger Penske's Porsche Can Am car on the same track in 1975. After initially planning to go back and reclaim the mark, Foyt decided against it when Donohue was killed, saying he wouldn't try to reclaim the record "as long as it belongs to Mark."[52]

But things changed when Mercedes-Benz moved the record to a new level in 1979. Company engineer Hans Liebold had turned a lap of 250.958 miles per hour at the wheel of the company's C111-IV prototype on the Nardò Ring, a 7.8 mile, high-banked circular track in northern Italy. Foyt saw the Aerotech not only as an opportunity to reclaim the record for himself but also America as well.

The project ran into difficulty right from the start. Foyt disliked the initial sketches of the car developed by a team of aerodynamic engineers and advanced stylists. As a result, Welburn, one of those who'd worked on the narrow-body NASCAR Olds, was asked to submit a design. He was a big fan of the Le Mans dominating Porsche 917 from the early 1970s, and it was reflected in Welburn's sketch. Although he'd never met A.J., he'd been a fan of the driver since his father took him to a race at Langhorne, Pennsylvania, back when the track was still dirt and Foyt virtually unbeatable.

"He was like a gladiator," Welburn remembered. "He was a young driver and winning everything. He became one of my heroes."[53]

Despite the fact Foyt "hated" the original design, a clay model was prepared for review along with several others, including one from Welburn's drawing.

"There was a meeting in a conference room at GM Design, and it was packed with people," Welburn recalled. "I kind of kept my distance because I knew his reputation. There was a large model of the primary design in the front of the room, and he was not happy. Then when he saw my model—all of a sudden, he was happy. He felt good about what we were doing. That was the very first time I'd been in his presence, other than watching him on the racetrack."

The decision was made to go forward with Welburn's design. Welburn also sketched a long-tail version of the car he felt was even better, but the powerful marketing group preferred the short-tail version because it was more "car-like." The marketers also insisted on a rear pedestal spoiler because it "looked sporty." Indy car expert Herb Porter, "Herbie Horsepower," was brought in to help with engine development. The production engine produced about 150 horsepower, but Porter's target for a turbo-charged version was around 800 horsepower.

Welburn and others spent long hours in GM's wind tunnel refining the design, especially the nose and canopy. A March Indy car chassis was used, and March also fabricated the Kevlar and carbon-fiber tub and body. Extensive use of adjustable underbody panels allowed the ground effects to be fine-tuned. The chassis, engine, and other components were eventually shipped to Foyt's Houston garage for assembly, with Starne overseeing the project.

By November 15, the prototype was finally ready for a shakedown run at GM's Desert Proving Grounds in Mesa, Arizona, which included a five-mile circular test track. Foyt's initial reaction was the car was too pretty, and after a few slow laps, he pulled into the makeshift pit. The rear of the car was smoking from insulation mounted too close to the engine. When Olds engineers reacted slower than he liked, Foyt stepped in and—barehanded—ripped away the offending pieces. The engineers recoiled in surprise and recognition that they weren't working with a normal test driver. It was the start of a sometimes-tenuous relationship between Foyt, his crew, and the corporate types.

"Foyt was probably the one who . . . had the most to consider," said Bill Porterfield at the time. He was GM's future systems and technology engineer and program manager under Louckes. "He was really being asked to commit to driving a vehicle that was going to be designed by some people at General Motors [and] constructed in England by March. He was familiar with March, but not in full-body type things, and it was going to have a lot of high-tech stuff in it that was put on there by GM engineers and technoids. The engines were going to be developed and fine-tuned by different engine camps that Oldsmobile was hiring, and Foyt's not used to operating that way."[54]

Foyt ordered the wing removed along with a flat surround panel that filled the space between the tub and bodywork. When speeds picked up, neither were seen again. They were the first of several changes A.J. wanted. "You're trying a lot of things at very high speeds that are unknown," he said. "It's very tricky, to be truthful with you. You hang it out just as far as when you're in competition. If you slip, you know you're gonna be in serious trouble, and you better be ready for it."

Even with a "highly detuned engine," Foyt ran a lap at more than 218 mph and raved about the car's stability. He said with a few modifications, they could go for the record, and the GM research crew that had been gathering data concurred.

The test proved to be a turning point for Foyt's relationship with Welburn, who would rapidly rise through the ranks during the next fifteen years to become GM's first-ever vice president of global design and the auto industry's highest-ranking African American.

"Once he started driving the car and saw how well the thing handled, we started to get along quite well," remembers Welburn.[55]

Like many designers, he was a stylish dresser, even at a dusty test track in the middle of nowhere. "A.J. used to joke with me about things, and he didn't joke with many of the others. He'd say, 'Eddie, you're a good ole boy,'—which kind of threw me—'but you're always wearing those damn Dee-troit shoes.' It just became a joke, so I would make sure whenever I was around him, I was wearing what he thought were 'Dee-troit shoes.'"[56]

After the run, Foyt talked with Sam Posey, a former driver and commentator on ABC's Indy 500 race coverage who was there to narrate a promotional film for Oldsmobile.

"Sam, this car was so easy to drive at 218 mph, even you could have done it."[57]

It would get harder.

CHAPTER 11

HAVING FUN AGAIN

1987

There was more action than there'd been in years in the Houston garages of A.J. Foyt at the start of 1987. The relationship with Preston Henn was over, and Foyt worked a deal to acquire a Porsche 962, worth about $380,000. The team was preparing it for the 24 Hours of Daytona, a race paying $50,000 to win.

"A.J. had a Ferrari, a Daytona or something like that—a valuable car, and wanted to get a 962," recalled Brumos employee and driver Hurley Haywood. "We had one and made a deal with him and told A.J. we would help him run it. A.J. was good friends with [Brumos executives] Bob Snodgrass and Dan Davis. Andial was the engine builder. Porsche knew the value of A.J. Foyt, and they were willing to give him stuff that was hard to get."[1]

Overseeing it all was Jack Starne, who was already shepherding the Aerotech program. Although he was anxious to cut back on his travel to spend more time with his family, he embraced the challenge of learning a new car.

"It's got four wheels on it," Starne said. "Basically, race cars act the same. You do a little research, do a little bit of background checks, and talk with some people here and there and get a little more knowledge. The 962 was a very, *very* nice car. You could get in the car, turn the key, and drive it away."[2]

Foyt assembled a dream team for the 24 Hours of Daytona, bringing in Danny Sullivan and Al Unser. The Porsche also carried sponsorship from Columbia Crest wines, which paid a million bucks to put its name on the Porsche for four races. The Washington winery was owned by U.S. Tobacco, and the company decided wine was more appropriate for the sporty car set than chewing tobacco. The sponsor couldn't have been too happy, however, when Foyt was asked how he liked the wine. "They sent me some but I haven't tried it," he responded.[3]

◀ Oldsmobile Aerotech. *GM Research and Archives*

Sullivan had been happy to hear from Foyt, fearing his chance to drive at Daytona may have gone away when Henn closed shop.

"A.J. just said, 'We'll figure out a way to do this, let's go racing,'" Sullivan recalled. "Foyt bought those cars himself and put the sponsorship on them and ran them. I never heard him complain about how much money it was costing him. He just got on with it. God love him—he was a racer."[4]

While Foyt set up the car and qualified eighth, Unser had trouble adjusting to the way A.J. liked the car.

"It was a good car and a good team," Unser recalled years later. "Foyt's a funny guy. He wants to set up a car to his liking, and not everybody can drive like he did. We just didn't match up."[5]

For the third straight year, the race turned into a battle between Foyt's car and the 962 of Porsche North America distributor Al Holbert, whose team of drivers included Al Unser Jr. The two cars traded the lead through the night, the two Unsers going head-to-head at one point. The Holbert team benefited from quicker pit stops, and with a little more than two hours left, held a lap lead. Foyt took over his car and ordered the engine's boost turned up, ignoring warnings it wouldn't make it to the finish at that level.

"I told A.J. if he wanted to go for it, go," said Alwin Springer, Porsche's top engine builder. "But I told him the engine would not make it. It was running bad and if he wanted to finish, he better just idle around the bottom of the racetrack. I guess for Foyt a win is everything and second doesn't count. I told him it wouldn't make it and he decided to try it anyway."[6]

Foyt managed to get back on the same lap as the leader before the engine started to run rough with little more than an hour remaining. It quit entirely with fifty minutes to go.

"We all had a lot of fun," a smiling Foyt said afterward. "All in all, we did a helluva job. This year they had the racing luck and we didn't. At least we made 'em run for it all day and night too." Then he went to congratulate the winning team, which left an impression on Holbert.

"I've never found a tougher competitor or a nicer gentleman in racing," said the winning car owner and driver.

Despite dropping out before the finish, the team was still classified fourth at the end of twenty-four hours. Unser said he'd often good-naturedly kid Foyt that they should have won the race.

"That was a hard race. It came down to the last hour, and dear Mr. Foyt screwed the boost to it and blew the engine," Unser recalled with a laugh. "That put us out. I always said if he hadn't turned the boost up, we would have won. He was always 'Argh, argh, argh!'"[7]

A month later, Foyt and Sullivan finished sixth at Miami, and for the Sebring 12 Hours March 21, they were joined by Porsche regular Haywood, although Foyt once again set up the car. Sullivan, involved with a promotional program for his sponsor Miller beer, missed the first day of practice, but wasn't concerned.

"I knew my way around Sebring, and they had the thing set up pretty well, so I wasn't worried," Sullivan recalled. "But after about five laps Foyt pulls me in. He tells me, 'Get out of the car. I'm getting back in.' I said I'd only done five laps, and he said he didn't care—he was getting back in. I walked over to the crew to find out what I'd done wrong, and one of the guys said, 'Ahh, you went quicker.'"[8]

Sullivan saw it as a compliment to both him and Foyt.

"The great thing was, he still had that competitive spirit. It wasn't just, 'Hey, I've won Daytona, Le Mans, Sebring, Indy—all that stuff.' He still had that very, *very* competitive drive in his genes. At that stage, my career was going along pretty good, and his was starting to wane, but he was still very fast. He was a competitor."

For Haywood, it was his first chance to drive with A.J. since they'd shared Preston Henn's winning car in the 1983 Paul Revere race at Daytona. He noticed a difference between driving with Foyt the co-driver and Foyt the car owner.

"He was very focused on what he was doing," Haywood recalled. "He was the kind of driver who demanded 100 percent from everybody around him, from the lowest person on the team to the drivers and the mechanics and engineers—everyone. He was always, 'We're gonna do it my way, or get out.' I understood that and stayed under the radar."[9]

Unlike some drivers, most notably Al Unser, Haywood didn't have a problem with Foyt setting up the car.

"A.J. was the boss, and it was his responsibility to set the car up. Whether it was right or wrong, that was something I had to adapt to. I wasn't gonna tell A.J. Foyt, 'No, you can't do this, or you can't do that, or maybe we should try this.' A.J. said, 'This is the way it is,' and you got used to it. So that's what I did, and it worked out. I was not somebody who was gonna argue the point with him."

Sullivan was involved in a pit road accident early in the event while the team was running third, and it did enough damage to knock the car out. It was Sullivan's last drive for Foyt, and they would later have their differences, but he looked back fondly on their time together.

"It was a lot of fun. Racing always has its ups and downs, and nothing is ever perfect. You're always asking, 'Why did we have this problem,' or, 'Why did we have that problem.' I drove for Roger Penske, as best prepared as anybody out there, and we still had shit that failed. I have a plate and seven screws in my forearm to prove that. Shit happens. It's racing."[10]

Starne also remembered the period fondly and the more relaxed attitude Foyt exhibited at the endurance races. "I really enjoyed Daytona and the Florida races," Starne said. "We had the [Indy] guys driving with us, and it was just a lot of fun. I really enjoyed the project."[11]

In between the sports car races, Foyt ran in the Daytona 500, and if there was any question about his desire to compete, it was again on full display. He was moving up through the field in the qualifying race when he was caught up in what was described as a "brutal" four-car accident. Foyt was briefly knocked unconscious and his car destroyed. Complaining of shoulder pain, he was checked out at the local medical center, and while X-rays proved negative, he returned to the track wearing a neck brace and with his right arm—the one he nearly lost at Michigan—in a sling.

Rick Wilson and his car owner Larry McClure stepped forward. "If A.J. wants my backup car, he's got it," Wilson said. "He sure has helped me over the years."[12]

Foyt immediately accepted. A "1" was added to the Wilson's bright yellow No. 4 car and Copenhagen added to the rear quarter panels and hood. Although he'd start on the last row and was still hurting, Foyt said, "I'll be ready. I've drove in a lot worse shape than this.[13]

"This is the biggest stock car race in the world, that's the reason I want to run," he said when asked why a driver who just turned fifty-two would bother. He also said there were no plans to have a relief driver standing by. "Relief? I've never had relief in my career."[14]

His race was over before it started, a crewman having left a spark plug wire loose, and by the time the problem was spotted, he was many laps behind. "This is nothin' but a big damned screw-up," he yelled at his crew surrounding the car. "Simply dumbness and stupidity. When I get back to my shop in Houston, some guys are gonna be fired."[15]

He managed only ten laps and finished last, but he came up with the quote of the race:

"I was flying," he said after passing twelve cars on lap one. "Nobody was running faster. The car was absolutely amazing.[16]

"I was just picking my nose out there."

If Foyt's thirtieth Indianapolis 500 was to be his last—as he'd announced two years earlier but now refused to confirm—the fans were committed to making it one to remember. Everywhere Foyt went, he was greeted by cheers and surging crowds.

"It's kind of getting embarrassing," he said. "I go out there, and they start hollerin' and cheerin.' Hell, I'm just A.J."[17]

He also admitted, "It's hard for me to believe I'm as old as I am, but there's no sense lying to yourself, I am. I get so doggoned sore. I think it's just arthritis setting in from all the knocks and bruises over the years. I'm like the race cars. They get old too."

He entered five cars in the race and would have his choice of a new Lola or March. An innovative V8 engine was making news, branded a Chevrolet and developed by Ilmor Engineering in England and Penske Racing, but Foyt and most of the field would continue to use a Cosworth.

Both Foyt and his cars were sporting a new look. The cars were now mostly black with Foyt Orange trim. A.J. wore a black uniform with Copenhagen emblazoned across his midsection, although his helmet was still orange. While George Snider was expected to drive one car, Foyt added a pair of rookies to the team, Stan Fox and Davy Jones, both of whom brought some sponsorship money. He collectively called them "the boys," and when asked if it was the start of his shift from race car driver to race team owner he answered, "It really is. I'm not getting any younger."[18]

The two first-time drivers couldn't have come from more different backgrounds. Fox was a driver Foyt could relate to, having proven himself in midgets and winning races at places like Phoenix, Milwaukee, and Ascot Park. He'd struggled in a handful of Indy car starts, although never in the quality of equipment Foyt was providing. At thirty-four, he realized he wasn't going to get too many more chances.

Davy Jones

Jones's background was mainly in road racing, and at twenty-two he was considered one of the top young drivers in the country. He'd tested for Brabham in Formula One and was coming off two successful seasons driving a BMW-powered prototype in IMSA, where he faced off against Foyt in several races and won at Watkins Glen. Jones was from a family of race fans who had been attending the 500 "for as long as [he] could remember." His father had wanted to name him Parnelli, although "mom axed that idea."[19] Jones explained,

> As a family, we went to the Indy 500 every year and had the same seats in the upper paddock penthouse right across from the pit lane. A.J. Foyt, Al Unser Sr., Johnny Rutherford—I mean those names were synonymous not only to the Indy car series—they were synonymous to racing in general. We always used to kind of pick our favorite drivers, and mine was always A.J., and my sister—her driver was Al Unser.
>
> So, growing up as a kid, A.J. Foyt was always a bit of a hero. I looked up to what he accomplished and what he was doing. I never dreamed I would end up on the starting grid, you know, many years later, driving for him and as a teammate.

Tony George, who knew of Foyt's desire to start building his team for the future, was familiar with Jones from the Super Vee series, recommended him to Foyt, and helped put together a four-race program for the young driver.

"I'm looking for someone young who wants to run seventeen or eighteen races a year and knock heads," Foyt said. "I want to run a team when I'm through racing."[20]

Jones soon discovered Foyt ran a different style operation than the very regimented BMW effort:

> When you drive for A.J., you're always wondering, *What's the plan for today?*" Jones said. "So, practice starts, and our cars are sitting in the garage, and it's like, 'Okay, when are we gonna go out?' At that time, A.J. didn't like to put a whole lot of laps on the cars. So a lot of times, practice would start, and we wouldn't go out. Then all of a sudden, he was like, 'Okay, we're gonna go out now.'
>
> A.J. was very nice and very calm until he hit the rev limiter—then look out. I think that's what made him a great race driver. You have to have that

drive and that desire to really, you know, to run down the person in front of you and pass 'em and get the most out of your car.

Jones compared Foyt to Bobby Knight, the mercurial University of Indiana basketball coach, and to his own father, who'd been a ship captain in the Merchant Marines. "We had a sign at home that read, 'The Captain's Word is Law.'

"They had that kind of air about them. They were leaders, and when they raised their voices, people jumped. They made things happen. Fast forward to today, and you raise your voice, and people just say, 'Fuck you.' If you're not massaging them and rubbing them, and kissing ass, then they won't do anything."

During the week of practice before pole day, Foyt spent most of his time with the rookies. He turned only a handful of laps in his Lola, failing to top 209 miles per hour, while Mario Andretti was running laps at 218. When things didn't improve in morning practice before qualifying, he ordered all the cars back to the garage and went to lunch.

When qualifying started, Snider went out to test the track before waving off a run. It wasn't until late in the day that Foyt gave the crowd what it wanted, telling his crew, "Put it in line, let's try and make the damn race." His first lap at more than 212 mph had the Speedway reverberating like the old days, and while his speed fell off, his four-lap average of nearly 211 mph was fourth fastest—good for his best starting position in five years. Watching from pit road and shaking his head in disbelief was the third-fastest qualifier, Rick Mears.

"How that man can do what he does with no more laps than he takes . . ." Mears said in amazement. "It takes me twenty laps to find out what city I'm in. That he takes only a handful of laps every year and runs quick, shows the ability he's got. I'm just glad he doesn't practice much."[21]

Foyt said he was "thrilled to be starting up there," and the enormity of the accomplishment seemed to set in.[22]

"To qualify for this race thirty years, I don't think I realize myself what it means. I don't think I'll see anybody break the record. It's been a lot of fun."

He also didn't sound like someone ready to stop at thirty.

"I have been disgusted enough to quit, but don't want to do it just because I'm mad at myself or mad at somebody. The day I feel like I can't be competitive here, I'll be the first one to admit it to myself. A lot of people say I should have quit ten years ago. Well, maybe I should have and maybe I shouldn't have, but I'm still having fun. You know, what's it about if you can't have fun?"

It wasn't much fun the following week as both of Foyt's rookie drivers struggled to find qualifying speed. Like many young drivers, they'd started the month running fast laps then slowed down as they pressed for more speed. Foyt took them back to square one and slowly let them build speed during the week.

"You could be going really fast around the Speedway and as comfortable as can be, and then all of a sudden, you just get a little twitch, and you get spooked," Jones said. "Then it becomes a mind game. You get in a rut, and you just couldn't get out. A lot of drivers went through it back then."[23]

Fox was the first to make the field, with an assist from his car owner.

"A.J. was adjusting the wing, and I mentioned that it felt like he was taking too much out," Fox said. "He looked at me and said, 'I'm working on the car and you're driving it.'"[24]

Fox added, "A.J. just told me to go out and run four smooth laps and run the car hard. [He said,] 'You can't do anything unless you run the car hard.'"[25]

While Fox was in the race, Jones brushed the wall during practice, and Foyt figured it was time for a refresher course, taking him out for a few laps in the Chrysler LeBaron pace car. "You got ten million people telling you what to do, and you just can't listen to them," Foyt said.[26]

"That was a huge help," Jones said. "I mean, A.J. *knows* the Speedway. I don't think there's anybody who has more knowledge on getting around that place. I took in all the advice that I could, and it worked out well. I also remember he got really close to the wall."

It wasn't until the final hour of qualifying Sunday afternoon that Foyt pointed at his head—the international symbol for "Think!"—and waved Jones onto the track. Four laps later, each one faster than the last, Jones was in the field as the race's youngest driver.

"I was a little worried, but A.J. knows just what he's doing," Jones said. "I just tried to do exactly what A.J. said. To concentrate on doing exactly the same thing through each corner on all four laps."[27]

When told Jones was the fastest rookie qualifier ever, Foyt shrugged. "He's supposed to be. I knew he had the ability to do it if he could get it all together."[28]

Right on cue, Snider went out and put the fourth Foyt car in the race. Another driver making the field on the last weekend was Al Unser. He'd been released by Roger Penske and sitting on the sidelines when the driver who replaced him, Danny Ongais, was involved in a crash and told by doctors he couldn't race. Unser jumped at the chance to replace Ongais, even though the car he'd be driving had been sitting in a hotel lobby display just a week earlier.

After twenty-one accidents during the two weeks of practice and qualifying, Foyt called the team together before the final Carb Day session and told Fox and Jones to be careful. It would be their first time experiencing so many cars on the track at once, and just as he'd been warned thirty years earlier, he cautioned them about the air turbulence caused by the cars at speed. "It's Carburetion Day," he reminded them, not race day. "Don't be out there racing cars in traffic. I told them some idiot would try that and get in trouble." It could happen to anybody, he said, even Mario Andretti had crashed.[29]

After turning laps at 205 mph during the session, Foyt was ready to pit when he saw two cars ahead. He decided to follow them for a lap and see how his car performed "in dirty air," exactly what he had warned the others against. He trailed them into the first turn when the rear of his car suddenly broke loose, did a half spin, darted up the track, and hit the wall broadside. The impact tore the rear wing from the car and lifted the right side off the ground as it started shedding parts and tires and sliding 320 feet down the track. He managed to get out of the car and hobble away a few feet before sitting down in the grass and waiting for the safety team. Foyt would later say a bolt broke on the wing and triggered the accident.

"It just took off," he said at the time. "The car was runnin' good, just a little loose. Then all hell broke loose. I felt we should leave all the cars in the barn. I wish we had."[30]

Foyt went to work alongside Starne and his crew, and the completely rebuilt car was ready by race day. Not surprisingly, Foyt made a tentative start. "I didn't know what the car was going to do. It wasn't acting perfect, but under the circumstances, it probably drove as good as any car I've had in a long time." [31]

Mario Andretti ran hard from the green flag, and by midrace Foyt found himself three laps behind. He tried to pick up the pace, but his engine soon began to smoke.

"I could have run harder, but I was just trying to keep my nose clean and keep out of trouble," he said. "All of a sudden, something went in the engine. Some days it's your day and some days it ain't."

He wasn't the only one to suffer engine problems. After leading 170 of the first 180 laps, Andretti pulled to the side of the track, his day done. Unser, who'd been a lap behind at one point, took over the lead and went on to win his fourth Indianapolis 500, tying Foyt and becoming the oldest Indy winner at forty-seven.

Of Foyt's four cars, only Fox finished the race, eight laps behind the winner in seventh. Jones made it only thirty-four laps before dropping out with engine problems, and Snider didn't even manage that, his engine catching fire on the pace lap and putting him out before the green flag. The team was again stretched thin, with family and friends pressed into service to fill out the race day pit crews. UNO had come on board to help with sponsorship of Jones's car, and it created a humorous moment when Huey Lewis, who fronted one of the era's most popular rock bands and had a relationship with UNO, was offered the chance to operate the fuel flow valve. Jones recalled,

> So, on my first pit stop ever in the Indy 500, I come in, and the crew's waiting for me, and I see Huey Lewis in his fire suit standing next to the tank," Jones says. "The car goes up on the jacks, and they put the fuel hose into the car, but nothing happens. Huey hadn't pulled the lever to allow fuel to flow. It probably cost us about five seconds.[32]
>
> After the race, Huey comes up and apologizes. He said with all the excitement of the race, he just froze. I told him not to worry about it. I couldn't get in front of 30,000 and sing.

Despite his seventh-place finish, Fox knew it might not have been enough.

"This was a one-race deal with A.J.," he acknowledged, saying he was looking for a ride for the rest of the season. "I'm sure this won't hurt, but it is awfully difficult. I was lucky I had a couple of sponsors. Without them I couldn't have run today. Without money, it's hard.[33]

He also knew it had been a rare opportunity.

"Learning from A.J. gave me a lot of confidence. For a new driver at Indy, being with Foyt was the best thing that could have happened to me. He knew exactly what you were talking about when you'd come in from a practice run and he really took the time to teach you about the track and what it took to race there. I couldn't have dreamed of a better introduction."[34]

In order to pay tribute to Unser, Foyt attended the victory banquet the next night, one of the few times he attended the dinner when he wasn't picking up the winner's check.

"Al did a hell of a job," he said. "If anybody had to tie my record, I'm glad it was Al. I hope people recognize that Al is still a race driver and he can get a ride." He also couldn't resist reminding Unser and everyone else that when it came to winning the Indianapolis 500 four times, "I was there first."[35]

He also continued to talk about building a team and looking to the future.

"I want to have a team I can run. I've got a couple of good boys running with me now." He was especially high on Jones. "He's got all the stuff it takes. I thought his first performance was excellent. We'll just have to see how things go."[36]

The following week, Foyt ran at Milwaukee, and although Jones wasn't driving, he attended the race to support the team and was asked to handle the pit board and pass on signals from the crew to the driver.

"They were getting around the Milwaukee Mile in about nineteen seconds," remembered Jones. "That's fast. I'm this kid, and they're radioing me what to put on the pit board, and I would write it on the board and put it out, just as A.J. went past. Then they'd tell me something else, and I'd be scrambling to write it down, and I'd get done just as he went past again."[37]

Foyt was running up front and led a lap as others pitted. He ran another lap with disastrous results as he ran out of fuel. The engine stalled three times before he was able to get back in the race, four laps back and in sixth place, where he finished. No one remembers if Jones's late signals were the cause of the late pit stop, but he was never asked to man the sign board again.

After teaming with Jones for a fourth-place finish at the West Palm Beach IMSA race, the pair entered the Michigan 500 August 2. Foyt had the fastest time and was in line for his first pole position since 1979 when Michael Andretti went a tick faster in the final moments of qualifying.

"He's supposed to," Foyt said when told Andretti had gone faster. "He's younger and he's braver." Andretti couldn't hide his surprise that it had been Foyt he had to beat. "It totally amazes me how he can do what he does with twenty to twenty-five laps of practice."[38]

In the final practice session, Foyt brushed the wall, requiring substantial repairs. In the race, he was out before the 150-mile mark, while Jones was tenth, ten laps behind Andretti at the finish.

A week later, it was Jones who crashed in practice at Pocono, his car too damaged to qualify. Foyt started seventh and was among the early challengers before he was penalized along with five other cars for entering the track after a pit stop above the yellow lines. He aggravated the situation when he stalled leaving his pits after the stop-and-go penalty, losing several laps in the process. After finishing seventh, three laps behind winner Rick Mears, he grabbed the CART official who levied the penalty and shoved him against the wall in the tech area.

"I think it was the maddest I've ever seen him," Anne Fornoro recalled. To no one's surprise, Foyt blamed CART.[39]

"As far as I'm concerned, they are completely wrong," he said. "They aren't going to fry me. I don't need 'em. They need A.J. more than I need them. If they don't want my cars to run, fine, I'm not going to lose no sleep because to me the only big race there is in the world is Indianapolis."[40]

New World Records

It wasn't until late August that the Aerotech teams—there were now two cars and two support teams—were ready for another assault on the world's closed-course speed record. Deciding the five-mile oval at the General Motors test track wasn't long enough, they gathered at Firestone's test center August 26 in Fort Stockton, Texas.

It was familiar territory to Foyt, who'd often tested Indy cars for Firestone on the 7.7-mile oval in the 1960s and had been the first to top 200 mph there. It featured a paperclip design with two 1.5-mile straightaways, connected by a pair of wide and sweeping 15-degree banked turns. Repaved in 1981, most of Firestone's testing had since been shifted to Mexico, and as a result, the track was available to rent. With Oldsmobile paying, it was free to use Goodyear tires on the Aerotech. One thing hadn't changed—the facility was so remote, a lady's organization from the local church was contracted to provide lunch for the group.

There was trouble from the start. It had been decided to build a second car, based on Welburn's long-tail design. A second engine, a twin-turbo version with a 1,000 horsepower target, was contracted out to Rocky Phillips, Herb Porter's former partner and now a competitor. In typical GM fashion, separate engineering teams were developed for the two cars and pitted against each other. When Foyt and his crew arrived, they found the two cars housed in separate tented areas.

It wasn't long before Foyt found himself caught in the middle. Porter and Phillips naturally favored their own engine. Computers said the engines would take up to eighty pounds of boost pressure, but Foyt didn't trust them at even half that level. In his first runs made in the original car, he ran flat out around the track while gradually turning up the boost level—just not fast enough for Porter.

"The Aerotech was kind of spooky," Foyt recalled years later. He'd approach 300 mph down the straights and then let the car slide up the slightly banked turns to scrub off speed, not wanting to lift off the gas and lose boost pressure. "Herb kept saying, 'Turn up the boost, turn up the boost.' I just knew it was gonna blow up, and—shit—that ain't no fun. But like a damn fool, I turned up the boost. A little more. A little more, then boom!"[41]

His average speed was short of 250 mph, and in addition to a new engine, Foyt said he wanted some aerodynamic changes made. Several of the engineering types had different ideas and wanted to try something else, which didn't go over well. Foyt started drilling holes himself and put in a call to his second cousin, Joe Foyt, who ran a precision machine shop in Houston. He described the pieces needed, and when Joe arrived to deliver them, he could tell something was wrong.

"Everybody was sitting on their butts, and it was real quiet," Joe said. "I asked Jack [Starne] what the hell was going on. He said they had started telling A.J. how to build a damn race car, and A.J. told them where to shove it."[42]

Even though the twin-turbo long-tail car had just been completed and arrived at Fort Stockton having never turned a wheel anywhere near the speeds it would need to run, Foyt took it out on the track. After two warmup laps, all action in the pits stopped. The car looked and sounded fast. Several radar guns were flashing 250 when it went by, the maximum speed they were calibrated to record. Then came word the USAC timers had clocked Foyt at better than 275 mph through the measured mile.

"I think the whole group was stunned," program director Bill Porterfield recalled. "That is when we knew we had a real hotrod."[43]

Someone pointed out the speed was more than enough to better the flying mile record of nearly 255 mph for 2-liter cars set in 1959 on the Bonneville Salt Flats by Phil Hill in an MG streamliner. Although Porterfield would say, "Our sights were set on the closed course record," and the flying mile mark was "not really" one of the team's initial objectives, the decision was made to turn Foyt around and try and top Hill.

To set an official record in the flying mile, a car must be timed going in both directions over the same portion of track, traveling both downwind and upwind, with the average being the official time. The two runs also needed to be done within sixty minutes of each other.

Virtually all flying mile records are set at places like Bonneville, where there is a nearly unlimited straight-line course available for a car to build speed—and slow down. Foyt, however, had to drive the track backward to build speed before starting the second measured mile. He'd never driven the track clockwise, and the Aerotech, its chassis set up for left turns, was a handful. Several times, the car bottomed out, and when the engine cut out in the turns, Foyt came in to refuel.

With the clock ticking, he ignored requests to get out of the car while the red-hot engine was refueled, an awkward procedure. There'd been no overheating problems with the engine, and he ordered several openings taped over, including the one bringing air into the cockpit. "Hell, I'm only out there for eight minutes," he said. "I can hold my breath for that long."[44]

Back on the track, the engine continued to cut out in the turns, causing the car to bobble, but he still came up less than one mile an hour short as the time limit expired. He realized the fuel pickup point in the gas tank was set for left-hand turns, and when he ran in the opposite direction, the centrifugal force generated at speed was pushing the fuel away from the pickup. Some wanted him to start another run, but he wanted the fuel pickup situation fixed first.

"It would miss in the turns, and I had to save it a couple of times," he said. "I came in and told Jack we'd do it tomorrow—we know what we gotta do. Tomorrow is when it counts. Today don't mean shit. I don't want no coyotes eating on me tonight."

A compromise of sorts was reached. The long-tail model would be set up for the flying mile and the short tail car for an attempt on the closed course record.

A.J. also made a call to Welburn, who'd been left off the list of GM personnel invited to Fort Stockton. He caught Welburn at home, having dinner with his family.

"My daughter came in and said some guy named A.J. was on the phone," Welburn remembers. "It sounded like he was in a bar. He was talking real loud, as if he wanted others to hear him. He wanted to know why I wasn't there. Then he said he wasn't gonna set the record until I got there. He put the PR guy on the phone, and he said, 'I think he means it. You better get down here.' So I went."[45]

The record runs were almost anti-climactic. Even with gusting winds of 25 mph, Foyt topped 278 mph running with the wind in the flying mile and 257 mph against it, despite losing an engine valve during the run. The average of 267.399 mph set a new mark. He followed that with a record lap of 257.123 mph in the short-tail car. Both records still stand nearly forty years later. Foyt returned to the pits to the cheers and obvious relief of Oldsmobile executives.

"The program was overwhelming at times," Porterfield recalled. "After we had the records documented, a magazine guy caught me at the motel that night. He said something like, 'This must have been a fun project for you.' I responded with something like, 'This has been a three-year project, and it finally became fun after we ran the numbers today.'"[46]

Back in the pit area, Foyt went directly to his team's hauler and retrieved a pair of custom-made cowboy boots and presented them to Welburn, who'd arrived in time for the runs. They were from Foyt's personal bootmaker, Rocky Carroll, who also provided boots for Presidents Reagan and Bush and celebrities, including Willie Nelson.

"Ed was a super guy and super smart," Foyt would say.[47]

"[Foyt] said, 'Here, Eddie. I don't ever want to see you wearing those damn Dee-troit shoes anymore,'" said Welburn, who at the end of a forty-four-year career at GM felt the Aerotech was the single most important car he worked on. "[The boots] sit on a shelf with other memorabilia, and they're very special to me. It's a priceless memory to have from that whole experience."[48]

Full-page newspaper ads touting the record runs appeared within a week and set the stage for Foyt to run the Aerotechs one more time, October 22 at Indianapolis Motor Speedway. The target was Rick Mears's one-lap record of 217.581 mph, although anything Foyt did would be unofficial. When told that computers said a lap of 240 mph around the track was possible, Foyt grinned. "Oh yeah?" he asked, "Who's gonna drive it?"[49]

Cool temperatures, high winds, and car problems combined to leave Foyt well short of 200 mph, let alone Mears's record. "I'm just kinda babying it," he said while jumping between cars. "I'm gonna give it all the room in the world. We don't learn nothin' if I stick it in the wall. In Texas I didn't have to worry about coming face to face with a concrete wall."[50]

Driving a closed cockpit car at the Speedway was a new experience for him, and he said a canopy was something Indy car designers should consider in the future. Driver Roberto Guerrero had recently emerged from a seventeen-day coma after being injured while testing at the Speedway when a tire came off and hit him in the helmet. "It's a safety factor for the future," Foyt said. "I feel more comfortable with the canopy."[51]

Despite the speed shortfall, Foyt said a top speed of 300 mph was possible and recommended the Aerotech be taken to Bonneville. "There is a lot more left," he said. "We're just breaking the crust."[52]

Welburn drew up several versions of a Bonneville car but "costs went over budget like a lot of racing programs do," Porterfield said. Olds management declared mission accomplished. The Aerotechs were relegated to the auto show circuit until five years later when a third car was built and all three fitted with Olds's new Aurora V8 engines. They returned to Fort Stockton, and although Foyt wasn't involved and the top speed records went unchallenged, eight drivers combined to break forty-seven endurance marks.

One of the Aerotechs used in the endurance effort was damaged when it hit a deer on the course at night. The car was eventually obtained by Larry Foyt, restored with Starne's assistance, and put on display at the Foyt Winery Museum in Fredericksburg, Texas.

Ready for a break, Foyt headed to his house on Lake Travis near Austin for Labor Day. A few years earlier, with son Jerry attending the nearby University of Texas, the Foyts had rented on the lake several times before deciding to buy a lot and build. While A.J. still preferred the ranch for his downtime, Lucy, who loved being near the water, insisted on spending a long weekend at the lake house.

The area was overrun by end-of-summer vacationers trying to avoid the even hotter than normal temperatures, and it was something of a relief for Foyt when Al Holbert called a few days before the holiday. IMSA was running its first race through the streets of San Antonio on Sunday, September 6, and hoping to jumpstart ticket sales, Holbert asked Foyt to drive in the event. Holbert would supply the car, set it up, and start the race. All Foyt needed to do was show up and drive—an offer too good to refuse. He invited his neighbor on the lake and a former racer, Jimmy Finger, to go to San Antonio with him. Of course, Finger said yes.

There was only one problem. He'd failed to check in advance with Lucy, who'd been part of the planning committee for Finger's surprise birthday party scheduled for Sunday afternoon. They'd all agreed not to tell A.J. because he'd repeatedly proven himself unable to keep secrets. As it was, Lucy waited until Sunday morning to tell A.J., saying she wanted him home immediately after the race.

Born and raised in Austin, Finger spent most of his racing career running modifieds on area short tracks. He also ran several bigger events, his best being an eighth place in a stock car race at Texas World Speedway in 1979—a race won by Foyt. He'd been introduced to A.J. by Gordon Van Liew, a longtime racing supporter and sponsor through his Vita Fresh orange juice brand. Finger was an "uneducated, still in twelfth grade type of guy who made a living working on cars" and just the type of person Foyt was drawn to. Finger helped Foyt find a lot and a builder for the lake home, and the neighbors often spent time together when the Foyts were there.[53]

Foyt's entry in the San Antonio race was announced two days before the event, and it did the trick, with more than 50,000 fans turning out. Holbert started the car, and Foyt took over for the last seventy-five minutes of the three-hour race. He finished second to Holbert's primary car, more through attrition than anything else, with temperatures in the mid-nineties. Then the fun started. As Finger headed for the winner's circle to watch the trophy presentation, he spotted Foyt coming in the opposite direction, still in uniform and covered with sweat and grime from the race. Finger recalled,

> He always goes and showers and puts on his street clothes right after a race. Always. He said he wasn't going to the goddamn podium and didn't want their stinking trophy. We fought our way through the crowd and got to his Suburban, and he's still got his driver's suit on, and he heads toward Austin.
>
> The drive home was a lot more exciting than the race. He's driving like a wild man. We're running eighty-five, ninety, a hundred, zigzagging through traffic. I thought he'd lost his mind.
>
> We get near Austin, and we're coming from a different direction than normal as he'd usually be coming from Houston, and we miss the exit. No matter. He cuts across traffic, drives through the grass and up over the curb, down a service road and back to the exit ramp. We get back to our house, and there must have been fifty to seventy-five people waiting there.

Finger became one of the small club of Foyt's close friends and would attend races with him. When the Foyts were at their lake house, they often dined together. He learned early the secret of getting along with Foyt:

> You got to put right back on him what he puts on you. If he starts jacking on you, just turn it around. Don't take any of his bullshit. And the last thing you want to do is try and impress him, especially with money. If you do, that will be the end of the relationship.
>
> He's good to people, real good to people. He always said he liked the lake because nobody knew him up there, it's nice and quiet here. Still, someone is always interrupting him when you go out to eat. He does real good with it, but he won't put up with a drunk. Not for long. Anything starts to get out of line, and it's over.
>
> We're at a restaurant and sitting close to this couple with a kid or two, and they recognized him. The guy waited until A.J. was finished eating and came over and introduced himself. The guy was very polite and says, 'Don't you live in Houston?' A.J. spills the beans and says, 'I built a house on Hudson Bend,' and one thing leads to another, and hell—he tells the guy to stop by. That's the other side of A.J. people don't see. Stranger walks up and thirty minutes later they're not a stranger, as long as they act right.

Foyt took Jones to two more Indy car races before the year was out, at Nazareth and Tamiami Park. At Tamiami, Foyt was involved in an incident with Emerson Fittipaldi, and afterward the Brazilian driver took a shot at him.

"I had lapped him three times and was going for number four," Fittipaldi said. "It's pretty obvious he didn't see me. I came inside of him and he closed the door on me."[54]

Discussions about Jones's future with the team continued through the end of the year. He'd been consistent but not flashy. Financing became an issue, and Foyt offered a partial slate of races. While Jones was a paid driver, he said, "It was everybody's intention to find money or bring on some sponsorship. We had a deal we were working on, but the money never really came through. We talked about [1988], but his team was looking for funding, and I didn't know how serious it was."[55]

Jones had offers from other Indy car teams but eventually he decided to join Jaguar, which was launching a major international sports car effort. "It was a multiyear program, and it was just a more solid program than what I'd been offered in Indy cars. In racing you gotta go where it takes you."

CAMEL
Copenhagen
RACING
SIMPSON
Copenhagen
Copenhagen
14

CHAPTER 12

MOST IMPROVED

1988

A.J. Foyt found several new excuses not to retire on his fifty-third birthday, although he did admit, "Hell, I'm getting up in age now."[1]

"I've never been to Long Beach," he said. "I've never been up to Elkhart Lake. I'd like to run there, run a few of the courses I've never been to. I just want to go to these courses because when I field a car with a new boy or someone who might not have been there, maybe I could help him a little. I'm going to run a full schedule with CART."

Foyt's decision indicated a realization that Indy car racing was changing. There were more road races than oval track events on the schedule, and half of those were on temporary tracks. Not everyone liked the changes.

"American oval tracks are becoming extinct—much like American drivers on the Indy car circuit," wrote Robin Miller in the *Indianapolis Star*. The oval tracks were being replaced by "makeshift Mickey Mouse road courses with no place to race and terrible vantage points," and the sport had become "a rich kid's hobby where money talks and talent walks."[2]

If Foyt went through with his plans to run all fifteen races, it would be his first full season in ten years. But he made one thing clear—it wasn't a farewell tour.

"I'm just running all the races this year is all I'm saying. After this, we'll see."[3]

His decision to add the road courses and street races seemed odd after letting Davy Jones, one of the top young road racers in the country, slip away. It was the start of a trend of up-and-coming young drivers spending a short time with the Foyt team before moving on. With Jones signing with Jaguar, A.J. dropped plans to run two cars for the season, although he left the door open to adding teammates for Indianapolis.

◀ Jack Starne and A.J. on their first trip to Road America. *Dan Boyd*

Foyt also realized the pace of technology was picking up and missing races meant falling further behind.

"I want to learn something about these new cars," he said. "I mean, there isn't a better place to get updated on that stuff than in the driver's seat. You look for weak points when you're out there driving. You just can't find them any other way. And that gives you practice in diagnosing problems before they come up."[4]

First, Foyt went to Daytona for the twenty-four hour race where he finally convinced Al Unser Jr. to drive for his team, although "Big Al" turned down the opportunity. Part of the winning team the previous two years, Little Al was the odd man out when Al Holbert cut back to three drivers.

"I'd known A.J. since I can remember," Unser Jr. recalled. "When dad would take us to the races, A.J. was always just super friendly. He's just an all-around great guy. When he called and asked me to drive in '88, of course the answer was an instant yes. It was such an honor."[5]

Unser Jr. quickly learned what others had discovered: It was Foyt's car, and he set it up like he wanted it. Unlike his father, it didn't bother Little Al.

"The cars were prepared super. He knew what he wanted, and he really did a great job with those endurance cars. He was fast—he was right there. It didn't surprise me. In an Indy car, it was a little bit tougher for him because he was starting to get up there in age, and they're shorter races, and you're driving hard the whole time. With the sports cars, you pick a pace that will take you the twenty-four hours."

Engine restrictions placed on the Porsches by IMSA caused problems for all the teams in the race, including Foyt's. They gradually fell further and further behind, coming home sixth more than fifty laps behind the winning Jaguar team. "We came into this race handicapped, but we still weren't worried about the Jaguars," Foyt said. "They still have to beat us. They kind of backed into a victory."[6]

That didn't sit well with Jaguar team manager Tom Walkinshaw, who'd lured Jones away. "For someone to make that comment, he'd have to be blind."[7]

The race did result in one humorous incident Unser Jr. remembered years later:

"I got up real early to take over the next shift and I'm walking towards the pits and someone handed me a sandwich. So I drove the first two laps eating the sandwich, and my first time by the pits, A.J. gets on the radio and says, 'I'm paying you to drive the race car, not to sit and eat lunch.'"[8]

Disappointed with his NASCAR effort the past few years, Foyt took a suggestion from the U.S. Tobacco Company and turned to another Texan to oversee the program, Tex Powell. He'd worked for a number of NASCAR teams, including Ray Nichels and Petty Engineering and most recently, a team sponsored by Skoal, a sister UST brand to Foyt's Copenhagen sponsor.

Foyt and Powell had known each other since high school, although not well. "I ran with a crowd that was a couple of years younger," Powell recalled. "We knew each other. We weren't the older guys' favorite people, but it was okay."[9]

He'd also raced against Foyt at Playland Park and other local tracks in the mid-1950s.

"I was running around at the back of the pack, and he was winning races," Powell said. "I thought, *Well hell—if this guy is that much better than me, I think I'd better work on cars and not try to drive 'em.* If I had known then I was driving against the best driver in the world, I might have tried a little harder. Instead, I became a mechanic."

Powell worked a short time for Tony Foyt before moving to the local Ford dealership. He never lost the racing bug, however, and by the late 1960s was working for the Bud Moore Trans-Am team preparing cars for Parnelli Jones and George Follmer and occasionally Foyt.

"They were both Firestone drivers and when we wanted to compare them to Goodyear tires, we called A.J. and I would work on his car." Their paths crossed often over the years in NASCAR, but they'd never worked together until the team's first test session at Daytona in mid-January.

"The talent was still there," Powell recalled from the test. "He was always over-blessed with talent. He'd also mellowed a good bit by then, and he and I always got along good. I wouldn't say he was always real happy with me or that I was real happy with him, but we never had any harsh words."

Much of the Daytona 500 prerace attention was focused on three aging drivers: Foyt, along with Richard Petty and Bobby Allison, who both had turned fifty. All three were running well just past the halfway point when Foyt and Petty were involved in an alarming accident.

Coming off Turn Four, Petty was being followed closely by rookie Phil Barkdoll. Foyt was running a car length behind and a lane lower on the track when the rear of Petty's car began to slide out. Barkdoll bumped him, turning him hard left, directly into Foyt's path.

"I was going under that whole group on the bottom side," Foyt said. "When [Petty's] car jerked sideways he come down across the track and when he did, I hit him real hard."[10]

The impact turned Petty's car backward and launched it airborne. It began pirouetting on its nose as the rear of the car ripped along the grandstand fencing for half a dozen revolutions. After damaging two of the posts holding up the barrier and sending debris flying into the stands, the car fell back onto the track then was hit again and sent spinning. An emotional Chris Economaki said Petty's career was over, and Foyt, his car too damaged to continue, went to the infield medical center to check on him.

"I think he's going to be alright and thank God for that," Foyt said. Although Petty had momentarily lost his vision and spent the night in the hospital, doctors eventually determined he didn't even suffer a concussion.

In the weeks after the wreck, reporters bombarded Petty, who hadn't won in four years, with questions about retirement. His answers sounded a lot like Foyt's:

> What keeps me going? To tell the truth, I just love climbing in a race car and driving it. When I'm strapped in that car, riding up along the high

> bank, ain't nobody in the world's going to bother me. It's my time, my private time, and I still enjoy doing it. I hear people saying maybe I ought to retire, that maybe I'm hanging on too long, but they don't understand what racing means to me. Sure, I'd like it better if we'd win again, but I sure wouldn't have a chance to win if I retired, so I'm sticking around a bit longer.[11]

Bobby Allison went on to win the race, edging his son Davey, the leader of the new generation of drivers. Petty missed the next race at Richmond but returned three weeks later at Rockingham, saying it was a matter of "mind over matter. If you don't mind, it don't matter." He would continue to race until the end of the 1992 season without winning another event. Bobby Allison would be involved in a terrible crash later in 1988 at Pocono, ending his career.[12]

Happy with the way his cars ran at Daytona, Foyt decided to enter the 12 Hours of Sebring and the Atlanta 500 on subsequent days, March 19 and 20—something he hadn't done since shuttling between the tracks in 1967. With the start of the Indy car season only a month away, the *Los Angeles Times* called him "the busiest major driver in America."[13]

"It feels great to be this busy," Foyt said. "I'd like to get back to winning like I used to, but I'm having a lot of fun."[14]

Heavy rains at both tracks and airport problems threatened to interrupt his fun as Friday qualifying at Atlanta was washed out and moved to Saturday. Juggling four rental cars and two airplanes and flight crews, he managed to pull it off, thanks to an assist from the team of Richard Childress and Dale Earnhardt, who recommended Foyt be moved to the front of the qualifying line. The other NASCAR drivers approved in a unanimous vote, and after posting a time, Foyt headed for Childress's plane and Sebring, where the race had already started.

"That's one thing about the NASCAR guys, they really pitch in and help you when they know you're in a bind," Foyt said. "We were off the ground seventeen minutes after I took the checkered flag (in qualifying). I didn't even know where I qualified until I was at Sebring."

His time was good for sixth, and Earnhardt took out the No. 14 Oldsmobile during the final practice session after the team converted it from qualifying to race trim. Powell recalled,

> Sometimes when Foyt was away doing other stuff, we needed someone to drive the car. He was pretty particular about who he would let drive his car, but it was okay to have Dale drive it. At Atlanta, Dale drove it and came in and said it run good, 'But you better put a round of wedge in it and tighten it up for the old man.'[15]
>
> A.J. and Dale senior were very similar. You had to handle them both the same way. If you wanted to do something to the car, it was best to talk to them when there was no one else around. And it helped if you could make them think it was their idea to begin with.

At Sebring, Hurley Haywood had moved his car from seventh to fifth by the time Foyt arrived, and they would go on to finish fourth. The Atlanta race didn't go nearly as well, as he dropped out after just eighty-five laps, with Earnhardt posting a dominating victory.

At Phoenix on April 10 for the start of the Indy car season, Foyt surprised many with a fourth-place finish in a race won by Mario Andretti. It was Andretti's forty-eighth Indy car win and pulled him to within seventeen of Foyt.

"I'm trying my best," he said when asked if he could catch Foyt. "I'm not knocking at his door yet. But I wouldn't trade my twelve Formula One victories for his. I'm still here and still grinding away. Tell him to keep finishing fourth."[16]

A week later, Foyt made his first trip to Long Beach, California, for the street course race to see what all the hoopla was about. The race, held only a few miles from where Foyt's race shops had been in the mid-1960s, had quickly become one of the most popular on the circuit—some said second only to Indianapolis.

He "pooh-poohed" his rookie status at the track, saying, "I've been around long enough to find my way around the racetrack," before clipping the wall during practice.[17]

After qualifying twenty-third in the twenty-six-car field, he soldiered on to an eleventh-place finish, although he was last among the cars still running in a race won by Al Unser Jr. He complained about back and kidney pain afterward, the harsh ride of the Lola chassis and bumpy city streets of Long Beach having taken their toll.

The following week, he was back in Florida to run his Porsche at a new track in West Palm Beach. When his car was delayed by transporter problems, he joined son Jerry in the Firehawk race to help learn the course. Starting last in a field of more than thirty cars, he drove the basically stock Oldsmobile Calais with a Quad 4 production engine to thirteenth. He turned the car over to Jerry, who wasn't as fortunate, as he was involved in an accident soon after.

In the main event, Foyt started eleventh and moved up to fourth before tangling with Oscar Larrauri, an Argentinian-born driver and regular on the international sports car circuit, who was making one of his occasional starts in the United States. Larrauri was also advancing through the field and bounced off Foyt while trying to make a pass, putting the Copenhagen car into the wall and badly damaging its nose. It wasn't the first car he'd hit.

"Larrauri decided to play ping-pong with a lot of us," said another driver, Bob Earl. "He knocked me in the wall in the beginning."[18]

As Foyt slowly drove back to the pits, he stopped and "played possum," waiting for Larrauri to come around again. When he did, Foyt attempted to administer some "frontier justice," using his race car as a battering ram. He only made glancing contact, which further upset him.[19]

"It was clearly Larrauri's fault, not A.J.'s," recalled co-driver Haywood. "He was furious, just storming mad. He went down and was gonna strangle Larrauri. It was serious but amusing to watch it all play out. A.J. wasn't gonna take shit from anybody."[20]

Foyt admitted, "I tried to nail his ass. He's got a lesson coming, a good lesson. I moved over to try and give him room but he's been driving like an idiot all day. He just went in where there was no hole. I've seen him at the track before. He was an idiot then and he's an idiot now."[21]

The 150-pound Larrauri said he'd followed Foyt for half a lap waiting to be let by before forcing his way past. After avoiding Foyt's ramming attempt, he'd been able to finish the race.

"He wanted to crash me," Larrauri said. "My English not very good. It was stupid. He's a very, very crazy man. He is stupid. Do you understand?"[22]

Foyt had the last laugh when Larrauri's car was disqualified for having an oversized turbocharger. Both drivers received warnings from IMSA about "inappropriate driving," but that didn't stop Foyt from leveling a threat as he left the track.

"There'll be another race. I'll get his ass next time. I'll get that son of a bitch. He's just lucky I didn't get another shot at him. If he had gone around another time, I would have hit his ass so hard it would have knocked him out in the parking lot."

For once, Foyt was wrong. There would not be another race. With his Porsche 962 damaged and IMSA rule changes he believed favored a new generation of cars coming from Nissan, Jaguar, Toyota, and others, the race marked his final IMSA appearance. His sports car driving days were over, and occasional co-driver Haywood would miss the opportunities to share a car with his hero. Haywood said,

> A.J. is such a fixture. I had not seen him in a while, and we were doing a vintage car race along with the Indy cars in Milwaukee. I walked down to their pits, and I asked if A.J. was around. The guy said he would check and asked who I was, and I told him. A minute later, A.J. came out of his trailer and gave me a big hug and asked how I was doing. I told him Bob Snodgrass and Dan Davis were at the track and asked if it was okay if I brought them back to see him. A.J. said no, he'd walk down to see them. This was after his big crash, and he was crippled up pretty badly. He wanted me to hold his arm while we walked. You could see he was in a lot of pain. It was an honor to lend him a hand.[23]

A week after the Miami race, Foyt was in trouble again—this time with NASCAR over his actions during the May 1 Winston 500 at Talladega. Running up front late in the race, he tangled with Alan Kulwicki during a caution period. Kulwicki was one of NASCAR's few remaining owner/drivers and among the series' most popular competitors.

As NASCAR attempted to align the field for a restart with six laps remaining, several cars were ordered around Foyt. As Kulwicki started past, Foyt swerved up the track, damaging the front of the other car. Kulwicki banged back.

While the race restarted, both drivers were black-flagged into the pits and held in NASCAR's "penalty box" designed to help cool tempers. After being released, Foyt nearly sideswiped Kulwicki's car while leaving the pits. Black-flagged again, Foyt raced through the pits, sending several officials diving over the wall. Black-flagged a third time, Powell was told to get the car off the track. Within minutes,

NASCAR announced a $5,000 fine and six-month suspension for Foyt for "conduct detrimental to the sport."[24]

"We're not going to have people running Winston Cup with the mental attitude that he had at that time," said Dick Beaty, NASCAR's series director.

Although Powell said Foyt had mellowed, "he would kind of unravel from time to time. At Talladega, he went back to the trailer, tore up his hard card, and threw it on the floor. I thought we would be out for the rest of the season."[25]

Things were even worse when Foyt arrived home.

"My wife said I was acting like a fool," A.J. recalled later. Eleven-year-old Larry Foyt had watched the race and wanted to know "how Pop got fined and suspended and didn't even win the race."[26]

Kulwicki said he had no idea what caused Foyt's tantrum.

"I don't know what he was thinking. We never touched before that. There was nothing at all, no precedent to something like that. All I know is he went down to the apron and came up into me. I hadn't touched Foyt, and can't figure out what I'd done to make him angry."[27]

It turned out to be a case of mistaken identity. After bumping several times with a car driven by Greg Sacks during the race, Foyt was lying in wait for what he thought was Sacks's car when he hit Kulwicki.

"Really, nothing happened," Foyt sheepishly said later. "It was blown way out of proportion. You couldn't blame anybody. I can see their point and I can't see their point. NASCAR held me on pit road, but wouldn't tell me why. I was sitting there like a goose."

In the sometimes-odd world of NASCAR justice, the suspension was dropped—allowing Foyt to race in the July event at Daytona—while the fine was increased to $7,500. Beyond debate was the fact that for the second week in a row, Foyt was involved in an on-track dustup that drew the ire of the sanctioning organization. Even more concerning, he again tried to take revenge on the racetrack, something he'd seldom done in the past.

When things didn't go well at Indianapolis, he did something else he'd seldom done in the past—blamed his luck. He'd often said he didn't believe in luck and "you make your own luck." But he blamed luck for his poor performance during the first week of practice at the Speedway and the failure to make the field on the first weekend of qualifying.[28]

"I just ain't had no luck," he said. "We're not running fast. Maybe that's a good omen."[29]

In this case, it was more a matter of making your own luck as he'd decided to stick with the well-tested Cosworth engine, winner of ten straight Indy 500s, rather than switch to the more powerful but unproven new Chevrolet Ilmor powerplant. He struggled to match the speeds of the Chevrolets during practice, although some said it was just Foyt sandbagging. There was no magical qualifying run, however, as he waved off two attempts and failed to make the field on the first weekend. Chevrolet-powered cars took the top-five qualifying spots, including a sweep of the front row by Penske Racing.

While saying the Penske team "did their homework," Foyt added, "It looks like I screwed up. I felt I'd get more reliability with a Cosworth. I did it for longevity. I guess I was conservative."[30]

Despite his problems, Foyt took time during the week to host Sean Callahan, a five-year-old Houston boy battling muscular dystrophy, whose wish it was to meet the driver. Naturally at ease with children, Foyt picked up the young boy and put him in the cockpit of the car and chatted quietly with him, saying afterward, "That's what racing's all about."

As the second weekend of qualifying approached, Foyt also moved to fill the seats in his other cars. Rather than go with a young driver, he offered a car to Rocky Moran, a sports car veteran with occasional Indy car starts, primarily on road courses. It was a matter of being in the right place at the right time for Moran, who stuck his head in the Foyt garage and asked if there were any cars available.

"I feel like an old man—a rookie at thirty-eight years old," Moran said. "You have a wealth of expertise when you're driving for Foyt's outfit. It's like going to graduate school for a race driver."[31]

The other car went to Stan Fox, who hadn't driven in a major event since his run with the Foyt team at Indianapolis a year earlier.

"Most of the guys come here with a lot of sponsorship behind them, and I come with a helmet bag," Fox said. "I just kept hanging around and bugging A.J. I had written off this year. Then came the page over the loudspeaker system telling me to report to Foyt's garage."

Foyt waited until late on the third day of qualifying before making another run, admitting, "I ain't never been this God-damned nervous." When both Moran and Fox qualified, Johnny Parsons then made a last-ditch effort to qualify Foyt's fourth car but bounced off the wall before completing his run.[32]

George Snider's absence from his traditional last-minute role started rumors of a rift between him and Foyt, but he scoffed at the suggestion.

"If we'd had a fight one of us would have looked like we'd had a fight," said Snider, who indicated he would handle the fueling on Foyt's car during the race. "There's no problem with me and him. I retired for the month. I just decided I wanted to sit around." The rumor was further put to rest a couple of nights later when Foyt brought Chuck Yeager, who again was driving the pace car for the 500, to watch Snider race in the Hulman Hundred Silver Crown event at the Indiana State Fairgrounds. He gave the fans—and Yeager—a thrill between heat races by turning hot laps in a pace car. Yeager said he wanted to return the favor and take Foyt up in a fighter jet, an offer A.J. declined.[33]

Despite his difficulty in making the race, or perhaps because of it, Foyt was again the center of attention once the field was set.

"It's unbelievable," said Foyt's godson John Andretti, making his first start in the 500. "To be in this race is very difficult and to do it thirty-one consecutive times is hard to believe. Everything changes so much. To move with the times says more than what all the record books say about A.J.[34]

"He'll probably be here when I do my thirty-first."

Race day track temperatures well over one hundred degrees turned the racing surface into an ice rink, according to Foyt, and caused a record fourteen caution periods involving nine accidents and eleven drivers. One of those was for Foyt, who was involved in a race-ending accident for the first time since 1966, when he'd been knocked out before it started.

"Eighty-eight? I crashed? I don't remember that. Oh yeah, I do too," he'd say years later when asked about it.[35]

"I was coming off (Turn) Two. I was tryin' to get under Emerson Fittipaldi, and I spun in dirty air. I got disgusted because he was outrunnin' me down the straightaway. I spun down the back straightaway. Nothin' got really hit."

Foyt ended up twenty-sixth, while Moran finished 159 laps before his engine gave out, good for sixteenth. Fox lasted just two laps before the engine quit in his car. That was still good for twenty-ninth as three cars crashed on the pace lap, and he split more than $100,000 with Foyt.

The crash and overall miserable performance of the team didn't go unnoticed and left one columnist wondering if it was "pasture time."[36]

"A.J. Foyt knows what it takes to win and it doesn't look like he wants to pay that price anymore," wrote Harold Lowe in the *South Bend Tribune*. "Car preparation left a lot to be desired. But the crowning blow was Foyt crashing out of the race for the first time since 1966. He doesn't have the reflexes or the concentration he had as a young man. Experience compensated for the eroding of the natural skills but maybe now even that isn't enough."

Despite the problems and criticism, Foyt remained committed to running the full Indy car schedule, including racing for the first time at Portland, Toronto, and Road America at Elkhart Lake. He also returned to Laguna Seca for the first time in twenty-three years and was the only driver undertaking the Fourth of July weekend doubleheader, shuttling back and forth between Daytona and Cleveland.

After qualifying in Daytona on Thursday, he'd flown to Cleveland for practice and qualifying on Friday, arriving back in Daytona at 12:30 Saturday morning. While most NASCAR regulars stayed at or near the track in Daytona to avoid traffic, Foyt preferred the oceanfront Hilton Hotel when he was in town. But with the race starting at 10:00 a.m., he got a late start for the track and was caught in prerace traffic. When he missed the 8:00 a.m. driver's meeting, he was fined $100 and more importantly—under a new NASCAR rule—moved to the back of the forty-two-car field.

"I guess because I'm A.J. Foyt they felt like the penalty would impress the rest of the big name drivers," Foyt said. "I think it was a rotten deal. NASCAR just wanted to show they were big dogs, that they can make A.J. Foyt start last. If I was at any other racetrack, I would have just left. It's really a shame they treat me like this because I just came here to try and help the show out. I flew a private jet clean across the country to get here. It was really a cheap shot."[37]

He ran well in the race until debris cracked his windshield, forcing a long pit stop while it was taped up. Despite his complaints about NASCAR, he returned to Talladega at the end of the month and ran all 188 laps, leading three. When he complained of back pain there were snide remarks about hurting himself squeezing through the window of his stock car, but in reality he'd been hurting since Long Beach.

When it reached the point back in Houston where he could "hardly stand up," Lucy forced him to see Dr. Gary Friedman, who checked him into Memorial Medical Center. A series of tests indicated a badly bruised kidney. He'd likely had the injury since Long Beach and had made it worse while continuing to race.[38]

Complete rest was the primary treatment, and Johnny Rutherford replaced him for the Michigan 500 CART race. Foyt returned three weeks later at Pocono a few pounds lighter and again showed good form. Using a new Cosworth, he qualified sixth, led fourteen laps, and was out front when he ran out of fuel, the new engine failing to deliver the expected gas mileage.

He ran the remaining five races on the CART circuit but finished only one, a surprising tenth at Road America. He ended the year November 20 at the Atlanta NASCAR race, where he raced from twenty-fourth starting position to the lead before engine problems knocked him out.

Years later, Powell discussed some of the struggles with the NASCAR program:

> Running the partial schedule was tough because you were always behind the curve on setup. You'd miss out on the little things that were being done with the tires and other stuff. We'd come in and work hard for three or four days before a race, always trying to catch up.[39]
>
> He was so well respected, if we were struggling, he'd go by and visit with some of the other teams and they'd share their setups with him. He'd come back with a collection of what some of the good cars were running, which was sometimes confusing because he'd want to mix and match. If you had time, you could work it out. But other times it was pretty confusing.
>
> I don't think we'd ever eat lunch. They'd shut down the track between noon and 1:00 p.m., but A.J. always had a bunch of stuff he wanted done. He was very demanding, but the crew never complained. In fact, they liked it. They weren't doing it for the money or the glory. They wanted a feeling of accomplishment. Foyt would hang in with them and work right alongside them. They liked that dedication.
>
> He was a hell of a mechanic. Very high mechanical skills. I don't think you have many drivers today with his overall understanding of machinery, and it wasn't just the chassis. He could be an engine guy, too. Just so much knowledge there.

The season over, Foyt had run twenty-six races in three major series. He started fifteen of the sixteen CART races and finished sixteenth in the final points standings.

It was still a surprise when Foyt was named CART's "most improved driver," a dubious honor Mario Andretti admitted later was "a joke that got out of hand.

When we were voting, everybody was cutting up and nobody took it seriously. Actually, there were no improved drivers this year . . . a couple of guys got worse."[40]

Foyt didn't take part in the voting, nor was he at the CART banquet in Miami to accept the award. At times during the season, he'd been amused by the encouraging words of others. At other times, he bristled. "I finish fifth (Milwaukee) and everybody says, 'A.J., you done run good.' I say, 'How do you figure. Four guys blew my doors off.' I'll tell you what, if you don't finish first, nobody gives a shit about you."[41]

It was left to Foyt's secretary in Houston to inform him about the award. She said later Foyt thought it was "cute." It's his only use of the word on record. "I don't care what they call me," Foyt joked. "Just send me the money that goes along with it."[42]

Others didn't find it cute or humorous. Racing historian Joe Scalzo wrote,

> It was supposed to be a joke. It was no joke. It was the biggest, most offensive insult Indy car racing has suffered—and making it all the worse, it was an insult shamelessly inflicted by Indy car racing itself. You aren't supposed to mock your very history. You don't assassinate your own father.[43]
>
> That A.J. Foyt is Indy car racing's father—the greatest, most dominating champion in all nine decades of competition—is recorded fact. But that is just the trouble. The drivers now ruling the sport have no concern for any history except their own.

Andretti also came to A.J.'s defense:

> If Foyt was really serious, put all the horses and other bullshit aside, I think the guy could still be the Foyt I know. He's at all the races this year, but he could care less. It's not that he's not capable. I don't think he has the desire to be there and devote the time. It's unfortunate in that sense because he's judged on that performance. If a guy is having a good time, maybe that's good enough but I hate to see a brilliant career forgotten.[44]
>
> My feelings for Foyt will never change. I've raced too much against him and I know his worth. Nobody was more intense when he was winning and I know what kind of racer he can be when he wants to.
>
> He'll always be at the top of my list as far as guys I've looked up to. That will never change.

Copenhagen
VALVOLINE
GILMORE
14
GOODYEAR
GOODYEAR

CHAPTER 13

AN OUTRIGHT EMBARRASSMENT

1989

For the first time since 1983, A.J. Foyt started his racing year somewhere other than Daytona. Unhappy with IMSA rules he felt made his Porsche 962 uncompetitive, he decided to race in USAC's Copper World Classic in Phoenix, held the same weekend as the 24 Hours of Daytona.

"Why go racing if you can't run to win?" he said. "I'm not going to take a half-million-dollar race car and not be able to set it up to where we think it can win."[1]

Sponsored by Skoal, the Phoenix event included races for midgets, modifieds, Silver Crown, and stock cars. Foyt entered the stock car race along with several NASCAR regulars also sponsored by United States Tobacco brands, including Kenny Schrader and Harry Gant.

Despite not having raced a stock car at Phoenix in more than twenty years, Foyt qualified fourth. Driving the winning car from the past two years, he battled Schrader for the lead before suffering a blown tire. He raced back through the field to finish third and said he was ready for another full season of Indy car racing.

"I feel like we should be a lot more competitive this year," he said of the CART series. "I felt like the only tracks we were competitive at last year were Phoenix and Indianapolis. At least 90 percent of the tracks were all green to us. Now that we've got some experience at some of those tracks, I'm looking forward to it."

As usual he added, "If I didn't think I could win I wouldn't be doing it."

He said there were no plans to run more than one car in CART, but he would enter one for Tony George (Tony Hulman's grandson and the executive vice president at the Indianapolis Motor Speedway) in the single-make America Racing

◀ Foyt was no fan of street courses. *Dan Boyd*

Series for March-Buicks. George had run Formula Fords and Super Vees in the past, and the ARS series was considered the final step before Indy cars. Foyt also said he would return to the International Race of Champions after a four-year absence, where he would race at Watkins Glen for the first time.

He also took part in Goodyear tire tests at both Indianapolis and Charlotte. Goodyear was facing a challenge from Hoosier Racing Tires in NASCAR and trying to introduce a new radial tire for the stock cars, similar to one used on Indy cars. The Charlotte test was a real eye-opener for crew chief Tex Powell, who recalled,

> It was a four-car, four-day test, and [Dale] Earnhardt and [Darrell] Waltrip were two of the other drivers. On the second day, we were making short runs, and Foyt came in, and I was listening to him talk to the Goodyear engineer. He was describing what the car felt like and what was causing it to act that way. He was very specific about the construction of the sidewall and tread of different tires.[2]
>
> I'd been doing tire tests with Goodyear for ten years but had never heard anything like that. And it was all from memory. Hell, I couldn't remember how many sets of tires we'd run the day before. To feel the difference between the tread and tire construction, I don't think many drivers can do that. They can tell you something about how the tire feels, but not about the construction of the tire.
>
> When [Foyt] went back out, I asked the engineer how close he was. The engineer said he was exactly right. He said, 'He's by far the best tire test driver we've ever had.'

According to Mike Babich, Goodyear's assistant director of racing at the time and top racing tire engineer, "A.J. would tell you immediately what was wrong. He didn't need a computer. I'll bet if you polled all of the engineers who work with A.J.—and who had a disagreement with him regarding compound or stagger or almost anything affecting the car—they wouldn't know of a time he wasn't right."[3]

The Daytona 500 had a different look and feel as former winners Cale Yarborough, Buddy Baker, and Benny Parsons had all retired during the offseason. Foyt had driven against Baker's father Buck, was helpful to Parsons when he was first getting started, and counted Yarborough among his closest friends in NASCAR and his drafting partner.

The cars were also changing, with aerodynamics and even ground effects playing a larger role. They were more stable at speed and safer as a result, "but they're getting rid of some of the fun," Foyt said.[4]

Despite the best efforts of Foyt and others, Goodyear withdrew its radial from competition after tire failures caused practice crashes by Bill Elliott and Dale Earnhardt. Only Foyt and one other driver started the 500 on Goodyear tires. Loyalty went only so far, however, as Foyt switched to Hoosiers (with the brand name blacked out) at the first opportunity, just four laps into the race. That helped Foyt take the lead when the rest of the field pitted. But it didn't last long—only four laps, before a busted shock tower ended his race.

At Phoenix for the start of the Indy car season on April 9, the track was celebrating its twenty-fifth anniversary and honored Foyt as the winner of the first race. It was an embarrassing start to the season, however. He qualified eighteenth in a field of twenty-four cars and finished twenty-second when the turbocharger literally fell apart shortly after the green flag.

The questions about Foyt's desire and abilities started anew.

"I can understand his wanting to stay in," said Chris Economaki. "I think A.J. just does not know how to retire. I think, inside, he wants to. He's a great, great talent and it's just a shame to see A.J. hang on too long."[5]

Bobby Unser, who'd been calling for Foyt's retirement for several years, chimed in.

"We've lost a tremendous amount of the old Foyt," Unser said. "What's really sad is that so many of the new drivers and the foreign drivers don't know just how good he was. His team don't really stay with it the way they used to. They don't work as hard as they used to at preparation."

Stung by the poor showing, Foyt fired the new crew chief he'd hired during the offseason to replace Jack Starne, who wanted to get off the road. Starne, who had planned to oversee George's ARS efforts, agreed to return and was named chief of operations. Foyt warned, "I'm going to eliminate people until I get the ones I want to keep.

"I'm back in the race shop now," he said. "I'm with the racing operation every day. I can keep an eye on it a lot closer now, and I hope I can get it turned around before Indy. I know they're saying the old man's over the hump. He can't do this, he can't do that. I'm saying, you think whatever you want, big boy. If I get things lined up, it might be a whole different ballgame."

It was too soon to see any changes a week later at Long Beach, where he spun twice during the first three laps of practice and said he "felt like a fool." He came back to qualify a respectable fifteenth but was running slowly in the race when he was hit from behind and pushed into a wall and out.

"I don't really care that much about street racing," he said. "I'll take Indy, and they can have all the rest."

He ran in the IROC race at Nazareth a week later. After finishing seventh in the series opener at Daytona, he dominated until forced to the pits with a flat tire. Danny Sullivan was a surprised winner, saying he'd been passed by Foyt and left in the dust. At Talladega on May 7, Foyt ran all 188 laps and this time stayed out of trouble with NASCAR.

It was a relief to get the races behind him so he could focus on Indianapolis. He entered five cars in the race, including two new Lolas. He balked at Chevrolet's reported million-dollar price tag to supply his team with engines and instead went with an updated—but still less powerful—version of the Cosworth. For a change, his team was ready to go when the track opened, and he had a new philosophy on running practice laps.[6]

"You've got to be like Penske. You've got to be ready when you get there and get out there on Monday and run it every day. That's the way to win."[7]

For the first time in years, he ran more than 250 miles in practice and focused on getting his primary car ready for the race. He qualified tenth at a little over 217 mph, his fastest qualifying speed ever, but it could have been better.

"I fell asleep and had forgotten I'd taken the green," he said of his first lap at 215 mph. It was a startling admission. "Jack (Starne) said, 'Don't forget dammit, the second time around we're on it.' I guess I didn't go far enough in school to count."[8]

He continued to work on race setup and when satisfied, let Rocky Moran, who'd come up with some sponsorship dollars, practice one of the cars. First, he put up a partition in the garage to separate the No. 14 from the others, wanting his crew to work only on his car. And he exuded a level of confidence not seen in several years.

"I think our chances are real good. Sure, I'm almost seven miles per hour off the pole, but that doesn't mean much in a 200-lap race. Oh, I can't do some things I could twenty-five years ago, but I think the older, experienced guys have an edge. You have to keep your nose clean and run a good, consistent pace all day."[9]

One car owner who agreed with Foyt was Roger Penske.

"Guys like Foyt and Big Al (Unser), with their experience, are going to be tough to beat in the right cars," Penske said. "I don't know when they decide not to run, I guess it's when they lose the urge to compete. But in this type of racing—a long race on an oval track—guys like Foyt and Al don't need to stop."[10]

Moran qualified despite blowing an engine as he approached the finish line, and Foyt offered a car to George Snider. After a few practice laps, Snider went looking for Starne.

"That damn thing wouldn't run over about five laps," Snider said after testing a car. "I figured, I'm tired of this. I'm taking up somebody else's spot that maybe could do some good. So I decided I was just gonna quit. I walked over to Little Jack and asked, how do I quit? He said, 'I guess you just say you quit.' I told him, 'Okay, I quit.' And that was it. Foyt never said nothing."[11]

Snider drove his and Foyt's Silver Crown cars for the next ten years, winning several major events and recording numerous top-five finishes. After finishing second at his home track, the California State Fairgrounds, in late 1998, he decided to retire as a driver at age fifty-seven. He would continue as a car owner and to work on projects for Foyt in the years ahead.

With Snider stepping away, Foyt decided to run just two cars in the race. That is until Johnny Rutherford was bumped from the race late in the final day of qualifying.

After a month of struggling to make his twenty-fifth 500, second only to Foyt's thirty-two starts, Rutherford seemed destined not to make the race. That's when Foyt stepped forward, as he'd done five years earlier, and offered Rutherford a car to make another attempt.

With just ninety seconds remaining on the qualifying clock, Rutherford took to the track and ran a warmup lap at 217 mph, easily fast enough to make the field. Shortly after taking the green flag, however, the engine began to smoke and then quit.[12]

"Words can't describe my disappointment," Rutherford said back in Foyt's garage, where A.J. apologized for the blown engine. "This is the biggest disappointment of my career."[13]

Although he'd make several more attempts to qualify for the 500 in the years ahead, he'd run his last race at the Speedway.

In the race, Foyt finished first in class, his fifth place highest among Cosworth-powered cars and his best finish since 1979. Emerson Fittipaldi won after making contact with Al Unser Jr. two laps from the finish, putting Little Al into the wall and Fittipaldi in Victory Lane.

"It was one of those years where they [Chevrolet-powered cars] were outrunnin' us," Foyt would say. "There wasn't nothin' I could do about it. They had the Ilmor Chevrolet. There was no way you was goin' to run with that."[14]

"I finished fifth, you can't brag about that. God willing, if I'm not crippled or hurt, I'll be back next year. I think getting back into the race shop has made a big difference."[15]

Any hopes that the Indy result indicated Foyt had turned things around were soon dashed. He failed to finish a week later at Milwaukee, then failed to qualify for the June 18 race on the street course in downtown Detroit—the day after being inducted into the nearby Motor Sports Hall of Fame. He was added to the back of the field as a promoter's option but at first tried to turn it down, saying Michigan driver Scott Brayton was more deserving.

"I don't feel like taking a spot if I'm not competitive," he said. A new fuel injection system was causing problems and had caught fire at one point, burning Starne's hands. "I'm not the type to race and not compete. I don't want to start just because I'm A.J. Foyt. It's embarrassing for the crew, it's embarrassing for me." [16]

He eventually relented and agreed to start, convinced by promoters he'd been a big a part of the prerace publicity and that many fans were turning out to see him.

"I'll do what I can," he said, "but you can't carry these cars." He lasted just ten laps before stopping, saying the Cosworth engine was overheating. He seemed to make the fans happy, however, as he stayed to sign autographs and pose for pictures for those near his pit.

A week later in Portland, he again failed to qualify and this time was successful in turning down the promoter's option, saying the fuel system "runs half a lap and just quits. I'm very sorry to have to withdraw but I'm not going to race if I can't be competitive."[17]

He decided to skip the next race at the Cleveland airport, running in the Firecracker 400 and a couple of stock car exhibition events instead. At Daytona, he was running well when two cars spun in front of him, and his Oldsmobile plowed into them, destroying the front of his car.

The exhibition races often featured other UST-sponsored NASCAR stars, including Harry Gant. It typically involved showing up midweek at a local short track, attending autograph and "meet and greet" sessions, and driving a car belonging to one of the track regulars. Early in his career it would have been the last thing Foyt wanted to do, but now he seemed to enjoy it.

"I haven't raced on short tracks like this since probably the mid-70s down in New Zealand," he said before one event in Columbus, Ohio, with a record crowd of about 10,000 fans packing the grandstands. "Harry was tellin' me how much fun this was and now that I'm here, I believe him.[18]

"It gives some people who've been your fans for years a chance to meet you. That don't happen at Indianapolis or Daytona. As for me, let's face it, it's fun. I just enjoy racing and in this kinda situation, you don't have that pressure. No politics, just plain old racing. But I've got to get back to work on my Indy car."

After the brief respite, he was back for the July 16 race at the Meadowlands, but the relaxed attitude was gone. Arriving at the track without his credentials, he roughly pushed aside a track security guard, Myron Hackett, a non–race fan who didn't recognize the driver. Arriving at his transporter, he warned Fornoro and Starne to be on the lookout for cops.

Foyt had already started the first practice session when a couple of New Jersey state troopers showed up at the team's trailer. Practice over, they escorted him to the Meadowlands State Police office, where he was charged with "simple assault." Foyt eventually went back to practice, and the state police tried to downplay the incident.

"It was a minor thing, just a misunderstanding," said a police spokesperson. "The young man decided he wanted to file simple assault charges." According to the official police report, "Mr. Hackett challenged Mr. Foyt, who attempted to get past. The guard told him to use another gate, at which time Mr. Hackett was grabbed by Mr. Foyt, pushed against the fence, and struck in the face."[19]

One local newspaper report cited an unnamed member of Foyt's crew saying the pair also were "exchanging racial insults."[20]

While an August court date was scheduled, Foyt said he'd be away racing and wouldn't be able to attend. It didn't become an issue when the charges were later dropped. He returned to practice but failed to qualify and was one of four drivers accepting the promoter's option to start, although he failed to finish.

The ongoing question at each race was becoming who would qualify last, Foyt or Guido Daccò, the Italian sports car driver in his first season of Indy car racing and renting a car from Dale Coyne. At Toronto a week later, the answer was Foyt, who failed to post a qualifying speed but was again added as a promoter's option. Starting twenty-eighth and last, he managed to finish the race in seventeenth—last among those still running—and twelve laps behind winner Michael Andretti.

The team was hopeful a return to an oval track for the August 6 Michigan 500 would turn things around, and the fuel injection problem at least seemed to be solved. Other issues cropped up in qualifying and the race, however, and although Foyt briefly challenged for the lead, he was out just past the halfway point. Before the race he'd said, "I could get better mechanics at a Shell station," and when *ABC Sports* pit reporter Brian Hammons tried to compliment him on a "tremendous run," Foyt went off.[21]

"Well actually, all I've had is mechanical troubles," he said. "The guys ain't got their heads together. They just got their heads up their ass. The car was screwed up from the third lap on." He recited a litany of errors made by the crew and started to turn away in frustration, saying, "They're just screwed up, that's all, I need to make a change."

On the ABC broadcast, Sam Posey cited the need "for a terrific team behind you," and while Foyt had some good people—especially Starne—he lacked "the total team." Paul Page thought the team was okay and said, "If A.J. Foyt would use that team and test a little bit more and spend more time in practice, he'd be up running with the likes of Rick Mears any day."[22]

Posey and Page had a point. Foyt ran a skeleton operation compared with the teams of Penske, Newman-Haas, Patrick, and others. The lack of a Chevrolet engine hurt, but he'd yet to embrace the need for engineers and other specialists. He was well behind the curve when it came to chassis setup—especially on road and street courses. And while other teams had been using professional pit crews for several years, Foyt often relied on pick-up crew members at the races.

Dick Mittman, the *Indianapolis News* reporter who'd been covering Foyt in a favorable light for parts of three decades, pointed out the obvious:

> A combination of age and uncompetitive equipment have made Foyt a back marker . . . You wonder what he's trying to prove.[23]
>
> His crew appears to have walked right in from some dirt track in the Midwest. There is no engineer like the top teams have today, and A.J. is the only driver who still climbs out of his car to work on it.
>
> Indy-car racing today is a sophisticated sport that looks for state-of-the-art technology to propel it into the 1990s. Today it's computers and telemetry systems that prepare the cars for the varying courses of CART. No longer will a ball-peen hammer against a balky suspension work.

While Foyt admitted, "It is my fault that I've got this far down, but I lost a lot of interest in it the last four or five years." He'd always been willing to share information about his car or a track when asked, and while the NASCAR teams had been helpful recently, the Indy car garage wasn't as open with its secrets—and Foyt was too proud to ask. [24]

"These guys aren't volunteering to come over and say, 'A.J., put this spring on,' or 'Here's the gear ratios you gotta run.' Uh-uh. I mean they don't feel *that* safe about me."

The Michigan debacle set off a string of five straight DNFs for Foyt on the Indy car circuit, including Road America, where he qualified last, an incredible thirty-two mph slower than the pole sitter.

He decided to go to Charlotte for the fall NASCAR event, always one of his favorite races and one of the few he hadn't won. He'd made a decent run at

Talladega, and Tracy Leslie, the defending ARCA champion and up-and-coming NASCAR rookie, had run the car in several races, mainly so the crew could try and stay abreast of the advancements other teams were making.

He arrived early at the track, and practice had just started on Tuesday, October 3, when his car veered into the fourth turn wall and hit it head on at an estimated 170 mph, raising the rear wheels off the ground. The car ricocheted about 300 yards down the track before coming to a rest at the entrance of pit road, the front end completely destroyed. Goodyear engineers later identified a flat right-rear tire as the cause of the accident.

Foyt was unconscious and slumped in his seat when the first emergency workers arrived and established he was breathing. It took about ten minutes to stabilize his head and neck and remove him from the car. There was a ten-inch crack down the front of his helmet, and the steering wheel was bent over.

It wasn't until medics rolled the gurney into the infield care center that Foyt began to come around, asking what happened. A helicopter was brought in to airlift him to Charlotte Memorial Hospital, where he was initially listed in serious condition. After X-rays turned out negative, and there were no signs of life-threatening injuries, he was shifted to fair and stable condition, although he remained in the intensive care unit.

Charlotte officials initially clung to the hope that Foyt—who still helped sell tickets—would be able to compete in the race, and the team made plans to ready a backup car. Others weren't so confident, including Charlotte promoter and longtime Foyt friend Humpy Wheeler.

Knowing Foyt's propensity for leaving a hospital before being released by doctors and concerned about the severity of the crash, Wheeler took Foyt's clothing, money, and other valuables and locked them in A.J.'s rental car in the hospital parking lot.

"You left me naked and broke," Foyt complained to Wheeler later.[25]

The next morning after checking with Foyt, Powell decided against bringing a backup car to the track.

"I think A.J. is going to be OK, but he's really hurting right now," Powell said. "He's got lots of bruises about the upper chest and a severe neck bruise. There's a lot of neck pain and he has a severe headache. A.J. is wanting out of the hospital, of course, but the doctor said it would be better to keep him at least another day in case he got a blood clot."

On Thursday, Foyt was moved to a regular hospital room and agreed to do a conference call with reporters at the track. Unsure what happened, he said he still wanted to race.

"It's just a little ol' bump," he said. "If they'll have a special session, I'll try to qualify tomorrow." It was a proposition no one took seriously, and then reality set in.[26]

"It's the first time I've had an accident where I don't remember what happened," he said. "Whatever I hit, I hit real hard. I would probably be ready today if I wanted to push myself. I feel pretty rough right now though, and my neck is pretty sore. I guess what made me sicker than anything is the car was really working good. I felt like I had a chance of qualifying good and running good."[27]

When released on Friday, he flew home, never to race at Charlotte again.

Back in Houston, he went to the hospital complaining of chest pains and a severe headache. It only took a couple of minutes for the doctor to realize Foyt was still in the throes of a severe concussion and ordered him to bed, which sidelined him for the year's Indy car finale at Laguna Seca. He would also require surgery to repair nerve damage on the left side of his face. He still fielded a car for Moran at Laguna, who qualified last and didn't start the race because of engine problems.

Foyt was cleared to run one race before the end of the year, a NASCAR event at Atlanta where he led a few laps but dropped out early. Despite missing several races with injuries, he'd competed in more events (including IROC) than he had in any of the past eight years. Of the non-IROC events, he had often failed to qualify and been added as a promoter's option and had failed to finish two-thirds of the races he started.

Under the headline "Foyt Losing Races, Touch with Reality," Robin Miller wrote in the *Indianapolis Star* that A.J. had "gone from one of the most respected race drivers to an outright embarrassment. He goes through mechanics like Hardee's goes through summer help. He doesn't have a test program or an engineer.[28]

"In his heyday, there wasn't anything he couldn't—or wouldn't—do. He ran his team with an iron fist and also ran off some good help with his tantrums. None of today's good mechanics want any part [of] the hostility in Houston. Testing is a must, but A.J. won't make the time."

Miller didn't question Foyt's desire to race or even his ability and suggested A.J. take his Copenhagen dollars to another team and concentrate on driving.

"I remember what a great racer Foyt used to be and it's sad to see what he's become. But all the yellin' and cussin' and excuses don't cover up the fact A.J. Foyt isn't racing anymore. He's just spinning his wheels."

Although Foyt admitted, "I could be getting pretty near the end of my career," he also said he had a new goal—to race in his fifth decade—and that he planned to race several NASCAR events and run the full CART season in 1990. He'd never been interested in driving an Indy car for anyone else and wasn't about to start now.

"A lot of people said, 'Well, if you would have drove for so-and-so, you would have won a lot more,'" Foyt said. "If you'd have driven for Roger Penske and not run your own team, you would have won so many more times.' Well, that could be true. But then again, Mario Andretti ain't no slouch as a race driver. He drove for Roger Penske and couldn't do nothing. And he's back running on his own."[29]

"I'll never have another year like I've had this year, I assure you that," he promised. "Even if I have to do everything myself."

Foyt also was becoming an increasingly vocal leader of the smaller teams and have-nots. The rift had continued to grow between the large and small teams over rising costs, the availability of the Lola chassis, and the now-dominant Chevrolet engine. A Lola minus the engine—available only through CART board member Carl Haas—cost $235,000 for a road course version and $255,000 for a speedway car. The Chevrolet engine, developed by Penske's team with Ilmor, was unavailable to many at any price. A.J. had plenty to say about the situation:

> Roger Penske, if he wants to run five cars, he can run five Chevrolets. That's his prerogative. It's the same thing with Carl Haas and Rick Galles. They are all on the board of CART. If they decided they want to run another team, they get another Chevrolet. Meanwhile, people who have been waiting in line for a Chevrolet can't get them because they say they can't build any more. Even though we have the money, we can't get the parts. Why should the board of directors get 'em when no one else can? I think that's a bad move, and it's gonna hurt 'em in the long run.[30]
>
> CART was formed because everybody was hollerin' about what USAC was doing. Well CART is just as bad as USAC was—if not worse. I don't think a man running a race car team or an owner should be on the board of directors. I think it's wrong. They make the rules their way. I could understand if a man put his money up to develop the Chevrolet engine, let him run one car but don't let him run two or three other cars.
>
> It's pretty hard to see a sponsor. He asks you what kind of motor you've got and you tell him you have a Cosworth. Why should they sponsor you when you can't run better than seventh or eighth. The way it is right now, if there are seven Chevrolets, you're running for eighth place, unless they break. They should give Cosworth more boost and hold the Chevrolet down: it's just no contest.

By the end of 1989, a series of events unfolded that would have long-lasting impacts on Foyt's future as a driver and car owner and the future of Indy car racing in general.

The revolt by the smaller team owners and the feelings by most that CART Chairman John Frasco and President John Caponigro had overstepped their bounds led to first Frasco and then Caponigro being forced out of their roles. A new board of directors formed, this time with each of the twenty-four regular Indy car teams represented.

In the middle of the CART palace coups came the death of Joe Cloutier, Tony Hulman's longtime right-hand man, who'd been running the Speedway since Hulman's death in 1977. Caught in the middle of the battles between USAC and CART, Cloutier had for the most part been able to maintain an uneasy truce with the two organizations by talking softly and carrying a big stick—the power of the Speedway.

At eighty-one, Cloutier had worked long past the normal age of retirement because of his concerns about who would replace him. Most thought it would be either Tony's daughter, Mari Hulman George, or her son and Tony's grandson, thirty-year-old Tony George. He'd spent the past year racing for Foyt's ARS team without much success and was the Hulman family's only male heir.

"It's no secret that Cloutier continued to 'mind the store' the past few years because he didn't think Mari or Tony was ready to assume control," Miller wrote. "And even if they have learned the ropes of the family business, neither seems to possess the leadership qualities this job demands."[31]

CHAPTER 14

THE ROAD TO ELKHART LAKE

1990

The New Year brought good news for A.J. Foyt Enterprises. Moving quickly to keep the peace in CART's ranks, Carl Haas said because of "A.J.'s standing in the sport," he would sublease Chevrolet engines to Foyt if a deal couldn't be reached with Chevrolet. As it turned out, Haas didn't have to dip into his supply because Chevrolet agreed to boost production instead.[1]

"The Chevrolet people asked me what I thought and I told them it would be the greatest thing because there's only one A.J. Foyt," said Franz Weis, who'd worked for Foyt in the past and was now Chevy's chief engine builder. "I was happy as hell because I knew the guy has it in him."

Foyt was one of ten teams slated to get a Chevrolet engine for 1990. Another went to the new team of Chip Ganassi, who had purchased Pat Patrick's equipment and brought in driver Eddie Cheever from Formula One.

"I was trying to get the Chevy for the last two or three years," Foyt said. "I'm just glad they accepted our team 'cause if you look at our track record, it's been very bad. I'm the first to admit it. I think sometimes you have to have your butt beat very bad to realize that you're not on top no more, you're on the bottom. Now we can't use the excuse that we don't have the power, 'cause we will have the power with the Chevy engine."[2]

The Ilmor came with a catch. In order to protect the company's technology, engines were leased to a team, and only an Ilmor-supplied engineer was supposed to work on the powerplant. But Foyt seemed willing to adjust to the new realities.

Saying, "I've reorganized my whole team," Foyt hired longtime family friend Phil Casey to work alongside Craig Baranouski and allow Jack Starne to once again spend more time at home.[3]

◀ Receiving an honorary degree from Rose-Hulman Institute. *David Nearpass*

"I've never been too good to change," Foyt said. "With all this technology, no one man can do it anymore. Those days are gone. Sometimes you've got to know how to lose before you can know how to win again and I think I do. I've embarrassed myself and I'm not going to be embarrassed this year."[4]

Phil Casey

Four years younger than A.J., Casey had been a family friend since the early 1960s. Growing up in the Fresno, California, area, he tried driving before going to work for George Snider as a mechanic. He'd worked for car builder Fred Gerhardt and later served as crew chief for a number of drivers, including Parnelli Jones, Al Unser, Johnny Rutherford, and Danny Ongais. His cars had won nine Indy car races, and he'd eventually be inducted into the Auto Racing Hall of Fame. Unser called him "one of the best chief mechanics I ever had."[5]

He'd become close to Tony Foyt early in his career and occasionally worked on A.J.'s race day pit crew. "His dad and I got along really well," Casy said. "He treated me like a son. When we needed something, he was always there. He did favors for me all the time."[6]

The friendship also gave Casey a front-row seat to view Foyt's often stormy relationship with Tony, George Bignotti, Johnnie Pouelsen, and Starne over the years. "I'd seen him get mad and knew that at times he was hard to get along with. He'd get after his crews and stuff."

As a result, Casey had been reluctant to work for Foyt and risk their friendship. That was until A.J. called in early 1990 and asked him to come to Houston.

"He said he wanted me to come and work for him, and I said only if we could get along—not if we're gonna fight. I said, 'We've been good friends for too many years.' He said, 'No problem,' and never once did we have a disagreement in the time we worked together."

Casey also remembered A.J. had been there when he needed help the most:

> It was at Phoenix in 1971. Roger McCluskey blew an engine, and there was a fire. Burned all the clothes off me. I was at Good Samaritan Hospital. You really don't know how bad you are for a few days and holy cow, I was really worried.
>
> Then here comes A.J. and Donnie Allison in the door. They'd been to L.A. and stopped on the way back to see me. He said I'd be okay. I'll always remember that. I had a lot of respect for him doing that, going out of his way to visit me at the hospital and reassure me.

Turning down a ride in the 24 Hours of Daytona, Foyt showed up at the Copper World Classic at Phoenix International Raceway for the second straight year to start the season. He was still recovering from surgery to repair nerve damage around his eyes suffered in the Charlotte crash and looked like he'd just gone a round with Muhammad Ali. He sported two black eyes, and his face was so swollen he had to switch to a larger helmet.

Looking to "get the season off to a good start and get the adrenalin running," he qualified eighth. When he was involved in a first-lap accident and dropped to the rear of the thirty-two-car field, it turned out to be just what the doctor ordered as he passed twenty-nine cars on his way to a fourth-place finish.[7]

After finishing sixth in his Daytona 500 qualifying race, he lasted until just past the halfway point in the main event before parking his car with an excuse no one had heard before: The new helmet had gotten him drunk.

"I'm so dizzy, I can't see," he said. "The fumes of the glue in the helmet got me drunk. I just got so dizzy I thought I better park it before I hurt myself or anybody else. I don't know how anybody can take drugs and drive."[8]

It didn't help the team when the new Lola chassis arrived too late for testing prior to the opening Indy car race of the year at Phoenix. The car had been delayed while Lola added an inch and a half more width in the interior to accommodate Foyt.

Simply qualifying at Phoenix and two weeks later at Long Beach were considered improvements compared to the previous year. He dropped out early in both races, but as the team headed to Indianapolis there was a feeling of confidence not yet justified by its on-track performance.

"We were passing people on the outside again," he said after Phoenix. "It's been a long time since I've felt this good.[9]

"For having a new car and new motor and then to unload and go racing—I'd like to see other teams do that. No one volunteered us a bunch of information. We've had to take our stabs in the dark and I think we've held our own."[10]

He skipped the May NASCAR race at Talladega to focus on Indianapolis but was still well behind the fastest Chevy-powered cars as qualifying approached. He drew a late qualifying slot, and—when rain played havoc with the first two days of action—saw his attempt delayed by a week. The added practice helped improve his times, but the weather didn't, changing from cool and still to hot and windy as his appointed run approached. A number of drivers had already turned in much slower times, including Al Unser Jr., who'd been among the fastest all month.

As Foyt's Lola moved closer to the head of the qualifying line, he went to work on his car, changing the front wings and removing the wicker bill—the small, upturned strip of metal at the back of the rear wing. The moves would increase straight line speed but make the car more difficult to drive in the turns.

"My crew looked at me like, 'What the hell are you doin?' I know they thought I was crazy. But we weren't working well so I said, 'What the hell.'"[11]

The crew weren't the only ones questioning Foyt's sanity. In line behind him was Cheever, a rookie at Indy but ten-year F1 veteran. He watched with increasing amazement as Foyt appeared to change the entire setup of his car. In Europe, mechanics didn't let drivers touch the machines.

Cheever was leery of approaching Foyt, having asked for some advice early in the month only to be told, "Go fast, stay off the walls and keep turning left." Curiosity finally got the best of him, and he asked Foyt if he was pulling the car out of the qualifying line to test the new setup. Foyt shook his head no. "You mean you changed all that and haven't even tried it?" Cheever asked. Foyt said only that he was going to "roll the dice."[12]

Although admittedly all over the track, Foyt ran his fastest laps ever at the Speedway, one at more than 221 miles per hour for a four-lap average over 220 mph, eighth fastest overall.

"The old man didn't want to let those Chevrolet people down," Foyt said, adding, "I'm disappointed with this run. I expected to start on the front row. Don't get me wrong, I'm happy where I'm at, but I am disappointed in not having run faster than we did."[13]

The performance was not lost on Robin Miller, who'd been critical of Foyt only a few months earlier:

> With the wind blowing and the track changing, the oldest race driver at the Indianapolis Motor Speedway showed the young generation a glimpse of his glorious past. A.J. Foyt, who's gone from the man to beat to a beaten man during the past decade, was back in familiar territory Saturday—up front. [He] put on a classic display of good ol' American, oval-track, seat-of-the-pants ingenuity.[14]
>
> I don't care if you like him or not, what A.J. Foyt did Saturday was one of those rare, unpredictable moments where a real race driver can still make a difference.

Jim Murray, the Pulitzer Prize–winning *Los Angeles Times* sports columnist who called Foyt "the greatest in the world at what he does" following his Indianapolis win in 1977, somehow upped the ante. Murray wrote,

> One thing hasn't changed at Indy in all these years—the driver in car No. 14, the honorable Anthony Joseph Foyt Jr., the terrible Texan. Technology has improved a lot of things at the Speedway, but they haven't figured a way to improve on A.J. Foyt. He's still the same cantankerous, get-out-of-my-way, lead-footed guy he was 32 years ago.[15]
>
> Foyt is driving an automobile through traffic on the most dangerous race course in the world at speeds up to 240 mph and he's on his way to being a great-grandfather. He is, by all odds, the most remarkable athlete of his time.

One person not surprised was Casey. "It was magic," he marveled. "He could get around there with his eyes closed."[16]

As race day approached, Foyt found himself back in the spotlight at Indianapolis, and at times he reveled in it. "I've always felt my good has offset the bad," he said. "I regret nothing.[17]

"Right now I'm enjoying it and still think I can hold my own under the right conditions. The Chevrolet engine gives me the best shot I've had at winning in years. This is fun again."[18]

At other times, he was uncomfortable with all the attention.

"I'm walking by Fittipaldi, who's sitting on the pole, and I never heard so many people scream for me. Here's a man who just set a new track record and they're screaming for me. That's embarrassing."

Mario Andretti, for one, thought the adulation was deserved.

"You know when he's coming into the pits," Andretti said. "The crowd really lights up when his car comes around the corner. I can't imagine the month of May without A.J. He's the most competitive racer I've ever known. Every time I hear his name, I know something exciting might happen.[19]

"Truthfully, without being corny, Foyt's tenacity and his competitive spirit overshadows everything else. He's been an inspiration to me and more often than not you use that to sometimes set your mind straight."

Scanning the starting lineup, Foyt admitted, "I'd be lucky to name probably half this field. Nowadays people just come out of nowhere and get a good ride. You hardly ever see someone pay their dues and work their way up the racing circuits anymore.[20]

"These days you got to sell, sell, sell. A young guy has to kiss ass to make it. Everything is done through promotions. Hell, promoting, that's what's screwing up the whole world. That, and lawyers."[21]

The day before the Indianapolis 500 found Foyt in Terre Haute at the Rose-Hulman Institute of Technology with his thirteen-year-old son, Larry. A.J. attended graduation ceremonies and received an honorary degree—doctor of technology. He was recognized for his self-taught engineering skills and as someone who "makes your career an example for all those who work to find innovative technical solutions." The irony wasn't lost on the high school dropout, who said, "Daddy would be turning over in his grave seeing me here."[22]

A.J.'s ability to find an innovative solution was on full display later when the helicopter that brought him to the campus and was supposed to take him back to the Speedway wouldn't start. Declining a police escort for the hour-long car ride back to the track, he stripped off his suit coat and tie and—surrounded by engineering professors and graduates—went to work in the engine compartment, eventually jury-rigging a way to jump start the whirlybird.

Despite the buildup, there was no magic for Foyt on race day. Saying, "I ran as hard as I could," he never challenged for the lead and eventually finished sixth, six laps behind winner Arie Luyendyk.

Foyt had his hands full throughout as the car bottomed out in the first and third turns with a full fuel load affecting its handling. When his shoulder harness somehow became unhooked during a pit stop, he ran the next segment holding the belts with his left hand to keep them from flapping in the wind, while steering with his right and reconnecting the belts on the next stop. He was also forced to take evasive action to avoid Danny Sullivan, who bounced off the wall while running in front of him.

Despite the problems, Foyt said, "We're not looking for excuses. I felt I drove as hard as was safe. We still might come back and look for number five. We haven't given up yet."[23]

While Jim Gilmore suggested Foyt might want to take some time off after Indianapolis, the team was at Milwaukee a week later and running again at the finish, this time in ninth. He struggled in qualifying for the June 17 street race in downtown Detroit but was moving up when he glanced off a wall, ending his day early.

"Everything was going so good," he said. "It was all my fault. It was stupid and ignorant on my part. I just drove the son of a bitch in there myself. I sideswiped the barrier and that bent the right-front arm of my suspension."[24]

Detroit started a string of five straight road course events, four of them on temporary circuits—never Foyt's favorite. He was again the only driver to undertake the Cleveland/Daytona back-to-back races over the Fourth of July weekend and the oldest driver in each. NASCAR's Richard Petty compared him to Bo Jackson, who was taking the baseball and football worlds by storm at the time.

"There's very few people that are that versatile," Petty said. "There might be a lot more who could do both, but they don't want to take a chance on messing up where they're already doing a good job. Foyt came along at a time when there wasn't all these fancy computers. It was just seat-of-the-britches running, working on cars and driving them too. From a professional standpoint, he'd be better off if he picked one (Indy car or stock car) and stayed with it. But if A.J. had to make a choice, I don't think he'd enjoy it as much."[25]

Foyt agreed:

> As long as I race, I'm going to race everything, because I've done it all my life. I'm not going to pick one car unless I feel I've lost the urge to win. Then I might do something like that. But until I lose wanting to win in both types, I'm going to continue. Through the years, a lot of people have said, "He's gone too far; he's just trying to live on his name." I'm not trying to live on my name. Hell, I'm not ashamed of anything, even if I don't win another race.
>
> I'll agree I'm at the end of my limit—we all know that. But I've still got something to prove to myself and to the world. If I can do it, fine. If I can't, I won't be too proud to step down.

After qualifying at Daytona, Foyt headed back to Cleveland, where he qualified twenty-first after spinning and hitting a tire barrier. While he was in Cleveland, Dale Earnhardt again agreed to take the No. 14 car out for a few laps in the final practice, but things didn't go well. Earnhardt was running in a tight pack of cars when the oil seal on the Oldsmobile came loose, touching off an accident that forced six drivers, including Foyt, into backup machines.

Starting in the rear at Daytona, Foyt was caught up in a first-lap accident that involved half the field and knocked him, Petty, and twelve other drivers out of the race. Returning to Cleveland, he drove through the field to finish seventh and a week later went from seventeen to fifth at the Meadowlands. It was his best finish ever on a temporary circuit and his best road course finish since winning at Silverstone in 1981. He was downright giddy afterward.

"I guess the old man isn't as bad as some think," he said. "On these type of courses you have to play a waiting game, take care of the equipment, and when you pass make sure it's a clean pass."[26]

The next stop was another temporary circuit, this time in Toronto. After qualifying twenty-third, he ran afoul of officials, who wanted to inspect his car. Typically, officials took the first couple of qualifiers and another vehicle selected at random draw to be checked.

"It seemed like every time we qualified, they'd take our car to tech and try and find something wrong," Casey recalled. "It wasn't like we were setting quick time. With his arm and all, it was kind of hard for A.J. to shift. At Toronto, Foyt said, 'Don't take it to inspection. Just take it to the trailer.'"[27]

At the trailer, officials said they spotted a crew member tampering with the pop-off valve and confronted the mechanic, but that turned into a shoving match. Foyt was soon in the middle of it, and when he refused again to present his car for inspection, he was disqualified.

"A.J. called their bluff and said we were going home—to load up the car," Casey recalled. "All of a sudden, they got real nice and put us back in the race."

Foyt was added to the field by the Toronto promoter and started twenty-eighth and last—then passed more cars than anyone else and finished sixteenth. But A.J. clashed again with CART officials nearly two weeks later before qualifying for the August 5 Michigan 500. Forced to change an engine, the team was late getting in the qualifying line, and officials said Foyt had missed his turn. He again ordered the car to be loaded on the transporter, and again CART officials relented.

"They kind of picked on A.J.," Casey would say. "He was real outspoken about CART and some of the things going on, and they used that against us. Some [officials] had a grudge against him. Most of the owners had a lot of respect for Foyt. Even though he hollered at them and gave them a hard time, they still respected him for all that he'd done."

Following a sixth-place finish at Michigan, Foyt finished tenth in a new street race in Denver and then went to yet another new temporary circuit in Vancouver, Canada, where things boiled over between Foyt and CART officials.

After qualifying twentieth, he was up to eighth just a third of the way through the race when he was forced to a stop because another car crashed and blocked the track. While the rest of the field was diverted down an escape road, Foyt sat and fumed as he fell several laps behind. He still finished thirteenth but was further upset when CART officials refused to hear his protest afterward.

He was still hot two weeks later at Mid-Ohio, where he finished fifteenth and was running at the end in his ninth consecutive Indy car race. He vowed he wouldn't be back if CART didn't "change the people who run the races." If not, "I'll drive one race," he said of the Indianapolis 500, "and go NASCAR." He also ripped into CART's move toward street circuits, noting a course worker had been killed at Vancouver at the same corner where he'd been stopped. "Temporary courses are fine, but the first time they kill a bunch of people that will be the end of it. They may be more difficult, but they're Mickey Mouse."[28]

Despite his threats and growing frustration with CART officials, Foyt decided to go ahead with plans to enter the next race at Road America in Elkhart Lake, Wisconsin. Not only was the team finishing races, they were eleventh in the season-long point standings—his best performance in more than ten years. A new 1991 Lola was already on order for the coming season, and the team was planning an off-season testing program for the first time in years.

41
Copenhagen
Copenhage

CHAPTER 15

ROAD AMERICA

1990

Elkhart Lake, Wisconsin, September 24, 1990

At more than four miles long, with fourteen turns and extensive elevation changes, Road America was the longest, fastest, and perhaps most challenging road course in the country. The front straight alone was nearly a mile long—4,440 feet—and featured a steep climb from Turn Fourteen before peaking near the start/finish line and rushing downhill into Turn One. The course put a premium on horsepower—and brakes. Many drivers considered it among their favorite tracks.

Foyt, who was making only his third start at the circuit, qualified twentieth while complaining about the car's brakes during practice. He was still complaining before the start of the race as the drivers gathered for introductions, where he struck up a conversation with pole sitter Danny Sullivan.

"I remember talking with him on the grid before the start," Sullivan recalled years later. "He was saying he'd been having brake problems all weekend. I thought then, *This is the worst track in the world to have a brake issue. If you don't have it sorted out, this isn't the place to go.* But I had my game face on, and they called us to our cars, and we never finished the conversation."[1]

For the first twenty-five laps, Foyt battled Dominic Dobson for position as they moved up through the field. They'd started the race next to each other, Dobson qualifying nineteenth. Now Foyt held a slight lead as the two cars fought over fourteenth approaching the first turn, a tight right-hander where the machines slowed from nearly 200 miles per hour to just sixty.

Up ahead, contending for the lead of the race and the CART series national championship, were Michael Andretti and Al Unser Jr., the sons of two of Foyt's

◀ On the road to Road America. *Dan Boyd*

contemporaries from the 1960s. Neither had been born when A.J. won his first Indianapolis 500 in 1961.

Dobson, twenty-two years younger than Foyt, had been trying to break into Indy car racing with minimal success. He'd been doing better in sports cars, finishing second in the 12 Hours of Sebring earlier in the year.

He could be forgiven for wondering why Foyt was still racing. The older driver had accomplished everything the sport had to offer, but it had been more than nine years since Foyt's last Indy car win. The only record he'd set recently was—at fifty-five—becoming the oldest driver ever to start the Indy 500.

Dobson had been trying to get around Foyt for several laps, creeping alongside the veteran's car on the long straight but unable to complete the pass. Now he was on the inside as they went by the exit from pit road, the perfect spot for passing as the cars went into the first turn.

Both cars were Lolas, jet black and hard to tell apart as they flashed past, differentiated only by their sponsor logos and the driver helmets. Foyt's car carried Copenhagen sponsorship on the side of his car. Dobson's hawked Texaco Havoline.

"I was trying to out-brake him, and I went as deep as I thought I could," Dobson would later recall. "I remember putting on my brakes, and he kept going. I wondered, *How the hell is he going to make this turn?* He shot across in front of me, and I saw a puff of smoke like his brakes locked up."[2]

Worried by Dobson's move, Foyt had waited a fraction of a second longer than normal to start braking. The added force he applied on the pedal momentarily locked up the front wheels and caused the tire smoke Dobson saw. The brakes locked only momentarily because the force Foyt applied pulled the *L*-shaped pedal mounting bracket from the floor of the car, eliminating any brake pressure. With no brakes, Foyt was rocketing toward the forty-five-degree right turn at about 180 mph. His first thought was similar to Dobson's.

"Ain't no way I can make this corner."[3]

His next moves were instinctive, based on four decades of experience. Trying to turn the corner at that speed would probably send the car into a barrel roll as it slid off the edge of the track and the tires caught on the turf. His only chance was to angle toward the gravel trap and hope it did its job.

The trap, at Road America an aggregate of stones, dirt, and sand—drivers sometimes called it "kitty litter"—was supposed to slow and stop a car going off course. It was designed, however, to grab a spinning car going less than one hundred mph, not one traveling in a straight line at nearly 180.[4]

As former driver and commentator Derek Daley pointed out on the *ABC Sports* broadcast of the race, "The great thing about the gravel trap is it can catch a car. Unless you're going straight into them. Then it can run right through it."[5]

The flat-bottomed Lola skipped off the gravel like a smooth stone on a glassy pond, the car's nose cone flying off at first impact. The car skipped again, launching it over the end of the trap and down a hill sloping away from the course.

"I saw him go over the side," Dobson said. "He just launched into the air. At that point, it looks like you're at the end of the universe."[6]

Foyt's car was hurtling downward toward an earthen embankment lining the outer edges of the property. Beyond the dirt wall was a stand of trees—the last line of defense before what was then County Highway 3.

"When it went off, I got airborne," Foyt recalled. He looked down on the treetops off in the distance and thought, *"Man, this ain't gonna be one of them I get out of and wave to the crowd. It's going to be rough."*[7]

The Lola hit the mound like a missile reaching its target and burst through, leaving a gaping hole in the barrier. But the mound ultimately did its job, bringing the car to a violent stop in the ravine, the front end buried in dirt.

Foyt's first concern was a fire he could smell but not see, the heat from the engine having ignited the brush. He often said fire could make a dead man walk, and he tried to push himself out of the car but couldn't budge. His feet wouldn't work. Then the pain started.

"I was in such severe pain, I didn't care about the fire," he'd say. It was more pain than he'd ever felt before.[8]

More than in 1965 when he broke his back in a stock car race at Riverside, California, and those first on the scene thought he was dead. At least then he'd been knocked unconscious. More pain than at Milwaukee in 1966 when he pushed himself out of an Indy car engulfed in flames, burning his hands so badly that "the skin slid off like chicken on a bone." And more than at Michigan in 1981, when his right arm was nearly sheared away and doctors wanted to amputate. He'd passed out then, too.[9]

It took a moment for the volunteer safety workers stationed nearby to react. They'd never seen a car reach that point before. Nobody had. One worker began frantically waving a yellow caution flag, warning the other drivers there'd been a crash and to slow down. Others ran toward the car. Several carried fire extinguisher bottles, and one went to put out the grass fire.

Initially, the workers weren't sure what car was involved but soon spotted the orange helmet—A.J. Foyt. The driver was alternately waving his arms and trying to lift himself out of the car, all the time yelling something. As they got closer, Foyt raised the visor on his helmet.

"Get me out of this goddamn car!"

Safety Two, a custom-built GMC crew-cab pickup truck loaded with emergency equipment, was parked at its normal location at the end of pit road, where vehicles merged onto the racing surface. "Pit Out" they called it. In the front passenger seat was Dr. Terry Trammell, CART's director of medical services. Alongside was the vehicle's regular driver, Dave Hollander. A third member of the team sat in the back seat and another in a jump seat in the truck's bed, alongside a fifty-gallon tank of water.

Nearby was CART's mobile hospital, a forty-by-eight-foot emergency room on wheels. It served as the command center for Dr. Stephen Olvey, the organization's medical director and Trammell's close friend. Safety One, an identical quick response vehicle, sat near the track's Turn Five, providing emergency coverage for the back portion of the long course.

It was an unusually chilly and damp morning, even for Wisconsin in late September, and Trammell wasn't feeling well. He'd made several trips for coffee and slipped on the yellow raincoat he'd just bought at L.L. Bean. Someone pointed out it didn't make much sense to put the highly flammable slicker over the fire suit all the safety workers wore, but Trammell said he didn't plan to be in any fires.

The safety team saw Foyt and Dobson go by but didn't think much about it. They knew going into the first turn at the end of Road America's long straight was the track's best place to pass, and cars often went by their position side-by-side, occasionally even three abreast.

Although it was nearly a quarter mile away, they could see the rear of the two cars approach the corner. The side of one car made the turn and disappeared from view. The other car also disappeared, but it seemed to go straight, over the horizon.

Trammell figured the car was in the gravel trap. Again, not unusual. Protocol on a road course calls for safety vehicles to hold their position until dispatched by race control. There was a chance the car rolled through the trap and returned to the track, in which case they wouldn't be needed. More likely, the car was stuck in the gravel, and a tow truck would be sent to pull it out.

Then they noticed the black smoke. Fire. Protocol or not, it was time to roll. Almost at the same moment Olvey was on the radio. He'd been watching the video broadcast of the race. "This is bad. Go!"[10]

As they got closer to the first turn, Trammell was surprised he didn't see a car in the gravel. The brush was on fire, not a car, and someone was already putting it out.

A light breeze came up and started to dissipate the smoke, and off in the distance, "way out there in the boondocks," he saw the rear of a car sticking up in the air at a weird angle. Through the smoke, he also spotted Foyt's orange helmet.[11]

Pulling up short of the trap, the crew of Safety Two ran toward the car, across the gravel, and through the remains of the brush fire. Trammell noticed the car's nose cone off to the side—not a good sign. He'd long advocated, without much success, for moving the driver's feet behind the front axle of a race car to help protect their lower extremities in a head-on crash. One concession the car designers made was for a longer nose cone, which would hopefully absorb the impact in a frontal collision. It obviously hadn't worked in this case.

When he reached the car, Trammell saw the remains of the front end buried under about a foot of dirt and what appeared to be the toe of one of Foyt's shoes. Nothing else was visible. A couple of course workers with shovels were plunging them into the dirt, trying to dig Foyt out.

"Hold on guys," Trammell shouted. "Let's find out where his legs are first."

Each member of the safety team had well-practiced duties upon reaching a crash site, and Trammell climbed on the front of the car and turned his attention to Foyt, who was in obvious pain. Hollander straddled the rear of the car and put his hands on both sides of Foyt's helmet, stabilizing his head while the doctor checked for neck or spinal injuries. It was quickly apparent Foyt's upper body wasn't the problem. Trammell started an IV, a simple saline solution, and indicated it was okay for Hollander to remove the driver's helmet. Foyt was bleeding from the chin where the helmet straps had cut into his skin due to the force of the impact.

"Goddamn it Doc, get me out of here," Foyt yelled. "Get me out of this fucking car!"

Foyt was relieved to see the doctor. It was Trammell who, as the junior member of an Indianapolis orthopedic practice, had been on call at Methodist Hospital in Indianapolis in 1981 and was credited with saving the legs of Danny Ongais following one of the most horrific crashes in Indy 500 history. And it was Trammell whom Roger Penske called to save the leg of Rick Mears following a terrible crash in Canada in 1984. The doctor had earned the respect and trust of everyone in the series and the nickname, "The Magician," for his ability to piece drivers back together.

Confident Foyt wasn't in immediate life-threatening danger, Trammell dropped to his knees and, with his hands, began dog paddling the dirt away from the exposed shoe, several other crewmembers joining in. It was slow work, and at one point—because of the unusual angles of Foyt's feet—Trammell thought one of his legs may have been severed. Yet the driver was becoming combative and boisterous as the shock of the crash wore off, and the pain spiked—an indication he wasn't losing massive amounts of blood.

"Get me out of here, Doc! Get me the fuck out of here," he kept repeating, thrashing around in the cockpit of the car. He was growing increasingly frustrated by the slow pace and abusive to those trying to help him. "Goddamn it, Doc!" he yelled. "I'll get out of the goddamn car myself."

Trammell had heard enough and told everyone to back away. "Mr. Foyt is going to get out of the car now."

Foyt put his arms outside the cockpit, his hands on the car's side pods and pushed for all he was worth. Even at fifty-five, he was perhaps the strongest driver in racing. He rose up "about two inches," according to Trammell, and dropped back in his seat. For a moment, the doctor thought he'd passed out, then the screaming started again, louder than ever.

"Alright, A.J., now we're going to do it my way," the doctor said, motioning the others back to work. He'd been in contact on CART's medical radio channel with Olvey, and now he keyed his communications headset and asked his colleague to go to their private channel.

"Steve, can you come out here?" he asked.

Trammell paused for a moment. Painkillers weren't carried on safety vehicles at the time. Doctors in the field didn't like to use them before a patient was fully examined because they could mask injuries and interfere with a person's breathing.

This was different. Well known for his ability to ignore discomfort and injuries, Foyt was in an increasing state of pain and agitation. He continued to move about in the cockpit and was in danger of hurting himself further.

Trammell keyed the headset again, requesting something he hadn't asked for in ten years of working with the CART safety team.

"And bring some morphine."[12]

Standing along the outside pit wall, across from where Safety Two was parked, Bill Luchow watched as Foyt and Dobson went past. He was part of CART's technical team and was responsible for overseeing half of pit lane and managing any situation that might come up with the teams on race day. *No way he's gonna make that turn*, he thought as Dobson slowed and Foyt kept going.[13]

In recent weeks, he'd clashed with Foyt, or—more precisely—Foyt's crew. Luchow had been the one demanding to see the team's pop-off valve after qualifying in Toronto and in the middle of the melee that followed. At six-four, 260 pounds, Luchow was one of the few guys Foyt couldn't physically intimidate.

Safety Two's rapid departure from pit road, along with the simultaneous "Yellow, Yellow, Yellow" call over Luchow's headset, confirmed a car was off the track. The black cloud of smoke was quickly turning gray, an indication the fire was already being put out. Luchow turned his attention back to pit road. It was about to get busy as cars took advantage of the caution to stop for fuel and new tires.

In the Foyt pit area, crew chief Phil Casey wasn't sure what was going on. The pit was too far away for him to see what happened in Turn One. He'd also been unable to contact his driver on the radio—not all that unusual at Road America, where the length of the track and elevation changes made communications difficult at best. But when the field came by slowly under a caution flag, and he was unable to spot the No. 14, he grew concerned. The concern heightened when the CART medical radio channel, normally accessible to the teams, went quiet—never a good sign. As Casey continued to try and contact A.J., a CART official came by. "There's been a big accident in Turn One," he said. "Looks like A.J.'s in it. It's a bad one."[14]

Jumping down from his perch in the pits, Casey set off on foot toward the first turn. He didn't get far before running into Luchow.

"A.J.'s been in an accident," Casey said. "I need to get down there."[15]

"Now, Phil, you know you can't go out on the track when there are race cars on it," Luchow said, blocking the crew chief. Casey ran back to the paddock area and, along with several crew members, piled into the Lincoln Town Car Foyt had rented for the weekend. He pulled out on pit road and floored the accelerator. No way would Luchow stop him this time.

Even after being told the wreck "was a bad one," Casey was stunned to see the car when they arrived. The workers had uncovered most of the mangled front end. He could see that the brass skid plate used to protect the bottom of the car was rolled back like the top of a can of sardines.

He spotted the pedal assembly and guessed what had happened. Lola had developed a sliding pedal designed to give way at impact so it would do less damage to a driver's feet. The Foyt team didn't think the mounting was strong enough and had strengthened the base further, although apparently not enough. Casey says he later learned there'd been a similar failure on another car.

Casey also spotted a large boulder embedded in the earthen barrier just a few feet from where their car burst through. If Foyt had hit that, he thought, they'd still be picking up the pieces.

Before the crew chief could get any closer, he was again confronted by Luchow, out of breath and sweating. He'd been ordered by race control to get Casey and his crew back to the pits and, with no transportation available, had lumbered down the track to the crash site.

"Phil, you guys have got to get out of here or it's going to cost you a lot of money," he warned.

Casey was tempted to try and push through but realized there was little he could do. The safety team was all around the car. The crew reluctantly returned to the pits and began the process of packing up their equipment.

Leading the line of race cars slowly around the track under the full course caution was Sullivan. The cars had been circulating for more than twenty minutes, and he was growing increasingly worried about the sport's icon. Sullivan would later say,

> I figured it must be pretty bad because it was taking a long time to get A.J. out of the car. Anytime it's a long process, everybody is worried because you know it's not a normal procedure. They must be cutting him out of the car or something. I was thinking, *Oh shit, the last thing we need is one of our heroes being killed or badly hurt.* It was just not good for the sport. I don't mean to be flippant, but you don't want to lose someone like that late in their career.[16]
>
> I got it about him racing at Indy. The guy was a legend, and he was still competitive. But as we drove by the crash site, I remembered having the conversation on the grid and wondering why, at that stage in your career, he was here.

Dr. Olvey had been chomping at the bit to go to the crash site before Trammell's call but knew his responsibility was to stay at the main medical unit in case of another emergency. Cars were still on the track, and although they were moving slowly behind the pace car, experience told him something could still happen requiring medical response. He also knew Trammell wouldn't request his presence and the morphine unless it was absolutely necessary.

Grabbing a vial of the pain drug and his medical kit, Olvey paused to request the track's helicopter be moved to the scene. Outside, he discovered all of the unit's emergency vehicles were gone. Spotting Jon Potter, the head of the driver's association and a friend of Foyt's, the pair commandeered a golf cart and headed off to the first turn at what seemed like an incredibly slow pace.

With virtually all of the track's safety equipment at the crash site and the helicopter on the way, it was decided to stop the race, and the red flag was displayed. The cars were directed onto pit road and stopped, the drivers climbing from the machines.

When Olvey and Potter reached the crash site, they found Foyt's car surrounded by more than thirty safety personnel and track workers, along with several photographers and a handful of spectators who'd somehow made it to the scene. As Olvey worked his way through the crowd, he had a hard time finding Trammell. He was looking for the red sleeves only the two doctors wore so they would be easily identifiable. Then he spotted Trammell, still with his yellow slicker on and working at clearing away the dirt. He'd later joke his colleague was conducting "the first archaeological dig in Indy car history." Foyt was obviously in great distress and demanding to be "knocked out."

The doctors exchanged a quick glance. Neither was licensed to practice in Wisconsin and weren't technically allowed to administer medication outside the medical center. But Olvey saw the same thing Trammell did. This was an extraordinary situation.

Olvey added morphine to the IV, and almost immediately Foyt began to calm down. He spotted Luchow among the people around the car and motioned for him to come to the rear of the vehicle.

"Hold him down," Olvey said. "Talk to him. Try and keep him still and focused." As Luchow reached down, Foyt's hands shot up and grabbed him. Now it was Luchow's turn to cry out as Foyt put a vicelike grip on his armpit.

"What the hell are they doing to my right leg?" Foyt wanted to know. "Jesus that hurts. What the hell are they doing to my leg?"

Luchow looked to the front of the car and could see no one working on the right side. All the attention seemed to be on his left leg. It wasn't long before Foyt started complaining about the pain again. He wanted to know why the doctors hadn't knocked him out and demanded more painkiller. Luchow looked at Olvey for help. The doctor shook his head no.

"I've already given him enough to stop an elephant."

"Then get a hammer," Foyt said. He was serious. "Just get a hammer and knock me out."

With most of the dirt cleared away from the front of the car and Foyt's legs secured, the Jaws of Life was brought in to cut away parts of the car not already ripped away in the crash. Trammell turned to Foyt and explained what would happen next. He was able to blank out the crowd and noise around the car.

"Regardless of what's happening around you, you're focused on a small orb around the driver," Trammell explained. "You can talk in almost a conversational tone of voice. Inside the bubble, everything's quiet. There can be a whole lot of stuff going on, but as long as it doesn't impact what you're doing with the driver, you don't even know it's happening."[17]

It would be painful, he told Foyt, but it was the only way to get him out of the car. They wedged an extraction board—a small aluminum seat designed specifically for the purpose of removing a driver—behind Foyt's back and under his butt. He was the biggest driver in the series, and the crew struggled to lift him out of the car, but given everything else that had happened, the process went relatively smoothly.

Once he was out, they moved Foyt to a backboard and then placed him on a gurney. The doctors decided there was no sense taking him back to the mobile hospital and transferred him directly to the helicopter for the sixty-mile trip to Milwaukee. The Flight For Life helicopter was better equipped to transport Foyt than the one at Michigan had been, but it was still too small for anyone else. Before taking off. Foyt grabbed Trammell.

"Doc, get my briefcase," he said. "You gotta find my briefcase and bring it to the hospital. Don't forget it. Bring my briefcase."

Potter said he'd get the doctor to the hospital and went for his vehicle. Trammell went for a change of clothes and found one of Foyt's crew to pass along the driver's odd and adamant demand for the briefcase. Then he climbed into Potter's van, and they set off for Milwaukee.

In Houston, Lucy Foyt heard the phone ring. She glanced at her watch and thought it was too early for her husband of thirty-five years to be calling.

She'd long ago stopped going to races, the two of them agreeing early on she would stay home and raise their children while he traveled the motorsports circuits. She'd still go to Indianapolis every year for the 500, but even those trips were getting shorter. At first, she'd gone for the entire month of May, leaving the kids at home to split time with their grandparents. In more recent years she'd fly in the morning of the race and depart soon after it was over.

A.J. was always good about calling home after a race to let the family know he was okay, and she always stayed close to a phone. She was getting ready to watch the race with son Larry when the phone rang. It was her nephew Tommy LaMance, who'd gone to work for A.J. and was part of the team that traveled to the races.

"We were waiting for the race to come on in Houston," Larry Foyt would say. "It was tape delayed. My mom and I were sitting there, and the phone rang and my mom was immediately upset and throwing clothes in a bag and getting ready to head for the airport. It was pretty scary."[18]

A.J. had been badly hurt in a crash, Tommy said, but was awake and being airlifted to a hospital in Milwaukee. Lucy had made the trip to Milwaukee in 1966 to help care for A.J. when he'd suffered extensive burns, and she wondered if it was the same hospital. LaMance called back and told her to stay put. The doctors said they would transfer A.J. to Indianapolis as soon as possible, so there was no sense in her coming to Milwaukee.[19]

Milwaukee Med

It's hard to imagine many places better prepared to receive Foyt that Sunday afternoon than Froedtert Hospital, part of the Milwaukee Medical Center. It was one of only two level-1 trauma centers in the state and handled hundreds of trauma arrivals each year. The other center, at the University of Wisconsin in Madison, was another twenty miles away.

On hand to meet the chopper was Dr. Charles Aprahamian, Milwaukee Med's chief of trauma and emergency surgery. At fifty-five, he'd devoted his career to emergency care and was the driving force behind the hospital's level-1 status. He'd eventually become president of the American Trauma Society and be credited with helping to define the standards of trauma care and education still followed today.[20]

Aprahamian quickly checked the driver's head, chest, upper extremities, and vital signs. All seemed in good shape. Foyt's pulse was strong, and he was alert and talking, although complaining about the pain. Aprahamian determined the driver was not in a life-threatening situation and upgraded him to satisfactory condition.

Foyt's legs and feet were another story. They would require attention and soon. That was obvious even before the X-rays, which showed a broken left tibia (the larger of two bones below the knee), a dislocated left kneecap, and a fractured left heel. His right heel was dislocated, and there was a broken bone in the foot. The X-rays also indicated a fractured vertebra already showing signs of healing. The doctor figured it was from a previous injury Foyt had apparently ignored. The technical description didn't do the injuries justice.

Next to arrive was Dr. James Stiehl, the hospital's well-known orthopedic trauma surgeon. He'd been contacted by Trammell prior to race weekend to make sure he'd be available if needed. He was on the golf course when his wife reached him and told him to get to the hospital. They were bringing in A.J. Foyt.

While growing up in the early 1960s in Champaign, Illinois, Stiehl often attended time trials for the Indianapolis 500 with his father. He'd been to the 24 Hours of Le Mans and Formula One races while studying in Europe and held Foyt in the same esteem as his favorite golfer, Arnold Palmer.

"Arnie made golf what it is in America—he popularized it," Stiehl would say. "Foyt did the same for auto racing."[21]

Stiehl had seen plenty of leg traumas but was still taken aback by Foyt's.

"There was a horrible injury to his left leg," he recalled. "Both feet were mangled—just crushed. You saw the X-rays, and it was, *Oh my god*. It was awful. I thought he might lose his foot. I didn't see how he could have those injuries and not tear the blood vessels. But his pulses were fine. It was amazing."

Both feet continued to swell grotesquely, and the doctors were concerned about compartment syndrome, where muscle swelling restricts blood flow, causing severe tissue and nerve damage. If that happened, Foyt could lose a foot or even part of his leg. They decided immediate surgery was necessary and called in the trauma center's foot specialist, Dr. Jeffrey Johnson.

Trammell soon arrived at the hospital in record time as Potter, a former Indianapolis-area sheriff, had arranged for a police escort along the way. Trammell had scrambled out of his smelly and dirty safety uniform and slipped on street clothes, hoping he looked something like a doctor.

The Wisconsin doctors agreed to overlook regulations and allow Trammell to join them in the operating room as an "observer," so he prepped for surgery. Potter went to find Foyt and was soon joined by Eddie Thrap, director of motorsports at U.S. Tobacco. Crew members, reporters, and even some fans began gathering in the waiting room.

Foyt was coherent enough to sign an array of release forms. He'd heard the doctors talking about the compound fracture of his left leg, how badly the main artery was twisted, and the possibility of amputation. He made it clear there were to be no amputations. If it came to that, he wanted it done back home in Houston—not in some hospital in Milwaukee. Ironically, both Stiehl and Johnson had done part of their medical training at the University of Texas. Thrap reinforced the point with the doctors, warning, "I'd hate to see you get your ass kicked by a one-legged man."[22]

As the nurses began to move Foyt to surgery, Thrap asked what he should tell the reporters and others in the waiting area.

"I'll be back," a defiant Foyt said. "Tell them I'll be back," After all, Foyt was the toughest, meanest, son-of-a-bitch in auto racing—and ready to prove it.[23]

Although Johnson wasn't on call that evening, he was at home when Stiehl telephoned and asked him to come to the hospital and examine an injured race car driver. He immediately recognized the name.

"Growing up in Minnesota, if you were playing football, everyone wanted to be [Vikings' quarterback] Francis Tarkenton. If we were playing a racing game, everyone wanted to be A.J. Foyt. He'd won the Indy 500. Everybody knew who he was."[24]

Foyt was already sedated when Johnson arrived and examined the driver's feet. A graduate of Duke and the medical school at Georgetown University, he'd done his orthopedic surgery residency at the Mayo Clinic in Rochester, Minnesota, and only recently moved to Milwaukee. He'd go on to become one of the top foot doctors in the country, chief of foot and ankle surgery at Washington University in St. Louis, Missouri, and president of the board of directors of the American Orthopedic Foot and Ankle Society. Johnson recalled,

> There was a serious fracture of the left heel bone. That alone can be a devastating injury. But the vascularity of the foot was good, and there appeared to be no major damage to nerves or arteries. When you have a nerve or blood vessel injury, you just don't have anything to work with. And there were no open wounds, which was good. If you get a deep wound infection, especially in the heel bone, there can be very serious complications. Obviously, he was beat up, but we had something to work with. There was nothing indicating, "Oh boy, that foot's a goner."

Johnson's real concern was the same shared by the other doctors—the potential for compartment syndrome. It wasn't an easy diagnosis. Wait too long, and severe damage could be done. On the other hand, the incisions necessary to relieve the pressure opened the door to infection.

Using an instrument that "looks like a large hypodermic needle," he conducted a pressure test, "like using an air gauge to test a tire." But the result was inconclusive. Johnson said,

> Sometimes you have to go with your gut. If you say, "Maybe he doesn't have [compartment syndrome] let's just watch him," and miss, by the time you figure it out, it can be too late. You can lose a lot of the muscles in your

> foot that turn into scar tissue, and you can lose a lot of function. We also considered what he did for a living.
>
> The key to avoiding damage from compartment swelling is to act fast. If you wait six, eight, ten hours, the damage is done. If you're going to do anything, you've got to do it early.

It was already more than six hours since the crash when Johnson went to work. Using a combination of plates, pins, and screws, Stiehl repaired the left kneecap and tibia. Johnson's job took longer. The muscles in the foot are more complicated than most, consisting of several smaller muscles rather than the single, large muscle found in the thigh or leg. It was a painstaking process taking several hours as Johnson made numerous incisions in each foot to relieve the pressure. He then applied a soft dressing to help control swelling and absorb drainage.

Convinced they'd made the right decisions, the doctors confirmed plans to return early the next morning to check on the patient. Trammell was already talking about moving Foyt to Indianapolis.

After four and a half hours of surgery, Trammell realized he was famished. He hadn't eaten anything since lunch at the track. Potter had anticipated as much and arranged a late dinner at an Italian restaurant, a local favorite of Foyt's and one they often ate at when in the area.

Trammell went to see Foyt before he left, and a nurse handed him the driver's briefcase one of the crew had brought in. Curious as to what was so important, he popped it open and was surprised to find it filled with cash. A lot of cash.

"It was like one of those scenes in a movie where they make you an offer you can't refuse," Trammell said. The first thing Foyt wanted to know when he saw the doctor wasn't about his legs or feet—he wanted to know where his briefcase was. "Right here," Trammell said, putting it down.

Foyt would later thank the doctor for "not making a withdrawal." He often took cash with him on race weekends in order to help with crew expenses and to take advantage of any opportunities where cash might help secure a better deal. He'd been planning to look at some racehorses the day after Road America.

While Trammell and Potter were having their late dinner, Foyt had another visitor—his father, Anthony Joseph "Tony" Foyt. A.J. always called him "Daddy."

"You're hurt pretty bad," Tony said. "But everything's going to be all right."[25]

A.J., his left leg hanging from a sling, his right leg in a cast from the ankle to just below the knee, was nauseous and lapsing in and out of consciousness—aftereffects of the morphine and anesthesia used during surgery. Having his daddy there proved to be a calming effect.

"It'll be all right," his daddy said again as A.J. relaxed and drifted back to sleep. It was perhaps the most comforting thing the late Tony Foyt had ever said to his son.

CHAPTER 16

I'LL BE BACK

1990

Despite A.J. Foyt's Terminator-like proclamation of "I'll be back" as he was wheeled into the operating theater at Milwaukee Med, there were many who doubted his return. Others hoped he wouldn't try.

Among the first to see Foyt Monday morning were Jim Stiehl and Jeffrey Johnson, the doctors who had worked on the driver's legs and feet the night before. Dr. Terry Trammell was already headed back to Indianapolis aboard Tony George's jet. He had a full slate of patients to see and needed to prepare for Foyt's transfer to Methodist Hospital, where additional surgeries were being planned.

"Sir, you've got some pretty bad injuries here," Stiehl recalled telling Foyt. "I think we've done a pretty good job, but I can't tell if you'll be able to race a car anymore."[1]

It was a typical doctor-to-patient comment following serious trauma surgery. They knew at the very least there was a difficult healing period ahead of Foyt, and how soon and to what extent he was able to recover would depend on the driver. The patient's response was anything but typical.

"He just gave me a real hard look and said, 'We'll see.'

"I'd never seen anything like it," Stiehl said. "He was different. He was not like a normal human being. You could see it in his eyes. This was not going to do him in."

Johnson wanted to inspect the incisions and wounds on Foyt's feet before releasing him to make sure there were no signs of infection. Everything looked good.

"Knowing what he did for a living, we were worried about whether he would ever race again," Johnson said. "Having never [raced], I didn't know how good

◀ A determined A.J. Foyt. *Anne Fornoro*

you had to be with your feet and ankles. I would think he'd have to be pretty good with [his] feet, but I didn't really know."[2]

Removing the dressings—some of which had dried on the wounds—was a painful process. Foyt didn't flinch. There wasn't a lot of chitchat either.

"He was really tough and able to take a lot of discomfort. The wounds were still draining and still bleeding a little bit. We took off his dressings, looked at his foot, and asked him to move around, did he feel anything, that sort of thing."

Johnson came away with similar thoughts to Stiehl:

"I remember thinking, *This dude is tough.* Nothing bothered him. This was going to be a nuisance for a while, but it wasn't going to slow him down. You could tell that in the short time I interacted with him.

"He was like, 'Let's go—I gotta catch a plane.'"

Although it was unusual to move a patient so soon after trauma surgery, neither doctor thought Foyt was at risk and agreed to release him from the hospital. As he was being rolled out on a gurney to the ambulance for the trip to the airport and a medical transport plane, there was one more task for Foyt.

"This nurse came running out calling A.J.'s name with a sheet of paper," recalled Anne Fornoro, who'd spent the night at the hospital. "I thought maybe there were more papers to sign, but it turned out she wanted A.J.'s autograph. I was really surprised at that and even more surprised when A.J., who was still pretty sedated, gave her one."[3]

Foyt's stoic reactions were fresh in Stiehl's mind as he answered reporter questions later that day.

"These are not the kind of injuries we feel will end his career," the trauma surgeon said, although he refused to put a time frame on the process. "Ultimately, we feel he'll gain a full recovery."[4]

At Indianapolis Methodist Hospital, Trammell went further, predicting Foyt would drive again, noting the injuries were similar to those of Rick Mears and Jim Crawford, two drivers who returned to the track.

"He could be behind the wheel of a racing car in four to six months. He should be able to walk within eight weeks and then he will have to undergo rehabilitation to prepare to race. I think he'll be able to drive again. He has had surgery to the extremities in the past and it hasn't slowed him. We're going to treat him like he wants to drive.[5]

"He's an awfully healthy person for his age. His physiology is not fifty-five years old. It's younger than that. His bones are like rock."

Even as the doctors were saying Foyt could race again, the media drumbeat calling for his retirement started. Some considered it a foregone conclusion and were already writing the final chapter to his driving career.

"For racing legend A.J. Foyt it appears over, his career almost certainly ended after a spectacular crash at Road America," wrote Robert Markus, a reporter who had been at the race, in the *Chicago Tribune*.[6]

"A.J. Foyt went out and hurt himself and that makes me mad," wrote Harold Lowe, the editor of the *South Bend Tribune*. "Since I've been an adult I've had only one sports hero. And I've worried about him hurting himself, or worse. Now he's gone and done it. And it makes me mad because he didn't have to get hurt. He doesn't have anything else to prove. Now's the time to retire, A.J., even if it isn't the way you wanted it to be."[7]

Robin Miller chimed in. He wasn't at the race, having been in Houston reporting on the Baltimore Colts getting thumped by the Oilers, 24–10. Having learned a lesson from his past dealings with Foyt, Miller used Bobby Unser for cover, quoting extensively from the three-time Indy winner. Unser's relationship had soured with Foyt after A.J. testified against him during hearings following the controversial 1981 race, and Unser didn't hold back:[8]

> He's not fooling anybody. He knows as well as we do he just isn't as fast as he used to be. A.J. is like (Richard) Petty. You hate to see two legends just stick around and my hat's off to them if they want to do it that badly. It just happens I don't agree.
>
> A.J. hasn't been a threat to win a race in a long time. And he knows it. He ought to be running better with that equipment and he knows it. He was a hero of mine growing up and I'd like to see him continue as a legend. But he can't do it, that is be a legend anymore, by racing himself. He doesn't want to hear that, but it's the truth.

One person who didn't question the will or wisdom of Foyt's intention to return was the one person who knew better than anyone else the challenges ahead—Mears. It had taken him more than eight months to recover from the severe foot and leg injuries suffered in the crash at Canada's Sanair Super Speedway in 1984. The injuries were so bad, Canadian doctors initially wanted to amputate before car owner Roger Penske spirited him back to the states.

Mears had spent several months in Methodist Hospital as Trammell conducted numerous surgeries to restore his feet. He had faced the same questions and doubts Foyt was now facing. And even though Mears was twenty years younger when he went through the process, he never questioned if Foyt could—or should—return. Mears recalled,

> When I looked down and saw my feet, I thought, *Okay, I [am] going to drive again*. That was a no-brainer to me. When people asked me how I could ever get in a car again, I'd think, *Why wouldn't I?* It's what I loved doing. Now if I didn't *love* what I was doing and didn't have that desire, it might be a little more difficult to do. But if the fire's lit and the desire is there, why not?[9]
>
> A.J. told me he still had the desire, and he still had the fire lit. I was always amazed he could keep that fire lit that long. People start asking when you gonna retire, when you gonna retire, like the media, and they're trying to tell you to retire, whether you want to or not. To me, it's not up to anybody else except the driver. Especially when A.J. was running his own team.

Beating Foyt back to Indianapolis was the team's transporter, and it went straight to Gasoline Alley. After unloading the destroyed Lola tub, which Foyt would keep, Craig Baranouski began unpacking the driver's personal items. Bell was already asking for the helmet to inspect the D rings that had cut into A.J.'s chin. But no one was getting the uniform.

The boss had always said if something happened to him, he didn't want his uniform to become some sort of morbid souvenir. Now Baranouski rolled one of the fifty-five-gallon trash barrels lining the garage area over to the transporter. He tossed the uniform and tattered remains of the shoes into the barrel, poured gasoline on them, and lit them on fire.

"Even a fire-resistant uniform will eventually burn if you pour enough gasoline on it," Baranouski says.[10]

When Foyt arrived at Methodist Hospital, he went into two hours of exploratory surgery, mainly to clean his wounds—the first of many such operations. After initially saying Foyt could be back in four months, Trammell changed his tune—six to eight months.

The doctor was planning to use a new type of external fixator called an Ilizarov apparatus to stabilize the bones in his left foot and lower leg. He'd used it on a handful of patients in the past couple of years, but Foyt would be the first driver.

The device was similar to a halo brace, used for years to prevent head and neck movement while allowing spinal column injuries to heal. It had been developed in the 1960s in the Soviet Union by orthopedic surgeon Gavriil Ilizarov. Due to politics, however, it wasn't until 1987 that it was introduced in the United States.

Ilizarov had received his medical degree during World War II, and—because he was Jewish—he was sent to Kurgan in Siberia to support the war effort. The city sat astride the Trans-Siberian Railway and was home to a critical tank plant. As the Soviets rushed to build the world's largest tank army, industrial injuries were common and often horrendous. Surgical facilities were limited and treatments crude, but Ilizarov did what he could.[11]

After the war, he dedicated himself to orthopedic surgery. He looked for ways to treat badly broken bones while avoiding traditional surgeries and incisions. Next to the tank factory was one for bicycles, and Ilizarov started using bike spokes to stabilize broken bones. He used the wheel to anchor the spokes, which could be adjusted to hold or move bones into place.

Over time Ilizarov developed the device that bears his name and founded the Ilizarov Scientific Center for Restorative Traumatology and Orthopaedics in Kurgan, which would one day become the largest orthopedic center in the world. He'd be named a laureate of the Lenin Prize and Hero of Socialist Labor—the Soviet Union's two highest civilian honors.[12]

Trammell was one of a handful of doctors in the United States using the device. He'd traveled to Kurgan as part of a State Department program and spent three days attending lectures at the Center and meeting with Ilizarov.

"The ability to correct deformity with the device is incredible," Trammell said. "Let's say you had a lot of previous surgery or an open wound. That makes it almost impossible to use a plate and screws under the skin, so the ability to cut the bone and move it around was fascinating."[13]

Trammell went to work crafting an Ilizarov device for Foyt. The circular apparatus looked as if it was made from an erector set, with girders holding the broken bones in place. Nuts and bolts were used to tighten or loosen the tension rods and adjust the alignment of bones as needed. Stabilizing the bones without a cast also provided access to the badly damaged soft tissues and nerves of Foyt's feet, allowing treatment to start immediately. Adjusting the device was often a painful process, however, and Trammell immediately ran afoul of Foyt.

"It's like a cage around the leg, and you have to adjust the cage periodically," Trammell recalled. "So, he's lying on the operating table, and I start to make adjustments. All the nuts and bolts for the external fixtures were metric, and I didn't have any metric tools, so I pulled out a crescent wrench."

"What in the hell are you going to do with that?" Foyt asked. Trammell explained he was going to tighten some of the bolts on the fixtures.

"You're not gonna use that Mexican fit-all on me," Foyt said. End of adjustment.

The next day Trammell received a complete set of metric wrenches, courtesy of A.J. Foyt.

"I don't want to see that Mexican fit-all in your hands ever again," Trammell recalled Foyt saying. "He was particular about his tools."

There was a constant stream of family and friends through the hospital, where a suite was set up to handle the overflow. Mario Andretti called and joked he wanted Foyt's Gucci loafers. As the follow-up surgeries continued, there was a need for blood transfusions, and a call went out for donors, although Foyt was picky about whose blood could be used.

It was less than a decade since HIV (Human Immunodeficiency Virus) and AIDS (Acquired Immunodeficiency Syndrome) had been identified, and concern and misinformation were widespread. When driver Tim Richmond was dying of AIDs and ostracized by most of the racing community, Foyt had been one of the few to visit him. He was shaken by what the disease did to the driver, who had died in August.[14]

Foyt knew it could be transmitted by sexual contact and blood transfusions and worried about several of his more active friends. Two years earlier, tennis player Arthur Ashe had been diagnosed as HIV-positive after contracting the disease from blood transfusions during heart surgery, and Foyt didn't want that happening to him.

Jimmy Finger and his wife Sharon came from Austin, as did Foyt's children. Tony and Nancy Foyt brought their children, which they knew would cheer up A.J., making the quick trip up Route 65 from Louisville. It wasn't long before six-year-old Anthony Joseph Foyt IV confronted Trammell.

"This little kid with cowboy boots and getup comes stomping up to me," Trammell recalls. "He's about three feet tall and squares off in front of me. 'Are you the guy that hurt my grandpa?' I tried to explain, but he cut me off. 'Because if you are, I'm gonna kick your ass.' There was no doubt whose grandson he was."[15]

Anthony didn't recall the incident with Trammell later but said seeing his grandfather in the hospital for the first time was "crazy. I remember walking in and his legs being up in a sling, all bandaged up. It was a pretty horrific scene, seeing his whole body bruised. It was pretty scary."[16]

There was also a problem with pain management.

"When he started getting up and moving around a bit, it was painful, and he wanted something, but he didn't want anything that made him groggy," Trammell said. "So all the usual stuff was out. I asked if he'd had anything before that worked and didn't make him groggy. He said he'd used 'that Stadol stuff,' and I thought, *Okay, let's try that.*"[17]

Shortly after he was given the pain killer, Foyt started complaining about not feeling well. He told longtime crew member Cecil Tindall he was fading fast and to get some help.

"He was having an allergic reaction, and I thought he was going to die," Trammell says. "It was a big deal. When it was all over, I was a little bit irked, and I said to him, 'I thought you told me you'd used this stuff before and that it worked.' He said it had worked—he'd used it on his horses."

Lucy Foyt took charge of her husband's hospital stay shortly after arriving in Indianapolis.

"That was a very trying time," she recalled. "It was a horrible accident. Painful. A.J. doesn't respond to pain like a lot of people do. Me, I'm a baby, I don't want to think about pain. It amazes me, all the pain that he's gone through. If that had been me, I don't think I would have ever put my foot in a car again."[18]

Trammell had also noticed a difference in A.J. when Lucy was around and tried to time his interactions with Foyt accordingly.

"Lucy was A.J.'s soft spot," he said. "She was the lady in charge, and whatever she said went. He never got crusty around her. There were times when A.J. was A.J.—when she wasn't in the hospital room—but I kinda knew his moods by then.[19]

"He'd defer to her. She'd tell him to do something, and he'd do it. I don't know how it was at home, but around me, whatever she said went."

Unlike Mears, who'd spent months at Methodist during his recovery, Foyt was soon lobbying for a return to Houston, and Trammell was hard pressed to find a reason to stop him. Before departing, Foyt agreed to meet with reporters on Tuesday, October 9, a little more than two weeks after the accident. Entering the room for the press conference a few minutes before A.J. was Lucy, who scanned the room of reporters and spotting Miller, walked over to him. She didn't like the article quoting Bobby Unser and let him know it.

"You're lucky he's in a wheelchair," Lucy said. "Or he'd kick your ass again." There was a smile on her face, but Miller didn't think she was joking.[20]

Trammell opened the event, saying, "Dr. Foyt has informed me that he's a Texan and Texans heal faster than normal people. He *is* going at a rate faster than you would expect him to, given the injuries he's suffered and his age. He's really coming around quickly."[21]

With A.J. propped up in the wheelchair and surrounded by pillows, his right leg in a cast from his toes to his knee, and his left leg surrounded by the

Ilizarov device, Miller wrote afterward, "The tough Texan looked like he never had before—vulnerable and helpless. His shattered feet, ankles and legs still grotesquely swollen and discolored."[22]

Foyt thanked those who had helped him.

"I don't think I would have a left leg today except for the doctors and the way they took me out of the car," he said. He also thanked the school kids of Indianapolis, who had overwhelmed the hospital with homemade get-well cards.[23]

For the most part, he was in a good mood—lighthearted and joking. When asked about the fifteen-stitch cut on his chin, he said, "It was like being in a Saturday night bar fight; someone hung one on me." He said he'd promised to take Lucy and the kids to Japan and Hong Kong at the end of the season, and that Lucy had warned him before leaving for Road America, "If you get hurt, I'll kill you. I told her, 'From now on, just go and leave me a note on when you'll be back.'"

In order to get a jump on the coming year, he said the team would race at Laguna Seca to close out the season, with Didier Theys doing the driving. It wasn't until he was pressed on retirement that it was apparent the chip on his shoulder hadn't been knocked off in the crash.

"I know it's a long road before it all gets healed. But I've been this route before. People have kicked me when I'm down and say I can't make it. I've got a point to prove."[24]

The next two oldest Indy car drivers, Andretti and Johnny Rutherford, were quick to weigh in and support Foyt.

"You can't impinge on a person who has been so strong-willed all his life," Andretti said after talking with Foyt. "For a guy who has been beaten down as hard as he has in this situation, he sure didn't sound like a guy who wants to do anything but get back in a race car."

Rutherford agreed:

> If A.J. wants to come back and race, it's great. I don't know if it is the era we come from, but we love to race. People tend to look at things the way normal people look at things. We're normal, but we're not. We know what's there (the risk), but we don't acknowledge it. It's human nature to think it won't happen to me. If it does, then it becomes a challenge to get back.
>
> If he's 65 and still wants to drive a race car, it's his business. People hope he retires, but it's his right. At times it gets infuriating. Under the right circumstances, A.J. and I could still win the 500.

Foyt cracked open the door to retirement later in a telephone interview with Ron Lemasters of the *Muncie Star Press*. He said plans were already in place with U.S. Tobacco before the Road America crash for him to retire after the 1991 season. Foyt said,

> We had discussed it before the accident ever happened. I really have nothing left to accomplish. I still have more victories than anybody. I really

> love the sport, but the technology and everything has changed so much. The days of unloading off the trailer and going racing are long gone. I kind of let it slide there for quite a few years, and I just want to be caught back up before I retire. We got caught up quite a lot [and] for what we accomplished in 1990, I can't holler. I just want to be back abreast of it so we could have a front-running team.[25]
>
> I have mixed emotions. I've been here long enough and I've had lots of fun. I think what I'll do is just enjoy managing my team and go from there.

During his time at Methodist Hospital, late at night after the crowded suite emptied, Foyt would say his daddy continued to visit him, as he had that first night in Milwaukee. While A.J. said he had a strong belief in God, he'd never been particularly religious or a spiritual person and couldn't explain his father's visits, other than to say he felt "like I talked to him. Like he was right there and he came and talked to me. I don't know—I can't tell you why."[26]

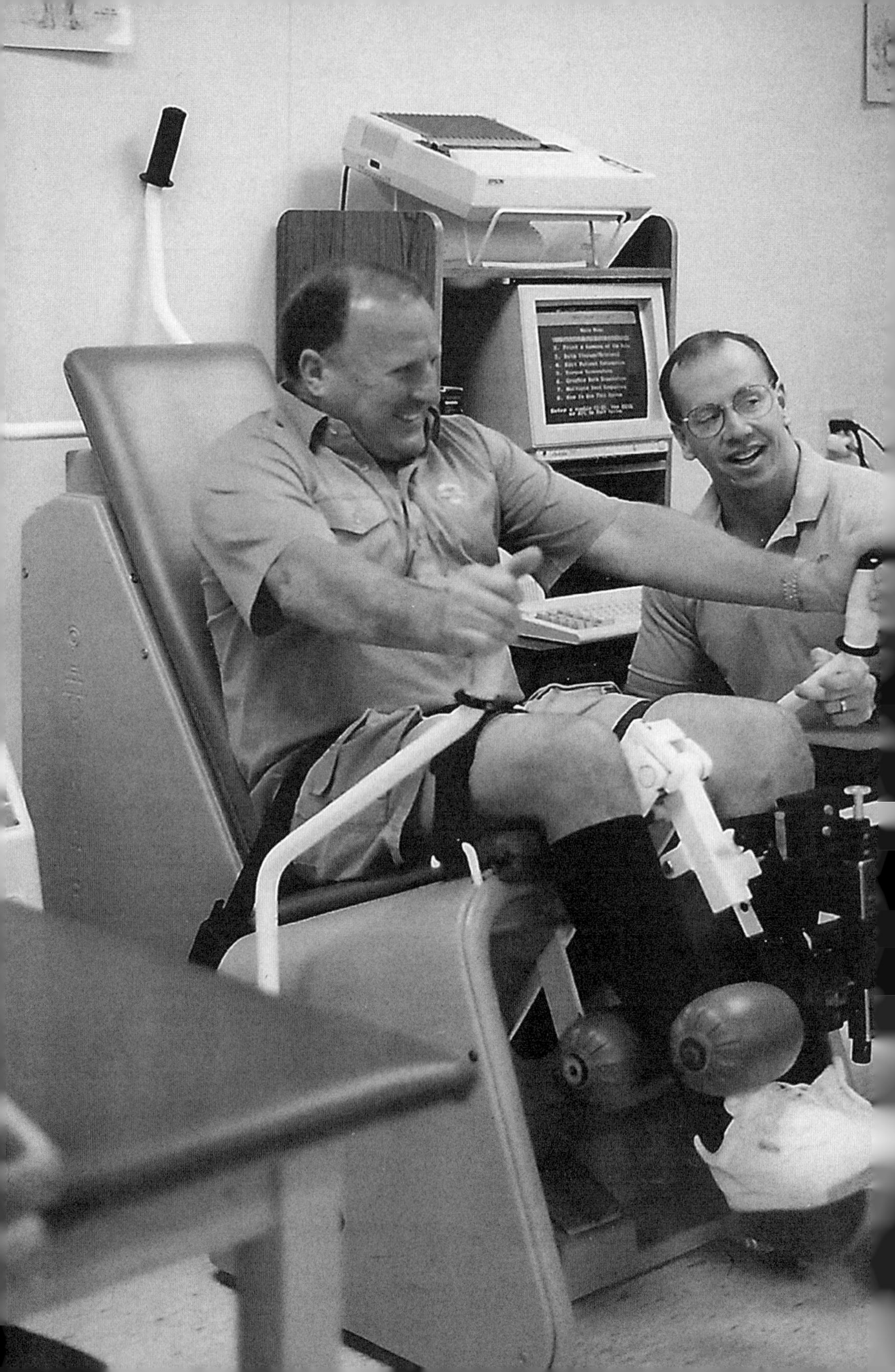

CHAPTER 17

REHAB

1990–1991

Back in Houston after three weeks of sheet time in Indianapolis—his longest hospital stay away from home—A.J. Foyt began putting together his support team. Faced with a long and uphill recovery, he realized—perhaps for the first time—he was going to need help and lots of it.

He knew simply working at his ranches and riding his machinery, his own prescription for getting back in shape following past injuries, wasn't going to do the trick this time around. Just taking care of the ranches and his other properties and businesses would be a challenge.

Son Jerry was already taking charge at the new Honda dealership. He'd still been running some races, but a hospital visit changed things.

"I remember A.J. lying in the hospital bed in Indy with his legs up in the air," Lucy said, "and Jerry was there. [A.J.] kept saying, 'Jerry, you don't want to do this. You just don't want to do this.'"[1]

The way Jerry remembers it, A.J. was pretty direct. "He gave me a lot of advice, like 'Get out of the business' [of racing]. He wanted me to concentrate on the business side of things. He wanted me to get a strong and solid business background. He told me racing was too rocky a business."[2]

For help managing the ranch and his other properties, Foyt turned to his oldest son. Tony's horse training career had continued to prosper, and he'd left Calumet Farm and was now running the Foyt Stables. While he was still looking to saddle his first Kentucky Derby starter, his horses continued to win their share of races. Tony recalled,

◀ Foyt works out with Houston Oilers' strength and conditioning coach Steve Watterson. *Anne Fornoro*

> He called and asked if I would be interested in coming home and helping him around the ranches. He couldn't look after things like he wanted. If I came home, he said he would help us build a house on his ranch property. It was a hard decision. I had a successful stable, and I still had a few horses for Calumet and a couple of other different owners.[3]
>
> It wasn't a forced deal or anything like that. It was totally our decision. He didn't lean one way or the other. He just told us to think about it and let him know what we wanted to do. That's when we made the decision to move.

The timing was right for a couple of reasons. Tony and Nancy's kids were getting older, and the vagabond life of a trainer moving from one meet to another was tough on them. Tonia, named for her great-grandfather, was talking about staying in one place for school.

"They were gypsy kids," Nancy Foyt said. "My family was looking for a place where we could settle down and stop living from apartment to apartment on the (horse) racing trail. It was probably a good time to settle down, so we came home."[4]

The timing was right for another reason. The "Bluegrass Boom" had turned to bust following the collapse in the oil markets and horse racing, like much of the American economy, was in the midst of a recession. The sport was also about to be rocked by a scandal beginning with the death of superstud Alydar in November 1990, leading to the financial collapse and bankruptcy of Calumet Farm.

While Tony had left as the farm's head trainer several years earlier and Calumet had last sponsored one of Foyt's race cars in 1988, both A.J. and Tony had remained friendly with Calumet President J.T. Lundy. What they didn't know was Lundy had taken the farm deep into debt beginning in 1983 when it first sponsored Foyt's team. Lundy had taken out a loan for $13.2 million, eventually adding a $20 million mortgage on the farm itself and continuing to leverage it ever deeper in debt.[5]

Without the millions earned from Alydar's stud fees, there was no way to pay the interest on those debts, and the farm was soon losing about $1 million a month. By the end of 1991, Lundy was forced to resign, and the farm and its assets were auctioned off. In an unrelated case, Lundy would be sentenced to four years in prison for bribery and, although he was never charged, implicated in Alydar's death as part of a scheme to collect insurance money.

Tony continued to train racehorses for a short time after moving to A.J.'s ranch, before deciding to focus on running the family properties.

"I told my dad I was done with the horses. I told him I wasn't gonna leave Louisville or Lexington to work horses here. That's like being at the Indianapolis 500 and then coming home to run the local dirt tracks. I just didn't want to do that. That's when we sold a bunch of them off. But he still piddles around and buys him a couple a year to run."

Tony ranks among the top-fifty all-time trainers at the track with 172 wins, five of them coming in stakes races. One of A.J.'s horses, Colonelsdarktemper, was winning races as recently as 2020.

The main ranch in Hockley covered about 1,000 acres with about 500 head of cattle and thirty horses. A.J. was always looking for land or a ranch in the area he could buy, renovate, and sell, which kept Tony busy.

"For a long time in my life, it was pretty much work seven days a week. My grandfather and my dad always taught me that if you work, you're gonna be able to make it. That was both of their goals—you gotta work to make it."

Next, A.J. went to see his long-time family doctor and friend Gary Friedman. He knew Foyt's injuries were severe but was taken aback when he first saw them.

"From the knees down, his legs were just a bunch of bone fragments," Friedman said. "A.J. had a very bad combination of severe bone injury and damage to the blood vessels that would supply the oxygen necessary to heal the bones and the area. Because of the nature and location of his injuries, the healing process was going to take some time."[6]

Not only were the broken bones and wounds severe, their location added to the healing challenge. The blood flow to your feet—the farthest part of your body from the heart—is at its weakest, and as a result, foot wounds often take longer to heal.

Foyt's goal was clear: He wanted to be back on his feet and walking in time to return to the Speedway for the next running of the Indianapolis 500. Just driving in the race wasn't enough. He was determined to walk to his car. No wheelchair, no crutches.

"He very much wanted to regain his mobility," Friedman recalled. "He knew he was never going to run a hundred-yard dash again, but he did not want to be confined because that's totally against his whole life ethic. A.J. has a will of steel. When he sets his mind to something, who knows what he can accomplish."

To help speed the process, the doctor recommended Foyt use the hyperbaric chamber at Memorial Hospital, which Friedman had helped bring to Houston years earlier.

The hyperbaric oxygen chamber originally was developed to help submariners and divers adjust to atmospheric pressure after being at extreme depths. The chamber forces 100 percent oxygen into the body, typically at about two times atmospheric pressure. Scientists also discovered the pressurized oxygen treatments were useful in healing wounds. Foyt immediately signed on for the treatments.

Each morning, Friedman would pick Foyt up, both figuratively and literally, manhandling him from a wheelchair into Friedman's car for the ride to Memorial, where he would oversee the treatment. Using the chamber and maneuvering Foyt and his halo-wrapped shattered leg in and out proved to be extremely painful. But it was during these daily treatments that Friedman saw another side of Foyt far different from the one who had flung food across the hospital room when they first met.

"There was a young boy receiving treatments at the same time as A.J.," recalled Friedman, who became emotional at times while telling the story: "The boy had severe diabetes, and diabetics are prone to infections. He had developed a fungus infection in his sinuses, which is extremely hard to treat. In addition to all the usual medication, they were using hyperbaric therapy.

"You cannot imagine how kind A.J. was to this little boy. He gave him all kinds of souvenirs and he'd always talk with him. I'd never seen this side of A.J. up close for as prolonged a period as his relationship with this little boy."

The boy's infections were severe, and he eventually died, his father sending Foyt a letter of gratitude for the kindness shown his son. While A.J. would speak frequently and at length about his recovery process to reporters in the months ahead, he never mentioned the child. He would get quiet years later when asked about the boy and say only, "He was crying and needed help," adding they'd been planning a deer hunting trip together.[7]

"There is a side of A.J. that has a heart of gold," Friedman says. "As much as A.J. gets publicity for his public life, sports endeavors, and what sometimes happens at the track, he can also be very generous and very private."

The wounds responded well to the hyperbaric treatments and while not completely healed, Foyt's focus shifted to physical therapy.

"I hate to say it was a great result when a guy can barely walk," Friedman said, "but at least he could barely walk. He exceeded my expectations for an ordinary patient. Under normal circumstances, I would have been absolutely surprised. But nothing surprises me about A.J."

Feeling well enough to venture out for something besides a hospital visit, A.J. went to check on his properties. He also went to one of his son Larry's church basketball games. Lucy had long ago banned her husband from the kids' sporting events after tangling too many times with officials, coaches, and other fans. But how much trouble could he get in at a church league basketball game with a halo around his leg?

Larry remembered,

> It was one of the first times for him getting out of the house after Elkhart Lake. He still had the Ilizarov on his foot and was on crutches.[8]
>
> I think I was on a fast break, and a guy kind of took me out from behind really hard, kind of a bad foul. I think the kid's dad said something like, "That's a great play." Next thing I hear, one of my friends is yelling, "Go A.J.!" and I looked over and dad is pointing his crutch up into the stands and yelling, "I can't walk—you come down here!"

Foyt shrugged when asked about the incident:

> It's one of those deals. I get mad and I don't give a damn where I am. He was a mouthy-mouth [expletive]. He was saying, "Foul, foul, foul." I said, "Well you mother [expletive], you come closer." He wouldn't, so I took the crutch and poked him in the chest. I don't know anything about basketball, but I knew more than he did. It was one of those deals where I was feeling bad, and I just wanted to see my kid play. I'll take a lot of stuff, but finally I'll just blow up.[9]

Foyt soon grew frustrated with the slow pace of the prescribed physical therapy, three times a week for thirty to forty-five minutes. Lucy had noticed a difference in her husband's approach to rehab.

"He did all the therapy, which he never liked to do," she said. "He hung in there and was determined to do it all. He worked very hard and went through all that time in a hyperbaric chamber, which nearly killed him. But it was taking him so long to get over it. Longer than any of his other accidents. He was determined to get back to the next race, the next Indy."[10]

Among those calling to offer their encouragement was General Chuck Yeager. If anyone knew pain, it was Yeager. Two days before his scheduled attempt to break the sound barrier, he'd fallen off a horse and broken two ribs. Afraid he wouldn't be allowed to fly the X-1, he'd gone to a civilian veterinarian to tape him up and then sworn him to secrecy. Yeager knew better than most what drove Foyt to get back in a race car.

"It didn't even enter his mind to quit," Yeager said after talking to Foyt. "When guys hang in there like A.J. or George Foreman or Nolan Ryan and do a good job, people have to admire them. Too many of our so-called athletic heroes let the public down, either on drugs or other ways. A.J. is not one of those guys. He's been at the top of the peak almost all of his career, and he's still trying."[11]

With the Ilizarov device scheduled to come off in mid-November, Foyt wanted to jumpstart his recovery and turned to an unlikely source.

Houston Oilers

Monday mornings were a busy time for Steve Watterson, the strength and conditioning coach of the Houston Oilers. He tended to player ailments from the previous game and worked with others to get them ready for the next contest. After losing their first two games of the season, the Oilers new "run 'n' shoot" offense led by quarterback Warren Moon had started to click, and the team was back in the playoff race.

He didn't have a lot of time for a phone call from Barry Warner, a flamboyant Houston sports radio personality known as the "Mouth of the South." Watterson tried to keep an arm's-length relationship with the media as they were often looking for comments on player injuries, which was closely guarded team information.

Warner was calling for a different reason. He wanted to know if the coach would talk with A.J. Foyt. The race car driver was back in town following his accident at Road America and unhappy with the way his rehab was going. Foyt had been doing local interviews, reinforcing plans to race one more year and then retire.

"This will be the last time," Foyt told KHOU-TV in Houston. "I hate that I've got to call it an end. But there comes a time in everybody's life that it's over with. I'll finish the 1991 season and then call it quits. I've had an enjoyable career."[12]

Watterson had seen video footage of the accident and was generally aware of the severity of the injuries. He was surprised Foyt was already back in

Houston, figuring he would have been bedridden in Indianapolis for several months. He agreed to talk to A.J., who called a short time later. Watterson recalled Foyt saying,

> "I got to get [rehab] going. I got to pick up the pace." He asked if I worked with anybody outside of the Oilers. I said, "Not really." I'd done some other stuff in my training and during my internship, but since then I'd only worked with football players. He said football players get bumps and bruises, too—could he work with me? I thought this was crazy. I had read about his comminuted injuries, and they were from a different world. But I was headed into a coaches meeting, so I asked A.J. if I could check a couple of things and call him back. He said, "Okay," but that he didn't have much time. He wanted to get started.[13]

The next morning, Watterson received a call from Jack Pardee, the Oilers coach. Pardee was from a small town in west Texas where they played six-man football. He'd gone on to play fullback and linebacker for Bear Bryant at Texas A&M and become an all-pro linebacker during his fifteen years in the National Football League while playing for the Los Angeles Rams and Washington Redskins. He'd missed one season during his playing days, fighting off malignant melanoma. To Watterson, a New Yorker, Pardee—the future NFL and college Hall of Famer—was Texas tough personified.

"He was a good guy but a hard-nosed personality," Watterson said of Pardee. "Old school. He was just like A.J. They came from the same genes."

Pardee and Foyt had met and become friendly doing charity work in the Houston area.

"Jack called and asked me to do whatever I could for A.J.—as long as it didn't interfere with team activities," Watterson remembers. "He said, 'If you're looking for a blessing, you've got one.'"

Tuesday was the players' day off, so Watterson went to visit Foyt's nearby race shop. He asked to see one of the cars up close, so he'd have a better idea of the physical challenges a driver faced. He measured the cockpit and foot-box area and studied the knee and ankle angles of a driver. He also brought a gauge he could attach to the pedals to see what kind of leg strength Foyt would need to operate his car. It was Watterson's first close-up look at a race car:

> I see this thing, and I'm stunned. I weighed about 210 pounds and wondered how anybody fit. I finally get in, and it's basically a box of tin. I'm trying to attach the gauge, and I'm having trouble just moving my feet around and wondering how anybody does this. I finally get it hooked up, and I can't budge the clutch. I put some oomph into it, and one of the crewmen said the clutch still wasn't engaged.
>
> Then I wanted to test for upper body strength. I could barely move the wheel. The crewman said, "Ah, coach—there ain't no power steering on this thing."

Foyt heard about the visit and called Watterson the next morning. "So, you're all in?" he asked. The trainer warned that while he'd worked with plenty of athletes facing career-ending injuries, this was entirely different. But he was willing to do everything he could to help. He told Foyt to contact him when he was able to move around, and they'd meet to evaluate the situation and establish a game plan.

A few days later, Foyt called back. He was still in a wheelchair but wanted to get started. Watterson, who'd been studying Dr. Terry Trammell's reports, was already having second thoughts.

"I thought I'd bit off more than I could chew, that this [was] way beyond my pay grade," he recalled. "When I read Dr. Trammell's medical findings, it left you verklempt. It was overwhelming."

Foyt's first appointment did nothing to ease Watterson's concerns. There were zippered horizontal scars across his right knee and a ten-inch scar down his left leg from the compound fracture. There was a red area on his right thigh where doctors had removed the top layer of skin to use as grafts on the incisions made on Foyt's insteps to relieve the pressure in the hours after the crash. He was also wearing a back brace.

Worst of all were his feet. Despite time spent in the hyperbaric chamber, there were still open wounds. Both feet suffered from sensory deprivation, and were black-and-blue and badly swollen, with his toes curling under.

"When Foyt arrived and I saw his injuries in totality, it was nothing like anything I had ever seen or experienced," Watterson recalled. "You can take the ten worst lower body injuries in NFL history at that point, combine them, and it wouldn't match what I was looking at. Nothing that I'd known compared to how A.J. arrived for that first evaluation."

Watterson went to work taking measurements and administering tests. Pin pricks to the feet revealed little or no feeling, and there was virtually no range of motion. He couldn't tell cold water from hot. Foyt did show his sense of humor was uninjured.

"Don't worry about the left foot," he told the doctor. "That's my brake foot, and I don't use it very often. I just need to flex this right foot."

Foyt compared his feet to those of a bloated cow and wondered if they'd ever look normal again. He repeatedly asked, as he had in Indianapolis, if he'd ever wear his cowboy boots again.

"I don't know what I'm going to do," A.J. mockingly complained. "My kids are standing in line to see which one gets my alligator boots, my ostrich boots and the ones with the Coyote on them."[14]

Despite his concerns, Watterson agreed to work with Foyt as soon as the Ilizarov device came off. Watterson estimated Foyt needed three or four hours of therapy a day, and as the players were typically in the facility from 7:00 a.m. to 7:00 p.m., he could work with the driver before or after. Foyt suggested they do both. He'd come in before the players in the morning and again at night.

"It didn't take long to see that his personality and his drive superseded everything else," Watterson said. "It is where *will* overcomes all obstacles. It doesn't matter how much damage there is—it's how are we going to fix it. It wasn't about when he could get back to walking—it was about, 'How fast can you get me back on the track?'"

Watterson and Foyt also came up with seven steps for getting him back in a race car by the 500, tying together his life on and off the track.[15]

Step One: Standing up and moving around without a walker or crutches.
Step Two: Driving his bulldozer.
Step Three: Playing with his grandchildren on the floor.
Step Four: Hot-walking his racehorses at the ranch.
Step Five: Hunting—enduring a long day and changing temperatures on his feet.
Step Six: Driving a race car again.
Step Seven: Competing and finishing well—like the old A.J. would.

"Each of those steps allows for a lower margin of error," Watterson warned. "Some of those functions will never be back the way they were originally, so we'll have to make modifications."[16]

During the appointment in Indianapolis to remove the device and the cast on the right leg, Trammell said he was happy with the healing process, but Foyt would be lucky to walk before April. The doctor said driving at Indianapolis was "a very realistic goal" and held out the possibility that "he could be back in a car as soon as the end of March or early April, but it'll take some doing. The brake pressure is going to be a problem." They scheduled a follow-up for mid-January, and Foyt promised to "walk in the front door."[17]

Foyt called Watterson from Trammell's office and said he was ready to go. Thanksgiving was only a couple of days away, and the trainer suggested they start on Monday after the holiday. That was a whole week, and Foyt didn't want to wait. He'd be back that night, and Watterson agreed to start the next day, Tuesday, November 20.

Initially, they focused on reducing inflammation and improving the range of motion of his feet. Part of the treatment included fluidotherapy—putting his legs into a machine with ground-up corn cobs heated to 112 degrees. The heat massage was done without water to reduce the risk of infecting open wounds. Watterson also spent hours massaging and working the tissues of each foot, toe-by-toe. The time passed quickly as Foyt mesmerized the coach with racing stories.

"There was so much inflammation and damage. The tissues had been completely torn apart. There was gauze on both feet where they had split them open to allow the extra fluids to drain out. We had to work around that. We were just trying to get passive movements back into the joints. This was all before he could move on his own.

"We spent hours talking," Watterson recalled. "He'd tell me about how he started and how the game had changed. He'd ask about the [Oilers] players."

Despite saying, "My feet are hurting twenty-four hours a day," Foyt began pushing to work on range of motion to get him up and moving around. Watterson started him picking up towels with his feet and then marbles with his toes. "It makes you kind of pissed off, but it's one of the best exercises for your toes," Foyt said. "If anyone told me that at fifty-six I'd be picking up damn marbles with my toes—shit."[18]

In darker moments, Foyt confessed there was something else driving him besides getting back in a race car—something he'd felt since visiting Jim Hurtubise at the military burn hospital in 1964. "If I was confined to a wheelchair, I don't think I could take it. I know I couldn't. I'd have to do something that would probably be embarrassing to the family." Asked if he was talking about suicide, Foyt said, "I don't know. Let's put it like this, if I ever get hurt to where I would be confined, I'd just as soon pass on. I'd rather not be a burden. I was such a burden (after his recent surgery)—I don't think my family felt like that—but I've always been too independent and like to do things for myself. I know a lot of people eat this up being hurt, playing sick. That's not my role."[19]

When Foyt pushed again to do more, Watterson stepped in to establish some ground rules. "I said, 'A.J., I don't tell you how to drive a car. Let me tell you how to get your body right. I'll push you hard, but if you push it too hard, too fast, you'll start having setbacks. The worst thing that can happen is to travel that lap a second time. You don't want to do something a second time because you've had a setback.'"

Eventually, Foyt was able to ride a stationary bicycle. The Oilers also had one of the first production versions of the Orbiter treadmill—a new ultra-low-impact piece of machinery developed by a Houstonian, with a "trampoline-like surface" and so named because it was like walking on the moon. It allowed him to start walking long before he would be able to walk on the ground. Even using the Orbiter, the pain was constant.

"If I walk too long, it feels like someone is jabbing a hot needle in here," Foyt said. The area around the incisions made in Milwaukee were especially painful. Through it all, Watterson kept a close eye on Foyt. With his sports shirt, shorts, and knee-high black compression socks, he looked like a typical old man at the gym. He was proving to be anything but.[20]

"You always worried about him doing too much. If I said, 'Let's go with six one-minute walks, he wanted to do twice that. If I told him five minutes, he'd want to do ten. When he was on a machine, he wanted to know what his last score was. He wanted to see a red line where that score was. And he was gonna beat that score. There was no status quo. Repeating what he had just done wasn't standing still to A.J.—it was going backwards. I know he must have been in excruciating pain."

Pardee would occasionally stop by to talk with Foyt during the sessions. Eventually, the head coach asked Watterson to schedule Foyt during the day, at the same time as the players.

"He thought it would be good for the team to see what Foyt was going through," Watterson said. "To see how hard an icon was working to get back. He'd achieved the pinnacle of success, yet here he is, giving it his all to get back on the track."

Once the workouts were rescheduled, it wasn't long before Watterson observed an interesting dynamic and understood why Pardee wanted the driver in the gym at the same time as his players. One of those impressed by Foyt was Oilers' offensive lineman Bruce Matthews, who was in his seventh season with the team. There wasn't a football player tougher than Matthews, who would never miss a game because of injury in nineteen seasons. A consensus all-American at the University of Southern California, he'd start 293 NFL games, trailing only quarterbacks Tom Brady and Brett Favre. He was selected to the Pro Bowl fourteen times and would be inducted into the Pro Football Hall of Fame in 2007. Years later, Matthews recalled,

> I was a little apprehensive when I heard A.J. Foyt was going to be working out with us. I mean, oh my God—A.J. Foyt. I wasn't a big race car fan, but I recognized him immediately. Everyone knew who A.J. Foyt was.[21]
>
> His legs were just mangled, much worse than any football injury I had ever seen. I remember thinking, *No way is he going to be able to drive again.* It was very, very impressive with what he accomplished. We talked about our injuries and other things. He'd ask me questions about football, and I'd ask him questions about racing. And he was just the nicest man—a real gentleman.

Watterson also observed a natural, easy banter between Foyt and the players:

> He was like the godfather in the training room. The guys loved being around him and were absolutely amazed by him. If there was ever a young guy complaining about things being too tough or that I was working him too hard in the weight room, the other players would use A.J. as an example. "You think you got something to cry about?" they'd ask. "You think you got it tough?" Then they'd point to A.J. and show the kid the scores A.J. was putting up while riding the bike. He was a great example of appreciating what you've got and what it takes to stay there.[22]
>
> He could needle you as well as anyone. He wouldn't hold back. A guy would be riding a bike next to A.J., and A.J. would be just kicking his ass. Foyt would turn to him and ask him if he was going on a milk run. He'd ask, "Is that dial even moving?"

Trammell came for a visit and was surprised when Foyt confronted one of the players. "He'd had a knee injury of some sort and was carrying on about something. A.J. stops in front of him and puts his hands on his hips. 'You pussy,' Foyt said. 'You're not even hurt.' He pulled his pants up and said, 'Look at these legs. *These* are fucked-up legs. And I've been doing ten times what you're doing.'"[23]

He took it too. "I'd be working on Foyt's feet, and one of the players would walk by and say, 'Come on, old man—how much longer you gonna be on *my* table?'" Watterson said.

When Foyt was ready to start upper-body conditioning, the strength coach ran a series of tests with him. The results were surprising.

"He was what I call country strong. I showed some of the players Foyt's results, and they were amazed at his upper body strength. And his leg strength started to return as he was able to handle more stress."

Only once did Foyt complain about pain, and Watterson had to hear about it from Trammell. Foyt's legs would swell up after workouts and a hard massage, and Watterson started putting his legs in big trash bags and then into an ice tub:

> Usually, guys get used to the cold tub after three or four minutes, but he was having a tough time with it. He never complained to me, but you could see it in his face. It was just killing him. He wasn't gonna admit anything, but he'd say, "God bless, coach—are you sure this is right?"
>
> After a couple of days, Trammell called me. He said it was a great idea, getting the scar tissue broken down and getting rid of the inflammation and that A.J. said things were going great. But then Trammell said, "You probably shouldn't put him in a cold tub. There are so many wires and pieces of metal in his legs and feet that the cold is being conducted to the core of the bone." I felt awful. I asked A.J. why he didn't tell me.
>
> "Hell coach, I didn't want to sound like a pansy," was Foyt's response.

Even after the Oilers were eliminated in the AFC Wild Card game in early January, some of the players came by the facility to work out and check in with the driver.

"There is an amazing fraternity and respect among elite athletes in the arena, regardless of what sport they're from, and I strongly came to believe drivers are athletes," said Watterson, who moved with the original Oilers to Tennessee in 1997, where he became an assistant head coach. He eventually retired as the longest-running NFL strength and conditioning coach with one team. "You saw a lot of incredible relationships develop. The guys were honored to have him there."

One of the players checking on Foyt was Moon, who'd had an all-pro year as the team's quarterback. Foyt mentioned that Moon was his son Larry's favorite player and that he'd like to get something autographed. A few days later, Moon came in and flipped Foyt a signed football.

"He'll like this," Moon said. "It's a special one."

Special indeed. It was one of the game balls from Houston's 27–10 December 16 victory over the Kansas City Chiefs in which Moon passed for a then Houston record of 527 yards. The football still has a place of honor in Larry Foyt's home office.

CHEVROLET

CHAPTER 18

COMEBACK

1991

As promised, A.J. Foyt walked into Dr. Terry Trammell's office in Indianapolis under his own power in mid-January of 1991. He propped his crutches outside the doctor's office and, mustering all his strength, hobbled in. Trammell was waiting for him.

"Hey doc, I'm here to get my physical for Daytona," Foyt joked. The doctor was impressed. Not only was A.J. moving on his own, he'd lost about thirty pounds and seemed to be in "superb cardiovascular condition.[1]

"I was really confident that he was going to be in great shape for Phoenix," Trammell said.[2]

After getting good marks from the doctor, Foyt altered his timeline. He scheduled a practice session at the Speedway for March to test the new Lola and his rebuilt legs. He said he would skip the first two Indy car races of the year—on street courses in Australia and Long Beach, California—planning his first start for Phoenix on April 21.

When the first of two new Lolas arrived on January 22, he gingerly lowered himself into the car. He spent time in the cockpit, watching a video of race footage and going through the motions with his feet on the pedals, an early version of the simulators now common in auto racing.

He was still on crutches when he went to Phoenix for the February 3 Copper World Classic, entering a car for George Snider to drive and hinting he might try it in practice. When Trammell heard that, he quickly nixed the idea, and Foyt drove the pace car instead. "Maybe the doctors don't think so, but I listen to them—up to a certain point," Foyt said. What Trammell didn't know was that Foyt was already driving a street car, using a cane to operate the gas and brake pedals.[3]

◀ A.J. and Al Unser. *Dan Boyd*

Saying, "I felt like I needed to be here, it's where I belong this week," Foyt then attended the Daytona 500 in mid-February. It was the first time in twenty-six years he wouldn't start the event, handing the consecutive race streak to Richard Petty. He'd always reveled in talking about his crashes, and he repeatedly told the mesmerized NASCAR media about Road America.[4]

He also began to hedge on his retirement pledge, saying he planned to race in the Firecracker 400 at Daytona in July and, "If I run good, I might come back next February and give [the Daytona 500] another try."[5]

The travel and work at the shop, however, cut into Foyt's rehab time. "He was pressing his team to get ready," Steve Watterson said. "That and his travel required him to be away from therapy. That's a hard thing to balance, and I'd seen it happen before to others. The one thing that was accounting for his advancement now took a back seat at times to working with his race team and other activities.[6]

"I asked if he talked to Terry (about Phoenix) and if he really thought they were going to clear him to race. He said, 'If you get me behind the wheel, coach, I can do anything.' But it wasn't that simple."

In March, Trammell stopped in Houston on his way to Australia for the CART race to check on Foyt and was disappointed. A.J. had put nearly all of his weight back on and the rehab pace had slowed.

"Sometime after [the previous exam], he sort of quit," Trammell said. "I really thought we had lost the battle. I climbed all over him. I started calling him every few days, making sure he was going to therapy."[7]

Foyt was notorious for his sweet tooth and admitted to "craving chocolate and Coca-Cola." He said he planned to take off at least fifteen pounds before racing at Phoenix, but Trammell wondered how Foyt put the weight back on in such a short period of time. Then he visited the ranch.[8]

"A.J. climbed up on one of his bulldozers, and he had a giant bottle of Coke and a box of candy bars," Trammell remembered. "Not *a* Coke and a candy bar—one of those huge bottles and a whole *box* of candy bars."[9]

Others tried to talk Foyt out of racing again. Louis Bantle, the president of United States Tobacco Company, urged him to retire but said the company would back him either way. A.J.'s friend Jimmy Finger pointed out Foyt had already made thirty-three starts in the Indianapolis 500, the same as the number of cars in the starting lineup, so it was a good time to stop from a numerology standpoint.

"Those 400,000 people in the stands, no matter what you do, they'll love you forever, if you race again or not," Finger said. [10]

Jerry Foyt knew better than to try and discourage his father. "That's something only he can decide for himself. Only that man can decide. It's like when any great athlete decides to retire. Logic can't make him do it."[11]

Another visitor to the ranch was crew chief Phil Casey. He saw a different Foyt than Trammell and left with no doubts about where they'd be in May.

"He was rehabbing up on his Caterpillar, knocking trees down," Casey recalled. "He was the most determined person you'll ever see in your life. Unbelievable. He never let it slow him down."[12]

Another urging Foyt to keep going was seventy-year-old Carroll Shelby, who would drive the flame red Viper pace car at Indianapolis. He'd won the 1959 24 Hours of Le Mans while chewing on nitroglycerin pills for an ailing heart and knew better than most what drove men to race.

"Knowing A.J., I'm surprised he's quitting at all," said Shelby, a fellow Texan and recent heart transplant recipient. "A.J. really loves to drive a race car. I've heard a thousand people say, 'What's that old goat still driving for, why doesn't he give it up?' I know why he doesn't. He loves to drive."[13]

Even NASCAR's Dale Earnhardt chimed in. "He's the most awesome old fart I know."[14]

The next time Trammell saw Foyt was when he limped into the doctor's office for another checkup prior to testing at the Speedway, which had been pushed back to the first week of April. A.J., who normally wore a size ten shoe, wore a pair of mismatched black adidas athletic shoes: a size thirteen triple-E on the still-swollen left foot, and a size eleven on the right. "I walked around in those big old shoes and I swear, I looked like a goose," he'd say.[15]

Adding to his problems, Foyt's toenails had started to grow back, but he'd waited too long to trim them, and several had become ingrown. Trammell cut back the nails and was forced to remove three entirely, including those on both big toes—a painful process.

"He told me it wasn't going to hurt, but I think he fibbed a little," Foyt would say.[16]

"Sometimes doctors don't know what hurt is. If somebody stepped on one of my toes right now, I'd probably faint."[17]

He agreed to talk with reporters before and after the test while asking for the track to be closed the first two days to the media and public. The first day was rained out, perhaps a blessing in disguise as the toes continued to give him a great deal of pain. He needed help on day two to struggle into his uniform, gingerly pulling it over his tender toes and feet. Much of day one was spent sorting the car, including bleeding air from the brake lines after the pedal went straight to the floor the first time he tried it on the track. He tired easily and could run no more than about ten laps at a time. Watching it all was Watterson, who was still impressed by Foyt's performance.

"It was very fulfilling to watch him drive again and I'm as honored now as I've ever been with any athlete," he told reporters. "A.J. has phenomenal pain tolerance and focus and I never doubted for a minute he'd be back here."

A large crowd of spectators turned out on Saturday for the final track day, and Foyt turned laps in the 215 miles per hour range before meeting again with the media.

"I ain't gonna lie to you, I had to talk to myself a little bit," he said. "Did I really want to run that fast and take a chance again? Getting in and out of the car was a chore. My feet were sore enough, but my toes really hurt. It was hard to concentrate on driving with all that pain down there."[18]

"I didn't go fast enough to make the hooligan [a race for last chance qualifiers], but I felt better than I thought I would. It's nice to be in the cockpit again. It felt real good and I worked hard to get there.[19]

"I've made up my mind that I'm going to accept the challenge," he said when asked if he'd be back. "I've had challenges before. I like challenges. I think that when May gets here we'll be in good shape."[20]

Much as he'd put together a rehab support team, Foyt assembled a team for the track. Casey had already agreed to return as crew chief. Jim Gilmore would be there, although for the first time in nearly twenty years, he was taking a secondary role. He'd invested heavily in several automotive dealerships, and as new car sales went through one of their periodic down cycles in the early 1990s, he was forced to cut back his sponsorship and would have only a small decal on the now completely black car. Copenhagen more than made up the difference in sponsorship dollars, and both Bantle and Eddie Thrap at UST became confidantes. None were closer than Copenhagen publicist Anne Fornoro, who'd noticed a change in her relationship with A.J. since the aftermath of the Road America crash. "When I gave blood and stayed with Lucy at the hospital in Indianapolis, I became like family," she said.[21]

Also returning was Bob Riley, the original designer of the race-winning 1977 Coyote. He'd become an in-demand engineer for Trans-Am and sports cars and had planned to work with Foyt in the offseason. That was before the Road America crash. Now he agreed to spend the month of May in Indianapolis with A.J. and help with the engineering challenges.[22]

Despite the tentative first laps at the Speedway, Foyt went ahead with plans to run at Phoenix and entered his car for the April 14 race at Long Beach to help get his crew back in the groove. A number of people contacted him about driving the Lola, including NASCAR car owner Felix Sabates, who was interested in putting Kyle Petty in an Indy car for a couple of road course events. Foyt had someone else in mind.

He reached out to Bernard Jourdain, a Belgium-born and Mexican-raised driver who'd earned co-rookie-of-the-year honors at Indianapolis in 1989. Jourdain appeared to have a promising career ahead of him before being involved in a big crash during practice for the 1990 500. A series of surgeries, including one to remove his spleen, had been followed by a lengthy recovery process. He'd raced in only a few minor events in Mexico since the accident, but Casey, who'd served as Jourdain's crew chief at the Speedway, convinced Foyt the driver deserved another chance. Foyt telephoned Jourdain, who was surprised A.J. knew who he was.

"I never thought in my life I would have a call like that one," said Jourdain, who became the first foreign-born driver to race for Foyt. "I thought, *Why is he calling me?* There are so many of his friends who are looking for something like this. I knew after a while he had meetings with several drivers, but he ended up deciding I was going to be the one. That was really amazing."[23]

Driving the No. 14 car, Jourdain qualified twentieth at Long Beach and was moving up through the field when the transmission broke. It was more bad news for Foyt, who'd already been told by Trammell he wouldn't be cleared for Phoenix. In many ways, 200 laps around the tight one-mile Phoenix oval was more challenging than Indianapolis. Drivers were constantly on and off the gas and hard on the brakes going into the first turn at Phoenix, all the while facing heavy traffic. During the Indianapolis test, A.J. had been able to cruise around the track with steady pressure on the gas pedal and only needed the brakes when he pitted.

"I knew I wasn't right and Trammell didn't want me to race to begin with," Foyt admitted. "We talked and he said, 'Let's not fool ourselves.' Phoenix is a very tough, physical track. Things happen a lot quicker there than they do at Indy. You have to be all there to drive it, and I'm not there yet. My reflexes are all right, but my feet and legs are not where they should be. My feet still hurt so bad in the morning I want to cry. A couple more weeks of healing will help and I'll be ready for May."[24]

Foyt reached out to Al Unser about driving his car at Phoenix, who immediately said yes.

"You've only got to ask once," said Unser, who didn't have a ride for 1991. Unser said he owed Foyt for giving him his first chance at the Speedway in 1965.[25]

"We've been good friends a long time," Foyt said. "He's one four-time Indy winner helping another four-time Indy winner."

At the track, however, Unser discovered one thing hadn't changed. He and A.J. liked different car setups, and Foyt was adamant about the way he wanted the car. Publicly, Unser said all the right things.

"Working with A.J. is great because he's a racer and he knows you can't carry the car, you've got to get things working," Unser said. They never did get the car sorted to Unser's liking. He qualified seventeenth in the twenty-two-car field, dropping out just past halfway. It would be the last time he drove one of Foyt's cars.

Even though Foyt wasn't driving, the Phoenix track went through with a fundraiser to mark the occasion. More than 400 people paid $75 to attend. It turned into a roast with Al Unser Sr. and Jr., Johnny Rutherford, Mario Andretti, and Parnelli Jones joining in.

"A.J. came out sounding like an ornery, fist-slinging, tantrum-throwing, woman-chasing carouser," read one report. When it was his turn, Foyt said he was glad Lucy wasn't there and that, "Paybacks are hell. But I'll stick to my story. I'm innocent of everything I've ever done."[26]

The dinner was part of a farewell tour Fornoro was coordinating, and at Phoenix they gave Foyt a rocking chair. She convinced A.J. to serve as co-grand marshal alongside Mary Fendrich Hulman for the upcoming 500 Festival Parade, an event Foyt often skipped in the past. He also agreed to promote the May 24 Hulman Hundred at the Indiana State Fairgrounds, renamed the A.J. Foyt–Hulman Hundred.

Although still concerned about people stepping on his feet, Foyt attended the Kentucky Derby, then headed for Indianapolis, where rain interrupted the first few days of practice.

"I feel pretty good," he told reporters at the Speedway. "I'm going to run here if there's any way possible. I'd say Al would do it if something happened where I couldn't run. That's if he wanted it. But I don't see any reason I couldn't run. My toes are a lot better and there's a lot less pain."[27]

The mention of Unser as a possible replacement driver surprised some. Tied with Foyt with four victories in the 500, Unser was the only driver with a chance to surpass the Texan. Unser wasn't interested in the ride, but he wasn't surprised by the offer.

"That wouldn't have bothered him," he said of the possibility he might win a fifth 500 in A.J.'s car. "He's a funny guy that way."[28]

Foyt's highly anticipated track physical conducted by the Speedway's head physician, Dr. Henry Bock, on Monday, May 6, turned out to be anticlimactic as he was approved in about twenty minutes.

"So much is their mental attitude," Bock said. "I wouldn't say A.J. is a stubborn individual, but others would. What he's got is a great mental attitude.[29]

The exam had its moments.

"They wanted me to stand up on my toes," said Foyt, who had converted one of the rooms at the Speedway Motel to a workout facility. "Of course I grinned when I did it but you can fake a lot of stuff. I did everything they wanted me to do. My therapist and all of us worked hard to get as much strength as I've got in my legs. The upper part of the body is good, but the bottom is still hurting a little bit. Like one doctor said, 'You've got a year-and-a-half worth of injuries and it hasn't been a year-and-a-half."[30]

Although he'd passed his physical, Watterson was asked if he thought Foyt could run 500 miles. He said that was still difficult to know:

> If this was just an average driver, take away the A.J. Factor, and a doctor looked at his fitness this soon after a major injury and asked would he be able to compete 500 grueling miles, I think maybe it would be questionable. I think you have to factor in A.J. When he gets into that car, his experience, his stamina, his determination, his adrenalin will be pumping. It's something you can't quantify.[31]
>
> I've worked with athletes both in the Philadelphia and Houston areas. I have a great feel for looking in their eyes and seeing something intangible in them. You look in the eyes of Nolan Ryan, Julius Erving, Larry Bird or a Warren Moon. These athletes hold something, an undaunted ability to keep things in perspective and what needs to be achieved. A.J. exemplifies that. He was unwilling to succumb to obstacles. Obstacles only strengthened and affirmed the commitment he had to continue. I learned to respect his focus. To him [the goal of returning to Indianapolis] never faltered.

Foyt turned his first tentative practice laps before the day was out and slowly built speed during the week, but not fast enough for some. When he failed to break 220 mph by midweek, he heard about it from Lucy. She'd been checking with Watterson and crew members in addition to nightly calls with her husband. When their nephew and team computer operator Tommy LaMance mentioned the telemetry indicated he wasn't on the accelerator as much as some of the other drivers, she called her husband.

"She called me and asked, 'What's the problem?' I says, 'It's no problem.' She said, 'Tommy says you have a little bit left. The computers show you're backing off quite a bit.' And I said, "Well that little . . .'"[32]

After telling LaMance he'd "whip his ass and then fire him" the next time he talked to "Aunt Lucy," A.J. topped 220 mph on Thursday and 223 on Friday, May 10, the day before qualifying. Not bad, but only fifteenth fastest.

With heat and humidity forecast to increase through the day on Saturday, he caught a break as Gilmore drew the third qualifying spot. When the first two drivers stepped aside, it was Foyt's opportunity for a dramatic return to the Speedway, and he didn't disappoint.

His first lap was just over 221 mph, and he later said he let the crew down by "tightening" up the car too much. He went faster each lap, and the last circuit of 223.469 mph was his fastest official lap to date at the Speedway. Waiting in the pits on his return was a crowd including Gilmore and Mari Hulman George.

"When A.J. pulled over, tears came to his eyes," Gilmore said. "And mine too. The way he qualified today is almost equal to a fifth win. You tell me what sport anyone could come back and do as well as A.J. did today."[33]

Rutherford was there too and saw the tears. "If you put anybody into that microscope and have everybody standing there with tears running down their faces, clapping hands for you, if you don't get caught up in that, then you've got no nerve endings in your body."[34]

After thanking everyone who had helped with his rehab and the crowd of 200,000 for supporting him, Foyt hinted for the first time it might not be his last Indy 500.

"Every time I've made decisions I've *tried* to stick with them," he said. "Do you understand what I'm saying? I just asked [UST's] Mr. Bantle for permission maybe to run one race a year, and I dearly love it here at Indianapolis. I'm not really looking at it as my last race, just kind of looking at it as being just another race."[35]

As temps went up and speeds went down during the day, it appeared Foyt's run might hold up for the pole position. Then the Rocket Man, Rick Mears, took to the track late in the afternoon and averaged more than 226 mph to take the pole away. What wasn't known at the time was that Mears had broken one of his surgically repaired feet earlier in the week in a practice crash.

"He's one of the guys who elevated the sport to what it is," Mears said after knocking Foyt from the pole. "We're good friends, but that's racing. If somebody had to do it, I'd just as soon it be me. To have all this happening and start next to him is very special."

The second-oldest driver in the field, Andretti at fifty-one, was third fastest, completing one of the most successful front rows in 500 history. Andretti said he was motivated by his longtime rival.

"To me, what A.J.'s doing is very inspiring. Whether he's twenty-five or fifty-five, with those injuries, it's still inspiring. And it's extra special because everybody looks at this as the twilight of his career. From my standpoint, knowing A.J. and certainly appreciating what he's done, I'm just happy to see him get back in the race and not walk away from his career with terrible memories. I think he's doing himself justice. I'm going to have to race him, but I'm hoping to hell he goes out with a good month."[36]

Danny Sullivan, Foyt's former endurance racing teammate, was another impressed by the qualifying effort. "He's a tough son-of-a-bitch. I was surprised, but then knowing A.J.'s character—not really. He wasn't gonna let it get him down. For mere mortals, that could have been something when most people say, 'Hey, I've had enough. That's good. I've made enough, and I've done enough. I'm going down to my ranch and watch this stuff from afar.' But that ain't A.J."[37]

Despite throbbing feet, aggravated by his refusal to use a golf cart on pit lane—"the guy could barely walk," Riley recalled—Foyt took the team to dinner that night. After posing for the traditional front-row pictures the next day alongside Mears and Andretti, Foyt lingered so additional photos could be taken with crew members and friends. Afterward, he escaped back to Houston for a few days away from the glare.[38]

With cooler temperatures for the second day of qualifying, four more drivers ran faster than Foyt, but it was too late to change the makeup of the front row. Jourdain qualified twenty-first in the second Foyt entry, but Unser was unable to land a ride and decided to watch the race instead. Of the thirty-three drivers, thirteen had not been born when Foyt qualified for his first 500 in 1958.

There was a constant stream of well-wishers flowing through the Foyt garage, including Dominic Dobson, who'd been racing alongside Foyt at Elkhart Lake when A.J. had the brake failure.

"He'd always been good to me, and I'd never had an issue with him," Dobson said years later as he recalled going to see A.J.:

> I could go see him, particularly at Indy, and ask him for some advice. He was always friendly to me, and we chatted a bit.[39]
>
> I was glad to see he was okay. I respected A.J. as an Indy 500 winner and multi-time champion. I wasn't surprised to see him still racing. I guess I had an opinion about whether he should be, but who am I to say what the great A.J. Foyt should do and what he doesn't get to do? The fact that he was racing didn't bother me a bit.
>
> Now if someone asked me in my mid-50s if given the chance, "Would you go race in the Indy 500 again?" I think my answer would have been, not just no, but, "Hell, no." I don't want to be going down into a corner with a nineteen-year-old knowing what I have to lose and what he's got to lose. I'm probably gonna lift first.

If there was anyone being asked about retirement as much as Foyt, it was Richard Petty, who stopped by the No. 14 garage while visiting the Speedway for a sponsor:

> We didn't talk a whole lot about retirement. He was pumped up, and I tried to keep him pumped up. As far as I was concerned, that was his business. He's like me. He's going to do what he wants anyway.[40]

> It's just a way of life. It's just like getting up and eating breakfast or eating dinner or going to bed at night. I guess it's hard for me to change because it's so much a part of me. It ain't hard to explain to myself but it's hard to explain to other people how dedicated I am to driving a race car. It's hard not to drive a car because I enjoy the driving part so much. Good, bad or indifferent, I'm satisfying my own needs.

With the field set, attention turned to Foyt. Despite a number of other prerace stories available for the seventy-fifth anniversary of the first running of the 500—Willy T. Ribbs had become the first African American to qualify for the race, Hiro Matsushita the first Japanese driver, and there were four Andrettis in the event—every reporter still wanted an interview with the retiring driver, and every cameraman needed a shot. *The National*'s Ed Hinton did a lengthy feature article entitled "The Last Ride of A.J. Foyt," an overwhelmingly positive tribute. ABC prepared a feature narrated by Sam Posey for its race broadcast answering a question from his young son, "Dad, who's the greatest racing driver ever?" The Associated Press put together a package of four ghost-written columns that appeared under Foyt's byline, along with a special graphic package. Even *People* magazine did an article on him.

"A.J. is a hero, he's the focus of a lot of attention," said Chris Economaki, who'd been covering Foyt for more than thirty years and seemed to do nearly as many interviews telling people what A.J. was like. "There's a certain charisma there that no other driver has. A.J. Foyt sells tickets. People do not get their friends together and charter a bus to go to a race to see some European nobody ever heard of. It won't be the same—there's no question about it."[41]

Foyt was happy with the way his car drove on Carb Day and seemed race ready himself when he ripped into his crew as they struggled during the largely ceremonial pit stop competition. Fornoro kept him busy, including a rare appearance at the 500 Festival Queen's Ball, where he arrived early and was "chatty and friendly."

He went from there to the Indiana State Fairgrounds for the Foyt-Hulman Hundred dirt track race, where he watched nineteen-year-old wunderkind Jeff Gordon score an impressive Silver Crown victory. He was the defending USAC midget champion and had won the opening sprint car race of the year at Phoenix. While Gordon had made it clear his ultimate goal was to race in the Indianapolis 500, he was also in his first season in the Busch Grand National NASCAR feeder series. The Foyt-Hulman win was the first of three races in two days in three different kinds of cars for Gordon, who some were already calling the next A.J. Foyt.

More than thirty years later, Gordon recalled meeting Foyt and receiving the winner's trophy from him that day:

> It was one of the most impactful experiences I ever had and one I'll never forget. I was certainly in awe of A.J. As a kid, I'll never forget, knowing who A.J. Foyt was and wanting to grow up to be like him and be as successful as him. To have an interaction like that was very surreal. It almost didn't feel like it was actually happening. It felt more like a dream.[42]

> I remember how complimentary he was, how cool he was. It really motivated me to stay on that path, and maybe one day it would take me to Indianapolis.

The next day, as promised, A.J. took a seat alongside Mary Hulman for the 500 Festival Parade. A number of his friends were coming in for the race, and one of the first to arrive was General Chuck Yeager. Their friendship had strengthened since their first meeting at Indianapolis five years earlier. "I'm not a polished individual and neither is A.J. That's the reason we got along so famously," Yeager said. He wasn't worried about Foyt driving because "he's got the reflexes and the eye-sight and the eye coordination.[43]

"He probably would have been a good fighter pilot. He's got courage, but he's not foolish. A.J.'s very competitive and aggressive, and he most certainly knows his job. That's what counts. He's funny and loves to joke around, but he's a level-headed straight guy. He's a real professional."

While the entourage gathered in Indianapolis, two of Foyt's closest friends and longest-serving crew members decided to remain in Houston. Jack Starne, who'd been with Foyt since 1967, and Howard Gilbert, who'd run the team's engine room since 1971, had both come off the road several years earlier and didn't want to get back on it. Neither was sure if Foyt was going to retire, although both hoped he would.

"I don't miss it," Starne said of the action at the track. "My son grew up without me being home and it's kind of nice now that we can do things together." Asked if the race would be Foyt's last, Starne said, "I don't think anybody that works for him knows. [Elkhart Lake] scared him. It did everybody. I'd be thrilled to death if he retired."[44]

With Chevrolet engineers handling the powerplant responsibilities, Gilbert found his role diminished at the track and no longer enjoyed his time there.

"Through the lean years you hate to see a man of his caliber go downhill. He's got nothing left to prove, so why keep going?"

Foyt himself seemed to settle the "will he/won't he" retirement question in his final bylined column for the AP that was distributed to media outlets across the country. "Win, lose or draw," the series concluded, "when the checkered flag falls, it'll be the last time I'll pass under it at the Brickyard."[45]

The only thing not cooperating as the big day approached was the weather, and Foyt awoke to a rainy and windy race morning. Knowing it would take time to dry the track, and the start would be delayed, he lingered at the Speedway Motel, preferring to spend time with his family and closest friends rather than face the hordes that were already ten deep around his Gasoline Alley garages. Gilmore, a staunch Republican, coordinated a call with President George H. W. Bush, who wished Foyt well.

Foyt took a golf cart for the quick trip from the motel to his garage, where he dressed quickly. After first saying he would take the cart to pit road, "to save my feet the wear and tear," Foyt then decided to walk. He'd been assigned two burly state troopers, and they took the lead, with Gilmore and Bantle guarding the flanks. As he prepared to leave, Foyt beckoned for Watterson, Hardy Allen, Eddie Thrap, and several others to join the group. ABC's cameras were on hand to follow his progress.[46]

The troopers were quickly engulfed by the crowd, and Gilmore and Bantle moved forward to help clear a path, pleading with the crowd to "give the man some room." Everyone wanted to shake Foyt's hand or pat him on the back. A.J. took his time, the limp barely noticeable, and he accepted the good wishes the best he could, although he seemed surprised by the commotion.[47]

"When I walked from Gasoline Alley out to the track, it was almost spiritual," Watterson recalled. "The power of the cheers, the power of the voices that were cheering for A.J., went right through me. I've been blessed to have been to the Olympics. I've been to sports festivals and to the Super Bowl. I've been to lots of big-time arenas. And I was absolutely stunned at the energy of those cheers for A.J."[48]

Foyt was one of the first drivers to settle into their car, more to get off his feet and avoid the crush of the crowd than anything else, but it didn't stop the steady stream of well-wishers. Only when the command was given to "start your engines" was he finally alone.

He slipped back to third at the start and then fourth as first Mario and then Michael Andretti got past. As the leaders moved into traffic, the turbulent air caused the front end of Foyt's car to "push" up toward the wall, and he slowed further, telling the crew to be ready to increase the downforce on the front end by changing the wing angle when he pitted.

Almost on cue, a caution flag came out, and Foyt stopped along with everyone else. One of the air wrenches used to loosen and tighten the wheel lug nuts malfunctioned, however, and when Foyt got back on the track, he found himself well behind the leaders.

He'd started to work his way forward when two cars he was chasing, Kevin Cogan and Roberto Guerrero, touched coming out of the first turn and slid hard into the outside wall. Foyt went low and seemed to get through unharmed when a shower of debris came raining down, a suspension piece off one of the cars hitting the front of the Lola. The impact broke the left-front wing and bent the suspension arms connecting the left-front tire, which now hung motionless in the air. Realizing his race was over, Foyt slowed the car to a crawl, raised his visor, and started waving to the crowd.

Reaching his pit, he paused for a moment before climbing from the car. Then the chant started, first in the seats near where he stood, then spreading through the grandstands. "Thirty-five, thirty-five." It was clear, the fans wanted him to come back. Too loud to ignore, he turned, grinned, and waved. He talked briefly with ABC's Jack Arute and refused to say he'd competed in his last 500. He started on the short walk to the passage back to Gasoline Alley and was intercepted by actor James Garner, who gave him a kiss on the cheek. Then he was gone.[49]

Back in the garage, Foyt struggled with repeated questions about retirement. It wasn't supposed to happen like this, he kept saying. He'd worked too hard to be out after only twenty-five laps through no fault of his own. He'd finished twenty-eighth, his second-worst finish ever in the 500. This was not the way he wanted it to end.

"We shouldn't have been back there where you can expect things like this to happen," he said of the crash. "I thought I had everything missed. A piece of suspension dropped out of the sky. I didn't want to go out with a wreck, but if it had fallen another two feet into the cockpit I probably wouldn't be talking to you now."[50]

Asked about the crowd's "thirty-five" chant and if he'd been waving goodbye on the last lap, Foyt was noncommittal.[51]

"Thirty-five would be a nice round number," he said with a smile. "I was just waving to the fans. They've always been a big part of my life and I think I've been in their life. I was just saluting all of them. If they want me back, you never know what I'll do if I'm healthy and healed-up 100 percent. A lot of my friends want me to quit. But it's part of my life. I love it."

"Probably I should come back. I know the Speedway, I feel I have a lot of savvy. So maybe we'll run just the big race. I still think I've got a win in me. We're going to do some more talking and see what happens the rest of the year."[52]

In an exciting end to the race, Mears passed Michael Andretti to become the third driver with four Indianapolis 500 victories.

"To be able to be here with A.J. on the front row for his final race, which we all won't believe until next year this time, it's just outstanding," Mears said at the awards banquet.

Among the amazed was Parnelli Jones, Foyt's chief rival from the 1960s, who hadn't driven an Indy car in twenty-five years. "A.J.'s my new idol," Jones said. "Can you imagine him coming back like he has, at his age? It's unbelievable."[53]

AJFoyt
Copenhagen
RACING
BOSCH
Spark Plugs
Copenhagen

CHAPTER 19

NO FEET, NO HEART

1991

A.J. Foyt's comments leaving the door open for a return to the Indianapolis 500 had Anne Fornoro scrambling to try and control the situation. Early in the month, she'd written off Foyt's evasive comments as, "Superstition, you don't say it's over until it's over." She said Foyt would be back but only as a car owner and that he was already looking for drivers, although, "he hasn't mentioned any names because then their price goes up."[1]

One driver had already taken his name out of competition to succeed Foyt—Bernard Jourdain. He'd run a clean 500 before dropping out on lap 141 with a broken transmission, finishing eighteenth. It had been enough to convince him his racing career was near an end. He said he was willing to stand by as a relief driver for Foyt in the upcoming races, but beyond that, he was done.

A week later at Milwaukee, promoters presented Foyt with a motorcycle. "I think this will be my last race here," he said. "There comes a time when you have to call it quits and I think it's that time. Hopefully I'll be back here next year as a car owner."[2]

Next came four road course races in five weeks, three of them on temporary circuits. Most were surprised when Foyt said he intended to drive in all the events. It had taken Mears a full year to return to the road courses following his injuries. Jim Crawford, who'd suffered injuries similar to both Mears and Foyt in 1987 and gave up road racing entirely, said, "I can't imagine why he's even trying."[3]

Upon arriving in Detroit, Foyt said, "I was disappointed in Indianapolis. I'd hate to go out being a quitter. I'd be lying to tell you I don't want to go back. I've been doing some serious thinking. I felt we were cheated a little bit.[4]

"I get so damned mad at racing. But I'm tired—the wreck took a lot out of me—and I don't know if I'll campaign the whole circuit. You've got to call it quits sometime."

◀ Foyt's still-recovering feet were a problem on the road courses. *David Nearpass*

Reality began to set in on the streets of Detroit, considered by many the most physically demanding course in the series. Saying "my feet are kind of retarded," he gave up using the clutch entirely, timing his gear changes the best he could. He managed to qualify nineteenth, although he was out of the race with a broken transmission before the halfway mark.[5]

"I had some pain," he admitted, "but I'm a race driver and you've got to expect some pain. That's no excuse."[6]

He managed to finish a week later at Portland, a traditional road course, although seven laps behind the winner. In a small concession two weeks later, he decided not to attempt the 4th of July double he'd run in recent years, the back-to-back Firecracker 400 NASCAR race at Daytona, followed the next day by the Cleveland Indy car race. He committed to running on the Cleveland airport circuit and hired Mike Chase, thirty-nine, who'd been running NASCAR's western circuit, to make his first Daytona start. Chase, who'd been recommended by George Snider, had named his son A.J. The moved kicked off rumors Chase would run for NASCAR's rookie of the year in 1992 driving for Foyt.

While in Cleveland, Foyt was visited by Jeff Gordon, the twenty-year-old driver he watched win the Hulman Hundred back in May. Despite his success in midgets and sprint cars, Gordon was having a hard time getting on the radar of Indy car owners. Instead, he'd spent the year driving in the Busch Grand National series, one step below NASCAR's premier Winston Cup.

"Indy car owners just were not hiring dirt track oval racers at that time," Gordon said. "That time had kind of passed, and the series had moved in a different direction. That was eye opening to me. It was disappointing because I really wanted to race at Indianapolis. But at the same time, I wanted to go where it was best going to suit me."[7]

Larry Nuber, the former ESPN announcer, was introducing Gordon to team owners and other drivers, including Foyt, who didn't paint a pretty picture. Road racing was becoming increasingly important. The politics of Indy car racing were getting worse, not better. And rapidly rising expenses meant a young driver needed to have financial backing to land a ride.

"Two meetings that really stood out were the ones I had with A.J. and with Al Unser Jr.," Gordon recalled years later:

> They both said to me something like, "With your background, with what you're doing right now, and with what's happening with Indy car right now, I think you need to think about NASCAR."
>
> I really appreciated their honesty. That was important. We needed that to know which way to pursue. It seemed like if you didn't have money to bring to the ride—which we didn't—then it wasn't going to happen. It was one of those things—could I train myself to be a road racer, could I figure out how to get a ride at Indianapolis? Maybe yes, but it was going to take money, and that was just something we didn't have. So when I left there, it was pretty clear the next thing to do was do the same thing in NASCAR, and figure out what the opportunities were there.

> A.J. and Rick Mears, and (Johnny) Rutherford—those guys will always be my heroes. But it was disappointing to hear the news of what it would take to get there.

Foyt also found time to call Tommy Kendall, who'd suffered serious leg and foot injuries in a sports car crash at Watkins Glen. Although they'd never met, A.J. helped arrange for Kendall to see Dr. Terry Trammell in Indianapolis, where Kendall underwent a nine-hour surgery to put his legs back together.[8]

Foyt may have been better off running the NASCAR race. He qualified next to last at Cleveland and was a lap down after ten circuits before dropping out with suspension problems. Chase didn't do much better, being involved in an accident and finishing thirty-third.

Two weeks later at the Meadowlands—one of his least favorite tracks—Foyt sounded like someone ready to hang up his helmet. After accepting a Stetson from the promoter as part of the Retirement Tour activities, he said,

> I told people I'd run all the races, but I've got to face the truth. I've got a problem. There's no sense of crying to myself or anybody else, it's just a fact. My feet burn and tingle all the time and I get a delayed feeling in them. The toes are so screwed up on my right foot. I've tried some different things, like braking with my left foot and I think running the road courses has helped a little, kinda like therapy. But I just can't do myself or my car or my crew justice the way things are. I'll be honest, these last few races have just been fill-in deals. We've got to turn this operation around and I want to do a good job for U.S. Tobacco.[9]

Despite the pain, Foyt managed to qualify eighteenth and was still running at the finish in thirteenth, although nine laps behind winner Bobby Rahal. Afterward, he faced the facts:

> Damn feet. The car was good enough to win the damn race. It wasn't the car. It was me. It just made me so mad. It's a shame to have wasted the car running so good. If I could have hustled it, we could have done a lot better. It wasn't the car that wouldn't hustle. It was me. It felt like my foot was sliding up and down. I couldn't do anything with them. I'd want to do something and I just couldn't. The car was running so good. Damn feet.[10]

A few days later, he seemed to indicate the August 4 500-mile race at Michigan International Speedway, the only 500-mile Indy car race he hadn't won, would be his last:

> The Meadowlands race is probably the last time I ever drive on a street course unless a miracle happens. It's like they say in horse racing—no feet, no heart. That's like I feel. I just don't have the coordination you need for some of these tight street courses and temporary courses. Dr. Trammell told

> me not to run the road courses, but bullheaded as I am, I had to find out if I could do it. Now my feet feel like they're on fire. I know the car is capable of running up front. I can run 4–5 good laps on road courses, then I can't do it no more. I've got a $700,000 race car and real good crew and it's no use just going through the motions out there. And I couldn't take the pain any longer. We finished thirteenth at the Meadowlands and everybody on the crew was real happy, but I wasn't. That's not the way I race. All I've been doing is trying to pace myself and not hurt myself too bad.[11]
>
> I figure I don't have too many years left in racing, so this is the right time to get started with somebody new. We'll get some time in together this year, see how we get along and, if everything is all right, we'll have that much of a jump on everybody for next year.

The line of people hoping to replace Foyt immediately formed. Roberto Guerrero, Scott Sharp, Jeff Wood, Johnny Rutherford, Raul Boesel, Didier Theys, and Mike Groff were all rumored as potential drivers of the No. 14. Parnelli Jones called to put in a good word for his son PJ, who was having a good year in the Indy car feeder series.

Foyt decided on Groff, twenty-nine, who'd set a rookie qualifying record at Indianapolis in May. He liked the fact the driver had started in quarter-midgets when he was ten and come up through the USAC ranks in midgets and on dirt tracks. He also had plenty of road racing experience in Super Vees and had won the ARS championship in 1989.

"My retirement plan was to come to all the races this year and race," Foyt said in making the announcement. "I hate to quit in the middle, but the way I'm running, I'm in everyone else's way.

"Mike has impressed me through the years and I felt instead of starting fresh with someone next year, if this works out, we'll have a jump on it. I'm not happy when I'm running in the back row and I won't be happy if whoever drives for me is running in the back row."

Groff said racing for Foyt was "a dream come true. I've known A.J. a couple of years. When I did ARS, I'd ask his advice now and then and he's always been helpful. Listening to the old pro, it helps a lot.[12]

"Those are some big shoes to fill, and I don't think anyone ever will fill them. There's not going to be another A.J. Foyt. I'm here to be me. It's an understatement to say this is a great opportunity. I'm here to make the most of it."

A second race was soon added to Foyt's schedule, the oval at Nazareth—and he again left the door open when asked about a return to Indianapolis.

"We'll see," he said. "A lot depends on my sponsors and on how I feel. Right now, I really don't know what I'm going to be doing next year."[13]

The new team got off to a good start July 21 on the streets of Toronto, where Groff qualified eighth, thanks to an assist from Foyt.

"I didn't know how involved A.J. would be with the car," Groff said during practice. "But this morning on pit lane, I was having a problem with understeer. He stuck his head in the cockpit and asked me what was going on. I told him, he made some suggestions on what to change and we picked up a second right there. I'm all ears right now when he comes around."[14]

Groff ran as high as fifth during the race before a botched pit stop dropped him to eighth. It still matched his best finish in two years of Indy car racing and the team's best result of the year so far. Foyt seemed pleased and repeated he was done with road courses.

A.J. was back in the car for the August 4 Michigan race and things didn't go well from the start. Forced to change the second engine of the day, the team was pushing the No. 14 onto pit road when the car in line behind Foyt was sent on the track. At first officials seemed to indicate Foyt would be able to qualify without penalty, but he was then told he would have to go to the back of the line and would be docked one of two qualifying laps. Four other cars received the same penalty. At that point, he ordered the car be pulled from the qualifying line and be put back on the transporter—he was going home.

The track had heavily promoted the possibility of the race being Foyt's last 500 miler and, along with Jim Gilmore, track and race officials talked him into waiting overnight before making a final decision. In reality, with only twenty-one cars on the grid, the smallest field for a 500-mile race in seventy-five years, it didn't matter much where Foyt started. But the exchange ripped the scabs off the old wounds between Foyt and CART that had festered since the Road America crash, and he left no doubt his crusade against the organization was back on.

"I'm here for my fans and sponsors," he said in the morning. "It's damn sure it wasn't for CART. It was a cheap shot. The whole deal is just the principle of the thing. It is so Mickey Mouse. Thank God we've got Indianapolis. I just hope [this is] not my last race."[15]

It took Foyt a little more than one hundred miles to move into the top ten, but he was out soon thereafter with recurring engine troubles. He spent the next week promoting the Hoosier Hundred at the Indiana State Fairgrounds and used the opportunity to keep up his attack on CART: "I want it like it was in the '60s, when it was a good time and everyone lived for it," he said of the dirt track event. "Most of the CART races I go to are cutthroat and everyone gets jacked around. I don't want any of that shit here. I want this to be a big race and a fun race."[16]

Then he uttered the ultimate threat. "Everybody is making me so damn mad, I might run for another ten years."[17]

Any momentum Groff created for the team at Toronto was destroyed two weeks later, along with his car, when he crashed hard early in practice for the race on the streets of Denver. While Groff complained of dizziness and headed for the hospital, Foyt ordered the team's backup car off the truck, only to be told it wouldn't be allowed to qualify as no official entry had been filed. Already mad about the crash, Foyt took it out on CART.

"I think it's time for a new organization to be formed because there's a bunch of idiots running CART. I helped start CART but not with some of the morons we've got running around now. Don't get me wrong. There's some good people in the trenches, but some of the guys making decisions, well a kid who went to grammar school has got more smarts."[18]

A.J. ordered the car put back on the truck and left Denver immediately. He spent the next day at his ranch on his bulldozer, trying to blow off steam, when Robin Miller reached him. It didn't take long to get Foyt riled up again, and he laced into CART and in particular Kirk Russell, its technical chief. He launched into an invective-laced tirade that Miller quoted at length in his Sunday *Indianapolis Star* column.

"I asked him (Russell), since when did we need two entries to run one car? Where does it say I've got to have two entries for one car. It's bullshit and nobody does it. Besides, we hadn't qualified so why can't you substitute your backup car?" Foyt said Russell made him an offer he could refuse:

> He said they had a full field and my car wasn't eligible. But if something happens and another car gets wrecked, then we could run. I told him to get serious. I'm not gonna sit around waiting for somebody to crash. What do you think would have happened if they'd only had nineteen cars? Think they'd have let me run? You bet your ass they would have. They have no cars, they're begging for cars and they are trying to pay people to show up. Then they pull this shit with somebody who supports all the races. I've never seen such a Mickey Mouse operation. CART has shit on all the people who have helped them.[19]
>
> I don't want to blow my own horn but they're jealous of me. I'm the only name they've got. I spent an hour and a half signing autographs Friday in Denver. I didn't see 'em lined up for anybody else. I'm also one of the few people who will stand up to them. I ain't kissin' nobody's ass and I never will. There's so much bullshit going on under the table with CART it's ridiculous.
>
> They don't have any common sense either. I'm quite sure after that comment I made at Michigan he [Russell] saw it as a way to get even. He likes to play the macho part. He'd love for some big name to beat the shit out of him. I'd love to but they'd suspend me and I might kill him. The problem is that he's stupid and ignorant. He's a chronic liar and he's dumber than whale shit. If CART don't run him off, a lot of people might leave. It hurt them (CART), it didn't hurt me. I'm embarrassed for championship racing. But if they don't need us, then fine. We'll stay home.

Miller added his own two-bits, writing Foyt could "be a bully and a baby at times but I've got to side with him in these situations . . . his treatment at Michigan was abominable . . . the Denver episode sounds like more petty thinking. Classy sports honor their retiring superstars—not deface them. As much as CART tries to ignore tradition, there's no ignoring Super Tex still draws more headlines and paying customers than anyone else."

The team skipped the next race at Vancouver, saying it was too risky to make the long haul without a backup car. While CART's battles with Foyt were escalating, the organization was also trying to make peace with Tony George and the Indianapolis Motor Speedway. CART wanted to form a joint series with IMS, working Indy into the name and doing away with USAC. Even though CART was apparently willing to part ways with Russell and put together a new technical team as part of the deal, Foyt wasn't having any of it.

"I think it's a big mistake for the Speedway to join anybody. It needs to stay independent. People respect the Indianapolis Motor Speedway, but there's no respect for CART at all.[20]

"I don't think Tony will get conned into anything, and I think he'll work with those people on his own terms. If not, he's made a bad mistake because CART needs the Speedway. The Speedway sure in hell doesn't need CART."

In another article he added, "I don't think Indianapolis should let [CART] use their name. Not unless all the races are going to be on ovals, like Indy, because that's what Indy stands for. It don't stand for those sorry street races CART puts on.[21]

"People have been misled about Indy car racing because of CART. Indy car racing is Pocono, Milwaukee and Phoenix—not Vancouver, Denver and the Meadowlands."

Despite everything going on, Foyt surprised many by entering Groff in the September 15 race at Mid-Ohio, where he immediately clashed with CART officials over the team's assigned pit. It didn't matter as Groff could do no better than twentieth in qualifying and dropped out early.

Foyt headed from there to Indianapolis, where he was slated to film a commercial for Craftsman tools, driving his stock car around the Speedway. George stopped by, and during a break in the filming, he took Foyt's car out for a few laps. It seemed innocent enough at the time but would lead to changes that would rock all of racing.

Two weeks later, Foyt was in Nazareth, Pennsylvania, for what many expected—and what he had indicated several times—would be his last race. He qualified fifteenth but collided with Jeff Andretti and was knocked out of the race. An obviously irate Foyt climbed out of his car and, after a few moments with his crew, approached ABC pit reporter Jack Arute, who asked Foyt what happened—not aware his microphone was open.

"Goddamn Jeff Andretti run right over me," Foyt said. "He's all over the goddamn track."[22]

In the control booth, Paul Page jumped in, calling it "Vintage A.J.," before sending it back to Arute for the formal interview. Foyt was still hot.

"A.J., it was Jeff Andretti that got you?" Arute asked.

"Well yeah, he's all over the goddamn track. He doesn't know where in the hell he's going," Foyt repeated.

"Was it the suspension . . . ?"

"Yeah, it kept me from sending him through the goddamn wall. I'm tired of this shit. You got people who shouldn't even be in a goddamn race car."

In his defense, Andretti said, "A.J. and I got into it a bit in Turn Three. I went up high to let him pass, but I can't stay up there forever with a loose-handling car. I guess I put him out. I'm sorry for that, but I can't see how I could have done anything different."[23]

Before he left the track, Foyt had calmed down enough to say he wasn't sure what his plans were for 1992. "I don't know what I'm going to do at the present time," he said, indicating a decision would come "probably the later part of January."[24]

Two more races remained on Groff's schedule, and he finished eighth at Road America before dropping out at Laguna Seca. But there was no more talk of getting a head start on next year.

With the season finally over, CART went out of its way to try and make amends with Foyt. The street race in Denver and race on Cleveland's airport were dropped, with the oval at New Hampshire added. The year-end banquet had been scheduled in Houston partly as a tribute to A.J. and partly as a launching pad for a new race being planned for Texas in the coming year.

After originally saying, "CART can kiss my ass, I will not be at that banquet," Foyt relented and agreed to attend. A seven-minute video was shown highlighting his career, and a congratulatory telegram from President George H. W. Bush was read. Foyt received both comeback driver of the year and special achievement awards. CART board members—the other car owners—presented him with a new Cadillac and a leather-bound, embossed copy of the series rulebook. It announced the No. 14 would be reserved for the Foyt team and would be retired when the team no longer needed it.[25]

"Coming in my hometown, this night has special meaning," an embarrassed Foyt said. "I've had some fun through the years." Trying to regain his composure, he turned to Jeff Andretti with what passed for a Foyt apology:[26]

"Jeff, you shouldn't always believe everything you hear on television. I've always said I'm innocent of everything I've ever done."[27]

Sitting at the table with the Foyt family was Gilmore, who was surprised when Foyt called him "my best friend in or outside racing." Also at the table was Steve Watterson, who'd received a last-minute invite from A.J. Watterson said years later,

> We had stayed in touch. He came by and got treatment now and then. But by then he wanted to get on his tractors, which wasn't always the smartest thing.
>
> So, he calls me—and this is vintage A.J.—says, "They have a little thing going on at the convention center tonight for the PPG awards. I'd like you to be my guest—sit with me and my family." He said, "The shindig starts at seven." Then he called back and said, "Anne says to wear a suit." So, I figured it was a little bit of a nicer thing. He wasn't into all the pomp that was part of the sport.
>
> After the dinner there was a tap on my shoulder. "Fine job, young man. You put an icon back on the track. Our profession owes you a debt of gratitude." I turned to thank the man, and it was Paul Newman. To see the inner mingling of the worlds, and the respect that A.J. brings, was overwhelming. I was honored to have had a relationship with him.

Foyt then took team members to his new hunting ranch in Del Rio, Texas, near the border with Mexico. It was a desolate area which would be used as a backdrop for the movie *No Country for Old Men*. But Foyt had turned the hunt club into an oasis, damning up a creek to provide water and turn the area green. He imported animals to hunt and surrounded the property with an electrified fence to keep the game in—and intruders out. While there, it quickly became obvious to crew chief Phil Casey and the others that Foyt was planning to come back for another year.

A few days later, Foyt made it all but official:

> It's possible I'll be back in May. I'm looking forward to it. If I get to feeling much better it's very likely I'll be back. My ankles are giving me a lot of trouble and I've still got the plates and all the screws in. They've put me in some different braces, to try and take out some of the pain. I'm going to try that for a while and maybe be operated on after the Indy 500.[28]
>
> That's the reason I ran Nazareth at the end of the season, just to see how the car felt. The car felt beautiful, and I had a lot of fun.

The announcement was news to Gilmore, who said, "I read about it in the paper. He had trouble just walking to the podium [in Houston] to accept recognition and I figured his most recent retirement statement was for real. But if he says he's going to race at Indy next May, more power to him. I'll be there to support him all the way."[29]

An indication it was more than just talk came when Foyt showed up for a winter test session at the Speedway, running only slightly slower than the fastest cars. Missing from the test was Groff, who had committed what would often become an unpardonable sin—he'd crashed one of A.J.'s cars.

With testing already underway, discussions continued between the Speedway and CART. Both George and Foyt said they were concerned about the rapidly rising costs and the impact it was having on field size and the number of teams competing. Foyt was supportive of stock block engines like the Buick V-6 that was proving to be fast but unreliable. Many of the CART owners, heavily invested in the Ilmor-Chevrolet, opposed any changes.

The CART meetings weren't the only ones George was attending in the waning days of the year. In a largely overlooked event, the Speedway's board of directors approved additional races for the track, specifically a NASCAR event.

It wasn't a new idea. Tony's father Elmer had suggested it to Tony Hulman in the mid-1960s, and A.J. himself had talked to Hulman about renting the track to stage a USAC stock car race there. Even Richard Petty, the King of NASCAR, had openly talked about racing at the Speedway while visiting Foyt earlier in the year. Now George reached out to NASCAR's Bill France Jr., who promised to arrange a test session at the track in the coming year.

AJ Foyt
Copenhagen
RACING
RACING
Copenhagen
RACING

CHAPTER 20

WILL HE OR WON'T HE?

1992

Those closest to A.J. Foyt already knew he was determined to race again in 1992, and he let the rest of the world in on his plans in early January at the annual USAC awards banquet. Rather than run one race a year—the Indianapolis 500—as he first indicated, Foyt decided to start the season as he had the past few, at Phoenix for the Copper World Classic stock car race then on to Daytona for the 500. His only change was to add a new race to his schedule—the season-opening Phoenix CART event.

"I'm feeling a lot better," he said. "It's almost scared me how much my feet and legs have improved over the last week or so. If everything keeps going as it has and I feel like I have lately, it's very likely I'll come back. Don't bet against it."[1]

"I'm ready to hang it up, but I'm not ready to hang it up. I probably shouldn't even have tried to come back last year. I should have waited. I feel like if I quit 100 percent right now, I would be cheating myself. I'd always feel like I'd had some things on my mind I never had the answers to.. I've always been the type of guy that I always want to know the answers."[2]

He accepted several awards during the proceedings and presented Rick Mears with the winner's ring for his fourth 500.

"I hope you get five, six, seven and eight," he said, then added with timing worthy of a comedian, "I do lie now and then."

Mears turned to Foyt when it was his turn at the microphone. "One of the highlights was to sit next to you on the front row in your retirement race," he said. "Now it sounds like you're blowing the whole thing."

Not everyone was supportive of Foyt's plans, especially his wife, Lucy, who had nursed him back to health several times during his career.

◀ Going, going, gone! A.J. at his auction. *David Nearpass*

"My wife was as upset as anybody," he said of his plans to race again. "She said she wasn't going to hand me any more bed pans. She said if I bust my ass, I'm on my own."[3]

After crashing during qualifying for the Copper World Classic and being forced to start forty-fourth and last, Foyt drove through the field to a sixth-place finish, passing NASCAR regulars Ken Schrader and Davey Allison in the process.

At Daytona, he was involved in a multi-car wreck during practice and forced to borrow the backup Oldsmobile of Rick Mast. Foyt wrecked that one in an eight-car crash just four laps into his qualifying race. When added to the field as a promoter's option, he went in search of a third car. He got it from Eddie Bierschwale, a perennial NASCAR backmarker who had turned in the fiftieth qualifying speed and failed to make the 500 in his qualifying race. In the main event, Foyt started thirty-ninth and was still running at the finish in twenty-first place, five laps behind winner Davey Allison. Afterward, he sold what was left of his car and his other parts and equipment.

The race also marked the final Daytona 500 for Richard Petty, who announced he would retire at the end of the season. He said he had learned what not to do by watching Foyt's "retirement" the previous year.

"When Foyt made his announcement, I hadn't made mine, but I'd already made up my mind," Petty said. "I was going to see how he did his deal and he didn't handle it too good. It's a hard thing to give up."[4]

While the number of drivers rumored to be on Foyt's short list of replacements for Mike Groff included Steve Kinser and Arie Luyendyk, Foyt surprised everyone by hiring Gregor Foitek, a Swiss driver and four-time touring car champion. He'd spent the past two years driving for second-rate Formula One teams and trying to qualify for races without much success, a seventh at Monaco his best result. He'd also earned a reputation for being a bit reckless.

In Australia for the season-opener, Foitek qualified a respectable thirteenth but dropped out early. Foyt himself was a surprise starter, qualifying the car of Derrick Walker but stopping after just two laps with an announced transmission problem.

Next on the schedule was Phoenix, and Foitek was a spectator as Foyt took the car out for the first practice session. He was still working up to speed when he lost control and slid into the second turn wall, his fourth crash in three races.

"I was getting ready to put down a hard lap when I felt like I hit fluids because the car went very slowly into a slide. It wasn't like it jumped out on me."[5]

Complaining of pain, he was taken to the hospital where X-rays revealed a hairline fracture of his right shoulder blade. Foyt scoffed at initial estimates that he would be out of action four to six weeks, jeopardizing his start in the Indy 500, saying, "Texans heal faster."[6]

Despite the injury, A.J. went from Phoenix to Indianapolis to oversee Foitek's participation in the Rookie Orientation Program. He'd emptied out his garage, entering five cars in the 500, including a new Lola Chevrolet and his team cars from 1990 and 1991. Although no drivers were listed, it was expected that Foitek would be in one of the cars.

After a day of meetings, however, the Swiss driver said he was headed home and wouldn't be coming back. His wife had reportedly given him an ultimatum—her or racing.

"I came over here and liked it very much, but I've got some family obligations that came up that won't allow me to finish out the season," Foitek told reporters. "I don't want to do just a partial season."[7]

"It was a surprise to all," Foyt said at the time, "but I do understand family obligations because I am very close with my family. It's just one of those deals."[8]

Years later he would say, "I brought the Frenchman here, and he just didn't like lookin' at the walls."[9]

After Foitek left, Foyt was visited by another F1 driver who'd had considerably more success: Nelson Piquet, a three-time world champion with twenty-three grand prix victories. He was a rookie at Indianapolis but had been turning impressive lap times.

"I had never met him, but I had heard so much about him," said Piquet, who was in Foyt's garage for less than a minute and was uncertain if A.J. knew who he was. "I wanted to meet him in person. Of course it's like meeting a legend."[10]

Foyt was at Churchill Downs on Saturday, May 2, for the Kentucky Derby when Jim Crawford stunned the first-day crowd at the Speedway with a lap of nearly 230 miles per hour, five mph faster than the track record. Cool temperatures and windy conditions on day two saw rookie Fabrizio Barbazza slam the wall. The stage was set for a month of unusual weather, high speeds, and drivers hitting the wall.

One of the first things Foyt did upon reaching the Speedway was to announce a surprising choice for the team's second driver: Jeff Andretti. The youngest son of Mario, it was Jeff whom A.J. had ripped on national TV at Nazareth the previous year. The rookie of the race in the 1991 Indy 500, Jeff had been left without a ride when his team folded. Foyt selected him over a number of veteran drivers looking for a ride, including Gordon Johncock and Tom Sneva.

"It was definitely a godsend," said Jeff, who was able to bring limited support from Gillette and Texaco. "It came at a time when I was trying to decide whether to skip Indy and concentrate on getting a ride for the rest of the season. He was getting calls from all kinds of drivers wanting the ride, so he wanted to announce it immediately. That was when we were able to get a sponsorship package going. It was a tremendous break for me."[11]

It was also a relief for Mario, who was teamed with his oldest son, Michael, and among the fastest cars in early practice sessions.

"It's a great opportunity for Jeff," said Mario, who watched his son's first laps standing alongside Foyt. "He had difficulty putting something together and Foyt saved him. This sport is like any other. You've got to be there when the opportunity presents itself. Somewhere the decisive break comes along that changes your whole career. For Jeff, it could be this. He is certainly a happy kid right now."[12]

Despite saying he'd be ready to go on day one when the Speedway opened, A.J.'s right arm, injured in the Phoenix crash, was still in a sling as Jeff Andretti made his first laps. One reporter made the mistake of saying he thought Foyt had retired the previous year.

"That's what you idiots in the media get for thinking," Foyt snapped.[13]

Through it all, U.S. Tobacco PR rep Anne Fornoro was able to keep her sense of humor, noting on the inside of the front cover of the AJ Foyt Racing media guide, "Last year A.J. Foyt had indicated that the 1991 season would be his last driving Indy Cars. He changed his mind."[14]

Although he claimed to be "about twenty pounds lighter," A.J. also admitted he'd lost more than that before his accident. "After I messed up my shoulder and couldn't drive, I started eating some ice cream and candy bars. I figured, what the heck. So I've put a little weight back on, but I still feel a lot better than last year."[15]

It wasn't until midweek that Foyt made his first laps, and by the end of the week, he'd still only run a handful of laps over 220 mph—more than ten mph slower than the fastest cars. But others were in worse shape. Mears, the defending race champion, crashed hard and was limping around the pits with a broken bone in his foot. Next it was Piquet, who'd been impressive all month until he slammed headfirst into the wall, sustaining injuries rivaling Foyt's from Road America. Dr. Terry Trammell spent eight hours in surgery and installed the latest version of the Ilizarov device he first used on Foyt.

One final practice session remained for Saturday morning before qualifying started, but the guaranteed thirty minutes of green-light track time took nearly two hours as one car after another crashed or broke on track.

"Talk about a zoo," Foyt said. "That probably was the most dangerous practice session I've seen in my thirty-five years of being here. It was like five o'clock on the L.A. Hollywood freeway. I just wanted to survive."

Never one to miss an opportunity for the dramatic and with the long practice session and occasional light showers playing havoc with the schedule, Foyt began working the clock like only someone with his experience could. He was set to be the last car on the track when qualifying closed for the day at 6:00 p.m. Just ahead of Foyt was Danny Sullivan, who was already on the track building speed when Roberto Guerrero, who'd just captured the pole at a record-shattering average of more than 236 mph, suddenly slowed, forcing Sullivan to abort his run. He was brought back to the pits and told he could refuel his car and go to the head of the line. But when he did, he found Foyt there, revving his engine.

"You think I'm going to bump A.J. out of line?" recalled Sullivan, who pulled to the side. "Think about what kind of problem that would have been."

Foyt ran his first three laps at more than 226 mph, good for the second row at the time, but it was all for naught as the engine let go coming down the backstraight on lap four. He cruised into the field the next day but would have to start well back in twenty-third, two rows behind teammate Jeff Andretti.

"A.J. has really been great to work with," Andretti said. "Some people said he would be tough, but he helped me get through these tough times. It's been a pretty productive month, but we didn't have all the time in the world to work on the car before qualifying. I'm not happy about our average, but A.J. thought it would hold up."[16]

The carnage continued the following week and reached a peak when Filipino rookie Jovy Marcelo was killed during practice on Friday. Two more drivers,

Hiro Matsushita and Pancho Carter, crashed heavily on the weekend and were also injured. In fifteen days of practice and time trials, fourteen cars had hit the wall. Mears joined several other drivers saying they wanted to see speeds cut back.

"I think it would be good if we could slow the cars down," said the defending champion, "so that 200 mph means something again."[17]

Foyt disagreed.

"Speed is not what kills you. Look at Rick's accident. He was at top speed and survived it. Look at Jovy. He was just coming out of the pits coming up to speed, but he hit his head. Tracks are made to run faster. This track is safer now at 220 mph than it ever was at 150. It's according to how you hit in the car. Like any type of race car or passenger car, if you hit wrong, that's it, I don't care if you're in a damn tank or on a bicycle."[18]

There was another problem on race day: the weather. A cold front had moved through Indianapolis overnight, and as the field moved away for its pace laps, the official temperature was forty-three degrees with a wind chill factor of thirty-nine. Race tires are designed to work best when hot, and it was apparent before the start that getting tires up to optimum temperature was going to be a challenge. Pole sitter Roberto Guerrero was swerving back and forth and trying to heat up his tires on the parade lap when his car veered hard left and into the inside wall, putting him out of the race. A second driver spun but was able to continue.

It wasn't just the inexperienced drivers having trouble. Tom Sneva, Mario Andretti, Emerson Fittipaldi, and Mears were all involved in crashes. Eight times the race was slowed by accidents involving thirteen drivers, nine of whom ended up at Methodist Hospital.

Jeff Andretti had the biggest crash, although it wasn't because of the tires. The right-rear wheel hub broke on his car in Turn Two, and he flew into the wall just below the Foyt family suite. It took nearly twenty minutes to extricate him from the car, and he was sent immediately to Methodist Hospital.

For his part, Foyt had told Jim Gilmore before the start he wanted to finish the race and, "I'm not going to push it. I'm just going to try to keep the car in." He did just that, and thanks mainly to the high attrition rate, picked up fourteen positions to finish ninth—although five laps behind first-time winner Al Unser Jr. It was his seventeenth top-ten finish at Indianapolis, far more than any other driver. Only ten drivers had even competed in seventeen 500s.[19]

When asked about retirement, he joked he might race for five more years until he could start collecting social security. He added he'd make a decision "when it's appropriate," but by the next night at the Victory Banquet, it sounded as if his mind was made up.[20]

"You're probably seeing A.J. Foyt coming to an end because I'm not the same A.J. Foyt I used to be. Thank you and God bless you. I love you all."[21]

One thing was certain: Foyt was not going to drive in the upcoming Detroit Grand Prix road race where he'd had so much trouble the year before. With Foitek in Europe and Jeff Andretti in the hospital facing a long recovery, he was in need of a driver for the No. 14.

"That was a shame about Jeff," Foyt said. "It wasn't his fault. We got along real well at Indy. He qualified good, he ran fast and I know we could have worked together real good. When that happened, it left us hurting."[22]

He picked Brian Bonner, who'd qualified twenty-sixth for the 500 in his first oval track race. Set to line up right behind Foyt, the two sat next to each other during the driver's meeting, where they met and chatted. Bonner, who'd spent most of his career in sports cars, then got around Foyt at the start and ran as high as seventh before crashing out near the halfway point. He had made an impression, however.

"Brian is clean cut," A.J. said. "He did a nice job at Indy. He's got some road racing experience and I felt I wanted to give him a shot at Indy cars."[23]

Bonner, thirty-two, said, "To think about the sequence of events and how fast it all happened, it's crazy. I guess I just happened to be at the right place at the right time. Obviously, I made some people pay attention (at Indy) but I put a lot of pressure on myself to do well there, because I could've smoked my career right there if I don't even qualify."

At Detroit, Foyt told him, "You don't have to be a hero. Do a respectable job, keep if off the wall and bring it back in one piece."[24]

After qualifying twentieth, Bonner worked his way through the field, passing more drivers than anyone else and finishing tenth behind winner Bobby Rahal. It was exactly what Foyt wanted—or so Bonner thought.

Unknown to Bonner, Foyt had already tested Ross Cheever, the younger brother of Eddie, at Texas World Speedway. When Cheever ran well, Foyt hired him to drive in the next road course on the schedule, at Portland.

In retrospect, Bonner said he should have been able to read the handwriting on the wall. He'd been surprised when the team showed up in Detroit with a year-old Lola rather than the car Foyt had driven at Indianapolis. His name wasn't on the car, and he also noticed a stream of drivers in and out of the team's trailer to talk to A.J. Bonner recalled,

> Going into that race I think they already knew it was going to be a one-race deal. I should have known when we met some people in the lobby of the hotel and he introduced me by saying, "This is Brian. This is the boy who's driving for me this weekend." It was like this is the boy who's driving for me this weekend, but not next weekend.[25]
>
> After the race I went around and shook hands with the crew, and there was a real sense of finality to it all. I had to look at the faces of my family and friends, who were smiling and happy, to get any kind of feedback.
>
> You have to love racing. It's not something you should do because it's a job and it's a paycheck. You have to love it, and I got the feeling it's become more or less a job to A.J.'s crew, and I don't ever want it to be that way for me.

It was another week before rumors of the Cheever signing began to leak out.

"They said they were going to call, and they never called me," Bonner said. "It wasn't until I called them that I found out. It would be easy for me to be bitter, but I feel everything happens for a reason. I believe in fate, and for whatever reason it wasn't meant to be. I feel like A.J. has a good team and good equipment, but he does things a little differently than I'm used to."

Bonner would run a few more races for Dale Coyne, but his tenth place at Detroit would be his best Indy car finish. He failed to qualify for Indianapolis the following year and then ran a few stock car events, including a failed attempt to qualify Foyt's stocker at Watkins Glen in 1994, ending his career at the end of that year.

Cheever, twenty-eight, had been successfully racing open-wheel cars in Japan with an eye on following his brother into F1. That's where Foyt contacted him and asked him to come to Houston. The test went well, with Foyt saying, "I was amazed he ran as fast as he did.[26]

"I'm still learning at this point," Cheever said of his first meeting with Foyt. He'd already learned one important lesson: "It's better if I just keep my mouth shut and listen and try to learn as much as I can from A.J. He knows what he wants and knows how to get it."

Cheever was working with a new team manager, John Anderson, who'd replaced Phil Casey. Foyt wanted to run more of his operation out of Houston instead of the team's garage at the Speedway, and Casey didn't want to spend that much time away from his family in Indianapolis. Besides, now that he wasn't driving, A.J. was the de facto crew chief. Anderson had overseen Guerrero's pole-winning team at Indianapolis but since that group had only run the 500 he'd been looking for work.

At Portland, Cheever qualified fifteenth and finished eleventh, a decent start. "He did a great job," Foyt said, "drove a heckuva race." He told Cheever to plan on making his first oval track start a week later at Milwaukee and that he would drive most of the rest of the schedule for the team. But A.J. already had other things on his mind.

NASCAR Comes to Indy

Many of NASCAR's top drivers, including Dale Earnhardt, Bill Elliott, Davey Allison, Rusty Wallace, Ernie Irvan, Mark Martin, Kyle Petty, Ricky Rudd, and Darrell Waltrip, were already making laps at the Indianapolis Motor Speedway on June 23 when Foyt arrived at the track. He made a beeline for the garage of Richard Childress Racing and its most famous employee, Earnhardt.

The relationship between the two drivers had improved light years since its inauspicious beginning in 1979, when Earnhardt was trying to make his first Daytona 500. He'd failed to follow Foyt when he pulled out to pass Waltrip on the last lap of a qualifying race, which cost both drivers a chance at victory. At the time, Foyt had been furious.

The two strong-willed drivers eventually gravitated toward each other, however, and became friendly. Most importantly, Earnhardt had learned to give Foyt's guff right back to him.

"A.J. and Dale had a mutual relationship because they respected each other," recalled Danny "Chocolate" Myers, who handled fueling duties on Earnhardt's car during pit stops and was at the Indianapolis test. "It all had to do with the way that they were. Both those guys were aggressive."[27] He continued,

> The first time I met Foyt was one of the coolest things ever. It was at a test at Daytona, and he was there. We had started to win a couple of races, but we were just a bunch of guys from North Carolina, and he was *A.J. Foyt.* When you were around Foyt, you knew that presence was there—that powerful personality. We looked up to that guy. He was the hero of all heroes. You wanted to be up close, but you were almost afraid to be around him. You didn't want to intrude. You didn't want to be in the way. But we were going to go to lunch, and Richard told me to ask Foyt if he wanted to go. That's how I got my foot in the door.
>
> The more you were around him, the more comfortable you got with him. Eventually, it got to the point it was okay to tease each other and say things to each other and just have a good time.

Now it was Foyt's turn. With the team on pit road, he went into its garage, grabbed a radio, and started telling Earnhardt what he was doing wrong—mostly that he was slowing down too much in the turns. "If you go down there and flatfoot it through the corners, you can make it," the voice said. "You've got to flat-foot it through there."[28]

It wasn't until Earnhardt questioned who was on the team's radio channel and the voice shot back, "We stopped backing off in the '60s," that Dale realized who it was—Foyt.

Back in the garage, Childress offered to unload the team's second car for Foyt to drive for a few laps. At first A.J. begged off, saying he didn't have a uniform or helmet. Then Childress volunteered the uniform of the six-foot-four, 250-pound Myers, if Foyt "could fit into it."

Fitting into the uniform was easier than getting into the car and then into the seat of the much smaller Earnhardt. Once on the track, A.J. struggled through a couple of laps before pulling back into the pits.

"It meant the world to him to be able to do that," Myers recalled. "You could tell how excited he was to go out there and make some laps. And I still got that uniform."

Earnhardt wasn't about to cut Foyt any slack, saying, "Not so easy, is it, fat boy?"

Foyt sounded later as if he would approve of a stock car race at the track.

"NASCAR and the Speedway need to look at the pluses and minuses, (but) the way I'm looking at it right now, I can't see that many minuses. Those boys put on a helluva show. People will pay to see good racing."[29]

Most of the Indy car drivers, however, spoke out against the possibility of a NASCAR race at the Speedway, including Mario Andretti. "I'd hate to see it happen because, to me, Indianapolis has always been sacred ground for open-wheeled, single seat thoroughbreds." Johnny Rutherford was even more blunt. "I think it's a big mistake."[30]

A.J. acknowledged, "Some Indy drivers don't like it because it brings their pedestal down. But if you're a winner you can adjust to different types of racing. A lot of guys running Indy cars don't know what they're missing."[31]

Foyt was kept out of a mock race by NASCAR officials who first said he "wasn't invited." They eventually altered their position, saying two No. 3 cars in the photos would be confusing. Later, at the bar in the Speedway Motel, a group of NASCAR drivers and crew members let Foyt know how they felt, greeting him with chants of "A.J., A.J., A.J."

The first oval track start of Cheever's career at Milwaukee got off to a rough start when he hit the wall in the opening practice session. Often the end of a driver's career with the team, A.J. joked about it as he worked to repair the car, saying, "If you're going to make me get my hands dirty, you're going to have to come to the ranch and plow soybeans and get yours dirty."

Cheever qualified twentieth in the twenty-two-car field and stopped after just thirty laps, complaining about the No. 14's handling. As far as Foyt was concerned, the experiment with the road race driver on an oval track was over. He hired Pancho Carter, who was still recovering from the arm he broke at Indianapolis, to drive in upcoming events at New Hampshire and Michigan.

Foyt had raced against Carter's father, Duane, in the late 1950s and early 1960s and later against Pancho when he was getting started running midgets and sprint cars. Carter had won the 1972 USAC midget championship and 1974 and 1976 sprint car titles. He hadn't fared as well in Indy cars, and it had been ten years since his lone Indy car victory in the inaugural Michigan 500 in 1981. Although a serious crash had left him with a badly injured leg that made it difficult for him to drive on road courses, he was still fast on ovals.

At New Hampshire July 5, Carter qualified fourteenth and finished eleventh. Jan Beekhuis drove Foyt's car on the Toronto street course, and Carter was back in it for the Michigan 500. Things, however, were not going smoothly. Thirty years later Carter recalled,

> He was going through a bunch of drivers at the time. He'd go with somebody he thought was a road racing specialist on the road courses. Then he called me because he knew I was really good on the ovals. I probably should have turned it down. It was only four or five weeks after I broke my right arm at the Speedway. I was supposed to wear a brace, but I couldn't drive with it, so I just went without.[32]
>
> I wouldn't say we hit it off great. We definitely butted heads in a lot of areas. My eyes are very light sensitive, so I wore a dark [helmet] shield. He used to flip my shield up so he could look me in the eye, and I'd flip it down. We must have done that half a dozen times before he finally just gave up. He also loved to put more wing in your car when you were in the qualifying line. So, when nobody was looking, I would back out some of

the wing, knowing full well what he was going to do when I was sitting in the car and couldn't do anything about it.

At Loudon there was a practice the morning of the race, and we had the car all set up from Saturday. I asked before I got in the car what changes were made, and everyone said, "We didn't make any changes." I made it as far as Turn Three, and the thing swapped ends on me—slapped the fence—and we had to repair the suspension. I found out later A.J. had told them not to tell me what changes they had made.

At Michigan the half shaft broke going into Turn Three. I got it whoaed down and into the pits. I got out of the car and walked by A.J. and told him, "I just saved you about $250,000 because this car should have crashed." And that was that.

Going, Going, Gone

Perhaps the biggest racing event of the summer took place at the Indianapolis Motor Speedway August 13–15, although the track itself was quiet. That's when Foyt took advantage of a rare off weekend in the Indy car schedule to stage a garage sale to empty out his Houston race shops. It was the only garage sale in America featured on page one of *USA Today.*

He stressed that he wasn't going broke and it wasn't a going out of business sale—only that he wanted to move to a smaller shop and he'd accumulated too much "stuff" over the years.

"I just don't want to mess with it," Foyt said. "If somebody wants this stuff, fine. If nobody bids on it, they can have it. It's not the money. I don't care if it brings in a nickel. I just don't have no room and I don't feel like keeping them up any more. I've had my fun with 'em for 35 years. Let someone else have some fun. The cars are too nice to sit in a barn with three or four inches of dust on 'em."[33]

Foyt said it took ten tractor trailer loads to haul everything to the Speedway, and initial estimates put the expected take at about $5 million. The star of the show was the Coyote he'd driven to victory in the 1977 Indy 500. Foyt had originally promised to give it to track owner Tony Hulman for the Speedway Museum. Now Foyt said the car that had been on display the past fifteen years was actually his backup Coyote, which was also put on the docket.

Another of the top draws was the 1964 Type 34 Lotus he'd acquired from Ford. He'd extensively modified it before capturing the pole at Indianapolis in 1965 and went on to win three races during the course of the season. A beautifully restored midget Foyt had driven during the 1960s also attracted attention. Other cars included a trio of Lola Indy racers, several NASCAR stockers, and the 1979 Camaro he drove to the USAC championship.

A number of personal vehicles were also set to be auctioned off, topped by a 1984 Ferrari 512 Berlinetta Boxer (or BBi, the "i" indicating it was fuel injected). Foyt had bought it as a personal driver, but it had just over 9,000 miles on the odometer as he'd kept it mostly in a barn on his ranch, afraid it might be damaged if he drove it. There was a 1959 black Ford Ranchero that once served as A.J.'s tow vehicle and a Rayson Craft drag/ski boat with a Ford 427 SOHC engine built by Holman-Moody. It was supposedly so fast it scared even A.J. and was only put in the water once. Other items included the remains of the Foyt/Ford engine inventory from the 1970s—along with the motor's tooling and casting equipment—thousands of spare parts, and one of the team's tractor trailers with a machine shop on board. There were plenty of uniforms and personal memorabilia, along with numerous trophies—most of which were in various states of disrepair—an estimated 7,000 auction lots in all, scattered under the Tower Terrace grandstands.

"To get all these cars in one place is unbelievable," said NASCAR team owner Richard Childress, who was in attendance and had his eyes on the midget. "I'd like to have one. As a kid I was an A.J. Foyt fan. I had to come here and see it myself."[34]

Foyt said he wasn't taking anything home, and as a result there would be no minimum bid. As the first day of the auction approached, however, he began to have second thoughts:

"In one sense, I've regretted I got it started," he admitted. "Now that it's getting close, I'm getting cold feet. They're going to have to tie my hands to keep me from buying some of that stuff back. I love all of it."[35]

"There's stuff here I hadn't seen in twenty-five years. I spent millions and millions of dollars to buy this. In today's dollars, it would sink the Queen Elizabeth. Probably, someday, when I go out to the garages and everything is gone, that's when it'll hit me. But the memories are in my heart. Those can't be sold and will never be lost."[36]

Joining Childress at the auction were a number of heavy hitters, including Tony George, George Snider, Jack Starne, Smokey Yunick, Dale Coyne, Arie Luyendyk, and longtime Indy car builders A.J. Watson and Grant King.

"I'm interested in them," Luyendyk said of the cars, "but I can't afford them. I collect memorabilia, like drivers' suits and helmets. I'll see what he has and maybe I'll bid on some of them. I've been asking A.J. to give me stuff, but he won't do it, so I guess I'll have to buy it."

Four uniforms were unavailable—the ones Foyt wore while winning the Indianapolis 500.

"My mom kept all of my driving uniforms I won here in," he said. "And there's not enough money in the world that would get me to get rid of them. They were never cleaned. She put them in plastic bags just like they were when I got out of the car."[37]

Victory Lane doubled as the auction block for the racers and passenger cars. Video and audio tapes helped introduce each car, and Foyt started things off by saying a few words about them.

- On the 1977 race-winning Coyote: "We designed and built it in Houston along with the engine—and that will never happen again."[38]
- The 1964 Lotus: "It was a great race car, but it was also the most dangerous. Sitting in the middle of all that fuel. If I knew then what I know now, I never would have climbed into the thing."

- The midget: "Parnelli [Jones], Herk [Jim Hurtubise] and I all drove this car and it won a lot of races. With that Offy engine and all the memories, it's probably my sentimental favorite. When you race a midget on a dirt track, bumping and sliding around with the rest of the guys, you get a feel for what racing's all about."[39]
- The Ferrari: "It was just too damn expensive to really drive. I was always scared somebody was going to hit the aluminum body and bend it. It's the kind of car you drive on weekends, and if you park it, you park it a quarter-mile away from everybody else so no one bangs the door."[40]

The personal introductions ended after just a few cars when it became apparent the process was more emotional than Foyt expected. It had the same impact on Yunick, who was watching from the grandstands.

"I watched closely and had a hell of a time to keep from crying," Yunick wrote in a story for *Circle Track Magazine*. "I really felt for him. For thirty-five years the man *was* Indy. I plan on going back next year [to the 500] and I hope I see him there. But my biggest hope for him is that he never drives an Indy car again, 'cept in old timers' races. Quit playing with live rattlesnakes and let the racing world enjoy what is left of you."[41]

Yunick added, "I truly believe him to be the greatest race driver that ever raced and probably the most onerous human being that ever strapped himself in a race car."

George was the big spender, outbidding Tom Ryan, a retired auto dealer and friend of Yunick's, for the 1977 winner. The $410,000 bid was less than expected but more than Foyt had earned for winning the race ($259,791). To ensure there was no confusion on which car was the race winner, George also bought the backup Coyote for $112,000. The Museum kicked in another $19,000 for a complete Foyt/Ford racing engine.

"It's always been an important car to us," George said of the race winner. "It was important to my grandfather. I think he would have wanted it this way, so I was here for him to make sure we at least had an opportunity to make its permanent home in the museum."[42]

George also bid on several other vehicles without success, including a 1976 midnight blue Cadillac El Dorado that had special meaning for him. Following the death of his father, Elmer George, in a shootout with the man who was having an affair with his mother, Mari Hulman George, Foyt had taken sixteen-year-old Tony to Houston to get away from the media coverage and memories. It was one of the cars in Foyt's garage at the time.

"I'd go out in the garage every morning and look at it," George said. "I thought it was the neatest car I'd ever seen."[43]

Ryan didn't go away empty-handed, placing the winning bid of $165,000 for the 1965 pole winner. It would change hands several times, most recently in 2017 when it was sold at auction for a reported $1,150,000.

Both George and Childress were outbid on the midget that went for $82,000 to Keith Elson of Cedar Rapids, Iowa. Although Foyt said he had turned down an offer of $375,000 for the Ferrari a few years earlier, it went for just $120,000—even with its "A.J. Foyt" license plate. A pit board sold for $1,200, and used tires were going for as much as $1,000. In all, an estimated 15,000 people attended over the three days with total sales of about $3 million.

With four consecutive road course races next on the schedule—Cleveland, Road America, Vancouver, and Mid-Ohio—Ross Cheever had returned to the No. 14 car. After dropping out early at Cleveland, he crashed in practice at Road America and again on the second lap of the race. When he crashed in practice at Vancouver, that was it. The car was withdrawn, and Ross Cheever's Indy car career was over.

"I'm looking at a lot of drivers but I don't know if I can afford them," Foyt said. "Every time they wreck, it costs me a $200,000 race car. I keep saying that if we can't get somebody, I'll get back in."[44]

To finish out the season, he turned to Mike Groff, the same driver he had dropped at the end of the previous year. The team showed an immediate improvement at Mid-Ohio and Nazareth, Groff racing into the top ten before a bad pit stop and blown engine dropped him back. In the season-ending Laguna Seca race, he posted the team's best finish of the year—eighth. Afterward, a frustrated Groff found himself back in the unemployment line, Foyt having already made other plans for the coming year.

"Team owners over here are enamored by foreigners and, while I think there's a place for a foreign driver, I really don't understand it," Groff said. "A lot of these owners don't know the true value that's under their nose. American drivers can't look good if they don't get the same shake as the foreigners. If I can get a race car that's capable, I assure you I'll be right there. I'm not a quitter."[45]

Have You Driven a Ford Lately?

Despite the dismal 1992 season, opportunity came knocking on the door of AJ Foyt Racing in the form of Ford Motor Company, Michael Kranefuss, and Robby Gordon.

After sitting on the sidelines of Indy car racing since 1971 when it sold the last of its engine program to Foyt, Ford had returned to the series on a limited basis in 1992, paying to put the corporate logo on the valve covers of the first all-new Cosworth engine since 1967. In the hands of the Newman-Haas and Chip Ganassi teams, the powerplant proved competitive, especially with Michael Andretti behind the wheel as he posted all five of the Ford-powered victories. In an effort to end Chevrolet's run of five straight Indy 500 wins, Ford was ready to make the engine available to additional teams for 1993, and given Foyt's prior relationship with the company, his team seemed like a natural fit.

The Ford offer came with one string attached—while Foyt could race at Indianapolis and anywhere else he wanted, the twenty-three-year-old Gordon would be the team's primary driver and compete for the Indy car championship. It was an offer Foyt couldn't refuse.

Gordon was the prodigy of Kranefuss, the director of Ford's Special Vehicle Operations, the company's worldwide racing group. Bobby Unser referred to Gordon as Ford's "golden-haired angel."[46]

The son of off-road racer Bob Gordon, Robby began racing dirt bikes when he was seven and won his first desert race in a four-wheel vehicle when he was sixteen, beating his father in the process. With Ford's pickup truck sales as the key to the company's success and off-road racing as an important promotional outlet, Gordon endeared himself to its racing brass, winning five straight off-road class championships from 1986 to 1990 and its two biggest races, the Baja 500 and Baja 1000.

Kranefuss had moved him to Jack Roush and Ford's road racing program in 1990, where he won both Trans-Am and IMSA GT races. He won the Daytona 24 Hours by driving fourteen of twenty-four hours when a teammate injured his eye, similar to Foyt's feat in winning Le Mans. Continuing his rapid advancement, he made a few NASCAR starts in early 1991, and then ran seven Indy car races for Ganassi during the second half of the 1992 season, with a pair of eighth-place finishes to show for it.

Ganassi, who once drove for Foyt at Indianapolis, had launched his own Indy car team in 1990 and was still looking for his first win. He'd made a smart move buying into the Ford Cosworth program through Newman-Haas, but his team was basically a one-car operation with Eddie Cheever as the driver, adding Arie Luyendyk for the 500-milers at Indianapolis and Michigan. The addition of Gordon at the end of the year had put a strain on the team.

At the end of the 1992 season, Ganassi had let Cheever go and hired Luyendyk as his regular driver. There'd been little chemistry between Ganassi and Gordon, and when Ford was unwilling to fund Gordon for an entire season, it reverted to a one-car operation. As a result, Kranefuss needed a new home for Gordon. Foyt's team was one of the few without a primary driver already in place, and a deal was quickly made. A.J. was on message at the Monday press conference to announce the partnership, held a few days before Thanksgiving at the Speedway Motel.

"Some of the best years of my life were with Ford Motor Company," he said. "Our main concentration is to try and win for Ford and Robby."[47]

When pressed about his own plans, Foyt said, "I really don't know. U.S. Tobacco doesn't want me to run anymore. I gotta take off thirty pounds and I don't know if I feel like getting in shape to run Indy. If I see a chance and I felt good, I might try to qualify on the second weekend, but I'd prefer to answer that question later. Right now we're going to give Robby 110 percent and try to get him going fast."

Gordon also said all the right things.

"A.J.'s always been an idol and I'm not replacing him, I'm just joining his team. I learned a lot this year and I feel I've got a lot more to learn next year. And what better teacher than A.J.?"

Foyt didn't mince words when it came to his team's recent performance on the track. "The last two or three years we haven't performed and we took a big you-know-what last season. I tried a lot of drivers last year and it got pretty expensive. I ran the team and it's my fault, but I guarantee you we're going to improve in 1993."[48]

Kranefuss hoped Foyt might be able to provide some desperately needed discipline and direction for the young driver. Gordon was outgoing, personable, and likable. He could also be hard on equipment, brash, cocky, and hot-headed, with more than his share of on-track encounters.

"Robby is almost like one of my sons, who also don't listen," Kranefuss said of his star pupil. "Young people wonder sometimes if they actually can learn from somebody who is much older, or has done the same stuff for maybe twenty years. It's up to Robby to tickle A.J. in the right places. Robby's got to realize, 'If I'm going to talk to A.J., asking him the right stuff, I'm going to learn.'"[49]

Kranefuss added that Robby "has two major faults. He has got very little fear and he's got no respect for other people. Any time he entered into a higher class of racing, if he didn't win right away, he was really upset. I mean, difficult to deal with. But if this combination doesn't work, I'll be surprised—big time."[50]

The Foyt/Ford deal wasn't the only major announcement during an unusually busy offseason as Indy car champion Michael Andretti signed with Team McLaren in F1 for the coming year, to be replaced by the reigning F1 champion, Nigel Mansell.

In a bit of odd timing, it was also announced at year-end that Mario Andretti, who surpassed Foyt during the season in career Indy car starts, had been named motorsports driver of the quarter century, spanning 1967–1992. He'd topped Foyt and Petty in a vote of twelve journalists and sixteen surviving drivers who'd won past driver of the year honors.

"This is the biggest thing that has ever happened to me," Andretti said in a ceremony at Charlotte Motor Speedway while a stoic Foyt looked on:

> I have an Indy 500 trophy, I have a Daytona 500 trophy, but I will never have a trophy that will be so big in my house as this one. Just to be asked to be in the company of people like Richard and A.J. and all the rest would have been honor enough. Every man on this stage has so many skills, I will be forever grateful, because the drivers participated in the vote. I know race drivers, and we're all a selfish group, and if we could have, every one of us would have voted for himself. To be chosen driver of the year is incredible enough. Only those of us who have received it knows what it means. But to be picked for twenty-five years, I owe you big time.[51]

The other announcement was a shocker: Rick Mears saying at Roger Penske's Christmas party that he was retiring from racing.

"I'd been doing it for fifteen years and I was tired," said the forty-one-year-old Mears. "It was burnout. When you get up in the morning, if that desire isn't there, you can't get in a race car like that."[52]

Andretti said he was "surprised" and "shocked" when he heard the news and, "I wish I could talk him out of it." But Foyt said he was making the right decision.[53]

"Rick has a lot of good years left in him to race, but if he doesn't want to, he did the right thing."

At the time of his announcement, Mears said the possibility of breaking his tie with Foyt for most Indy 500 victories never entered into his decision process. "I don't care about records. The opportunity to win that fifth at Indy had no bearing." Thirty years later, he'd say otherwise:[54]

> The possibility of a fifth win was the hardest part of the decision. I struggled with that. I knew how much the team wanted it. I knew how much they would have loved to have gotten that fifth win. Same as me. I felt like I was letting the team down if I retired.[55]
>
> So I struggled with it and struggled with it and finally woke up one morning and thought, *You idiot, if the desire is not there, you're not gonna get the fifth win. You're not gonna do what's necessary to win.* So I decided if I was not gonna get the win for them anyway, and if I'm not gonna get the job done, it's not fair to them. It's just time to go.

Copenhagen
RACING
Copenhagen
RACING
AC 120V

CHAPTER 21

IT'S TIME

1993

The stories comparing A.J. Foyt and Robby Gordon started immediately after the announcement of their pairing. The brash Gordon would be twenty-four when he started his first Indy 500 if all went well, while a brash Foyt had been twenty-three when he first qualified for the race.

"He's cocky, he's a little arrogant and he wants to win," Foyt acknowledged. "That's the way you have to be to be a winner today."[1]

"I stepped into some pretty big shoes," he said, recalling how he'd taken over the Dean Van Lines Special from two-time champion Jimmy Bryan in 1958. "I felt pretty cocky too, like nobody could beat me. You've got to have that attitude. You've got to feel you're the best and you can beat anybody."[2]

Also joining AJ Foyt Racing was Kenny Anderson (no relation to team manager John Anderson) who'd worked well with Gordon at Chip Ganassi Racing.

"A.J. and Robby are both very talented," Anderson said. "They're two peas from the same pod. Very self-assured and very selfish. Don't take that wrong. I just mean they want it all. They want to win everything. All the great drivers are like that."[3]

The arrival of Ken Anderson as technical director was a major addition to the team. He was part of a new breed of specialized racing engineers taking advantage of the latest technology when setting up their cars. They were also rapidly replacing the jack-of-all-trades, shoot-from-the-hip chief mechanics that had reigned over Indy cars for years.

Like Gordon, he had an off-road racing background, having worked with Roger Mears, the older brother of Rick. He'd had an important role with the success of Fox Racing Shox (shock absorbers) in the off-road arena. When Mears moved to Indy cars in the early 1980s and found the performance of shock

◀ A.J. tells Tom Carnegie, "It's time." *IMS Photo Archive*

absorbers wanting, he contacted Anderson. Fox shock absorbers quickly became an alternative to the traditional Monroe shocks that had dominated Indy car racing, and Tom Sneva won the national championship in 1983 using them. Anderson also had become acquainted with Foyt during the period, doing some work for A.J.'s Porsche 962 team, so he wasn't a complete unknown.

"He was always very nice—when he wasn't pissed off," Anderson remembered from his first stint with Foyt.[4]

Through Rick Mears, he'd met Roger Penske, who hired him to play a key role in the development of the team's proprietary shock absorbers. He also served as race engineer for Mears from 1985 to 1988, including the fourth Indy 500 victory. He'd left for a shot at Formula One with the Ligier and then Onyx teams. The demise of Onyx returned him to the U.S. and Ganassi. Left without a job following Ganassi's decision to run just one car, he followed Gordon to Foyt.

The addition of Anderson marked a much-needed concession by A.J. With engine manufacturers maintaining strict control over the powerplants and most of the teams using the same basic Lola chassis, engineers like Anderson were becoming increasingly critical to a team's success. He wasn't concerned about Foyt's reputation for being tough on mechanics and especially engineers. Years later, Anderson recalled what working with Foyt was like:

> A.J. ran a really good little team. He probably had half the number of people that other teams had. But they were a great group of guys who'd been with him a long time and the cars were always immaculately prepared.
>
> He was also way more accepting of technology than people thought. Here's a guy who started in dirt, then roadsters, embraced Lotus, motors in the back, and fat tires. He was always looking for something new. He was open to technology as much as anybody.
>
> What A.J. doesn't like is stupid. If you did something stupid, he'd call you on it. You tried not to do too much stupid.

Foyt purchased the car Gordon drove at Ganassi in order to start a testing program while awaiting the arrival of two new 1993 Lolas. It was another departure for a team that had done very little testing in recent years.

Somewhat surprisingly, Gordon, a fun-loving California boy, melded easily and quickly with the team. He adapted to the good-natured banter the team shared and helped around the shop where he could. He bonded with Tommy LaMance, who was about the same age and worked for the team. Gordon lived most of the year in Houston, staying at A.J.'s ranch or with LaMance.

Testing was interrupted when Gordon was called to run one last IMSA race for Jack Roush and Ford, the season-opening Daytona 24 Hours. He led the Mustang team to a class victory and second place overall behind the winning prototype. It was Gordon's fourth straight class win in the endurance race.

Foyt himself tried to qualify for the Daytona 500. Having sold off his stock car inventory at the garage sale, his new relationship with Ford helped open the door to a team being formed by Bobby Jones, a former crew chief for

Junior Johnson. The group struggled to get the new car through the inspection process, however, and Foyt posted the forty-ninth and slowest qualifying speed. Any hope he had of making one more Daytona start ended with an overheating engine in his qualifying race.

Foyt's performance was in stark contrast to that of Jeff Gordon, the now twenty-one-year-old driver starting his first full season in Winston Cup. It was Gordon who sought career advice from Foyt two years earlier and was steered away from Indy cars and toward NASCAR. His Daytona debut in NASCAR's premier series began in dramatic fashion as he won his 125-mile qualifying race. The contrast did not go unnoticed.

"While Jeff Gordon blossomed, A.J. Foyt withered," wrote longtime Foyt supporter Dick Mittman of the *Indianapolis News*. "It's embarrassing to watch a driver you have admired for three and a half decades refuse to accept that his best days are behind him. Why can't this man who once was the greatest driver in the world give up?"[5]

Dale Earnhardt, the winner of Foyt's qualifying race who would go on to finish second in the 500, admitted he had mixed feelings watching his friend try and make the field.

"I love him to death and I support him if he wants to race," Earnhardt said. But "it's pretty tough. Sometimes you hate to see him run bad. It's something he has to come to grips with."

Foyt himself couldn't help but reminisce about his years driving stock cars, while taking a shot at the new breed of drivers, especially Indy car drivers.

"I've enjoyed the people here as much as anything," he said. "Some of the guys in our type of racing are so snooty.[6]

"In the old days we drove so many different cars just to try to make a living. These guys today are spoiled. In their first year they make more money than I won when I won the championship. I'd like to see some of these guys try to run in the dirt at the Hoosier 100. They wouldn't even know where the clutch pedal is."

The first Indy car race of the year was in Australia, and Foyt—whose feet had given him trouble during the long flight the year before—elected to stay in Houston, turning the event over to the Andersons and Gordon. The rough street circuit at Surfers Paradise put a premium on chassis setup, especially shocks and dampers, and Ken Anderson immediately proved his worth as Gordon set fast time on the first day of practice.

"*We* were even surprised how fast we were," Anderson would recall. Gordon was fastest again in Saturday morning practice, but something broke in the transmission as he headed down pit road for the final practice session, and he failed to make a lap, the team barely getting the car repaired in time for qualifying.[7]

The weekend's big story, however—as it would be all year—was Nigel Mansell, the defending F1 world champion. He was paired at Newman-Haas with another world champion, Mario Andretti, and replacing Mario's son Michael. It was the first time in history the reigning F1 champion had come to Indy car for a full season.

Born in England, Mansell, the BBC's Sports Personality of 1992, was enormously popular in Australia. Race organizers distributed more than 800 media credentials, more than any race other than Indianapolis. The Indy car media even gave it a name: "Mansell Mania."

Mansell proved the mania wasn't just hype when he qualified on the pole, with Emerson Fittipaldi alongside, putting two former world champions on the front row. The second row was made up of the twenty-four-year-old young guns being touted as the future of Indy car racing. Paul Tracy, starting his second season with Roger Penske, qualified third, with Gordon fourth.

Gordon made his presence felt right from the start, forcing his way past Mansell with a daring move and then passing Tracy for second. He went back and forth between second and third throughout the race, losing any chance at victory when the clutch failed and he stalled the car leaving the pits on his final stop. He may have been able to get past Fittipaldi for second late in the race but was blocked by Eddie Cheever who'd been lapped by the first two cars.

Although overshadowed by Mansell's victory, it was a heady experience for Gordon, standing on the podium with a pair of World Champions and having beaten a third, Mario Andretti, in fourth. It was also the best finish by an AJ Foyt Racing entry in twelve years, and for the first time the team proved itself capable of competing with the powerhouse Penske and Newman-Haas entries. Gordon made it clear he wasn't conceding anything to the world champ.

"He's a great driver," he said. "But Mansell is beatable."[8]

It was a quick turnaround for the teams to get ready for the one-mile track at Phoenix. Rather than the expected praise from Foyt when they returned to Houston, they were grilled instead.

As Anderson remembered it, "We got back, and Foyt was pissed. He wanted to know why we didn't do this or didn't do that. Turns out a zillion people called A.J. and told him he should stay home more often. That got up his nose pretty good."[9]

Foyt got another reminder that things were changing early in practice.

"The garages are open at Phoenix, and Foyt was sitting on a table and facing outward, talking to Robby and several members of the team," Anderson said. "Somebody in the crowd kept yelling, 'A.J., A.J.' and he kept ignoring him. Well, the guy kept yelling and finally A.J. looked up and kind of acknowledged him. And the guy yelled, 'A.J., will you get Robby for us?'"

Foyt was on hand to help Gordon, who was making just his second oval track start in an Indy car, having run twenty-nine laps the year before at Milwaukee. A preseason Phoenix test session had been disappointing.

Mansell noted Foyt had also given him some advice, saying, "A.J. told me, 'Don't turn right, boy, or you'll be eating concrete.'"[10]

He should have taken the warning more seriously. After a few practice laps faster than the track record, Mansell did a half spin and backed into the wall at more than 180 miles per hour, punching a hole in the concrete barrier. He was lucky to escape with nothing more than a mild concussion, but it was enough for doctors to rule him out of the race.

Gordon fared only slightly better. After five practice laps, the turbocharger blew, and the backup car had a fuel pickup problem. When Gordon finally got on the track, he spun and could do no better than twentieth in qualifying. In race morning warmups he spun again, hitting the wall and causing enough damage that the team was still working on the suspension as drivers were called to their machines.

While Tracy dominated early, ABC commentator Bobby Unser called Gordon "the driver of the day" as he moved through the field and eventually into second place. "He's been the shining star, the class act," Unser raved. "He's been the class act all the way around."[11]

That was before Gordon spun again, this time in Turn One, backing into the wall and breaking off the rear wing. Gordon climbed out and stomped around the car, slamming his helmet down in disgust, before being led away by the track medical staff.

"Robby was plenty quick, but rather than work at it and try to get a little more out of the car, he'd hold his breath and drive in a little deeper," Anderson said. "He had great reflexes, but he counted on them too much. Phoenix was a classic example. We were telling him, 'Slow down, slow down.' But he had a bee in his bonnet to catch Tracy. Went in a little over his head and stuck it in the wall."[12]

Tracy soon spun in nearly the same spot with similar results. Andretti went on to victory, his first Indy car win in seventy-three races covering a span of nearly five years. He became the oldest series race winner at fifty-three, in what would also be his last victory.

Foyt was surprisingly lighthearted and philosophical, saying, "I'm just glad we got out of here alive."[13]

"It's one of those things we knew we were gonna go through this year. He did a hell of a job. I told him to take it easy baby, we're doing good, take it easy. It hurts, but I know it hurts him too. But we'll be back at Long Beach. We'll be tough there."[14]

Gordon chalked it up to another lesson learned.

"If I could have just kept my nose clean, we'd have had a shot at winning. But I learned something. I must have gotten into dirty air. It just spun around on me. This is just my second oval race and I know I've got a lot to learn."[15]

Foyt had a quick comeback. "Boy, I was driving before there *was* air."

The team had high hopes as it headed for Long Beach, California. It was another rough street circuit like Surfers Paradise, putting the emphasis on the chassis setup. And it was one of the few tracks on the circuit where Gordon had previous experience, having won the Trans-Am event the year before. He was also happy to hear Mansell would be back.

"I came away from Australia confident I can run with Mansell, or anybody else, on the street courses. I like my chances. He's coming to my territory when he runs Long Beach. I might have a little edge on Nigel because I've been there and I've won there. He's beatable and I'm not in awe of him. I respect him for what he's done, but when I put my helmet on he's just another driver, someone I've gotta pass."[16]

Foyt could do little more than shake his head when told Gordon's comments. "He's a little cocky, but so far he's backed it up."

A transmission problem slowed Gordon in practice and qualifying, and he ended up thirteenth on the grid. He moved up quickly in the race before the bulky transmission slowed him again. He found himself in a battle with Cheever for ninth—the same driver he felt blocked him in Australia and cost him a chance at second. Cheever moved to block him again as Gordon attempted to pass, running him right to the wall on the straight.

"Eddie and Robby had been teammates at Ganassi the year before and Eddie hadn't been too pleased about it," Anderson explained. "He had the Formula One mentality that above all else, you've got to beat your teammate. Winning races was almost secondary to beating your teammate. Robby had beat him a couple of times at Ganassi the year before, and even though they were on different teams now, he still wasn't happy."[17]

Somehow Gordon made the pass but ran wide on the next turn, allowing Cheever to close in. The two cars touched, and Cheever's left-front wing punctured Gordon's right-front tire. While Cheever motored on, Gordon was forced to limp around nearly a full lap back to the pits, losing two laps in the process.

Gordon returned to the track in front of a pack of cars racing for position in the top ten, including Cheever. As they approached the final turn on the course, a tight hairpin, Gordon pulled to the inside before accelerating and torpedoing Cheever broadside, sending a number of cars spinning. Gordon added an exclamation point, giving Cheever the finger. Cheever was able to continue, however, while Gordon was out of the race.

"I passed Eddie clean on the front side and there on the back side, I was totally committed to the corner and he got into me and gave me a flat tire," Gordon said. Not surprisingly, Cheever saw it differently.[18]

"He got me, I got him," Cheever said. "Then I see him on the back straight and I know he is at least a couple of laps down, and he blocks me. But I get by him. Then bang! He hits me. In all the years I've raced, I've never seen another driver so blatantly wait for another car and then hit him. What a chicken move. This is like having an argument with someone then hitting them in the head with a pole after they turn their back. Unbelievable."[19]

The other young gun, Tracy, broke through for his first win. Later in the media room, Mansell and Teo Fabi, who finished third and fourth and were running just behind the Gordon and Cheever incident, shared a knowing laugh when asked what they saw. They refused to comment but the message was clear—the brash rookie had received his comeuppance.

CART agreed with Cheever, disqualifying Gordon, stripping him and the team of its championship points from the race, fining the driver $5,000, and placing him on a year's probation for unsportsmanlike conduct and unsportsmanlike driving. Cheever also received six months of probation for unsportsmanlike conduct.

After the penalties were announced, the team released a statement from a seemingly contrite Gordon. "It was unfortunate the two of us got hooked up again. Once it's all said and done, it's a shame."

Foyt held his temper publicly and eventually would take partial responsibility for the incident:

> The guy jacked us around for two races, then he runs into us and blew a tire. Robby said he was sick and tired of it. I said, "Well eliminate it." So I guess I had a little bit to do with it. You just don't let people run over you on the racetrack and then go home and drink tea. I wasn't brought up that way. Everybody got mad at me for saying that. Hell with it. You show me somebody that don't ever get in trouble while he's racing, and I'll show you somebody who's never won. If you've never won, you never know what it feels like.[20]

Gordon said, "I know A.J. was mad. Real mad. He was obviously disappointed because it was an event we thought we had a shot at winning. . . . Looking back, we fired off so good and had such high hopes, but between Phoenix and Long Beach, we kind of let it slip by."[21]

The team created a stir when it arrived at the Speedway with three cars, with Gordon listed as driver for the No. 41. No driver was named for Foyt's traditional No. 14, which Gordon had driven in the first three races of the year. Questions started immediately about A.J.'s plans. A crew member smart enough not to be quoted by name said, "Only he knows for sure. We've got everything ready in case he does."

Jim Gilmore told reporters, "I haven't the slightest idea," when asked if Foyt would race. For the first time since 1972, Gilmore had no role in sponsoring the team. "Copenhagen objected to my involvement in the publicity surrounding the team," he'd say years later. "So I backed off."[22]

First up for Gordon was his rookie test, held on the opening weekend. Foyt wasn't in attendance, but he'd already spent valuable time with the driver during an earlier visit to the track. The test went without incident, and Robby gave the credit to his car owner.

"He's definitely got me up to speed on the ovals," Gordon said. "You need to drive one line and be smooth, and that's where A.J.'s real good. He tells me what to do with the throttle and where to do it.[23]

"This is a place I've wanted to be all my life and I'm really excited. Besides that, I'm going to run it like I run any other race. Just concentrate and get toward the goal. And the goal here is to qualify good and finish the race."

Foyt arrived late on Monday, May 10, and learned Gordon had already brushed the wall without damaging the car. On Tuesday, Foyt ventured out himself, running forty relatively slow laps, topping out at 212 mph. Afterward he said he'd been testing "experimental stuff." He remained coy on if he would attempt to qualify, expressing more concern about his legs than he had in the past couple of years. He said he was uncomfortable in the car, and because of the tight fit—especially on his shoulders—he was forced to hold the steering wheel differently. As a result, in case of trouble, he told Anne Fornoro he wasn't sure he could "snatch it" back.[24]

"I don't care who you are, you get a bit rusty. Last year I ran 500 miles here, but I haven't run a race car since. I'll let people know in a day or two. Last year I ran, but I was just here. All I did was fill the field, and I was fortunate to finish ninth. But that's not my style or racing. If I qualify, I'm qualifying for one reason, and that's not just to make the race, believe me."[25]

He added, "I'm just gonna play it by ear. I'm not gonna do nothing at this late stage in life. I already screwed up three years of my life, but not as bad as a lot of my friends are. If everything works good, feels good, I'll do it. If it don't, I'll just sit there and watch it. I can't afford to injure my legs real, real bad again. I'm very glad for what Dr. Trammell did for me. Like I say, I have good days and bad days with 'em. It's something that's hard to explain to somebody."[26]

He ignored questions about Gordon's brush with the wall but acknowledged there was plenty of work to do with the young driver.

"I think he's gonna be real good. This is something new to him. We've asked a lot of him. I just have to sit on him a little bit, you know, to try and calm him down a little bit. But he's up here with the big boys, and this is what separates the men from the boys, right here. Like I said, I'm giving Robby 110 percent."

Some asked if he was still considering qualifying the second weekend if Gordon got in the field. At first, he said he wouldn't, then surprised everyone by adding, "I would consider the second weekend, but if everything goes well, I'll try the first week. You start back there nowadays, you can get in a lot of trouble."

Gordon immediately benefited from Foyt's arrival at the track, picking up speed and moving above 220 mph.

"He knows his way around here so well," Gordon said. "This place is different from any other track, and he knows what works here and what doesn't. We were stuck at 213–214. A.J. comes in and says do this on the straights, do this in the corners, do this front-wing angle. All of a sudden, we're running 222."[27]

While Foyt contemplated his future, Gordon continued to pick up speed, and by Thursday turned in one of the fastest laps of the month. Moments later, he was in the wall along the short chute between the first and second turns, causing enough damage to park the car for the day and force the crew to work late on repairs. This time Foyt was a little more outspoken, both with Gordon and the press.

"I'm glad he's okay, but I got on him," he told reporters after chewing out Gordon. "I told him he's got to back off and drive to his ability because he has what it takes to be a star. But if he keeps doing this, that won't happen. He just lost the front end. He was trying too hard. The car was pushing and he was trying to make it do something it didn't want to do. You've got to make the car do the work."[28]

Late Friday, Gordon nudged 222 mph again, and while the pole position was probably out of reach, the fastest rookie honors were possible. Mansell was the quickest of the first timers, and Gordon had become increasingly obsessed with beating him. That evening he convinced the Andersons to reduce the Lola's downforce by "trimming" the wing angles, allowing the car to run faster down the straightaway.

"We were very, very fast the day before qualifying," Gordon remembered. "We were near the top of the chart. Overnight we all got a little overzealous. We decided to go ahead and drop a little more rear wing out of it."[29]

The next morning, Foyt got wind of what Gordon and crew was doing.

"A.J. warned us not to go in that direction," Gordon says. "He said we didn't want to try that."

Foyt, however, was busy finalizing the setup on his own car. With Gordon showing plenty of speed, he had decided to go ahead and try to qualify on the first day. He ran a lap of nearly 222 mph in the No. 14 car, easily fast enough to make the race, and pulled back into the pits to make a few more minor adjustments.

"A.J. was crazy quick," Anderson recalled. "He wouldn't put a whole lap together. He didn't want to show everyone what he had. He'd run Turns One and Two one lap and lift through Three and Four. Then he'd lift through One and Two and run hard in Three and Four. You never saw a full lap from him. But I saw the data [one radar gun had Foyt at 239 mph entering Turn One] and I'd bet my house we would have been on the pole with A.J. that year. He was just so smooth."[30]

Back on the track for a final run before qualifying started, Foyt was just getting up to speed when the yellow caution light came on. He radioed the team to find out what happened, trying to figure out if there'd still be time to get in some laps before practice was over.

"It's for us," Craig Baranouski told him on the radio. "It's Robby again."[31]

Exiting Turn One, the back end of Gordon's car had come around 180 degrees. He rolled backward next to the wall, before the car swapped ends again, glancing off the barrier this time. The nose cone was knocked off but otherwise the damage was minimal.

As he headed toward pit road, Foyt remembered his trip to New York City after winning the 1961 Indianapolis 500. He had appeared on the television show *I've Got a Secret* along with Ray Harroun, the winner of the first 500 in 1911. He'd asked Harroun how he knew when it was time to quit.

"You'll know when it's time," Harroun told him. "It will come to you."

He thought about the conversation with Gordon's team in the garage that morning and was upset his warning had been ignored. He also blamed himself, realizing he'd been too absorbed with his own car to give full attention to what Gordon's team was doing.

It's time, he thought as he rolled to a stop. *It's time.*

Back in the garage, he spotted Fornoro. He had told her the night before he would decide in the morning about qualifying, depending on how he felt. When he saw her in the parking lot that morning, he'd told her he felt "icky."[32]

"What do you think?" Foyt asked the PR rep. She had talked with George Snider minutes earlier who told her he didn't think A.J. wanted to run but might feel he needed to in case Gordon failed to qualify.[33]

"I think the time has come for you to get out," she said.

"How would it work with the press," he asked.

"It'll work fine," she assured him. Both were near tears.

U.S. Tobacco's Lou Bantle and Eddie Thrap arrived in the garage a few minutes later. Foyt was already having second thoughts and said the car was capable of winning the race. Bantle sensed A.J. was on the edge of retirement, however—something he'd been pushing for—and decided to give it another push. He told Foyt they would continue to provide support no matter who the driver was and urged him to devote his full attention to running his team. He suggested A.J. take a farewell lap.

"He was ready for me to concentrate on the team and let him [Gordon] drive the car," Foyt would say. "That's how the situation was finalized."[34]

Gordon's first stop was the infield care center for the mandatory checkup. He'd inspected the car after climbing out, and it didn't look too bad. He thought it could be repaired in time to qualify later in the day. If not, there were a couple of backup cars in the garage. As soon as A.J. got in the race, Gordon was hopeful of getting another chance in one of the backups.

"Are you injured?" a nurse asked when he entered the care center.

"Ah, not yet," Gordon said, knowing Foyt wasn't going to be happy.[35]

Back in the garage, Foyt was laying into the team, but nowhere near what Gordon had expected. The garage, which was always crowded, seemed even more so than normal. The head of U.S. Tobacco was standing against a back wall, and executives from Ford, Goodyear, and the Speedway were there. Foyt approached Gordon.

"I thought it was going to be one of those things where he was going to tell me to go to my room and not to come out until he told me to," Gordon said at the time. "Then he tells me he's made the decision to retire."[36]

Everything happened quickly at that point. The Speedway ran on a tight schedule, and the start of qualifying was fast approaching. Tony George came into the garage, and Foyt told him of the plan to retire and asked if he could run one more lap "for the fans." Both men got emotional and embraced.

"I didn't see how there was any way we could deny him that honor," George said. "He wanted to say goodbye to his fans for the last time."[37]

Mary Hulman was next.

"A.J., is it really true this time?" she asked. Foyt hung his head. "Yes, it's true."

Crew members for the various teams were already pushing cars into the qualifying line when Foyt came back onto pit road. Some wondered what he was doing as he started putting on his helmet, at first forgetting he was still wearing sunglasses. Then the word started to spread: A.J. was going to retire.

Tony George dropped a green flag, and as Foyt pulled onto the track, Tom Carnegie began informing fans over the track's public address system. The normally boisterous qualifying day crowd of nearly 200,000 grew eerily quiet, and the sound of a single engine echoed off the grandstands.

Foyt waved to the crowd in the first turn, where he had sat and watched his first 500. He waved again as he slowly passed the family suite in Turn Two, his eyes too fogged by tears to see if anyone was on the balcony waving back. There hadn't been time to alert them about his decision to retire.

The lap seemed to pass as quickly as any 200-mph run. As he pulled out of the fourth turn and headed toward pit road, he saw the entrance was jammed with people awaiting his arrival and veered back on the track. People surged to the short wall between the pits and the track, saluting him as he drove slowly past. He stopped near the yard of bricks start/finish line, and in front of the University of Purdue marching band, which was already on the track for pole day opening ceremonies. With the crowd chanting, "A.J. A.J," he climbed from the car, pulled off his helmet, and was handed a white ballcap and his sunglasses. Bantle shook his hand and then began wiping tears away. Aware that qualifying was on tap, Foyt moved everyone over the wall and onto pit road so his car could be rolled away.

Breathing hard and already emotional, Foyt was approached by Carnegie, who'd handled the Speedway's PA chores since the resumption of racing following World War II and was as well known around the track as Foyt himself. He'd say the finish of Foyt's 1967 victory was the most dramatic of his career.

"It's a hard decision, but it comes a time," Foyt said, his voice rising and cracking, tears streaming down his cheeks. It was a Foyt fans had never seen or heard before. "I don't . . ." For a moment it appeared he wouldn't be able to continue. Carnegie moved closer to the driver he had interviewed hundreds of times and put his arm around him.

"He said, it's a hard decision, but there comes a time," Carnegie repeated, giving Foyt a moment to regain his composure. When Foyt started again, his voice was normal and calm:

> The fans have brought me back as many years as I've been back. But I felt like, if I'm gonna run a team, I can't be in a race car. Seems like every time I'm not with the car something happens. I realized that this morning. Just as I went to get the green, the yellow come out and it was my other car. So, if I'm gonna be a successful car owner, I've got to spend 110 percent of my time with the car and not think of A.J.
>
> So Mr. Bantle and Ford Motor Company, this decision was made when, well when Robby hit the wall, is when I made the decision. I intended to qualify, and the car is a very fast car I got out of, and I would have made the race very easy. I'd have no problem putting it in the show and I think, like I said, there comes a time. I love all y'all a lot. You've been great fans. I love you and I'll still be back and we'll still be up in the winner's circle. Thank you very much.

He stopped to see his friend and former teammate, Roger McCluskey, who was battling cancer and would die before the year was out. Then he went to talk with reporters and teared up again. He felt bad that everything had happened so quickly but said it was, "typical A.J., spur-of-the-moment.[38]

"Believe me, this wasn't planned. It's like a damn nightmare. I've always been known to do things on the spur of the moment. This is typical A.J.—bang, bang, bang.

"I had to make a decision. I just thought, 'It's time A.J.' This is the place that made A.J. Foyt and it's hard to give up what you love. It's hard to give up racing. I've been here for thirty-five years and this has been my life. This was the hardest thing, damned near as hard as losing Mother and Daddy. I can't put it in words. It hurt."[39]

George also spoke with the reporters:

> I think A.J. epitomizes what this race is all about. He, more than any other driver, transcends five decades of racing. Everybody can identify with him, even young kids. We're all happy he finally decided to stop rolling No. 14 out of the garage. He *is* family.[40]
>
> You know, he's running one time a year, there are a lot of new guys he's not familiar with and they're not familiar with him and you've got a comfort level you have to deal with when you're driving 220 miles an hour and he obviously didn't feel comfortable in this environment. I was emotional. We got choked up, trying to talk to one another. It was pretty garbled.

Up in the Turn Two suite, Larry Foyt had been excitedly awaiting qualifying. He had become a big Robby Gordon fan, and both Gordon and his dad were running well. He didn't think Gordon's car looked bad after the accident and expected both to try and qualify. Then he heard the announcers talking about A.J. Foyt's last lap and watched as his dad drove slowly by, waving up at the suite as he had done many times before.

"To watch him take that last lap was very surreal, very emotional for everybody involved," Larry recalled. "To hear his raw emotion talking with Tom Carnegie—when you look at his life, his body of work, the years he'd been at Indianapolis, I can't imagine what he was feeling, let alone what we were feeling. I was a little sad. I loved watching him race at Indy. I was the little kid running around the suite all the time. Always proud to be wearing the gear and just proud of him. It shaped a lot of my childhood."[41]

Gordon wandered out onto pit road and embraced Foyt. Then he was quickly surrounded by reporters.

"I'm happy and I'm sad," he said. "A.J. was one of my heroes growing up. He knows his way around this track better than anyone. I can't say enough about how happy I am for him to be sitting on that stand and helping me with what's right and what's wrong. He's accomplished so much in his career. To be driving for A.J. in the year he retired is really special. I'm just happy to be the guy in his car. A.J. will be in the winner's circle for a long time as a team owner."[42]

Foyt's retirement ceremony bumped plans for Richard Petty to donate one of his cars to the track museum and intruded on plans to honor Rick Mears. "Rocket Rick," whose six pole positions remains an Indy record, was set to take a ceremonial inspection lap with Chief Steward Tom Binford in the pace car before the start of qualifying. While the tribute lap went forward, few noticed. Mears, always a class act, realized the moment belonged to Foyt.

"He set the standard in this industry for a lot of years," Mears said. "He's made racing what it is today. You hate to see him go, but if that's his decision, that's what he should do and he needs to do. We're not losing A.J. by any means. He's going to be around."[43]

"It's good to see him get out in one piece."[44]

Snider caught up with Foyt on pit road.

"It was a pretty emotional deal for him at first," Snider said. "He had a hard time getting it out, but he did. Then everything was fine. It was just like another day for him. I guess when you're ready, you're ready."[45]

For Mario Andretti, who was waiting to qualify, Foyt was one of the last drivers who'd been active when he first started racing.

"It's time, obviously. He's done everything everyone could expect. I'm sure he's happy with his career. As a competitor, I'll miss A.J. I'll miss Mears, my contemporaries for sure. I feel left alone more and more. There's a personal feeling there when you grow up and do battle with these guys for more than half a lifetime. You become very close in many ways. But the cycle must go on. That's life. That's the way it is. One by one we'll all be following him."[46]

For another contemporary, Parnelli Jones, who hadn't driven at the Speedway in twenty-five years, it was about time:

> It's not for me to say when somebody should quit. I've hinted at it a few times to him over the years, but to each his own. I know everybody was disappointed he kept racing after he got hurt. But I remember how tough he was. He always went at it hard, and it was that extra 10 percent that made him so good. That, and he was from Texas of course. He always had that extra little edge, that will to win that makes a great driver.[47]

Not everyone thought they'd seen the last of Foyt on the racetrack. He'd "retired" too many times in the past.

"I don't believe him," Tracy said. "I think he'll come out next week after they get their other car in. He ran too fast this morning to quit now."

Qualifying was underway, and Andretti was on the temporary pole when Foyt finally made it back to his garage and spoke with the team. Gordon said he still wanted to make a qualifying attempt and wear Foyt's helmet as a tribute. His own car still needed to be repaired from the morning crash, but there were two others to choose from.

"Boss, let me have that car," he said with a wave. Either the No. 14 or the No. 84, it didn't seem to matter. "I know I can get you the pole."[48]

Gordon was pushing his luck. Foyt was in no mood to allow him to go back on the track.

"Robby, you'll probably get the pole, but it'll be the flagpole," A.J. said.

"The worst thing in the world I could do for you would be to send you right back out there. I know you're not scared, but you've got to think about how lucky you've been."[49]

Then Foyt took it a step further. His first decision solely as team owner was to put off any qualifying attempt until the following weekend. It meant Gordon would start further back in the field—never an ideal situation, but it was preferable to putting another car into the wall.

"He basically told Robby to sit down and shut up," is how Anderson remembered it. "Robby was pissed because A.J. wouldn't keep throwing new cars at him until he put one on the pole."[50]

Foyt also indicated the No. 14 he'd carried in twenty-one of his thirty-five Indy 500 starts would never race again, telling a reporter, "That last lap is the last time you'll see that number." Both USAC and IndyCar quickly said the number would be reserved for Foyt or retired.[51]

Any hope Gordon had of talking Foyt into allowing him to qualify on the second day or at least to practice ended when A.J. left on a 6:20 a.m. flight for Houston Sunday morning, leaving the team strict orders not to put a car on the track. There hadn't been time to talk with Lucy or anyone else about his decision to retire, and he needed some alone time to regroup.

"He'd talked about it before he left for the Speedway," Lucy said, recalling her husband's retirement years later. But she'd heard it before. "I wasn't sure he would go through with it. He knew he was getting older. He knew that the competition was getting a *lot* younger, and it was just time. He'd had so much success; it was time to relax a little bit. Not that he did. He came home and got on a bulldozer. But that's relaxation for him. Doing his farm work and driving his farm equipment, that's his relaxation."[52]

His daughter Terry, who'd help write the country-western hit "The Ballad of A.J. Foyt" years earlier, wrote a poem trying to sum up the family's feelings:[53]

Dad you're a winner, there is no doubt, in everything you do,
It's not how fast your car runs, or the races that you've won,
It's the spirit inside your body, that shows you're number one.

The Belief—you have in your abilities and how you use them,
The Pride—you take in yourself and all that you have,
The Caring—you have inside for the people that you love.

Seeing your eyes filled with emotion, my heart goes out to you,
I wish I could take the pain away, make your dream come true,
You may not think I've learned, but you did teach me well,
The qualities of life, I hope my children will instill.

Remember we are proud of you, no matter how fast you run,
We would rather have a dad and grandpa, it's time to relax and have fun.

My children need to learn what a winner really is,
In all my aspects of life, your time, is the best gift you could give.

A.J. would start 1978 with two of his longest-tenured crew members, Jack Starne (left) and Howard Gilbert (right), but for the first time since 1966, he'd drive an Indy car not of his own design before the year was out. *Foyt Family Collection*

Foyt continued to race his 1977 Indy 500–winning Coyote (above) into 1979 while transitioning to the VPJ (below) built by former rival Parnelli Jones, winning in both. *John Mahoney*

A.J. was still driving the occasional sprint car race in 1980. *John Mahoney*

Jack Starne checks on the new Coyote entered at Indianapolis in 1981. It was badly damaged in a crash at Michigan that July in which Foyt's right arm was severely injured. It was the last Coyote to be built. *Dan Boyd*

Foyt joined Preston Henn's Porsche team in 1983 to win the 24 Hours of Daytona and Paul Revere 250 at Daytona. *Dan Boyd*

Two years later he won the twenty-four hour race again for Henn (left) along with teammates Thierry Boutsen, Al Unser, and Bob Wollek (not shown). *NASCAR Archives and Research Center*

A.J. ran his own Porsche 962 in 1987 (above) and 1988 (below) with co-drivers including Danny "Hollywood" Sullivan and Al Unser Jr. *Dan Boyd*

Two of Foyt's longest and closest friends in racing, Jack Starne (above, middle in 1986) and George Snider, who worked on, drove for, and co-owned cars with Foyt. *Dan Boyd*

They watch proceedings during the 1992 auction of Foyt equipment and memorabilia at the Indianapolis Motor Speedway. *David Nearpass*

Foyt set the world closed-course speed record at the wheel of the short-tail Oldsmobile Aerotech. *GM Research and Archives*

A.J. had a love-hate relationship with Les Richter's and Roger Penske's International Race of Champions (IROC) series, winning it twice, but also refusing to race some years and pulling out another time. He is pictured below with Penske and Danny Sullivan in 1989. *Dan Boyd*

The 1990s saw a new generation of drivers. At left, Linda Vaughn and Foyt presented the winner's trophy to a young Jeff Gordon after the Foyt-Hulman 100 in 1991. At right, posing with Tony Stewart after he took USAC's Triple Crown in 1995. *John Mahoney*

By the end of the 1990s, both Larry (left) and Anthony were competing.
Anne Fornoro

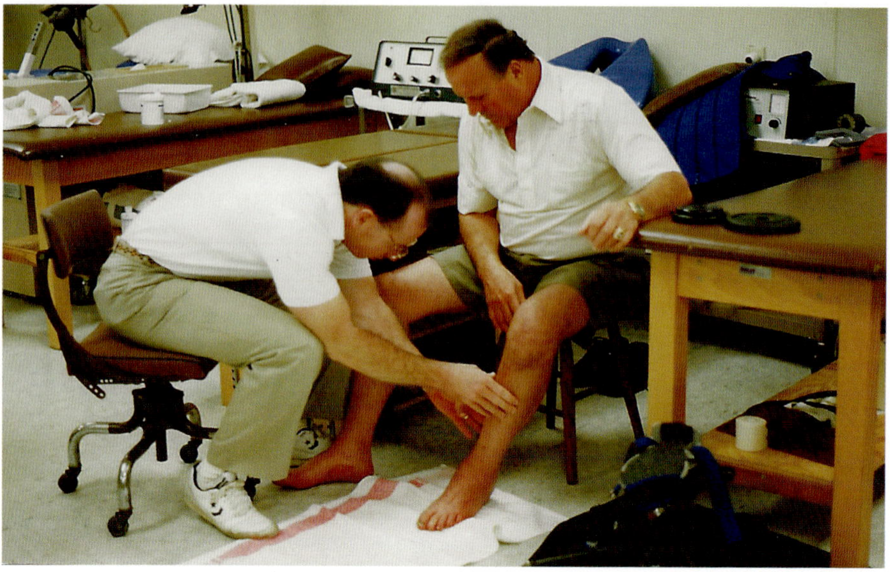

Houston Oilers strength and conditioning coach Steve Watterson checks on the progress of Foyt's feet and legs in early 1991. *Anne Fornoro*

Foyt was ready to go when practice started at the Speedway. *Dan Boyd*

Foyt's friends rallied around for his return to Indianapolis in 1991, including longtime supporter and close friend Jim Gilmore (top left), crew chief Phil Casey (top right), and Tony George (bottom). *David Nearpass* (top left) / *Dan Boyd* (top right and bottom)

A.J. took a liking to Rick Mears (top) early in the driver's career. In 1991, Mears spoiled Foyt's return for the Indy 500 by knocking him off the pole for the Diamond Jubilee running of the race. Mario Andretti was third fastest. *Dan Boyd*

After deciding to retire in 1993, A.J. added his godson John Andretti to the team for the Indy 500. Below, teammates Andretti (No. 84) and Robby Gordon (No. 41) run together. *John Mahoney*

Davy Jones (top) signed to drive for A.J. at the start of 1994 but left the team when they couldn't agree on car setup. Rookie Bryan Herta (bottom left) took over at Indianapolis. *Dan Boyd*

Billy Boat (top) and Kenny Bräck (bottom) made a formidable one-two punch for AJ Foyt Racing from 1998 to 1999. *David Nearpass*

For the first time since 1977, Foyt drank milk in Victory Lane following Kenny Bräck's Indy 500 triumph in 1999. *IMS Photo Archive*

A.J., Anthony, and Larry. Their early years together were not always happy ones.
IMS Photo Archive

Foyt started the 2000s with two new drivers: Jeff Ward (left) and Eliseo Salazar, who finished fourth and third in the 2000 Indianapolis 500. *Foyt Family Collection*

Larry (left) started the new century by driving stock cars in the American Speed Association series while Anthony (right) was on a fast track from go-karts to Indy Lights to Indy cars. *David Nearpass* (left) / *Don Figler* (right)

After losing Conseco and Harrah's sponsorship, Foyt was approached by ABC Supply Company about the 2005 racing season. A.J. said company co-founder Ken Hendricks (top), "Came up the same way I did. It was the hardworking street. It wasn't an easy street." Far from a traditional sponsorship, ABC saw the relationship as a way to bring employees together and in Foyt, "The kind of guy that fit our culture." Pictured at bottom (left to right): President David Luck, Foyt, Anne Fornoro, and Ken Hendricks. *ABC Supply Company*

Felipe Giaffone (top) drove for the ABC Supply team in 2005–2006. In 2007, Al Unser Jr. made his final Indy 500 start and marked the fiftieth anniversary of A.J.'s first Indy car race. *Grindstone Media Group*

Takuma Sato and A.J. hit it off from the start. *Grindstone Media Group* (top) / *Anne Fornoro* (bottom)

A.J. and Joe Namath trade helmets as Lucy Foyt looks on. Joe inscribed his "A.J., You are one of my main heroes, Joe Willie Namath." Foyt signed his, "To Joe, It's hell getting old." *ABC Supply Company*

Scott Dixon has come closest to Foyt's IndyCar victory and championships records. A.J. says records are made to be broken. *ABC Supply Company*

A.J. and friends. With Air Force General Chuck Yeager, whom A.J. took for a ride around the Indiana Fairgrounds dirt track in the pace car (top). Parnelli Jones at the Speedway (bottom left). Touring the spectacular Foyt exhibit at the Speedway Museum with Robin Miller in 2017 (bottom right). *ABC Supply Company* (top and bottom left) / *Dan Boyd* (bottom right)

A man and his office. A.J. at the race shop in Waller, Texas. Many of the items have been given to him by fans and supporters. *ABC Supply Company*

A.J. would come to the race shop most mornings. Afternoons he'd often move to one of his ranches to do what he liked best. *ABC Supply Company* (top) / *Anne Fornoro* (bottom)

Takuma Sato's 2017 Indy 500 win was popular with Foyt and the team (top). A.J. in his typical perch on the front lines (bottom). *ABC Supply Company*

Foyt fielded "Team Brazil" in 2018 and 2019 for drivers Matheus Leist and Tony Kanaan. A.J. and Larry (bottom) struggled to replace ABC Supply as a full-season sponsor. The relationship between A.J. and Tony was strong at first, less so after Kanaan departed following the 2020 season. *ABC Supply Company*

The ROKiT sponsorship (Sébastien Bourdais at top) went from a godsend to a nightmare. Longtime friend Marlyne Sexton stepped in to help keep the team going. *Grindstone Media Group*

Mario Andretti (top at right) was one of the first to call on the Foyts at the Speedway in 2023 following the death of Lucy Foyt. Lucy and A.J. (below) with Larry's wife, Kelly Foyt, and baby Lucy. *Grindstone Media Group* (top) / *Anne Fornoro* (bottom)

Even as A.J. began to play a smaller role at the racetrack, Larry says he checked with him on every major decision. Michael Cannon (below) joined the team in 2023 and received much of the credit for the team's improvement at the Speedway. He left the team prior to the 2025 season. *Grindstone Media Group*

When Santino Ferrucci joined the team in 2023, he hit it off with A.J. They soon had things to celebrate when he qualified fourth at Indy (bottom) and went on to finish third in the race. *Grindstone Media Group*

A.J. and his four Baby Borgs. *IMS Photo Archive*

Also in Houston, Dr. Gary Friedman, the longtime family doctor for the Foyt family, let out a sigh of relief when he heard A.J. had retired but admitted years later to having mixed feelings:

> I had my own emotions, and it was a very melancholy moment when he announced his retirement. He'd had a great run and given his all. At his age, with his injuries and reflexes, I was scared to death that it was not going to end well. I was relieved just because I didn't want to see him get hurt anymore.[54]
>
> I think everybody was sad to see him retiring because it was so great to watch him race. On the other hand, it was selfish of all of us to wish he would race forever. But as a person that had been through some of these events with him, I was so happy he could get to a part of life where he could still enjoy the fruits of his labor and was still a young enough man to enjoy his retirement. I think that was my sentiment.
>
> It reminded me of a song by Chris LeDoux, who'd been a professional broncobuster before he was forced to retire after breaking just about every bone in his body. It has a line that goes, "I'd rather spend ten seconds in the saddle, than a lifetime in the stands."
>
> That will always remind me of A.J. He loved racing and everything that went with it. He loved the competition, and he loved the fans.

OAKLEY
COSWORTH
GOODYEAR
BOSCH
Spark Plugs
PPG
RACING

CHAPTER 22

TEAM OWNER

1993

Robby Gordon showed up at Indianapolis Motor Speedway late Monday afternoon after the first weekend of qualifying hoping he'd be able to talk his way back into a car. No dice. Car owner A.J. Foyt had said he'd be back Wednesday, and there was to be no track action until then. There was nothing Gordon could say to John Anderson or Ken Anderson or anyone else to convince them otherwise. He was quickly surrounded by reporters, and for the most part, Foyt's weekend message appeared to be sinking in. Gordon said,

> He doesn't want us to run while he's gone because it seems like every time he was not on pit road, something happened. I need miles at this track. The speed was there, but I'm not used to running that speed. If you look down the list of speeds and laps, I'm the highest up the list with the least laps. It just comes down to miles and experience on the track.[1]
>
> I guess I need to slow down and concentrate a little bit more on what I'm doing. I've never had to do that before. They're keeping me out of the car a couple of days to give me some time to think about what happened. I'm ticked off with myself, because we had a good car and could have been in the field already. We had some good speeds. I just couldn't put them together and got into the wall. It set us back for a couple of days, but I'm sure we'll be fine for the race.

Asked how his relationship with Foyt was going, Gordon was upbeat. "I think I get along with him better than any driver he's ever had. We fight some. He yells at me and I yell right back at him. Then we shake hands and say, 'Let's go get 'em tomorrow.'"

◀ A.J. with Robby Gordon. *Dan Boyd*

Another article quoted him as saying, "He's still A.J. Foyt, but I think he's going to really work with this team, put all his effort into it and build more pride within the team. He wants to be more like Roger Penske as a car owner and rise to the next level. That's why he went back to Houston for a couple of days. He's got to come back with a different hat on, a different mental approach. He loved driving the cars, but now he's a team owner."[2]

At other times, the talkative Gordon would tread into dangerous territory. Foyt bristled when Gordon said he worked for Ford's Michael Kranefuss, and A.J. made it clear it was *his* race team. Another time he implied Foyt hadn't been at ease on the track and was trying to do too much off it:

> He wasn't very comfortable in the car and that could as easily have been him (spinning) in the car as me. We were just trying to do too many things with not enough people. Now we've put all the effort into a one-car deal. He's out of the race car permanently. I really don't expect him back in there.[3]
>
> The worst thing about it is I'm not afraid of the speed. I'm not intimidated by this place, but it keeps biting me. I just don't know what to think. Maybe I'm trying to carry the car or maybe I need to slow down a little bit and work on the setup a little more. I'm trying to do something that isn't there right now. Maybe in a couple of days it'll be there.

Gordon also received an encouraging visit from Smokey Yunick, longtime Foyt friend and master mechanic. "He said when A.J. came here in '58 he wasn't afraid of the place, he wasn't afraid of the speed," Gordon remembered. "He crashed twice in practice and spun twice in the race. It's almost the same story all over with me."[4]

When Foyt finally returned to the track, he had more bad news for Gordon, imposing a 216 mph speed limit. Rather than sheer speed, he wanted Gordon to focus on running a smooth line through the corners. But it didn't take long for Gordon to run a lap of 219 mph, and as soon as he did, Foyt pulled him off the track. The message was clear: If Gordon wanted to run laps, he'd do it A.J.'s way. Foyt explained,

> The biggest thing with Robby is trying to control him. I'm not trying to embarrass him. I'm not trying to do that at all. I'm just telling you what we talked about. He wants to win, he wants to win real bad. But I've got to tell him to win a race, you've got to finish a race first of all. And secondly, to calm down a little bit. He gets himself hyper.[5]
>
> I'm glad he's making some mistakes and I think Robby's realizing it. The biggest thing, like I told him, is this track is 71 or 72 percent turns. A lot of people forget that. It's not just straightaways. And it's not really how hard you get into that corner, it's how hard you get *off* that corner. I think I've finally gotten that beaten into his head. Of course, on race day, we'll just have to wait and see.

By Friday, Foyt's speed limit was raised to 219 mph, and Gordon was lapping smoothly and easily. When he turned a lap at more than 221 mph, Foyt called him into the pits—but for a different reason. Gordon was ready for qualifying.

Robby's re-found speed also started Foyt thinking about adding a second car to the field, and he called his godson, John Andretti. The son of Mario's twin brother, Aldo, John had driven in five straight 500s, with top-ten finishes running for Jim Hall the past two years. But Hall had cut Andretti loose at the end of 1992, too late to line up a ride for the coming year. He didn't get on the track until late Friday afternoon and pulled back into the pits after only a few laps. Andretti would say,

> The Speedway had some small bumps in Turn Three, little ripples that made the front-end chatter. When I'd been there with different teams, I spent hours asking the engineers for ways to keep the tires from chattering and I got nowhere. After one practice in A.J.'s car, I mentioned those bumps and he knew *exactly* what I meant. He said, 'I can fix that.' He took a little panel off the nose of the car, reached in and made an adjustment to the shocks, and sent me back out. Problem solved. In five years I'd never been able to get an engineer to *understand* this problem, let alone fix it.[6]

After reaching the Foyt-imposed 219 mph speed limit, A.J. asked if there was more speed in the car. "Oh yeah," Andretti said, "I could go a lot faster."[7]

Publicly, Foyt was noncommittal about adding Andretti to the team, saying, "The big thing is that we're still on the outside looking in with Robby."

Privately, he told Andretti he had the ride but asked him not to say anything. He wanted to make the announcement on Saturday so it would be in the Sunday newspapers. Andretti had been around the Speedway long enough to know nothing was certain and wasn't sure he had the ride until Saturday morning when he saw his name on the car.

Then Foyt made the official announcement:

> We had three beautiful cars and Robby couldn't use them all up that quick. All three were ready to run and I felt like John deserved to be here. I'd known John, his family and his Daddy. I knew he had a lot of experience here, had run a lot of test miles and was running the kind of cars that I have. He's run sprint cars, midgets and he's a race driver. I think race drivers need to be at this joint. There's a lot of people going to be in this race who shouldn't be here, but they're here because of sponsorships. The cars kinda carry some of the drivers. I'm from old dirt track days and if you work hard enough, it'll pay off. I think he needed a good shot here.[8]

Foyt put both cars in line to qualify, Andretti behind Gordon. It was a blustery day with wind gusts adding to the challenge. Gordon ran his warmup laps and two of his four qualifying laps when he suddenly veered into the pits, screaming at the crew on the radio that he was out of gas.

Both Foyt and Gordon were furious about the fuel mix-up, but Foyt made it clear he'd handle the crew—it was Robby's job to drive. While this was going on, Andretti started his qualifying run and turned his first lap on the clock at more than 223 mph, a speed topped by only three other qualifiers. He then settled down to post a four-lap average of 221.746 mph, the sixth-fastest speed of the month.

"You always have to keep coming out and proving yourself," a philosophical Andretti said. "Racing's a tough sport. The only way to be in it professionally is to do the job well and keep coming back. When '94 comes around, this month will be forgotten and we'll be starting all over again. It's the same for everybody. You've got to fight hard to get into this race. It's the way it's supposed to be. It's the best thirty-three. I don't look to the past, I only look to the future. And the future looks good."

In the time it took to refuel Gordon's car and get it back in line to qualify, the weather conditions had grown even more challenging. He ran over 220 mph on the first lap and 221 mph on the second before a gust of wind nearly tossed him into the wall in Turn Two. He was able to maintain control, and while his speed on lap three dropped to 216 mph, he finished with a lap over 220 mph and put his car solidly in the field. Still steaming about running out of gas and being dressed down by Foyt, he snapped at the PA announcer who asked in the traditional post-qualifying interview what it was like driving for the master.

"It's a tough job, want to try it?"[9]

Gordon, Andretti, and Foyt then went to the media center to face reporters. Sitting between his two drivers, Foyt was clearly enjoying himself. He joked about Gordon running out of gas and rolled his eyes when Robby said it had taken a "couple of days" to figure out the Speedway.

"You flirt with the wall three times, we're fortunate to have a car left—and that Robby didn't have his butt skinned," the team owner said. "He's going to spend a little sheet time if he keeps that up."[10]

"Robby's learned a lot and still has a lot to learn. He won't let the car do the work and he tried to make up for it. I told him he couldn't throw the car around like Phoenix or some off-road deal. He finally listened today and I'm proud of him."[11]

With both drivers securely in the field, Foyt couldn't resist teasing reporters.

"The No. 14 car's still in my garage, and nobody's gotten into it since I got out of it," he said. "You never know what'll happen tomorrow." When a moan went up from the media, he quickly reversed course, saying, "The show's theirs. A.J. Foyt's gone."

The shtick, however, was beginning to get a little old for Gordon. Normally light-hearted and chatty, Gordon wasn't having nearly as much fun as the other two and sat stoically through much of the session. Not only had he fallen well short of his goal of being the fastest rookie, he'd been outqualified by his new teammate who'd been driving the car for only a day. Like Foyt in 1958, however, he said he was happy to just be in the field. Foyt joked about the repair costs Gordon had rung up so far in the season, something the pair had good naturedly bantered about in the past, but now Gordon sat unmoving, staring straight ahead. Asked about race day strategy, Foyt didn't let up:

"I'll probably have to holler at this one on my right a little more than the one on my left," he said referring to Gordon. Everyone laughed except Gordon. "Like I told Robby, that canvas [the wall] is going to skin your butt if you keep flirting with it."

The media piled on, the Automobile Racing Writers and Broadcaster Association presenting Gordon with a special plaque.

"To Robby Gordon, who crashed and made A.J. retire," it read. "He did what the media couldn't do for the last 10 years." Ironically, the group, which had called for Foyt to be sanctioned following his slapping incident with Robin Miller in 1979, also presented A.J. with its annual sportsmanship award.[12]

After initially telling ABC's Jack Arute the buildup to the race was, "very hard. Like a nightmare to be honest with you," Foyt found himself too busy to dwell on it as the 11:00 a.m. start approached. He didn't even notice when fans unfurled a banner in the grandstands that read, "It isn't Indy without A.J. Foyt."[13]

He was especially concerned about the first laps of the race with his two drivers starting well back in the field, Andretti on the outside of the ninth row and Gordon on the inside of the tenth.

"There won't be any escape room if somebody pulls a Watusi at the start," Foyt warned. When Andretti jokingly said maybe they should start from the pits, Foyt responded only half in jest, "The pit lane would be about as good as anything on that first lap."[14]

Ken Anderson showed Foyt a couple of signs he'd had printed up for the pit boards that would be used to signal drivers. One read, "Use Your Head," and the other, "Watch Your Butt." Foyt had another idea for Gordon: "Better have a ball bat. It may be the only way to get his attention."

As a result of the added focus on his drivers' success, Foyt said, "I didn't even think that much about not starting. I was more worried about the cars and the guys staying out of trouble. I knew we had a big job to do, and I was worried about Robby quite a bit."[15]

Both drivers used their heads at the start and avoided making any wrong moves. Foyt's first big decision as the team owner calling the shots came shortly after the start, when an early caution flag on lap sixteen brought most of the field into the pits to refuel. Foyt elected to leave his two cars out, gaining track position and banking on a second caution before Andretti and Gordon would need to pit for fuel. He looked like a genius ten laps later when Danny Sullivan crashed, and most of the cars pitted again. For the rest of the race, Gordon and Andretti ran near the front of the field and both would lead two laps.

"Everybody wanted to stop, but I rolled the dice," Foyt said of the decision. "Starting back there, I felt like we had to take a chance. That's what kept us from being lapped. I figured I was either gonna be a hero or a jerk and it turned out we were heroes. I was more worried about our cars and the guys staying out of trouble."[16]

Foyt was on the radio constantly with Gordon, trying to talk him through the race.

"He talked a lot about when to go and when not to go," Gordon said. "He just kept saying, take your time, take your time, it's not time to go yet. He kept saying you've got to make it to the end. That there was no reason to risk it early."

Just when it was about time to turn Gordon loose, his transmission failed on lap 165. Andretti went on to finish tenth in his lone Indy car start of the year, on the same lap as winner Emerson Fittipaldi. Andretti's finish might have been even better except for a flubbed pit stop when Foyt was forced to hold him for nearly forty seconds while the team made a quick repair. Someone else calling the race may have sent his driver back on the track without making the repairs.

"One of the boys just flat screwed up," Foyt said. "I made him stay there until we fixed it proper. My boys did a good job. I can't really holler. I thought all-in-all Robby used his head real good, and considering where we started, I thought we did a heck of a job."[17]

The following week marked Gordon's first trip to the Milwaukee mile oval, and he was back in the No. 14 car, Foyt saying, "No. 41 doesn't mean anything to the fans."[18]

Gordon soon discovered what Danny Sullivan, Rick Mears, and others already knew: Nobody was better on the short ovals than A.J. Foyt. Between Foyt and Ken Anderson, they came up with the right setup for the rough track.

Saturday morning, Foyt walked Gordon down to the corners and talked about how to run the tricky oval, warning him the second turn was particularly challenging. Gordon told Foyt that Sullivan had also given him some advice.

"Nobody else will tell you this, but there's more room in the first turn than they say," Gordon said Sullivan told him. "You can race into that corner." Foyt told Gordon to ignore those words of advice and set off looking for Sullivan.[19]

"I've got my hands full keeping him under control," Foyt told him, "without you revving him up even more."

Gordon qualified eighth and immediately began moving forward once the race started, leading laps while other drivers made their pit stops. Tracy was in command as he had been at Phoenix and preparing for his final stop when he was involved in a four-car accident not of his making.

Gordon was entering the pits when the caution light came on and confusion reigned. The previous week at Indianapolis, the pits were closed by USAC as soon as the yellow was shown. He started to accelerate back onto the track when Foyt came on the radio shouting, "Pit, Pit, Pit." At Milwaukee, run under CART regulations, the pits remained open.

Gordon slammed on his brakes after hearing Foyt and slid sideways at a ninety-degree angle into the pit, sending tires and crew men flying. A normal twenty-second stop stretched to a minute as the crew scrambled to recover and mount tires and the refueler struggled to stretch the hose to the car. Despite Foyt screaming on the headset for the team to get the car back on the track before the pace car came around, Gordon went a lap down.

On the restart, Gordon got back on the lead lap and started racing through the field. He was gaining on fourth place Bobby Rahal with six laps left when he spun coming out of Turn Two and hit the wall.

"My fault, I just screwed up," Gordon said when he saw Foyt. "After Indy I thought the pits were closed under the yellow so I was going to blow by it and then I heard you yelling, so I jammed on the brakes and got sideways."[20]

Foyt jumped to his driver's defense.

"It was our fault because we screwed you up in the pits. It was like an airplane crash because about four things hit us at once. Our right-front guy should have been out there to signal you in, but he wasn't. Then I was yelling to push you out before the pace car came around but nobody listened to me. It cost us the race."

Gordon said the crash was like the one he'd experienced at Phoenix:

> I know I was running a little over my head after I lost that lap and it got me. We were the fastest car on the racetrack. I could pass Mansell inside or outside. I thought I was in control all day. I could stay on the same straightaway as Tracy and nobody else was in my mirrors. Then he crashed and I had the race won.
>
> I was driving the car, but it was A.J.'s experience, it all came down to A.J. I'm a road racer, but I'm really starting to dig these ovals. I was scared to death of 'em last year, but I'm starting to feel more comfortable. We're gonna win one of these races with this car.

Foyt had nothing but praise for his driver: "I can't holler at him. He's trying hard and he's learning."

The next race, held on Detroit's Belle Isle, was the annual matchup between Ford and Chevrolet in their corporate backyards and a race Michael Kranefuss wanted badly to win. Held on the island's tight, bumpy park roads, it again seemed perfect for Gordon and Anderson to do well.

Despite hitting the wall in practice, Gordon qualified eighth and stayed out of trouble early in the race as more than a third of the field was eliminated by accidents. On the last lap, he moved up to challenge leader Sullivan, whose Chevrolet engine was losing power. The two cars appeared to touch, and Gordon spun when his left-rear tire shredded. He was able to keep going, however, and crossed the finish line on three tires.

"The game is to run hard," Gordon said. "Danny did a little rough driving. When I got up alongside him, he ran me into the wall. That's part of the game, but what comes around goes around. I knew I could go by him, and I really wanted to win this one for Ford. When I spun, I was disgusted.[21]

"We're real close. Pretty soon we'll be in front."

Belle Isle was followed by three more top-ten finishes on road courses—the natural track at Portland, the airport circuit at Cleveland, and on the streets of Toronto. He'd gone from twelfth at the start to sixth on the first lap, holding that position as the top Ford finisher.

Despite the four straight top tens, there was trouble afoot. During an off weekend for the Indy cars and at Kranefuss's behest, Gordon went off to drive a NASCAR race at Talladega as a temporary replacement for Davey Allison, who'd been killed in a helicopter crash. Rumors started that Gordon was going to drive in the coming year for Kranefuss in everything from NASCAR to Formula One. The following week at Michigan International Speedway for its annual Indy car 500-miler, Kranefuss said he would start his own Indy car team with Gordon as the driver.

"I felt it was time to do something else and I have a couple of options, one of which is setting up my own team and that is what I'm pursuing," Kranefuss said. "Most likely it will be an Indy-car team and right now I'm hustling to get the funds together. It's not a question of if, but when I can pull it together. I think there's a 50 percent chance right now that I'll be making it in time (for 1994). I already told A.J. I'm going after Robby just like everyone else. Everyone in my position would be foolish not to go after him."[22]

Foyt was upset with Kranefuss, not only for tampering with Gordon, but also for the Ford engine situation. After watching Chevrolets dominate the mid-season results, winning six of seven races, including the Indy 500, Cosworth had developed a new camshaft for the Ford engine producing an added fifty horsepower, critical for the high-banked, high-speed track at Michigan. There were enough parts for only two upgraded engines, however, and both went to the Newman-Haas team. Ford blamed a problem with customs for the lack of parts.

Andretti and Mansell qualified one-two, led every lap between them except one, and finished one-two with Mansell out front. No other driver was on the lead lap. Like everyone else, Gordon struggled to keep up, finally blowing his engine with twenty-one laps remaining. Foyt had the good sense not to say anything to detract from Ford's win after the race, waiting until later in the week to make it clear he wasn't buying the customs story.

"That's such a load of crap," he said. "They lie, they make excuses and it's a bunch of bull. Robby is supposed to be Ford's fair-haired boy and my deal was that he was supposed to get what everybody else had—not have two or three cars with special engines. You can't compete with fifty less horsepower."[23]

At the next race, August 8 in Loudon, New Hampshire, where Gordon finished fifth and moved into the top ten in points, Foyt made it clear he wasn't letting the driver go without a fight.

"My contract with Robby is for this year, but I have an option on him for 1994 which I plan to exercise," Foyt said. "When I hired Robby I knew he'd have a lot to learn, but I accepted that because I felt like he has what it takes to win. I have invested a lot of my time and money in him this year and I feel like it will pay off next year."[24]

Relationships continued to deteriorate after two straight mechanical failures.

"It was definitely awkward," Ken Anderson recalled. "When Michael announced he was going to start a team and have Robby as a driver, that caught A.J. off guard. And it was definitely premature. If he'd had a sponsor ready to go and it was a done deal, that's one thing. I don't know if he thought someone was going to throw ten million dollars at him or what, but it never got past the talking stage."

The team's problems and potential were never more evident than at the next race at Mid-Ohio. Anderson and Gordon had wanted to run a certain setup and qualified fifteenth. Foyt gave them a list of changes to make for race day, and despite turning in fast time during the morning warmup session, they wanted to change back to their original setup for the race. This time Foyt put his foot down.

"You're gonna run it like this and if you don't like it, park it," A.J. remembered telling Gordon.[25]

Gordon started with Foyt's setup, and despite knocking off the front wing in an opening lap skirmish, drove through the field for a second-place finish—his best of the year. Afterward, it was apparent Gordon would be on the move. "The team's got places to go," he said. "And I've got places to go."[26]

He complained the team was shorthanded, and he became increasingly vocal about the lack of testing and the fact he would be relegated to driving the 1992 version of the Lola in the year's remaining races.

Anderson said the need to use the backup car "was partly the result of having to fix busted up cars Robby kept sticking into walls. There's two sides to every story.[27]

"On paper, we were probably three or four guys less than what a comparable team would have. Robby started saying, 'If I'm staying, I want you to hire this guy and hire that guy,' and he started telling Foyt how to run his team. Which didn't go down well. And to be fair, Foyt didn't need it. We were good. It's quality, not quantity when it comes to people. But Robby had all that in his head."

One place Gordon wouldn't be going was a team run by Kranefuss. The soon to be ex-Ford exec had discovered promises of sponsorship dollars often aren't worth much in auto racing. Instead, he brokered a deal moving Gordon to the team of Derrick Walker, the former team manager at Penske Racing, who had landed a big sponsorship package from Valvoline and Cummins.

It was a "a very, very, *very* well-funded program," said Gordon, who flew to Houston to tell Foyt face-to-face he wanted to leave. He may have been fortunate Foyt's right arm was in a sling following carpal tunnel surgery.[28]

"It was a business decision and I think A.J. understood that."[29]

"I don't regret going to him. I learned a lot from him. If you can make it through a year with A.J., I think it toughens you up for reality."

Robby Gordon

Years later, Gordon shared more about working with Foyt:

> When I was a young kid, growing up in Southern California and watching Indianapolis for years, A.J. was an idol of mine. A.J. was phenomenal. He was the man.[30]
>
> To go there with A.J. and John Anderson and Ken Anderson, those three guys really taught me a lot and helped me get through the Speedway.

> As a young rookie coming in, I wouldn't have wanted it any other way. Here's a guy who has won there. He knows the Speedway. He knows the way the air blows. What the car will do. His experience equaled their engineering. He'd say you need a half turn of the wing, a little bit of this, a little bit of that. It was good. Really, really good.
>
> A.J. was also hard, and I was young. It really didn't bother me too much. I was young and needed to be directed and trained. The biggest thing A.J. taught me about the Speedway was that the corners were as long as the straightaways. From the time you arc into Turn One to the time you exit Turn Two, it about equals the straightaway. If you exit Turn Two a couple miles an hour faster than normal, it's a couple miles an hour faster at the end of the straightaway. The speed you can carry through the corners is probably more important than the speed at the end of the straight.
>
> We had a good run. We worked well together, had good chemistry, and were a force to be reckoned with. When I left A.J.'s team, I was still a fan. I respected the man, and I respected the organization.

During his first two years with Walker, Gordon would win twice, finish fifth in the season-long championship both years, and post two fifth-place finishes in the Indy 500. In 1996, the final year of Gordon's contract, Walker would side with CART at the start of the Indy car civil war, Gordon missing the 500 as result. The final season was disappointing, and Gordon left Walker and Ford at the end of the year for a chance to drive a Chevrolet in NASCAR. He would bounce from team to team during the years ahead, finishing out driving his own car in NASCAR before founding and driving in the highly successful Stadium SuperTruck series. He never reached the level of success many had predicted for him, but like Foyt, he did it his way.

For his part, Foyt decried drivers that want "to jump from here to there. They don't normally do much in the long run. I've never jumped around." He seemed to forget jumping from Clint Brawner and Dean Van Lines in 1960 to George Bignotti and the Bowles Seal Fast team, after which his career took off.[31]

"I knew Robby was going to need a lot of help. I felt like we helped him as much as we could and if he wanted to change ships—I never hold nobody back. I'm not going to stand in nobody's way. I never have, I never will. Nobody ever stood in my way. So that's the way I think a driver should be treated."[32]

With Gordon out, Foyt started looking for a replacement driver. Ken Anderson lobbied for Stefan Johansson, whom he'd worked with in F1 and was now driving in Indy car for the underfunded team of Gary Bettenhausen. Foyt met with Johansson, who'd won CART rookie-of-the-year honors in 1992, but there was no connection. Another young driver, Jimmy Vasser, was available, as were veterans Danny Sullivan and Arie Luyendyk.

Foyt decided to go in a surprising direction, signing Davy Jones for the 1994 season. After driving several races for Foyt in 1987, he'd spent the past six years driving for Jaguar in sports car racing, where he'd won eleven races, including the 24 Hours of Daytona and a second place at Le Mans. His success had landed him a ride in the 1993 International Race of Champions series, and he'd been at Michigan for an IROC race in conjunction with the Michigan 500 when the rumors started about Gordon. He'd been close to signing a NASCAR deal when Foyt reached out to him.

"I always wanted to give the full IndyCar season a chance," Jones said. "I've had a lot of respect for A.J., and I've gone to him for advice even when I wasn't driving for him and he's always steered me in the right direction. This is a great career opportunity for me."[33]

Foyt seemed ecstatic to have reunited with Jones, saying they had signed a long-term contract: "Davy was a lot like Robby when he was younger, but he's grown up and matured and he's married and settled down now. This isn't like starting over. He's driven for me before, and I know what he can do. He has all the qualifications."

"I really respect this boy. I've watched him with the Jaguar team; he did a fantastic job. Since I happened to get in this owner bit, I figured I needed somebody to push the gas.

"We had three or four names in the hat and it kept coming up Davy, Davy, Davy."[34]

With Foyt's decision to hire Jones, Ken Anderson elected to join Johansson on Bettenhausen's team.

"I was good friends with Stefan, and it just worked out that I went with him," says Anderson, who would work with Foyt during the formation of the IRL and again in 2003.[35]

"I was happy at Foyt and disappointed that it had fallen apart. We had a pretty decent year in '93. I think if we'd all stayed with Foyt, the second year would have been even better. We showed a lot of potential we could have built on.

"But Robby was hellbent on going elsewhere, and it took a lot of air out of the blimp. He was really keen to get on a team that—in his mind—was a better team."

John Anderson also left after receiving a substantial offer to serve as vice president of race operations of the new PacWest team. He stayed at PacWest for several years before moving on to guide Dan Wheldon to an Indy 500 victory in 2005 and Dario Franchitti in 2007. He died of a heart attack in 2010 at age sixty-five.

The year ended with Foyt receiving the Sports Legend Award, an occasional honor presented by the American Sportscasters Association. He was only the third athlete to receive the award, joining Muhammad Ali and Arthur Ashe.

A.J. Foyt, Jr.
Ford
50

CHAPTER 23

HELP WANTED

1994

The departures from his team at the end of the 1993 season left A.J. Foyt confronted with a situation he would face often in the years ahead, with a new driver and in need of technical and mechanical assistance.

For help on the technical side, he turned to an old friend, former Coyote designer Bob Riley. "It's not easy to say no to A.J.," said Riley, who was already plenty busy overseeing his flourishing race car building business.[1]

Although the team struggled in their first event together at Australia, Jones felt it "was a good learning race for all of us." Two weeks later at Phoenix, he was third quickest in a Thursday practice session, although Foyt didn't arrive at the track until that evening.[2]

The next morning, Jones "was just bringing the car up to speed and it swapped ends and went into the wall," he recalled years later. The car was badly damaged, and he sustained a deep thigh bruise. "I went to talk to Bob Riley, and told him the car was completely different from the day before. I'd gone out expecting to pick up where I'd left off, and it was completely different. Bob checked and came back and told me A.J. had the crew make some changes to the car."

Jones said he didn't object to trying different things, only that no one alerted him to the changes. "That was concerning to me. There was a lack of communication. We didn't get the message."

He qualified seventeenth and finished twelfth. A week later at Long Beach, Jones struggled in practice and felt Foyt listened to everyone but his driver when trying to find an answer for their problems.

"We had a lot of other people coming and saying, 'The car is doing this, the car is doing that,'" Jones said. "We were taking in more information from what we were hearing from other people rather than trying to focus on our own program."

◀ Ready to run the first Brickyard. *David Nearpass*

They never got the car straightened out for qualifying, and Jones could do no better than twenty-fifth in the thirty-car field. He managed a fourteenth-place finish, mainly the result of a high attrition rate. With the Indianapolis 500 next on the schedule, Jones flew to Houston to discuss the situation with A.J. When they failed to reach an agreement, Jones announced he was leaving the team. Foyt said he fired Jones.

"A.J. more or less said it was his way or the highway," Jones would say. "So I chose not to go to Indianapolis with the team."

At the time, Jones said, "He's awfully, awfully hard to get along with. No matter what goes wrong with the car, it's always the driver's fault."[3]

"The Foyt team just doesn't have the proper engineering to be able to get the most out of the car. Basically, I had three of the worst races of my life. Without 100 percent confidence in the technical side, you can't go out and do your best."[4]

It wasn't an easy decision for Jones to make. This was different than in 1987, when he'd left the team for a better opportunity. He had nothing lined up. He'd also spent time with Foyt at the ranch and lake house.

Jones said,

> He was always good to me. He's really personable, and he's got a big heart—especially when you're one-on-one. But as soon as somebody steps into the room, and it becomes more than just you and him, he's got to put on this big, kinda Texas-like, "Rrrrr." You know, "Don't do that, why are you doing that? Why are you doing this?" That's just the way A.J. is.[5]
>
> I love the guy. He's an absolute icon. What he's done and what he's accomplished really, you know, made the sport. He is the stepping stone for what the sport is today.

Jones would try his hand at NASCAR before returning to run at the Speedway and in sports cars. He'd win twenty-nine major events over the course of his career and, in 1996, win the 24 Hours of Le Mans two weeks after finishing second at Indianapolis, nearly matching Foyt's 1967 accomplishment of winning both races in the same year.

"Davy is a good friend, but I couldn't do him no good, and he wasn't doing us any good," Foyt said when they parted. "We tried everything but nothing clicked. I'm not saying he won't get going with somebody else, but this is like a marriage that didn't work and we agreed to call it quits."[6]

Foyt wasn't completely back to square one, he'd already made a deal to field a car again for John Andretti at Indianapolis, with sponsorship from Jonathan Byrd and longtime Indy supporter Bryant Heating & Cooling. Andretti, who was doing most of his racing in NASCAR driving a No. 14 car, also announced plans to be the first driver to race at Indianapolis and later that same day in the Charlotte 600 stock car race. Although Foyt had raced in many Indy car/stock car same-day doubleheaders over the years and won both races on two occasions, he wasn't thrilled about Andretti going back and forth to NASCAR events while practicing and qualifying at Indianapolis.

"I know John's in pretty good physical shape, but he is a small boy," Foyt said. "And stock cars you rassle quite a bit. I've never seen him jump from Indy cars to stock cars. The transition is a big transition. I was very fortunate, but still it was tough for me. You've got to be careful right at first, or you'll stick 'er right in the wall. I don't care who you are, if it's A.J. Foyt or anybody."[7]

With only a week until practice started at Indianapolis, Foyt was still looking for a driver for the No. 14 car.

"Right now, I don't know what I'm going to do," he said. "If worse comes to worst, I'll drive it."[8]

One person reading about Foyt's situation was rookie driver Bryan Herta, who'd won the 1993 Indy Lights championship in dominating style, taking eight poles and winning seven races, including the last five. Herta was looking to make the jump to the top series, but the car he was supposed to drive in the Rookie Orientation Program hadn't shown up, and his sponsorship was shaky. Although he'd never met Foyt, he called and left a message, asking to borrow a car for the rookie test. Herta recalled,

> There's two guys everybody in the sporting world knows: A.J. Foyt and Mario Andretti. As a kid, I wasn't an Indy 500 fan per se. I remember listening to it on the radio with my dad. But what really got me into the Indy car was the Long Beach Grand Prix at the end of A.J.'s career. So, while I didn't have a lot of firsthand experience watching him race, I knew he was a legend of the sport.[9]
>
> So, he called and said, "Bryan, this is A.J.," but I didn't believe it was him. I thought it was a prank call. So, I questioned him a little bit at first, but he was like, "No, this is A.J." He said Carl Haas and some other guys told him I was a good driver, and he wanted me to come to the Speedway and do the rookie test. He took me to the Outback Steakhouse, and we had a nice dinner. The next day, I did the rookie test, and it went really well. It was easy.
>
> I think the minimum at that time was four phases and ten laps a phase. They were focused on seeing me do that. I think it took me forty-one laps, and I know that pleased A.J. because I didn't need time to get up to speed for each phase. He just wanted you to go out and drive hard. He was a racer and, you know, he didn't want somebody who was building up speed. He wanted somebody who was going to get in and drive the race car, because if you couldn't, then he was going to go get someone else who could.

Foyt was impressed.

"He went almost 190 miles per hour right out of the box," he said at the time. "That's pretty good for never being here. We drove around the track this morning, me and him, and I was showing him what to do and what not to do. Of course, that's got to grow on you a little bit as time goes on."[10]

When Herta's car never materialized, Foyt signed him to drive the No. 14 in the 500.

"He knows how to win and I think he might be a sleeper," A.J. said.[11]

He added, "They said I was going through drivers like a racoon through a garbage can. But if you're hungry for victories, you can go through that garbage can pretty quick."[12]

Herta couldn't believe his good fortune. He was immediately exposed to the advantages of driving for Foyt. All engines were equipped with a pop-off valve supplied by USAC to manage a turbocharged engine's boost levels. Buick engines were allowed fifty-five inches of boost, and the Ford Cosworth engine like the one used in Foyt's cars was limited to forty-five.

Herta recalled,

> On my very first day of official practice, I somehow ended up with a Buick valve on my engine, and it made my car a lot faster. I thought, *This is what it's like to drive at Indy for A.J.* But then that valve went away, and I never saw it again. I think they just wanted me to have a good first day of practice.[13]
>
> A.J. looked after the valve himself. There was a boost-control switch in the car. I wasn't allowed to touch that. He told me many times that it wasn't for me to touch. He adjusted it.
>
> Then there was the time the valve we got wasn't very good, and we were struggling to get as much boost as we should. So, I walked into the garage, and A.J.'s got the valve on the bench. He's got a hammer and [he's] beating that valve. He looked terrifying. He's a big, strong guy, and he's swinging this hammer. He heard me walk in the door, and he didn't say anything. He just smiled and gave me a wink. And he hit it again. Then I watched him walk out of our garage into the N1 garage, which is where they used to hand out the valves. The door was open, and he took that valve, and he threw it through the door, and walked in behind it. Our next pop-off valve was a lot better.
>
> A.J. has this reputation for his fiery temper, but I saw very clearly that he was very much in control of what he was doing, and he knew how to use it to get what he wanted. It was an example of the aura and gravitas he carried. And that's probably part of why he was successful as a driver. You've got to fight for yourself and get the tools and the things you need to be successful. And I'll never forget it. He was such a character.

Herta also discovered there were benefits to driving for Foyt off the track:

> It was hard to get reservations at St. Elmo's or some of the other places in town, especially on the week of qualifying or the race. Very early on, I picked up a trick. Every reservation for dinner I made, if there was four of us, I made a reservation for party of five for Foyt. And we'd get to the restaurant and say, "A.J. will be here in a minute. Go ahead and seat us." Then we'd say, "Oh, you know, he got tied up. He can't make it." I don't think I ever told him I made all my reservations under his name.

While Herta built speed, John Andretti picked up where he left off the year before, running laps at more than 222 mph. That's where his speed leveled off, however, while other teams began running faster. And as qualifying weekend approached, Foyt wasn't happy when Andretti flew back to Sonoma, California, to practice and qualify for the NASCAR Sunday race at Sears Point Raceway. There was more of the same on tap for the following week, with Andretti scheduled to shuttle between Indianapolis and Charlotte.

With Andretti in Sonoma on Thursday and Indy qualifying just two days away, Foyt told Herta he was going to change the setup on their cars.

"I'm going to change your car completely," Herta says Foyt told him. "'It's going to be a lot different than you've driven it.' It wasn't a small change. It was a humongous change."

Foyt was never one to give much in the way of details about the adjustments, but Herta had learned to keep an eye on his car owner and what he was doing to the No. 14.

Herta says,

> I was a struggling rookie, at times because he was changing the car a lot. Every time I'd go out, he was doing something different. I was trying to keep the car the same so I could learn to drive it. I was just trying to get comfortable.
>
> I noticed that he'd walk by the car in the garage and adjust the front wing. He'd know the track temp was coming up or whatever. Once I figured that out, I would literally sit in the garage all day, and when he would walk by and put a turn in the front wing, when he walked away, I'd walk over and take the turn out. When they would make a spring change or something, I would just sit there and watch, so I at least knew what was happening. A.J. didn't keep anything secret. He would answer any question I had, but I didn't even know the questions to ask at that point. I was drinking through a firehose.
>
> Especially at Indy, he knew in his mind what he was trying to accomplish when we went out and made a run. He just communicated differently than the traditional driver-engineer relationship, where they might tell you, "We're gonna go out and do this or that." He didn't tell you all that stuff. He'd just say, "Hey, I want you to run twenty-five (laps)." That was because he'd set the car up to run at race pace. He knew what he was trying to do, and you had to learn to figure out the why. He didn't really give you the why. But he was always very clear in what he expected of you when you got in the car—what the goal was, what he wanted to see you do.

Herta wasn't entirely comfortable in the revamped car but, after running his fastest laps of the month, said he would use the setup for qualifying. Then Foyt ordered the same changes made to Andretti's car.

"They changed everything," Andretti would say. "I mean everything. The shocks. The rocker arms. The wings. Everything."[14]

After qualifying thirty-eighth for Sears Point, Andretti returned late Friday night. Rain was in the forecast for Saturday, which could further upset his plans. Foyt was insisting they qualify on the first day, and if Saturday was rained out, it would be pushed to Sunday—in direct conflict with the NASCAR race he was committed to run.

Andretti arrived early at the track for the practice session before qualifying started, just as rain began to fall. When the track was eventually dried, and the teams told to get ready for practice, Andretti's crew didn't budge.

"A.J. was not in a great mood," John recalled, saying Foyt told him, "You can just sit there and watch. You haven't been here all week."

Foyt and Andretti had what John described as an "animated discussion" about his absence, but the car stayed in the garage.

"You can win ten of those races [Sears Point] and nobody would know," Foyt told Andretti. "You do something here and the whole world knows about it."[15]

Foyt said, "I told him 'I'm not happy about it, but you're a big boy and I'll let you make your decision.' Naturally, I'm going to do everything I can for John. (But) when a guy wants to go out and race and he goes somewhere else and busts his butt, don't come back crying on my shoulder."[16]

Watching it all play out was Herta.

"John had some similarities with A.J. in that he was also just a very tough-as-nails type of personality," Herta said. "He and A.J. would butt heads because neither one of them was going to back down.[17]

"John was a great teammate to have because he had a lot of experience, and he was very good to me as a rookie and gave me some good advice. I set up his car for qualifying, and he said 'Good job—that's a good car.' That meant a lot to me because I didn't know what a good car was supposed to feel like, and John did."

Rain played havoc with the schedule throughout the day, and it wasn't until after 5:00 p.m., less than an hour before the track was to close for the day, that Andretti drove out of pit lane for his qualifying attempt. The warmup laps were his first of the day, and the first two circuits on the clock were over 224 mph, among the fastest so far. The car began to bottom out on the third lap, however—something that might have been caught if Andretti had been allowed to practice. His next two laps were closer to 222 mph, although he still managed to record the tenth-fastest time among first-day qualifiers. The next day he would finish a respectable nineteenth at Sears Point.

Herta also posted a first-day speed. His first qualifying lap was slow, just under 219 mph. He'd been too cautious on his warmup laps, and his tires weren't up to optimum temperatures. His next three were better, well over 221 mph. Second day speeds were faster, however, and when others began running quicker in practice the following week, it became apparent Herta was in danger of being bumped from the field. He started practicing the team's backup car, the year-old Lola he'd driven during the rookie test. The team also went to work completing a new car.

As concerns about Herta being bumped mounted, rumors started that Foyt would get in the backup car to check it out, perhaps qualify it if necessary and turn it over to Herta, or even race it himself. Foyt added to the rumor mill when he took a physical and was cleared to drive.

"That was A.J. being A.J.," Herta said later. "He joked about that with me. He just liked toying with people. So, he went and got a physical and was joking about, 'Maybe I'm gonna get back in.' He was never gonna get back in. He had that sort of mischievous sense of humor. He liked keeping people off guard, not knowing what to expect from him. So, he was joking, but then again—it's A.J., and I also wouldn't have put it past him. I wasn't completely convinced he wasn't going to get in it."

Under a scorching sun and with track temperatures hitting 134 degrees—Foyt said it was "one of the worst days I've ever seen here"—Herta found himself on the bubble as the slowest car in the field with more than an hour remaining. At least four other cars were expected to make a run, and the pair debated if they should withdraw the already qualified car and make a preemptive run in the backup machine. Herta had run nearly 223 mph in the car earlier in the day. At one point, Foyt gave chief steward Tom Binford a note withdrawing the original car but told him not to open it until A.J. gave him the final nod.[18]

"I was hollering and shouting now and then, but that's A.J.," Foyt said. "Bryan had a helluva lot of pressure on him. I felt he could do it. We had run 222s and just needed 221 [to make the field], so it was a cakewalk for him. But then again, there's no guarantee it'll run four laps. I'd hate to withdraw a car and then something happen in the last minute. I've gambled all my life, so why change now?"[19]

"Like I say, race cars are like women, they're unpredictable. It was a big gamble. I rolled the dice."[20]

Ultimately, Foyt decided not to withdraw the car, and all four attempts failed to bump Herta from the field.

"Waiting was tough," Herta admitted, "but I think it was tougher on A.J. (He) may be as great a team owner as he is a driver. He's been great to work with. I don't have a negative thing in the world to say about the experience with the team."[21]

Foyt was happy to have both cars in the field and seemed especially pleased with Herta's performance. Asked to compare Herta and Robby Gordon, A.J. said, "Bryan knows what he wants; he doesn't just stab and steer. Bryan's going to use his head, which gives the whole team feedback. You can compare them to Mario and me. I used to be a little bit conservative but still run just as hard as Mario. He would always go out real quick and really stand on it. It's just as fast, but it's two completely different styles to work with."

For his part, Gordon refused to talk about Foyt, saying, "I'd rather not answer any of those kinds of questions." Instead, he referred reporters back to the press conference where he'd shared the stage with Foyt and Andretti and been the target of A.J.'s jibes as an example of their relationship.

Rutherford Retires

Earlier in the day, while Foyt was wrestling with the decision on whether he should withdraw Herta's time, another driver had finally reached a decision. Like Al Unser earlier in the month, Johnny Rutherford was ready to officially retire.

He'd last qualified for the 500 in 1988 and hadn't competed in a race of any kind since 1989. Yet each May he'd come to the Speedway, helmet in hand, looking for a team in need of a veteran driver—not to mention a three-time Indy winner.

"I was hoping to catch on with another team, but it just wasn't available to me," Rutherford said. "There comes a time when you have to do this sort of thing. I've had my day. Now I've got to move aside and let the young guys come along."[22]

Once the decision was made, it was time to go see Foyt, his old friend and rival, with one last request.

"I went over to A.J.'s garage and walked in and stood right in front of him," Rutherford recalled. "I said, 'Have you got a car I can take a last lap in? I'm going to retire.' He didn't say a word, just turned around to his chief mechanic and pointed to a car and said, 'Is that car ready to run?'"

Foyt was pointing to the No. 14T, the team's backup machine, and the same car he had driven his final laps in the year before. It had been prepared for Herta to drive if the decision was made to withdraw his primary car or if he was bumped from the field.

"When the mechanic said yes, A.J. said, 'Well, get it ready for Rutherford. He's gonna take a couple of laps in it.' That was it. No questions asked, no nothing. Now, I'm sure the eyes of the young guy who was in the car got real big, and he probably thought, *Well there goes my ride.*"

Herta did, in fact, wonder what the heck was going on.

"It was never really explained to me," he recalled. "Johnny Rutherford shows up, and the next thing I know, he is getting belted into my backup car. But I didn't understand why. I didn't know what to think at that."[23]

Rutherford went through the same emotional roller coaster that Foyt had experienced the year before:

"I asked A.J. before I went out, 'If I can run this thing fast enough, could I make the race with it? He just said, 'Whatever you can do.' But I knew better.

"The memories come flooding back when you make those, you know, semi-fast laps around the speedway. Going out of the pits and into the first turn with the fans waving was awe inspiring. I just made a couple of laps and did the interview with Tom Carnegie and that was it—the end of my Indianapolis career. It was not easy. It's never easy."

Rutherford told Carnegie,

> I really want to thank A.J. for caring enough to do that. A.J. knew what it was about and he didn't hesitate to let me take that car and run it around here. When I came in, he was the first one there to shake my hand. I did ask him if I could put it in the qualifying line if I got up to 222 mph. Believe me, it was tough to not put it into fifth or sixth gear.[24]
>
> I was pretty much the last of our group. A.J. and Bobby Unser had retired, and Al announced he was retiring a couple of days earlier. Mario said he was retiring at the end of the season. That was our gang. A.J. and I were talking about it, there will never be a group of drivers that have that

much fun. These young guys don't know what they missed. Being able to run midgets three or four nights a week and sprint cars on Saturday and Sunday. Running on dirt. It's not like that anymore.

With the field set, attention turned to Mario Andretti, who had qualified ninth for his final 500. John Andretti was asked what would happen if the race came down to a last lap battle between him and Mario.

"I would do exactly what Mario would do and that is I'd do everything in my power to win the race," John said. "I'd rather be scolded by my uncle than beat up by my godfather."[25]

For once, Foyt was politically correct and gracious:

"What I always respected about Mario is that he's a racer. He liked to run midgets, sprints, stocks. He's done it all."[26]

Mario's plans and Rutherford's retirement were billed as the last rides of the "Magnificent Seven." The departures of Foyt, Rutherford, Andretti, Al Unser, Bobby Unser, Gordon Johncock, and Rick Mears would take years for Indy car racing to overcome and perhaps never has. Robin Miller wrote elegantly about this changing of the guard in the *Indianapolis Star*, calling the drivers "the backbone of American auto racing for four decades.[27]

"They chased each other around the country, tested their limits, thrilled thousands of fans and endured the best and worst times of Indy cars. They were the last link to the old days, when bravery caught an owner's eye, ability earned an instant ride and racer's life expectancy was week-to-week."

The race itself was controlled by the Mercedes-powered cars of Roger Penske. Al Unser Jr. emerged victorious after teammate Emerson Fittipaldi crashed sixteen laps from the finish while trying to lap the field. Estimates gave the Mercedes a 200-horsepower advantage over the Ford engines used by the Foyt team and most of the field.

"It reminded me of a glorified Formula One race," Foyt said of the lack of passing and the domination by the two Team Penske cars. "I've been saying all month they'll play with us on race day. That nobody would touch them if they finished and we'd all be running for third.[28]

"But I also respect Roger because he's done a helluva job and I guess everyone else should get off their ass and quit crying."

Foyt was the only owner to place both his cars in the top ten, with Herta in ninth and Andretti in tenth.[29]

"There's no doubt A.J. has really helped me out," Herta said. "We brought the car home in one piece, ran our pace and did the best job we could. It's tough to come here with the Indy 500 being my first [Indy car] race, and driving with A.J. there was a lot of pressure on me. We just wanted to respond to that by running all day and finishing the race. We had a great car in the middle of the race, but lost the handle a little on it at the end, but that happens."[30]

Foyt said, "I think Bryan did a hell of a job for this being his first race in an Indy car. There were a few mistakes made, but no more than I've made. You've got to remember this is where all the big daddies are and to run in the top ten, he did a hell of a job."[31]

After running as high as third at Indianapolis, Andretti answered a few questions then left for Charlotte, arriving in time for driver introductions. Starting ninth, easily his best start to date in a regular NASCAR event, his race was cut short by a broken crankshaft after 220 of the 400 laps. He completed 820 miles on the day.

"We didn't run as good at Indy as I would have hoped," he said, "but it's not from a lack of effort from my guys." He blamed the inability to adjust to changing track conditions for falling back. "I knew the car was going to run all day. At the beginning we had a pretty good race car, but we couldn't get it straightened out to go fast all day."[32]

It would also be the last time he raced for his godfather.

"I never had the sense that I was just another driver to him," Andretti said of his relationship with Foyt. "I was someone he felt a bit closer to. To this day, wherever A.J. introduces me to someone, he'll say, 'Hey, you might not know this, but I'm John's godfather.' That means more to me than A.J. will ever realize."[33]

While there was a great deal of backlash against the Mercedes engine, it didn't seem to matter a week later at Milwaukee when Unser led the Penske team to a one-two-three finish with all the teams using the same engine specs. Like others before him, Herta benefited from Foyt's guidance on the one-mile oval, finishing tenth. A week later, he was ninth at Detroit. Herta had learned to listen to what Foyt had to say.

"They had a team guy on the radio with me, but every once in a while, A.J. would pipe in. It was always funny because he'd say, 'Bryan, this is A.J.,' and of course, with that big booming Texas voice, he didn't have to say that. I knew who it was. But I think it was his way of saying, 'Okay, this is important.' But he always had something good to say, and I learned a lot."[34]

After the Detroit race, it was Foyt making news in the driver's seat turning laps at Indianapolis in apparent preparation for the upcoming Brickyard 400. He was driving the same Ford Thunderbird he'd failed to qualify at Daytona the year before. He was sharing the track with Rusty Wallace, who had a fleet of four Team Penske T-Birds, trying to decide which two he would keep for the race. By the end of the test, Foyt had run consistently over 168 mph, which Wallace thought would be fast enough to qualify. Foyt also enlisted NASCAR point leader Ernie Irvan to drive a few laps and doublecheck the car's setup.

Foyt said driving a stock car at the Speedway "reminds me of when we ran the roadsters here and they kind of slipped and slid and you had to thread the needle. It's kind of what it felt like—like the old Indy cars." When asked if he would run more races, he replied, "I think it's possible, but after I get through with this and my wife gets through with me, I probably won't have enough money to get out of town."[35]

While grandstand seats had sold out in two days for the inaugural Brickyard, and more than 300,000 were expected, many Indy car drivers continued to be upset about a second race at the track. Foyt was one of the few to come out strongly in support of the event.

"I'm not a prima donna," he said. "A race is a race and a driver is a driver. But there are a lot of people in this garage who don't feel that way."[36]

Wallace said, "It would be great for the sport," if Foyt were to qualify, but warned, "He will have to take it serious. He will have to be out there at 9 a.m. [for the start of practice] ready to run."[37]

Paul Page, set to call the race for the ABC broadcast, said having Foyt in the field would "go a long way toward validating the event."[38]

Darrell Waltrip was another who hoped Foyt would be in the field.

"The Indy car guys were all up in arms because that's Indy car country and an Indy car track. Who the hell do we think we are running these stock cars. So having A.J. be a part of the program, a part of the show, that was a good thing. Anytime A.J. showed up—I don't care if it was today—everybody would be glad he's there and probably try to help him."[39]

Team Penske was having almost as dominating a year in NASCAR as it was in Indy cars, Wallace having already won five races during the season, the last three in a row. The team agreed to provide Foyt with a couple of engines and help with shock absorbers and chassis setup if he decided to enter the race.

Foyt delayed his departure for the June 26th Portland Indy car race to run another day of tests at the Speedway and also had his son Jerry drive the car. Jerry had given up his dream of a driving career to help with the family auto dealership during his father's recovery and rehab from the Road America crash. With the recovery complete and his dad supposedly retired, he'd tried to jumpstart his career, running in a number of ASA and ARCA stock car races.

When Jerry turned in the eighth-fastest time and outran several NASCAR regulars in an ARCA race at Atlanta—his first superspeedway start—A.J. was asked if he would consider entering a car for his son in the inaugural Brickyard 400.

> I don't know what I'm going to do there. He's done all that on his own. I got to give him credit, never having gone to a superspeedway before in his life. He improved his time by over a second and out-qualified [Dick] Trickle. I don't know about the Brickyard. He does such a hell of a job in the business, but I don't know what I'm going to do there. If he's going to run, I'm going to see that he does it right. I'm not going to let him get hurt in some junk. So I might have to put one together, I don't know.[40]

It wasn't just Jerry A.J. was worried about. His sixteen-year-old grandson/adopted son Larry Foyt had caught the racing bug. And ten-year-old Anthony Joseph Foyt IV, the son of Nancy and Tony Foyt, who most called Anthony, was part of the National Hot Rod Associations (NHRA) junior dragsters program and finding a fair amount of success.

"He ordered go-karts from California and he done got my wife to agree to all that," A.J. said of Larry. "He's got a trailer and he goes out and runs his go-kart.

Him and this friend haul them. I told her she was going to have to run that race team with the boys. That's the one we're going to have trouble with. He just loves racing. And Jerry's a little jealous of him because at a young age we wouldn't let him mess with none of that stuff. And now he's kind of done it on his own. I don't know. I've got my hands full."[41]

At Portland, Herta saw his string of three straight top-ten finishes end when he spun after tangling with another car. He was fourth fastest in early practice a week later on the Cleveland airport circuit, where he had captured the Indy Lights pole and won the race the year before. But the team made a number of changes to the car prior to qualifying and went the wrong way. They never recovered as he started sixteenth and finished thirteenth.

In general, however, Foyt seemed pleased with Herta's results.

"He's a very smart race driver," A.J. said. "He's a hard race driver and when I make a little change, he can read the change. And when somebody's outrunning him real bad, he don't get excited. He's just got a pretty level head. I think you'll hear a lot about Bryan."[42]

Herta seemed to be equally happy with Foyt.

"I guess to me he's like two different people. I can't really put together the A.J. Foyt I race with, or that I'm working with, and the guy who won the Indy 500 four times and was a legend, because when you get to working with him, he's just a normal guy. We work very well together.

"Yeah, I guess I am in awe of him in one sense, but when you're working one-on-one you forget he's A.J. Foyt. He's just A.J."

From there, it was on to Toronto, where Herta had also won the Indy lights race the year before. He was one of the first on the track for an early practice session and quickly pitted, complaining the steering felt "sloppy." Back on the track, he rounded a blind corner on the tight 1.78-mile street circuit and slid up into the wall. Foyt was furious with officials, saying a slow-moving safety vehicle had been on the track and forced Herta high coming out of the turn. Herta, who never lost consciousness, emerged with a fractured upper-right thigh bone and two pelvis fractures. Years later, he said he wasn't sure what happened.

"I went back out, and I think the second lap around—in the last corner, a flat-out, fourth-gear corner—I went straight into the wall. I think something broke in the steering. I think something failed on the car. But I'll never know for sure.[43]

"There was a safety truck that had gone on course and had pulled some dirt onto the track. And A.J. was really mad about that. I don't know if that was a factor. I don't really 100 percent know what happened."

The badly damaged car was withdrawn from the race, and Foyt went to visit Herta in the hospital. The driver had been fitted with a large exterior exoskeleton device to hold his badly broken pelvis in place. Herta recalled,

> A.J. just pulled the sheet up and looked at me and said, "We might make a race car driver out of you yet." Wow. He'd been through it many times himself, so he knew. And he was wonderful to me. He was supportive, and

he told me that the car was there as soon as I was ready to drive—that the car was mine to come back to.

In Indianapolis he got me a van with hand controls when I got out of the hospital so that I could drive myself to my therapy appointments because I couldn't use my legs yet. He bought it from one of the auction places in town. He looked after me.

With the Michigan 500 two weeks away, an upset Foyt's first impulse was to drive the car himself. Cooler heads prevailed, and he hired Eddie Cheever to finish out the year, although Foyt stressed it was Herta's car in the future.

"I liked the kid early on," Foyt said of Herta. "He's going to be good, and it's a damn shame he got hurt."[44]

Foyt added, "I was wanting to run (at Michigan) real bad after Herta got hurt, but I made U.S. Tobacco a promise I'd get out of racing Indy cars. But I never said I'd get out of stock cars."[45]

Foyt then indicated he would drive in the Brickyard 400 with sponsorship from UST's Copenhagen brand. Not everyone was happy with the apparent compromise.

"My wife is awful damn mad at me," he said of Lucy. "She says if I bust my butt she's pushed me for the last time in a wheelchair. She says, 'You damned old man, going to try to run with twenty-year-olds, who do you think you are?' She's really been hard on me. But I knew going into it that some people were not going to be happy. I would just like to be able to say I ran in the first (Brickyard), to tell the grandkids."[46]

With more than eighty cars entered for forty starting positions (plus three cars added as promoter options), just qualifying for the Brickyard would be a challenge. He fell short on day one, turning the forty-fifth fastest time. Overnight he installed another engine provided by Penske Racing, reminiscent of 1980 when Foyt loaned an engine to the Penske team for Rusty Wallace's first NASCAR start.

"It's come full circle," Foyt said. "They borrowed two motors from me and finished second. So they always felt like they kind of owed me a favor. I shouldn't be hurting in that department."[47]

Foyt made it by the skin of his teeth, qualifying in the fortieth and last regular spot, setting off the sizable crowd's biggest roar of the day when he told them he just wanted "to be part of history.[48]

"I was probably playing it a little too close. I was sliding around a lot out there and I didn't feel like I could gamble today. I was nervous as hell. I should have stood on it a little harder. I was just trying to get it close and not screw up."

Foyt also had a hand in the qualifying run of pole sitter Rick Mast.

"We were up here testing," said Mast, who was sponsored by Skoal, another UST brand. "He drove my car a little bit and gave me his opinion. Then when we came back here this week, I went to him again a couple of times. This track changes more than any track I've ever seen. For that reason, I felt good that I could ask someone like A.J. what he thought the weather would do to the track.

It's not Indy cars, but, the track has its tendencies and a man like that you've got to listen to."[49]

In the race, the NASCAR drivers were greeted on the pace lap by a banner unfurled in the first turn grandstand reading, "Welcome to the House Foyt Built." He made an early pit stop for gas and then tried to stretch his fuel mileage, hoping to lead a lap when other teams pitted. He made it as high as second before the engine sputtered and he had to coast slowly back to the pits—out of fuel.

"It was one of those days that nothing went your way," said Foyt, who had run out of fuel more than once in the 500. "We didn't get the mileage like everyone else did. When I got back in, I knew I wasn't going to win, so I just tried to stay out of the way of the leaders. On restarts I didn't try to go racing. I figured, why race. The race was over. I was three or four laps down. I could have run with them, but you know you're not going to make up three or four laps, so I just decided to keep my nose clean."[50]

He finished thirtieth, four laps behind winner Jeff Gordon, who at twenty-three was the youngest driver in the field. Foyt was noncommittal when asked if he would return to race in the Brickyard.

"You could drive these cars until you're eighty years old, they don't tire you," he said. "That's one reason I wanted to own my own car. We can run it whenever I want. I might let my son Jerry run it a race or two.[51]

"But I don't know. I don't want to make that prediction. Next year I'll be sixty years old and these kids are pretty young. I'd have to be in a lot better shape."[52]

Eddie Cheever

Cheever's father was a race fan, and family lore had him attending the 1958 Indy 500—Foyt's first—along with his expecting wife. Eddie was born in Phoenix less than eight months later. The couple moved to Italy, where they raised a family, and Eddie attended a race at Monza with his father at an early age. He caught the bug and started racing go-karts, winning the European championship at fifteen. It was during this period that Cheever learned about the Indianapolis 500 and its most famous driver. He recalled,

> When I was growing up, probably the most important sport in Italy was Formula One, so I was very focused as a kid on following Ferrari. My father had spent most of his life in the states and always followed the Indianapolis 500. He was a big fan of Foyt. So, I learned about the Indy 500 through my father.[53]
>
> My dad made a big deal about that race. He was always comparing the Indianapolis 500 to Formula One. We would spend long hours driving from one go-kart track to another, and we would talk about racing. We'd talk about [Jimmy] Clark and [Jackie] Stewart, and Foyt. I have great memories of us having these long, drawn-out discussions about which drivers were better. It was almost like a kid playing baseball with his father in the backyard talking about who was the best pitcher in the World Series.

Cheever quickly rose through a series of European development programs, including Formula Two, where he won at the demanding Nürburgring, and finished second in the 1977 world championship. The next year, the twenty-year-old Cheever entered his first F1 race, although he failed to qualify. He then competed in F1 through 1989, driving for nine different teams and racking up a number of podium finishes but failing to score a victory. He had more success driving for Jaguar in the World Sportscar Championship, where he recorded several major victories.

With his F1 career coming to a close, Cheever joined Chip Ganassi Racing for the start of the 1990 Indy car season. His first experience with Foyt had not gone well.

> I found Turn One at Indy to be incredibly difficult. There was a gap there, and the wind—how much and the angle—always affected it. And there was a big bump in the middle of it. I thought, *I've got to ask somebody here to give me a hint what we're trying to do.* I mean, you approach the corner at 230 mph. So, there's Foyt sitting there before practice—the guy who's won four times, and he's still going incredibly quick. So why not just go over and ask him? I was very deferential. I asked if I could sit down and talk to him, and he said, "Yeah, sure." I said, what's the trick in Turn One? Can you tell me just one thing? And he looked at me and paused as he always did, took a deep breath and said, "Just keep turning left." I actually got a little flustered and angry. I thought, *Come on, man—just turn left?* He changed subjects, and that was it.

Cheever's first year with Ganassi was the best, but after three seasons without a victory and the team needing to cut back, they parted ways at the end of 1992. Since then, he'd raced for a hodgepodge of owners and only once in an Indy car in 1994, at Indianapolis where he finished eighth. As one motorsports columnist noted, "Eddie Cheever's continued sad slide down the IndyCar ownership chain has come to Foyt's door."[54]

The team struggled from the start, and after four races had only a pair of seventeenth-place finishes to show for their efforts. Herta showed up at Road America, and the rumors immediately started to spread that he was talking to Ganassi and Newman-Haas about a ride for the coming year—rumors the driver soon confirmed.

"I have a lot of opportunities and I want to look around and see what's happening," Herta said. "The accident hasn't changed my philosophy or my love for the sport. It hasn't changed my goals."[55]

Foyt didn't like the way that sounded, and with the pool of available drivers dwindling, he signed Cheever less than a month later. Despite the lack of success on the track, both sides seemed happy with the arrangement.

"I know the results don't show it," Foyt acknowledged, "but we got stronger at each race. Eddie is smart, he can drive and he's very professional."[56]

Cheever said he was looking forward to working with Foyt, especially at Indianapolis.

"A.J. knows so much about that place and it's so important to him. I'm going to try and suck all that knowledge out of his brain. It's tough coming into a team at mid-season but by Sundays we were running pretty good, especially on the ovals. A.J. has every intention of getting back to where he'd like to be and I'm proud to be on his team."

Herta eventually signed with Ganassi and had nothing but good things to say about his time with the Foyt team:

> It's the greatest thing I've done in racing, driving for A.J. I really enjoyed it. I learned a lot from the man. However long my career lasts, someday I'll be able to look back and say I drove for A.J. and got to know the man and learned some things from him.[57]
>
> I think the thing that happened was, it just worked out best for everybody this way. There wasn't a desire not to work together with A.J. He's done things in racing that will probably never be done again. His records will probably never be broken just because racing's become so specialized now.

Years later, Herta had more to say about the split with Foyt:

> If I could go back to one thing I would have changed in my career when I got better, I would have gone back and continued to drive for A.J. because I was still learning. I still needed time. I wasn't ready for the next opportunity at that point. I didn't know that. A.J. was the right place and the right environment. It was a smaller team, but it was a family environment. So probably the biggest mistake I made career-wise was not sticking with A.J. and not repaying the loyalty that he had shown me. Like, if there's one thing I'm sorry for, that's it.[58]
>
> I had half the paddock calling me—Carl Haas and Chip Ganassi and Jim Hall—and all these guys saying, 'We'd like to hire you.' And I got ahead of myself. A.J. caught wind that I was talking to other owners, and he didn't like that. He got mad and called me up and basically said, 'You're fired.' I don't blame him. He was good to me, and I was young. I was in a hurry to get somewhere, and it was the wrong thing to do.
>
> I think my career maybe would have gone better if I had just stayed with him a little longer. There was going to come a time that I would have needed to leave. But not yet. I wasn't ready for all of it. A.J. would have had the patience, he would have understood. He knew what it was like to come back from injury. He'd been hurt. A.J. cared about his drivers. He always did. Even though he's tough on you, he cared. You knew that. You knew he was tough, but you also knew he cared.
>
> A.J. didn't talk to me for years—many years. He was mad at me. I knew that. But now, you know, he's come around, and he's friendly again. You know, time heals all wounds, but it was probably never the same.
>
> A.J.'s the guy that gave me my break and he did that for a lot of drivers.

He put a lot of drivers in a car. And I'll be forever grateful to A.J. for giving me that break and giving me a shot to become an Indy car driver.

I had a really good time. He was so funny. I was young—twenty-four, which is not young to be an Indy car driver now—but at the time, that was pretty young. And to just be able to spend time around him. On a rainy day, you'd just sit in the garage and people stopped by all day long, and those guys would just tell story after story, and it all seemed so unreal to me. Each one was sort of crazier than the last. He was very warm and welcoming to my family.

Imagine coming into the sport as a rookie, making your debut in Indy car racing in the Indy 500, and driving A.J.'s No. 14. I mean, it was pretty heady stuff. I understood it at the time, but I didn't understand or appreciate it in a way that I do now, because I didn't have any context. I didn't know enough and didn't really have as much of an appreciation for the history of Indy car. I knew A.J. won the 500, and I knew all the stuff he'd done, but, you know, as I look back now, it's a tremendous source of pride to me to have said that I drove for A.J. at Indy and drove that iconic No. 14. Everyone knew that's *his* car. It's A.J.'s number.

We had so much fun. It was just such a great chapter in my life and in my career. I probably had as much fun as I ever had in my career. It was short, but I have so many memories.

Before the year was out, Foyt attended son Jerry's ARCA test session at Atlanta, his first opportunity to watch him on a superspeedway. A.J. still had very mixed emotions about his sons and grandson racing. He'd been shaken when he called Parnelli Jones after hearing Jones's son Page had been in a bad sprint car crash. Foyt learned Page was paralyzed and in a coma. At least Jerry was driving a stock car and not an open-wheel race car.

"He wanted me to come see him test and I'm really glad I did," A.J. said. "There's too much politics in Indy car racing now. I'd love to start a Winston Cup team."[59]

GOODYEAR
DieHard
COPENHAGEN
GOODYEAR
DieHard
COPENHAGEN
RACING
COPENHAGEN
RACING

CHAPTER 24

A GATHERING STORM

1995

The politics threatening Indy car racing A.J. Foyt warned about at the end of 1994 had been simmering for nearly a year since Indianapolis Motor Speedway President Tony George resigned from the board of the Championship Auto Racing Teams, a move Foyt supported.

"Indianapolis has always been independent and it should stay that way," A.J. said. "They will run a race in May, even if it's with go-karts."[1]

George argued car owners shouldn't run the series and said he wanted to control costs, cut back on the number of races, focus on Indy car racing's traditional oval tracks, and include more American drivers. Although expressing concern about the impact of a second series, Foyt eventually left no doubt where he stood.

"Whatever way Indianapolis goes, I will go," he said, reciting the familiar, "Indianapolis made A.J. Foyt" theme. "They've been awfully good to me through the years. Indianapolis made Mario Andretti. Indianapolis has made all the American drivers.[2]

"What Tony would like to see—now this is A.J. talking—I think Tony would like to see more oval racing and permanent facilities. I think Tony is looking for the long-time security like Mr. [Tony] Hulman, his grandfather, did. That is the reason Indianapolis looks as great as it does."

Foyt immediately offered to resign his seat on the CART board but was talked out of it by other car owners. Most still saw Foyt as the key voice in open-wheel racing and desperately wanted to keep him involved with CART. Foyt agreed to stay for the time being, saying, "A war or something like that, fighting each other, never settled nothing. I think that would be the worst thing."

The controversy surrounding Mercedes's dominant engine in the 500 had further escalated calls by the smaller teams to do something about spiraling

◀ A.J. and Eddie Cheever. *Dan Boyd*

costs. USAC amended its rules, rendering the engine noncompetitive, but it was too late for George. By midyear, he'd announced the formation of the Indy Racing League, a series of oval track races centered around the Indianapolis 500 beginning in 1996 with new cars. It was to be managed by a five-person board of governors, none of whom would be team owners. No other tracks were named, nor were the rules the League would operate under released. Despite the scant information, Foyt seemed to support the organization, already being called the IRL.

"He's a big boy, he can make his own decisions," Foyt said of George. "I talked to Tony on some things, but if I thought he was going the wrong way, I'd raise hell and say something to him. But he's been around and knows what's going on."[3]

Saying, "Indianapolis cars were meant to perform on ovals, not street courses," Foyt indicated his team would compete in the IRL but left open the door to running in some CART events. He then reinforced his commitment to the new league, standing next to George in Orlando, Florida, when plans were announced to stage the inaugural race at a yet-to-be-built track at Disney World.

"I know the Indy Racing League and Tony George have the best interests of racing at heart," he said. "I'm glad to see an effort to get racing back to Indianapolis and championship-style events—which are on ovals."[4]

"We're definitely going to run the IRL series, but it's just according to how the schedule falls. I've always loved oval racing, and I like some of the road courses. But I've never been a fan of the street courses. Oval racing is my first love."[5]

The racing season was barely underway, however, when George announced a major change to his plans. The 1996 IRL races would be run under existing rules. George said he would continue to work toward establishing the new organization but for the moment, it seemed peace would prevail.

Eddie Cheever started off the year on a couple of street races about as well as could be expected, coming from twenty-second to fourteenth at Miami and from seventeenth to seventh at Surfers Paradise in Australia.

He finished fourteenth April 2 on the Phoenix oval, but the real story was a pair of ex-Foyt drivers who dominated the event, Bryan Herta capturing the pole and Robby Gordon winning the race. Afterward, a reporter went by the Foyt transporter wanting to know what A.J. thought about the performance of his two former drivers. Fortunately for the reporter, Foyt had already left for the airport.

"If you wanted a blackeye, that would have been the question to ask," a crew member told him.[6]

A week later at Long Beach, the team recorded their best finish yet. Although Cheever qualified eighteenth, the car worked well in traffic and good pit work and strategy put him in third on the last lap. Even though he ran out of gas and rolled to a stop short of the finish line, he was still awarded fourth place.

Next up was Nazareth two weeks later, a tight one-mile oval. The track surface was causing havoc with tires, and Cheever qualified a disappointing twenty-first. Afterward, Foyt said he wanted to make major changes to the car.

"The track was shit—excuse me—and the tires were getting a lot of pickup," Cheever recalled twenty-five years later. "So, our normal setup was not going to work. He said, 'I'm just going to make these changes. You okay with them?' and I said, 'Yeah, fine with me.'"[7]

Cheever continued,

> He changed everything. It was all him. Now they'd probably have three engineers working on it—one guy in charge of the shock absorbers and two other guys doing stuff. This was just Foyt. He looked at the track, looked at the tires, looked at the conditions, then said, okay I'm going to do this crazy thing.
>
> He took all the tires and changed all the toe-ins. When I went out on the grid, my steering wheel was crooked, and not one of the wheels was pointing forward. I thought, *Oh my God, what have we done. This is going to be impossible.*
>
> I'll be damned—after five laps, it was wonderful. It was perfect. He had done something to the toes to make sure all of the rubber pickup wouldn't stay on the tire. I was going by people like they were standing still. I had far and away the best car on the track, and we were leading. Throughout that race, his voice (on the radio) would always be this monotone. It was just always the same, like, 'You're leading. Coming up on traffic.'

When Cheever passed Jacques Villeneuve for the lead, it was his first time out front in an Indy car race since 1992. After a couple of caution flags, the computers said they were good on fuel. Cheever led by more than a second with just over a lap to go when the car sputtered and slowed to a stop, out of gas again.

Cheever said,

> We ran out of fuel. We ran out of fucking fuel. Can you imagine that? Two races in a row. A week later, we got a memo from Lola telling us that there was an issue with the fuel tanks. When you filled it, you had to do something different to get the last gallon and a half.
>
> I'm really sorry I didn't win Nazareth because that would have brought us to a whole new level. I think winning a race for Foyt in Indy car would have been exceptional, and I would have been very, very proud to have that on my resume.

Foyt, who hadn't won an Indy car race as an owner since he drove to victory at Pocono in 1981, said, "I feel bad for Eddie, I've had many wins over the years."[8]

Despite the disappointments, the momentum generated at Long Beach and Nazareth carried over to Indianapolis, and everyone wanted to talk about Foyt and Cheever. Cheever had come up driving European open-wheel and sports cars on road courses, while Foyt had spent his formative years on ovals in midgets and sprint cars. While Cheever spoke three languages, Foyt had mastered only one:

Texan. And while Cheever preferred pasta and a glass of good red wine, Foyt was strictly a steak and potatoes man. The combination seemed to be working, although there were still moments.

"Everybody has this idea A.J. and I have this calm relationship but that's not true," Cheever said before practice started at the Speedway. "Working with A.J. is not easy and I've been told working with me isn't either, but I've got to say we've developed a pretty good relationship. It can never be calm and peaceful, but it can be successful. The man is a walking technical library and if you can get through all the Foyt-isms, he's got such knowledge. I've learned things on how to approach a race, little nuances I'd never thought about.[9]

He continued, "A.J. is unbelievably determined. He will plow through things to get what he wants. We both want to be successful, and A.J. is not going to change. I could see why he would enjoy having new drivers work for him because he could bend them to his will. But I think A.J. is enjoying our relationship as much as I am. We have very eventful weekends, but I can see renewed vigor in him. The challenge for me is to try to modernize what we're doing and merge my experience with all the winning he's done."[10]

Foyt said, "We may have different personalities but I think people read too much into that. When I hired him, I didn't want a yes man. I also didn't want to take any guff from someone. I wanted someone with the credentials and experience to win. I think Eddie gives us that. Sure, we like to jab each other all the time. But I get along with him just fine."[11]

The No. 14 car ran well in practice, especially in traffic, and even a disappointing qualifying run—Cheever was fourteenth—couldn't dampen the team's spirit as the race approached.

"The car kept bottoming in turn three [in qualifying trim] and we never found a way around it," Cheever recalled years later. "But with full tanks and running in race trim, the car was great. We focused more on getting it well balanced so that it would be good for 500 miles as opposed to going out and trying to get the pole. That made a lot of sense to me."[12]

With Cheever in the race and running well, Foyt looked at adding a second car to the field. He offered a ride to 1975 500 winner Danny Sullivan, who had just signed with another team. Then he turned to Scott Sharp.

The son of six-time SCCA champion Bob Sharp, Scott had come out of the sports car ranks where he'd won sixteen Trans-Am races, and the 1991 and 1993 series championships. He'd competed in the 1994 International Race of Champions and ran most of the Indy car season for PacWest, a new team in the series with no experience on ovals. He'd failed to crack the top ten, however, and was dropped near the end of the year.

"My first year in Indy cars, I didn't know a thing about ovals," Sharp recounted. "I didn't know a thing about aero cars. I was like a deer in headlights. PacWest was a brand-new team, and it was only our third or fourth race. We were trying to figure things out at the track, and it was my first time there. It didn't go that great. I had some moments that looked good, but it didn't pan out that well."[13]

Twenty-seven at the start of the 1995 season—ten years younger than Cheever—he'd been serving as an occasional test driver for Penske Racing but otherwise without a ride. Sharp said,

> I was really good buddies with Robby Gordon from our days in Trans-Am, and he invited me to Indianapolis. He had talked to A.J. about running me in a second car. When I got there, I was just sort of hanging around, and I got to spend some time with A.J. He threw me in the car literally on the Friday afternoon before bump weekend.
>
> I had minimal running time, but I got my first taste of A.J. working his magic. It was amazing. Typically, you work with engineers and crew chiefs, and you make one change and then go see if it worked. Then make another change and see if that worked. I'd come in after a few laps in A.J.'s car, and he'd tell the crew do this, do that, and put a set of tires on it. I'm thinking, *Oh my gosh.* Then I'd go out, and the car would fly.
>
> With A.J., I went immediately faster than I'd gone the year before and at a whole 'nother comfort level. I very quickly developed a confidence level and trust in him. A.J. didn't like to run more than just a few laps at a time, and after we did about four or five practice runs, he was like, "Put it in line to qualify."
>
> He was good on the radio. He was a driver's driver. He was aggressive, short, sometimes expletive filled. But you knew you were with someone who just had immense amounts of experience. You learned pretty quick that whatever he said, you do what he's telling you to do. It's the way to go.

A bad pop-off valve ruined his first run, and a bad cylinder the second, but Sharp finally made the field on his third and final attempt. Failing to qualify were the three Penske cars that had dominated the year before, which Foyt seemed to enjoy.

"I'm very proud of Scott," he said. "He did exactly what I asked him to do. I've probably qualified for this race more than Roger Penske or anybody. I know how hard it can be."[14]

"Who'd have ever thought Penske would have two 500 winners [Emerson Fittipaldi and Al Unser Jr.] and can't qualify for this race? I can truthfully say we've been in the back before, but we have never missed this race."[15]

Both Foyt cars ran well on Carburation Day, and both drivers were excited about their prospects.

"The car was good," Cheever would say. "If you have a car where you can put it anywhere you want on the track regardless of conditions and how much fuel you have, you're looking good. That's something we worked on together throughout that whole month to make sure that we had a very wide window of drivability. The car really was good."[16]

Sharp said, "A.J. has just a wealth of knowledge. When he leans his head in the car and tells you the kind of changes he's making and what he's trying to do, you know it's going to work. He's given me a really great setup and if I keep myself out of trouble and keep working my way up to the last 100 miles, I think we're going to finish solidly in the top ten."[17]

The race was over for both before it started. The field was badly jumbled behind the front two rows, and Cheever, who lined up directly behind Stan Fox, jumped to the outside of the former Foyt driver coming out of Turn One. Fox was low on the track when the car suffered a broken half shaft, suddenly turned hard right, and shot up the track into Cheever.

"Stan made a sharp right and hit me and hit the wall," said Cheever, who was unhurt. "He had a big hit. Something must have broken on his car or somebody bumped him because he came across the track at such a sharp angle. Stan is one of the better drivers out there. I am very concerned for him."[18]

Fox suffered internal head injuries and was in a coma for five days. He would eventually learn to walk again and recover, but his racing days were over.

Sharp had just finished a pit stop when his right-front tire either exploded or came loose, tossing the car into the wall while working lap seventy-five. He was lucky to escape with nothing more than a badly bruised arm.

"It all blew up in a couple hours," Foyt said as he surveyed his two wrecked cars. "It's a shame because I felt like Eddie had probably one of the best chances of winning. We've been on a good run but things happen in this game. I've had days like this before. You got to fight your way back up.[19]

"At least neither of our drivers are hurt. You can replace the cars. Drivers are hard to replace."

Years later, Cheever would look back on the race fondly:

> The experience I had racing for him at Indy was phenomenal. It was magical. Foyt would sit down and describe every bump on the circuit; where they were and how the car should feel. And I think having Foyt on the radio with you at Indianapolis would have been like having an extra fifty horsepower.[20]
>
> To this day, I'm disappointed that I did not get to run the whole race with Foyt hooked up to my helmet. I'm convinced there were things that he could tell you that were going to happen before they actually happened. But I never made it past the first corner.

It also proved memorable for Sharp.

"The contrast between my first year to when I got some time with A.J. was just immense," he'd say. "I don't think I ever would have gotten there without him. The only other way you could get comfortable fast would have been to be on the best team, with the best teammates and a really good engineer who could explain what to do. A.J. supplied all that. He quickly got me up to speed and really made me love driving those cars."[21]

Another person who had their first experience with Foyt that day was a young driver named Tony Stewart, who'd been pressed into service by A.J.'s friend George Snider to work the so-called deadman's valve in Cheever's pit. Snider had been racing against Stewart in Silver Crown cars and talking him up to Foyt.

Stewart's job was holding open the valve handle on the fuel tank during a pit stop, allowing fuel to flow to the car. Should there be any problem, he was to release the valve, cutting off the flow of fuel.

"Normally I have a midget race to run in Wisconsin that day, so I always listened to the race on the radio," Stewart said. "Working in the pits is a neat opportunity to do what a lot of people would love to do. The only thing that I would change is that I'd like to have a different job."[22]

As bad as it was, Indianapolis turned out to be the team's high-water mark. At Milwaukee the following week, Cheever crashed in practice and was forced into a backup 1994 Lola due to a lack of spare parts. He was the first out of the race, parking the older model after complaining about its handling. He crashed again in the next race on Belle Isle in Detroit.

Cheever acknowledged the accidents beginning at Indianapolis, "Really set us back. Not being a large team, that really affected our ability to respond in time to whatever problems we would have later."[23]

By the time the team arrived in Cleveland for the July 23 race, they'd managed to finish only two events since the 500, and the frustration had turned into tension. Foyt's ability "to do it all" that had amazed Cheever at Nazareth was now adding to the challenges in the driver's eyes as he thought the owner had too much on his plate.

"He's capable of doing every single piece that makes up a race team," Cheever acknowledged before the start of practice. "He's capable of doing it unbelievably well. [But] in modern racing you cannot do that anymore. You have specialists that just focus on one thing. It's become so competitive, if you have a crossover with certain people doing more than one job, you're not going to get the maximum of their time."

Not surprisingly, Foyt didn't see it that way.

"We've had engineers and they didn't show me nothing I hadn't forgot, so I decided to start doing it myself," he countered. "We peaked and looked like one of the ones to beat at Indy. But after the accidents, we've been down since then. We've done a lot of changing, a lot of checking, and we're probably going to do more changing and checking. I really can't understand why, and it's disgusting as hell. You think you've turned it all around then all of a sudden, bang, it slaps you back in the face."

In addition to more engineers, Cheever said the team needed more equipment and to do more testing. He felt the intensity the team had shown early in the year had waned.

"A.J. always put a lot of effort into starting the season," he'd say. "We had some really good cars. Like any race car driver, I always thought we needed a little bit more. I wish we'd had better engineering."[24]

Again, Foyt disagreed.

"That ain't the problem. Eddie—a lot of times, I feel—beats himself because he feels that someone's got something he doesn't have. I never felt that way as a race driver. And I think that's what separates your No. 1 guys from your No. 2 guys.[25]

"It kind of looks like he's got a black cloud over his head."

Cheever qualified poorly again at Cleveland and dropped out of the race with engine problems. He wasn't ready to give up, however, pointing to two upcoming races as a last chance to turn the season around.

"A.J. is able to put together very competitive cars for ovals," he said. "And we have two ovals [Michigan and New Hampshire] coming up. If we can focus the way we were focusing before all the mishaps, I think we've got a definite shot."

Rather than turn things around, the situation on the team reached a boiling point at Michigan. Cheever qualified eighteenth but was running near the front and had led a couple of laps when his transmission let go on lap 163 of 250.

Foyt immediately recalled the race when asked about it twenty-five years later. "I love Eddie, but I could have killed him a couple of times," he said with a laugh. "At Michigan, we could have won the race, but he kept arguing with me. I wanted him to stop shifting, and Eddie would say, 'I'm not shifting.' But I'm watching him on the computer, and he's shifting. He said he needed to turn more rpm, and I kept telling him to stop. Finally, he broke a shift bar."[26]

Cheever admitted, "We had a really bumpy Michigan race. I had started becoming more demanding, and he started getting tired of me asking for more. I probably said the wrong thing afterward. You could always tell when you said the wrong thing because he'd call you a cowboy. Whenever he called you cowboy it was like a fifteen-second warning. You better shut up or get out of the room—or both."[27]

In the midst of the turmoil surrounding his Indy car team, Foyt decided to try and qualify again for NASCAR's Brickyard 400 at the Speedway. He'd been able to line up sponsorship from Motorola although the car—the backup machine from the previous race—was the only year-old model entered. He hadn't driven since the last Brickyard, and—now sixty—he struggled getting in and out of the car for an early practice session. But that didn't seem to dampen his enthusiasm.

"I didn't have the results here last year that I wanted," he said in making the announcement. "But I've never been a quitter and I'll never be a quitter. As this race got closer and closer I got more itchier and itchier."[28]

He said running the Indy car team "hasn't been much fun for A.J. Foyt. That's why I'm looking forward to this week. It'll be the most fun I've had in a long time. I still want to race. I just think that when I stepped down out of Indy cars, I stepped down a little early.

"I'll tell you what, I just want to start racing a little bit more, get back in shape, take off about twenty pounds. It's something I enjoy and what's life all about if you can't have fun?"[29]

The sponsorship from Motorola came with a catch: The car was painted the company's shade of purple. While Foyt declined to wear a purple driver's uniform, he and the car were quickly labeled "Barney" after the purple dinosaur on a popular children's television show.

He was second slowest of the forty-eight cars that made a run on the first day of qualifying and afterward crawled under the car to work on the suspension. As he had been the year before, he was joined by members of Rusty Wallace's Penske Racing crew. They wouldn't find out if they fixed the problems as day two of qualifying was completely washed out. Under NASCAR regulations, the field was set based on series points, with the provisional spots reserved for series regulars. It was a defiant Foyt who took the blame and said he planned to try again and might even start his own NASCAR team.

"I'm very embarrassed that I did not produce like we had hoped. It was my call. I screwed up. The next time I will not be caught with my britches down.[30]

"I'm going to do what I want to do. I will continue to do that 'til I die. That's A.J. If I decide I want to race, I'm going to race."

The off week did nothing to help Foyt's Indy car team, and after a poor overall performance at New Hampshire, Cheever turned in his notice with two events still on the schedule. Several reports said the pair nearly came to blows.[31]

"It was no longer good for either of us," Cheever told reporters. "He wants to continue without engineers and I don't, so we decided to get on with our lives."[32]

Despite the less than amiable parting, Cheever has no regrets about driving for Foyt.

"Of all the people I have raced for, I would say that Foyt was just an exceptional experience," said Cheever, who would go on to win the 1998 Indianapolis 500 driving for his own team. "It was really cool to spend that much time with somebody of his caliber who achieved so much in his life. In racing, you have a lot of time waiting for something to happen, like when it's raining. I spent so much time with Foyt just talking about racing. It was a great experience."[33]

Foyt looked back on the relationship with similar feelings. "We got along pretty good. He's just hardheaded. And I guess I'm hardheaded. And when two hardheads get together, well, you know. We're still great friends."[34]

Taking over at Vancouver for the penultimate race of the year was Brian Till, who hadn't driven an Indy car in more than a year and had never seen the course. Foyt skipped the race to promote a dirt track event, and it was just as well because Till crashed out after twenty-six laps. For the final race of the year at Laguna Seca, Foyt brought in Swedish sports car driver Fredrik Ekblom, who was making just his second Indy car start. He was still running at the finish in twenty-first place as the checkered flag mercifully came down on the season.

As Foyt began his seemingly annual search for a new driver, there was one name at the top of his list—and everyone else's for that matter: Tony Stewart. The twenty-four-year-old who'd been ready to operate the deadman's valve on Cheever's car at Indianapolis had gone on to win USAC's first Triple Crown, capturing the national midget, sprint car, and Silver Crown championships.

He was coming off a sprint car victory at Salem Raceway, the same place Foyt credited with launching his Indy car career. He'd also led all one hundred laps in winning the Hut One Hundred dirt track race at Terre Haute, where Foyt had often dominated. If ever there was a driver cut in the mold of A.J. Foyt, it was Tony Stewart. And Foyt was Stewart's hero.

"I would watch the Indy 500 with my dad, who drove in SCCA," said Stewart, who was born May 20, 1971, in Columbus, Indiana. He continued,

> It was the year when A.J. got out of the car and grabbed a hammer and was beating on the right-front suspension. That was the first time I ever saw anybody get out of a car and take a wrench to it, let alone a hammer, and beat on the suspension, then get back in the car and go racing again. That was my first memory of him catching my eye.[35]
>
> My love for him developed as I'd go back and watch the four races that he'd won. To be able to see the Dick Wallen videos of A.J. running the Silver Crown cars and sprint cars and the midget in the Astrodome. I was young when I watched those videos, but that was really when I became a fan of A.J.

Now Stewart had his eye on running the new IRL circuit and also trying his hand at NASCAR.

"The IRL opened up the opportunity for me to get with A.J. If it wasn't for the formation of the IRL, the guys who came from midgets and sprint cars through that time period never would have had those opportunities. I doubt if I would have."

Foyt was also looking at starting a NASCAR program and building a Ford F-150 for the new SuperTruck series and a new car for Winston Cup. He'd been badly embarrassed while trying to qualify for the Brickyard 400 and was determined not to make that his final race, hiring veteran NASCAR crew chief Barry Dodson to oversee the effort.

Foyt announced he'd race in NASCAR's season-ending events at Phoenix with an eye toward the next season:

> I've always been the type that if somebody kicks me when I'm down, it makes me want to fight back. I love a good challenge. I might be sixty, but my heart feels like it's twenty. I feel if I give up, I might as well roll up and die.[36]
>
> I know I don't drive like I'm twenty anymore, but I feel I can be competitive. That's why I'm out here testing. I want to get in a groove. I've got fifteen or twenty pounds of excess I'm carrying, but I think I can get rid of that. I'm still trying to put something together where I can run all the big races next year, like at Daytona, Talladega, Charlotte and Atlanta. That's what I'd like to do. Racing is my life. It always has been.

Foyt brought both his NASCAR vehicles and a pair of Indy cars to Phoenix for a week-long test and invited Stewart and Ekblom. He talked of running Stewart in IRL races and Ekblom on the CART road courses. Most of the first two days was spent standing around as Foyt and Dodson tried to fix an oil leak on the truck. When Stewart finally got a chance to drive the Indy car, Foyt allowed the young drivers to run only a few laps at a time and imposed strict speed limits.

Years later, Stewart recalled,

> We went out in the rental car and rode around with him a little bit. Didn't say a whole lot about the line, it was more about the speed and lap times he wanted us to run. He was really strict about that. As soon as you started

> creeping up in speed over the bracket he wanted you in, he brought you in right away. There was no hesitation with him. He'd tell you to go run ten laps at a certain speed, and if on lap five you went over the speed, he'd pull you in. He was very picky about that speed bracket.[37]
>
> He wanted to make sure you had control of what was going on. The hard part was, that speed was just slow enough that it was hard to modulate the throttle and maintain the speed. You'd get in that bracket and start to build momentum and the next lap would be faster and felt more comfortable and you just kept building momentum. You weren't really trying to go faster, but he'd pull you in right away before you could slow down. But I really liked A.J., I liked his guys, and I was really excited and hoping we would get an opportunity to work together.

There was another problem. Stewart had become a target of Foyt's sharp needle, and while he enjoyed bantering with drivers as much as anyone, he'd been reluctant to engage A.J. When he finally did (see foreword), Stewart said, "It strengthened our relationship for the rest of our lives.

> That's what it was like the rest of the trip, and that's what our relationship has been like ever since. The bigger the group, the more grief he gives you. He loved to put on a show. Now if he's got an audience, we go toe to toe with each other. When those people leave that conversation, they'll never forget it.

Despite the banter, Stewart never questioned whether A.J. should be getting back in a race car:

> I don't think it's anybody's decision when you retire, as long as you're not a danger to everybody else on the racetrack. A.J. had racked up enough credentials to make that decision on his own. People don't realize it's a passion and a life style—it's what you eat, breathe, and sleep every day of your life—and it's not easy to walk away. Even when you're not running as well as you like and not winning races like you used to. But he was still A.J. Foyt. He had a right to be there and do whatever he wanted to do.

When Foyt finally turned Stewart loose for a few laps, he got within a second of the Phoenix track record. But when Foyt offered him the No. 14 car for the Indianapolis 500 and the full five-race IRL season, Stewart hesitated. He'd also been offered a ride in the NASCAR Busch series, the stepping stone to Winston Cup, by Harry Ranier, who'd been supportive in the past. Ranier had owned cars driven by Cale Yarborough and Buddy Baker to victory in the Daytona 500 and had also been friendly with Foyt at one point, although that relationship had soured.

Foyt said he wanted Stewart focused on the Indy car ride, which seemed odd as A.J. himself had often raced in both series on the same weekend, flying back-and-forth between tracks. But the experience with John Andretti trying to run in both series had been difficult for Foyt the car owner. Like Foyt had in the past, Stewart was headed to Australia to race his midget or "speedcar" during the offseason and wanted to make a decision before he left.

Stewart remembered,

> I went to Texas with A.J. to his ranch. It was a really hard situation because I had to talk with A.J. about trying to do both. I was used to running multiple cars and racing a lot, and the IRL was only going to be five races the first year. Ranier wanted to run me in eight or so Busch series races. The Raniers also said they'd make sure none of the Busch series races conflicted with my IRL races.
>
> But A.J. did not want me to run that stock car. He would not allow me to run both. I had to do the Indy car or nothing. I'd already been working with the Raniers for a year and a half trying to put this deal together.
>
> I don't know if there was a beef between them or if it was just A.J. wanting to be in control of everything and just wanting me to run only Indy car. I don't know the answer.

Foyt would only say, "Tony would probably have been driving my race cars if he hadn't had a contract with a guy that I didn't want to deal with."[38]

Longtime Foyt crew chief Craig Baranouski went a little further. "A.J. didn't like the guys he was going to drive the stock car for. He felt they were crooks, and if Tony was going to be involved with them, he didn't want to be involved with Tony."[39]

Stewart said, "At that point of my life, that was the toughest decision I'd made. Here I had an opportunity to race in the IRL full time for my hero and also had an opportunity to go race in NASCAR for a team that had a great reputation and a great track record. I just felt loyal to the Ranier family because of the time they invested in me."[40]

Stewart committed to the Raniers and turned down the Foyt ride. He was soon snatched up by John Menard to run the IRL races.

"There were no hard feelings when I went and did those deals. A.J. never treated me any different. He wasn't happy that I didn't take him up on his offer at the time, but once we got racing again, we were back to being friends. That always impressed me about him. I would have fully understood if he was upset with me and didn't want to be my friend after that. But he understood it was a business decision and that I had been working with those guys and we went back to being friends again."[41]

Foyt went ahead with plans to try and qualify for the October 28 NASCAR SuperTruck race at Phoenix and the Winston Cup event scheduled there the next day. He'd won the first Indy car race staged at the track thirty years earlier, before many of the drivers in the field had been born. The SuperTrucks was a new series NASCAR had launched a year earlier in an attempt to take advantage of the booming pickup truck market in the United States, and Foyt had commissioned a truck from Hutcherson-Pagan.

Initially, Jerry Foyt had hoped he might be the driver of the truck, saying, "It will be A.J.'s re-entry into NASCAR as an owner."[42]

As race day approached, however, it became apparent A.J. would make the qualifying run himself. A new father for the first time, Jerry didn't press the point. "If there's somebody out there who's more competitive than he is, I don't know him. He's got the endurance of a young man. He still has a lot of drive."[43]

After qualifying a respectable ninth in the forty-truck field, Foyt faded to eighteenth at the finish, the first truck one lap behind winner Mike Skinner. That was the highlight of the weekend as he came up one position short of making the forty-four-car Cup race. There'd be no more talk about running the major NASCAR races in the coming year.

The faceoff between the Indy Racing League and the Championship Auto Racing Teams had continued to spiral out of control through 1995, and the only thing that was certain as the year came to a close was that Indy car racing in general would suffer.

"There's going to be a lot of blood spilled before this thing is over," said Les Richter, a respected NASCAR official who tried and failed to broker a compromise.[44]

When CART teams threatened to boycott the new series, Tony George—"the little rich kid who brings the ball and says he's going to be the pitcher or the game's over," wrote veteran motorsports journalist Shav Glick in the *Los Angeles Times*—further escalated tensions when he announced plans to reserve twenty-five of the thirty-three starting positions in the Indianapolis 500 for IRL teams and drivers. It was an early form of the franchise system now commonplace in auto racing but unheard of in 1995.[45]

CART countered by announcing plans to stage the U.S. 500 at Roger Penske's Michigan International Speedway in direct opposition to the Indianapolis race. Glick was equally hard on the CART move, calling it a "spiteful and mind-boggling decision that defies logic."

Through all the skirmishing, there'd been one constant: Foyt was committed to running the entire IRL season, although he said he was "kind of neutral" on the idea of guaranteed starting positions in the 500.

"Tony wants to get it where the normal guy can come up and race," Foyt said. "Right now it's getting so high tech and so expensive, that a guy needs so many sponsors that it's just unbelievable. He is trying to get the costs back in reality where you can still have a good race."[46]

"Right now, I think it's beyond the point of resolving it. There's too much friction both ways."[47]

CHAPTER 25

THE SPLIT

1996

With the first race of the inaugural Indy Racing League season slated for January 27 at the new Walt Disney Speedway in Orlando, Florida, A.J. Foyt moved quickly to shore up his driver lineup. He said he wanted to run two cars in the series and signed Davey Hamilton to drive the No. 14 car, poaching him away from another IRL car owner, Ron Hemelgarn, who thought he had already secured Hamilton's services.

Hamilton was a good example of the type of driver the IRL was hoping to promote. He'd made his name driving super modifieds along the West Coast before moving to midgets and Silver Crown cars. At thirty-three, he'd all but given up on an Indy car ride before the IRL came along. A.J. had first spotted him when Hamilton won the 1989 Copper World Classic in Phoenix, driving a car painted Foyt Orange and wearing No. 14. George Snider introduced the pair, and Foyt said maybe they could work together in the future. It took seven years, but then things came together quickly.

"It's amazing how fast things have been happening," Hamilton said. "Getting a call with that offer from A.J. was like a dream come true, but it put me in a tough spot. Ron and I had an informal deal for '96 but that was based on proper sponsorship, which wasn't totally assured. Foyt's deal was a rock-solid two-year contract with the biggest name in Indy car racing and I just couldn't pass it up."[1]

He told another reporter, "I'd been trying to get an Indy car ride since 1991. But the [Championship Auto Racing Teams] guys wouldn't even talk to me unless I had a pocketful of money. Well I may not be rich, but that doesn't mean I can't drive a race car. I'm not saying I'm the best out there, but I felt like I

◀ Foyt and IMS President Tony George in deep discussion at the Speedway. *David Nearpass*

deserved a shot. The IRL gives me that opportunity. This series is a dream come true for me."[2]

The second seat was proving more challenging to fill. The Clinton administration was pushing to ban tobacco companies from sponsoring sporting activities, and with the handwriting on the wall, Copenhagen had notified Foyt the Indianapolis 500 would be the last race with the company's name on the side of one of his cars. So A.J. was also looking for sponsorship dollars along with a driver.

Willy T. Ribbs, the first African American driver to start the Indianapolis 500, was rumored to be in line for the second car at one point, but the hoped-for funding never materialized. Mike Bliss, who was driving in the SuperTruck series that Foyt had his eyes on, tested at the Disney track but elected to stick with NASCAR. Dirt track star Steve Kinser also tested a Foyt car and was offered the ride but decided to stay in the World of Outlaws sprint car series where he had won fourteen championships.

"It's flattering whenever A.J. Foyt asks you to race for him," said Kinser, indicating it would take two or three years to feel at ease in an Indy car. "I just thought it was better for me in terms of my career to stick with what has been good to me."[3]

It wasn't until a week before the Disney event that Foyt announced he was bringing back Scott Sharp to drive for his team. In a reversal of his stand against Tony Stewart driving in NASCAR, Foyt agreed to let Hamilton compete in modified races and Sharp, who was just coming off a victory in the 24 Hours of Daytona, to drive in sports car events.

Foyt also raised the stakes against CART, filing a Sherman Antitrust Act federal lawsuit against the organization in a Houston court, where he'd won previous cases against *Sports Illustrated* and the *Indianapolis Star*. The suit said CART was trying to monopolize Indy car racing by scheduling the U.S. 500 directly against the Indianapolis 500 and pressuring companies to stay away from sponsoring his IRL cars. Foyt was seeking a minimum of $5 million in damages plus additional court costs.

In part, the fourteen-page suit read, "This action arises out of the wrongful and tortious acts of CART and various other individuals and entities, which were committed in an attempt to interfere with and restrain free competition and trade in the Indy Car automobile racing industry.[4]

"The overriding purpose (of scheduling the U.S. 500 against the Indianapolis 500) was to restrain trade, monopolize the sport of Indy Car Racing and to prevent competition in the IRL events."

Foyt also claimed the organization was preventing him from competing in CART and IRL races through intimidation. "Certain individuals, acting in concert with CART, contacted representatives of Texaco in Houston, Texas, in order to discourage them from approving sponsorship to IRL or to anyone who had expressed a desire to race in an IRL event. As a result, Texaco advised Foyt that it would not provide financial sponsorship for the 1996 season, nor would it associate itself with any IRL event."

Hamilton found out during his first Orlando practice session about the A.J. Foyt way of doing things. Hamilton admitted,

> A.J. was my hero and I was intimidated by him. But I'd already learned how to build my own cars, and I was doing my own setups. We were really good even though I was scuffing off speed, probably fourth or fifth quickest. It's my first practice session, so I'm feeling pretty good. I tell A.J. I'm scuffing speed, and he makes some changes, and I go out, and it's kind of doing the same thing. Now he never had the intercom on. He'd always come and sit down on the car's A-frame, and we'd just talk. He's sitting there, and he's thinking. And I go, "What spring we got in the right front? Because it feels soft." He said, "Boy, you just drive this car. You don't worry about what spring's in it." So that kind of set me back.[5]

Tony George was hoping to have twenty-five cars start the race at Orlando, and when it looked like the field would fall short of twenty, Foyt added a third car for Mike Groff. The last-minute addition caught even Groff by surprise, who still had a CART patch on his uniform as he climbed in the car for the first time.

Sharp qualified fourth, Hamilton sixth, and Groff twelfth after just a few laps in the car. As the race approached, Hamilton realized just how big a jump he was making. He said,

> There are a lot of things I've yet to do. I've yet to make a pit stop. I've yet to get out there and pass cars. I've been out there in traffic, but I haven't been really racing. So it will be a new experience. I'll have A.J. walking me through it on the radio, telling me when to charge a little bit, telling me when to just ride, telling me when to pit. He's one of the main reasons I came to this team. I mean, who has more experience than he does? He's been on both sides of it. I'll leave the strategy part of it up to him. Whatever he says is whatever I'll be doing.[6]

With all eyes focused on Orlando, Foyt was asked if there was still time for a peace treaty between the IRL and CART.

"I don't think it can ever be hashed out," he said. "It comes down to ego. People want to be drunk with power. Andrew Craig [CART president] knows nothing about racing. All the things he's said are bald-faced lies. I don't like nobody who don't talk with a straight tongue. I'll go head-to-head on a talk show with any of them."[7]

Told Mario Andretti was considering a comeback to race in the U.S. 500, which was being promoted as "The real cars, the real stars, The Real 500," Foyt promised, "If that SOB comes back, I'll be back. I'll match that SOB any day of the week in anything he wants to run." He added that comparing the Indy 500 to the U.S. 500 was like "comparing chicken salad to chicken shit. Will people remember the winner of the U.S. 500 or the Indy 500? I guarantee you one week later if you ask who won the U.S. 500, they ain't going to know. Ask who won the Indy 500 and they'll tell you."

The race itself was one of survival as only nine cars were running at the finish, just two on the lead lap. Groff led the Foyt contingent in sixth, five laps behind winner Buzz Calkins. Hamilton led a couple of laps, but both he and Sharp crashed.

The next race was at Phoenix, where Foyt had always found success. The team looked good from the start.

"We'd gone testing and were one of the first to go flat all the way around the track in an Indy car," Sharp recalled twenty-five years later. "I was just flying, and it was due to A.J. of course. The car was on rails. I felt like I could put it anywhere I wanted. But we had a problem in qualifying, and we didn't start well (sixth). Then at the start it was *boom*—we went straight to the front."[8]

The combination of fast cars and good strategy had the Foyt trio running one-two-three at one point, although Hamilton dropped out about halfway through the 200-lap race. Sharp and Groff put a lap on the field when a timely caution flag seemed to be just what the two leaders needed. That is until Foyt ordered the drivers to pit immediately. While Groff responded, Sharp hesitated. He knew that although CART regulations allowed cars to pit immediately after a caution flag, the pits at Indianapolis were closed as soon as a yellow flag waved. The rule had been carried over to the IRL, although enforcement had been shaky so far in the race.

"A.J.'s telling me to pit and I'm like, 'I don't think we're supposed to pit. We'll get penalized,'" Sharp remembers saying. Foyt said other cars had pitted without penalty. "There was a lot of talking back and forth, and finally he just said, 'F-ing pit!' You don't argue with that. So, I pitted and we got a one-lap penalty."[9]

Sharp and Groff raced back through the field, and Sharp nearly caught winner Arie Luyendyk at the end, but they had to settle for a two-three finish.

"That just showed how good a car A.J. would give you on a short oval and my level of confidence in it," Sharp said, adding with a laugh that after the race, "A.J. was steaming and throwing things." Foyt chased down Tony George and gave him an earful but decided not to protest the penalty.

"We got screwed, they took it away from us," Foyt complained, making it clear he was going to continue to speak up when he felt wronged. "Hell, some guys came in under that one yellow and we stayed out and lost six spots. How are you supposed to know when to come in after you see that? It's a bunch of bullshit and it stinks."[10]

"When the yellow came out he told me the pits ain't open. I told him to come in anyway. Then they penalized me a lap. It's like Bobby Knight says, 'We're always right and those damn officials are wrong.'"[11]

While some expressed concerns early on that the split between the IRL and CART would leave an Indianapolis 500 with less than the traditional thirty-three starters, seventy-seven cars were entered, although only thirty-five drivers were identified. Prior to getting the Foyt ride at Orlando, Groff had already committed to drive for Derrick Walker at Indianapolis. At the behest of his sponsor, Walker was one of the few CART loyalists who was entering a car at both Indianapolis and Michigan. The deal was for the Indy 500 only, but Groff had run his last race with Foyt, who was critical of Walker "for stealing Robby Gordon and Mike Groff."[12]

A new sponsor was found for Sharp's car, Conseco, an insurance and financial services company that served as the IRL's insurance underwriter. With Groff's car available, Foyt tried to talk Al Unser into coming out of retirement, saying he could be the first driver to win the 500 five times, an offer Unser was able to refuse. Many hoped A.J. would give a test drive to the country's best midget driver, Billy Boat, who had broken Foyt's record for midget victories in 1995 with eleven.

Despite citing his own background in midgets and sprint cars and saying, "People are going to see some young, great race drivers that are going to be the future of racing," Foyt elected to go with Marco Greco for his third car. The Brazilian had run in Formula 3000 in Europe and spent the past two years racing Indy cars but was still looking for his first top-ten finish. Greco, however, also brought $500,000 worth of sponsorship with him.[13]

Or as Robin Miller in the *Indianapolis Star* put it, Greco gave Foyt "a big checko."[14]

With the team unloading at Indianapolis, Hamilton and Sharp soon discovered the Foyt team operated in a somewhat different manner.

"I was excited to get to the Speedway with A.J. and to get going," Hamilton says. "Then he said, 'Tomorrow we're meeting early in the morning. We're going to Kentucky.' I asked about practice, and he said there was plenty of time to practice—we were going to the Derby. So, Scott and I went to the Derby with A.J. and had a great time, but as a rookie, it drove me crazy. I knew everybody else was on the track—they were running. But he knew two weeks was plenty of time. He knew—I didn't know—but he knew."[15]

It also worked out for Hamilton. He knew one of the jockeys, Gary Stevens, a two-time Derby winner (at the time—he'd later win a third) who was from his hometown of Boise. Rather than bet on him, Stevens suggested Hamilton bet on the stable of his trainer, D. Wayne Lukas, who had five horses entered. It turned out to be a winner, as Grindstone came home first.

Back in Indianapolis, Foyt was busy not only running his own team but helping anyone who asked for it. Richie Hearn, one of many IRL rookies at the track, was one of those drivers.

"A.J. put me in his passenger car and took me around the track about ten times," Hearn said. "Believe me, it was quite an experience. I'm a talkative guy, but I don't think I said more than ten words the whole trip. A.J. talked about the track, the entry point into the turns, how high to go on the straight, and a little about horse racing. I just tried to take it all in."[16]

Foyt was enjoying the new atmosphere in Gasoline Alley, noting, "It feels better. Everybody's more friendly. Everybody's working together. It's kind of like racing used to be. It's gotten so much politics here in the last three or four years, it was really sickening. You couldn't go in anybody's garage. You couldn't talk to anybody. They were scared you'd steal their secrets and all that. To me that isn't racing."[17]

Sharp ran a lap of more than 235 miles per hour the Friday before qualifying, and Hamilton was nearly as fast in the Saturday morning practice session. Both thought they might have a chance at the pole. But Sharp blew two of the Ford Cosworth engines and Greco one as neither were able to qualify. Hamilton qualified in eleventh and wondered where his speed had gone.

"I came in after practice, and the car was so good, I said, 'A.J., we're gonna sit on the pole,'" Hamilton recalled more than twenty years later:

> I go out to qualify, and I'm ducking to get out of the air, and I'm turning the wheel—no scuffing, man, it's good. And I ran 230 something. So, I'm wondering *What happened? Where's my speed?* I mean, the car still felt great, but it was just slow.[18]
>
> So I went to A.J. and said, "I'm not sure what happened." And he goes, "You were getting ready to crash my shit, so I pulled some boost out to slow you down a little bit." I guess I can appreciate that because I was on the edge. But I'm still A.J.'s fastest rookie ever. I just felt like I could have been a little better.

Both Sharp and Greco made the field on day two, and, egged on by journalists, Foyt took the opportunity to unload on CART again, in what one reporter called "an extremely profane tirade." He was incensed to learn CART had wiped his Indy car records from its new media guide.[19]

Calling the CART board "a bunch of assholes," Foyt said, "This is the biggest racetrack in the world and the world knows it after eighty years. You can't replace tradition."

He went after two of CART's biggest names in Michael Andretti and Roger Penske. Andretti had been critical of the quality of drivers running at Indianapolis and the speeds they were turning. Foyt said,

> I hate to hear Michael. He's like his daddy [Mario]. He's been a crybaby all his life. I'm not telling you all something you don't already know. I'll tell them to their face. I heard that statement and it really pissed me off.
>
> They're all jealous. It's like Roger Penske. *Big Roger Penske!* Where in the hell was Roger Penske made? Right here at this damn racetrack. He damn sure didn't make this place—like A.J. Foyt didn't or Wilbur Shaw didn't. I'm sick and tired of hearing the crap. Like Mario, like they made Indianapolis. They made crap.
>
> You don't know me from winning Daytona three times. You don't know me winning Le Mans, you don't know me winning Ontario, you don't know me winning Pocono or Nassau and all them places. You know me from one place and that's right here. Them people start saying they made Indianapolis. They have a bad problem. They're forgetting where

> they came from and what made their name. That's what I'm getting disgusted about.

Asked about Penske and Bobby Rahal releasing statements saying they wouldn't race at Indianapolis, Foyt exploded. "Who gives a crap? They weren't here last year (when the Penske team failed to qualify) and Rahal wasn't here the year before (when he failed to qualify). But the damn race went on pretty damn good."

The racing world was stunned a few days later when pole sitter Scott Brayton was killed in a practice crash. His car cut a tire, spun around, and slammed into the wall. The well-liked Brayton had been one of the most experienced drivers in the field, with fourteen starts in the 500. He was the sixty-sixth Speedway fatality, the first since 1992.

"I sold his father his first Indy car and Lee and I have been good friends," said an emotional Foyt, his voice cracking. "I've watched Scott come up and naturally it's a very, very sad moment.[20]

"The hell of it is, I guess, in racing you've got to expect this. You never want to see it. It's terrible, because I just feel for his father, his wife and also his mom. I know we all got to go someday, but it's terrible when you're starting on the pole and have a misfortune like this. I guess we all got to go some way, somehow, you never want to expect it to happen to friends of yours."

With less than an hour remaining in qualifying, Foyt struck a deal with Hemelgarn to loan him a car for Boat, who'd been bumped from the field. It went for naught when the rookie driver bounced off the wall, badly damaging the car and landing himself in the hospital.

With the field set, Foyt put pressure on both Hamilton and Sharp to suspend their extracurricular racing activities until after the 500, which both reluctantly agreed to do. For the first time, Foyt expressed some concern about the seventeen rookies—the second most ever. It was also the first time since 1919 that rookies outnumbered previous race starters. Only four drivers had started more than six Indy car races.

"Usually by the time you get here, you've run with most of the guys and you know what they're likely to do," Foyt said. "With all the first-timers, the race could go two ways. It could be wide open, with more holes than ever to run a car through, or guys could spend all day running up each other's backs."[21]

At the same time, he remained upbeat about his own team's chances, saying,

> Any one of 'em can win the race. The way Scott's been running, he's got a hell of a chance. He's run some 235s and ain't but a couple of guys running better than that. He wanted to let it out a little more but I had to rein him in. It's like playing poker out there. You just don't show everything you've got 'cause a lot of times you do and it's hard to back it up.[22]
>
> Davey's a good all-around race driver. That's what I like about him. He's won a lot of races in other cars so he knows how to win, and he's already proven he can run fast at Indy. He understands that the car's got

to do the work. That's what I keep preaching to my guys and they know they'd better listen too.

If there wasn't enough on A.J.'s plate, he was at the Indiana State Fairgrounds the night before the 500 overseeing the Foyt Group's promotion of the Hulman Hundred Silver Crown race. For a while, it seemed like old times as George Snider drove Foyt's car to victory, and the pair posed for photos in Victory Lane, Foyt saying he was going for a doubleheader victory the next day. Then came the bad news. The winning car was disqualified for being six pounds underweight.[23]

In the 500, Sharp was running a lap back in fifth with five laps remaining when he slid on oil entering Turn Two and up into the wall, dropping him to tenth at the finish. Hamilton finished twelfth after twice running out of fuel, and Greco twenty-sixth after dropping out with an engine problem.

"The first time A.J. gets on the radio and says, 'These dumb asses don't know how to do fuel mileage.' He said they didn't get the warmup laps," Hamilton recalled. "Whatever, I'm just driving. Then he says, 'But don't worry, we've got it figured out.' Then we run out again, coming off at four, and I couldn't get in. I barely got back, and we lost a bunch of laps. That's when he really went crazy."[24]

"It's a shame Scott couldn't have run four or five more laps," Foyt said. "It was just one of those days when everything you did was just backwards. Today we just couldn't catch the yellows."[25]

Buddy Lazier, whom Hemelgarn had hired to replace Hamilton, went on to win the race. Foyt's fingerprints were all over the standings, Davy Jones finishing second with Hearn in third. Eddie Cheever was eleventh after starting fourth, and Groff ended up twentieth. Tony Stewart led forty-four laps before dropping out with a sour engine.

The winning car owner couldn't resist a final dig. "The biggest break I got was when Davey Hamilton broke his contract with me last fall so he could run with Foyt," Hemelgarn said. "That gave me the opportunity to hire Buddy."[26]

At CART's U.S. 500 in Michigan, a twelve-car accident before the start created chaos in the race eventually won by Jimmy Vasser. Foyt certainly wasn't going to let that go by without comment, saying, "They've made themselves look like fools as far as I'm concerned."[27]

"For the world's greatest professional drivers, they sure have made a lot of mistakes. I'm sick and tired of them running their mouth about how great they are. Almost every race they've had this year there's been an accident on the first lap—and it wasn't the rookies."[28]

Although the action on the track was over, it carried on to the Indianapolis Victory Banquet, where Foyt confronted Walker about stealing his drivers. Foyt then flipped off Walker several times during the proceeding.

"I laughed at the time," said Walker, whom one reporter called "among the nicest and most approachable owners in motor sports" and who was the only CART owner in the room. Walker added,

> I don't know what in the world I've ever done to that man. I mean, I've barely said two words to him.[29]
>
> He always accuses me of stealing his drivers, but any drivers that have come to me after driving for him are free and clear of contracts. But he seems to single me out, along with a few other distinguished owners. So I'm flattered to be associated with such an esteemed crowd. But I don't know what it is. There's just something I'm doing he takes exception to.

Robby Gordon, who wasn't at the Indianapolis banquet, later came to his new car owner's defense:

> I did learn a lot with A.J. But if you look at where A.J.'s team is now, they can't win against IRL cars. I mean, how are they going to compete against Indy cars. I have nothing against A.J., but it's a team that has not caught up with technology. This is a very technology-oriented business and if you're not up on the latest computers, and the latest, greatest ride-height control sensors, all the stuff that makes it competitive, you can be fifteenth on the grid. Well, they say they take all that stuff out in IRL—and he's still fifteenth on the grid.[30]

Years later, Foyt recalled the incident with a laugh, saying he had "a couple too many glasses of wine" and regretted what he said, "especially in front of the ladies." Then he added, "But he [Walker] was an asshole then, and he's an asshole now."[31]

One thing was clear as the month of May drew to a close: Neither side was ready to back down. And the battle wasn't going to be decided in court either, at least not a Houston court. While the judge denied CART's request for outright dismissal of Foyt's antitrust lawsuit, she also ruled her court did not have jurisdiction, saying too few of the organization's activities took place in Texas.

Indianapolis marked the end of the IRL's abbreviated 1996 "season," and Sharp was crowned co-champion with Buzz Calkins. With the 1996–1997 schedule slated to start in mid-August, Foyt decided to pull the plug on the Hoosier Hundred set for the same timing.

While the number of entries for the Silver Crown dirt track races at the Indianapolis State Fairgrounds had remained strong, spectator attendance had fallen off in recent years. A night race and several different dates had been tried in August and September without much improvement. Foyt, a six-time winner of the race, then canceled the event about which he once said, "I'd settle for winning the 500 and this one and to heck with the rest." Some thought it an odd decision given his support of the IRL, which was looking to promote the very drivers who competed in the Hoosier Hundred.[32]

Others thought the real reason had something to do with Snider's disqualification by USAC after winning the May race. Foyt had reportedly threatened to replace the USAC event with a World of Outlaws race.

Freed from promoting the race, Foyt turned his attention to once again trying to make the Brickyard 400 field. He bought a Ford Kenny Wallace drove to victory in a Busch race at Pocono earlier in the year and updated it to Cup specs.

After running a lap at more than 172 miles per hour in practice, fast enough to qualify for the race, inspectors said the front of his car needed to be raised. He got slower each time he returned to the track and finally posted the forty-sixth qualifying time among forty-eight cars, too slow to make the race. He'd had a garage full of support, including his son Jerry, John Andretti, Hamilton, and Snider, but nothing the group tried could find the needed speed.

"It just hacks my ass I'm not running that fast," Foyt said. "It's terrible, absolutely terrible. We'd run fast this morning, but it seems every time the temperature would go up, we'd die out there. I don't know exactly what happened today, but to be this terrible is awfully tough."[33]

"Winston Cup racing is not easy," Hamilton said. "For a guy to come one time, even though he is the world's best race driver, is extremely tough. Maybe he'll come back and try it again."[34]

Afterward, it sounded like Hamilton's wish might come true.

"I've never been a quitter, but you know, it gets kind of disturbing. I made it here the first year, and that meant more to me than anything. But I don't care where I go to race, I don't like missing no race."[35]

After tying for the driver's championship in the IRL's inaugural season, Sharp was awarded the No. 1 for year two because the Foyt team captured the owner's championship. Sharp stayed busy for the nearly three months after Indianapolis, racing at Le Mans and in the Trans-Am series, where he was in the running for the championship. He also won a major IMSA race at Sears Point Raceway in Sonoma, California.

At New Hampshire for the start of the second season, he qualified in the middle of the pack but quickly moved forward and eventually into second place. There was only one problem. Tony Stewart was light years faster than everyone else and was two laps ahead when a short rain delay paused the race.

"I almost didn't mind if they stopped the race then," Sharp would say. "I don't think we could have caught Tony. He went by me like a freight train."[36]

Stewart picked up where he left off on the restart before he darted into the pits with eighteen laps remaining with an electrical problem. His race was over.

"Tony is a great race driver and an asset to the series," Foyt said. "But anytime you race, you can have problems. It's happened to me before and I feel really bad for Tony. But Scotty worked as hard as he did and may the best man win.[37]

"He drove just as I was trying to coach him on the radio," Foyt said of Sharp. "Being there at the end of the day, keep chargin', that's how you win races."

Foyt made the call to hold Sharp on pit road during the last stop to get as much fuel in the car as possible and then to have him stay out at the end of the race when others thought he would need to pit. The car finished with four gallons of fuel in the tank.

"When A.J. gave me a chance to drive for him in '95 at the Speedway, I knew right then going in it was really special," Sharp said. "Every step of the way people would say, hey, this guy's long overdue for a victory. It's an honor to drive for him, but it's an even bigger honor to win a race for him."[38]

It was Foyt's first Indy car win since Pocono in 1981. He took exception with those saying it was his first victory as a car owner with another driver, pointing out Jim McElreath had won the Ontario 500 in 1970 driving one of his Coyotes.

"I don't care if you go there one time or 1,000 times, it's great," he said of his return to Victory Lane. "Show me somebody who's not happy to win a race, and I'll show you somebody who's never won one."[39]

The final race of the "old IRL" took place September 15 at Las Vegas, and while both Sharp and Hamilton showed potential, both were out before the end. It was the final race for the turbocharged engines and the previous year's chassis, which were to be replaced when the series started up again in January with new four-liter engines and chassis specifically designed for the IRL.

Although the season was over, Foyt decided he wasn't through yet and announced plans to run in the two season-ending races of the increasingly popular NASCAR truck series at Las Vegas and Phoenix. He decided to go old school, leaving the team's transporters at home and using a fifth-wheel trailer to haul his unsponsored F-150 to the tracks. He showed up with a handful of crew members and a cadre of buddies and spent most of his time sitting next to the hauler and bench racing.

"We don't have no lounge, no air conditioning," he said of the low-key approach. "I think all of racing, all phases, is all blowed way out of proportion. That's what kind of happened to CART. That's not real racing. Look what we came out here with, and we run pretty good for not being on the circuit. It goes to show what you can still do on your own without big money."[40]

At Phoenix, he qualified twenty-first in a field of thirty-six but dropped out early. At Las Vegas, he started thirty-second and was still running at the end in twenty-eighth, although twenty laps behind the winner.

Those were the final laps of A.J. Foyt's driving career. From that point on, he was strictly a car owner.

To celebrate the end of the season, Foyt took the entire IRL team to his ranch near Del Rio, Texas. Sharp recalled,

> That was just a fun time all the way around. Me and Davey were running around on quad runners. We were out deer hunting, although we didn't get anything. We came across a deer that was stuck in a fence, and A.J. had to kill it. Then he showed us how to skin it and prep it. It was the first time I'd ever hunted and first time I'd ever seen someone prep an animal.[41]
>
> Those were some of the most fun times—when you got away from the track and saw some of the things he really enjoyed doing. Running around on his bulldozer, constantly fixing things, or building things on his ranch. It was really fun spending that time with him.

> We just sat around the house, had some beers, and heard the stories. It was just a blast. You felt like you were in real special company when you [had] the chance to be able to do that. Just to hear him talk about the racing and the rivalries. He obviously took it very seriously when he was driving—did whatever he could to win. But I think he had a pretty good time too.

Hamilton also fondly remembered the trip, especially when the deer "peed all over Scotty." Hamilton had shuttled back-and-forth between his home in Las Vegas and Houston throughout the season, staying at one of the Foyt homes whenever he was in town. He got to know Lucy on those trips:

> Lucy was great. She was absolutely the perfect Texas lady that you expect. She had that little Texas drawl and was so polite. I would go, *Gosh, she's with A.J.?* They were just opposites. She was always asking if you needed anything and really made you feel at home.
>
> She was friends with everybody on the crew and just a pleasure to be around. Nancy too [Nancy Foyt, the wife of Tony, who worked with the team]. They treated me like family, and even when I wasn't driving for A.J., they were there with open arms—welcoming and happy, you know, and always trying to make you feel good.

The Texas trips and gatherings reflected Foyt's vision for his race team. For better or worse, racing was rapidly evolving into big business with massive super teams. While Indy car racing was being ripped apart by a civil war, A.J. was desperately trying to cling to the past, to a time when he and his father raced with a tight-knit group of family and close friends. And he was losing the battle. The handwriting was clear for all to read, but A.J. was determined to fight it—to keep doing things his way.

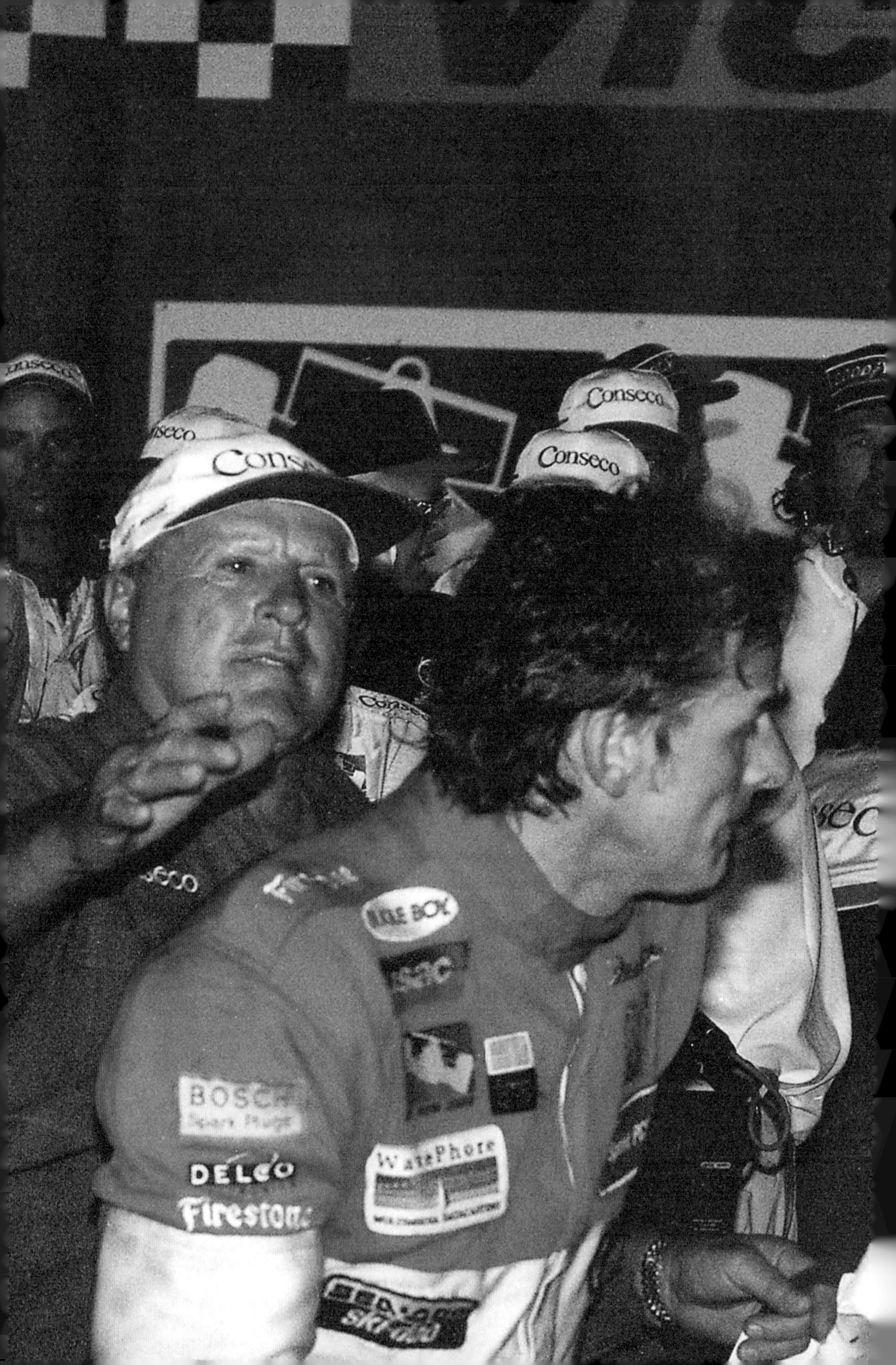
Conseco
Conseco
Conseco
BOSCH
DELCO

CHAPTER 26

TEXAS SHOWDOWN

1997

For the first time since A.J. Foyt had retired from driving at Indianapolis in 1993, his race team was beginning the year with the same two drivers it started with the year before, Scott Sharp and Davey Hamilton.

The Indy Racing League was introducing two new chassis makers—Dallara and G-Force—and two new engine suppliers—Nissan's INFINITI brand and Oldsmobile. A complete chassis was priced at $263,000, about half the cost of a chassis in the CART series, with an engine going for about $75,000, compared to CART's $1.2 million lease program. The non-turbocharged IRL cars were also expected to be about fifteen miles per hour slower than the CART racers.

The war between the IRL and CART had cooled somewhat as the U.S. 500 was rescheduled, with a smaller race in St. Louis planned for the day before the Indy 500. But that didn't stop Foyt from taking his shots at the group.

"I read in the newspaper that the Andrettis and Bobby Rahal said they made [Indianapolis Motor Speedway] great, and the 500 couldn't go on without them," he said, citing one of his popular refrains. "They are full of shit. They must be smoking some dope. CART is nothing but a glorified Formula One series."[1]

Foyt was designated as one of the Dallara test teams and ordered four chassis from the company. Renewing a relationship that dated back to his NASCAR and Aerotech days, he announced plans to run Oldsmobile engines. There was also a new sponsor for the No. 14 car, PECO Power Team, a company that bought and sold excess electricity and whose president was a race fan. Sharp acknowledged that as one of the premier teams in the IRL and the defending champions, there were high expectations.

◀ A.J. goes after Arie. *IMS Photo Archive*

"Nobody has more experience working successfully under pressure than A.J. and his guys," said Sharp, who was focused on winning the IRL driver's championship outright. "So we're not worried about the job ahead of us. But I know I need to carry my share of the load too. A.J. made it possible for me to win the first championship and that makes me responsible for the No. 1 staying on the car."[2]

The new era got off to a rocky start as the teams had little to no prerace practice before the January 25 opener at Walt Disney World. Sharp was able to do some testing, but Hamilton said he had only thirty miles on his car. The three Nissan teams were in worse shape, with the company flying in a replacement engine the morning of the race.

"It's really too doggoned early," Foyt said. "But the racing season is here. It's going to be a tough year for all of us. But you crawl before you walk."[3]

Tony Stewart was the first to walk, qualifying on the pole and dominating the event, even lapping the field at one point. He spun in oil from his own engine, however, three laps before rain stopped the race. Eddie Cheever, who had joined the series as an owner/driver, emerged victorious—the first win by an Indy car owner/driver since Foyt's at Pocono in 1981. Sharp finished fourth and Hamilton seventh.

"All in all, I think it was a decent show," Foyt said. "These engine people have had to scramble and a lot of us didn't get much testing. But it wasn't bad and it's gonna get better."[4]

Orlando also marked the F2000 debut of Larry Foyt, and Lucy Foyt made her first appearance in years at a racetrack other than Indianapolis. The nineteen-year-old Larry qualified tenth but lasted only two laps before he was sidelined by a blown engine. When he began to show his displeasure at his quick exit, his father stepped in.

"When he got out of the car, he started to throw a little temper tantrum," A.J. said at the time. "He started to holler, and I said, 'Hey, boy.' I told him not to do as I do, but as I say."[5]

As for Lucy being at the race, "She said, 'You can replace a husband, but you can't replace a kid.' I said, thanks a lot."

Following Stewart's domination and Cheever's victory, both using G-Force chassis, Foyt ordered two for his team and sold off one of the Dallara's. In early tests at Phoenix, Sharp turned the fastest lap, topping even Stewart.

"It wasn't in the budget to buy these cars, but I didn't want to be caught out," Foyt said.[6] "It's not that I'm unhappy with Dallara, I just want to make sure my drivers have the best equipment. We owe it to our sponsors to be at our best."[7]

Testing at Indianapolis didn't go as well the following week when Sharp crashed his Dallara twice. The first was relatively minor, but the second time he spun in Turn Four, hit the wall, and was knocked out, regaining consciousness as the safety team worked to remove him from the car.

Back in Phoenix for the race, things continued to go poorly for Foyt's team as Sharp blew two engines in practice and qualifying and was forced to start at the back with a borrowed powerplant. It took Sharp just sixty laps to drive to the front, and he was leading when the borrowed engine let go. A record nine caution flags resulted in the slowest race in Phoenix history, slower than the inaugural 1965 event won by Foyt.

As the team arrived in Indianapolis, Foyt said he would leave it up to the drivers to choose between the Dallara and G-Force chassis. Both elected to start the month with the G-Force as their primary car while the Dallaras carried the "T" car designation. Foyt also added a third driver after arriving at the Speedway—Billy Boat—the midget champion who had crashed his car in a last-ditch attempt to qualify for the 500 the year before. Boat was surprised to get the call—wrecking one of his cars was often the end of a relationship with A.J.—but Foyt told him the crash had been caused by a faulty wheel bearing. Boat shared,

> A.J.'s initial experience with me was not probably the greatest. But I always had one of those reputations of a guy who was never afraid to push the pedal. So I think he respected that; I think that's one of the reasons why I got a second opportunity.[8]
>
> I was sitting at the restaurant at the Speedway Motel, and George Snider walked in. He said, "A.J.'s looking for you—you better call him." I immediately walked outside and found him, and he said to come over to the garage, "I want you to get fitted in the car to go practice."
>
> My father was always a big A.J. Foyt fan. So, when you're growing up, and your dad's a big fan, you obviously inherit some of that admiration. He was always my favorite when I was watching Indy car races and the 500. I remember when he won his fourth 500 vividly, it's one of my earliest memories. So, it was obviously a huge opportunity when I got to drive for him and got to know him on a personal level.

By midweek, Sharp was at the top of the speed charts, but not for long. Coming out of the fourth turn—where he had crashed in preseason practice—his engine locked up, and he lost control, backing into the wall. There appeared to be minimal damage, and he was examined and released from the infield care center.

Two days later on the eve of qualifying, Sharp was second fastest in the Dallara to Arie Luyendyk when he entered Turn Four too low on the track. He lost control, looped twice, and slammed the wall hard, pancaking the right side of the car. The impact pushed the right-front tire back into the cockpit where it hit Sharp, knocking him out with his foot still jammed on the throttle. The Dallara rode the outside wall nearly the length of the front straight before it ground to a halt. This time he didn't regain consciousness until he was being loaded in an ambulance.

Sharp was diagnosed with a concussion at Methodist Hospital and held overnight for observation. There was no such thing as concussion protocol in 1997, and he pulled a Foyt, leaving on his own early Saturday morning. He headed for the track where he told the team he was ready to go. Before he could get in a car, however, he was intercepted by Speedway medical director Dr. Henry Bock, who ordered further tests. A CAT scan revealed a small brain contusion, and Sharp's return was put on hold.

"I'm no doctor but [the contusion] has kind of settled it," Foyt said at the time. "It takes a while for the brain to mend itself and it's just not worth taking no chances."[9]

Foyt later blamed himself for not realizing Sharp had been hurt worse in the crash earlier in the week than originally thought.

"When he crashed he was hurt a lot more than we all realized," Foyt recalled, saying Sharp gave contradicting feedback in later practice sessions. "We was trying to get him right back out on the racetrack. He came in with the new car and said everything was all right. He talks fast anyway, but I should have caught it when he turned around and said, 'The car's bouncing. No, it's pushing. Maybe the back end's loose.'"[10]

With Sharp out, Robin Miller reported in the *Indianapolis Star* that Foyt, despite being in and out of doctor offices with an inner ear infection, seriously thought about driving the car. He went as far as sitting in both the G-Force and Dallara to see which was most comfortable before being talked out of the idea by his crew.

"I really considered getting back in, probably more than you ever thought," Foyt would say. "[Then] I said, 'You're just kidding yourself, A.J.' I knew I wasn't in shape to drive."[11]

Foyt had earlier in the year talked with his godson about running the double—Indianapolis and Charlotte—but those plans were scuttled when the Talladega 500 was rained out and rescheduled for the same weekend as qualifying at Indianapolis. Billy Boat had been added to drive the third car.

"It was all set," Andretti said of Indianapolis plans. "We were going. Talladega kind of jumped in there and ruined everything."[12]

When Sharp's crashes pushed qualifying for the No. 1 car to the second weekend, however, Foyt decided to try again. Saying, "I'm asking him a big favor," Foyt called Cale Yarborough, Andretti's car owner on the NASCAR circuit. He promised to have one of his jets standing by for Andretti's use. But Andretti, who had qualified on the pole at Talladega and finished fourth, was having his best NASCAR season to date and Yarborough was reluctant to agree to the last-minute proposal. Andretti also ran a Ford in NASCAR, and the company wasn't excited about having Andretti drive a Chevrolet-powered car at Indianapolis.[13]

"I haven't told John 'No' and I wouldn't consider doing it for anybody else but A.J.," Yarborough said. "I feel his first obligation is to the Winston Cup ride."

They soon decided it was too late in the planning process to make the double work, and Foyt turned to Johnny O'Connell, who'd spent most of his career driving sports cars with a handful of Indy car starts. His time with Foyt lasted only three days, however, when an oil line came loose prior to the second weekend of qualifying and the car spun, hit the wall nearly head-on, then spun again and backed into the wall. It was the Speedway's hardest crash of the month, and O'Connell was shipped to the hospital for surgery on a dislocated arch. With some wondering if there would be enough cars and drivers to fill the field, Foyt's crew went to work repairing their machines, and A.J. went looking for a driver.

He found one in thirty-eight-year-old Paul Durant, who'd made two IRL starts the previous year, including a thirty-second-place finish at Indianapolis. He'd spent most of his career driving super modifieds, often as a competitor to Hamilton, who recommended him for the ride.

While Hamilton worked with Durant to get the third car ready, Boat finally changed the team's string of bad luck when the Indianapolis rookie turned in the fastest time on day three of qualifying. It wasn't easy as he blew an engine in early morning practice, and the team was forced to install yet another powerplant for the attempt.

"So many freak things happened, it's just been one of them months," Foyt said. "Regardless of what we did, it seemed like it was backwards. I felt we could have run a little faster but I told him, 'Just go out and get four good, solid laps.'"[14]

The next day, Durant needed just fifty-two minutes and twelve laps of practice before he easily qualified. It really didn't matter what speed he ran as long as he hit the 203-mph minimum, as the No. 1 machine had a guaranteed starting position under current IRL rules. Durant also said he was ready to give the car—which Sharp had dubbed "Christine" because "she's mean"—back to the other driver if he was cleared before race day, an offer A.J. appreciated.[15]

"He won't be one of those crybaby drivers if that happens and that's why he's in the car," Foyt said. "I just told Paul to get real comfortable and don't take no chances. He didn't."[16]

Foyt now had three cars in the field, which was at thirty-three drivers, but he wasn't finished yet. He still had a Dallara in the garage, and he agreed to make it available to driver Scott Harrington—variously reported as loaned, rented, and sold—and to help try and get him into the race. Harrington ran a lap at more than 214 mph, which would have easily bumped his way into the field, when he spun and hit the wall hard in Turn Two.

With qualifying over and Harrington on his way to Methodist Hospital, Foyt learned that Tony George and Leo Mehl had decided the field would be expanded to thirty-five in an effort to make sure the fastest thirty-three cars were in the race. That allowed the two cars bumped because they didn't have an IRL-guaranteed position to start the race. The announcement came too late for Harrington, and Foyt was livid to discover the driver had been put at risk for no reason. He shifted from livid to enraged when rumors started that some owners had been alerted to the change in advance.

"That boy belongs in the race, it's bullshit," Foyt said. "He's out there busting his ass when he didn't have to."[17]

Mehl, who was normally on good terms with Foyt, acknowledged, "He's very upset right now and I understand that. I'd be upset too. At six o'clock [the end of qualifying] we tried to do the fairest thing."[18]

Despite everything that had gone on during the month, Foyt felt his team still had a real chance at victory as the race approached.

"We've had drivers hurt, equipment torn up, just about everything you can imagine," he said. "But we've come through it all, and we're excited about race day. I think we've got three guys who have a chance to do well.[19]

"I feel like I'm really back into things as an owner. I don't care what anybody says, this is a great place and a great race. No matter what all the talk is before the race, it still takes your breath away. I've had lots of firsts in this place. I'd love to get another one this year."

The race was delayed two days by rain, and when they finally waved the green flag, both Hamilton and Boat moved forward, the rookie actually leading a lap. But then both teams stumbled on pit stops. In the end, neither could challenge race winner Luyendyk, who edged teammate Scott Goodyear in a chaotic finish. Hamilton finished sixth and Boat in seventh, the first cars a lap back.

Durant ran well, moving from his thirty-third starting position to sixth before being involved in an accident just past the halfway point. He also became the fourth driver to end up in the hospital after crashing a Foyt car, with a concussion and a broken pelvis.

"We got behind and could not get it back," said Foyt of the team's efforts. "But hell, that's racing. I just told them to stay out of trouble. But you're never satisfied with anything but finishing first. No one is ever satisfied with sixth or seventh. You show me who is satisfied and I'll show you someone who has never won a race."[20]

With Indianapolis in the rearview mirror, Foyt turned his attention to the 500-mile race June 7 at the new Texas Motor Speedway. He'd won the last two Indy car events held in Texas back in 1979 and was committed to making the inaugural Indy car race at the new track, and the first night race in Indy car history, a success. He even agreed to do one of his least favorite things—prerace promotion. As a result, he found himself having dinner with a group of journalists, including Mike Harris of the Associated Press, probably the most influential reporter on the racing circuit at the time. Harris recalled,

> Foyt could be every bit as charming as he was difficult to work with. I was always telling my wife about working with A.J. and what a bastard he could be. That you never knew what he was going to be like.[21]
>
> They had this party and my wife, Judy, and I were invited. They had a little private room for only ten or twelve people. We were sitting at a table with A.J. and Anne Fornoro and another writer and his wife. A.J. turns into this bon vivant, just as charming as he could be, telling stories about his family and how his grandson [Anthony] was gonna be a great driver. He's going on and on about family and everything like that. That night we're driving home and Judy says, "I don't know what you were telling me about A.J. Foyt. He's a charming man."
>
> The next morning, I walked up to him and said, "A.J., you definitely charmed the ladies last night." He looked at me, winked, and said, "Did a good job, didn't I?"
>
> He has so many facets to his personality. He could be gruff. He could be friendly. He has a great smile, and when he decides to smile and be friendly, he can be a lot of fun to be around. I've seen that side a few times, but not many.

Sharing the spotlight with Foyt was Luyendyk, the now two-time winner of the Indianapolis 500 and holder of the track's one- and four-lap speed records. While the Netherlands native's dreams of a Formula One career had never been fulfilled, they'd led to a successful sports car and Indy car career in America, and he was fast becoming the face of the IRL. A full-page feature in the *Fort Worth Star-Telegram* noted, "Luyendyk methodically has gone about placing his mark on the racetrack where A.J. Foyt, Al Unser Sr., Rick Mears and Johnny Rutherford transformed themselves into legends of 'The Brickyard.'"[22]

"In America, they like to see winners and achievers," Luyendyk said. He also noted a difference between himself and the other drivers. "I'm a lot more non-confrontational, let's put it that way. I've always been accused of being too calm."

Despite getting the green light from a number of doctors and being declared "crystal clear" by Methodist Hospital after a complete neurological exam, it was decided to hold Sharp out of the race on the high-banked Texas track. Foyt again turned to Boat, whom he'd taken a liking to at Indianapolis.[23]

"I was very impressed with the way Billy ran," Foyt said. He reinforced his commitment to Sharp while adding he was working on a third full-time car for Boat. "The kid knows how to win. He gasses the car pretty good. I think a lot of him and he's one of my top priorities right now."[24]

The fact Boat was still a rookie became apparent in a unique qualifying session at Texas that incorporated a pit stop. Boat turned in the second-fastest lap on the track but overshot his pit, dropping him to the back of the field for the start.

An announced crowd of 128,000 and an ESPN television audience watched Stewart dominate as he had all year, leading from the pole and a race-high one hundred of the 208 laps. He seemed to be home free with less than one hundred miles to go when a challenge from Buddy Lazier ended with engine problems. Boat, Hamilton, and Luyendyk—now listed as second, third, and fourth—were a lap or more behind, and Foyt ordered his drivers to use only sixth gear in an effort to safeguard their engines.

At the same time, USAC officials breathed a sigh of relief. Before the race was twenty laps old, they'd discovered several scoring discrepancies. Then they were alerted by Luyendyk's team following his first green-flag pit stop on lap sixty-three that it had not been scored. Officials discovered the electronic transmitters on the cars of Luyendyk, Boat, and three others had not been working properly on at least two early pit stops. Still, they were hopeful the issues would be worked out by the end of the race, and with only thirteen of twenty-six cars still running, they were confident Stewart was well ahead of the others. That confidence faded when Stewart blew an engine and hit the wall less than three miles from the finish, and the race ended under caution. Boat was waved into Victory Lane, where he was joined by Foyt and excited team members. Hamilton and Luyendyk were parked nearby, and all three drivers were expected in the media center for post-race interviews.

Both Luyendyk and Hamilton were mad. Both thought they should have won the race—Luyendyk because of scoring errors, and Hamilton because of team orders. Hamilton had been leading early in the race and told to move aside so

Boat could lead some laps, then Boat would return the favor. Hamilton recalled the events twenty-five years later:

> I was leading, and Billy was in second. I was told to let Billy by because his sponsor, Conseco, paid lap money to the team and Power Team [Hamilton's sponsor] didn't. I didn't want to let him by, but it was getting a little heated on the radio. So, I made it pretty obvious. I pulled up and let him by. He was supposed to let me back by. Well, it never happened. We were so close on speed, I couldn't get past. I just happened to be in front of him at first, and then I couldn't pass him back. It wasn't Billy's fault. Conseco always paid bonuses for wins while Power Team didn't. I think A.J. wanted that extra money for the win, and those were the team orders.[25]
>
> So, Billy's in Victory Lane, and they park Arie and I outside. I'm pissed at A.J. because I just think I gave up an opportunity to get a win. Arie's going, "I won that race," and I don't know what he's talking about. So, we're walking to the media center, and we're both mad—not mad at each other, we're just mad because we both think we should have won. I stop to do a radio interview, and he goes into Victory Lane. I didn't know what happened next. I didn't see it. But I hear everybody going crazy, it's just chaos.

One account said Luyendyk "tossed aside his helmet and stormed to Victory Lane. He shoved his way through the throng, bellowing and gesturing" when he "came toe-to-toe with A.J. Foyt. After Luyendyk crashed the victory-lane party, Foyt charged like a grizzly bear."[26]

Arie's verbal barrage surprised and startled everyone in Victory Lane, including Tony George, Boat, and A.J. and his team members. Having said his piece, Luyendyk turned away about the same time Foyt realized what was happening and went after him.

"I called out to him because I wanted him face to face, but he didn't want any part of arguing with me," Foyt would say ten years later. "He started walking off. I moved toward him and called again, but this time I slapped his head to get his attention because he seemed hard of hearing at that point. He half-turned around and I grabbed him by the head and gave him a little shove, and he stumbled into the flower bed. By then the sheriffs and guards had hold of me and I couldn't do much else."[27]

Years later, both Boat and Foyt remained adamant they'd won. "We got flat-ass screwed out of the race," Foyt would say. "I don't give a crap. Have you ever seen NASCAR do anything like that? Right or wrong, if they caught you cheating, they'd take the points and money and all that, but not the victory."[28]

Right or wrong, Foyt had a point. NASCAR policy at the time made the driver who took the checkered flag the winner, even if they went home without the points or the money.

"I had no idea what was going on," Boat said years later. "I was caught completely off guard. I remember standing right next to [A.J.]—I remember it clear as the day—there was words exchanged. A.J.'s not the kind of guy you come into his Victory Lane kind of mouthing off. He's going to react. His face turned red, and you could see smoke come out of his ears. It didn't take him two steps to have Arie in that flower bush. I definitely had a ringside seat."[29]

Hamilton was wrapping up the radio interview and still mad at Foyt: "Arie comes out, and he's messed up. I didn't know A.J. had bitch-slapped him. A couple of minutes later, A.J. comes out and tells me, 'I think I'm going to jail.' I go 'Good.' That's what I said—'Good!' But I still didn't know what happened."[30]

At the time Foyt said, "You don't come in here and start mouthing someone in Victory Circle. I guess because he won Indy, he thought he won this damn race. He was never in the hunt all day. I just wanted him to get out of there and leave us alone and let us have our day. To have the first Indy car race in Texas and my drivers go 1-2, I couldn't be happier."[31]

Foyt may have wished he had gone to jail before the night was out as he got an earful on the drive home from his wife, Lucy, who'd made another rare appearance at a race.

"She was chewing me out royally," Foyt recalled. "Our little fight had made the news and all these people were calling into the radio station saying how great it was. Just like the old days of Saturday night racing where you watch the race, then you watch the fights afterward. That's when my wife got upset with me all over again and said, 'Aren't you proud of yourself?' I told her I wasn't proud of nothing, but I wasn't going to take nothing either. I finally turned off the damned radio."[32]

At first Luyendyk said he wasn't going to protest the finish, asking, "What's the point?" Then he changed his mind. After an all-night review, USAC officials ruled Luyendyk actually completed two more laps than he was credited for, and the IRL declared him the winner.

"We were busy trying to audit the best we could while running the race. . . . We just weren't able to get on top of it to determine there was an error," USAC chief steward Keith Ward said. "We feel very badly. We've never had a problem of this nature. Certainly, this is a magnitude we have never seen. We're embarrassed by it."[33]

Luyendyk said, "I have to commend them for stepping up to the plate and admitting, OK, we were wrong. We've corrected it now. All I know is I got hit from behind and almost got choked by somebody and it turned out to be A.J. Foyt. I never did talk to him at all. And I don't have to talk to him."

At first Foyt stuck to his guns, issuing a statement "that we feel we are right." But by Monday, he called Luyendyk to apologize.

"A.J. called and apologized and I think he genuinely meant it," Luyendyk said. "He said, 'It was stupid of me to do that' and said his wife told him he was stupid to do it. But A.J.'s a fierce competitor. He's a hothead. He does things a lot of times before he really thinks about 'em."[34]

In another interview Luyendyk added,

> I was prepared to fight tooth and nail for what I knew was mine, but I didn't want to physically fight anybody. I'm not controversial. I came out of my car expecting to see USAC officials, but nobody was there.

> I was surprised to see they had a victory celebration. We were led to believe everything would be sorted out a half-hour after the race. But I didn't go down there to crash their party. If I wasn't 110 percent sure I'd won the race, I wouldn't have gone looking for officials.[35]
>
> People told me I should sue, but I'm not going to sue anybody. What's the point? I'm still breathing and that doesn't belong in racing.

Robin Miller wrote that A.J. had "ambushed" Luyendyk, who had become the newest member of an exclusive club—"'Victims of Foyt,' a national organization for many racers, mechanics, media, officials, or gate guards who have been assaulted, tackled, threatened, swung on or slapped by Anthony Joseph Foyt during the past four decades."

It was a sometimes repentant, sometimes defiant Foyt who eventually spoke with the Associated Press.

"I know it looked awful bad on TV from my part, which was shown throughout the world. It was one of those misfortunate things.[36]

"I guess you'd have to say, that's A.J. I've never seen a winner not one time or another blow up, and I just blowed up. I've been known through the years to have a temper and all of a sudden I guess I lost it a little bit. It just looked bad. I want to apologize for my actions. It was not the proper thing to do."

Still, he believed they'd won. "Whatever it takes, we're going to follow through. We're going to carry it that far. If it goes to court, it goes to court. We're not going to take this as a loss."

"I've known Arie throughout his racing career and have the utmost respect for him. He's got a temper, I've got a temper. In the heat of the moment you don't know what goes on. What else can you say? It's got to be put aside."

To try and help put it aside, Foyt and Luyendyk posed for photos together three weeks later before the next race at Pikes Peak, Colorado. Arie also was wearing an "Indy Rasslin' League" T-shirt. The IRL wasn't ready to forgive and forget, however, fining Foyt $20,000 and Luyendyk $14,000. Foyt protested, saying, "I didn't start anything. To me it's senseless."[37]

The big loser, however, was USAC. The IRL announced it was immediately taking over all sanctioning and officiating responsibilities for the series, a move supported by Foyt, who'd had more than a few run-ins with USAC officials in recent years.

"This is a smart decision by the IRL," he said. "It makes them more like NASCAR, there's no third party involved."[38]

To this day, both Foyt and Boat believe they won the race. Foyt refused to return the trophy, and it sits on display in the team's showroom along with other artifacts from his racing career.

Years later, Luyendyk would receive a duplicate trophy, and the track would continue to highlight the fight when promoting new races. Luyendyk said if it had been a younger driver attacking him, it would have been game on.

"There was never an issue between Foyt and Boat and me," Arie said. "The issue was the scoring. If it had been a guy my age or younger, I would've totally gone after him. But because it was A.J. who, although he's quite the bully, I do respect him. I was not about to start hitting A.J. I probably would have lost that battle anyway because he's as strong as an ox.[39]

"But we buried that hatchet a long time ago."

Sharp was back for Pikes Peak to help ease Foyt's pain, finally getting everyone's approval to drive again. After a disappointing Friday practice, Foyt completely reworked the chassis overnight, and Sharp turned in the fastest qualifying time the next day, edging Stewart.

The race, however, was another story. Stewart pinched the pole car down tight going into the first turn, and Sharp lost control, backing into the outside wall. Sharp was knocked unconscious by the impact, and while Stewart went on to his first Indy car victory, Sharp went to the hospital where he was listed in serious condition with subdural hemorrhaging. Although he'd recover, his racing season was over. It wasn't an entire loss for the team, however, as Hamilton's third-place finish allowed him to maintain his lead in the season-long championship battle, although Stewart moved into second, just five points back.

With Sharp sidelined, Boat returned and qualified third a month later at Charlotte with Hamilton alongside. Foyt urged Hamilton, who was working on a string of five straight top-five finishes, to see the big picture and focus on the championship. It seemed to be having an impact.

"Obviously I want to win a race," Hamilton said. "Tony (Stewart) has one now. At this point, I'm not so much looking for a win as the championship. If it's a risk of crashing or running second, we're probably going to run second."[40]

Boat was part of an exciting fight for the win before finishing second to Buddy Lazier while Hamilton was involved in the race's only incident and ended up sixteenth. Stewart's seventh-place finish was enough to move him into the championship lead, seven points ahead of Hamilton with two races remaining. Both dropped out of New Hampshire, and Hamilton went into the finale at Las Vegas with a ten-point lead.

Foyt decided to pull out all the stops and brought in Ed Nathman to work on Hamilton's car for the race. Nathman had been a championship winning team manager at Newman-Haas before becoming fed up with the sport's politics and quitting, although he still did occasional freelance work. Hamilton had been told he could "work magic."

Hamilton recalled,

> A.J. said he was gonna get an engineer to help us out. We go to Vegas, and we were fast by a ways in the first night practice. The race would be at night and so were the practice sessions. We're P1, and I go, man, this guy *is* magic.
>
> So I'm all excited for the next night, and I go, "We just gonna do like long run stuff tonight? I just want to do race stuff because we're fast—we proved that—so let's do some long runs, let's try and win the race." And Nathman goes, "Do you think we were fast last night? Wait 'til tonight."

> So I pull out of the pits to do my normal warmup, and they must have changed something—probably the ride height—and it bottoms out. *Pow.* I go into the fence—knocks me out. I remember A.J. knocking on my helmet: "You okay?"
>
> I go get checked out. I'm all good. But that was the end of Nathman. A.J. goes, "Well, that ain't working."

Nathman laughed when trying to recall the event nearly twenty-eight years later. "I always admired A.J., what he did and what he could do. He just knew so much. But he gets impatient when he has to work with somebody with lesser talent—like me. The car was probably too loose to actually race, and he knew it."[41]

Hamilton switched to the Boat/Foyt setup and was still in position to pick up a point on Stewart when he posted the fastest time early in qualifying. When Stewart moved into a backup car to make another run, however, Foyt told Boat to go for the pole. He responded and posted the fastest time, with Stewart in third.

The point never came into play as Hamilton struggled to a seventh-place finish. Stewart, in what he called "the longest night I ever had in a race car," simply kept Hamilton in range throughout the event and finished ninth, easily enough for the championship.[42]

Stewart was clearly a star, just the type of driver the IRL was established to showcase. And while a few others showed potential, no one had stepped forward to share the spotlight. His versatility reminded everyone of Foyt, and he joked about becoming the first driver to win the Indianapolis 500, Daytona 500, 24 Hours of Le Mans, and the Knoxville (sprint car) Nationals because, "A.J. has won three of those, that's why I threw Knoxville in there. He's never won that."[43]

A week later, Stewart was back in Victory Lane in Las Vegas, this time driving the Silver Crown car of Foyt and George Snider to a win on the half-mile dirt track. Stewart had already won midget and modified races earlier in the year. He'd just signed to run the coming NASCAR season with Joe Gibbs Racing and would continue to drive the Snider/Foyt Silver Crown car whenever he could. Foyt couldn't help but think how things might have been different if he'd signed Stewart when he had the opportunity.

"Tony Stewart is the A.J. Foyt of our era," said Larry Curry, Menard team manager. "When Tony went to Orlando, he did so well a lot of doors were kicked open for other drivers. This guy is just a natural. He's going to win whatever he races. I think at the time we got him, he was a breath of fresh air for our organization."[44]

Most considered Stewart's championship and the performance of the new cars and engines examples of a successful first full IRL season. New races at Texas and Charlotte had drawn the second- and third-largest crowds of the year behind Indianapolis, more than 200,000 combined. The number of entries had gone from eighteen in the first race at Orlando to thirty-two in the finale. The series also was expanding from eight races to eleven in 1998, and Pep Boys had signed on as the sponsor, offering a $1-million bonus to the championship winning team. Throughout the season, Foyt had remained the most outspoken advocate for the new series.

"I like this league because it gives the American guys a chance to race," he said. "It's definitely not an easy league. It's tough and it's going to keep getting tougher.[45]

"[CART] can do their things and we're going to do our thing. One thing about this league, it makes no difference how much money you have. You can have the same kind of equipment and if everything falls your way, you can win. Well, you can't win over there. To me racing should be the team, the mechanics and drivers and not a bunch of engineers who come out and say my motor's better than yours, but you can't get my motor. Who cares if Roger Penske leaves? Chip Ganassi? I mean, let's face it . . . his daddy is the finest guy I ever met, but what does Chip Ganassi know about racing? Nothing."

The season over, all three of Foyt's drivers were contacted by other teams about their plans for the coming year. His hopes of fielding a three-car effort evaporated when Pennzoil backed away from a possible sponsorship package after the Texas Victory Lane incident. With Foyt unwilling to make commitments while he struggled to find additional sponsorship, Sharp was the first to make a move.

"It was a very amicable breakup," Sharp said at the time. He'd been approached by a new team with solid sponsorship from Delphi, a major automotive parts supplier. "I'm very appreciative of everything A.J. did for me. He certainly gave me a shot a couple of years ago when no one else was stepping up to the plate. That's not something you forget. Unfortunately, a lot changed this year with the accident and everything. I just felt it was time to move in a different direction."[46]

Years later, Sharp recalled his time with Foyt:

> Billy Boat had replaced me when I was out, and he'd done a really good job. He and A.J. got along well. The thought was he was going to keep running along with Davey Hamilton. There was some talk about running me in a third car, but at that point things were certainly up in the air. About that time, Delphi called, and it came together pretty quickly.[47]
>
> A.J. and I always got on great. There were no problems. He played a huge role in how I drove an Indy car. I had immense confidence and belief and trust in him and I had a really good run with him. Even those times when I wasn't driving, when I was out, I was still able to spend a bunch of time with him. That guy just had so much experience and so much success and so many really entertaining stories.
>
> Everybody looks at him as legendary—and he is. And very generous. It was a great run for me with A.J., and that ended up propelling me to Delphi and Kelly Racing and on and on in my career.

Hamilton's departure was more contentious. The second half of 1997, beginning at Texas and followed by the Charlotte crash and Las Vegas events, had caused some friction between Hamilton and A.J. When Rick Galles's team reached out to Hamilton with an offer and was pushing for an answer, he called A.J., who never liked to hear that one of his drivers was talking to another team.

"A.J. just decided he wanted to make a change," Hamilton said in 1997. "It shocked me actually."

Hamilton would later say his first choice was always to stay with Foyt:

> I called A.J., and I go, "I'm loyal, I want to come with you, but I gotta know, cause I gotta give Galles an answer." He said, "You tell him to mind his own business." But I had to give [Galles] an answer because he was gonna go a different direction. It was another good car, a good opportunity. A.J. would never commit. I had to make a move.[48]
>
> I'll be honest with you, it was touchy for a while. I think he was kind of trying to test my loyalty, which I'd told him my loyalty was there, he just had to say yes. But I couldn't wait forever. I do feel like we probably would have moved on and stayed together, but as a racer, I just wanted an opportunity to race. It wasn't money or anything, honestly, I just wanted to make sure I was in a car.

In retrospect, Hamilton said the breakup was for the best:

> We never really got into any big battles, and we're still friends today. But A.J. was my hero. So I was really intimidated by him. Like I didn't wanna mess up. I didn't wanna wreck his cars. I didn't wanna disappoint him. So, I felt like I wasn't getting 100 percent out of myself being a little too conservative. I look back at that and go, *I had more in me. I was close, right?* My confidence was there and all that stuff, but I didn't get that win. That's what I wanted for A.J.—I wanted to win for him. In hindsight, I just think, honestly, I would have been better off to drive for somebody that I didn't have on such a high pedestal.

Throughout the year, it became increasingly apparent that Foyt was going to have to deal with at least a couple of his children/grandchildren continuing to race. Both Larry and Jerry drove in a number of F2000 events, although without much success. Twenty-year-old Larry seemed intent on trying to make a career of racing. Jerry, thirty-five, no longer held career aspirations but still enjoyed the sport. Both were slated for another season in the series. It was Tony and Nancy Foyt's thirteen-year-old son, Anthony, that seemed to have the most potential, having reached the finals of the NHRA Jr. Drag Racing League for his age group.

"The best young talent in America is coming out of this series," Foyt said of the Formula Ford–based F2000 competition, which included both oval track and road course events. Anthony would continue in junior drag racing, and A.J. asked his most trusted and longest-serving team member, Jack Starne, to oversee all their efforts.[49]

11
TEXAS
CONSECO

CHAPTER 27

CHAMPIONS AGAIN

1998

Adding Billy Boat to his team full-time for 1998 was a no brainer for A.J. Foyt. The pair talked the same dirt tracking language and even though Boat said, "To be able to drive for your hero is a dream come true," he didn't have the same problems as Davey Hamilton did while driving for a man he'd placed on the highest pedestal.[1]

"I couldn't be happier," Boat said after the announcement. He celebrated by winning a third Turkey Night Grand Prix midget race in California, something Foyt had accomplished only twice. "A.J. and I have pretty good chemistry and we get along. We actually do."[2]

Kenny Bräck (pronounced "Breck"), tabbed by Foyt as the team's second driver, was more of a surprise choice. A road racer with limited success to show for his one season driving Indy cars, in many ways he was the opposite of Boat.

Born in Arvika, Sweden, in 1966, he "grew up in the woods, in the wilderness. There were no racetracks, nothing like that." He'd started driving the family's passenger car at age seven and learned car control on the area's frozen lakes and roads.[3]

He started karting at thirteen, and from there he moved to various open-wheel and touring cars. He made his first trip to the United States in 1993, driving in the Barber Saab series and winning four of six races. When no Indy car opportunities materialized, however, he returned to Europe and started competing in Formula 3000. He won three races in 1996 and took the checkered flag first in the final race of the year, which would have given him the series championship, but he was disqualified in a controversial ruling for ignoring a black flag regarding avoidable contact.

◀ Foyt drivers—Billy Boat on the pole at Indy and Kenny Bräck on the outside of the front row—would battle for the IRL championship, which Bräck won. *David Nearpass*

Although Bräck received offers to serve as the test driver for several Formula One teams, he saw no way forward with them to competition. With nothing left to prove in F3000, he returned to America in early 1997 and began hounding IRL and CART team owners. When Davy Jones was badly injured in the first race of the season at Orlando while driving for Rick Galles, Bräck did a test for the team at Phoenix and—after nearly breaking the track record—was offered the seat. He'd often qualified well and occasionally led laps, but two fifth places were his only top-ten results, and he'd crashed out on the pace lap at Indianapolis. At the end of the year, his future with Galles, who was having financial problems, was in doubt. That's when Foyt called. The two had never spoken at that point.

"Everyone had quite a lot of respect for A.J.," Bräck recalled. "You didn't just walk up to him and start jacking. He was a bit larger than life."[4]

Bräck added,

> I get this phone call, and he says, "Hi, this is A.J. Foyt." He said he was in Las Vegas and if I was interested in driving for him, could I come there so we could discuss it. I said I was in Florida and would go to Las Vegas, "But only if you decide to sign me now. Then I will come, and we can discuss the details." He said he needed to check with his sponsors. He called back and said, "Get your ass to Vegas."

Bräck took the red eye to Las Vegas but had neglected to find out where A.J. was staying. He went from hotel to hotel before tracking him down at Harrah's. That's where they had breakfast, which created another problem.

"A.J. was having steak and eggs and said, 'What's that you're eating?' I told him yogurt. He said, 'I don't like that.' I thought I'd ruined the deal. I would eat steak, but I never saw A.J. eat yogurt."

Hamilton eventually signed with Galles, replacing Bräck. While A.J. was initially upset about Galles and Hamilton talking, there was no apparent bitterness about Bräck joining Foyt's team.

"A.J. didn't steal Kenny. It just didn't work out between us," said Galles, who would sell his team before the season started. "Kenny had an investor, but the guy didn't show me anything. Kenny is a great kid and a fine driver and there are no hard feelings. I don't think he had to take any money to A.J."[5]

Bräck, who'd been living in Albuquerque, New Mexico, where Galles was based, moved to Houston in order to be close to the team.

"I wanted to do everything in my power to make things as successful as possible," he said. "I thought being in the workshop with the guys preparing cars and building those relationships, getting to think the same way they did, was very important. I believed I'd do that best being next door to the team and not just seeing them at races. A.J. was still downtown that first year, and it was quite nice to see his original workshop where he had been with his dad and everything. It wasn't modern by today's standards, but we got the job done there."[6]

Bräck drew the line, however, on riding a horse. "No," he said, "I'm real grateful for the opportunity he gave me. I couldn't think of a better way for a foreigner to come over here and race with the greatest name in the United States. But no, I don't want to get hurt."[7]

Despite increased offseason testing and impressive qualifying results, the team struggled through the first two races of the season. At Orlando's Disney World Speedway, Bräck and Boat qualified second and third. Boat crashed out before the halfway point, however, and while Bräck was still running at the finish, he'd been involved in a pit incident and finished thirteenth, twenty-six laps back of race winner Tony Stewart. At Phoenix, Bräck was running second with fourteen laps remaining when he crashed while lapping several cars. Boat was close behind and barely avoided wiping out both Foyt cars in one accident. Larry Foyt added to the team's challenges, wrecking his F2000 racer in practice. Jerry Foyt took over and qualified third, his best—and last—start in the series.

With Indianapolis next on the schedule, Foyt entered six cars, two each for Boat and Bräck and another driver listed as "TBD." In an effort by the IRL to trim expenses, there would be only one weekend of qualifying, preceded by a single week of practice. Despite the compacted schedule, Foyt kept his cars mostly in the garage early in the week.

"The racetrack changes so much," Foyt said, "I'd rather wait until Thursday or Friday to run fast, because it don't pay nothing this first part of the week."[8]

> We're going to be qualifying and racing in the heat of the day, so there's no reason to go out and run fast at 5:30 because that don't prove anything. There's no sense in chasing the racetrack. I've done it before and these kids don't need to be doing that. I'm very pleased with how they've been running. You always want to run faster, but we are kind of happy because we've been going out in the heat of the day. If we can stay where we're at for qualifying, that will be good, but we're here for the race. That's why we've been doing so much running in the middle of the day at race time.[9]

As if to prove a point, Bräck and Boat ran a combined total of just fifteen hot laps early in the week but were near the top of the speed charts, running identical laps of 222.080 miles per hour. It also was enough for Boat to get his groove back.

"The one thing A.J. stresses is to be patient and not make mistakes," Boat said. "That's why you see him put us out there for only a few laps and then take us back to the garage to think about it."[10]

"I felt like I had lost my line around here a little bit. You know, A.J. isn't real shy about telling you if you're doing something wrong and he'll point that out. A.J. is so good about knowing what the car wants, and he makes you feel real comfortable."[11]

Although he was running fewer laps than he had the year before with Galles, Bräck noticed an immediate difference. Bräck said years later,

Galles gave me a chance, and I'll always be grateful for that. But the first year at Indianapolis had been very difficult. It was the first time where I was praying to God every morning and happy to be alive every afternoon. It was a really tough experience. My first engineer was a great guy, a really good engineer with good road racing credentials. But he was also new to ovals, and I couldn't help them get the car where it needed to be with the experience I had at the time.[12]

A.J. provided that car to me. That was the difference. When I came to A.J., it was a proper race car. At a totally different level. I could control it, and I could do with it what I wanted. The confidence you get from that is a whole 'nother thing.

He was like my first and only racing dad. He didn't tell me how to drive, but he was really good at knowing what setup to put on the car. I'd say I had this feeling, and he'd say, "Well then, I think we should do this." He was like a super computer today. Not only the setup on the car, he knew the external elements. When the weather was great, the cars are good. On shit days, the cars are terrible. And when a car is terrible at Indy, it's not just terrible, it's life threatening. A.J. would see the trees in Turn One blowing from a certain angle and say, "There's no sense running today. We're not gonna learn anything. Let the others run and have their crashes." He had this enormous ability to map out the weekends. He taught me stuff from all these different areas that I didn't know, and I was really grateful for that. It made a lot of difference to me, my confidence, because I didn't grow up on oval racing. So, to get this education from someone who had been living on ovals for forty or fifty years, that was invaluable.

Boat and Bräck had moved to the top of the speed charts on the last day of practice before qualifying. The plan went awry when Stewart countered with the fastest lap of the month and Boat crashed while trying to regain the top spot. Stewart and car owner John Menard were clearly enjoying the competition.

"Foyt's going to have to work harder if he wants the top spot," Stewart said.[13]

Within an hour, Boat was in his backup or "T" car, which had actually been quicker at times than the primary machine. After some fast laps, Foyt ordered both his teams back to the garage, saying, "That's it for today. We're going home." Boat, who'd wanted to keep running, said he was looking forward to matching speed with Stewart and predicted the condensed schedule would have an impact.

"It's always good to have a great rivalry in the pit area, but I don't think you'll see A.J. as excited about going out and trying to post the fast speed as Menard is. He's been here a long time and he knows what can happen. I think it's important, but the pole doesn't win you the race. A.J. would like to see both of his cars on the front row, and I think we have the speed to do that."[14]

Bräck and Boat would face one of their own engines in qualifying, Foyt having loaned it to Eddie Cheever.

"I came into the Indy 500 after having exploded every engine I owned (at Phoenix)," Cheever would recall. "I had to borrow an engine from Foyt to make the race. I just walked up to him and said, 'I need an engine,' and he said, 'If it breaks, are you going to pay for it?' I said 'Yup,' and that was it, he lent me the engine. I'm still grateful for that."[15]

To celebrate his fortieth appearance at Indianapolis, Foyt started off qualifying day activities by driving his 1961 race-winning roadster around the track, joking afterward, "It felt a little tight." He wasn't talking about the car's handling, noting, "Back then it was a little big. Now I'm seventy pounds bigger."[16]

In the final practice before the start of qualifying, Boat surprised even himself with a lap of 223 mph, followed closely by Bräck. As a result, Stewart, who was fourth in line to qualify, felt he needed to take a chance to find more speed and changed his car's setup. The move backfired, and he turned in a four-lap average of a little more than 220 mph. Bräck went a few spots later and was quicker at nearly 221 mph. Boat made his run in the heat of the day, a little before 1:00 p.m., and blew everyone away with a first lap of 224.573 mph. He turned in three of the four fastest laps of the day for a four-lap average of 223.503 mph and a new track record for a car with a normally aspirated engine. Greg Ray qualified second, splitting the two Foyt cars.

"We've been running in the heat all week, so that was never a concern," said Boat, who received a hug and a "thank you" from Foyt. "A.J. has told me over and over that you're just kidding yourself when you run at 5:00 p.m. and the track is a lot cooler. You have to be ready for when it counts."[17]

At times, Foyt seemed to downplay the pole run, the first for one of his cars at Indianapolis since 1975. "It's nice to be the fastest, but all we really wanted to do was get in the race and worry about winning the race. Starting from the pole is great, but I don't think I ever won it from the pole."

At other times he was, "Fired up! This IRL has really grown to be competitive. The way it was in the other circuit, you couldn't really do the work yourself. And now it's back to racing, back with the teams. That's what fires me up more than anything. Now we can do our own motor work, and we have a lot more input on what we run. It's back to racing like it was in the '60s and '70s."[18]

Among those who noticed the change in Foyt was Hamilton, whose eighth-place qualifying spot had helped him overcome the bitterness of splitting with A.J. the year before.

"He has been doing this for a long time and he told me several times that he was just tired," Hamilton said. "I think these cars are back to his style. They took a lot of downforce away from them and took the turbochargers off. They're doing a lot of things A.J. was used to in the days he did this. He needed to be reckoned with before, but I think he's really on a mission right now."[19]

While Foyt might have been fired up and excited after the field was set, some questioned whether a front row of Boat, Ray, and Bräck—all three making only their second 500 start—would fire up race fans. Six years since he had last raced in the 500, Foyt was still the IRL's biggest name. When CART owners and drivers criticized the 500 field, Foyt, who'd bought a single share of CART stock when the organization went public, "So I could keep track of how much money my old buddies are spending," struck back.[20]

"Who are we familiar with in CART?" he asked. "I don't know 'em and I've been in racing all my life. The average race fan knows a lot more of these (IRL) boys than they do CART drivers. You see these guys weekly. That's the way A.J. Foyt made his name."[21]

He went after Bobby Rahal, who'd been outspoken in his criticism of the league.

"There are so many people who bad mouth this place, but who won Brazil?" Foyt asked in reference to the most recent CART race, won by Greg Moore:

> In the other circuit you couldn't do the work yourself. Now you do your own motor work. Before you had no choice. Now it's back to the way racing was in the '60s and '70s. Your hands are not tied.[22]
>
> I know Rahal and a lot of people know Rahal. But the average laymen do not know Rahal. His name, to me, has never been a name that catches you like the others. Certain names just, boom, you get it, and other names just don't.

No matter what Foyt said, however, there was no denying the Indianapolis 500 had lost some of its luster since the split. The shift to a single week of practice and weekend of qualifying was an admission of the changing landscape. Race tickets, once handed down from generation to generation and sold by scalpers at significant markups, were now widely available at face value. While more than 400,000 spectators were expected, local hotels said they had rooms available and that fewer people were coming from outside the city. Those that did were staying for shorter periods of time. The Daytona 500 earned a higher TV rating the previous year, and while the numbers were partly skewed by the rain-delayed Indianapolis race, many predicted it would happen again. The big-dollar sponsorship deals were going to NASCAR teams, and even the IRL's top driver—Stewart—had announced he was moving to NASCAR full-time in the coming year.

Not only were Foyt's cars back on the front row, an old friend was back in his garage. For the first time in six years, Jim Gilmore returned as one of the team's associate sponsors. He'd been the team's primary sponsor much of the time from 1972 to 1992, before stepping away as Copenhagen took on a bigger role. He'd been an associate sponsor of the Menard team the past couple of years. Gilmore said,

> A.J. called and asked about getting our team back together for this year's Indy race and I was pleased with the invitation. A.J. and I had a great relationship and have always kept our friendship. There's no one like A.J. My loyalty to him is total and I feel his loyalty to me is the same—it's total. We're going to give it our best shot.[23]
>
> A.J. wants me to work in the pits. I'll just try and stay out of the way. But I'm so happy to be at Indy for another year and to be teamed with A.J., in my opinion, the greatest race driver in history.

Gilmore was blunt when asked about the IRL/CART split.

"The battle between (Tony) George and (Roger) Penske, neither of whom I'd spend any more time with than I had to, has hurt Indy car racing and opened the way for NASCAR to reach an all-time high in popularity."[24]

Joining Gilmore in the Foyt pits for the race would be Danny "Chocolate" Myers, the regular fueler on Dale Earnhardt's NASCAR team. He was hoping to become the first crew member to do "The Double" and plans were for him to fuel one of Foyt's cars in the 500 then head to Charlotte and his regular job for Earnhardt.

"It was quite the experience to be with A.J. Foyt at Indy, walking around the garage area and spending time with him," Myers recalled. "You couldn't have been with a king or queen and gotten more attention. When you go to Indy, he is the guy. He is the man. The fans are hanging on the fence and they're going, 'A.J., A.J.,' and he'd say he wasn't gonna mess with that, that he had things to do. Then after a little while, he'd go over there to the fence and sign autographs and stuff. I think he wants everybody to think he's a hell of a lot tougher than he is."[25]

Overseeing Foyt's fourteen-member team and race day crew was Tommy LaMance, A.J.'s twenty-eight-year-old nephew. LaMance's parents had divorced when he was seven, and A.J. had taken on a greater role in his upbringing. He began bugging his uncle to go to races as a teenager, and when A.J. repeatedly said no, he stowed away on the team transporter headed for a 1985 stock car race at Talladega. Although Foyt was livid, LaMance was on the transporter headed for the next race at Michigan, and he'd been with the team ever since.

"I was nothing more than a go-fer but it sure taught me the dedication racing demands," LaMance said of his early days with the team. "When you ride that truck day after day it's a grind, but you understand everyone on the team. Those were some of the best years of my life."[26]

LaMance stuck with it and worked his way up, serving as a mechanic and using his schooling from Texas Tech to drag the team into the computer age. When John Anderson departed along with Robby Gordon in 1994, LaMance had been promoted to team manager at twenty-four, sharing the role with Jack Starne, who coordinated activities from the team's Texas base.

"[A.J.] guides me twenty-four hours a day, sometimes in ways he doesn't realize," said LaMance, who focused on Bräck's car on race day while Foyt worked with Boat. "There's nothing I enjoy more than making Uncle A.J. happy. I love to see him be 'The Man' in racing. Maintaining the image and reputation of A.J. Foyt is very important to me."

Foyt said, "If the boy couldn't do the job, he wouldn't have gotten the job. Tommy's been there every step of the way. I know he looks at me like his father, and that's good. I see him as one of my sons."

Serving as crew chief on Bräck's car was John King, who had moved from Michigan to Houston to join Foyt and had been with the team for six years. He'd also received the inaugural "True Grit" award and a $5,000 check acknowledging a "dedicated mechanic."

"When A.J. asks you to join his team, you don't question it," King said. "You just say, 'Yessir.' There's no one like A.J. I've never met anyone like him. When things don't go his way—look out. He yells at everyone. He yells at me all the time, but the only time he really gets mad at me is when he wants to know when one of my crew screws up and I won't tell him who. We're a team here, and we're going to stay a team."[27]

"Working for A.J. puts a lot of pressure on you. He demands perfection. If you can't perform, then you're not the right person for the job. He knows what's happening all the time. You can't fool him, so don't even try."[28]

With LaMance focused on crunching the team's fuel mileage calculations for the 500, King was taking a lead role on the radio with Bräck.

"I don't talk to him constantly. When he's battling for position and he's busy, I don't bother him. But I'm there for him and I can see some things in traffic that he can't. A.J. says every race he won't go on the radio, but he always does. But it's rare—maybe two or three times during the race."

Admitting, "I'm the old hardass on the team," Foyt seemed to be happy with its makeup and direction. "I think the whole atmosphere of this team is great. These kids did a hell of a job and we're having fun."[29]

Foyt added,

> Maybe I ask too much out of my guys, but I don't think so. What's changed is the drivers. I guess it's the same way in everything. It's a different breed today. There are some guys you have to treat real tender. If you say something harsh to them, they pout. I guess I'm like (Chicago Bears coach) Mike Ditka. When I came up, if somebody did you wrong, you got out and whipped their ass and went on about your business. Or they whipped your ass. Today you can't do things like that. I kinda think that's hurt the sport a little bit. There's just too many prima donnas today.[30]

As race day approached, Bräck, who had picked up the nickname "Whitewall" for grazing the walls coming out of the turns in practice, admitted to feeling additional pressure from all the prerace attention on the team.

He said of Foyt's No. 14,

> It's hard to drive that car. You've really got to do well because it's a big difference being A.J.'s driver than being someone else's driver. It's good to be with him here because he has so much experience. You can always ask him because he's been in the cockpit and knows exactly what goes on inside the car. He's very, very straightforward. He tells you what he thinks, and maybe it's not always what you want to hear, but at least you know where you are with him. . . . He's the best I ever worked for.[31]

For his part, Foyt said, "Bräck is one of those guys you don't have to tell things to twice. He gets real quiet and real intense when he's in the car. He's a real good driver."[32]

One of the things Foyt told Bräck was to stay away from the wall. "He kept brushing the wall, rubbin 'Goodyear' off his sidewalls," A.J. recalled. "I told him if he kept rubbing the wall like that, the wall was going to get him."[33]

Going into his second 500 with Foyt, Boat was more at ease with the pressure and added attention and joked he was serving as a "translator" for Bräck and Foyt.[34]

Foyt repeatedly told reporters,

> As far as I'm concerned, Billy Boat is just as good any day as Tony Stewart. I've known Billy since way back when he was racing midgets. He was quite a bit wilder then. He got in a lot of trouble. He was too brave when he first started. Here you've got to be on a fine line and control it and not cross that line too often. That's when you're gonna win it.
>
> It makes me feel good that I can do things for Billy and other young drivers. I get a kick out of working with the young kids. To be here after forty years or so and have both my cars in the front row, it's a story you could write that would never end that way.

After turning in the two fastest times during the final Carb Day practice session with Bräck leading the way, Foyt was as confident as he ever allowed himself to be before a race.

"We feel pretty good going into it. We might not run but one lap, but we're feeling pretty good. I hope I'll be talking to y'all on Sunday evening. But I want the notoriety to go to my race drivers, more than to A.J. I had my glory days. They're the boys that's got to win in that race car."[35]

Following his boss's orders to "bring the field down nice and smooth," Boat jumped out to an early lead as the caution light almost immediately flashed on for a first-turn crash. When the race restarted, Bräck missed a shift and fell back to tenth. Boat also lost ground and the lead after burning away his right-rear tire, which affected his car's handling.

Boat dropped further back on his first stop. As the team went to change the car's handling characteristics, Foyt jumped on the radio, yelling, "Go, go, go!" at the same time a crew member was telling him to hold. Boat hesitated a moment and then stalled the car when he started to pull away. Those problems seemed minor when his transmission stuck in second gear. The team changed the transmission and got Boat back in the race, although twenty laps back.[36]

With Boat hopelessly behind, Foyt's attention turned to Bräck, who had worked his way back to the front, leading twenty-three laps. At one point, Bräck thought he had a tire going down and wanted to pit, but LaMance said the computer telemetry indicated it had full pressure and convinced him to stay out. Bräck was running in a tight pack with the top four, as pit stops approached a little more than ten laps before the halfway point.

As the other leaders stopped, Foyt went to LaMance and wanted Bräck brought in. LaMance insisted the computer said they could go further, and the two were jawing back-and-forth when Bräck suddenly broke in on the radio:

"I'm out of fuel."

Not only was he out, he'd run out at the worst possible spot as he crossed the start/finish line. Making it worse, Bräck's pit was at the end of pit road.

"Sorry about that, Kenny," Foyt said as Bräck finally rolled into his pit. The team then struggled to restart the engine, and he was two laps down when he finally got going. With Bräck headed back on the track, Foyt ripped into LaMance then walked down to the No. 14 pit, picked up a $7,000 laptop computer, and slammed it down.

Despite running some of the race's fastest laps, Bräck couldn't make up the deficit as Cheever went on to win, becoming the first victorious owner/driver since Foyt in 1977. Although he spent less time on the track than anyone except the winner, Bräck finished sixth, with Boat in twenty-third.

Afterward, both Foyt and LaMance refused to talk to reporters. Bräck said he "wasn't exactly happy," but was surprisingly controlled, especially when compared to Foyt. "I try to keep as calm as I can in the car and just drive. That's the best I can do. It won't change something if I get upset. It may affect my performance. We had a good race. Some things put us down, but we're happy. It's a long race and it was nice to do 500 miles. Last year I didn't even make the first lap."[37]

Years later, Bräck still wasn't ready to point a finger at anyone.

"Who knows. Somebody had to get the blame. Tommy (LaMance) called my races, and he was a good guy, and we worked good together. He was eager to win and eager to do what was necessary to win. It was done with the best of intentions, to give us better control of the fuel than we had before and allow us to run closer to the absolute limit. But something obviously went wrong, and in the end, it didn't work out for us."[38]

Next up was a return to the Texas track where Foyt and Luyendyk had tangled a year earlier. A.J. added to the prerace publicity with charges that Boat's car had been sabotaged before the start of the Indy 500. He claimed a secret seal had been broken on the team's garage door, proof someone had broken in overnight.

"Everything was fine with the car on Saturday afternoon. But when we got to the track Sunday morning someone had been in the garage. We found out the last two butterflies on the left-bank injectors [on the engine in Boat's car] were locked up solid. When we opened things up, we saw someone had put Red Loctite [a sealant] down the throttle shaft. The butterflies froze up like they were welded together. It was sabotage. There are a lot of jealous people out there, but it's still hard to believe anyone would do that."[39]

The team discovered the problem before the race, and it had no impact on the outcome, but the tale made for a great story. Robin Miller couldn't resist doing a tongue-in-cheek column in the *Indianapolis Star.* He listed the possible suspects, everybody from Luyendyk to Penske to George Bignotti. "Bottom line," Miller concluded, "A.J. needed some attention."[40]

Boat provided all the attention Foyt needed at Texas as he led a race-high 108 laps. He passed Ray with six laps remaining and won by less than a second, with Bräck in third. It was an emotional victory, especially coming after the disappointments of Indianapolis.

"I was hungry for this win," Boat said. "I wanted to win real bad. It's real satisfying [and] a little bit of a vindication for what happened last year. I didn't leave any doubts this time. But standing there in the winner's circle, it felt a little bit like deja vu. Been here, done that. It was really great for the team, a real pick-me-up and we needed it. A.J. was smiling all night."[41]

Foyt said, "I felt we won it last year and I hope nobody hollers this year." Later he told Boat that Victory Lane, "was more fun last year."[42]

The celebration in the Foyt household lasted less than a day. A.J. and Lucy had returned to their lake home in Austin after the race, and she started complaining about back pain and feeling nauseated. By early morning, she was sweating and said her chest hurt. It was about 6:00 a.m. when Foyt called Dr. Gary Friedman, their longtime family doctor, and told him about Lucy's symptoms. A.J. thought it might be a bad case of indigestion but wanted to bring her to Houston.

"That's not the typical history for heart disease, and I can't tell you why, but I told him I'd meet him at my office in about an hour," said Friedman. He was also aware Lucy's father had died of a heart attack and her brother had previously suffered one.[43]

Saying he averaged "probably eighty, maybe a hundred" on the drive over, A.J. had Lucy at Friedman's office in record time.[44]

"I immediately hooked her up to an electrode cardiogram," Friedman recalled, "and sure enough, she's in the middle of having a heart attack. A.J. gets excited and says he's going to drive her down to the medical center. I said, 'No, it's Houston traffic, and I've already called an ambulance. No matter how good a driver you are, you can't make it through this traffic.'

"Five minutes after she arrived [at the hospital], she went into full cardiac arrest. They resuscitated her, and she went into V-TACH [irregular heartbeat], and they took her into surgery."

Foyt says he heard the "code blue" call and had spent enough "sheet time" in hospitals to know it indicated a critical medical emergency and that the life of a patient was in immediate danger. As family members began arriving, they saw something they'd never seen before—tears in their father's eyes, although he was doing his best to hold them back.

Finally, a nurse told Foyt a doctor wanted to talk with him. He feared the worst. "In my mind, I knew what he was going to tell me," Foyt says. "Then the doctor said, 'We lost your wife, but we got her back.' All that happened in about thirty minutes. Bam, bam, bam."

"It was a miracle," Friedman says. By the end of the long day and with Lucy out of danger in the ICU, he talked Foyt into going across the street to a steak house. Friedman looked up from his menu to find Foyt in tears. Despite everything they'd been through together, he'd never seen Foyt cry.

"It's the only time I ever saw A.J. really tear up," said Friedman, who was emotional while telling the story.

"You know, sometimes she's a pain in the ass," Friedman recalled Foyt saying, "but I love that old woman."

The win at Texas moved Boat into third in the season-long championship behind Stewart and Sharp, who were tied for first. With a three-week break until the next race at New Hampshire, he felt the team was poised to go on a run.

"I feel like things can only get better," he said. "This team is right on the verge of doing some good things. We still haven't peaked. We're still climbing and still coming together.[45]

"We're coming up to the point in the season where there's a lot of races on 1.5-mile tracks. Last year we were really strong at those places. We're only five points out of the lead and I think we've got a shot at the championship."

At the time, Boat's teammate didn't share his opinion. Despite his third-place finish at Texas, Bräck wasn't happy and let Foyt know it.

"It wasn't always smooth sailing with A.J.," he'd say years later:

> There were two drivers on the team, and I didn't always feel I had the equipment in the beginning to win. That was clear to me in Texas when I was leading, and my teammate just blew by me, and I finished third. I was really not happy about that. A.J. congratulated me on finishing third and said it was a good result. I said, "It's a shit result, A.J.—a shit result." And we got into it because he thought I was a little bit ungrateful. I told him I'm here to win, and this is not a winning car. A.J. was a bit unhappy with that comment.[46]

When Foyt called a couple days later and asked Bräck to come to the team's office, the driver figured he was going to be fired.

"But he sat me down and said, 'You're right. The engine isn't right in your car. We're gonna put that right.' And he did. I think that was the moment when our relationship became really tight."

Boat seemed ready to make his prediction of a team breakout come true when he qualified on the pole while setting a new track record for the June 28 race at New Hampshire. One reporter noted that Boat "was fast becoming the rage of the IRL."[47]

Once again, the euphoria lasted less than a day. Bräck hit the wall on the race's opening lap, and Boat struggled from the start. He was already two laps behind when he was hit by a spinning car and knocked into the infield, where he was rammed by a third car. Boat suffered a broken pelvis and left thigh and was taken to nearby Concord Hospital, where Foyt arrived soon after with the driver's wife.

"When I crashed in New Hampshire he went to the hospital with my wife," Boat recounted. "I think it's unfortunate that a lot of people really didn't get to know the teddy bear side of A.J. Or the side of him that had a big heart. A.J. is the guy that no matter how hurt you are, he's probably got a better story. So, he starts telling stories about when he crashed at Road America or different things that happened. He's a good guy to have in your corner in those instances."[48]

Adding insult to Boat's injuries, John Menard, owner of Stewart's car, said he would not enter the car of Robbie Buhl in the upcoming two races at Dover and Charlotte to protest the IRL's apparent favoritism toward Foyt's team when it came to rule enforcement. He implied Foyt was using nitrous oxide to boost his team's qualifying speeds.

"Some people don't have to follow the rules," Menard charged. "I ought to go where the playing field is more level."[49]

Foyt's close relationship with Tony George didn't help appearances, nor did the fact he had two brothers of Brian Barnhart, the IRL director of operations, on his team.

"It's an incestuous deal," Menard said. "I don't think Jesus could be neutral if his (family members) were involved. You have to appear to be fair when you're the policeman. You have to be above reproach. It appears (the IRL) is trying to hide something and that's a foolish position to take."[50]

Others noted Menard didn't have sponsorship for Buhl's car for the next two races. Foyt said Menard's charges "shocked me because I never thought he was that way. I guess if you're getting beat, you cry about it. Maybe he wants publicity."[51]

Menard gave Buhl permission to seek another ride for the two races, but when Foyt indicated he had Buhl come to Texas to be fitted for one of his cars, Menard blocked the deal. Ray, who had called Foyt's shop and been told he was 150th in line, then got the surprise call to drive the No. 11 car. It had been Ray who split the two Foyt cars and qualified on the front row at Indianapolis and then nearly beat Boat at Texas.

"The first thing that comes to mind is getting to drive for A.J. Foyt," Ray said following the announcement. "A.J. is one of the few true legends in racing. He has an uncanny ability and feel for race cars, especially in oval racing. If people like what they see, it could bode well for me in the future."[52]

Ray, who was only expected to run two races, also received a quick wakeup call when Foyt declined to share any of the team's setup or engine information with him.

"I sat down with A.J. and said, 'A.J. let's go over the starting setup.' He goes, 'It's got four springs on it, it's got four tires. Just drive the thing.'"[53]

Ray struggled in qualifying and then tangled with Cheever before the race had reached the halfway point. Cheever blamed Ray, who responded with Foyt-type gestures indicating he thought Cheever was the one. Bräck wasn't much better, finishing tenth, as former Foyt driver Sharp won his second race of the year and moved into first place in the championship battle.

A week later at Charlotte, things began to turn around. Stewart was fastest, followed by Ray and Bräck. Even though his driver was on the pole, Menard repeated his charges about the Foyt cars using performance-enhancing substances, which set A.J. off again.

"What I have found out is that when somebody is hollering that you're doing something, it's because they're doing something and getting beat," he said. "They can't stand it. They say, 'Here I am cheating, and this guy is outrunning me.'

There's no way. If I am going to accuse somebody of cheating, I am going to know exactly what I am talking about. I've never accused anybody of cheating that I know of. If I have, I went to them face to face and told them if you don't quit it and if they won't let me do it, I am going to blow the whistle. You don't go holding a press conference."[54]

Stewart, Ray, and Sharp all dropped out early as Bräck overcame several problems during pit stops to lead a race-high seventy-six laps and put the No. 14 back into Victory Lane. Foyt had been furious when Bräck didn't get the message to pit under a yellow with the other leaders, dropping to the back of the field for the restart as a result. Bräck made up for it, making a daring three-wide pass around the outside to take the lead for good with twelve laps left.

Foyt said, "We might have blown the race. We went from first to last, but he made us all look like champions. I have been racing many, many years and I have never seen this many mistakes in a race and still come out with a win."[55]

There was more drama for the August 16 race at Pikes Peak Raceway. Boat was back after a quick recovery and though hobbling around on crutches, he qualified on the pole. In the race, he faded to ninth as the injuries sapped his strength. Bräck didn't stop for fuel when everyone else did and, in a reverse of the Indianapolis fiasco, ran out of gas as he came to the start/finish line for his second straight victory.

"I guess we can keep this computer," said LaMance, who had borne the brunt of Foyt's anger at the 500. Bräck could barely control his laughter when asked if his back-to-back wins made him a hero on the racing circuit.[56]

"It takes more than that I think," Bräck replied. "A.J. has got sixty-seven and he's an American racing hero. I have sixty-five to go."

The victory moved Bräck into third in the championship race, ten points behind Stewart, with Sharp in second. He moved into second without turning a wheel on the track when Menard's cars were penalized for problems with their rear wings, dropping Stewart to third. Bräck was suddenly very much in the championship race—only a point behind Sharp, with Stewart another five back. When the teams arrived in Atlanta two weeks later, Boat noticed a difference:

> When we left Texas, I was leading in points, and then of course I got in my crash at New Hampshire. I was out of the car for six weeks. Then I was coming back from an injury, and I probably wasn't 100 percent either.[57]
>
> I had been the A-team guy, and when I came back, most of the focus was on Kenny. Kenny became the guy that got more of the attention. When I was gone, he kind of picked up the slack, so it was his opportunity at that point, and he made the most of it. It was one of those kinds of things that happens in racing—we're still fast, and we still had good cars but I think at that point Kenny had most of the focus on him.

It was a big weekend for the team, with Foyt—who had driven in the last Indy car race on the track in the mid-1960s—serving as the grand marshal. Boat again earned the pole, with Bräck starting fifth. Bräck played it conservative in the race after a botched pit stop dropped him to the rear of the lead lap. Boat was up and down before being involved in a late accident. Riding around in tenth place during the caution period, Bräck decided it was time to make a move.

"On the last yellow we were not sure if we should go for the lead or stay in third for the points," Bräck said. "I guess I'm not that kind of driver. I've never driven defensively. If anything, early in my career, I've maybe been too aggressive. I think I've got a handle on that pretty well right now."[58]

It didn't take him long to move to the front, and Bräck took the lead with thirteen laps remaining. He'd led just seventeen of the 208 laps, but he led the last one. The win, combined with Sharp's failure to finish, moved Bräck into the championship lead. The spotlight remained on Foyt, however, which was fine with Bräck.

"It's not a one-man show," he said. "It's the whole team. The driver is an important part, but it's just as important to have a quick car and good people. It's up to the driver and team to adjust what you have to make a good race car.

"A.J.'s really good doing that. A.J.'s a big reason for the success because he has so much experience setting the cars up for oval tracks. Whenever there's a problem with the car he can easily relate to it and make necessary changes. He has a tremendous amount of experience with these things, so he's a big help."[59]

Foyt said, "I like working with the young drivers. They want to learn and I want to teach them. That's the fun of it."[60]

Bräck seemed to be enjoying the streak almost as much as Foyt.

"One reason I race is to have fun. And I have fun going to a race knowing I have at least the same chance as my competitors. You're not going to win every race, but at least you want to feel that you have an opportunity to win. Once you win, it boosts everyone on the team and everyone puts out that little extra effort that it takes to win."[61]

Back in Texas where Boat had won earlier in the year, he earned his third straight pole—fifth of the year and sixth of his IRL career, all series records at the time. Stewart, who qualified second, was left shaking his head, but refused to comment when asked if he thought Foyt was cheating.

"The guy's a genius," was all Stewart would say, with more than a hint of sarcasm.[62]

By now, Foyt had come to relish the cheating charges and implications. As he had during his driving days, he was clearly winning the psychological competition.

"Anytime you're winning, people are going to point the finger at you," he said. "That's fine, let 'em point. What I've learned over the years is that when people are accusing you of all this crap, you need to go catch them. They know they're cheating and you're still beating them so they figure you must be cheating too. They just can't accept that you're working harder."[63]

The race was marred by tire troubles throughout the field, and nine cars suffered blowouts. One was Boat, who hit the wall but returned to finish fourteenth, nearly fifty laps behind the leaders but still good enough to collect a $100,000 bonus for the best combined Texas finishes.

Bräck cruised to fifth place and took a commanding lead in the championship battle, thirty-one points ahead of Hamilton and forty-one ahead of Stewart. Bräck needed only to finish eighth or better at the Las Vegas finale to capture the title, no matter who won.

It wasn't as simple as just making laps, however. The championship paid $1 million, but Bräck was also eligible to earn another $600,000 in bonus money if he won the race. Foyt made the call, saying Boat would serve as the rabbit, while Bräck kept the leaders in sight. Foyt said,

> I told Kenny I'm not going to let him ding-dong for the lead and maybe have him break. I'll send Billy out early. He doesn't mind, he wants to win the race and he figures if he's out front early, that might be the way to do it. They're both very competitive, they want to race each other, but I'm the boss and they'll do what they're told.[64]
>
> The hardest thing about being an owner is trying to tell one of your drivers to take it easy. It goes against all their upbringing. But sometimes you've got to do it. All Kenny needs to do is finish ahead of two drivers to win the championship and that's what we want most of all. If it comes down to backing off to save the engine or keep out of trouble, that's what Kenny's going to have to do. Then if Stewart and Hamilton are out of it, he can go for the win.

Boat did his part, qualifying on the pole for the fourth consecutive race and taking an early lead before crashing out at the fifty-lap mark of the 208-lap race. Neither Hamilton nor Stewart were able to challenge the leaders and after Bräck suffered early electrical problems, he took it easy—finishing tenth, six laps behind the winner, Luyendyk.

"I'm really proud of my boys and my team," said Foyt, who picked up his twenty-first major championship as a driver and owner. "At the start of the race, everything looked pretty good. Then everything went to hell, but we didn't panic. We knew Davey and Tony were having their problems too."[65]

Foyt was once again on top of the racing world. One of his drivers was the national champion, he was the championship car owner, and—week in and week out—his team had the fastest cars on the track. His photo was on page one of every sports section in America, and the Associated Press, *USA Today*, and *Los Angeles Times* all did lengthy features on him. At times, he tried to deflect the attention. At other times, he embraced it:

> I really love working with these young guys, seeing them figure it all out. The other thing is I have a good young crew working very hard. When they win, it's new to them and you can see it change the way they look at things. When Boat won earlier this year they found out what it feels like. It's like giving candy to a kid. They get a taste of it and they want more.[66]

> I had my fair share of glory through the years. I couldn't have had a better career. I wouldn't change anything I did. There's a lot of stuff that comes with owning a team that's just hard work. But my daddy taught me never to be afraid of hard work.

It was clear Foyt's relationship with Bräck had evolved during the year.

"I liked Kenny because I saw that he was a very smart racer, but he had a car-control problem. He makes smart moves. Now and then, he still makes me pucker, the way he tries to get away with things he shouldn't have tried. He does things you aren't sure he can do. He's tough that way. He wants to learn and he wants to win. What more can I ask."[67]

The season over, Bräck said, "I'm going to stay with A.J. next year. I still have a lot to learn." Boat didn't sound nearly as confident. He was aware that sponsor Conseco was conducting a review of its motorsports marketing programs and was pulling back its sponsorship, concerned about the IRL/CART split and its impact on the Indianapolis 500.[68]

"I would suspect I'll still be with A.J. again next year," he said. "There's not much chance I'll be doing anything different. We've got a good team and we all like each other. We've had some success and I think we'll have even more. A.J.'s not looking to make any changes, and I'm not either. Everybody seems pretty happy."[69]

While talks continued between CART and IRL leaders throughout the racing season, by the end of the year little had been accomplished. CART had continued to do well, and the share of stock Foyt had spent sixteen dollars for at the start of the year had nearly doubled in value. Despite crowd sizes and television audiences continuing to decrease, leaders of both groups—while acknowledging they'd be stronger together—still insisted publicly they could coexist.

"We're sticking with our basic principle," said IRL's executive director, Leo Mehl. "The equipment has to be available to everyone; we're going to run on oval tracks and cost contain as much as we can."[70]

By his presence alone, Foyt was able to help the upstart IRL hold its own against the established CART series, a fact not lost on Mehl.

"Put it this way," he said. "Competitively, having [Foyt] involved is a great plus. You beat A.J., you know you did a good day's work. Administratively, well, let's just say he keeps everybody on their toes."[71]

With Stewart (the prototypical IRL driver who'd led a third of all the laps run during its first three years) moving to NASCAR for 1999, and Luyendyk saying he would race only at Indianapolis, the IRL was losing two of its biggest names. Some series car owners thought there might be room for negotiation. Not Foyt, who, despite the warnings from Conseco and other sponsors, thought the negotiations were "pointless."[72]

> I'd love to have everyone back, don't get me wrong. But you can't ask guys who have spent millions of dollars here to give that investment up. I can't

see it. We're two different leagues with two different cars and two different types of engines. We're too far apart.

I don't see much chance of each side getting together, but if they did, our guys would surprise some of their hotshots. There are some drivers in the IRL who are very good, good enough to race with anybody. I just don't see how it can be worked out. If they want to run, they can come and run with our rules any time they want.[73]

GOODYEAR
POWERTEAM
INVINCIBLE
POWER TEAM
POWER TEAM

CHAPTER 28

THE KING OF TEXAS

1999

Despite his proclamation he would be back with AJ Foyt Racing for 1999 following the championship race at Las Vegas, Kenny Bräck fielded a number of offers from CART and Formula One teams in the brief offseason. Several offered more money than the notoriously tight-fisted Foyt, but Bräck stood firm.

"Sure, I could have had another ride," he acknowledged. "And then I could have been somebody's backmarker."[1]

"If you have offers from other winning teams, you have to consider them. It would be stupid otherwise. But I really appreciate the situation I have with this team and with A.J. We are winning races, so it's not that hard a decision for me to make."[2]

One thing was clear: The year before, most considered Billy Boat to be the team's best driver at the start of the season. His injuries at New Hampshire and Bräck's championship had changed that. Now Bräck, who'd been voted by the American Auto Racing Writers & Broadcasters Association as the open-wheel all-American, was clearly the team's number one driver, and Foyt would be in his corner come race day.

"People that don't know A.J. think he's got a reputation of being difficult," Bräck said. "If he takes a liking to you, he treats you very well. Our backgrounds are somewhat similar. We both started with zero—no family money—and we both made it on our own. The first priority for both of us is we want to win. The will to win is everything. It helps us communicate."[3]

The defending Indy 500 winner, Eddie Cheever, was among those noticing a difference in Bräck.

"Kenny was a lunatic the first two years," Cheever said, "but Foyt's schooling and his European upbringing really made him difficult to beat last year. He

◀ Bräck and Foyt share the spoils at Indy. *IMS Photo Archive* was especially tough the final fifty miles. And now he's one of the best guys to race with."[4]

Boat had sensed the changes in the team's makeup after returning from injuries the year before and realized what he needed to do. He also decided to curtail his outside racing activities to focus on the IRL:

> For us to be championship contenders, we need to finish more races. That was the biggest downfall of our program last year. We just flat didn't finish enough races. After I came back, I felt like I was way behind and I was always trying to play catch-up. At times I probably pushed the car too hard. I definitely crashed too much.[5]
>
> We never had any trouble going fast. Our trouble was finishing races. A.J. and I had a conversation during the off-season, but it's not like there's any pressure on me. It's not like I have to prove anything. But the bottom line in racing is you want to take the checkered flag. If you're not doing that, you have a lot of room for improvement.

Despite losing Boat's sponsor, Conseco, Foyt ordered two new Dallaras—one for each driver. When the first arrived, Bräck gathered A.J. and the team around. It was only the cockpit or "tub," still in carbon black. Bräck talked about how his goal the previous year had been to win his first race and how if you win enough races, championships follow. Now he wanted more.

"Listen guys," Bräck recalls saying. "This is the car that will win the Indy 500. We just need to execute everything to every little detail."[6]

He explained,

> It was a totally different situation my second year. It was a good energy that was created. At the end of the day, it's all about teamwork. You have to have the greatest car to win. You have to have good strategy, a good driver. All those things. A lot of pieces have to come together. Good pit stops. Crazy stuff happens every year. People lose wheels. They run into each other in the pits. They miss the pit box. There's a lot of stuff to keep track of. Of course you have to deal with the external challenges, but those are the same for everyone—the track, the weather, the other competitors. But at least we had really good control of the things we could control. To do all those things gives you the confidence to perform when it comes time.

Bräck also wasn't shy about sharing his target outside the team. "This year our goal is to win the Indy 500," he said before the first race at Walt Disney Speedway.[7]

A rejuvenated Foyt had also been pointing toward the new season since Las Vegas:

> If you're going to be in this game you don't rest on your laurels of what you did before. To stay on top of it, you're going to have to work with the crew

> and the drivers. I've always been the type that has had hands on. I could have rested on my laurels and probably had a lot more fun.[8]
>
> After that first victory [by Boat] these guys got a taste of it and they've worked that much harder. Everything's falling our way, and it's not given to us. The guys are working night and day. We've got a good engine program, and the drivers are pushing the right buttons.

The team's title defense got off to a rocky start in the season opener. Bräck had warned, "At Disney the key is staying out of trouble. Normally, at the first race of the year, guys come back and tend to get a little excited and things happen. And the traffic at this place is unforgiving."[9]

Which is exactly what happened to Bräck. He was coming up to lap Gualter Salles, who was already running fifteen laps behind, when the engine let go in Salles's car. Bräck hit the oil and slammed hard into the wall. Boat stayed out of trouble but finished ninth, two laps behind the leaders. A month later at Phoenix, both Bräck and Boat failed to crack the top twenty in qualifying. Boat came through the field to lead laps before getting unlucky during a pit stop sequence and eventually finishing fourth. Bräck, however, first bumped with Robbie Unser, Unser sliding into the wall. On the restart, Bräck missed a shift and was hit from behind, sending him into the wall and badly damaging his car.

The Charlotte race, where Bräck had scored his first victory the year before, was moved to a May 1 race date for 1999. Bräck and Boat were running tenth and eleventh when tragedy struck on lap fifty-nine of 208 as two cars collided and debris flew into the stands, killing three spectators and injuring eight others. Promoters and officials decided to cancel the remainder of the event, a decision Foyt agreed with.

"It was absolutely the right thing to do," he said. "Racing is one big family, and that includes the fans. This was done out of respect for them."[10]

Despite his early-season pep talk, Bräck arrived at Indianapolis twenty-seventh in points, having crashed out of two of three races and failing to break the top twenty in qualifying in the last two events. A new engine rev limiter had been developed by the IRL, and opponents pointed to it and the poor times posted by the Foyt team as proof they'd been able to "cheat" the limiter the year before.

Foyt entered six cars for the Indianapolis 500, and for a while it looked as if he would need them all. Boat crashed hard on successive days to start the week of practice, badly damaging one of the new cars and his pole-winning car from the year before.

"He's probably a little embarrassed but it's just one of them deals," Foyt said after the second crash. "He's in good shape, that's what's important. We can replace cars."[11]

Making matters worse, while Bräck was back with Power Team sponsorship, Boat's poppy-red Dallara was devoid of corporate logos, an expected deal with Budweiser having fallen through. Only small decals for Conseco and Harrah's graced the car.

"The worst thing about crashing A.J.'s car twice in two days is you still have to go to dinner with him," Boat said. "He makes you buy and then he eats your ice cream."[12]

The crashes also dimmed Foyt's hopes of putting a third car in the race but not his sense of humor. To win a one-hundred-dollar bet with Eddie Cheever, he wore a hat emblazoned with "Viagra Tester" through Gasoline Alley, "but the cheap SOB only paid [him] $20."[13]

Foyt wasn't laughing, however, when Boat crashed again on his qualifying warmup lap. He slammed down the green flag used to signal the start of the run and then stomped back to Gasoline Alley where he led the repair effort. The car and Boat were not only back on the track four-and-a-half hours later, he turned in the second-fastest time to Arie Luyendyk and was one of only two drivers to average more than 225 miles per hour.

"It was a stupid incident," Boat said of the morning crash. "You've got to look at yourself in the mirror and say, 'What's going on?' I knew we had the race car, and I knew we had the setup, but it's been a really tough week. I don't think you can appreciate qualifying for this race until you go through something like this. There's nothing given to anybody here, and my boss told me that. Never once did he say anything negative to me. He's been there for me and I'm very fortunate he believes in me. It's times like this when you look at a guy like that to pick you up."[14]

Boat also showed his sense of humor was intact.

"A.J. chased me around the shop just a little bit to try to kick me in the butt," he told the public address announcer after his run. "I can still outrun him though. I only got a couple of bruises on my butt."[15]

Outside of his quick display of temper following the warmup crash, Foyt remained cool throughout. "I told him shit like that happens," Foyt recalled. "There's no sense jumping all over Billy and raising hell. The worst thing you can do is bring his morale down. If you want someone to push the button, you have to expect stuff to happen."[16]

Flying under the radar all week was Bräck. He wasn't particularly fast, qualifying in the middle of the third row. He remained confident, however, despite his early-season troubles.

"I'm not feeling any more pressure because of the crashes I've had," he said. "I'm confident in my abilities. Sometimes you're just in the wrong place at the wrong time. And sometimes maybe you make a little mistake.[17]

"I have a very good car and a very good crew and I'm in very good shape. I mean, look at my results. I know I can win. We have a focused group right now and we'll be strong in this race. They're going to have to beat us."

With his two primary cars in the race, Foyt decided to try and qualify a third. Marco Greco tested late Saturday and seemed ready to go when Foyt heard that Robbie Buhl, who had crashed his own car in a qualifying attempt on Saturday and then blew the engine in his backup machine on Sunday morning, didn't have time to install a new motor. It was Buhl whom Foyt had tried to hire the year before to replace the injured Boat, only to be blocked by car owner John Menard.

Foyt was friends with Buhl's new car owners, Jeff Sinden and Joe Kennedy, and offered a choice of his backup cars to the team.

Rain was in the forecast as Buhl sat in both cars and picked the one with the best-fitting pedals. While electrical tape was used to add No. 84 to the sides of the car, Boat told him what to expect from the setup and how to make minor changes from the cockpit. He said it would easily run the needed 220 mph. After a handful of practice laps—one at full speed—and with storm clouds looming, Foyt said it was time to make a qualifying run.

"They buckled me in the car back there [in the garage area]," Buhl said. "I thought they were fitting me up. They said no, let's go to the line. I thought, this isn't perfect, but we got a job to do. It's the 500."[18]

Although Buhl's helmet protruded from the cockpit and was buffeted by the wind, and a few raindrops began to fall on lap two, he was still able to bump his way into the field in thirty-second place. Moments later, the skies opened up, and qualifying was over—Buhl had made the race.

"I think it says a lot about A.J.," Buhl said. "He does things like this for people all the time. The more you're around, the more you hear the stories about the good things he's done for people on and off the track."

Foyt said the last-minute scramble brought back fond memories of earlier times at the Speedway.

"They were just in trouble. To me, that's what the IRL is all about. If somebody's in trouble, just like we used to do in the midgets and sprints, we help each other out. Tomorrow, if I need that help, I know they'll give me 110 percent. It's like old times. It's like open-wheel racing used to be. Money doesn't call the shots here. This is about giving guys a chance to show their abilities."

Most of the prerace attention was focused on Luyendyk starting from the pole in what he said would be his last 500. Greg Ray and Tony Stewart were the other prerace favorites while Foyt kept a tight rein on his cars. None were among the top fifteen on the speed charts during the final Carb Day practice session.

"A.J. keeps on telling me to take my time," said Boat, who had picked up Compaq computer as a late sponsor. "And I do need to be patient. That's the biggest key. But knowing it and doing it are different things. It wasn't something that came naturally and I still struggle with it. The fastest man doesn't always win this race. It takes a lot of luck and it takes a lot of patience."[19]

Bräck differed from his teammate, saying, "I don't believe in bad luck. I think you make your own luck. I'm a race car driver and it's my job to overcome things. But it ain't easy sometimes."[20]

It wasn't luck, but Foyt considered it a good omen when Jimmy Sills won the Silver Crown race on dirt at the Indianapolis State Fairgrounds the night before the 500—a race Foyt had sometimes driven in. Sills was driving a car owned by George Snider and sponsored by Foyt, who also supplied the engines.

As the 500 began, both Boat and Bräck seemed to have been listening to Foyt's lectures on patience as Boat dropped back at the start and Bräck was content to hold his position. About a quarter of the way through, Bräck moved up to pass both Luyendyk and Ray just to make sure he could, then dropped back to watch the two front-runners.

By the halfway point, the leaders began to run out of patience. Luyendyk picked up the pace and began running laps much faster than the field as he moved out to a two-second lead over Ray. But trying to pass a slower car on lap 117, he was pinched low on the track and spun up into the wall, his race over. Three laps later, Ray darted into the pits during the ensuing caution. In the team's haste to get him back on the track in the lead, they waved Ray out of the box before pit road was clear. He collided with another car and nosed into the pit wall, breaking the car's suspension. The drivers who had led ninety-five of the first 120 laps were out.

Bräck immediately passed Cheever on the restart to take the lead on lap 125. The defending champion tried to stay in the leader's draft, but it proved too much for the motor in his car, and Cheever was out with a blown engine fifteen laps later. Coming fast was Robby Gordon, who'd returned to run the 500. He'd lost a lap early in the race but was now the fastest car on the track. He passed Bräck to get back on the same lap and took advantage of caution flags to close up even more.

Bräck led to lap 150 when all the leaders pitted, and again from 154 to 170, when he pitted under caution with the rest of the cars on the lead lap to top off his fuel tank. All except one. Menard ordered Gordon, who was one of the few to pit on lap 164, to stay on the track.

Running twenty-five laps was considered safe with a full tank—completing thirty laps was a possibility if the driver conserved fuel. Gordon had never done better than thirty-one laps on a full load, and no one had stretched a fuel load to thirty-five laps. But it was clear Gordon—who wasn't running for the IRL championship and had nothing to lose if he ran dry—was going to try.

Bräck was blocked by a slower car on the restart, allowing a steady Jeff Ward to get past into second as Gordon moved out to a good lead. Bräck reclaimed second with thirteen laps remaining but was running in high gear to conserve fuel about five seconds back. That's when Foyt, who only occasionally talked to his drivers, broke in on a transmission.

"I thought Robby was going to run out before he did," Foyt said later. "Then I started getting a little concerned." Foyt told Bräck there was enough fuel to run hard to the finish and emphasized he "didn't want second." Which was exactly what Bräck wanted to hear. He started cutting into Gordon's lead by half a second a lap, enough to catch the leader with a lap or two remaining. Bräck, who had been run out of fuel by his team the previous year said he was now confident in the team's calculations:[21]

"We had better control of the fuel situation and I knew I could barely make it to the finish line if I saved and we thought it was impossible for Robby to make it," Bräck recalled. "But then if there was a yellow, maybe, just maybe, it would be possible. Then I got the message from the team to go full rich."[22]

"The car was slipping and I was driving as hard as I could. I hung on and I knew I would have to pass Robby if he didn't pit. I wasn't going to take second. Second is not good for a race like this."[23]

The last lap battle didn't materialize as Gordon's engine stuttered coming to the white flag, and he ducked into the pits. Seeing the leader coasting down pit road, Foyt, whose voice rises an octave or two when excited, was on the radio again. "Bring it home, you've won it."[24]

Bräck, who was a straightaway ahead of Ward, backed off when he heard Foyt's message, thinking he'd won. Then he realized he hadn't seen the checkered flag and accelerated again to finish the lap. Years later, he had a more colorful explanation of what happened.

"So A.J. comes on the radio and says, 'We're winning it, baby, we're winning it.' I'm like, 'Was that the finish line? Did we just win?' A.J. goes something like 'No, no, no. Keep coming.' So I told him, 'Shut the fuck up.'"[25]

It was a chaotic Victory Lane with the crowd chanting "A.J., A.J., A.J.," just as it had after his 1977 victory. Foyt and Bräck shared the bottle of milk. On Bräck and Foyt's victory lap around the track in the pace car, it was more of the same. "I don't think I heard my name screamed once," Bräck said.[26]

Asked how he felt, an excited Foyt blurted out, "I'm so wonderful!"

Boat finished third, and Buhl put on the drive of the race, coming from thirty-second to finish sixth. At times, A.J. tried to deflect attention to his drivers, without much success.

"I can't say enough about Kenny Bräck, Robbie Buhl and Billy Boat. You qualify one car in the front row and one in the back row and all three finish in the top six. What else can I ask for? All my drivers drove a great race today. They can't all win, but they all drove a hell of a good race."[27]

"It's not A.J.'s day," Foyt said when the interviews moved into the media center. But when reporters tried to direct a question to Bräck, Foyt broke in, saying, "Let me finish," which drew laughter from the crowd and Bräck.

Bräck was proud he and the team had met the challenge he made at the start of the year.

"We ran this race perfect from the green flag to the checkered flag. My goal was to drive a perfect race. If you drive a perfect race, then that's all you can do. You don't want to take any chances in the middle of the race. You wait to see who's your competition. Obviously, some things had to fall into place, and some guys fell out of the race."[28]

"I'm happy for A.J. and for myself. I think I'm more happy for me. He has won it four times already."[29]

After several hours of celebration and sponsor and media responsibilities, Foyt was ready to go. Bräck had promised to join him for a steak dinner "to make him happy." That's when King Carl Gustaf of Sweden called. No Swede had ever won the Indianapolis 500, and Gustaf was a race fan.

"I asked Jack Arute to tell A.J. to wait a minute because the king of Sweden was on the line," Bräck recalled. The pit reporter was friendly with both men. "Jackie comes back and says, 'A.J. says to tell him the king of Texas is waiting, and he's tired!'"[30]

While Foyt had made at least a half-hearted effort to share the spotlight with his drivers immediately after the race, he was centerstage the next night at the annual Victory Banquet. Bräck picked up checks totaling nearly $1.5 million, doubling the amount Foyt had earned for all four of his Indy 500 victories—combined. Boat and Buhl added to the team's coffers and brought the total take to nearly $2.5 million.

"Everybody laughed when I brought a foreigner to America, but I brought him to Texas and he's not too bad," Foyt said. "He's a good racer."[31]

The press had taken to calling them the "Odd Couple," but both men said they had much more in common than most people thought.

"We both have the same basic desires and same basic values," Bräck said. "I think that's what ties us together. Obviously A.J. has had a lot more success in his career and if you look at his record, no one comes close. He's been through all of this so many times that when he talks, I listen."

Foyt said, "they call us the Odd Couple, well if that's what it takes to win, I want to be the Odd Couple." But A.J. also thought they had much more in common than most people believed. Bräck "wasn't raised with a golden spoon and he knows if you work hard your rewards will eventually come." Foyt said, "I guess you'd have to say my part now is kind of coaching. It seems like we work very good together and when I see that I can help him on the racetrack, I get on the radio and start talking to him."

In addition to putting Foyt back at the center of the racing world, the success of the Indianapolis 500 also quieted rumors about a possible merger between the IRL and CART that had been rampant in the leadup to the event. Despite the talks, the two groups remained far apart—the IRL sticking to its low-tech, low costs, and oval track philosophy—the opposite of everything CART stood for.

NASCAR's Bill France Jr. had become so concerned about the state of open-wheel racing prior to the 500 that he took a leading role to try and broker a peace treaty. There wasn't anything altruistic about his efforts. It was strictly business. After buying a number of racetracks from Roger Penske, France needed a united Indy car series to make races at his new facilities viable.

Those efforts ended when Gordon ran out of fuel. What looked one moment to be a disaster for the IRL—an outside driver showing up, throwing together a part-time crew, and coming from a lap down to win the race—instead turned into a showcase for the series, providing a much-needed jumpstart for the struggling IRL and its biggest supporter. As Robin Miller noted, "Foyt is the official spokesman, recruiting officer and George's best public relations machine."[32]

Veteran motorsports reporter Shav Glick wrote in the *Los Angeles Times* that it had been "one of the most tantalizing races in modern Indianapolis 500 history." He estimated the crowd at 350,000—within shouting distance of the 400,000 that jammed the Speedway during its heyday. Foyt also noted the size of the crowd, sarcastically saying, "It's a shame there wasn't a lot of people here today."[33]

ABC/ESPN quickly signed a three-year deal to televise every IRL race. "ABC is going to let everybody know what Indianapolis racing is all about," Foyt promised. While he repeatedly said, "It'd be better to have one series," he made it clear any merger would be on his and the IRL's terms. "I can't see where the IRL would gain nothing with them coming over here. To me, they're not a series like we are. We're on oval racetracks. All they're wanting to run is road courses and street races. I can't see where the two series are really common any more. To me, I wouldn't walk across the street to see a street race."[34]

Boat mimicked his bosses' words. "The future looks bright for us and if CART wants to come run with us, I think that would be great," he said. "I think the IRL has reached a point where we have the most competitive open-wheel series in the world."[35]

Not only was the IRL finding success off the track, so was Foyt's team. Harrah's, with twenty-one properties in seventeen locations and one of the largest gambling companies in the country, stepped up to become the primary sponsor on Boat's car, signing a three-year deal worth a reported $10 million—a big number in the IRL.

"What I always wanted was a primary sponsor, where I don't have to have a bunch of little sponsors and four million decals on the car," Foyt said. "It wasn't that we couldn't get sponsors interested, but I'm very funny about the type of people I work with. If I like 'em, fine. If I don't, I don't have nothing to do with 'em. I've always done my own thing."[36]

A.J. also heard from his former sponsor, Conseco. The company had signed on to be the official financial services provider of NASCAR and wanted to go stock car racing to further promote the relationship. Foyt had often talked about starting a NASCAR team in recent years, and when the opportunity presented itself, the offer was too good to turn down.[37]

But where to start? Foyt initially considered purchasing one of several existing teams that were for sale but elected to start from scratch. It was an enormous undertaking. He had no shop, no team, no car manufacturer, and no driver. The Daytona 500 was a little more than six months away. And just to make things a little more challenging, after forty years in downtown Houston, Foyt was in the process of moving his Indy car team into new shops in Waller, about twenty miles west of the city and close to his ranch. Tommy LaMance, who'd been overseeing the IRL team, was dispatched to Charlotte to pull things together.

Conseco announced the program with full-page ads in newspapers across the country. Foyt quickly acquired a 30,000-square-foot building in Mooresville, North Carolina, the booming heart of NASCAR country just outside Charlotte, although it was little more than an empty shell with electricity.

Foyt said he was starting the team because, "I can do it right. With all new equipment and a shop. Conseco does everything first class and we're going racing again. Before when I ran down here it was hit or miss, never full time. This is something different. I sold my car dealerships and I don't have that much to do and I'm looking forward to it. I'm also getting up there in age and I want Tommy to have some things for his future."[38]

"I'll just be doing a lot of commuting. We're not getting into this just to run. We want to go out there and finish in the top ten. I know it's tough, and it was even when I raced here. But if you hire the right people, you can make some things happen."[39]

While all this was going on, Foyt's Indy car team began to struggle on the track. Sometimes it wasn't the team's fault. The first race after Indianapolis was Texas, and all the Goodyear-shod cars fell victim to tires that wouldn't last fifteen laps. A Goodyear loyalist, Foyt refused to change brands.

At other times, the team's performance was off. Boat, who had qualified on the pole six times the previous year, had only one to show for his efforts.

"It's not good," Boat said at one point. "We have no speed and no handling."[40]

He'd also crashed twice, failing to complete a lap at Pikes Peak, and knew he was on thin ice with Foyt when asked if he would be back with the team.

"You never really know when you deal with A.J.," he said. "You have to take it as it comes. We haven't performed probably to anybody's expectations the last half of the season. I don't know the reason for that. But I like this team. I like working with A.J. The team knows how to win."[41]

Bräck hadn't qualified in the top ten since Indianapolis and led only one event. At least he was finishing races, however, and he was still within striking distance of another IRL championship.

"We had decided to concentrate on Indy, and I think it showed," Bräck would say. "There's an old saying that if you chase two rabbits at once, you're going to lose one or the other. Our focus wasn't 100 percent at those other tracks."[42]

The 500 winner was hounded about his plans for the coming year amid rumors he was jumping to CART, rumors he didn't exactly deny.

"I think that A.J. has given me the best two years of my racing career and we work well together," he said. "I think I have given him something, too, so it has worked really well. We just have to wait and see for the future, what happens."[43]

Foyt acknowledged, "There's a lot going on, but we'll be okay. There's going to be days and years when everything's not perfect."[44]

The season hit a low point at Atlanta on July 17. Boat was on the pole for the Indy car race and watching on pit road alongside A.J. when Larry Foyt was involved in a frightening crash in the F2000 support race. Now twenty-one, Larry had qualified sixth and finished a promising fourth in the opening race of the season at Phoenix but had failed to come close to matching those results in the three events he'd run since.

Larry was running in a big pack of cars midway through the race when two of the cars touched. One car veered into the right rear of Foyt, launching him into one complete roll through the air, before landing right side up. The car then slammed backward into the outside wall and was hit by another car, catching fire and sliding down the track. The fire was out by the time he came to a stop, and Larry struggled out of the car, fell once, and then staggered to the grassy infield where he collapsed and laid on his back.

"I remember being very concerned," Boat said. "It was an intense few minutes. Obviously, any father would be very concerned."[45]

With the remnants of eight cars strewn along the front straight, a red flag was displayed to stop the race. When safety crews were slower responding to his son than he liked, Foyt took off on the run. He covered several hundred yards and reached Larry before any of the safety crews, leaving a startled Boat in his dust.

"It's amazing what a little adrenaline will do," Boat would say.

A.J. dropped to his hands and knees and quickly established that Larry wasn't seriously hurt. Larry, who was examined and released from the infield care center with minor bruises and burns, joked later that when he opened his eyes and saw his father, he thought he must be dreaming—or dead.

Despite the team's problems, Bräck put together a string of five top-ten finishes and was able to pull himself back into the championship chase. At the Texas finale, Bräck was leading when a wheel bearing went out thirty laps from the finish, ending his longshot hopes at the title, which was won by Greg Ray.

"I have never lost one of those before," Foyt said of the wheel bearing failure, "but like I said before the race, if it is your day, it is your day, and if it's not, it's not. That ain't the first time I have lost a championship."[46]

With Foyt having decided to drop Boat, and Bräck's future uncertain, he moved to shore up his IRL driver lineup, hiring Jeff Ward, who'd finished second at Indianapolis.

"Pound for pound and lap for lap, Jeff Ward is the best driver in the Indy Racing League," Miller had written about A.J.'s new driver. "Ward is going to trash the competition and win a Pep Boys championship."

The rest would have to wait, however. Foyt had a NASCAR team to get on its feet. His first step was to hire longtime NASCAR engine builder, crew chief, and team manager Waddell Wilson to serve as general manager. A year younger than Foyt, Wilson had been one of the top engine builders in the sport dating back to Holman-Moody in the 1960s. His engines had won more than one hundred NASCAR races and three series championships, and as a crew chief he helmed drivers to three Daytona 500 victories. Most recently, he'd served as general manager of Cale Yarborough's team. Wilson brought in Terry Wooten as crew chief, who'd worked for Junior Johnson, Robert Yates, Bill Elliott, Ricky Rudd, and Michael Waltrip. They considered leasing engines from another team before deciding to have Greg Wilson, Waddell's son, set up an engine room. Even a new transporter had to be built. By the end of October, Foyt had hired twenty people and was looking for another ten.

"We're building a team that can pull off the near miracle we need to get Team Conseco ready to qualify and run strong in the Daytona 500," Foyt said.[47]

It was certainly a veteran group, but some warned it might be too "old school" in a rapidly changing racing environment. "Racing has changed tremendously since they were in their prime," noted the *New York Times*. "Some wonder whether they can adapt."[48]

"I know people say I can't do this because I'm behind the times," Foyt countered. "Let me tell you, once you've been a winner, you know how to do it, even if you have to change with the times. We know how to win and we're going to win."[49]

After striking out with Ford, Foyt signed a deal to run Pontiacs and ordered a dozen cars from Hutcherson-Pagan, whom he'd worked with decades earlier. Finding a driver was proving more difficult as more than a dozen were rumored to be joining the team at one time or another. The most interesting name was Al Unser Jr., who had announced he was leaving Roger Penske's CART team at the end of the year so he could race in the Indy 500. Other names in the mix included Rudd, John Andretti, Wally Dallenbach Jr., PJ Jones, Kenny Irwin, Joe Nemechek, Johnny Benson, Scott Sharp, Ted Musgrave, and Rick Mast.

"We'll find somebody who knows how to drive a race car and who wants to win," Foyt said. "That's all I've ever asked for in a driver and I know there are still guys out there like that."[50]

Veteran NASCAR drivers, however, even ones who had never won a race, typically came at a premium, and Foyt found himself behind the curve when it came to salaries. He'd always paid on performance, offering a larger share of the winnings than most owners, but a smaller salary. He was surprised by the new NASCAR pay structure, where even mid-pack drivers were making millions of dollars.

"Paying three to four million up front is silly," he said. "I'll pay somebody a bit more money if they win, but I'm not going to pay a big salary for somebody to sit on his ass. I'll pay my driver based on incentives."

Wilson was more realistic and knew how hard just qualifying for NASCAR races would be. A typical Winston Cup race often saw five to ten cars fail to qualify.

"We're a new team with a new sponsor," Wilson said. "We need to make all the races. We don't need to be loading up on Saturday (after failing to qualify). We need someone who's not going to tear cars up. But that's a big task. And boy have we worn that conversation out."[51]

Foyt stood firm on salaries, and as a result, the experienced Cup drivers turned him down. He finally reached an agreement with Mike Bliss, a five-year veteran of NASCAR's truck series, who had a handful of Cup starts. Bliss was also a former modified and Silver Crown driver whom Foyt had once tried to hire for his IRL team.

"We're trying to do over a year's prep in six months," Foyt said in making the announcement. "We have put together a first-class team. I watched Mike in some of the truck races and he ran strong. I thought, 'He could be kind of a dark horse out there and I think he'll take people by surprise next year."[52]

But even Bliss was surprised to get the ride.

"It's pretty scary coming to Winston Cup, especially with a new team," he said. "I have nothing to bring to the team. I would have thought A.J. would have been looking for a veteran to start with. But I've known A.J. for years and what I like is he knows what it takes to win."[53]

Although he said he'd probably spend 90 percent of his time in Charlotte, Foyt insisted he was capable of overseeing both his Indy car and stock car teams. Afterall, Roger Penske had done it, and other Indy car owners like Chip Ganassi and Cal Wells were also starting NASCAR teams.

LaMance, who'd done much of the initial work on the stock car effort, would run the Indy car program in his absence.[54]

"I'm going to be playing both roles and I'm going to be jumping around like a rabbit," Foyt said. "I will spend most of my time in Charlotte, go to practice and qualifying at the IRL races and then come to NASCAR for race day."[55]

Foyt was still in Charlotte following the announcements when he was surprised to find Bräck waiting in his hotel lobby for him. The driver had decided to sign with Bobby Rahal's CART team, but before he did, he insisted on telling Foyt face-to-face:

> I got an offer from Bobby to drive for him. I told him I would do it, but that I wasn't going to sign any contracts until I spoke with A.J. I knew that other drivers wanted that seat and it could be risky to wait, but I couldn't sign before talking to A.J. So, I flew down to Charlotte and showed up at his hotel.[56]
>
> It was really a very emotional moment in my career because we had such a good relationship. To leave something that was so good was not easy for me. I think we were both close to tears. It was probably the only emotional meeting I ever had in racing.
>
> Some people were saying the IRL was best, and others were saying CART was best. I felt that after winning the Indy 500 and the championship, it was time to go to CART and to compete in that series. If I was successful there, it didn't matter what people were saying—I was good in both.
>
> He didn't try to talk me out of it. He understood I needed to go and do another thing because there was nothing more to win in one league. He'd been a driver longer than anyone, and I think he understood where I was coming from—that I wanted to compete against everybody.

Foyt recalled, "Kenny said he'd like to run more road races. I said fine, no hard feelings. If that's what you want to do, go do it. I've always felt that way. No hard feelings either way. I hated to lose him, but we weren't running the road races the other group was."[57]

Rahal said it was Foyt's tutoring of Bräck that attracted him to the Swedish driver.

"A.J. has done a great job of maturing Kenny on the ovals. That seemed to complete the picture to me."[58]

The impact of an IRL champion and defending Indy 500 winner jumping to CART could not be overstated. "Think of any athlete who has abandoned the uniform of one team for that of a bitter rival," wrote one columnist, "and you have some grasp of the luscious irony at work in Bräck's move."[59]

Despite the outside pressures, Bräck and Foyt remained lifelong friends.

"The relationship with A.J. was a very special one for me," Bräck said more than twenty years after they split. "He added a missing piece to me as a driver that was very important. He made me much, much more complete. And that's thanks to A.J. He's like a living encyclopedia. Nobody knows as much about racing as him. A computer might come to a more precise calculation about one aspect, but to win races, it takes a lot of aspects, and A.J. had that all inside of him due to his skill and experience. I had never met anyone like that."[60]

Boat also had nothing but good things to say about his time with Foyt:

> We weren't having the results we wanted, and this is a result-based business. When you don't have results, you make changes.[61]
>
> In '98, I was on top of the world: driving for your hero, and you're winning races, and you're fast every week—I don't think it gets much better than that. That was the pinnacle of my career right there. And then I got in the crash [at New Hampshire]. If you look at my career on a bell curve, I can go back and point to that day and say, "This is when I started going the other way."
>
> I still had good opportunities in '99. We sat on the front row and ran third at Indy. Any time you're in the last twenty laps of the race, and you can see the leader, you have a chance to win.
>
> A.J. and I actually got along fantastic. He never gave me a lot of direction on how to drive. He always respected guys that he never had to try to jack up. I was always the guy that he maybe had to slow down sometimes. He respected that.
>
> Our relationship was always very good. You see a lot of the version of A.J. where he's throwing a computer, or he's yelling at somebody or something like that, but the reality is, there was a few times when I tore up his race cars and never one time did he ever say anything to me. The only thing he'd say is, "Are you all right? What happened?" He gave me my biggest shot. I owe him a debt of gratitude for allowing me to drive for him.

Foyt said Bräck and Boat "were both good boys, and I enjoyed working with both of them.[62]

> When I picked up Kenny Bräck, he was running fast, but always seemed to get in trouble. I think Kenny had a lot of respect for me and he listened to me. We had a good combination going. Kenny would rate right at the top out of the best drivers we had. He was very fast.
>
> Billy Boat was a real good driver too. He drove awful hard and liked his car setup completely different from Kenny. A lot of times, Billy would outqualify Kenny, but come ten laps into the race, Billy's car would start getting loose, and Kenny would get by and go on.

With the twentieth century coming to a close, the Associated Press decided to name its athlete of the century in a number of sports, including auto racing. Longtime motorsports writer Mike Harris was put in charge of the process.

Harris assembled a panel of voters that included NASCAR President Bill

France Jr., Tony George from the Indianapolis Motor Speedway, Roger Penske, Jackie Stewart, and several others.

"We voted twice," Harris explained. "The second time, we culled it down to a couple of names, and Foyt and Mario Andretti came out in a dead heat." Each had forty-seven points. The closest challenger at forty-two was Juan Manuel Fangio, who'd won five Formula One championships in the 1950s, with Richard Petty another point back."[63]

"I don't think anybody can really argue with picking Andretti and Foyt as the top drivers," Penske said of the vote. "They were the epitome of racing. Tough, competitive, ready to do whatever they had to do to win. And they won in every form of racing they entered."[64]

Harris was tasked with informing each driver and obtaining a quote for his article. His first call was to Andretti, whom he'd known and covered as long as Foyt and was friendly with. He called Mario "my little quote machine." Harris told Andretti he'd been named Driver of the Century by the Associated Press.

"He was very appreciative about it, just so kind," Harris recalled. "He went on and on, typical Mario. Then I told him I also had some bad news. He was tied with A.J. Foyt."[65]

"That's not bad news," Harris remembers Andretti saying. "Anybody mentioned in the same breath with A.J. Foyt has to consider that a true honor. That man is one of the greats of all time. If you can just carry his helmet, that's a great thing."

In the article he filed, Harris quoted Andretti as saying of Foyt, "He was the yardstick that you measured yourself by. No one will appreciate more than me Foyt's qualities as a race driver."[66]

Harris's next call was to Foyt, whom he couldn't reach, and wouldn't return his calls. With the end of the year and his deadline approaching, he called Larry, whom he'd gotten to know.

"I need to talk to your dad," Harris said. "I got something to tell him. He's been given an honor, and I need to tell him about it.[67]

"Larry said he was going to try and get him on the phone, and I can hear them talking in the background. His son says, 'Mike Harris from AP is on the phone, and he wants to talk to you.' And I hear A.J. say, 'Oh, fuck him.'"

Larry finally convinced A.J. to take the call. Harris told him about being voted Driver of the Century and about being tied with Andretti.

"That goddamn little whop," Harris remembers Foyt saying, "He's always getting in my way—"

Harris broke in and told him, "Mario said some really nice things about you." He mentioned how Mario said he'd have been happy to carry A.J.'s helmet.

"He did?" A.J. responded. "Well, in that case, he's one hell of a good driver."

"I had a lot of fun when I was racing," Foyt said in the article. "I tried to be as competitive as I could be over the years. I never did want to settle for second."

He didn't want to settle for a tie with Andretti for Driver of the Century honors either.

"Put us in a car and let us settle it on the track," said Foyt, who would turn sixty-five in January.

A reporter for Andretti's hometown newspaper, the *Allentown Morning Call*, reached out to Mario to see if he had any response to Foyt's comment.

"I'll do that all day," said Andretti, sixty years old. "All he has to do is name the car and the place. We'll go on his terms . . . a match race on this planet or on Mars."[68]

There was no such ambiguity when *Sport* magazine released its list of the century's best athletes. When it came to auto racing, Foyt was number one followed by Andretti and Richard Petty. Leave it to Robin Miller at the *Indianapolis Star*, ever the contrarian, to come up with a different ranking. He had Andretti number one followed by Dan Gurney and then Foyt.

AJ Foyt
Racing
cons
14

CHAPTER 29

GRUMPY OLD MEN

2000

A.J. Foyt ignored the Y2K warnings about a possible technology meltdown and spent the first day of the new century in Tulsa, Oklahoma, watching Anthony Joseph Foyt IV compete against the country's best go-kart racers. His fifteen-year-old grandson was competing against others in his age group, and after starting fifteenth, worked his way up to seventh by the end of the race.

Foyt had already moved Larry into a stock car series for the coming year with an eye on eventually reaching NASCAR. He had promised to support Larry's racing efforts when he graduated from Texas Christian University, which was coming up in May. The handful of Larry's F2000 starts the previous year had been the first steps in that direction. After Larry passed his IRL rookie test at Texas Motor Speedway at the end of 1999, it seemed he might replace Billy Boat in the team's second car. But the crash at Atlanta had frightened everyone, especially Lucy Foyt. To keep the peace at home, A.J. arranged for Larry to drive in the American Speed Association (ASA), one of the most competitive short-track stock car series in the country. NASCAR drivers Rusty Wallace, Mark Martin, Kenny Schrader, and others had come from the ASA ranks.

Foyt said,

> I told him that if he went to school and graduated from college, I'd fulfill my obligation. So that's where I got caught. I definitely didn't want him to race. I raised him and told him that anything could happen at any time. I said I'm crippled up because of racing and I should have quit earlier. When you get in them race cars, there's no guarantees.[1]
>
> Larry drove Indy cars and ran very fast. But I felt like right now, the one big Indy car race is the Indy 500. The other races are fill-ins. It's a

◀ Going NASCAR. *NASCAR Archives*

> household word, NASCAR is, and I felt that if I'm going to be his father and try to direct him in the right way, this is where I think he needs to be.

Tommy LaMance, who'd been shuttling between Houston and Charlotte trying to oversee both the Indy car and NASCAR teams as they prepared for the new year, thought he understood what his uncle was doing.

"I think he's doing it for us—me, Larry, Anthony and everyone here," he said. "He wants to put a solid foundation under us."[2]

A.J. seemed to agree. "I'm here because it will be fun and because my children and grandchild are starting to race. As long as I feel healthy and I feel like I can do it, I'll do it. But I have a lot of the younger generation behind me. When I start backing off, they will take over. We're in this for the long haul."[3]

It was disappointing news for Larry, who would look back and say, "My heart was still dead set on Indy cars. But the crash had been pretty scary. A.J. was already starting a stock car team, and I think he wanted to keep Lucy happy. So, he put me in something with a roof on it."[4]

From Tulsa, Foyt went to Charlotte, where his team was working around the clock to finish its first Pontiac in time for the initial test session at Daytona. One reporter compared the task to "NASA trying to send men to Mars this summer." Despite the time crunch, Foyt set the bar high for the team:[5]

> We're going 100 percent to compete in all the NASCAR races, and it's going to take a lot of my time. I've surrounded myself with pretty good people, so that should make it a lot easier. Even when I was driving Indy cars myself and running the occasional NASCAR race, I was able to make the field, so I think it's not going to be a problem.[6]
>
> We're not scared of nobody. They can't do anything I can't do. I guess that's what made me what I am today. Anything I do, I want to be competitive. You can't rest on your laurels. What you've done in the past is over. What I want to do now is give young drivers the same opportunity that I had. Giving them the chance to win is the big thrill. A.J.'s time is past.

The first test days at Daytona served as a wake-up call for Foyt. It had been seven years since he'd last been to the track and nearly thirty years since he'd won the Daytona 500. Much had changed. Rules and regulations were tighter, and computers and engineers were nearly as prevalent as in Indy car racing. Three- and four-car teams dominated, while the one-car teams from Foyt's days were at a decided disadvantage.

The GM teams brought more than fifty cars to the track, and after the first day, Foyt's rookie driver, Mike Bliss, was at the bottom of the speed charts. Bliss did pick up nearly three miles per hour on day two, moving him into the top twenty.

"This was a shakedown test to see where we were," Bliss said and added,

> We've got some work to do. We're trying to find out what we can do to get over this hump. We're stuck right in the middle. If I could find something that could gain me a half second, I'd feel a lot more comfortable.[7]
>
> One thing about A.J. is people over here respect him. He's here to make a statement. He's here to win races and a championship. I mean, it's going to happen for him some day because he knows what it takes. Some of the other teams coming over, they might think they can just bring their money and engineers and think they're going to turn it around overnight. A.J. knows it's not going to happen overnight but he knows it's going to happen.

Afterward, Foyt acknowledged it was going to be an uphill battle. There hadn't been time to do a wind tunnel test of the new Pontiac before the track session, and now the team was planning on cutting the body off the car and replacing it.

"We're doing things that probably should've taken a year of planning, but Conseco wanted to come out in the year 2000," Foyt said. "It's a big campaign for them. But I told 'em don't expect miracles. We're gonna do the best we can and in the second year I'm looking forward to being competitive with everybody."[8]

Foyt's next stop was only a short hop away—the year's opening IRL race at Walt Disney World Raceway. After considering running a single car team, he landed another sponsor, the Rio Hotel in Las Vegas, owned by Harrah's. As a result, he added Eliseo Salazar, a forty-four-year-old driver from Chile who'd crashed out of three of the past four Indianapolis 500s. But he'd been one of the few remaining unsigned experienced drivers.

"I've heard all kinds of good horror stories," Salazar said of Foyt when he was introduced. "I'm just going to listen to what he says and do what he says. Who can argue with him with all his wins?"[9]

Jeff Ward added, "There's no more pressure because I'm driving the 14 car, but it's going to make it all the more special when I win my first race."[10]

"To hear my name and A.J. Foyt's name together, it's still overwhelming. He's like a coach. He'll throw his hat down if you make a mistake, cuss at you on the way in. Hey, that's what a coach should do."[11]

Foyt said, "Our goals this year are very simple. Come back and win again at Indy and win the IRL championship."

The IRL team got off to a modest start at Orlando, Salazar finishing fifth and Ward seventh. Foyt's frantic pace was already taking its toll, however, and he was limping badly by the end of the weekend. As a last resort, he tried DMSO, a painkiller cream sometimes used to treat arthritis. Foyt used the high-strength version normally reserved for the legs of racehorses without much relief.

For years, he'd been putting off doctors who wanted to remove much of the hardware installed in his legs after the Road America crash. He'd had one leg done, and now some of the screws were finally working their way loose on the other. He couldn't wait any longer. Doctors at Memorial Hospital in Houston removed a steel plate, two connecting bars, and twenty-four screws.

"My wife always said I had a few screws loose, but she can't say that anymore," he quipped afterward.[12]

Having turned sixty-five at the start of the year, he checked to see if Medicare would pay for the surgery, which led to one of his least favorite things to do—dealing with the government.

"I tried to get Medicare and the sons-of-guns turned me down," he said as part of a story he delighted in repeating often in the days ahead. "They asked me how much I make and I said, 'What's that got to do with it?' That pissed me off. I said, 'I don't know, it might be zero, it might be a million dollars.' Finally I told them the government could take it and shove it where the sun don't shine. That was terrible the way they treated me. Finally I said, thank you very much. The government needs it more than A.J. Foyt."[13]

He ignored doctor requests to stay home and was on crutches when he arrived in Daytona, carrying a plastic bag so he could show off the hardware he'd had removed. Most in the series officially welcomed Foyt and his team into the sport.

"It's good for the series, and obviously, the series is good for him," said his godson, John Andretti, who was now driving for Richard Petty. "A.J. is really good about working with things. And he wants things to be headed in the right direction more than anything. If they stop going in the right direction, that's when his patience runs out."[14]

Jeff Gordon said, "A name like A.J. Foyt carries a lot of prestige and respect, and I certainly was a big fan of his when I was growing up and going to Indy and watching him. I'm going to make sure I know whether I've won the race or not when I go into Victory Lane."

Not everyone welcomed Foyt, however.

"He brings a well-known name and a following of both NASCAR and Indy car folks and once upon a time the sport needed people like that to draw attention," said Rick Hendrick, Gordon's powerhouse team owner. "Now, the sport is so much bigger that people hardly notice."[15]

Another owner, Bill Davis, said Foyt wouldn't be receiving any favors. "A.J. Foyt was one of the greatest drivers of all time. That probably won't get him any spots or anything in here."[16]

Former driver Bobby Allison, who'd had his differences with Foyt over the years, warned, "I think he will be in the toughest situation he's ever been in, because I think NASCAR will make him abide by everything everybody else has to abide by. Apparently, with his sponsor's money he can buy anything for the car. It will be a case of how his people come together as a team. NASCAR is the ultimate team requirement.[17]

"Foyt will demand performance out of his people. He is at the top of the line among people who demand a lot. A.J. certainly is a unique individual."

The team found out just how hard it was going to be at Daytona when Bliss finished a disappointing twentieth in the first qualifying race, probably not high enough to make the 500. As they watched the second race, "We just had to hold our breath and wait," said Bliss, who celebrated with the rest of the team when they snuck in to the last qualifying spot based on speed.

In the 500, Bliss picked up a few spots in the early going but was then hit by an old Foyt team problem: The car ran out of gas as it was going down the backstraight. He lost two laps before getting back on the track and would finish thirty-third, four laps behind winner Dale Jarrett.

The next week at Rockingham, Bliss nearly spun on his qualifying lap and missed the race. They weren't alone, as three other new teams came up short. But when Bliss failed to qualify for the next two races at Las Vegas and Atlanta, then crashed two minutes into a special practice session at Darlington and said, "I still don't understand it," Foyt had seen and heard enough. [18]

"I've never been known to be missing races my whole career," A.J. said. "We'd like to evaluate the team and it seemed like we tested and things weren't progressing. We've got good equipment. I think he's a good driver. But we've got to see if he needs more time to step over here or what."[19]

Although no one took him seriously, Foyt hinted several times he might drive the car. Still, it was enough that when Wilson went to Mike Helton, NASCAR's chief operating officer, to tell him they were making a driver change, he responded, "Anybody but A.J.!"[20]

Instead, they announced that Dick Trickle, a fifty-nine-year-old veteran of the Busch Grand National series, would take over the car for the next two races at Darlington and Bristol. Foyt also said he would stay at Darlington and skip the IRL race at Phoenix. One reporter noted that between Foyt, Wilson, and Trickle, the team had more than 190 years of experience and labeled the trio "The Grumpy Old Men."[21]

The impact was immediate. A past Darlington winner in the Busch series, Trickle muscled the car to a surprising twelfth place in qualifying, turning in a lap faster than a host of Cup regulars. The race was another story as Trickle quickly dropped back and finished five laps behind the winner in thirty-first.

That was still enough for Foyt to dismiss Bliss afterward and start looking for another driver. Trickle was set to race the next week at Bristol but was not an option for the season. He was committed to running for the Grand National championship, and there were several conflicting dates that wouldn't allow him to do both.

"I knew Dick Trickle," Foyt said after Darlington. "I knew he had a lot of experience. I knew he was up in age. I didn't expect him to run all day like a twenty-year-old boy, but I felt he would be competitive and help me understand what's going on.[22]

"Any time you see A.J. Foyt's name on something, I'm 100 percent there. I've got a good reputation. People know that when I go into something I'm not going in there just to say I've got a team. That's not my way. I go in there because I love challenges."

Foyt made his first trip to Bristol the following week, the high-banked half-mile that epitomized NASCAR short-track racing. Trickle qualified in twenty-first and faded again to finish twenty-seventh as a new reality began to settle in.

"When I raced I never worried about making races," Foyt said. "But I'm in a little different position today. I'm not behind the wheel. Not that I wouldn't have missed a race, but I was always worried about trying to sit on the pole.[23]

"I knew this was going to be bumpy. I knew it was going to be hard. I wasn't worried about our car. I wasn't worried about our equipment. But I didn't know how Mike would adapt to the deal. We missed three races and I was kind of upset."

Those comments upset Bliss, who had remained quiet since being released by Foyt.

"I think if you look at my past in the truck series, I know how to qualify," said Bliss, who'd won fourteen truck poles, second in series history. "When we went into this, I thought they'd understand that I was a rookie and with a rookie team, we were going to have trouble and work through it. They felt they could point fingers more at me than anyone else. I don't feel bad. It wasn't going to work. I don't like to miss races. And I don't think it was my fault."[24]

Bliss added, "Waddell pretty much screwed things up and I tried to tell A.J. he needed to get to Charlotte and see what was going on. Our motors (stunk) and our cars weren't any good, but I'm just a rookie so nobody took me serious."[25]

Looking back on his time with the Foyt team Bliss would say, "The way my year went, I wish I wouldn't have gone to Cup. I thought I had it figured out, I thought I was ready to go. But I didn't have a prayer there. I was pretty much out of the seat before I got in the seat."[26]

With Bliss gone and Trickle headed back to the Busch series, Foyt hired Rick Mast to take over the car. He was one of the drivers who turned Foyt down at the start of the season when offered the ride. Now Foyt realized he needed to up the ante. "A.J. Foyt made Rick Mast an offer he couldn't refuse," said Larry Hedrick, Mast's previous car owner.[27]

Foyt had met Mast ten years earlier when both drove for U.S. Tobacco and Mast was a rookie starting out in Winston Cup. He'd also provided some tips that helped Mast win the pole for the first Brickyard race.

"I've known Rick for a long time and I've got a lot of respect for his driving," Foyt said, indicating he hoped to keep the driver for the following year. "I'm not the type of guy that likes to jump around with drivers if I don't have to. One of the things I like about Rick, if he tells somebody he'll do something, he lives up to his word."[28]

Mast was still looking for his first series victory but was the only driver running at the finish of every race in 1999. He was also "Foyt tough" and would be driving at Texas with two broken ribs suffered in a crash at Bristol.

"I just want to run well, race well and win. And everybody in this garage area knows that when it's all said and done, this team's going to be very, very competitive. I know A.J. and I know what he is, what he does, and he doesn't like to lose. He's not going to tolerate it, and I'm at the point in my career where I'm not going to either."

Mast qualified thirty-fourth at Texas with an engine borrowed from Richard Childress and Dale Earnhardt. It became clear just how difficult simply making the field every week would be for the rest of the year as Kyle Petty, Robby Gordon, and Wally Dallenbach Jr. went home, and even series contenders Tony Stewart and Jeff Burton were forced to take provisional starting positions. Mast spun in the race to avoid crashing cars and still finished twentieth, the team's best result to date.

When Mast failed to qualify for the next two races at Martinsville and Talladega, however, Foyt struck again and fired crew chief Wooten. He dispatched LaMance, "my right-hand man [who] knows how I want my race teams run," back to Charlotte to take charge. A week later Wilson was gone, along with the shop manager and engine department.[29]

"What we heard [from Wilson] was that we had a beautiful ship," LaMance would say. "What we didn't hear was that it was sunk."[30]

Mast went into greater detail on the challenges the team faced. "Basically, we had three problems. We had some geometry problems with our chassis; we had aerodynamic problems and we had horsepower problems. The team has a lot of plans. They have a lot of things they are going to do. It's just going to take time to get there. As long as A.J. Foyt owns it, at the end of the day, no matter how long it takes, it will be a successful race team."[31]

Foyt said he felt burned. "I put a lot of faith in Waddell and that turned out to be a mistake. I told Waddell this was not going to work. It looked like things had passed him by and the things he tried to do were way behind. We spent a lot of money building eleven cars and, after Waddell got through with them, everything had changed."[32]

LaMance said, "The biggest thing that I am coming over here to do is to coordinate all the different departments that we have and lead the employees in a more focused manner. We have a lot of energy and a lot of resources, and I need to direct that."[33]

Foyt and LaMance raided Hedrick's team again, hiring away crew chief Philippe Lopez (who had also worked for Earnhardt) and engine builder David Evans. Those moves provided a certain amount of stability as Mast qualified for all but two of the season's remaining races.

"As the team faltered early, the thing that bothered me more than anything was seeing the hurt on A.J. He wasn't really upset, he was hurt. And that motivates me because I know that A.J. Foyt needs to be in front. He deserves to be in front."

At Talladega, one of the races where Mast failed to qualify, Foyt was forced to stick around for another day to participate in induction ceremonies for the International Motorsports Hall of Fame. It was a stellar class, with Foyt joined by Mario Andretti, Don Prudhomme, Ayrton Senna, Craig Breedlove, and Nelson Piquet. In typical Foyt style, he skipped the pre-induction events and media obligations and showed up for the black-tie dinner in a sport coat and open-collar shirt. "At my age, I've the right to dress how I want," he said. His absence at the pre-event festivities had not gone unnoticed.[34]

"A.J., I want you to know Mario and I covered for you the last two days," Prudhomme said in his remarks. "You know I have two dogs. One is a good dog and I named him Senna. The other is the meanest dog you'd ever want to see and I named him A.J."

Before the ceremonies, Andretti and Foyt said hello, the first time they'd talked in five years—the result of the split between CART and the IRL.

"We have different personalities and we don't agree on a lot of things," Andretti acknowledged. "A.J. has his theories on things and I have mine. So be it. But I always respected him as a driver and always will."[35]

A reporter asked Andretti if he and Foyt could work out a reconciliation between the two racing organizations.

"That would be wonderful and I would love it, but I don't think it serves A.J.'s purpose. The IRL is much less sophisticated racing. When it comes to state-of-the-art, pushing-the-envelope engineering, Foyt doesn't like to be involved. That's what it comes down to. We totally disagree on the nature of racing."

Andretti was right about one thing: Foyt saw things differently.

"There's no talking to those people in CART," he said when asked the same question. "They think they invented racing. As for Mario, I think he has forgotten that it was the Indy 500 that made him famous. All he wants to do is talk bad about Tony George."

It had been George who introduced Foyt at the ceremony, saying A.J. was "the son my grandfather (Tony Hulman) never had, the man my father loved and the man my mother argued with like a brother."

While LaMance settled in Charlotte with the NASCAR team, Foyt headed for Indianapolis, where he had already caused a stir. He'd entered six cars, two each for Ward and Salazar, and two more for "Foyt-Bräck Motorsports." No driver was listed, and Foyt only smiled when asked if the defending race champion might return. Kenny Bräck later said he first heard about the entry from his new car owner, Bobby Rahal, who wasn't happy.

"Bobby came to me and asked, 'What the hell is this?'" Bräck recalled years later. "I told him I didn't know anything about it. So, I called A.J. and asked what he had done, and he just started laughing."[36]

Rahal, who'd considered a 500 entry then decided against it when Ford objected, issued a carefully worded statement. "As a former Indy 500 champion, I understand how unique it is for the defending champion to not race at Indy. It is a great gesture on the part of A.J. that he has offered Kenny a symbolic means to be involved."[37]

Bräck eventually warmed to the possibility of having a car in the race, saying, "A.J. is like my mentor. We have a special bond that I think will always be there. I learned so much from him. It is a lot different working for Bobby. It's like opposite poles of a battery. They are completely different, but they get the job done. A.J. is very hands on and gets involved with every aspect of the team. Bobby is more like the CEO of a corporation. Of course they are a lot different emotionally, too. But the point is both ways of doing things work for them. There is more than one way to be successful."[38]

The IRL team showed potential through the first three races of the season. Salazar already had a pair of top-five finishes and was leading at Las Vegas before being caught up in someone else's accident. Ward was fast but more inconsistent. At the Speedway, Foyt followed the successful format from the past couple of years: limiting the number of laps early in the week and increasing them as qualifying approached.

With Foyt jumping back and forth between the IRL and NASCAR, Craig Baranouski took over the day-to-day operation of the Indy car team. He'd been with Foyt since 1987, after working with the teams of Lee Brayton and then Pat Patrick in CART in the early 1980s. Over the years, he'd risen to his role of chief mechanic and was one of Foyt's closest and most trusted team members.

"It was different back then, because it was a lot of small teams and the little guys could survive," Baranouski said of his early days in the sport. "Then it went for a spell where there were virtually no small teams. Now, with the IRL, it's more like it was back in the beginning. It was more like being on a smaller team again, more of a family-type atmosphere. It's where I belong.[39]

"The man's mellowed a lot in the days from when he was a driver and owner," Baranouski said of the man he always called "boss." "But he's still very competitive and that's where you'll see those big mood swings of his. He doesn't want to lose. And when he loses his temper, it's just from wanting to win so bad. But when he settles down, usually you get to the bottom of the problem. And usually, we won't let that problem happen again."

Foyt seemed unconcerned about the upheaval. "We've got a veteran team that knows what it takes to win. We've got good drivers and the right equipment. We're in good shape."[40]

Receiving most of the prerace attention was Al Unser Jr.—who was hoping to make his first start at the Speedway since winning in 1994—and Chip Ganassi's four-time CART championship team with drivers Jimmy Vasser and Juan Pablo Montoya. Ganassi reportedly was working with a budget of $2.5 million for the race from sponsors Budweiser and Target department stores, more than half of what Foyt was getting from the casinos for a full season. The fact was not lost on A.J., who said, "I guess if them boys don't whip us, they're going to be pretty disappointed."[41]

Also at the track was Andretti, and while Ganassi tried to stay low-key and avoid IRL versus CART discussions, Mario lashed out at the quality of the 500 field.

"When I raced here, if you won you knew you had beaten the best in the world. But these guys can't say that because there's another series with great drivers that aren't here. The IRL is not a viable series."[42]

Not surprisingly, those comments drew an immediate response from Foyt.

"Mario is full of bull. It amazes me that he even has the gall to show his face here after all the terrible things he has said about this place and this league."

The two Ganassi drivers and Greg Ray topped the speed charts through the week of practice. On Friday, Foyt turned his team loose, and Ward and Salazar responded with the second- and fourth-fastest laps of the month before A.J. pulled them off the track.

"You know my boss," Salazar said. "As soon as we got in the top five [in practice speeds] he'd say, 'Ok, that's it.' He wouldn't let me practice anymore."[43]

While PJ Jones and Bryan Herta were among the drivers who contacted A.J. about the Foyt-Bräck Motorsports entry, he chose veteran Roberto Guerrero for the third car. Guerrero, age forty-one from Colombia, had four consecutive top-five finishes in the 500—back in the 1980s when Foyt was still driving. Since then, he'd finished last twice, including once when he crashed from the pole on the race's warmup lap in 1992.[44]

Ward was one of the first to qualify and ran four consecutive laps of 222.6 miles per hour, good for sixth on the starting grid. Both he and Foyt were happy with the run, although both said it should have been faster. "The gearing was just a little off," Ward said, as he used only third gear on the run, while Foyt felt he should have upshifted to fourth.[45]

Salazar was even faster and qualified on the outside of the front row behind pole-winner Ray and Montoya. Salazar said he might have been the fastest if he hadn't noticed his third lap speed was 223.7 mph and then overshot his marks going into Turn One. "I'm happy but I think Eliseo is disappointed because he felt like he could have run faster," Foyt said. "He looked at the damn computer and all of a sudden he got in the corner and he lost concentration and then he just had to get out the best he could."[46]

Not so fortunate was Guerrero, who had two runs waved off by Foyt when his average fell to 218 mph. After sleeping on it, Foyt decided to pull Guerrero from the car, saying, "I just couldn't get him going. I really felt bad about pulling him out. Sometimes it don't click."

That set up one of the most dramatic bump-day scenarios in 500 history.

Billy Boat had been one of the first on the track for day-two qualifying. He'd struggled all week trying to find speed and crashed during the run, badly damaging the unsponsored car. There was no backup machine.

When Foyt heard Boat might miss the race, he passed word to the driver that the Guerrero machine had one more qualifying attempt available, and he was welcome to try. With less than an hour remaining, Boat took to the track—or at least tried to. The car stalled three times leaving the pits, and when the run started, the engine cut out momentarily and the instrument panel went black. His posted speed was well off the pace and would certainly be bumped.

When Boat returned to pit road, he found only Foyt, who'd sent the crew running back to the garage to get Salazar's backup car ready to go. The car had not turned a lap at speed all week, but there was no time for practice. It was pushed into the qualifying line, and Boat clambered in. It still looked as if Boat would miss his chance, however, as another car took to the track with only minutes remaining in qualifying. They caught a break when that car aborted its run, and Boat took off with only seconds to spare.

"I didn't fit in the seat, and the crotch belt was too short," Boat recalled years later. "I couldn't reach the pedals. They put me in line, and we pulled out on the racetrack as the gun went off. I used my toe to push on the toe strap to put the throttle down, and away we went. It's a testament to his team at that time that we were able to do that—a testament to A.J.—and for me for being dumb enough to hold the gas down."[47]

Boat ran four pressure laps at 218 mph, enough to eke into the field in thirty-first position. Or did he? Robin Miller, who was increasingly critical of the IRL, questioned in a column whether Boat had really got on the track before six o'clock or if "officials looked the other way because the car belonged to Foyt."[48]

Brian Barnhart, IRL director of racing operations, said, "We didn't give anybody a break. The car has to pull away from the pit box before 6 p.m.—it doesn't have to be on the track. Billy's car crossed the pit exit line at 5:59.35."[49]

Both Foyt and Boat were emotional and near tears after the run.

"The kid's one hell of a good friend of mine and when I see a good friend struggling, I have to help," Foyt said. "That takes guts to do what he did. The car never had a hot lap, he never was in it. That's unbelievable."

Boat said, "Sometimes careers go in different directions. I feel very fortunate that A.J. and I maintained the relationship we did and that I still felt that I could walk into his garage and say, 'I'm in trouble. Can I get in one of your cars?'"[50]

Foyt was optimistic in the leadup to the race, saying, "I've got three great race cars, I've got three great drivers and I've got three great crews. If we can top last year, we'll have done something."[51]

The surprise story was Salazar. After spending two years in Formula One from 1981 to 1983, often failing to qualify, he took a step back to F3000, where he recorded two top-ten finishes over the next two years. He had more luck driving sports cars, winning at Le Mans in 1990. He'd won three races and finished second four times on the IMSA circuit in 1994. He started running Indy car races in 1995, first in CART and at Indianapolis, then adding IRL races the following year. His best performances came on high-speed tracks including Atlanta, Texas, and Las Vegas, where he'd won his lone race. He'd finished fourth and sixth at Indianapolis but also crashed there several times. He had limited sponsorship support and without a good ride to start the 2000 season, he'd been prepared to step away from the series.

"I really love the IRL, but if I wasn't going to be with a top team, I didn't want to be here," he said. "It took a long time for us to make the deal, but I thought I had to have patience because I didn't want to drive for another small team. I didn't want to drive just to be there. I wanted to win races. Sometimes when you get an opportunity like this you are too young to take advantage of it. This is the best chance I've ever had."[52]

At times, Salazar seemed as surprised as everyone else on how well he got on with Foyt.

"We get along great. I had heard so many horror stories about him. I used to say we were still on our honeymoon, but now it seems like we've been married for a few months. It took me awhile to understand him because of his accent. As for my language, he can say chili con queso but that's about as far as he can go."[53]

The race was delayed by rain, and when it finally got underway, Ray led the first twenty-five laps. After that it was all Montoya, as he led 167 circuits, giving up the front spot only briefly on pit stops. He finished seven seconds ahead of Buddy Lazier with Salazar in third and Ward in fourth. Boat finished fifteenth and passed more cars than anyone else as the team won more than a million dollars. Both Salazar and Ward ran in the top five all race and had a run at Montoya late.

Ward recalled being in second to Montoya with only thirty laps remaining:

> I had a good jump on him on the restart, but he's a smart guy. He knows I can't pass until it goes green, so he just lifted and he made me lift. If he would have kept going, I would have had a good run on him. But he knew to check me up because they hadn't yelled green yet. So I had to let off and he stayed ahead of me. The truth is he had such a fast car today that even if I had gotten ahead of him, I'm not sure how long I could have held it. I think this showed how competitive we were.[54]

Salazar also got as high as second. He waited until the last one hundred miles until making his move, before getting blocked while passing a slower car.

"I thought this was going to be a race where you had to be aggressive all the time. But A.J. wanted to wait. The strategy was perfect, but Raul [Boesel] got in the way—he was impossible to pass."[55]

Foyt seemed to be happy with the results. "I thought it was a great race. Any time you finish all three cars in a 500-mile race, you've done well. We didn't have things fall our way today. Every time they went to make a move, traffic was in the way."[56]

He also was impressed with Montoya, saying, "The kid is a hell of a driver."[57]

Indianapolis proved to be the team's best race of the season. Foyt's interest often waned after the 500 and he spent less time with the IRL team as he turned back to the NASCAR effort.

"A.J. really gets focused at Indy," LaMance said. "For some reason, he gets in a zone like you can't believe. It's what carries him in life, makes him work all those hours in a day, what defines him. He's driven by it."[58]

Two weeks later at Texas, Salazar and Ward qualified well and ran up front before they dropped out with engine problems. That set the trend for the rest of the year. Both drivers would qualify well, run up front, and lead some laps—but everything that could go wrong did. By the end of the season, the team was still without a victory with Salazar fourth in the final point standings and Ward in eleventh. Neither driver felt secure about their ride for the coming year.

While the Indy car team seemed to plateau, Foyt's NASCAR program showed steady improvement. The team continued to build new cars, and its own engine shop finally came online. After Memorial Day, they missed only one race—on a road course. Mast also posted three top-five qualifying efforts and an eighth-place finish at Pocono—his best of the year—and was optimistic about the coming season.

"I knew when I took this job we were going to have bumpy roads," Mast said after qualifying third at Michigan in August. "I knew it was going to take a while to fix it, but I didn't know how deep the problems were. I knew that at the end of the year, next year or whatever, I would be better off with A.J.'s team. I went there with that mindset. I went in knowing it was going to take a while, but I also knew, without a doubt it my mind, what the end result would be. We're not there yet, but we will be. Believe me."[59]

After a twelfth-place finish at Darlington on Labor Day, it seemed a forgone conclusion to all involved that Mast would be back the following year.

"I'm very happy with the turnaround," Foyt said. "We've still got a long ways to go. I'm just looking at this year as a learning curve. I think by next year at this time we'll be in the top ten consistently. Everybody knows even though I may lose every now and then, that's not the way A.J. likes it."[60]

LaMance added, "Our race program is not where we need it to be but we're getting there. We've run better and better. We just haven't had a complete weekend yet. But we've been very happy with Rick Mast."

After Darlington, Foyt was looking forward to attending the first F1 race to be staged at the Indianapolis Motor Speedway three weeks later. After experiencing chest pains, however, he underwent surgery in a Houston hospital where doctors used five balloons and three stents in a minimally invasive angioplasty surgery to clear blocked arteries. He spent the night in the hospital and a few more at home before heading for Indianapolis, where he joked about the surgery.

He said it was, "kinda like a valve job. They showed me a map of my heart, and I had like 98 percent blockage in one (artery) eighty-five in another and seventy-five in another." When his blood pressure showed significant improvement, he said, "it's like they retarded my spark."[61]

Asked if he planned to change his diet—which had always been heavy on meat, fried foods, and ice cream—he shook his head. "What do you think? I've lived this many years eating like this and I'm not going to change now. The doctors tried to explain that diet stuff to me and I stopped 'em and said, 'save your breath.'"

Larry Foyt showed improvement throughout the ASA season. He'd never raced on a track shorter than the mile at Phoenix, and most of the series was run on short tracks he'd never seen before. The other series "rookies" were often the champion at their local quarter-mile bullring. Many of the races were on tracks where his father had cut his teeth in his early years, and fans often brought him newspaper clippings about A.J.'s exploits, including stories about his first sprint car win on the high banks of Salem.

Larry acknowledged,

> Being a race driver named Foyt gets you a lot of attention and yes, there is a certain amount of pressure with it. But the good far offsets the bad. My dad didn't like the idea of me racing at first. He has lost friends in racing over the years and he has been seriously injured in several crashes. He always told me he hoped I wouldn't get involved in the sport. But eventually, when he saw that this was what I was determined to do, he got behind me and has supported me. He expects you to win. He has a very competitive nature. He demands a lot, but I don't mind it.[62]

For the most part, he qualified well and stayed out of trouble. "The neat thing about Larry is that when you watch him, you can't tell what the car is doing because he is so smooth," said his driving coach, Butch Miller—a series champion. Larry also was finding the rough-and-tumble world of short-track racing far different than his open-wheel past.

"The closed-wheel car is very different. It weighs twice as much. My impression is it's an easier car to drive than an open-wheel car, but it's a harder car to race. The racing is tougher. The rubbing, the beating, the banging and the closeness. The hardest thing to adapt to is the way you pass people and use the car to maneuver yourself. In an open-wheel car, you don't even think of touching wheels with somebody."

Near the end of the season, Larry captured his first pole position on the high-banked Winchester track, breaking a record set by Mark Martin twenty years earlier. Afterward, he called his father, who had finished second but never won a feature race at the track.

"The first thing he did was ask me if the throttle stuck open," Larry recalled years later.[63]

When his son finished fifth in the last ASA race of the year—his best result to date—and with Harrah being anxious to move into NASCAR, A.J. made a surprising decision. Dale Earnhardt had told A.J. his son, Dale Jr., was moving up to Winston Cup and that his Busch Grand National team was for sale. Despite the challenges still facing Foyt's Cup team and his son's relative inexperience, he decided to buy Earnhardt's Busch cars for Larry to drive in the coming season.

"I threw him out on his own in ASA," Foyt said. "He pretty much handled his team himself and he did a great job. He's got a good head on his shoulders, and he doesn't do anything stupid. If you watch him this year, I think you'll see how smooth he is on the racetrack."[64]

Larry had hoped to spend a second season on the short tracks but was game for the challenge.

"That was between A.J. and Harrah's," Larry said twenty years later. "I worried about getting away from Indy car, but I was also starting to enjoy stock cars and was getting a little more comfortable. We were starting to run pretty good toward the end of the year, and I was really looking forward to another year in ASA. But things moved pretty quickly, and I was moving up to the Busch series. It was a big jump, and I was pretty nervous about it."[65]

The one thing Larry said he wasn't worried about was comparisons with his father.

"There can be only one A.J. Foyt, and there will never be another one like him. This sport is different today. What he accomplished will never be done again. Sure there is pressure to compete and pressure to win, but I feel no pressure to be another A.J. Foyt. But if I can have an ounce of his success, then I will be happy."[66]

AJ Foyt
Harrah's
Racing

CHAPTER 30

SURPRISE, SURPRISE

2001–2002

A.J. Foyt's surprise decision to buy Dale Earnhardt's Busch Grand National team for son Larry to drive was followed by another surprise move. He released Rick Mast, his Winston Cup driver who'd been credited with helping turn his team around, and hired Earnhardt's Busch driver, Ron Hornaday, to replace him.

Hornaday, forty-two, was a two-time NASCAR Craftsman Truck series champion, held the record for most truck series wins, and had won several races as a rookie in the Busch series, almost all driving for Earnhardt. He'd been passed over for a Cup series ride by Earnhardt, who nevertheless put in a good word with Foyt for the driver.

"I was chasing my dreams and I got the phone call from A.J.," Hornaday said when the announcement was made.[1]

"To do what I've done in the truck series and the Grand National (Busch) series and have A.J. Foyt look at me and give me the opportunity to drive a Winston Cup car has definitely fulfilled my whole dream in auto racing."[2]

Although he'd only been working with Foyt for a short time, Hornaday was asked the difference between A.J. and Dale, considered to be two of the most notoriously difficult guys to work with in the garage area. He answered,

> Dale's Dale and A.J.'s A.J. Only when I call A.J., I don't have to go through ten secretaries. A.J.'s got his ways of doing things, but it still goes back to the basics—it's still a race car, still a piece of metal. He's not just a guy who comes to the shop, he goes *through* the shop. As long as you're up front

◀ Harrah's moves to NASCAR. *David Nearpass*

> with him, you know where you stand. But we're not foolin' ourselves, you ain't gonna teach him nothin'. He's still got his set ways. I'm just looking forward to a season of learning and keeping A.J. happy.[3]

After saying he thought he had a shot at the pole for the Daytona 500, Hornaday stumbled on his qualifying run. He was running fourth in his qualifying race before he "may have made a rookie mistake" and spun, losing a lap in the process. He finished twenty-first, and the team was forced to take a provisional starting position. In the 500, he raced through the field to run as high as second before he made another rookie mistake, stalling his car after a pit stop. He compounded the problem by speeding down pit road, leading to a stop-and-go penalty, and he finished seventeenth, one lap behind the leaders.[4]

Larry Foyt had a slightly better time of it in his inaugural Busch series run. After qualifying thirty-sixth, he finished all 120 laps on his way to a nineteenth-place finish. He even led a lap when the team had him stay on the track during a caution flag while everyone else pitted.

"He held his own pretty good," A.J. said of his son. "A couple of times I could see some things he was doing wrong. One time he got down low and lost seven or eight spots. I told him to 'Get up high and stay up high.' I had to holler at him a couple of times."[5]

Larry acknowledged he'd heard from his dad during the race.

"He's definitely tough on me. He has expectations. He knows this is just my second year in stock cars. He realizes how tough this is."[6]

The big story at Daytona, however, was the death of Earnhardt, who was involved in a last-lap crash while his cars driven by Michael Waltrip and Dale Jr. went on to finish first and second. His was the fourth in a series of NASCAR deaths over the past year that were the result of head injuries. Discussions started again about the use of the recently developed Head and Neck System (HANS device) designed to reduce such injuries. Earnhardt had refused to wear one, and only seven of the forty-three drivers who started the race did. Foyt said he was against mandating use of the device.

"Dale's crash was like Scott Brayton's (who was killed in practice for the 1996 Indianapolis 500), it didn't look that bad," he said. "But it's not necessarily the speed that kills, it's how you hit the wall.[7]

"In certain incidents, it could work, but I don't think it would have made any difference in Dale's death. Personally, I would never want to be constrained like that. I always wanted to be able to move my head around in the car."

Just over a month later, when some drivers started talking about a possible boycott at Talladega because of the high speeds and close racing, Foyt spoke out again.

"It's ridiculous," he said. "I never worried about getting killed in a race car. If you are worried about it, you need to do something else. That's the problem. We got too many plastic drivers."[8]

"He [Earnhardt] wouldn't want them to be whining or crying over him. Sure, I hate it. Sure, they'll have it on their mind and know what happened, but a lot of people died at Daytona. Dale's not the first person to die there."[9]

It would take until nearly the end of the year and the death of another driver in an ARCA stock car race before NASCAR mandated that drivers use a form of head restraint. It was more than a year before the IRL created a similar requirement.

The first race of the IRL season wasn't until March at Phoenix, the traditional opener at Disney World Speedway having been dropped from the schedule. The year had already started on a sad note with the death of Jim Gilmore in a snowy car accident. Foyt's close friend and sponsor since 1972, Jim had said his most cherished possession was the 1977 Indianapolis 500 winner's ring Foyt had given him.

With Gilmore gone and Harrah's shifting some of its sponsorship dollars to NASCAR, Foyt was down to a single car to start the season. After some discussion, he retained Eliseo Salazar, shifting him into the No. 14 car.

"Eliseo did a great job for me last year," he said. "I think we surprised a lot of people who thought this combination wouldn't work. But I like his attitude because he wants to win as much as I do. He stands on the gas and never gives up."[10]

Like others before him, Salazar understood the significance of the No. 14 car.

"Anyone who knows the history of A.J. Foyt knows the No. 14 is very special. I feel honored to be driving that car this year."

Salazar got off to a good start, with a second at Phoenix on March 18. Three weeks later, he led at his home track, Homestead-Miami, but was passed by Sam Hornish and Sarah Fisher near the end of the race, something Foyt made sure Salazar knew.

"You just got passed by a girl!" A.J. said over the radio for the whole world to hear.[11]

The one-two finish by Hornish, twenty-one, and Fisher, twenty, also was an indication of a new generation of drivers moving into the sport, many moving up through the karting ranks. "Both of them are younger together than I am," Salazar noted.[12]

After a fifth at Atlanta, Salazar trailed only Hornish in points as the series shifted to Indianapolis. Foyt offered to run a second car for Billy Boat, who turned it down when a full-season ride came available. "Not running A.J.'s car at Indianapolis is the hardest decision I've ever had to make," Boat said.[13]

Another deal with Scott Pruett fell through, and the rumor mill had Donnie Beechler, Richie Hearn, Roberto Guerrero, and Marco Greco all under consideration. That's when Foyt made a pick that surprised even his own team—Robby Gordon—who'd had a messy divorce from Foyt eight years earlier. Gordon had been fired from his Winston Cup ride for not being able to work with the team, similar to the problems he'd originally had with Foyt. Earnhardt's former car owner, Richard Childress, who was considering Gordon as a possible driver for his team, signed on as co-owner of the entry with Conseco sponsorship. A.J. also offered a car to Beechler if the other two made the race.

"Robby isn't a bad driver," Foyt said. "All he really needs to do is keep his mouth shut. Both Eliseo and Robby will have the equipment to win Indy. I'm shooting for a one-two."[14]

Gordon laughed when told of A.J.'s comment.

"I guess I will need to put a zipper on my mouth," he said. "When I drove for A.J. in '93, I wanted to be quickest every session. I learned a lot from him that year. He retired from driving Indy cars so he could baby-sit me. He taught me it doesn't matter how fast you go if you're not there at the end. You have to finish the race."

Chip Ganassi was back with four cars, including one for Tony Stewart. CART's Roger Penske returned to the 500 for the first time since the split as did Michael Andretti. CART had just been forced to cancel a race at Texas because of the high speeds and "driver dizziness," and Foyt poked fun at the returnees, passing out bumper stickers that read, "Real Men Race at Texas."[15]

Both Foyt drivers were consistently turning top-ten times in practice until the Friday, when Salazar crashed hard. He blew an engine and crashed again before qualifying on Saturday and was unable to make a run. Gordon said he thought he had a shot at the pole, and A.J. ended up telling him, "I told you so," when Gordon's fastest lap turned out to be his warmup lap. He still ended up third fastest.

"The last thing I told Robby was to not wear out his tires with too fast a warmup lap, but you know Robby," Foyt said.[16]

In some ways, it was like old times for Gordon—the good old times.

"He still doesn't even use notes," he said of Foyt. "We did like six or seven changes on our car at once, and you'd think we were going to crash. But it was exactly what we needed. He's forgotten more about this place than most people know."[17]

Things went from bad to worse for Salazar on Sunday when he blew another engine coming out of Turn Four on the final lap with a time that would have easily put him in the race. He'd have to wait a week for another chance.

"If qualifying at Indianapolis is somebody's idea of fun, they're pretty messed up," said a clearly shaken Salazar. "We'll have to rebound. I don't know how, but we will."[18]

Foyt spent the week rebuilding Salazar's confidence and getting Beechler ready for a potential run. Beechler was Foyt's kind of driver, having come up through the midget and sprint car ranks with wins at some of Foyt's favorite dirt tracks, including Terre Haute and the Indiana and California state fairgrounds. He'd run a couple of years in the IRL with several top-five finishes while driving for second-tier teams and had finished twelfth in the previous year's 500. But with the return of several CART teams and drivers, he'd been unable to bring any sponsorship dollars to the table and was left helmet in hand. That's when Foyt said he would fund the ride for Indianapolis.

When Salazar finally made it in the field, it was Beechler's turn. He qualified faster than Salazar, with the fifth-fastest overall time.

Gordon took the lead at the start of the race when he dodged spinning pole sitter Scott Sharp in the first turn. He led the first twenty-two laps, most of them under caution, until the first round of pit stops. Plans for Gordon to pace himself in the early going went out the window when the stop dragged on because of refueling problems. He worked his way back to fifth, and as Beechler and Salazar also moved up, all three Foyt cars were in the top ten with 200 miles remaining.

At one point, Beechler passed Gordon on the track only to be knocked out by an oil leak with forty laps to go. Gordon suffered a similar fate with fifteen laps left.

Salazar finished a lap back in seventh, the top IRL finisher. Hélio Castroneves led a one-two Penske finish, followed by Michael Andretti in third and then three Ganassi cars—clear domination by the CART entries.

Afterward Foyt surprised Beechler, saying he was being added for the next race at Texas.

"I really don't know how to thank a guy like that," said an emotional Beechler. "He's stepped up to the plate and given me the opportunity of a lifetime. I'm just very grateful."[19]

In another interview he added, "I thought that Indy was it. I don't think we're going further than race-by-race right now. He's been more than generous to fund this out of his own pocket. If we land some money in the next month or so, I'm sure we'll continue for the rest of the year."[20]

Foyt said that if Beechler had been able to qualify on the first day at Indianapolis, "he's somebody the leaders would have had to contend with. This is my money, so we're going to have to do what makes sense. But I really like him."[21]

There was still a big problem as the team headed to Texas—there was only one pit crew. Foyt said he would pit the cars on different laps under the green flag. But if a caution came out, he would pit the car that was ahead first—even if it meant hurting Salazar, who was battling for the points title. "I race for wins, not points," he said. "We'll help the driver who has the best chance to win."

Eventually, a pit crew of volunteers and draftees, wearing a hodgepodge of old team uniforms pulled from the souvenir trailer, was cobbled together for Beechler. Foyt's grandson Anthony was one of the draftees and was assigned the left-front tire. When Beechler outqualified Salazer and finished one spot ahead in sixth—good for $45,000—Foyt said Beechler had a ride for the rest of the year.

Texas may have been the high point for the IRL season. After a couple of races where the cars ran well but neither driver challenged for the lead, Foyt got mad. When Beechler said he wanted to protect his equipment, Foyt told him Salazar was going 200 yards deeper into a turn before braking. Beechler responded with a third place at Richmond, his best IRL finish to date. Then it was Salazar's turn.

"I was very disappointed with him in the way we started the season," Foyt would say. "He was just there. And that's not what he's paid to do. I want a driver to race like me. You're not going to win 'em all and you're going to have bad days. But I just want us to try hard.[22]

"Salazer came into 2001 with the wrong attitude. He came with the attitude of trying to win the championship that was, 'If I can finish every race, I can win the championship.' Championships come along with wins."

Foyt made it clear going into the final race of the year that Salazar's job was on the line, and he responded, running with the leaders before finishing fourth. When Greg Ray, the early favorite for the No. 14 car, took another ride instead, saying, "A.J. wasn't far enough along in his plan from an equipment and sponsor side (to) make a commitment"—Salazar found himself back with Foyt, only not in No. 14—that was going to Beechler.[23]

"No driver has ever stayed with A.J. three years," Salazar said, who would be the first. "And we know why. He's a tough boss to please.[24]

"A.J. told me he wanted to see aggression on the racetrack. Sometimes if I didn't have a chance to win and I was running fifth, rather than risk everything to go for fourth, I would settle. A.J. has a different philosophy. He says you have to go for the win, and the championship is going to come by itself. I don't have any problem with that."

As much as Foyt's IRL team struggled, by midyear the NASCAR operation was in even worse shape. After a ninth place at Las Vegas in the third race of the year, Hornaday had raced from last to first and led twenty-four laps at Martinsville before a poor pit stop dropped him back. However, he recorded only one top-twenty finish in the next fifteen races and by the time the team rolled into Daytona for the July 4 Firecracker 400, they had already used up their allotment of provisional starts. When Hornaday failed to run fast enough for one of the top thirty-six guaranteed spots and was subsequently bumped by cars still having a provisional, Foyt turned against the system.

"All this provisional crap is a bunch of crap," he said, to the consternation of NASCAR officials. "If you're fast enough to make it, fine. If I can't make it, I don't want a provisional. Sure, we've used a couple, but I would just as soon have it open to the world—even if you've got 100 cars."[25]

The team brought a new car to Indianapolis for the Brickyard, the home of sponsor Conseco, and averted further embarrassment when Hornaday turned in a banzai qualifying run. His twenty-eighth-place finish was considered an improvement to many, but Foyt just wanted to get the season over.

"It's not as much fun being an owner," he admitted. "I miss (driving). I really do. I know that time has passed me. As you get older, you have to slow down. I don't want to slow down, but I know I have to.[26]

"I hope we get it turned around. We're just a year and a half old. You've got to crawl before you walk. I'm not happy but a lot of people don't realize guys like Penske and Childress had twenty years in this league."

A series of crew chief changes didn't help matters. Although he denied plans to fire Hornaday, he was growing increasingly frustrated.

"There's no reason we should have missed this race and we did," he said after Homestead-Miami, with two races remaining. "Yeah, we've had some bad luck, but I'm the type who believes you make your own luck. I don't know what we're going to do. We've gone through three chief mechanics, guys Ron wanted. We really have to evaluate the program and figure out what we're going to do."[27]

When the team failed to qualify at Atlanta for the next race and was added to the field in the finale at New Hampshire only because rain wiped out qualifying, Foyt knew what he had to do. He released Hornaday. The driver was upset Foyt waited until the end of the season when most of the rides for the coming year were already taken. Hornaday did find one good thing about being released, though: "(Team manager) Tommy (LaMance) has a big nut to crack," said Hornaday, who had bragged at the start of the year about being able to get A.J. on the phone.

"He's got to talk to A.J. every day. Now when the phone rings and they say, 'Ron, it's A.J.,' I can say, 'I'm not here.'"[28]

While the Winston Cup program floundered, Larry Foyt was having a surprisingly solid year in the Busch Grand National series. He finished the season twenty-second in points and fourth in rookie-of-the-year standings, and A.J. seemed to be happy with his progress.

"I've been telling Larry to take it easy," he said. "This is a big step for him. He has to learn the tracks a little bit and learn about the drivers that he's running against."

Larry typically qualified better than he finished and was involved in more than his share of accidents—eight in all, often when he was running best. Not all were his fault, and at times he felt his last name made him a marked man:

> This is a tough game. You're going to have people that hate you. And you don't have to do anything to 'em. You're going to have your fans, and you're going to have people that boo you. It's very cutthroat, because the competition is so close and you have to perform. Maybe that's another reason A.J. didn't want his kids in it.[29]
>
> I think sometimes last year maybe I got spun out a few times because I was Foyt's kid. And I was trying to earn some respect and race clean. But like my dad said, "You got to root 'em right back or they're just going to keep doing it." It is a different style of racing.

Larry wasn't the only younger Foyt having a good year—so was Anthony. The Waller High School junior won five national karting events in a row and branched into Formula Fords, where he set the class track record on the three-mile road course at Texas World Speedway. He even climbed in A.J.'s Silver Crown car for a couple of dirt track races late in the year, although without much success.

As the 2002 racing season approached, Foyt hired thirty-five-year-old Stacy Compton to take over the No. 14 Pontiac stock car. Compton had finished five spots better than Hornaday in the final 2001 NASCAR standings. He had one top-ten finish but had also failed to qualify for several events. After splitting with the Cup team and signing to drive in Busch before being approached by Foyt, he now planned to drive in both series. One local newspaper said Foyt was "trading one so-so driver for another."[30]

The initial test was promising as Compton turned in the second-fastest time to newcomer Jimmie Johnson.

"Stacy has certainly shown that he has the ability to be competitive on the Winston Cup level, and I'm pleased that he'll be driving for us this year," Foyt said. "More important than that, my team is excited about working with Stacy. I don't care if it's Indy car or NASCAR racing, a team has to find the right chemistry and pull together to be successful. For the past two years we've been laboring to put the right people in the right places to take this team to the next level."[31]

A week later, one of those key people was gone: Tommy LaMance, whom Foyt had called his "right-hand man" two years earlier. The team made the announcement in a one-sentence statement saying LaMance had left to "pursue other opportunities in the sport." Others acknowledged there'd been a falling out between the two. A month later, Foyt made another change of crew chiefs.[32]

Compton's honeymoon with the team lasted until April. He arrived in Texas for the seventh race of the season thirty-ninth in points, the same place Hornaday had finished the year before. His best showing was a twenty-seventh at Daytona, and Foyt's patience was wearing thin.

"Our first year we did better than we did the last two," he said. "I think the crew expects him to give a little more, and I expect him to give 110 percent. We've got a good engine program and I've got good equipment. We had to make some changes with the crew chiefs, and I had a couple general managers who weren't telling me the truth on everything. Now everything is approved by me, I can be in China and I have to approve it."[33]

"It's been very hard for me to swallow. I've never had a dry run like this in my whole career, even when I ran only two or three NASCAR races a year. I know the competition is close, but we have the resources and the equipment to be in the top fifteen."[34]

Compton indicated he was hopeful of turning things around.

"On a scale of one to ten, one being the worst, our season is about a two. That being said, I feel like we're on the rise to a five or six or seven pretty quick. I think the season is about to turn for us. We feel that on any given day, we can go out and win a race. We just can't go and compete every week and be a threat to win races, not at this point."

There was at least a semblance of stability on the Indy car team as Salazar and Beechler, the two drivers from the previous season, were returning. That lasted until practice started for the first race at Homestead-Miami Speedway when Beechler crashed, suffered a concussion, and was ruled out for the race. A call was made to Airton Daré, a Brazilian driver who lived in the Miami area and had lost his IRL ride from the past two seasons.

"When A.J. called me I was ready to buy tickets for the grandstands," Daré said. With minimal practice and an underpowered engine, he qualified twenty-first then raced his way into the top five before being pushed into the wall by another car with three laps remaining. He still managed to finish tenth while Salazar was fifth.[35]

"He did a great job for us," Foyt said. "For me being new (to him) and he being new with the team, I thought everybody did a great job. He gave me 110 percent, so what else can I ask for?" When Foyt was asked if Daré might be a long-term replacement for Beechler, he said, "I think so. I have to talk to Harrah's, but I think Harrah's would be real happy."

When doctors told Foyt that Beechler would miss at least another race and maybe more, and Foyt recalled Scott Sharp's multiple concussions and lengthy recovery, he released Beechler and hired Daré for the remainder of the year.

Beechler, who felt he was ready to return and argued with doctors, was upset and said he'd never race for Foyt again.

The team struggled through the next two races at Phoenix and especially on the high-speed California track, where drivers battled aerodynamic challenges. Hoping to correct the problems before practice started at Indianapolis, Foyt scheduled a private mid-April test session at the Speedway.

Salazar was driving Daré's car and had just completed a run and started a cooldown lap when the car suddenly did a half spin and slammed backward into the Turn One wall. He was knocked out in the crash and rushed to Methodist Hospital, where he underwent emergency surgery to repair a torn vertebral artery. Salazar, who said his last memory was going down the front straight, was not wearing a HANS device, and the new softer walls ordered by the Speedway for the 500 had not yet been installed. The impact force was measured at 109 Gs, and doctors theorized the force of his head snapping back at impact tore the artery.[36]

"It was the loudest crash I ever heard," Foyt said at the time. "He just cremated the car and the engine."[37] He admitted the crash and Salazar's injury "really shook us up. It's been tough on our team because he has become a friend. We were really looking forward to running with him but the main thing is that he heals up and takes the time he needs to do it."[38]

Doctors told Foyt that Salazar was through for the season, and Foyt offered the ride to Beechler. The driver had been cleared by doctors to race but was still upset over how he'd been treated earlier in the year and turned Foyt down.

After a one-race drive by Richie Hearn, Foyt hired Greg Ray, who'd been released by his second team in six months. A five-time IRL winner, 1999 series champion, and fellow Texan, he'd qualified on the front row of the Indy 500 the past four years. He was also a driver who had developed a reputation of being hard to work with, and some wondered if his best years were behind him. One reporter described him as "a combination of unbelievable talent and questionable judgement." He'd driven three races for the team in the past, and Foyt seemed to have ignored or not to have heard the recent reports.[39]

"He is a talented driver," A.J. said. "He's a great spokesperson, but what I like about him most is that he knows how to get a car to the front. That's what I'm looking for."[40]

While Foyt may not have heard the stories about Ray, the driver obviously had.

"No doubt I've made my fair share of mistakes, and had the wrong game plan on race day," he said. "I probably can say I've won some Indy 250s, but nobody cares about that. I can't think of a better coach on the planet than A.J. Foyt. He has that magic touch.[41]

"There's three ways to do it at AJ Foyt Racing—his way, his way, and his way. I think we'll do it his way."

The number of CART teams and drivers returning to the 500 continued to grow in 2002, and Roger Penske shifted his entire team to the IRL. Chip Ganassi was fielding teams in both series, with Kenny Bräck making his first appearance in the 500 since his victory. Bobby Rahal, who'd been one of the most outspoken critics of the IRL, Foyt, and Tony George, also entered a car.

Looking back more than twenty years later, Rahal would say,

> I think A.J. understood better than I did at the time the value of the 500. He had a very strong relationship with all the George family and the Speedway. I don't know if it meant everything to him, but it meant a hell of a lot.[42]
>
> I thought, *Well, it's great, but there's other races.* And now, if you ask me, it's like—well, the 500 is *the* race. It changed my life, too, right? So when you get older, you get a little smarter. But having said that, I still felt that CART was the way to go. But it could never survive without the 500.

Once at the Speedway, nothing went right for the Foyt team as it continued to look for the answers to their handling and aerodynamic problems. With LaMance gone, A.J. tried to juggle both the IRL and NASCAR operations. He combined the Busch and Winston Cup teams into one location and asked Larry Foyt, twenty-five and in just his second NASCAR season, to take on a management role in addition to driving.

When Foyt arrived at the Speedway for qualifying, he was disappointed with what he found. He waved off the first qualifying run of both Ray and Daré, and rain wiped out a planned second attempt later in the day.

"We acted like a bunch of damn idiots Saturday," he said early Sunday while the rain continued. "I don't know what happens at Indy. Sometimes you come here and everything goes good. Other times you come here and, I mean, I found things that were wrong—nothing that was dangerous—but stupid, crazy stuff."[43]

After an "old-fashioned team meeting" behind closed doors in which he ripped into the team, Foyt calmed down—somewhat. "We just screwed up. And I am the CEO, I take the blame."

Rain canceled Sunday's activities, which meant the team would have to wait until "Bump Day" to try and make the field. Foyt, who had often joked about the entire Penske team failing to make the race in 1995, now found himself in a similar predicament. After having a driver on the front row in each of the past four years, he was now trying just to get them in the field.

Bräck, who'd remained friendly with Foyt since his departure and spent time with his former boss at the Speedway, saw how fast things were changing with the return of the CART teams.

"A.J.'s team was built around him," Bräck would say. "He had all this information in his head. The IRL at the time was such that you could still do well like that. CART was more computer-driven already. Bigger teams. More technology. That was the main difference."[44]

Foyt said, "I've been doing this longer than some of these drivers have been alive. Sure the cars and engines have changed, but the basic principles of racing have not. In the end someone still has to get into the car and drive it."[45]

Despite the already-uphill battle he faced getting two cars qualified, Foyt approached Beechler again (who'd been unable to find a competitive ride) and asked him to put aside his "hurt feelings," swallow his pride, and rejoin the team. This time he relented.[46]

"It's time to put silly stuff aside and not be an idiot," Beechler said. "I made my point to A.J. and everybody else. But this is too big of a race to miss, the biggest race in the world. And it's a good opportunity for me."

As the final day of qualifying approached, the team was able to find its speed. Foyt spotted trouble with the shock absorbers and made several aerodynamic tweaks that had Daré and Ray posting the fastest times of those not yet qualified. Daré qualified thirtieth and Ray thirty-first, although the clock ran out on Beechler before he was able to make an attempt.

Ray posted the third-fastest lap during the final Carb Day practice session. Foyt stressed the lap showed the team had the speed to compete and that the drivers needed to be patient. It didn't last long as Ray had a tire go down, and he spun and hit the wall before the first pit stops. He finished thirty-third and last for the second time in three years. Daré went on to finish thirteenth, one lap behind winner Castroneves, who drove to his second straight victory and led another podium sweep by former CART teams.

Although CART continued to win the battle on the race track, it was losing the war. Honda announced it would shift its engine program to the IRL, and Toyota followed soon after. The series also announced it would stage its first race outside the United States, at Honda's Twin Ring Motegi north of Tokyo.

While the returning drivers and owners for the most part were gracious, Foyt couldn't help but gloat at times. And when two of the returnees—Penske and Ganassi—started talking about slowing the cars down, Foyt was quick to react.

"What's racing all about?" he asked rhetorically. "Who runs the fastest. It doesn't matter how fast you're going. When it's not handling so well, it scares the hell out of you."[47]

Even though Indy car racing was slowly beginning to reunite, the stock car series continued to boom. "NASCAR didn't make NASCAR, big sponsors did," said one former CART official. "Those companies put the drivers in the marketplace by putting them all over cereal boxes."[48]

NASCAR drivers Richard Petty, Dale Earnhardt, Bill Elliott, and David Pearson had all been featured on a Wheaties box, but the last Indy car driver to grace the cover had been Wilbur Shaw in 1936.

Until now. Ironically, the driver selected hadn't raced at the Speedway in ten years, but if there was any doubt who was the biggest name in the sport, A.J. Foyt's picture on the Wheaties box erased them. "I didn't realize I was ever that young," said Foyt of the mid-1960s photo that turned him nostalgic. "That was before I got full of battle scars. I won't lie. If I could roll back to the younger years, I would. I miss it." He also became part of the new bobblehead collection craze, joining other four-time Indy 500 winners Al Unser and Rick Mears.

A week later at Texas, Daré was third in a close finish—his first top-ten result. Ray was still having problems, and a frustrated Foyt agreed to bring in the driver's former crew chief.

"They're doing their own deal on the car, their own setups," said Foyt, which was a major concession on his part. "I have a little bit of input, but I want them to see if they can pull together. If not, I'm going to be stepping in pretty quick and I'm going to call all of the shots. I have faith in Greg. If I didn't think he could do the job, I wouldn't have him here. I like somebody that's fast and I think if conditions are right, Greg can be very fast."[49]

After Ray failed to finish the next three races, however, the crew chief was gone.

As the July 7 IRL race at Kansas approached, so did the major league debut of another Foyt. A.J. had surprised his grandson on his eighteenth birthday, announcing that a car would be entered for him at the track in the inaugural race of the Infiniti Pro Series—a new training ground for Indy 500 aspirants. Longtime righthand man Jack Starne was overseeing preparations.

"There may be a little more pressure on me because I'm his grandson, but I don't think he'll be all that hard on me," said Anthony, who had already tested one of the team's Indy cars. "I'm not expecting anything different from how he treats his drivers. I know everything he tells me—or hollers at me—will be just for the good."[50]

It was an impressive debut, with Anthony qualifying on the pole and leading sixty-three of sixty-seven laps to take the win.

"He'll be hard to live with now," said the proud grandfather, "but I thought Anthony did a great job. I couldn't be more happier than I am today. We came here with a brand new car. He had no testing and no experience on a track this size."[51]

Despite the victory, Anthony still handled the right-front tire duties on Daré's Indy car for the main event, and it turned out to be another winning effort. Daré caught a break when Tomas Scheckter, who'd led most of the race, crashed with nine laps to go when a tire went down. Daré then got the jump on Sam Hornish on the restart with three laps remaining to post his first Indy car victory and the team's first in more than three years.

"A good team never quits," Foyt said. "And if they start to lay down, they go out the back door. Airton is young, he's eager, and he gives 100 percent all of the time. That's the type of race driver that I want."[52]

It was the end of a big week for the Foyt family as two days earlier Larry had finished eleventh in the Busch series race at Daytona. He'd already finished eighth at Talladega, and it was clear he was making progress, especially on the high-speed tracks. A.J. was already talking about moving Larry up to Cup in the coming year, something his son wasn't too keen on. Larry said,

> My dad's always been one to think that if you stay too long in one place, you're going to get stuck there. I know he wants me to go to Winston Cup next year, but I really don't want to move up that fast. I'd like to have another year in Busch. We've had some pretty heated arguments. He's got his views on what worked back then and, I guess you could say, I've got my more modern views.
>
> I've always trusted his judgment on where my career is headed. It's allowed me to live a dream, so I'm not going to buck him anymore than I

have to. He's got a lot of experience, and wherever he wants me to go, I'll probably go.

More good news followed a few days later when Foyt learned Salazar had made a quick recovery and was being released by doctors to go racing. Rather than bump one of the other drivers from a ride, A.J. went into his pocket again and entered three cars for the July 20 race at Nashville. Just how quickly the fortunes of racing can change was on full display as all three crashed out early in the event, Daré while battling for the lead. The team worked around the clock, and three cars were ready for Michigan a week later. It took its toll, however, as the team's best finish there was seventeenth by Ray.

The next day at New Hampshire, Compton drove his last race for AJ Foyt Racing. The team was forced to take a provisional to make the field—its fourth in six races. He'd qualified sixth for the Busch race and was in contention for the series championship.

"I didn't feel like the finances were there that we needed to be competitive," Compton said of the Cup effort. He pointed out his Busch team had twenty-nine employees while the Foyt operation only had twenty-six. "It wasn't a nasty splitting. I felt like I needed to tell them that I would be better off to concentrate on the Busch program and he'd probably be better off to find someone else. And that's what happened. It wasn't a bad parting. I mean I'm still friends with everybody over there. I'd do it (again) in a heartbeat."[53]

It was something of a surprise however, when the official letter of dismissal arrived at Compton's Virginia home the day after the race. It had been post-marked the previous week.

"I think he's really frustrated and it's easy to see why," Compton said. "My daddy always said that if you want something to be successful you've got to be around it all the time. He can't and he can't run the team like it needs to be run."

Foyt seemed to agree with Compton's daddy. During his career, he often said he had no regrets and wouldn't change a thing. Except once. Shortly after releasing Compton, he admitted,

> I wish I would have not built my shop in Charlotte. I should have built it in Houston or even Indianapolis. Before when I was down there [in NASCAR from 1973 to 1991] I did everything at home. That's what worked for me. I was around the thing all the time. I knew my people. They were loyal to me and if we had a problem, we fixed it right there on the spot. You hire a guy down there and all of a sudden he gets in an argument with another guy and says he'll go somewhere else. And you're paying guys $100,000 that could not make $20,000 working (in the IRL).[54]

While most of the administrative functions had been returned to Foyt's Waller operation, Larry Foyt was overseeing car and engine development in Charlotte along with engine builder David Evans. Compton did have high praise for what Larry was accomplishing.

"Larry Foyt has done an outstanding job with what he's got to work with and I'm really impressed with what he's done. But it's a difficult job to be competitive in Winston Cup and he needs help. He needs A.J. around more, but of course A.J.'s got his IRL team to worry about. That's his baby."

Planning to run two cars in the upcoming Indianapolis Brickyard 400, A.J. had previously tested both Compton and Mike Wallace in preparation for the race. Wallace had finished a career-high second at Phoenix the year before driving for Penske, and Foyt now moved Wallace into the No. 14 car. When NASCAR threatened the team with a $25,000 fine for testing two cars but only trying to qualify one, he brought in PJ Jones, son of his old rival Parnelli, to drive the second car.

In what became one of the most embarrassing race weekends in the team's history, Wallace and Jones turned in the two slowest qualifying times among the fifty cars entered. Wallace was added with a provisional and started last—right where he finished after crashing ten laps into the race.

Jones provided some redemption the following week when he took over the No. 14 on the road course at Watkins Glen and drove to fourth place, the team's first top-five finish.

"I hope I brightened his day," Jones said. "He gave me this opportunity. I didn't know if he was going to give it to me or not. I had asked a few times, or tried to get him to put me in his IRL cars at Indy and other places. But he always came up with I'm too big or something. I always felt like maybe he was holding it against me . . . you know, my dad beat him too many times or something. But I love A.J. He was good to me the last couple of weeks."[55]

It also provided some relief for latest crew chief, Mike Hillman, who said the performance on a road course provided a good example of the challenges the team faced. Hillman said afterward,

> You can't believe how unhappy [Foyt] is that we haven't performed better. Monday morning phone calls are pretty tough to take sometimes. He asked me about three weeks ago, "All right, what is it? Is it you? Is it the cars? Is it the driver? How are we going to fix this? We need to run better."
>
> I explained to him that we've got to get on top of our game. He understands we don't have the big engineering department, we don't go to the wind tunnel all the time, and that's why at places like [Watkins Glen] we can race with 'em. This is about shocks and springs and setting your chassis up and not making an adjustment all day long. This is about racing. That's what we did.

Ironically, Foyt wasn't in attendance at Watkins Glen. He was in Kentucky for the IRL race and to watch Anthony win his third Infiniti series event in four attempts. He'd also won on the high banks of Michigan, where A.J. had experienced three major crashes and expressed concerns about his grandson beforehand. But so far Anthony had met every challenge.

The same couldn't be said about the Indy car program. Ray blew an engine thirteen laps into the event, and Daré crashed out before the halfway point. Only Salazar finished at Kentucky, in fourteenth.

Ray would drive only one more race for Foyt, at Gateway Raceway near St. Louis, where he dropped out citing handling problems. His best finish was twelfth in eight starts, and he had led only one race. Afterward, he turned in his notice, sounding a lot like Compton.

"The reality of the situation is that we are a three-car team operating on a single-car budget," he said. "The mechanical failures and other problems we've encountered are due to the limited supply and excessive demands we have put on our people and equipment, and that puts a strain on the entire team, from top to bottom. This is the most appropriate thing to do in this situation—for Foyt Racing and for Greg Ray. The IRL is so competitive that it's nearly impossible to be successful when you're operating beyond your resources."[56]

Cutting back to a pair of cars didn't help in the final two races of the season as both Daré and Salazar failed to post a top-ten finish. The NASCAR situation was a little better as Wallace finished tenth at Bristol and posted seven top-twenty finishes in the final fourteen races, and most expected him to be brought back for 2003.

Things had gone in the opposite direction for Larry Foyt's Busch series program. As his management responsibilities increased, the team's on-track performance suffered. After the eleventh at Daytona in July, Larry posted only one more top-twenty finish in the remaining sixteen races. It was still good enough for twentieth in the final point standings, judged by most to be a solid second season, and Larry was looking forward to the coming year.

Anthony continued to be the success story as he won four of seven Infiniti races and the series championship. There were difficult moments, however, especially after he finished sixth at Chicagoland Speedway.

"I chewed on his butt from Chicago to Houston," A.J. said. "It's the first race I think he'd have rather rode home in the truck than on the airplane with me. But you live and learn through your mistakes."[57]

Questions soon started about the possibility of Anthony moving up to Indy cars in the coming year. He'd be nineteen on race day of the next Indianapolis 500, and if he qualified, he'd be the youngest driver in race history. A.J. made it clear how he felt while leaving the door open for other possibilities.

"I'd rather see him in college right now," he said. "But he's run real good and he's focused 100 percent on driving. I don't want to rush him because he's doing a great job."[58]

century21cr.com
costa rica
foytracing.com
ABC
Supply Co. inc.
ABC
Supply Co. inc.

CHAPTER 31

ALL IN THE FAMILY

2003

A.J. Foyt always paid close attention to the business news, and he'd known for some time that Conseco, the Indianapolis-based insurance and financial services company and his major NASCAR sponsor, was in trouble. The race-loving CEO of the company had been removed shortly after signing the four-year sponsorship deal with Foyt in 2000, his aggressive acquisition strategy judged a failure. The problems were worsened by the worldwide financial crisis created by September 11, 2001.

Despite the company's worsening situation, it had fulfilled the first three years of the four-year commitment to Foyt. That was about to end. After missing its massive interest payment in the fourth quarter of 2002, failing to restructure more than $6.5 billion in debt, and facing a federal investigation into its accounting practices, Conseco filed for chapter 11 bankruptcy protection in mid-December—the third-largest bankruptcy filing in US history at the time.

Foyt estimated he'd already put about $5 million of his own money into the NASCAR program, and if it was to continue, he needed to find more funding for the team elsewhere—with the first tests at Daytona only a month away.

A.J. had already been talking to Harrah's, and the gaming company was agreeable—even preferred—to consolidate its sponsorship dollars from Busch, Indy car, and Infiniti around a Cup program. It was still much less than Conseco's deal and well under most Cup team budgets. Foyt was going to try and run a Cup program with Busch series dollars, and as a result, he was unable to pay the million-dollar-plus rate for Mike Wallace or any other veteran driver. Plans to run a second car were scrapped. Ready or not, Larry Foyt was the team's driver.

In an attempt to save money and take tighter control of the program, A.J. moved much of the operation to Houston, although he kept the facility and a

◀ A.J. with Larry and Anthony (A.J. Foyt IV). *IMS Photo Archive*

skeleton crew of about a dozen employees in Charlotte. He also switched manufacturers from Pontiac to Dodge, which was increasing its involvement. Developmental engines, parts, and technical assistance would come from Ray Evernham's factory team—although with Roger Penske, Chip Ganassi, and Richard Petty all fielding Dodges, Foyt would be well down the food chain.

Foyt shared his big plans for improvement:

> The last couple of years, I didn't want to go to the races because I was so embarrassed. I'm not used to running in the back row. You're going to see an operation completely different than you've ever seen before. It's going to be like an A.J. operation should be.[1]
>
> It's going to be back to "my way or the highway." I have been really nice to some people and it didn't pay off and you've seen where we were—we were in hell running last, and that's not my way. I've got some good people that I believe in. If they make a mistake, they tell you. That was one of the big problems—they kept trying to cover up things like some of these big corporations in Houston.

Foyt said he understood and appreciated the challenges Larry had faced the previous year.

"I threw him in there with a pack of wolves, maybe on purpose. It will be easier now because he has a lot of supervision to lead him the right way. He's had a hard road coming up here, but now he doesn't have to worry about hiring and firing."

Larry also understood the situation his father had been trying to deal with. He'd shown gradual improvement as a driver during the two years of Busch Grand National competition but admitted it had been difficult learning how to run a team at the same time.

"At times I had some doubts about keeping my head above water," Larry said. But I got through it and I'm stronger and smarter for it, as a driver and a businessman."[2]

"I'm just glad I get to focus on driving this year. Running the day-to-day operations was a lot for me, especially not having been in the business that long. My dad has worked really hard to turn that around. We've hired a lot of new people, and I'm super excited and a bit nervous."[3]

"I wanted to stay in Busch another year, but my father really didn't like the pay scale. He was losing money on it, and A.J. doesn't like to lose money. It's an uphill battle, I'll be the first one to say. It's something he feels like I'm ready for. Whether other people think I am or not, he really doesn't care."[4]

Years later, Larry would look back on the decision to move to Cup with a mixture of regret and reality:

> I had some calls from other teams that offered me a chance to stay in the Busch series and run for another year. But I was like, *If this is what my dad wants me to do, this is what I'm going to do. He's the only reason I'm here,*

> *and I owe that to him.* I knew long term I didn't want to do something that wasn't what he wanted me to do.[5]
>
> I was nervous. We were pretty underfunded, and we were going up against some big race teams. You knew, *This is gonna be tough*, but at the same time, *If I can have some good races, maybe we can turn this into something.* It was a great opportunity. You never know as a driver if you're going to get to that level. So just getting the opportunity, I said, "I've got to go for this."

There were also major changes afoot for the IRL program. Foyt arranged a special test for Anthony at the end of 2002 at Phoenix and for help he called one of his former drivers, Davey Hamilton. Hamilton had suffered severe leg injuries in a crash at Texas Motor Speedway in June of 2001. He'd undergone more than twenty surgeries to rebuild his legs, and Foyt heard he was looking to get back in a race car.

Years later, Hamilton recalled Foyt reaching out to him:

> When I first got out of the hospital, A.J. called because he'd gone through some bad leg injuries too. And when he came to Indy, he came to see me. I was still wheel-chairing it. We were trading stories on who had the worse injuries, but at the same time, he was always encouraging me.[6]
>
> Anthony was getting ready to get into Indy cars, and A.J. called me and asked if I was able to drive. He goes, "You're so good at Phoenix, would you shake down the car before Anthony gets in?" So we went to Phoenix, and I'm still on a cane and he goes, "You okay, boy?"
>
> He gave me my first chance to get back in a car after my injuries. I liked being able to help Anthony out and make sure the car was right. But to be honest with you, it probably helped me more than it helped him. It felt so good to be back in the car, and it gave me the confidence that if the opportunity came again, I'd be able to do it.

The setup was to Anthony's liking as he turned laps faster than Airton Daré had in the same car. That was enough to convince Foyt to move forward with preparations to run his grandson in the upcoming IRL season. He estimated it would cost about $4 million a car, and if he had to, he'd pay for it himself—which was bad news for Eliseo Salazar.

"He's been super for us," Foyt said of Salazar. "But if I'm going to run out of my own pocket, I'm going to do it with my own family."[7]

"I know we probably could get some other guy to run for us and win right off. But it will be more important for me for [Anthony] to win for us. We know the first year is going to be a learning curve."[8]

From Phoenix, the team shifted to Texas Motor Speedway, where Anthony earned his IRL competition license in a test conducted by Johnny Rutherford, series special projects manager.

"He had to struggle a bit to go slow enough," Rutherford said. "I can see a great deal of his granddad in Anthony."[9]

Anthony sounded confident he was ready for the move.

"I wasn't expecting to have the success I had last year in the Infiniti Pro Series," he said. "So I'm not really going into the IRL thinking I'm going to win all the races and the championship like that. I'm going to do the best I can, hopefully maybe win a few races and stay in the top-ten in points."

A.J. asked him, "What's your salary?" Anthony, who was working at the team's shop, said, "It's $383 every two weeks," or about $10,000 a year. Foyt had found himself a driver.

The team was also in the midst of changing its engine supplier. Both Toyota and Honda were deserting CART for the IRL and bringing new engines with them. Toyota already had several teams in the fold, including Penske and Ganassi, but agreed as part of its three-year contract with the IRL to supply engines to two or three cars that had been running in the league.

"I just felt this is what we needed to do," Foyt said. "Toyota has done a lot of testing on their engines with impressive results. They seem to be ahead of everyone else at this point. The bottom line is we're trying to put together the best program possible for my grandson."[10]

Toyota had an eye on NASCAR from a marketing standpoint but was still at least three years away from a possible program with that organization. The IRL agreement was seen by the company as a way to keep its racing workforce active and operational.

"We're thrilled to be partners with A.J. Foyt, a name synonymous with Indy car racing," said Jim Aust, Toyota's vice president of motorsports. "A.J.'s team is a proven winner, and his talented grandson shows great promise for the future."

What wasn't announced at the time was that Foyt was taking on a Japanese driver, Shigeaki Hattori, who had backing from Epson, a major Japanese electronics manufacturer. He was signed through Indianapolis. Daré would join the team at the Speedway if all went well and finish the season in the second car.[11]

Foyt also announced Conseco would return as sponsor of the No. 14 Indy car as the company worked through the bankruptcy process. With the Toyota engine program and Epson backing Hattori, Foyt seemed comfortable with the Indy car team's financing.

"If I didn't think I had the money to run beside Penske I wouldn't be here," he said. The news surprised Daré, however, who hadn't been told in advance about the arrangements.[12]

Finally, Foyt said he would keep his Infiniti program going with Ed Carpenter (Tony George's stepson) moving into the driver's seat. He'd finished third in the series' first season behind Anthony and Arie Luyendyk Jr.

As the racing seasons approached, the early optimism was replaced by reality. More than fifty cars showed up for the first Cup race of the year at Daytona, and Larry had no illusions about how difficult it would be to make the field.

"Qualifying is going to be a lot tougher," he said. "The Busch Series wasn't too bad once I had my points. We probably won't have provisionals with where we are in the [Cup] points."[13]

Larry soon discovered just how challenging it would be. After starting seventeenth in his Daytona qualifying race, he drafted his way into the top ten before being shuffled back prior to pit stops. That's when an old Foyt team problem struck again—he ran out of gas coming into the pits. He was a lap behind by the time the engine was restarted and out of the 500.

There'd been an even bigger wakeup call for Anthony. In an early test session at Homestead-Miami Raceway, where the first race would be held, he was still running warm-up laps when he slid up the first turn and into the wall. The car was badly damaged, although Anthony walked away from the crash.

The team had to scramble to build a new car in time for the March 2 opener, and when it arrived at the track, Anthony promptly crashed it. Hélio Castroneves had been following him and dove underneath in the turn to pass. The move surprised Anthony, who moved up the track and out of the groove, sliding into the wall and badly damaging the right side of the car and transmission.

"I knew he was on my bumper (going into the third turn), but I didn't think he was going to dive in on me like that—not in practice anyway," said Anthony, who admitted his confidence was "pretty low."[14]

Castroneves took the blame, saying, "It was not his fault. I was on the inside and he let me go. He went a little off line (into the excess rubber) and there was no turning back. From then on, I don't do that. I told [Anthony] not to be such a nice guy next time."

A.J. agreed with the two-time Indy 500 winner and series defending champion but added a more aggressive suggestion for his grandson: "Next time just turn left and blast him and let both of you go to the wall. That will break him of that habit."

Anthony still managed to qualify seventeenth of twenty-one cars, making him the youngest driver ever to start an Indy car race. But of the non–Chevrolet powered machines, only teammate Hattori was slower. In the race, Anthony stayed out of trouble and finished where he started, six laps behind first-time IRL winner Scott Dixon. Anthony and Hattori were the last two cars still running. There was no mention that "a girl," Sarah Fisher, had beat them both.

"He ran the whole race and did what I asked," A.J. said. "He's on a learning curve, but I think he's off to a good start."

At Phoenix, he collided with Sam Hornish, knocking the other car out of the race, and he was soon sidelined with handling problems. At Motegi, he ran as high as eleventh thanks mainly to attrition before he wrecked by himself on the main straight. He wasn't the only one as eleven of the twenty-four cars crashed out of the race. Fortunately, there were three weeks for the team to rebuild its cars before practice started at Indianapolis.

Larry Foyt was finding things even tougher than expected, having used up his allotment of provisionals and failing to qualify at Bristol. But when the NASCAR circus reached Texas for the March 30 race, the team seemed on the verge of turning things around, qualifying thirtieth.

Larry said,

> I hate that we have struggled as much as we have. It kind of wears on you. It wears on your confidence. These drivers out here are the best in the world at stock car racing. So it makes it tough when you've got a rookie driver like myself. The team has been really great, they've really been behind me. We've got a big uphill battle to fight, but I think days like today, where we qualify on speed, are the little victories we've got to be proud of. Hopefully we can get a good race here and just get a top twenty-five.[15]

It wasn't a top twenty-five but it was thirtieth—his best Cup finish to date. Next on the schedule was Talladega, a track where Larry had posted his only top-ten NASCAR finish. Instead of continuing to improve, however, everything unraveled. The team brought a new Dodge Intrepid and it was judged to be too low. A.J. was upset the team wasn't given a second chance and pulled Larry from the Martinsville race the following weekend.

After a week steaming about his treatment and a long flight to Japan for the Motegi race, A.J. unloaded on NASCAR to a group of Indy car reporters who were only too happy to pass on his diatribe. He attacked NASCAR leadership on everything from racing back to the yellow flag, restrictor plate racing, and not enforcing the rule against passing below the yellow line at the Talladega. And he was just getting warmed up:

> More people are waking up to NASCAR, but they are afraid to speak out. I have nothing to lose. NASCAR is so crooked. Whoever you are, I don't care what you say, if you can't see that, then you are blind.[16]
>
> All it is anymore, restrictor plate cars, is a glorified IROC race. If you are going to go racing, then go racing. But if you want an IROC race, then just call it [that]. I've never been for plate racing and I never will be.
>
> After what NASCAR did to me at Talladega last week, we didn't see any point in going to Martinsville and tearing something up. The deal they did to us at Talladega was a big (expletive deleted) deal.

None of which was going to help Larry Foyt.

There were, however, advantages of having a four-time Indianapolis 500 winner as your grandfather at the Speedway. A.J. and Anthony spent time during a break in a mid-April practice session for the Infiniti Pro Series running laps in a passenger car around the track.

"I ran about twenty laps and showed him the line," A.J. said. "I let him drive about sixty laps while I talked to him. I think some of it soaked in pretty good. He was very smooth. He might never run as smooth again, but today, he ran as smooth as anyone could."

Even though he already had three Indy car races under his belt, Anthony admitted to being nervous in advance of the Speedway rookie test. The smoothness carried through, however, and he became the youngest ever to pass. Yet there were some who still wondered if he was ready. No one was more concerned than Nancy Foyt, Anthony's mother and the wife of A.J.'s son Tony.

"Being around racing like we have, we have seen what can happen," Nancy said. "You don't want to think about it. That's why I'm always checking him out, to make sure it definitely is his passion. I ask Anthony every day, 'Do you really love it?' He always says, 'Yes mom.' All we can do is everything possible to help him. He doesn't want to fail anybody—us, himself and especially A.J. I told him he's going to have to grow up a lot faster than his friends. He has a lot of responsibility to his team."[17]

Anthony had been six when his father gave up his successful horse training career and moved the family to Hockley, Texas, to oversee A.J.'s properties. Slight as a child—A.J. called him "pee-wee" at times—and an excellent rider, most thought he had a future as a jockey. He'd even practiced starts on horseback at Churchill Downs as a child. That started to change when he underwent a growth spurt, and his uncle, Jerry Foyt, bought him a junior dragster. That kicked off a rapid ascent through racing's minor leagues.

At times, he was still very much a teenager, into video games and hanging out with his friends. He'd also continued to impress his family and the race team with his skill on the track and willingness to learn and do just about anything at the race shop.

"I was nervous, but everything went so smoothly right out of the box," said Anthony, who shared his grandfather's good looks and had an even deeper Texas drawl. "It kind of took all the nervousness and pressure away. It's a tough place, and I've got a lot to learn about it."[18]

He was soon turning laps at more than 228 miles per hour, within sight of the previous year's 231 mph pole speed. A.J. was on the radio as he pulled into the pits.

"Congratulations," he said. "You went faster than I ever did at Indy."[19]

The celebration didn't last long as Hattori and then Anthony became the first two drivers to crash in practice. Hattori suffered a concussion and a broken finger. Anthony spun coming out of the fourth turn and brushed the wall then skidded down the track and hit a second time. His confidence shaken, it was clear Anthony was feeling the pressure as qualifying approached.

"It would mean a lot to me and my whole family, because the Indianapolis 500 has meant so much," he said. "He tells me to make sure the car is doing what I want it to do, to make sure it feels good every moment, and if it doesn't to come into the pits right away. At these speeds, too much can happen too quickly to take chances."

Qualifying was a wild affair. The first day was rained out, and while day two was dry, it was cold, with wind gusts of up to thirty-eight mph. Both Penske drivers initially parked their cars and eventual fast qualifier Castroneves called the conditions "brutal." Former pole sitter Scott Sharp crashed in Turn Two and said it was "one of the hardest days I've ever gone through driving here."

Anthony went ahead with his first run as planned but coming out of the second turn on his first lap, he did a 180-degree spin. He regained control and was rolling backward down the track when his grandfather came on the radio.

"A.J. was watching on the big screen and he saw it happening," Anthony explained years later, saying it was one of his most memorable experiences at the Speedway. "I was going backwards, but under control, trying to catch my breath. I was wondering why or how I didn't hit anything. Good and bad. Bad that you spun, good that you didn't hit anything. I was thinking how thankful I was for that, just letting it coast."[20]

"Then A.J. comes on the radio and says, 'Press on the damn brakes.' He'd been watching me roll down the back straight and wanted it to be fully stopped before he could relax. That's definitely a moment I'll never forget."[21]

He returned in the backup car, and neither Anthony nor the car had the same speed as he turned in a four-lap average of 224 mph, slower than he'd been running all month and the second slowest speed of the day. He blamed himself, saying he had used the wrong gear for the run.

"I'm not happy with him and I know he's not happy with me," A.J. said, although he later blamed the spin on a loose bolt and apologized. Anthony insisted he had nothing to prove:[22]

> I was definitely disappointed in my run because we ran so much quicker earlier in the month and we had been running pretty consistent times before then. It seemed like we got here and everything was going good and then it kind of got a little worse day-by-day. We know we can do better than that.[23]
>
> I think some people may look at my last name being Foyt and they expect me to come out and do really well right off the bat, but I think those people around the racetrack and around racing know I've got a lot of learning to do and know it's going to take time. I'm not really worried about trying to match A.J. It would be awesome to accomplish some of the stuff that he has accomplished, but he's the best race-car driver in the world so it's kind of hard to say I'm going to match that.

Both Hattori in thirtieth and Daré in thirty-third made the field on the second weekend. There'd been little drama as the biggest question was would there be enough cars to fill the traditional grid of thirty-three starters. The excitement was provided by Anthony, who crashed again during practice.

With the lineup set for the 500 and no action taking place on the track until Carb Day, a new controversy erupted. Bobby Unser—in town to promote his new book and looking to create a little news coverage—took Foyt, George, and the IRL to task, saying Anthony Foyt wasn't ready to drive in the 500.

Unser said Anthony "is going to hurt himself and someone else if he's not careful. The kid is not a bad kid. He's healthy, he's strong, he's got a good brain—he just shouldn't be here yet, that's all. He just needs more experience, in my opinion. I think someday he may be a really good driver. But this is not the place to start."[24]

Unser added, "He is, best I can tell, one to three years ahead of himself. It's simply a matter of somebody pushing too much. He knows that. You can tell by looking at him that he knows he's not experienced enough to be here. He needs to run a lot of races. It's all a matter of Foyt's power with Tony George. I tried to talk with Tony about this the other night. He didn't want to hear it."

Once friends, Foyt and Unser had parted ways years earlier. The split started when Foyt testified against Unser in the legal case with Mario Andretti to decide the 1981 Indy winner. Unser called A.J. a bully on national TV, and his calls later for Foyt's retirement only made things worse. Several other drivers reportedly agreed with Unser about Anthony, although they asked that their names not be used. That was enough to set Foyt off.

"Can you believe that crap? It's a damn good thing they didn't give their names 'cause I'd beat the crap out of each and every one of them. There's a lot of drivers walking around like, 'Why do you want that young punk in that car?' But everybody has got to start somewhere. And I think he's better than most of them. That's the reason they are walking around, because they never amounted to too much in a race car."[25]

"I was always beat down by the press or media. I couldn't do this or I couldn't do that. That made A.J. Foyt work harder. And I think he's got the same attitude as that. He doesn't really show it like I used to, but I think that's one thing that ticks him off pretty bad—when they start saying things about him. Because he knows how to win. He's won a lot of championships, and he's thinking, 'Just wait and see. I'll have my turn.'"[26]

Rick Mears was one who spoke up in defense of Anthony.

"He's OK. From what I've seen, he's precise and consistent. But he's learning. He needs a little time. You don't get the time when you're a junior, though. If you're a junior everybody's watching."

Andretti, who'd praised Anthony after the backward run, was more critical after the most recent crash. "If the crew (screwed up) as A.J. said, Anthony should have felt that coming out of the pits. That's experience and that's what he doesn't have yet." Andretti indicated the IRL's chief driver evaluators—Al Unser and Johnny Rutherford—might be too close to A.J. "Who's going to tell A.J. Foyt his decision is not the right one?"

Finally, IRL vice president of operations Brian Barnhart had to deny reports the organization was prepared to park Anthony or confront A.J. about his driver's readiness:

> Believe me, if Anthony didn't deserve to be out there or have credentials to be there, he wouldn't be running. But Anthony has very good credentials. He's had a rough go. But I've seen guys with all the experience in the world get lost around here. That kid's got a lesser amount of experience and this is a very difficult track. It's critical for him to have confidence and have his head in the game, but my concern for him is no more than for anyone, and no less.[27]

There was finally some good news for the Foyt teams as Carpenter, twenty-two, won the pole for the inaugural Infiniti Pro series race at the Speedway and went out and led all but one lap on his way to victory. Afterward, he got a handshake and a "good job" from his car owner.

"A.J. is a man of few words," Carpenter said at the time. "I know he would have said a few more to me if I messed up."[28]

In many respects, Carpenter was family. He'd been around the Foyt garages since Tony George drove for the team in the ARS series and worked on the pit crew. His mother had handled timing and scoring on the team's pit stand.

"I was very fortunate to be around him at a young age," Carpenter said twenty years later. "Obviously, I knew he was a legend and a hero, but I was lucky to have access to him that other people didn't have. I remember visiting him at Methodist after he had his accident at Elkhart Lake. I'd had a quarter midget crash and somehow come out of it with a black eye. He was pretty beat up, but he was giving me a hard time about crashing."[29]

Carpenter said of the Infiniti Pro ride,

> It was great to get my first experience at the Speedway driving for A.J. because he was very hands-on with that program. He talked about the flow and the rhythm and what parts of the track you need to focus on to be successful in passing.
>
> I've always been a very inquisitive guy when it comes to the mechanical aspects of the car and probably asked more questions than he wanted to answer. At times it was, "Don't worry about the car, just go out and drive it." I've always built confidence from understanding what was on it, but at the same time it was good for me because it simplified my focus.
>
> I think the program was fun for him too. It was more like racing used to be. We weren't using engineers like the Indy car team, and it was me, A.J., and Jack Starne. It probably took him back a little bit, and he probably enjoyed it more.
>
> I remember before qualifying, Jack and I were having a discussion about what ring and pinion to have in the gear box, because this was by far the fastest place we raced. Everyone was going to a taller ring gear for more top speed, and that's what we were thinking. A.J. convinced us to go with the shorter gear because he thought we'd get better runs in the short chute and that momentum would give us more top-end speed at the end of the straightaways. We trusted him and ended up sitting on the pole and winning the race, and I think that was why. That's something I think about regularly, even as we pick gears today.
>
> Winning the first Freedom 100 was a big springboard and put me on the map of Indy car owners and got me my opportunity to break in to the Indy car series. And I wouldn't have won that race without him, that's for sure."

For the most part, Anthony tried to keep a low profile, finally opening up a couple of days before the race. He sounded a lot like his grandfather:

> I passed my rookie test to get my IRL license. I came here and passed my test to try to qualify for the Indy 500. You know, we got great guys out here testing us and if they didn't think I was ready, I wouldn't be in the race. Everybody else can say what they want to say, it doesn't mean nothing.[30]
>
> I knew a couple of times it was a car problem when things just happened out of the blue and there's nothing you can do about it. You come in and find out what's wrong and say it. If nobody wants to believe it—drivers and Robin Miller and who else—that's their problem.
>
> I'm just a rookie, just like everybody else was at one time. I made the mistakes they made. It's easy to look at somebody and criticize a rookie making mistakes, but they need to think about what they did as a rookie.

The race did not go well for any of the three Foyt entries. Hattori finished right where he started, in thirtieth, the victim of a broken fuel system before the race was a hundred miles old. Daré ran as high as second early because he stayed on the track when most others pitted. The strategy fell apart when he had a long stop, and his race ended on the wall in Turn Two on lap 126 as he tried to catch up.

Anthony lost several laps at the start when he was forced to pit to have his radio earplugs replaced. He'd started with new fitted high-tech earplugs, which included sensors designed to measure g-forces. He'd been unable to hear, however, and A.J. called him in to have them switched out for an old pair. In a move reminiscent of his past battles with computers, Foyt ripped the earplugs apart, tossed them on the ground, and let everyone know what he thought of radios.

"It was just some of that new crap they've come out with, typical computer (bleep), excuse my language. I finally stuck some old ones in him.[31]

"I hate radios. I've had trouble with radios my whole racing career. I wish they'd outlaw the damn things. Everybody wants them, but there's just so much garbage out there."

The old earplugs were too loud and worked only on the front straight. On lap forty-seven, A.J. called him back to the pit and held him there for nearly four minutes while the team went over the car. Hopelessly behind and slow on the track, Anthony drew the attention of race control.

"I need the fourteen to pick up the pace or he doesn't stay out there," Barnhardt radioed A.J. He said Anthony was running laps at 219 mph, while the leaders were running 225. "I need more speed out of the fourteen."[32]

Foyt radioed his grandson: "You gotta get moving or they'll park you," and Anthony added enough pace to stay on the track.

"The best thing was coming off Turn Four, seeing the checkered flag and knowing the race was over," Anthony would say. "It was such a long, tough day. I was just glad to get it over with."[33]

Afterward Foyt said, "I'm proud of him," and called it "a huge learning experience.[34]

"He was kind of up and down on his speeds, but it was the first time the kid has ever run a 500-mile race. But all and all, you can't fault him. You look at a lot of guys that kind of badmouthed him early in the week. A least he stayed out of trouble and I don't think he got anybody in trouble."

Or so he thought at the time. Scanners had picked up numerous drivers complaining during the race that Anthony was a hazard on the track and going much slower than anyone else. At one point, Eddie Cheever, handling the television commentary, called him a "moving chicane." Other drivers came in for their share of criticism too.[35]

Anthony also was involved in the race's key pass. Castroneves was leading with thirty laps remaining and seemed on his way to winning his third straight Indy 500, something no one else had ever done. Teammate Gil De Ferran was about two seconds behind when they came up on Foyt IV entering Turn Two. Having already had one close call with No. 14 earlier in the race and unsure what Anthony was going to do, Castroneves said he slowed and then downshifted before making the pass at the start of the backstraight. De Ferran never hesitated and swept past both cars to take the lead for the first time. Castroneves would close to within a car length, but was unable to pass his teammate.

"That was the move of the race right there," the defending champion said. "Second place isn't a bad place at all. It's better than third. I'm happier—or I guess you can say I'm less upset—because it's my teammate up there."[36]

While Castroneves didn't blame Anthony directly, others did, and A.J. felt the need to step in and defend his grandson.

"They all came out and said they were going to go by on the outside, and then they dive under you. You're going to have crybabies all your life. They ain't got no room to talk. They forgot when they started all the mistakes they made and all the crap they tore up, so let 'em cry."[37]

The rest of the IRL season was one to forget. Daré replaced Hattori as planned, but that lasted less than two weeks as he crashed in practice for the next race at Texas, breaking both his right leg and arm. Jaques Lazier stepped in for four races and placed tenth at Kansas, his final for the team. Anthony continued to struggle, crashing hard at Richmond and having numerous run-ins with other drivers.

The NASCAR team wasn't doing any better. Going into the Brickyard 400 on August 3, Larry had qualified for just twelve of nineteen races. His best finish was twenty-eighth at Dover, and he stood forty-second in points. PJ Jones tried to recreate his success from the year before on the road course at Sears Point but also failed to qualify. The frustration was beginning to show.

"It's tough trying to build a team around a rookie without a lot of experience," Larry said. "It seems like every time I get used to a car, we go to something else. It's been a big jump, but my dad felt that if you have to take that learning curve sometime, you might as well do it now."[38]

Another rookie, Casey Mears, was quick to come to Larry's defense.

"Out of the whole rookie class, everyone knows Foyt has a very low budget," Mears said. "He's not in the best equipment and you can't gauge his talent based on what he's driving. Maybe looking in from the outside people are saying, 'He's a Foyt, he should be running like this or that.' But we understand the situation. If Larry runs exceptionally well, you know he's driven a heck of a race."

Larry's first laps around the Speedway prior to the Brickyard 400 were special. "I think the only time I had been around the track before was when I was about five years old and Dad took me around in a station wagon." He told his spotter to watch his back because he was going to take a slow lap and enjoy it. "I looked all around going by Turn Two where I used to sit and watch the race and my Dad would wave at us. I'm not sure if I'll be able to contain my excitement on Sunday, and a good run would mean so much to me and the team. I got the chance to race at Daytona in February and July and it was absolutely thrilling. But, to compete at Indianapolis for the first time, I'm not sure if words can accurately describe what it really means."[39]

He almost didn't get the chance. After running speeds fast enough in practice to qualify, he was slowed on his first official lap by a few raindrops that didn't draw a caution flag. He was surprised on the second lap when the right rear of the car slid out in Turn One and hit the wall, then did a half spin and hit it again. He told reporters, "We just took a gamble and it just didn't pay off," but back in the garage he wanted to know what had been done to the car.[40]

Twenty years later, Larry recalled,

> The thing jumped loose so fast, and I hit the wall, and I thought, *Oh my God, what was that?* A.J. was like, "You turned in too early." I went back to the garage, and I was looking at the crew chief and said, "I don't understand. The car hasn't turned in like that all weekend." He wouldn't look me in the eye, and I said, "Hey, what's the deal?" He finally said, "Well, A.J. came down this morning and made some changes." I said, "You've got to give me a heads up that something's different." I had been struggling with some push or some understeer. A.J. made some changes and made it turn, but I wasn't expecting it to turn that well and that fast.[41]

The team still made the race, thanks to a move by A.J. the week before at Pocono. Down to their last provisional for the No. 14, he'd entered the car as No. 50, the number entered the year before at Indianapolis and which he still had rights to. The move saved the No. 14's provisional for the Speedway if needed and it was, although Larry was forced to start from the rear in his backup car. The race itself was uneventful as he moved up ten positions to finish thirty-second, four laps behind the winner, Kevin Harvick.

After Indianapolis, things started to go downhill quickly. The team went through a series of crew chiefs, and Larry failed to qualify for six of the next eleven events. A crash at Talladega resulted in a broken wrist that wasn't diagnosed until after the next race at Kansas. Mark Green subbed for the next races, but also failed to qualify.

"That was my lowest point," Larry would say. "There were races you didn't qualify for, and you were doing it in front of such a big audience. You start to doubt yourself. When you're struggling in front of so many people, it's really easy to lose confidence."

If there was a saving grace, it came in the last race of the year at Homestead-Miami Speedway. As a thank you for the development work and testing Larry had done during the year, Evernham provided one of his team's cars for the race. Larry qualified twelfth, eight spots ahead of Evernham driver Bill Elliott. He ran on the lead lap all day and finished sixteenth.

"Doing the testing for Evernham was great," Larry said. "It was really cool because they were on the cutting edge of technology. I learned a lot doing that, and he really helped me. That was a little bit of vindication."

Rumors started immediately that A.J. was shutting down his NASCAR program. Larry seemed resigned to the possibility—even open to it—and shared just how difficult the season had been:

> At the beginning of the year, it was the first time in my life that I wasn't enjoying racing. I didn't want to go to the track. I dreaded waking up on Friday morning and having to go out there. It's not like you've just failed at a job. You're failing in front of lots of people and its embarrassing.[42]
>
> I've let my dad know I can't go racing again next year the way we've done it this year. This year could ruin my career. There's a very good possibility I could never get another ride. But I don't feel like this year I've gotten a fair shake. What's kind of tough is that I knew it would be like that going in. People said at the beginning of the year that I didn't want to go to Cup or I wasn't ready. It wasn't really that, but I knew the way we were going to Cup and I knew it was going to be a struggle.
>
> There are a lot of things up in the air right now. I feel like if I am able to get into something that's very competitive, I think I will be OK. If I have to go back to the Busch Series or do whatever it takes to get in something I have a chance in, I'll do it.

Just when it seemed things couldn't get any worse, they did.

"We had a two-year deal with Harrah's and even though the deal wasn't a whole lot of money, we were still trying to honor that contract," Larry said. "They bailed on us at the last minute after one year."[43]

14
ABC
foytracing.com

CHAPTER 32

ABC FINDS ITS MATCH

2004–2005

After Harrah's withdrawal, A.J. Foyt's NASCAR program—already in critical condition—went on life support. It was a refrigerator-white No. 14 Dodge Intrepid that showed up for the 2004 Daytona 500. With no sponsorship, the team skipped preseason testing, and the car hadn't seen the inside of a wind tunnel—normally a must while preparing for the high-speed track.

"This is all out of A.J.'s pocket," Larry Foyt explained. "My father really wanted to come here and give me a chance to be in the Daytona 500. We've struggled and it's been frustrating. We're hoping to get some [sponsorship] to keep us alive as long as we can."[1]

Larry missed advancing in the qualifying race by one spot, but the team was able to use a provisional to get in the field while landing last-minute sponsorship from the Ladies Professional Golf Association (LPGA). The team struggled throughout the race, although Larry was still running at the finish, twenty-four laps back in twenty-eighth place—still good for more than $200,000 in prize money.

That was enough to take the team to the next race at Rockingham. Larry was again a provisional starter and running at the finish, thirteen laps behind in thirty-second. Afterward, it was Larry who pulled the plug. NASCAR had moved to a new type of tire, and he said until he had an opportunity to test, there was no sense trying to continue.

"I said, 'I don't want to go run around last all day,'" Larry recalled. "We need to test on these new tires and get caught up. Let's test somewhere and try to do it right."[2]

It was more than a month later when the team decided to go to Bristol. They'd done less testing than hoped for but updated their short-track car. It was promptly

◀ ABC Supply livery. *ABC Supply*

seized by NASCAR for having an illegal roof and rear window, typically of no consequence on a short track. The car of Chip Ganassi was impounded for the same reason.

Down to only their speedway car and rather than risk it on the notoriously difficult Bristol track, the team went back to Texas, where Larry qualified on speed and finished thirtieth. That was enough to get them to Talladega two weeks later, but Larry was out of provisionals, and when he failed to qualify, A.J. stepped in. Enough was enough. He was shutting the program down.

The news came with a carrot for Larry—a chance to qualify for the Indy 500. At first, he thought his dad was kidding.

"Maybe it started as a joke," Larry said, "But when he asked me if I wanted to come give it a try, I said, 'Definitely.'"[3]

"I learned a lot last year," Anthony Foyt said at the start of the IRL season. "My goals are to be competitive at every race and to finish in the top ten in points."[4]

After three races, it was debatable how the team was doing. Anthony was running at the end of the events leading up to Indianapolis, finishing fifteenth, fourteenth, and fifteenth. In two of the races, he'd been many laps behind the winner, and in all three either the last or second-to-last car running.

One thing was apparent in the early going—the performance advantage the Toyota engine had enjoyed the previous year was gone. The company had announced it was shifting to NASCAR beginning in 2006, and it was clear its focus was elsewhere. The Honda engine was now the powerplant to have, and Honda-powered cars won two of the first three events. Foyt started referring to the "pokey-hontas Toyota," and at one point, A.J. confronted company executives and engineers on their pit stand.[5]

"He was upset, visibly upset," recalled Jim Aust, Toyota's motorsports vice president:

> He slammed down his fist and said he wanted to make "damn sure he was getting the same horsepower" as the other teams and wanted some kind of proof. He had a tendency to do that. That's his personality, and everybody understood it. That was just A.J. being A.J.[6]
>
> We assured him that was the case. We built the engines by hand, and they had to be within a certain tolerance horsepower-wise. Engines weren't assigned to any specific team. His engines were put together just like all the other ones, and they were within a certain variance of horsepower, and that's the way they were sent out to the teams. He wasn't totally convinced and went off in a huff, but nevertheless, that's the way the program operated.

Although exempt from the Speedway's rookie test as a NASCAR Cup driver, Larry participated anyway, anxious to get his first laps in at the track driving an Indy car. He was the slowest of the cars making laps, but that didn't bother Larry or A.J. Larry said,

> It's everything I thought it would be. This place is obviously so special. I've been here every year of my life, and this is just the coolest day yet. It's amazing.[7]
>
> I was real impressed with how well the car handled. I was just out there trying to get laps and I was pretty happy. My dad didn't want me to push the speed too much. I could have gone faster, but I think that was plenty fast for what we wanted to do today. This whole time, I haven't been nervous. As soon as I went out and got up to speed, everything seemed really good. Today was great, because there was no pressure.

On the first day of qualifying, the two Foyts posted the two slowest times. Anthony was twenty-first after brushing the wall during his run in the green-and-white Conseco No. 14 Dallara. Larry was twenty-second in the No. 41 poppy-red G-Force reminiscent of A.J.'s cars in the 1960s and 1970s and devoid of sponsorship. On hand for qualifying for the first time anyone could remember—A.J. said it was the first time ever—was Lucy Foyt.

A.J. had dialed in plenty of downforce on both cars that limited top speeds but provided more secure handling in the corners. There was little concern about being bumped, as once again the main question seemed to be if there would be thirty-three starters. Only twenty-seven car/driver combinations had turned laps at the track so far.

"I was flat out on the gas, just trying to be smooth," Larry said. "My dad's thinking was that it's plenty fast to be in the race. He's been here a long time and he knows the big pay day comes on race day.[8]

"The speed I ran today, I'm not content with. At the same time, it's the greatest day in my life."[9]

The top-seven qualifiers were all Honda-powered with Toyota engines occupying five of the bottom-eight positions.

"We just don't have the horsepower with the Toyota engine," A.J. said. "We're just down. I knew the first two races that we were down, but I didn't think we'd be off this far. We're just short of power. Honda is the one with all the power and the same is true for Chevrolet. I'm not going to say Toyota won't win the race, but right now, as far as on the high-speed stuff, they're hurting."[10]

Another rookie driver making the field was Ed Carpenter, who'd joined Eddie Cheever's team.

"You've got to remember I worked for A.J. last year," Carpenter reminded everyone. "So this is definitely going to be easier than that was."[11]

The happiest person of all may have been A.J. Foyt himself, who had often talked in the past about trying to discourage those in his family from racing. He'd also talked about how just qualifying for the 500 was one of his proudest moments, and it was clear he felt the same way about his son and grandson making the race.

"I think this will be one of the biggest thrills of my life, getting both boys qualified for the most important race in the world," A.J. said. "It is a thrill of my lifetime to have both of them follow in my footsteps."[12]

Both boys, however, knew that no matter how proud A.J. was, he expected them to perform better in the race.

"If we don't," Larry said, "we'll hear about it from the man himself. He's a tough old Texan . . . Dad can be intense and very driven. He's always told me that second place is the first loser."

Anthony added, "A.J. is very, very, *very* tough. As good a race driver as he was, he will sometimes bite your head off when you make a mistake. When you start out, that can be rough. Once you learn how to deal with that, and take the message from it, then it's no problem."[13]

Anthony tested his grandfather's patience when he spun through the third turn and backed into the inside wall, slightly damaging his backup car—a car A.J. already had plans for.

It had been nearly ten years since Foyt had offered Tony Stewart a chance to drive the No. 14 car at Indianapolis. Stewart had since won both Indy car and NASCAR championships, and they'd stayed close over the years. When Foyt heard Stewart would be in Indianapolis on the final day of qualifying, he called Tony and left several messages inviting him out to the track.

"I thought he was joking at first," Stewart said. "But there's only so many times a guy can call you before you call him back. I got tired of listening to his voice mails."[14]

"I knew he was in town and he didn't report to me, so I said, 'Damn it, you gotta call me back,'" Foyt recounted. "He's a friend of mine. I stay in trouble. He stays in trouble, so we enjoy trouble together. That's why we're friends."[15]

When Stewart arrived, he headed for the Foyt garages. Rain was starting to fall, and it seemed doubtful any more action on the track would take place. With nothing else to do, the two concocted a plan to spice things up.

"I went and saw Hank Bock (head of the Speedway's medical operation) and asked him to give me a physical," Stewart recalled years later. "We was just kind of messing with everyone. When a driver completes his physical they have to call the media center and tell them. We figured that would get everybody riled up."[16]

News of Stewart passing his physical had the expected results. When the rain stopped, Foyt and Stewart decided to rachet up expectations even further.

"It started out as kind of a joke," Stewart said. "A.J. said, 'Why don't you go run Anthony's [backup] car? Might as well go out there and run a couple of laps and stir everything up a bit.' Of course I said, 'Okay.'

"I didn't have anything with me. I was just there to see everybody. I went to Simpson and got a helmet rigged up. I borrowed a uniform and shoes, and Simpson gave me a pair of gloves. I got all the gear I needed."

With the track dry and open for practice, Foyt's No. 14T backup car was pushed to pit road. The seat had been set for Stewart, and his name was emblazoned on the side. Stewart arrived shortly afterward in his starch-white uniform. That's where he was intercepted by Cary Agajanian, the son of J.C. Agajanian and a lawyer used by many of the drivers to draw up their contracts. Word of Stewart and Foyt's plan had spread like wildfire, including to Charlotte, and Agajanian had heard from several people wanting to keep Stewart off the track.

"A.J. and I did what A.J. and I do best—we stirred the pot up," Stewart said. "Got everybody riled up, including Brent Dewar [General Motors racing head]. He was at a picnic with his family, and he was not very happy when I talked with him on the phone. He said under no circumstances would I be allowed to drive that car with that engine in it. That squashed things really quick. We were just gonna run some laps. There was zero intention to try and qualify it."

The Toyota engine in Foyt's car was the stumbling block. Everyone was especially sensitive since the company had announced its plans to go to NASCAR racing but had yet to identify the teams it would be working with. Stewart was also under contract to Goodyear, and all Indy cars ran on Firestones. Ironically, Stewart would eventually drive a Toyota in NASCAR for Joe Gibbs.

Foyt said, "When Agajanian got into it, I said, 'Tony, I'll see you. I'm going to the garage.' Hell, all the General Motors lawyers were running around. That's not racing anymore with all these lawyers."[17]

The day's events were yet another reminder how racing had changed from the time when Foyt would race sprint cars the night before the 500 and midgets the day after. Sponsors and money now controlled when drivers raced, what they raced, and for whom they raced.

As race day approached, attention again focused on the two drivers named Foyt and whether or not they were ready to run in the 500. A.J. was quick to jump to their defense:

> That's a pain in the butt, that name. I mean it's great to have it. It's great to do what I did. But let's face it, A.J. Foyt is not racing no more. The boys are. That's their name, that ain't mine. I just hope they have half as much fun.[18]
>
> I could name you four or five guys who pulled a lot more stuff than Anthony did last year and nothing was ever said. You never read a word about it. Why? Because their name don't mean anything to the world. But any time it's "A.J. Foyt" it means something. I'm still ticked about it. I told some of 'em don't even come around anymore. Mario Andretti? I told him where he can go.
>
> I think both boys are kind of a sleeper. I wouldn't be here if I didn't think they could do something. I'm not here just to see another race. I've seen enough of these damned races.

Foyt probably wished he had skipped this one. Both cars handled poorly from the start, and announcers on the television broadcast noted Anthony was running extremely high coming out of the turns. Working lap eleven, he brushed the wall in Turn Four and then lost control going into Turn One, did a 180-degree spin, and hit the outside wall going backward. He slid back across the track and hit the inside wall. After confirming Anthony wasn't hurt, A.J. reminded him, "I told you about going up high."[19]

"The biggest problem is when he's pushing like that, he won't give up and back off," A.J. told reporters. "I've done all I can do. Maybe he'll learn from this. He just ran out of brains."[20]

Anthony said, "It wasn't anybody's fault but mine.

"I'm just really disappointed right now. I don't know what to say. It's been a long month and it just ended too early for me. I was pushing pretty good and it was just stupid on my part not to be more patient and wait for our first pit stop and make the changes to fix the car. Just really stupid. I'm disappointed in myself."

During the ensuing caution flag and pit stops, Larry Foyt first missed his pit then stalled his car. With his dad screaming at the team to restart the car, he was eventually moved back on the track but in last place.

When rain stopped the race a short time later, Anthony's crew took advantage of IRL rules and repaired his car. It was for naught, however, as he parked it for good after another fifteen laps, complaining of handling. He'd finish thirty-third and last.

Larry was next out. He made it until lap fifty-four, when he slid up into the wall on the exit of Turn Two, just past the family suite.

"We were just really struggling with the cars," Larry said. "I think Anthony and I both missed the setup a little bit. The leaders were coming and I just tried to stay out of the way. Got up a little bit too high and into the marbles."[21]

Larry said his dad was disappointed and "didn't really say much. He said it's been a bad day for us, but we already knew that."[22]

For Lucy, who'd lost her stepfather earlier in the year and was in the family suite for the race, it was a nightmare come true.

"The worst time I ever had in racing was when my sons were driving," she said. "With A.J., it never really bothered me. I knew this was what he was going to do from the get-go. But let my kids get out on that track, and I would literally get sick. I couldn't take it. We didn't discuss it at home much. I didn't want to make them miserable. That was what they wanted to do."[23]

Years later Larry would say, "I get it now. Mom was scared. At the time I didn't really understand it, but when you have a child of your own, you get it. Unfortunately, between Anthony and I, we gave her some scares."[24]

Anthony finished last again two weeks later at Texas when Carpenter moved up in front of him and pushed him into the wall. He managed to finish seven of the next eight races with an eleventh at Richmond as his best result.

"It would be very easy to deal with the bad if you've never won," A.J. said at one point. "But when you're used to winning no, it ain't worth a damn. I hate it. It eats on me bad. I can't wait to get back in there."[25]

With a little over a month left in the season, something seemed to click. After a season and a half of failing to qualify higher than fourteenth, Anthony turned in the sixth-fastest time at Chicagoland and ran up front before being taken out in an accident. He followed it with a seventh starting position at California but hit the wall twenty-two laps from the finish. In the last race of the year at Texas, he qualified eleventh and finished tenth—the first top-ten finish of his IRL career. He finished seventeenth in points.

"The first half of the season wasn't what we wanted," Anthony said. "But the last five races have come together a lot better for us. We've been a lot more competitive and Toyota definitely has improved the engines lately."[26]

Anthony's late-season surge did not go unnoticed. Only twenty years old, several teams in the IRL and NASCAR expressed an interest in talking to him about his future plans.

"It's a possibility," Foyt IV said when asked if he would change teams. "We'll see what happens. I'd like to stay with my grandfather. But this sport is all about money. I have to do what's best for my career."[27]

Ganassi was one team that expressed some interest, and Panther Racing—looking to replace Sam Hornish Jr. who had moved to Penske—was another. He went to a private test at the Texas track but thought better of getting in the car, having not told his grandfather.[28]

"I've had better teams than that one talk to me about Anthony," A.J. said. "A lot of people want him, including some big NASCAR teams. I've talked to Richard Childress several times. They know how good he is. He's won in everything he's ever driven, but he's still a young kid."[29]

With his driver attracting interest and A.J. seemingly willing to let him go, some wondered if it was the end of AJ Foyt Racing.

"No way," Foyt said. "We'll work it out somehow. If worse comes to worse, we'll just pass the hat in church."

"I guess it's the challenge. You need a challenge in life. Life's very short, and when you lay down and give up, that's usually when you go to the cemetery."[30]

After the Indy 500, Larry returned to Charlotte in hopes of somehow resurrecting his NASCAR career. He knew it would be an uphill battle.

"I still really like racing NASCAR, and I'm really happy there," he said. "I had a lot of fun [at Indianapolis]. I wasn't planning on having that much fun. But I still think, right now, I'd like to have a home in NASCAR full-time."[31]

"I feel I've hurt my name enough running the way we have. I still want to race NASCAR full time. But we've got to find a sponsor and make it the right opportunity."[32]

Sponsorship dollars were hard to find, and by midyear, A.J. released use of the No. 14 in NASCAR for his godson, John Andretti, to use. It wasn't until the end of the season that Larry caught on with BAM Racing, the independent team of Beth Ann Morgenthau and her husband, Tony. The team had also struggled without sponsorship for much of the season, although primary driver Ken Schrader had started every race and was thirty-first in points. Several "multibillion dollar companies" had been lined up as sponsors for the coming year, and BAM was hoping to run two cars in 2005. Larry failed to make any of the last three races, however, and when the sponsorship fell through, the team dropped plans to add a second car. With it went Larry's hopes of running another season. He'd try to qualify for an occasional race at Daytona or Talladega in ARCA and all three NASCAR series, but with little success.[33]

2005

A.J. Foyt turned seventy years old on January 16, 2005. The demise of his NASCAR team meant he had more time to do what he enjoyed most: work on his ranch or one of his many properties in the area. At a time when most people his age and means were traveling the world, you could find Foyt at his ranch near the race team's shop in Waller, Texas. His last true vacation had come more than forty years earlier when he and Lucy were joined by crew chief George Bignotti and his wife for a cruise to Hawaii and a week on Oahu. He'd been so "island crazy" that when it came time for the cruise home, he and Lucy flew back instead.

Despite his growing frustration with the Toyota engines in his Indy cars, Foyt often joked with company officials about driving one of their trucks in the NASCAR series it had entered. At least, most thought he was joking. Larry Foyt knew otherwise.

"I think it kills him that he's not out there doing it himself. I know in his heart he still believes, right now, that he can go out there and whip everybody's butt."[34]

The IRL season opened March 6 at Homestead-Miami, and Anthony finished ninth—his best yet. Hidden in the result was that he finished four laps behind winner Dan Wheldon and was the second-to-last car still running as nine others were taken out in crashes. Two weeks later at Phoenix, he finished fourteenth, five laps back.

The next race was at St. Petersburg, the IRL's first road course event and Anthony's first-ever street race. The team missed the series' initial road course test session when the chassis conversion kit didn't arrive in time, and they'd had only a short break-in session on the road course at the old Texas World Speedway. Most of the other drivers, especially those coming over from CART, had extensive road race experience. Although Anthony said he "really enjoyed the road course test, he acknowledged St. Pete "will be a challenge for me on several levels."[35]

After struggling in practice, including one off-track excursion, it was decided to skip qualifying and start at the back of the field. He fell back rapidly at the start and was being overtaken by the leaders on lap eleven when he collided with pole sitter Hélio Castroneves.

"Hélio ran up on me in the bad part of the kink and we made contact," Foyt IV said. "I'm disappointed for both of us, because I needed experience and he had a chance to win the race."[36]

Although Castroneves said nothing, one writer called Anthony "hopelessly slow." Tim Cindric, Penske team president noted that Anthony was "a good guy, but he needs a little more time under his belt."[37]

At Motegi in Japan, Anthony again finished fourteenth, four laps back. Wheldon was winner of three of the first four races, but the big story early in the year was Danica Patrick, the twenty-three-year-old rookie driver. Driving for the Rahal Letterman team, she'd qualified second in Japan and led thirty-two laps.

ABC Supply

While the team struggled on the racetrack, there was good news on the sponsorship front as Foyt reached an agreement with the American Builders and Contractors Supply Company to sponsor the team. The company had been founded by Ken Hendricks and his wife, Diane, in 1982 and had grown to 300 branches in forty-five states. A high-school dropout, Hendricks had started shingling houses on weekends with his father. Forbes now estimated his personal wealth at $2.6 billion and listed him among the 400 richest Americans. The company and its self-made owner were just Foyt's kind of sponsor.

"When I first started racing, I can remember sleeping in the back seat of a car," Foyt said at the announcement ceremony. "Ken Hendricks came up the same way I did. It was the hardworking street. It wasn't an easy street. That's the problem in the world today. Some people have it a lot easier, but when you start from the bottom and work your way up, you really appreciate it."[38]

Foyt and his team were just what the company had been looking to get involved with.

"We were a national company and we were really starting to come along," said David Luck, ABC president and COO at the time. "Our people were dispersed around the country and I wanted to find something to bring them together."

Luck had been a sales executive at Firestone when the company returned to Indy car racing in 1995 and saw firsthand how the sport helped rally employees and rebuild the brand after several down years.

"We weren't looking for advertising," Luck said. "The average consumer doesn't buy our products. We sell to contractors, roofers and home builders. That's a small number of people. But it was a tool to create excitement for our employees."[39]

Critical in the search for the right "tool" was finding the right match for the company's core values.

"Our values were built on respect, opportunity, hard work, have fun, entrepreneurism, spirit, family, give back, and American pride," Luck said. "Anybody can succeed with hard work and the right opportunity.

"There was also an attitude among some that those in the construction business were viewed as kind of a lower class of professions. It's just not true. These people built America with their hands, and we had tremendous respect for them. We wanted something and someone who fit those values."

When Luck read that Foyt had lost his sponsorship, he went to meet with the team owner. He knew of Foyt's history and had met him several times at Firestone, but only in passing.

"We immediately connected," he recalled. "He was the kind of guy that fit our culture—hard work, pull yourself up by the bootstraps, you know, proud to be an American and loves the country where everybody has an opportunity to do great things. I knew he would resonate with our people. I knew that he had the same values that we did. He was a guy that represented all the things that's great about this country."

Six cars were entered for Indianapolis: two each for Anthony (No. 14) and a little-known rookie driver named Scott Mayer (No. 41), and two "TBD" (No. 48)—although most thought Larry was set for the ride.

Hendricks had asked Foyt to consider Mayer for Indianapolis. Mayer ran one of the largest employment firms in the Midwest and, like Hendricks, was from Janesville, Wisconsin. He had little experience or success on the racetrack, however. He'd run three IRL events at the start of 2003, crashing out of all three, and failed to complete his rookie test at Indianapolis that same year. Over the next two years, he'd run three Infiniti Pro Series events. He wanted to try again, and Hendricks was all about making dreams come true. Not even Foyt's magic touch could help, however, as Mayer again withdrew before completing the test. That moved Larry into the No. 41 car and left the No. 48—meant to mark A.J.'s forty-eighth trip to Indianapolis—without a driver.

Near the top of the speed charts from the first day of practice at the Speedway was Patrick. She was already being called "arguably the best female driver ever" by many, and Foyt was clearly impressed by her—in more ways than one.

"I'll say she's beating the boys pretty bad. I don't care if you're a boy or a girl, you have to take your hat off to her. I think she's great. She's got ability and she's a very good-looking girl. She's waking up some of these little deadheads."[40]

At one point, A.J. turned to Anthony and asked, "How does it look to have a beautiful lady like that outrunning you?" He responded the only way he could. "It's kind of embarrassing."

Foyt's comments weren't politically correct and raised a few eyebrows, but he wasn't exactly a male chauvinist pig either. Ed Hinton, one of the best motorsports reporters who'd been covering Foyt for fifty years, came to his defense.

"Foyt's best words of praise for her might be taken as double-entendre, though Foyt didn't mean it that way at all. He spoke in old racers' terminology, which is largely unprintable today. In this era of all G-rated journalism by public demand, Foyt remains as profoundly profane, and as profanely profound, as ever."

Foyt's comments on Patrick distracted from his team's on-track coverage, which was just as well. The Honda engine was now dominant, and even the revitalized Chevrolet-powered cars were outrunning the Toyotas. Both Anthony and Larry failed to make the field on the first weekend of qualifying. It meant little as only thirty-three cars were expected to make qualifying runs, but no one dared to tell A.J. that.

"It's killing me," he said of the team's performance. "It's eating my heart out. I've never been in this position in my life here."[41]

Anthony blew an engine on his second qualifying warmup lap, and A.J. was forced to borrow a powerplant with 400 miles on it from Chip Ganassi. Anthony finally qualified in twenty-eighth and Larry in thirtieth, both cars now painted ABC's red, white, and blue colors. Foyt claimed Penske and Ganassi were getting the best Toyota engines and bristled when asked if he was happy to make the field. "Hell no, I didn't come here to run in the back."[42]

"For the crap he was driving, he did a hell of a job," he said of Anthony. "Our hands are tied. The Toyotas are all different motors, and I think the Hondas are all better than the Toyotas. You can see the difference in the straightaway speed."[43]

The day's big news was made by Kenny Bräck, who was back in a racecar for the first time since a massive accident at Texas Motor Speedway in 2003. Replacing an injured Buddy Rice, Bräck put together the year's four fastest laps. Foyt, his former car owner, was one of the first to greet him.

"I'm real proud of the boy," an emotional Foyt said. "He's just an awesome driver. He was hurt pretty bad. To come back the way he did, it's great."[44]

When it appeared on the final day of qualifying that for the second year in a row there would be no bumping on "Bump Day," Foyt again took it upon himself to try and create some excitement. Larry had driven the No. 48 the previous week and set it up for qualifying just in case it was needed. Sunday morning, Foyt decided it *was* needed, although it wasn't until about 2:00 p.m. that the team caught up with driver Felipe Giaffone, who'd started the past four 500s, finishing third in 2002. After spending a couple of days trying to land a ride without success, he was getting ready to head home to Brazil and shopping for baby clothes when they finally reached him. He grabbed his helmet and uniform and headed for the track, where—without credentials—he had to bluff his way past the famous "yellow shirt" security guards. He still had time for nearly fifty practice laps and then bumped Arie Luyendyk Jr. from the field with less than thirty minutes remaining.

"He did a wonderful job," Foyt said after the run. "It was just hard for me to understand him. But we'll get better communications before the race."[45]

When reporters started asking if bumping Luyendyk Jr. had been some sort of retaliation for the confrontation at Texas in 1998, A.J. set off in search of the driver's father.

"All these idiots are trying to say there's a grudge between me and you," Foyt told Arie. "Your son is a great young driver. You're going to hear a lot more from him. This is just one of those things that happen. I know he feels bad, but he's a super kid."[46]

In the race, Larry Foyt made an early pit stop complaining about the car's handling. The crew went the wrong way on the wing adjustment and when Larry got up to speed entering Turn One, the car swapped ends and backed hard into the outside wall. He suffered two broken vertebrae in the crash and got credit for completing eleven laps and finishing thirty-third.

Next it was Anthony's turn. He was running five laps behind and being passed again by the leaders on lap seventy-six when his left front clipped the right rear wheel of Bruno Junqueira, who'd been running sixth. Junqueira spun hard into the outside wall and would suffer a concussion and two broken bones in his back. Foyt IV was able to limp back to the pits with a broken left-front suspension. That's where ABC pit reporter Jamie Little found him. A shaken Anthony said,

> You know, it happened so quick. I was slow coming out of Turn One because I had a car go underneath me in that corner. Bruno came up on me real quick and went underneath me. I don't really know what happened.

> I feel sorry for him. I'm sure he was running a lot better than I was. It was a lot more unfortunate for him than it was me. He was pretty much by when we touched. I don't know if I tried to turn in to stay out of the marbles or he waited a little bit late to turn in. When you're getting passed in the short chute, you can't get up and give them too much room 'cause you'll get in the marbles and hit the wall yourself.[47]

Broadcast race analyst and former driver Scott Goodyear pointed his finger squarely at Anthony. "I just think that A.J., being off the pace like that, has to give him some room. When a guy's closing in on you at twenty, or twenty-five or thirty, miles an hour faster, you know something—there's not a whole lot of room for error."

The broadcast then showed and rehashed Anthony's crash with Castroneves at St. Petersburg. Goodyear said the crashes were similar with Anthony, "just not giving him enough room, much the same situation as here right now, and, you know, something that's going to weigh a lot on A.J. the fourth."

Goodyear added, "I want to say that I think he is a very talented young driver, but unfortunately, he just doesn't have the equipment that's gonna actually get him up to the front right now. I'd like to see him get something underneath him that might give him the opportunity to really show his talent."

Giaffone in the third Foyt car struggled at the start and at one point was black-flagged for running too slow. He got back on the track and ended up fifteenth—a race-best eighteen places better than he started, although five laps behind the winner Wheldon.

After the race, Goodyear wasn't the only one critical of Anthony, and it didn't take long for A.J. to jump into the middle of the discussion. Not surprisingly, he felt Junqueira had pushed Anthony up the track, and not surprisingly, he took the criticism personally:

> A lot of people are saying the press is getting even with me 'cause I spent a lot of time telling them to go to hell in my day. They tell me that they're writing these things about Anthony just to get even with me. Fine. Our day's coming. It's a two-way street.[48]
>
> I've been up and down that ladder so many times, it's like a yo-yo. I've won championships. I've been at the bottom—if you're on the bottom and you give up, you're a loser. And we're not losers. It's what kept me going every time I got hurt. People would say, "He'll never come back from this one." I came back every time. Quitting, that ain't A.J. Foyt. I've never quit and I never will. Once we get back. I'll laugh at all of 'em.

Unlike the previous year, Foyt's racing team was getting as much criticism as the young driver.

"People say we don't have the computer stuff everybody has," Foyt responded. "That's all bull. I've got the same computers as everybody else has. Most of these engineers I know. I can get help from any of them I want. I've had a couple of them come over and say, 'Hell A.J., you know more than we'll ever know.' It's just what people want to write. I laugh about it."

Two weeks later at Texas, Anthony blew an engine during his qualifying attempt and started last. He moved up four spots to eighteenth, two laps behind the winner Tomas Scheckter, who was using one of the new Chevrolet Cosworth engines. The relationship with Toyota had hit a new low.

"It is tough when you get out and you want to run with everybody and your car is handling well, and you're still three or four miles per hour off the pace," Anthony said. "Toyota says they're working hard, but we also heard that last year and at the beginning of this year. Hopefully, they'll find something to get us up there where we need to be. I know they know we're down, but it doesn't make it any easier on us. What we need to do is get on equal footing."

Two weeks later, Toyota announced it was pulling out of the IRL completely to focus on its NASCAR program. Uncertain about the future of the family IRL team, Anthony ran a stock car test with Ray Evernham and signed on to his driver development program with an eye on running several Busch series races before the year was out.

"A.J. [IV] was very fast in the car and we were very impressed with him," Evernham said. "The kid's been struggling a little bit in the IRL, but he has a lot of people who believe in him. Who knows what's going to happen in the IRL shuffle?"[49]

With the IRL taking two weeks off in early August, A.J. was back on his ranch and on his bulldozer clearing brush when he disrupted a nest of bees. He jumped from the dozer and started running the best he could for a nearby stream about 150 feet away. He fell twice and was swarmed by an estimated 200 Africanized killer bees. He recalled, "When I fell the second time I was ready to give up right then. It's a good thing I didn't because [I was told] that the bees will keep stinging you until they kill you."[50]

He finally made it to the stream, and a man working nearby saw what was happening and called 911. Foyt had been stung dozens of times over his face and in his ears, mouth, and throat, but after being treated at the scene, he refused to go to the hospital. Having read about the incident in the newspaper, a team from nearby Texas A&M University visited the ranch and collected an estimated 60,000 bees.

A.J. Said, "This doctor tells me later, 'First of all, you should never slap at them. That makes them mad.' I said, 'Well, they made me pretty damn mad, too.'"

His face was too swollen to watch the Brickyard 400 the next day, won by Tony Stewart, although Stewart sent him a cell phone message afterward reminding him it was a race Foyt had never won.

"When I see him, I'll have to remind him that I had won Indy three times by the time I was his age," said Foyt, who was back in his office on Monday. He was finalizing a deal to immediately switch his team to the new Chevrolet powerplant. The move paid instant dividends as Anthony ran lap times on par with the other Chevrolet-powered cars. He qualified twelfth at Kentucky and ran as high as sixth before finishing ninth and on the same lap as the winner.[51]

"It's all motor," A.J. said. "We've got that. I feel better. I was tired of fighting to be dead last like we were."[52]

Two weeks later, A.J. made another move prior to the race on the Sears Point road course, replacing Anthony with Jeff Bucknum. The son of a former Formula One driver and one-time Foyt teammate Ronnie Bucknum, Jeff had been driving primarily sports cars. He started seventeenth and finished tenth, which was good enough for A.J. to bring him back for the next road course event at Watkins Glen, where he finished eleventh. A.J., however, missed the race, electing to stay on his ranch and ride out Hurricane Rita.

The following week, Anthony announced he would be moving to the NASCAR Busch series after the final IRL race of the year at California Speedway. Evernham had lined up the same car Kasey Kahne had driven in the Busch series before moving on to Cup.

"I'm not going to hold him back," said A.J., who didn't totally agree with the move and went through the formality of releasing his grandson from his contract. "Anthony wants to try his hand at NASCAR. He's still young and I'm sure some of the advice I've given him will start to sink in when he hears it from someone else. I admit I'm a little nervous about trusting him to the world because he is so young. At the same time, I think we both realize it's time for him to spread his wings. I'll still keep an eye on him no matter where he goes because he is my grandson and that will never change."[53]

Anthony said his biggest disappointment was the inability to win for his grandfather, saying, "We thought we could do it with the team we had. Unfortunately we couldn't." He also understood the challenges ahead. "I'm going to have to pay my own bills and get my own normal paycheck. I've grown up a lot in the past few months, and I'm looking forward to doing this. It's definitely going to be nerve wracking though."[54]

In another article, Anthony added,

> I had to go to him and get permission to put my name out there. I told him that I wanted to try to see what happens. He supported me. My grandfather did the best he could with the sponsors we had and the money we had to operate. He did what he could to put me in the position to win. At times we felt if everything went our way on a certain day we could maybe run in the top five and maybe even win a race. We just never got everything together to do that. I tell everyone this: I wouldn't be here without him.[55]

Anthony crashed out of the final IRL event of the season and then got his NASCAR career off to an inauspicious start, crashing four times in his first three races. He qualified eleventh in his last race of the year at Miami-Homestead and was still running at the finish in twenty-fourth, two laps behind the winner.

Larry, recently recovered from a back injury suffered at Indianapolis, was trying to get his NASCAR career back on its feet. He formed Foyt Racing, using the same facilities he'd started the year with. He hired Brian DeHart, NASCAR's former Busch series head, to serve as general manager. But the challenges remained the same: no sponsor, no cars, no crew chief—in reality, no team.

The end of the year also marked a new low point in the career of A.J. Foyt—team owner. In the ten years since the split between the IRL and CART, AJ Foyt Racing had won pole positions, races, championships, and the Indianapolis 500. But the attempt to form a NASCAR team from scratch beginning with the 2000 season had been a dismal failure and created a major drain on the team's resources, both financially and in terms of manpower. It had also been a major distraction for A.J. himself. The strain of trying to get the program up and running destroyed relationships between Foyt and longtime friends and drove a wedge between him and nephew Tommy LaMance, whom Foyt had been grooming to eventually run the team.

The return of CART's leading teams showed just how far Foyt's Indy car program had fallen behind. It was partly the fault of sponsors, partly the fault of drivers moving on to other teams, and partly the fault of Foyt himself, who was slow to modernize and still insisted on doing things his way—which was often the old way. He'd badly overestimated Anthony's readiness for the IRL and hampered both Anthony and Larry with his overly protective car setups.

The future of the team itself was very much in doubt. Anthony and Larry were off on their own, and A.J. was back to square one with no crew chief other than himself and no driver.

ABC
ABC
Supply Co. inc.
TOYOTA
IMPACT
BOSCH
A.J. Foyt IV
TOYOTA
Firestone
AJ Foyt Racing
IMPACT
BOSCH
Larry Foyt

CHAPTER 33

ANTHONY MOVES ON AND LARRY MOVES HOME

2006–2007

A.J. Foyt's first step to rebuilding his team was to hire Felipe Giaffone, who'd been a last-minute addition at Indianapolis the year before. The thirty-year-old Brazilian driver had spent six years in the Toyota Atlantic and CART Indy Lights training grounds before making the jump to the IRL in 2001, earning rookie-of-the-year honors. His best season was 2002 when he won at Kentucky, posted twelve top-ten finishes in sixteen races, and finished fourth in the series championship. He'd struggled since then, however, losing his ride at the end of the 2004 season and making just the one start in 2005.

"After working with Felipe at Indy last year, I was impressed," Foyt said. "Coming in to qualify on Bump Day, for the biggest race in the world, in a car you've never driven before, for a team you've never worked with before, well, you're either crazy or a real race driver. He proved to me he's a real race driver."[1]

"It's going to take us a little time to get our communication working the way it needs to. He's from Brazil, and I'm from Texas. He's hard to understand sometimes and, from what I hear from my crews, so am I. I know the more we work together, the better our understanding will be."[2]

Both Toyota and Chevrolet had pulled out of the IRL after the 2005 season, which meant all the teams would be running the same Honda engine, something Giaffone noted. He was also realistic about the team's goals:

"I'm glad to be coming back to the IRL with a good team that has a good engine package. The little time that I had to work with A.J. last year, we had a good race setup. And now that we have a strong engine, I am excited about our chances for the season, especially Indianapolis.[3]

◀ Anthony (left) and Larry. *IMS Photo Archive*

On another occasion Giaffone added,

> Any driver's goal is always to win, but we know the competition is going to be really hard out there. My goal is to finish the most races that I can in the top ten and top five. To win a race, you've got to be in the right place at the right time. I've been there, and I think there's no reason why we couldn't do it again. First, you've got to finish to win, and sometimes you have to take chances to win a race. But I think my goal is to finish races strong and then I think we can build ourselves to a win later in the season.[4]

Tragedy struck the first IRL event of the year at Miami-Homestead before it started. Driver Paul Dana was killed in the final warmup session the morning of the race when he slammed into the spinning car of Ed Carpenter. Dana's Rahal Letterman team withdrew its remaining two cars of Buddy Rice and Danica Patrick from the race "out of respect," and there was talk of canceling the event. Foyt adamantly opposed the idea, saying, "Drivers know things can happen every day" and that the ultimate sign of respect would be to continue. The race went on as scheduled, Giaffone finishing eighth.[5]

Afterward, Foyt addressed the question on why people race on the team's website:

"It's hard for people who have never driven a race car to understand. Fans can appreciate, crew members may think they know, but when it comes down to it, only fellow drivers really understand the feeling that racing an Indy car gives you. Lord knows I've come close to being killed several times in my career. Every time I recovered, I got back in the cockpit. Why? There is no other feeling that can compare to racing cars. I loved it."[6]

Giaffone recorded his second straight top-ten finish at St. Petersburg but then backed into the wall at Motegi in Japan. Foyt entered three cars at Indianapolis with Larry Foyt being listed as the second driver. No one was listed for the third car, although it seemed unlikely Anthony Foyt would get the call.

Anthony's Busch season was off to a rough start. He was involved in a crash not of his making at Daytona and finished forty-second—next to last. He then put together a string of five straight races where he finished, although only once was he able to crack the top thirty. Ironically, that came on the road course in Mexico City and was his only lead lap finish. As his home race at Texas Motor Speedway approached, he'd already been through three crew chiefs and was thirty-fourth in the point standings.

"I definitely thought we'd be doing better than we're doing right now," he said. "We've just kind of been struggling. Every team has changes, and our team is going through some changes right now. Crew chief-wise and car-wise, we just have to adjust to it as quick as possible."[7]

His new crew chief was Trent Owens, the nephew of Richard Petty, who showed up at Texas with a new car for Foyt IV to drive.

"I'm pretty sure his confidence is pretty beat up," Owens said. "He definitely needs to come here, run the entire race and get a good top-twenty finish and get his confidence up. Confidence means so much to a driver. If you don't have confidence in the people around you, you're only going to be that good."

The race didn't go as hoped, with Anthony being taken out in a three-car crash and finishing forty-first. Afterward, sponsor Great Clips announced it was cutting back its support of the team, which was then forced to merge with another group and switch from Dodge to Chevrolet. Anthony's deal was with Evernham and Dodge, and he was moved to another team for the upcoming Richmond race. When he failed to qualify, however, his brief NASCAR career was over. Asked if running Indianapolis for his grandfather was an option, he sounded hopeful.

"It's still early enough," he said. "We haven't talked about it yet, but I'd love to do it again."[8]

When reporters caught up with A.J. and put the question to him, it was obvious Anthony hadn't talked to his grandfather about the possibility.

"No, he definitely won't drive for me," Foyt said. "He wanted to go down on his own, which I gave him my blessing. If that's what he wants to do, I'll never hold nobody back. Some of the people that he signed with and some of the other things he's got going, there's no way I'd work with them. He definitely will not drive for us at Indy."[9]

At the same time, A.J. denied he and his grandson were on the outs.

"No, no, no, no. I love him like my own son. I love him to death. He's the one that wanted to go do his thing. I'm putting a team together. The last two-and-a half years, we've kind of had our butt kicked pretty well. I don't like that. I'm working too hard to get us back to the top."

As Indianapolis approached, so did the seemingly annual discussion about the IRL's reunification with Champ Car (the former CART), and it brought the annual rebuke from Foyt:

"Every year before the Indy 500 this stuff picks up," he said. "I don't think it's going to happen. You've got certain people over there as bullheaded as some of us are over here. Besides, what do they have to offer? They're in completely different equipment with a whole different formula. One way or another, it's going to cost one group of teams a lot of money to switch. I'd quit racing before I'd go to that concept. The IRL was in a slump for a few years, but we're good now, so why screw it up?"[10]

He also made it clear he wouldn't be returning to NASCAR anytime soon: "Stock cars? I wouldn't walk across the street for them."[11]

Despite the movement to Honda engines for the entire field, Foyt's team showed little improvement, slower than most of the IRL regulars, while ahead of the other teams and drivers making a one-off appearance at the Speedway. Giaffone qualified twenty-first and Larry twenty-third. Much of the attention was focused on Michael Andretti, Eddie Cheever, and Al Unser Jr.—three drivers making a comeback.

"They're kidding themselves," Foyt said. "I've always felt (driving) is like flying an airplane. If you don't do it every day, you get behind. It's not that you don't have the ability to do it, it's just that you let things slow down and slide by you, and that makes it very easy to make a mistake. The urge never leaves you, and it hasn't left me yet. But you can't kid yourself. Time passes you by and no matter how much you hate to admit it, you have to know those days are over."[12]

He also took exception with the number of drivers buying rides and bringing sponsorship dollars.

"I would say in today's market, 75 percent of them bought their way in. You would have never heard of A.J. Foyt if I had to buy my way in because I didn't have two pennies to rub together. I had to do it on my ability. But if it would have come to me having to go out and get sponsors, I'd still be standing outside, looking in."[13]

The race went poorly as in both cases the car setup let the team down. Larry immediately started to fall back, and not long after the one-hundred-mile mark, he pulled in and parked the car.

"We weren't handling very well out there," he said. "We were way in the back and there was no sense in us doing that. We missed the setup and we couldn't get it back."[14]

Giaffone was still running late in the race, although ten laps behind, when he moved high on the track to let the leaders through between Turn One and Turn Two and bounced off the wall.

"We'd been struggling so much, it was really a tough day," he said. "I thought that I actually crashed so many times today. I got into the marbles trying to stay out of the way of the guys, and I brushed the wall. We were just having a really bad day."[15]

A week later, Giaffone put on his drive of the year, going from nineteenth at the start to a fifth-place finish at Detroit. However, that was followed by a trio of oval track events where he failed to finish in the top fifteen. When he brushed the wall and subsequently parked at Kansas with handling problems, Foyt—who was at home recovering from left knee replacement surgery—decided to make a move, noting the next four races were all on oval tracks.

He released Giaffone and replaced him with Jeff Bucknum, the driver who had subbed for Anthony the previous year on road courses. It was an odd choice as Bucknum, forty, was primarily a sports car driver with limited open-wheel experience. He'd only run two previous oval track events, finishing twenty-second at both Motegi and Indianapolis the year before.

"I know he hasn't got much experience on the ovals, but I think he can adapt to them," Foyt said. "The next two ovals (Nashville and Milwaukee) are the hardest on the circuit, so if he can adapt to them, I think he can adapt to any oval. By the same token, I'm not expecting miracles. I told him to just go out and get some experience and try to come home clean."[16]

Bucknum said he was counting on Foyt to help get him through the upcoming races.

"I don't have a lack of confidence when it comes to ovals, but I'm smart enough to know I need someone to tell me the things that I don't know because of my lack of experience. A.J. is one of the best when it comes to oval tracks and teaching drivers to run the ovals. This is the best opportunity I could ask for. In the long run, I think it will pay off for both of us."

Foyt, however, wouldn't be at Nashville as his knee rehab continued. Much as he had turned to son Tony for help during the recovery from the Road America crash, he now turned to another son for help with the race team.

After the Indy 500, Larry had headed back to Charlotte. He was still looking to land a ride in one of the NASCAR series and was doing an occasional test session for Evernham. But he was finding it difficult and frustrating to land a ride. That's when A.J. called. Larry remembered the conversation fifteen years later:

> He said, "You know, son, I'm getting older, and if you want the race team to keep going and stay in the family, you really ought to think about moving back home." I'd always thought that I'd want to keep it going. But I was still in my late twenties at that time and not ready to give up on my racing.[17]
>
> I was a little lost right then, to be honest. I didn't want to give it up—I didn't want to stop racing. I was trying to find money to get back into the Busch series or to get back into the truck series and try and do a reset and work my way back up again. But it wasn't going well, and I was just stuck floundering, still trying to make it happen.
>
> I was also nervous about trying to run the team with my dad just because he's very strong-willed. I don't want to say he's set in his ways, but he has his way of doing things. In my mind, if I was really going to do this, I'd have to be able to modernize the team and take it to where I thought it needed to be to be competitive in the racing landscape, and I knew that was going to take a big financial investment.

Despite his concerns, Larry agreed to go to the upcoming Michigan race to talk about the prospect of joining his father's Indy car team in a management capacity.

"I always wanted to do right by him," Larry said. "I felt like everything I had was because of his help, and if he wanted me to do something, I would try my best to do it. So, I went to Michigan. He had a press conference [to announce Bucknum's sponsorship] and I was there. At the end he said, 'Oh, yeah, Larry is going to start being the team manager.' I was pretty shocked. I thought, *Well played, Dad—well played.* I told myself, *All right, it's time to move on to the next phase of my life.*"

When newspaper accounts implied Larry was taking over, however, A.J. was quick to clarify the situation.

"I'm not stepping down," he said. "I'm just getting Larry back home to help run the operation. To be more competitive, we need to have more people. We're working hard at it, to turn this operation around, and we're going to continue to make changes. This isn't the way A.J. Foyt made his name. We're not going to continue to run that way. We will be back on top. It's just a matter of when."[18]

Larry still hoped to drive again but was realistic about the possibility:

> At first it was tough to swallow, knowing that I may never race again. If a great racing opportunity came up, my dad and I would talk about it. But what are the odds of me really getting a good ride? If you have one bad year it's hard to sell yourself. But it's kind of a misnomer to say that I'm retired.[19]
>
> I'm going home to learn that side of the family business. It's a family business I want to keep going. This is an amazing opportunity, and it's something I've known I've always wanted to do. We need to try and get some more money to get our team to the next level. Hopefully we can grow the team and expand it into a multi-car operation. The more heads you have making the decisions the better. You put all those heads together and make it stronger. We have to keep this thing growing. We want to keep A.J.'s legacy growing for many years to come.

Both Foyts moved quickly, putting the Mooresville shop on the market and auctioning off the remaining NASCAR equipment, parts, and memorabilia. While A.J. said, "The plan is for Jeff [Bucknum] to be here next year," Larry had other ideas. But he was also treading lightly in his new role:[20]

> I didn't think that was my place [to come in and make major changes]. I wanted to come in and start learning the lay of the land, start to see what Indy car was like again. I knew I was going to have to pick some battles of what I wanted to do and which battles were most important to me. Some of the bigger ones included what drivers I thought were available. At that time, A.J. was still doing most of the engineering himself. It's amazing how good he was at that. But computers were becoming more and more involved in racing, and I knew we were going to need some more engineers.[21]

It didn't take long for Larry to become more assertive, and when he said he wanted to bring in a new driver "to push the button a little harder," A.J. agreed. They replaced Bucknum with Darren Manning, an English driver with extensive road racing and oval experience. Ten years younger than Bucknum, Manning had driven in CART and the IRL from 2002 to 2005, most recently for Chip Ganassi where he recorded thirteen top-ten finishes in twenty-four races. He'd been unable to break through to Victory Lane, however, and Ganassi released him midway through the 2005 season. He'd been racing primarily in Asia since then and jumped at the opportunity to get back in an Indy car.[22]

"Getting Darren was my first big move. I always thought he was better than he had a chance to show. I liked what he had done in junior formula over in Europe. I felt like Darren was a great chance for us to have a pretty solid driver that would surprise some people."[23]

At the time A.J. said, "Next year is a big year for our team. We're doing everything we can to get our program where it needs to be. Larry is a great asset on the management side, and we've worked hard to put together a solid plan for 2007. He's got a hell of a lot more youth than I've got. I'm getting up in age. I may back off a little bit, but I'll keep my hands on things, probably 100 percent and not the 110 percent like normally. We'll start him off with 10 percent and let him go right up to 100 percent."[24]

Years later Larry would say,

> Most people probably think A.J. was hard to deal with, but he really wasn't. As hard as he was on me at times as a driver, he was the complete opposite with the race team. There were tough days when we had some arguments on the way things should be, but I could also see the big picture, and I felt like this was my future. I also felt like, if we could just start getting competitive again, he's gonna enjoy it again.[25]
>
> The ABC deal had just started, and some of the funding was still coming out of his pocket, so I knew if I could get it to where we could make this thing break even, he'd give me a little leeway on what I wanted to do with the team.

With concerns the IRL might have fewer than what many considered the minimum eighteen cars competing in the coming year, the Foyts said they would consider running a second car. Anthony wouldn't be the driver, however, as he signed on with Tony George's Vision team.

"I just could never get him settled down," A.J. said of Anthony. "He was just a little too brave for himself. He's my grandson, and a lot of times your own kids and grandsons, they don't want to listen to you like they'll listen to some stranger."[26]

2007

The falling car count was just another indication of the damage the IRL-CART split in open-wheel racing continued to do to the sport. Even though many of those who'd left the IRL were now back in the fold, attendance continued to fall, television ratings continued to plummet, and major sponsors continued to desert the sport for NASCAR, which was now clearly the most popular form of motorsports in the United States. When ESPN asked sports fans what their favorite form of racing was, 60 percent said NASCAR, 6 percent the IRL, and 1.5 percent Champ Car. NASCAR television ratings were triple that of the IRL. While the IRL was formed to highlight American drivers and manufacturers, five of the series champions since 2000 were foreign drivers, and the lone American—Sam Hornish—was headed to NASCAR. The sole engine manufacturer—Japan's Honda—was as concerned about the sport's future as anyone.[27]

"Open-wheel racing is on life support, and its disappearance is not out of the realm of possibility," said Robert Clarke, president of Honda Performance Development (HPD). "We need unification; there's nothing more important to the growth and survival of the sport in this country."

Desperate to restore interest in the series, the IRL turned to a driver who hadn't won an open-wheel race in twenty-five years and opposed reunification—A.J. Foyt. The series launched a yearlong celebration to mark the fiftieth anniversary of his first year in Indy car racing. Foyt was to be featured prominently in prerace promotion efforts for upcoming events, where an eighty-foot timeline documenting his career would be on display. Things didn't always go as planned—like the time he told reporters there wasn't a single open-wheel driver he'd pay to see.[28]

"Don't ask me why I still love it," he said when asked what kept bringing him back. "When you start getting beat like we did the last couple of years, that's what inspired me. I told our sponsor, 'We will be back this year.' And we will. I feel like we can be competitive again."[29]

His team had already made progress simply by appearing at the January preseason test session on the road course at Daytona International Speedway, something it hadn't always been able to do in recent years. Even a thirteenth-place finish in the season opener at Miami-Homestead was considered progress.

"There was a fast pack and a slow pack," Manning said, "And we were the fastest of the slow pack, which was good for us."[30]

A week later on the streets of St. Petersburg, Manning turned in the fifth-fastest qualifying time, the team's best since 2001. Although he lost power steering early in the race, he was up to third with less than ten laps remaining when he spun. He managed to continue for a thirteenth-place finish, and after seeing Manning's blister-covered hands, former Ganassi teammate Scott Dixon said he "deserved a trophy."[31]

"At least they knew we were here," Foyt said. Manning tried to manage expectations, noting, "It's a fine line between being there and not being there. On a road course it's a little bit easier to climb that curve.

"Sometimes we'll go backward before we go forward and A.J. and I both know that. When we go backward, we're not getting upset; we're working it out."[32]

With the Indianapolis 500 approaching, Foyt made an unusual pick to drive his second car, the No. 50 commemorating his anniversary. There was also a certain synergy to the choice of forty-five-year-old Al Unser Jr. His father had been a rookie in 1965 when Foyt picked him to drive the team's second over the objection of crew chief George Bignotti. "Without him taking a chance on me, I would have never made it," Al would say repeatedly over the years.[33]

Foyt was now taking another chance with Al Jr. as his battle with alcoholism in recent years was well-known. He'd been arrested in January near his home in Henderson, Nevada, and charged with driving under the influence, misdemeanor hit-and-run, failure to render aid in an accident, and failure to report an accident. He had pleaded not guilty to the charges and a trial date had been set for July. "Little Al" realized the charges would scare away most Indy car owners and he'd all but given up hope of driving in the 500.

"I wanted to drive, but I really hadn't contacted anybody through the winter months," Unser Jr. said. "Then that issue I had in Nevada came up and I thought, 'That's it for '07.' At that point, I knew I had to come to grips with it. I said, I've got to come out of it, treat this disease seriously and admit I can't pick up one more drink. I started down that road and, blam, A.J. Foyt calls me."[34]

Year's later, Al Jr. would say, "It was a dream come true. For him to give me a call, especially after I had gotten in trouble, he totally looked past that and gave me the opportunity. He wasn't concerned about it, and we didn't talk too much about it. He said people make mistakes and they deserve second chances. He was really, really good to me. No matter what, he was really good to me."[35]

The move also surprised "Big Al" Unser. "Maybe he looked at Al and said I can help him," Big Al would say years later. "Straighten him out. That's Foyt's attitude. When he likes somebody, I don't think anything bothers him to make a decision. Foyt is a big gorilla. He's got a huge heart. He might yell at you and cuss at you, but then he turns around, and all of it is forgotten. If he likes you. But if he's ticked at you, you better hold on. He's man enough to whip whoever stands in his way. But he's a big-hearted man."[36]

For Foyt, who called himself a social drinker and would have an occasional beer, glass of wine, or a Crown Royal and water, Al Jr.'s battle with alcohol didn't enter into his decision.

"He just got in a problem with his drinking," Foyt would say. "Drinking kind of ruined his life, and it was a shame to see that happen to someone who had the talent he had. I've known a couple of people—brilliant people—who are like that. You hate to see that happen.[37]

"I still liked Al. He was a great race driver, and he knew how to drive the hell out of a race car. He was super."

The first day of practice at the Speedway was dubbed "A.J. Foyt Opening Day" and was kicked off by a lap around the track in the pace car by A.J. and Tony George. Then they watched as Foyt's five race-winning cars made a parade lap. George Snider, Foyt's longtime friend, teammate, and car co-owner was in the 1961 winner. Al Jr. drove the 1964 winner, Anthony the 1967 car, and Larry the 1977 Coyote, while Manning was in the 1999 car Kenny Bräck drove to victory.

Bräck, who had fully retired following the 2005 race and was now focused on a musical career, wrote a tribute song called "Legend of the Speedway." A video to accompany the song was filmed at the track. The opening lyrics went, "Hey, hey A.J., we love you / There'll never be another driver quite like you / Some of us had to find out the hard way / You just don't mess with A.J. / The Legend of the Speedway."

Foyt said the event "brought a lot of memories back":

> I didn't realize just how fast time flies by. When I first started, everybody said I wasn't going to live to be twenty-two years old. Hell, it's a big, big deal to me. I'm still looking down at the grass and not looking up at it, while a lot of my friends are.[38]
>
> I'm not one of these guys who's a hero race driver. The guy who tells you that is fooling himself. There's not a man alive who wants to go out and break his arms or legs or back, and I've had all that happen to me. When you get right down to it, every individual body has a little fear in it. Unless he's a complete idiot, and they don't last very long.

Under a new qualifying format aimed at adding some excitement missing in recent years, only eleven cars would qualify each day. Manning was hopeful of making the field on day one but just missed bumping Michael Andretti before coming back on the second day to qualify fifteenth.

"He was a bit upset that we didn't bump Andretti out of the field, I can tell you that," Manning joked, only half in jest. "I was kind of dodging a few bullets as soon as I got out of the car. He wasn't mad at me, just frustrated."[39]

Anthony qualified George's car just three spots back of Manning in eighteenth. He admitted, "It's like a fresh start. We never really got accomplished what we wanted to when I drove for my grandfather. I'm not blaming it on nobody. It just never really got accomplished."

He said any animosity that may have existed when he left A.J.'s team for NASCAR was long gone. "We're on the best of terms, I think, we've ever been on. You know, I don't care if you work for your grandfather or father in a lawn mowing service, you're always going to be butting heads more than if you just worked for somebody you're not related to. It's great to have him for a grandfather, it's great to be back in the IRL, spending a lot more time with him. I missed him last year."

Unser Jr. had to wait until the second weekend to qualify, and when he did, Larry took a physical, hopeful of trying to qualify the third car. A.J. put the brakes on that, saying Larry's job was to run the team.

Despite the monthlong fanfare for Foyt's fiftieth year, little went right in the race following another lap of the Speedway in the pace car alongside George. Manning and Unser Jr. were both running at the finish, although both had had their problems and were more than thirty laps behind, with Manning in twentieth and Unser Jr. in twenty-sixth.

"That was my last 500," Al Jr. recalled. "I was ready to get out of the car, and I was ready to retire. We didn't have a great deal of speed, but we finished the race, and it was a great honor to be driving for such a legend."[40]

The rest of the year had its moments, including a fourth on Detroit's Belle Isle street course and a fifth on the oval at Iowa. Manning finished thirteenth in the final points standings, one position better than Foyt IV, who had a pair of third-place finishes to show for his efforts.

The rest of the year didn't go nearly as well for A.J. On August 2, nearly two years to the day after tangling with the bees on his ranch, Foyt was back on a bulldozer. He was moving dirt around a pond on a recently purchased thirty-acre piece of land when the bank gave way under the weight of the 35,000-pound machine. The dozer rolled down the bank and turned completely over, trapping Foyt in the mud and water.

The bulldozer was equipped with a steel cage around the driver's area that protected him during the rollover but then nearly trapped him in about fifteen feet of water.

"It was such a helpless feeling when that dirt broke away and I was going down and down," Foyt said shortly afterward. "The steel cage probably saved my life, because without it the dozer would have crushed me. But the cage also made it hard to escape. I had to crawl through the front of it and it was hard to do under water with all my clothes on and with my bum legs. [41]

"I'll be honest, I panicked a little bit. If I hadn't made it to the top of the dozer, they would never have found me because it was completely under water. I didn't want to swim to the bank 'cause it was covered in vines and steep and I was already out of breath from getting out.

"I knew I'd get too tired trying to haul my big butt outta there. But as I was calling for help, I saw a water moccasin [snake] swim by. I started splashing like hell. After about 15 minutes someone heard me and stopped to help. I came awful close this time. I was probably the most scared in my life. I was like, 'Just finish it off.'"

Once on land and despite bruises on his face and head, Foyt refused a hospital visit for an MRI, telling medics, "If you're going to die, you're going to die." Instead, he spent the next four hours overseeing the removal of the bulldozer from the lake, finally accomplished with the aid of three massive wreckers. Two days later, he was in Michigan with his team.

"That was some bad stuff," he told Manning. "You don't want to do that. I'd be better off in a racecar. I think I need to go racing again."

Instead of allowing him in a car, Manning and the crew bought Foyt a remote-control bulldozer toy and a facemask and snorkel set.

"I thought I was going to see the undertaker right then," Foyt would tell Robin Miller years later. "Everybody wanted to know how I got out. I said I wasn't no Houdini, I needed some damn air and I needed air quick."[42]

At the end of the year, Larry picked up the option on Manning's contract for a second season and continued to work to modernize and update the team. A.J. had begun shifting some of the team's operations during the season to Indianapolis for the Midwest races and Larry planned to do it again in the coming year. He'd also found working with his father easier than expected:

> It was a work in progress, and A.J. was very much a part of it. People always seem to think he's set in his ways. But when you look back at how much change he went through, it amazes me. He started driving front-engine roadsters, went to rear-engine cars, then ground effects cars—while having success in all of them. That shows you that he's not someone who is averse to change.[43]
>
> A lot of times when we'd start talking about something, he got it. I'd be thinking, *This is gonna be a hard 'no,'* for what I was wanting to do, and he was actually really good about it. He knew how important the computer systems on the cars were. That the young drivers were growing up with computers on their go-karts and expected data, and that's just the way things were.
>
> There were little things we would argue about. Like higher-quality food for the crew because it was an added expense, and he was still putting some of his personal money into it. I thought it was one of the little things we needed to do to attract the best people. So, I just tried to pick my battles.

Another issue was a day off for crew members after working and traveling on the weekend.

"He'd talk about having to tow his car on an open trailer, race it, and then drive it home, and, 'Now the guys need a day off because they've been traveling?' He was just being old A.J. But when I'd go into his office and say, 'Hey, Dad, let's give the guys a long weekend. They've been working hard," he's like, 'Yeah, absolutely. Give them a long weekend.' He likes to play the tough guy, but he's got a big heart."

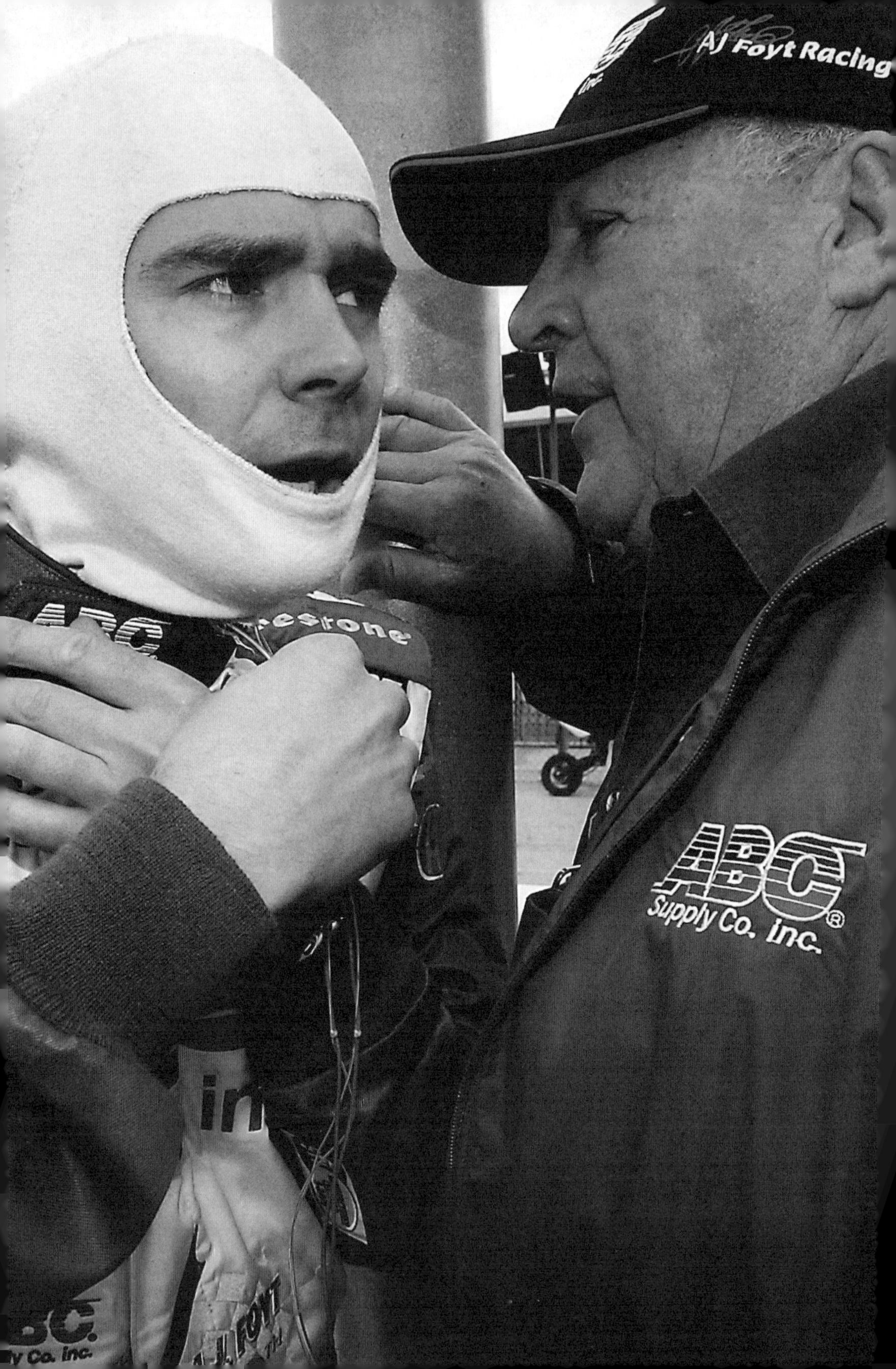
AJ Foyt Racing
ABC
Supply Co. Inc.

CHAPTER 34

REUNITED

2008–2010

For the first time in twelve years, open-wheel racing at its highest level in the United States was united to start the 2008 racing season—the Indy Racing League had "merged" with Champ Car.

Initially, A.J. Foyt balked at the proposed deal that had the backing of Roger Penske, Chip Ganassi, and most of the sport's other leading names. He'd been the IRL's staunchest supporter and opposed making concessions that included providing each Champ Car team committing to the IRL with a one-year Honda basic engine lease, two Dallarmana chassis from a pool of new and used cars for up to two seasons, and $1.2 million per car from the series support fund. The schedule also was growing from sixteen to eighteen races with the addition of three Champ Car road course events, including the Long Beach Grand Prix.[1]

"I would throw a damned fit and would want to damn near pack my bags," he said when told the terms of the deal while attending the Daytona 500. "And I think a lot of people that have been loyal would do the same because it wouldn't be right to people who had to spend a lot of money."[2]

A week later he'd been convinced that a merger—and whatever was necessary to make it happen—was in the best interest of open-wheel racing. He was arguably on the winning side, but he was also the lone team owner still operating from the original IRL. In some respects, he was more of a survivor than a winner.

"I'm glad that they were able to get it done," he said. "It'll eliminate confusion for race fans and the sponsors because there'll be just one type of car, and everyone will be running together. May the best team win."[3]

◀ Darren Manning, Larry's first big hire for the team, got along with A.J. too.
ABC Supply

Foyt was now at the age where almost everything he did marked some sort of anniversary, and he'd been in Daytona for the fiftieth anniversary of the first 500. Despite having said he wouldn't "walk across the street" to attend a stock car race just a year earlier, he joined other winners of the race for the "Drivers, start your engines," call. He also took the opportunity to bemoan the changes he saw happening in racing.

"When I raced back in my heyday, I always tried to have fun," he said, repeating a past theme. "Nowadays it's so much more cutthroat, and who can steal each other's sponsors. It wasn't all that in my day. The guys racing today do not know the fun it was back yonder. All it is now is money and who can run under somebody else."[4]

In a bit of unusual timing, ESPN picked its best twenty-five drivers of all time, just eight years after it put together a similar list to mark the end of the twentieth century. Not much had changed as Foyt once again occupied the top spot, followed by Mario Andretti, Dale Earnhardt, Michael Schumacher, and Ayrton Senna. Richard Petty, David Pearson, Jim Clark, Juan Manuel Fangio, and Jeff Gordon rounded out the top ten on a list lopsided by its American representation.

Foyt was one of nineteen who took part in the voting, although he said, "I can't remember" when asked who he voted for. It didn't matter, he said, "I knew I was going to end up No. 1 anyway."[5]

The team got off to a mediocre start to the season with Manning running at the end of three of the first four races and an eighth-place finish at Motegi as the best of his efforts going into Indianapolis. Larry had hoped to drive the team car at the Speedway, but his father again quickly put the kibosh on that.

"I'm not letting him in it," A.J. said of the second car. "He's more important to me as (the team director) than he is as my driver. His future is running this team. He's a good driver and knows what he's doing, but doesn't have a killer instinct. He's also broke his back once, and I don't want that to happen again."[6]

It wasn't the first time Larry had heard his father say he didn't have the killer instinct, and he didn't necessarily disagree with him.

"It's really hard when you're related to A.J. and you drive for him," Larry said. "He's always afraid you're going to get hurt.

"I just miss driving a race car," he said. "I love some of the days in the morning when no one is there and you get in the race car and know you are just going to go fast. It is nine o'clock in the morning and you are going 200 miles per hour. There are not a lot of people that get to do that and I always enjoyed all the aspects of competing, but I just enjoyed driving a racecar. Who doesn't want to drive fast?"[7]

The team hired Jeff Simmons instead. He'd driven for Foyt's Indy Lights team in 2004 and for Rahal Letterman the past two years.

Manning qualified fourteenth, but Simmons missed out on his first attempt when the car owner forgot to wave the green flag to start the run. "Guess I had a senior moment," an embarrassed Foyt said as Simmons went out a short time later to qualify twenty-eighth.

As part of the team's new setup, Larry was overseeing Manning's car while A.J. focused on Simmons. Which was fine with Simmons.

"I love the fact I'm racing here with A.J. Foyt. He's been engineering me, and it's been a privilege. I'm really looking forward to working more with him."[8]

In the 500, Manning quickly moved into the top ten and was running sixth, less than three seconds from the lead, when a caution flag brought the entire field to the pits on lap sixty-four. Manning was released onto pit road by a crew member as other traffic approached, and Larry's cries to "stop, stop, stop," were too late to keep the right-front wing endplate from being clipped off.[9]

"I made a mistake," Manning said, although most thought he wasn't to blame. "I didn't listen to Larry. I was thinking, 'Go, go, go.'"

Manning was forced to return to the pits, where a new endplate borrowed from George's team was fitted to the wing. Manning dropped to twenty-fourth and spent the rest of the race fighting his way back for a ninth-place finish on the same lap as winner Scott Dixon.

Simmons had also moved up and was running in the top twenty and on the lead lap when, during a caution period, his car suffered a broken half-shaft and swerved right and into the outside wall, then slid across the track and hit the inside wall. His race was over.

In the next four events, all on ovals, the team failed to score a top-ten finish. At Watkins Glen on July 9, however, Larry pitted Manning early. He took the lead when everyone else pitted and held it for ten laps. He was forced to conserve both tires and fuel near the end, and Ryan Hunter-Reay got by for the win, with Manning finishing second.

That was the high point for the season, and Manning's future with the team was clearly in doubt late in the year when A.J. brought in another driver to run a second car in the last race. Afterward, the team decided to go in a different direction and released Manning while hiring Brazilian driver Vitor Meira.

On paper, the two drivers appeared to be a toss-up. Meira had finished thirteenth in the point standings, with one more point than Manning in fourteenth. Manning had seven top-ten finishes compared to six for Meira. But even though Manning had provided the team with some badly needed stability when it needed it most and ran strong at Indianapolis, Meira had been one of the race's sensations. He'd led twelve laps and finished second, his second runner-up spot and his fifth straight top-ten finish at the Speedway. A.J. saw it as a chance to get them both into Victory Lane.

"I've always admired him because he's a hard racer who charges all day long. He should have won a lot of races but he hasn't had the best of luck. I believe we can change that and I'm looking forward to working with him."[10]

The move was harder for Larry, who'd made Manning his first hire.

"We had a good relationship with Darren and I appreciate everything he did with our team," A.J. said in making the announcement. "Towards the end, I felt like things had come to a standstill and we weren't getting the best out of each other. It was time for a change and I was the one who needed to make the changes as hard as it was for us. I really like Darren and wish him well. I hope he remains my friend."

The easygoing Manning seemed to understand. He'd run a couple more Indy car races on road courses and a number of sports car events before retiring at the end of the 2010 season.

"There's no hard feelings," he said at the time. "We had a good couple of years of improvement. Getting me on board was part of making his team better and I think we did that. I wish him well. We had a good relationship and I expect that to continue no matter what I end up doing."

Meira had been racing in the IRL for eight years and had a record ninety-three starts without a win. Twenty-three of his races had ended in accidents. He was generally considered the best driver without a victory, and he saw it as a chance to break through as others had before him, including Scott Sharp, Billy Boat, and Kenny Bräck.[11]

"Many people would give an arm and a leg just to meet A.J. and I am getting to work with him, I think that says it all. My goal is to come out and win, and by that I mean to give 100 percent no matter what is happening. I finished second many times but there were races where I finished fourth or fifth and I felt good about them because I gave 100 percent and we got the most out of the car that day. Whether it's in races or in the championship, if we are getting top-fives, it's because we are putting ourselves in position to win which is what you have to do before you can win. The wins will come."[12]

Foyt also announced that ABC Supply was not only returning as the team's sponsor, it was extending through 2010 with an option for 2011. It was still on the low end as sponsorships went and only for a one-car team—with a second car added for Indianapolis—but it helped provide badly needed stability. It had been anything but a sure thing as ABC company founder Ken Hendricks, one of the supporters of the original sponsorship, had died in a construction accident.

"Our company and their company are similar," Larry Foyt said. "Ken Hendricks was a self-made man who built his company the same as A.J. Foyt did. Our two companies together have meshed well. We are two family companies."[13]

Fortunately, ABC management, including Diane Hendricks and David Luck, had seen the value of the relationship, believing it provided a rallying point for company employees.

"We spent as much on ABC Racing logo wear as the gross national product of a third world country," Luck would joke. "Our people loved that stuff. We had an old show car that traveled around for open houses, and A.J. was always accessible and open to our people. It really helped us become a big family."[14]

Meira wasn't the only new driver headed for a No. 14 car. Tony Stewart announced he was leaving Joe Gibbs Racing at the end of 2008 to start his own team, Stewart-Haas Racing.

"I had to call NASCAR to see what numbers were available," Stewart recalled. Sterling Marlin had been using the No. 14 for a couple of years—the same number his father Coo Coo Marlin had used—but it was surprisingly available. "They started going through the list and as soon as they got to fourteen I said, 'I'll take it.' Like literally someone was standing in line to take it if I didn't take it right then. I went to tell A.J. and he was pretty excited about it.

"It was pretty easy to decide on the number that my all-time hero had."[15]

The announcement was made before the Brickyard 400 when Foyt was away attending an Indy car race in Canada. They exchanged phone calls beforehand, and A.J. took the opportunity to give Stewart a hard time about a recent altercation Tony had with track officials.

"Just because you've got No. 14 doesn't mean you have to act like me," Foyt said. "I told Tony, that ain't helping the reputation of No. 14. That's just living up to it."[16]

It wasn't until Stewart invited Foyt to Daytona Beach for the 500 that he saw the car. One of the first things he noticed was a "Heroes Drive Us" decal honoring Foyt. "What's it pay?" he asked Stewart. The pair were obviously enjoying themselves.[17]

"What I see in Tony is, he calls a spade a spade, and I think that is kind of what made A.J. what he is today because I think so many people sugarcoat so [darn] much. That is one thing I really respect Tony for. Somewhere down the line some genes must have crossed."[18]

Stewart said using No. 14 was a way of paying Foyt the ultimate compliment. Stewart also invited Foyt to sit on his pit stand to watch the 150-mile qualifying race and gave him a radio to use in case he had any suggestions. Or so he told Foyt.

"It had the button on it and everything," said Stewart, who finished second in the race and thought he was getting the last laugh. "But it didn't do anything when you pushed it. Can you imagine trying to sit there and drive with him yelling at you?"[19]

"He run second," was all Foyt said when first asked what he thought of the race. Then he warmed up—a little.

"We cut up with each other all the time, give each other a hard time. I'm proud to see him doing what he's doing. We'll have to deal with him for a few more years, unless he gets too fat."[20]

To which Stewart replied, "Hello pot, I'm kettle."

Meira had high hopes to start the season. "Maybe I'm not being too realistic, but a very successful weekend would be a top-five finish, and a successful weekend would be a solid top ten."[21] Larry had also brought in a new chief engineer, Adam Schaechter, who specialized in street and road course setups. The combination immediately clicked with a ninth-place finish on the same lap with the leader on the streets of St. Petersburg and followed it with a fourteenth at Long Beach. Their first DNF came on the oval track at Kansas when Meira was forced to slow for another car and was rammed from behind by Hélio Castroneves.

Headed to Indianapolis, Meira was fifteenth in points, and the team added Anthony for its second car. His contract had not been renewed at the end of the 2008 season as Tony George looked to cut back the size of his team. Both drivers were second-day qualifiers, Meira in fourteenth and Anthony in nineteenth. And while Anthony had a relatively uneventful 500, completing all 200 laps for the first time and finishing fifteenth. Meira's was anything but.

He was running twelfth when the field headed for the pits under a caution flag on lap 134. The team had struggled through several previous stops, and this time Meira pulled away before the fuel hose had been removed, ripping the nozzle out and dousing the car, which burst into flames. Meira tossed the steering wheel out of the cockpit but had not yet undone his belts when water was poured over the car, extinguishing the fire. Amazingly, the car was pushed back into its pit and restarted, Meira rejoining the field without losing a lap.

He was still on the lead lap and running in the top twenty on lap 174 when, in a move Eddie Cheever on the television broadcast called "just too risky," rookie Raphael Matos approached Meira on the outside going into the first turn. The left-front tire of Matos's car clipped the right rear of Meira's, turning the No. 14 hard right and headfirst into the Turn One wall at more than 200 mph. The impact tossed the car onto its side, and it rode the wall backward before coming down on its remaining wheels. Meira was taken to Methodist Hospital, where X-rays indicated two broken vertebrae in his lower back. His season was over.[22]

"I don't know what the kid is doing," Foyt said of Matos. "There are too many damn road racers who don't know how to run ovals. He should have seen that Meira had the groove. That's just driving with your head up your ass. I hate to say it, but it's pretty stupid what the kid did."[23]

Matos said he wasn't trying to make a pass and that Meira drifted high.

"I don't care what A.J. says about me. It was a race incident. I don't think it was my fault. If A.J. wants to blame me and say that, that's his right. And I'm not surprised he's saying that. He always talks a lot."

The next day, Foyt went to the hospital to talk to Meira.

"Don't worry about it," Meira recalled Foyt saying. "You've got your seat."[24]

The next race was a week away at Milwaukee. It was being sponsored by the ABC Supply, which was headquartered nearby, and called the "A.J. Foyt 225." Paul Tracy, who'd finished ninth at Indianapolis and was a four-time Milwaukee winner, was hired to drive the No. 14 car. He finished sixteenth, six laps behind the winner, and last among the cars still running.

Afterward, Tracy said, "A.J. called and said, 'Look, I'm embarrassed about the car we gave you in Milwaukee. I can't afford to be putting you in my equipment until we've got ourselves up to par. Having you in the car puts our team under the microscope, and I want to get our team better before we do that again.' I'm sad not to continue with Foyt. I was looking forward to traveling to races again and helping a little team punch big. But ultimately it's the team's decision."[25]

Anthony returned for the next race at Texas, a track he'd run well at in the past. But he was involved in an accident, and with five road courses still on the schedule, the team moved again, bringing in Ryan Hunter-Reay.

Hunter-Reay had driven mostly in CART and Champ Car while posting a number of victories. He'd been a victim of the recession's impact on sponsorship, however, and had been driving for George since the start of the year. With George continuing to try and pare down his team, he agreed to release Hunter-Reay to Foyt. Despite the problems the Foyt team was going through, it was a move Hunter-Reay welcomed.

"I'd always wanted to work with A.J., and Tony George allowed me to fill that role," Hunter-Reay would say more than ten years later. "It was an experience I'll never forget—to be able to sit in the same room as one of my heroes growing up and discuss driving his race car, getting his feedback, and having him being on my timing stand."[26]

He got off to an inauspicious start, crashing out on the second lap of his first race. In practice for the next event at Richmond, Hunter-Reay discovered what it meant to have Foyt on the radio.

"There's no filter with A.J.," he said. "If he didn't think you were getting on with it, he'd tell you right over the radio, 'Let's go, get your act together.' At Richmond the car was really loose. I described it as nervous. And he came over the radio and was like, 'What do you want me to do, get you a Tylenol?' I even laughed about it in the car."

The biggest test didn't come on the racetrack, however. Hunter-Reay's mother had been battling colon cancer for more than a year, and it had continued to get worse. When Foyt heard about it, he made arrangements for her to see the specialists at the world-renowned MD Anderson Cancer Center in Houston.

"A.J.'s pulled strings with his contacts from day one," Hunter-Reay said at the time. "MD Anderson was our glimmer of hope, but they can't do anything."[27]

With Ryan's mother too weak to travel home to Florida by commercial airline, Foyt took charge and arranged to fly her home in his jet. Hunter-Reay would later say,

> I will forever be so grateful for that. He very quickly said, "I'm flying your mom home." That peace of mind—I can't tell you how much that meant to her and to our family. It was more than just a flight. It was that somebody went way out of their way—obviously it was very nice and obviously very expensive—but he went way out of his way to make sure she was in a place of comfort in the final days and months of her life. I will forever be grateful. That man—A.J. and the entire Foyt family—are very highly regarded in my book.[28]

Hunter-Reay would score a pair of top-ten finishes including a fourth place at Mid-Ohio for Foyt before the season was out and perform well enough that by the end of the year he was signed by Michael Andretti. Hunter-Reay would win often in the years ahead, including the 2014 Indianapolis 500. But he wouldn't forget his days with the Foyts.

> It was great to work with [Foyt] and the team. It had a very raw, old school feel to it that I liked. It was all A.J. He was my engineer and crew chief during that time, and that was kind of a throwback. We did have an engineer on the team, but A.J. was the one calling the shots, the setup changes, and

everything else. He was the one I was working with. I was debriefing with him, discussing race strategy with him, and he was on the radio. It was one of the highlights of my career, for sure.

2010

Meira was cleared to drive before the year was out and immediately began testing. Larry brought in another new engineer who had worked with Meira at Rahal Letterman.

"All along the way, A.J. and Larry Foyt kept telling me to just get better, do what I had to do and that my job with them was safe," Meira said. "That was such a relief. A.J. also assured me there's no crash I could ever have that he hasn't already tried. I am easily the record-holder for longest distance traveled on top of the wall, but A.J. says until I flip completely outside of the track, to stop bragging."[29]

A.J. seemed happy with the team's progress and—with Meira back in the fold—was looking forward to the new year.

"We thought we had a good year going at Indy and then everything went to hell on race day and we never recovered," he said. "The racing the last few years has been very, very good. Good close racing. Very fast racing. But we need some different winners and that's what we've been working toward. But you've got some of the old teams out there that still got some bulldogs behind the steering wheel and hell, they're hard to beat."[30]

The year got off to a good start, Meira driving to a third-place and podium finish in his home country on the street course in São Paulo, Brazil. It was a wild race interrupted by dust clouds and heavy rains that stopped the event at one point and turned it into a timed, two-hour event. Meira survived an early collision and came from his sixteenth starting position to challenge for the lead late and was elated with the results.

"It was a real confidence builder for our team, A.J., myself and our sponsors," he said. "It makes everyone believe more in themselves and makes us all prouder to go to work."[31]

Unfortunately, Meira struggled during the next three road course events and a tenth place at Kansas did little to restore the team's confidence as it headed to Indianapolis.

Anthony was back to drive the second car in his first race since Texas the year before. A third car was entered, No. 16, in honor of Anne Fornoro's father Russ Klar, who was a standout midget driver in the 1950s and early 1960s. Jaques Lazier was expected to get a chance to qualify the car once Meira and Foyt IV had made the field.

Much had changed in Anthony's life since his last race. In July, he'd married Casey Irsay, the daughter of Indianapolis Colts owner Jim Irsay. The following year the couple announced they were expecting their first child in mid-September—a boy to be named Anthony Joseph Foyt V. Anthony was also working for the Colts as a scouting assistant, an entry-level position that allowed him to take the month of May off.

"If you're comparing this to racing," he said of his job with the Colts, "I'd be a helmet carrier."

Even though it was nearly a year since Anthony was last in a race car, A.J. didn't seem concerned.

"He'll catch on pretty quick," he said. "I'm not worried about him getting back up to speed. We'll have a good car for him. I'm looking forward to working with him again."[32]

Anthony turned in mid-pack times during the first couple days of practice, but as speeds began to increase, neither he nor Meira were able to keep up. The Speedway was trying a new qualifying format in which only the fastest twenty-four cars would make the field on the first day. Anthony was first in line to post a time but was bumped from the field before the day was out. Meira nearly made it but was the last driver bumped out. Others on the outside looking in included Tony Kanaan (who'd crashed twice), Paul Tracy, and John Andretti.

It set up a tension-packed "Bump Day." Meira would make the field in thirtieth, but Anthony was upset after the day's first practice session. He recalled the events a decade later:

> The day before, the car was good—we were just slow. Overnight, they changed the whole car—every single bolt on the car setup-wise. I get it. They were trying to find more speed out of the car. But I couldn't drive it. I couldn't drive it 200 miles an hour, much less what I needed to drive it in order to make the race.[33]
>
> It was a frustrating time for everyone. Finally, [A.J.] told me to, "Drive it like this, or get the fuck out." At that point I said, "Fuck it," and I got out. I couldn't drive it like that. That was the Foyt in both of us coming out. I was at the end of my road. I knew there was nothing more I could do to make the car go faster. So, I just decided to get out.

Anthony made a quick call to Davey Hamilton, whom he'd remained close to since their first practice session together at Phoenix. Hamilton had already qualified and was at church:

> I see Anthony's calling me, so I excuse myself and go out and take the call. He just didn't know what to do. He was broken. He and A.J.—they're at each other's throats. He didn't feel comfortable in the car, and A.J. wouldn't change it—he's blaming Anthony. It was a bad deal, and I felt for them. It was a father-son thing, though in this case, it was grandfather-grandson. Obviously, I can't get in between those two, but I tried to support Anthony and tried to encourage him. I think we were both half crying. It was a tough situation. A tough, tough call.[34]

Watching it unfold was Larry Foyt, who was trying to hold the team together.

"It was very stressful," he admitted. "Things had been going fairly well, but then Anthony started struggling with the car, and I think A.J. was upset, and tensions just boiled over. That's the Indy 500. There's a lot of pressure—a lot going on. I don't want to say I was stuck in the middle, but I didn't want Anthony upset, and I didn't want A.J. upset. It was just hard for all of us. There was just a lot of pressure on all of us, and it finally just boiled over. But I knew it wasn't something that would last."[35]

Anthony left without talking to reporters, and the team tracked down Lazier in a nearby suite. He made two qualifying runs, the second being 0.197 seconds too long. Anthony couldn't hide from reporters two days later when he and Larry held a media event to launch the family wine label.

"No, I haven't spoken to him," Anthony told Derek Daly of Channel 8 television in Indianapolis. "Everybody knows my grandfather. He's a bit hotheaded, a bit hardheaded, and maybe I got that from him too. So, maybe that's why we haven't talked. But, hopefully we'll work it out pretty soon. It's been a tough couple days just having to sit back at home and not going out to the track anymore. I've turned into a spectator."[36]

A.J. said the argument with Anthony was, "No big deal. Things like that happen." He also said he should have made the move to Lazier—who hadn't started an IndyCar race since October—sooner. "I tried to do something in a couple of hours that's hard to do when you haven't run here in a year."[37]

Eventually, Anthony reached out to his grandfather, although he never got back in a race car. He'd focus on raising a family of five children with Casey as well as his roles with the Colts and the Foyt Winery. Anthony recalled,

> We didn't talk for a month or so after. I just finally called him, and he called me right back. He's always been like that. Even when we've had our bad times—crashes and fights—it would always be over. This one went a little longer. But when we talked, it was over right then and there. One time, and that was it. Absolutely back to normal.[38]
>
> I've looked back of course, to think what [I] could have done differently. Maybe come up a little bit different way. More training here or there, whatever. But in the end, everything kind of worked its way out. That's how life is. You can't go back. Hopefully, you just try to make some adjustments from the past for the future.
>
> He's a lot . . . calmer now. When I was racing, he was not very calm at all. He was on everybody all the time. Now he seems really calm. All the crew knew it was nothing personal. That's just how A.J. was when it came to cars and racing. He wanted it to be perfect, and he expected to do well.

Nancy Foyt provided a mother's perspective. Her husband, Tony, refused to wear a radio headset during a race because he didn't want to listen to the conversation between his father and his son.

"He didn't want to hear anything. I had to wear the radio," she explained. "It was tough on the whole family. You never want to see your children upset.

But it was toughest on A.J. and Anthony. I think A.J. probably didn't want him racing. It was hard on him, and in turn, he was hard on the kids. I think he was so relieved when they both stopped driving."[39]

Meira began advancing slowly after the start of the 500 and moved into the top twenty just past the halfway point. That's when he was forced to take evasive action to avoid another car then slid up into the Turn Two wall, knocking him out of the race.

The team posted four more top-ten finishes before the year was out, capping the season with a sixth place at Homestead-Miami in the last race of the year. Meira finished twelfth in total points, the team's best finish since 2002, and they earned a solid "B" from the *Indianapolis Star* in its annual rankings, making "a nice comeback."[40]

The end of the year also saw the IRL present its first A.J. Foyt Award to Dario Franchitti as the top oval track performer, while Will Power picked up the Mario Andretti Award for his prowess on road and street courses. The awards were part of an effort by the IRL to build on the legends of the sport.

"I don't know about 'legend,'" Foyt said at the announcement. "I'm just old A.J., too old and too fat to get in (a race car)."[41]

ABC
Supply Co inc.
COYOTE
A.J. FOYT ENTERPRISES
SUNOCO
5
14

CHAPTER 35

LIFE AND DEATH

2011–2012

A.J. Foyt missed the first race of the 2011 IndyCar season on the streets of St. Petersburg, but he had a good excuse. He'd had a stent placed in his main heart artery two days earlier.

With his wife Lucy scheduled for a triple bypass, doctors took advantage of the timing to conduct an angiogram on A.J. Not to be upstaged, the test revealed a 95 percent blockage of his primary heart artery, and doctors decided to try and install a stent. Adding to the challenge, they were forced to work through several previous stents to get to the blockage and then open the artery enough to install the new stent. With Lucy's bypass successfully completed, her team of doctors stood by if needed.

"It was touch-and-go according to Dr. (Andrew) Civitello," Foyt said, employing the same flair for the dramatic he often used while describing racing accidents.[1]

"I watched on the machine while they did it. After what seemed like an awful long time, my doctor stepped back and said, 'We got it, A.J.' I can't tell you how happy and relieved I was. I think he was, too."[2]

Foyt was back at his ranch within a couple of days and back at the track two weeks later for the Grand Prix of Alabama. It was just in time to assume his leading role in the buildup to the one hundredth anniversary of the first running of the Indianapolis 500 in 1911. Foyt's first 500 victory had come on the fiftieth anniversary in 1961.

The celebration was being orchestrated by IndyCar CEO Randy Bernard, who was in his second year as series head. He'd been running the Professional Bull Riders Inc. and had never been to an Indy car race before assuming his role. But he had instituted a number of changes and rebranded the series "IndyCar."

◀ With Jack Housby. *David Nearpass*

He also announced a $5-million bonus for another driver outside of the regular IndyCar ranks that could win the last series race of the year at Las Vegas. Foyt was one of those impressed by Bernard's first year on the job.

"I think he's brought 100 percent improvement from where we were a year ago," A.J. said. "Even though he knew nothing about racing, he knew promotion and that's the secret to anything."[3]

Doing his part to help, Foyt's No. 14 carried a new paint scheme reminiscent of the car he ran in 1961. ABC was back as sponsor as was driver Vitor Meira, returning for his third season with the team. The year got off to a good start, with a pair of top-ten finishes and Meira running at the end of all four races as the series headed to Indianapolis.

It seemed not to matter that A.J. was somehow the second choice to drive the pace car for the 500. The first choice was Donald Trump, star of NBC's *The Apprentice.* The announcement created significant blowback and a Facebook recall campaign as Trump increased his attacks on President Barack Obama and implied he might run for president himself. When Trump eventually withdrew from the role, Foyt agreed to step forward and make everyone happy:

> I ran second in a lot of races (as a driver). I was just glad I won this race. As long as you wind up first, who cares? It will probably be as nerve-wracking as it was when I got in a race car before each race. Everybody's going to be looking for me to screw up. It's been a few years since I've ran around there, but I think I still know my way around. This is just a great, great honor, and I'll do everything I can to make the Indianapolis Motor Speedway and the Hulman-George family proud.[4]

"I'm quite sure fifty years ago, if I would have had this car, it would have been a hell of a lot better than the one I drove," he said of the Camaro SS pace car. "Probably could have won and listened to the radio. I'm just glad to be able to say fifty years later, I'll lead this race one more time."[5]

To cap things off, he was voted number one by the fans on the list of "greatest thirty-three drivers in Indianapolis 500 history." As he often did, he deflected the honor.

"Who's gonna say that *waaay* back I could beat them guys?" he said. "Who right now can say I could beat these boys? Way I look at it, to be truthful with you, it's nice for people to say that. But I'm A.J. I'm glad to be named amongst 'em. It's not that I'm any better."[6]

All the activities and promotions were having an impact on Meira, thirty-four, who was beginning to talk quietly about retirement. He was up to 118 Indy car starts without a victory. He said,

> I've been thinking about what it would mean to win here even more this year. Every driver out here thinks they deserve it, but I think I've paid my dues. It'd be really nice to have payback on those dues here this year. There's a reason I'm here. It's because I deserve to be here. I don't have to

prove I can win. Everybody knows it. If people want to be negative because I haven't won, that's their choice, not mine.[7]

Winning it for A.J. would just take it to the next level. There's a reason he was picked to drive the pace car. To be there together with him would be really cool. I've been thinking about that a lot lately.

The team added a second Brazilian driver for Indianapolis with Bruno Junqueira signing on for the No. 41 car. Meira ran well all month and qualified eleventh, with Junqueira in nineteenth. Shortly afterward, however, Junqueira found himself being bumped out of a ride in the 500 for the second time in three years.

It had been a wild Bump Day with six drivers failing to qualify. One of those was Ryan Hunter-Reay, whose first-year sponsorship from the delivery services company DHL was one of the most lucrative in Indy car racing. Looking for a way to get into the 500 and keep their sponsor happy, it was suggested team owner Michael Andretti talk with Foyt.

Hunter-Reay knew from his time with Foyt that the team's second car was typically funded out of A.J.'s own pocket. A deal was eventually worked out, and even though it wasn't the first time such an arrangement had been reached—not even the first time Foyt had worked out such a deal—the announcement created a great amount of controversy. Most felt Junqueira had been sold out and wronged by Andretti and Foyt.

"Before I did anything, I talked to [Junqueira] about it," Foyt countered. "And he said, 'I understand clearly.' He said, 'If you wouldn't have given me a ride, I'd have been home in Brazil.' I'd guaranteed him X amount of dollars to come here."[8]

Foyt added, "I know it's a tough deal for Bruno but he understood the situation. I appreciate that more than anyone knows. This is going back to the way racing used to be, where if people were in a lot of trouble, you tried to help each other out. We've been competitors for many years but still it's the kind of relationship when someone is really down and out, you can't turn your back on them—at least I can't."[9]

Michael Andretti was obviously appreciative, saying, "I can't thank A.J. and his team enough for giving us an opportunity to put Ryan in the Indy 500. Obviously, this is a unique circumstance for our team, but the thought of A.J. Foyt joining forces with the Andrettis for the Indy 500 could result in something special. It's a credit to A.J. for being willing to help us with one of our full-season IndyCar entries at a time when we need it."[10]

Caught in the middle were the drivers.

"It's an awkward position to say the least," Hunter-Reay said. "I feel absolutely horrible for Bruno. But this whole deal is not about me."[11]

"Nobody on our team wanted it to go this way, trust me. This is not about 'Let's go get Ryan a ride.' That's not what this is about. It's about keeping the doors open on the twenty-eight car. It's about keeping the jobs of sixty people."[12]

Junqueira showed plenty of class, saying, "I always respected A.J. before, but after working with him, I respect him even more. He has a lot of knowledge and

I learned a lot from him. I had a great time working with him and Vitor and I hope my work helped them this month. I also hope the team has a great race."[13]

Hunter-Reay's only opportunity to drive the car came during the one-hour Carb Day practice session. The No. 41, decked out in Foyt Orange and yellow DHL colors, turned in one of the top-ten speeds, as did Meira. Race management and pit stops would be handled by the Andretti team, and although Hunter-Reay would start last as a replacement driver, his fast practice laps created an interesting question: Would Foyt go to Victory Lane if Hunter-Reay were to win?

"I'll be there," he said. "To Mario I'll say, 'Keep your ass out.' Cause Mario ain't got nothing to do with this deal. This is all me and Michael. Let's face it, Michael is a lot different from his daddy."[14]

As it turned out, Foyt didn't have to worry about keeping Mario out. After driving the pace car for the start—with Mario right behind driving the two-seat Indy car—Foyt was back in the pits overseeing Meira's run. No. 14 never threatened, finishing fifteenth. Hunter-Reay struggled to a twenty-third place finish. "We just missed the balance," he said. "I almost lost it at least twelve times."[15]

In a finish reminiscent of Foyt's 1967 victory, Dan Wheldon maneuvered around the wrecking car of J.R. Hildebrand for his second Indy 500 victory. It was an especially important win for Wheldon, who was looking for a ride for the rest of the year.

Over the next ten races, Meira picked up five top-ten finishes, a fifth at Toronto being the best result. Only a pair of mechanical DNFs kept him out of a possible top-ten position in points. But a disastrous trip to Japan saw him qualify twenty-fourth in the twenty-six-car field and then crash out early to finish twenty-fifth.

After initially indicating Meira would be back for a fourth season, possibly as part of a two-car team, the Foyts decided to see what other drivers might be available. "It's not working," A.J. said.[16]

At Kentucky, the penultimate event on the schedule, Larry talked with Wheldon, who was back in a car for the first time since Indianapolis.

"I didn't know him that well," Larry Foyt recalled. "He seemed liked a nice guy, and we talked to him about driving for us."[17]

They'd already decided to stick with Honda power for 2012, despite the return of Chevrolet to the IndyCar series giving car owners their first choice of engines since 2006. The move surprised some, given A.J.'s past relationship with Chevrolet, but he was banking on Honda's past experience to give their engines an edge to start the season.

"The people at Honda have been very good to us through the years and when I asked them a question, they always answered honestly," he said. "So you want to stay with people who are truthful with you. I did talk to Chevy and they have been very good to us through the years, too, but we have to find a way to get back to Victory Circle."[18]

Larry Foyt cited the team atmosphere at Honda for a reason to stay. "You could tell all the Honda teams kind of worked together. They were all part of the Honda family and I think that's something else Honda brings. I feel like we'll have a lot of great teammates now, too. We're racing against them, but we're racing with them too."[19]

By the time the series reached the October 16 finale at Las Vegas, Wheldon was off the board. He was set to drive in 2012 for Sam Schmidt, part of his Indy 500 winning ownership team. He was also driving at Vegas for Schmidt with a chance to win $2.5 million. When no driver had stepped forward to make an attempt for Bernard's $5-million Las Vegas bounty, he had adjusted the rules to allow Wheldon to run for half the initial offering, with the other half going to a lucky fan. There was one caveat—Wheldon would have to start last in an expanded field.

It was the first time the Indy cars were racing at the Las Vegas track since it was significantly reworked in 2006. At that time, the racing surface was repaved and narrowed and the twelve-degree banking changed to progressive banking with each turn at twenty degrees. That compared to the nine-degree banking at Indianapolis and eighteen-degree banking at Michigan, both longer tracks. And while a race's starting field outside of Indianapolis typically topped out at twenty-eight, thirty-four cars were prepared to start in the last race for the current generation Dallara racer.

"As crazy as that whole thing was, that was something Dan wanted to take on," recalled Doug Boles, who had been one of Wheldon's car owners at Panther Racing and the public relations director at Indianapolis Motor Speedway in 2011. He would go on to become Speedway and IndyCar president. "He wanted to win that race because I think he believed it was helping grow the sport."[20]

Driving the same car that sat on the pole at Indianapolis, Wheldon could do no better than twenty-ninth in qualifying. It didn't matter that much as he would start last anyway, but the lack of speed was concerning. The car was completely rebuilt the night before the race, and when the green flag fell, he immediately began moving up and was on the radio to his team.

"This thing is fantastic," car owner Schmidt remembered Wheldon saying. "I don't know what you did to it, but the speed is back. I can go anywhere and do anything. I can drive around any of these guys."[21]

As the field started lap eleven, it was divided into several tightly bunched groups of cars. Two drivers in the first group, traveling at more than 220 miles per hour, touched wheels and lost control. One car became airborne, went into the outside wall, and exploded into flames. Drivers in the second group tried to take evasive action, but the track was too narrow and the speeds too high. Meira—running in the middle of the track—tried to go low to avoid the carnage near the outside wall, started to lose control, and was hit by E.J. Viso.

Close behind and low on the track was Wheldon, who had hit 224 mph on the front straight and already passed a third of the field. With nowhere to go, his car climbed up the back of Viso's and launched skyward nose first. The car began to roll in the air, flying over Meira and bouncing off the track into and on top of the SAFER barrier and into the catch fencing. The cockpit was facing the fencing, and as the car slid backward, the rollbar was sheared off, and Wheldon's head hit at least one of the support poles. The impact caused "non-survivable blunt-force trauma injuries to Dan's head," according to the official Indy Car report that referred to the accident as a "perfect storm." It all took less than three seconds.[22]

Fifteen cars were involved in the crash, and after another slow caution lap, the red flag was displayed. Those still running were brought down pit road, and at first drivers were told to stay in their cars for a restart. However, when damage to the wall and fencing where Wheldon hit was discovered and it was determined it would take some time to repair, the drivers were allowed to get out of their cars. As Wheldon was airlifted to the nearby University Medical Center, drivers, car owners, and team members began to congregate, joined by others returning from the crash site.

Many of the drivers were close to the outgoing and upbeat Wheldon. Several, including Dario Franchitti and Danica Patrick, were openly in tears. It had been the first on-track fatality in five years, and times had changed since the early days of Foyt's career when he said he learned not to get close to other drivers for fear they would be killed in a crash.

"I didn't have a lot of friends," Foyt had said. "Well, I had a lot of friends, don't get me wrong. But not ones I was close to. I'd say I'd rather be your friend—close but not *that* close—so if you got killed, it didn't bother me that much. I knew a lot of people got upset by that."[23]

After more than an hour, series CEO Bernard called the drivers together and told them what they already knew: Wheldon had not survived the crash. He also announced he was calling off the race. There was little discussion or protest among the drivers. Those with cars still running drove a five-lap tribute to Wheldon, running three abreast like at Indianapolis, while "Amazing Grace" and "Danny Boy" were played over the track's public address system.

Foyt said he was stunned by the decision:

> I'd never heard of such a thing. I'd seen so many people get killed. You hated it, but you didn't end the race. Look at Indy in '64. Look at Indy in 1973. I'd never heard of ending a race. It put me in shock, to be truthful with you.[24]
>
> You know when you get in there it's possible you'll get killed. There were so many mixed emotions. But to me, when I talked on that, I said, 'Man, it don't even make sense to me.' You know when you get in that car you can get killed. You get in a passenger car, you can get killed. You can get in an airplane and get killed. You don't know. But I'd never seen them end a race.

Larry Foyt says there was a generational split on how to proceed:

> You had A.J. and Mario definitely say, you know—let's continue the race. That's just what they did. I was in a middle generation. I'd been in races with some horrible accidents and we carried on.[25]
>
> But I think there was definitely a shift where the drivers at this time had gotten to where they were all a lot more friendly with each other, probably

> than any previous generation. And we weren't used to having deaths as frequently as the older guys. So I think the drivers just felt very strongly about it and the league went with that.

Bernard would say, "I didn't really care about tradition on this. I felt like no driver in their right mind could have a clear head knowing that one of their friends had just died, and I felt this is where I needed to make a stand and say, 'No.'"[26]

At the time Franchitti, the new series champion, told the Associated Press that Bernard had earned "an immeasurable amount of respect by canceling the race when grief-stricken drivers were unable to decide if the show—by tradition—should go on."

Years later, other drivers and car owners would agree with Bernard and Franchitti, including several who drove for Foyt. Bryan Herta, who by 2011 was a car owner and had run Wheldon's car earlier in the year at Indianapolis, recalled,

> The accident at Vegas was so big and so catastrophic, it was unlike anything else—a very unique situation. And I think that they actually did the right thing in that case. It was such a big crash. So many cars were eliminated. Everybody was out of the car, and by the time it was time to restart the race, everybody knew that Dan was gone. And I think that's a hard position to put the drivers in—take them out of the car, tell them, "Hey, one of your colleagues, one of your friends, somebody you were close to, [has] died. Now, get back in and drive." I think that's what was different. You know, when you're out there racing, you finish the race, I think that's the difference.

Davey Hamilton, who had returned to racing after career-threatening injuries, retired from IndyCar immediately after the event. He was one of the last drivers to make it through the crash site, and at the time he said he wasn't sure what to do:

> I mean, do we go, do we not go? Young drivers of that era were stomp and steer. I hated the way I had just seen them race. They just held it wide open and just kind of banged their way through. There was no respect.[27]
>
> Then they made us go through it a second time. They didn't just go red. You know, I made it through, and then I ran the caution lap, and there were cars and debris everywhere. I thought, *Oh my God, this is real.*
>
> We'd lost fifteen cars, but because I was still going, I felt we had a show to put on. I'm from Vegas. I'd [helped] build the racetrack. I wanted to race on the track. It wasn't the track's fault. It was just the combination that we had for that day, and the craziness of some of the drivers.
>
> But it took so long to fix the speedway, fix the fence, and by then we all knew Dan had passed. I think that's what played into it.

Many were critical of IndyCar after the event, including NASCAR champion Jimmie Johnson, who was quoted as saying, "I have a lot of friends that race in that series, and I'd just rather see them on street circuits and road courses. No more ovals."[28]

Foyt was quick to respond, noting his two worst crashes had come on road courses:

> I don't think Jimmie Johnson knows what he's talking about. He's never drove one, and he's pretty stupid to make a statement like that. You could say the same about stock cars. I've drove both, and I've been hurt real bad in both.[29]
>
> People like speed, so there ain't no sense (fooling) yourself. They want to see speed, and they want to see records being broken. You always hope you can make (the cars) 100 percent safe but this ain't going to be the last time things like this happen.[30]

Johnson later called Foyt, Mario Andretti, and others to clarify he was only talking about the high-banked ovals such as Las Vegas.

While the Indy car season was over, there was still one major auto racing championship to be decided. NASCAR's title was coming down to the season-ending race at Miami-Homestead in what many were saying was the most exciting title battle in NASCAR history, with Carl Edwards holding a slight points lead over Tony Stewart. Stewart, who was in his third year of running the No. 14 car—of which one columnist wrote, "may well be the most storied number of all time"—did his best A.J. Foyt imitation, keeping up a constant barrage of banter going into the race.[31]

At one point he was asked if he'd talked to Foyt. He said no, but added, "He'll call me after we win on Sunday."[32]

Edwards did nearly everything he could, capturing the pole and leading the most laps, but Stewart came back to win the race with Edwards second. The season ended in a tie, with Stewart earning the championship on the strength of his five victories to one for Edwards.

After watching the race on television, Foyt said, "I think Tony drove the best race of his life," which brought tears to Stewart's eyes when the message was relayed to him.[33]

"When someone wants to win like that, they aren't going to give up," Foyt said. "Tony was not going to quit. Now I knew Carl Edwards wasn't going to lay down. But I'm pretty certain Carl Edwards didn't know Tony's will. Come hell or high water, Tony was winning the whole thing."[34]

Stewart could only say, "Not many people can hear your lifelong hero say that. Just really, really flattering."[35]

President Barack Obama would later use the same words and quote "the great A.J. Foyt" in honoring Stewart in White House ceremonies.[36]

Before the year was out, the Foyts signed Mike Conway to replace Meira for 2012. After moving up through the Formula Three and Formula Two ranks in

Europe, Conway had spent the last three years in Indy cars, most recently driving for Michael Andretti's team and winning on the streets of Long Beach. Andretti had lost sponsorship for Conway's car at the end of the year, however, and had been forced to release the English driver.

After a halfhearted effort to find another ride in IndyCar, Meira announced he was returning to Brazil to drive stock cars.

"Everything has a beginning and an end," Meira said. "I just have to thank all [the] teams in Indy for the whole fantastic experience I have acquired over the past ten years.[37]

"I had some proposals to continue racing in the United States, but I strongly believe it's time for a new start, and I saw that it was the right moment to return to Brazil."

It was in sharp contrast to Foyt, who had been asked during the year when he might retire completely. His answer?

"When they lower that casket."[38]

2012

The year started the same way the previous one had, with A.J. Foyt in the hospital. This time the surgery was to remove bone spurs around his artificial knee and to repair a rotator cuff.

He was already being featured in a full-page newspaper advertisement titled "A.J. Foyt still has the Heart of a Champion" for Texas Heart Institute at St. Luke's Episcopal Hospital, where he and Lucy had been treated a year earlier.

He'd put the surgeries off until mid-January—after the holidays—but still planned to attend the 24 Hours of Daytona at the end of the month. He was scheduled to serve as the grand marshal for the fiftieth anniversary of the race—an event he'd won twice. Those plans were waylaid when a staph infection developed in his knee. What he thought would be a couple of days in the hospital turned into ten, and at one point, doctors were concerned he might not recover.

"I've broken a lot of bones in my life, but this was the hardest and scariest ordeal I ever went through," A.J. would say. "Unlike broken bones or even heart surgery, the doctors can't really predict the outcome with staph infections. And I heard a lot of stories from friends about people who died from it or had to have amputations. I did exactly what my doctors said to do and through it all, my wife, Lucy, took great care of me. The good news is that I was so worried about my knee that my rotator cuff healed just fine."[39]

With A.J. sidelined, Larry Foyt continued to work on rebuilding the team. He was instrumental in landing Conway, and now he brought in Don Halliday, a veteran chief engineer. He'd reached out to Halliday at the suggestion of Kenny Bräck, who'd worked with him for two years at Rahal Letterman Racing. Bräck also put in a good word to Halliday about the opportunity with the Foyts. Larry then hired a shock expert and Raul Prados, a young Spanish engineer who'd been working in GP2—the primary development series for Formula One. They represented the largest engineering staff in team history.

"I'd heard stories about A.J. from Kenny, and that's really why I went there," Halliday recalled. "Kenny thought I could give them a bit of a hand, and I really liked the idea of a David and Goliath sort of battle. What I knew of A.J. was that he was a highly respected guy who called a spade a spade."[40]

Halliday, originally from New Zealand, started in open-wheel racing in the late 1970s working for the McLaren and Brabham F1 teams, before moving to Indy cars in 1985. He'd worked with a number of top drivers including Scott Pruett, Dario Franchitti, Paul Tracy and—of course—Bräck.

"The chief engineer is obviously a very important piece of the puzzle when you talk about building a race team, so getting to know him and watching him interact with our group as we started to work together makes me very optimistic," Larry said. "I really enjoy his approach to engineering a race car and his methodology, and I think it's going to fit in really well with our team."[41]

"What I've tried to do is get us back up and modernize all the computer systems that A.J. doesn't care about."[42]

The team was facing the same challenge as everyone else in IndyCar racing, sorting out an all-new Dallara race car, named the DW12 in honor of Dan Wheldon. The level playing field seemed to help the Foyt squad as Conway turned in the fourth-fastest time at preseason testing. Using a cane, A.J., who'd lost about forty pounds during the staph infection ordeal, was back in the pits for the first race of the year on March 25 at St. Petersburg, where Conway dropped out early. A week later at Barber Motorsports Park in Alabama, Conway qualified a surprising fourth and raced to a seventh-place finish. He followed it with top-ten qualifying runs at Long Beach and Brazil but struggled to put together a complete race. Still, it was enough to impress A.J.

"When I got sick in January, Larry stepped up and did a great job. He's been here awhile and is running the team now, making more and more decisions. He hired Mike Conway, a talented young guy, to be our driver. He hired Don Halliday who has the same kind of competitive drive I do."[43]

Halliday was enjoying his time with the team, especially when he was working with A.J. at the Waller race shops. In advance of Indianapolis, a second car was added for Wade Cunningham, increasing the challenge. Halliday recalled,

> Raul was new to Indy, and he and I were the engineering group. We'd bounce ideas around with A.J. He loved to be involved. That's what it was all about when we were working down there in Texas. When you're a small band of folks as we were, up against the bigger teams—Roger's team and such—you really bond together and support each other through thick and thin. It was one of the reasons I joined them. I liked that situation. I'd probably been in that situation where you're fighting the big boys most of my career.[44]
>
> A.J. saw how much we were up against it. He was very much a realist about what we were trying to do and was always very supportive. As long as you're straightforward with A.J., he returns the favor. Absolutely straightforward.

Cunningham was from New Zealand and a 500 rookie, although he'd won three Indy Lights races at the Speedway and had five podium finishes in six starts at the track. Conway had last raced at the Speedway in 2010 when he'd led fifteen laps before being involved in a vicious crash two laps from the finish. He'd been close behind the car of Ryan Hunter-Reay when it ran out of fuel, and Conway rode up over it, sending his own car pinwheeling into the catch fence. The car disintegrated around him, and he was airlifted to Methodist Hospital, where he was treated for multiple fractures to his lower left leg and a broken back. He'd been in one of the Andretti cars to miss the 2011 race but didn't think the accident had anything to do with it.

"It was different coming back after the crash and I had to get rid of some of the cobwebs," Conway said. "The first time I went through Turn Three, I thought, *This is where I nearly killed myself*."[45]

"It doesn't really come into it [now], thinking about the accident. I kind of have a love-hate relationship with this place. I love being here, but after last year, not making it, you kind of hate it. I've seen a few sides of it now. But I'm coming back here."[46]

Both drivers struggled in the five days of practice before qualifying, although it didn't really matter as the introduction of the new car and lack of engines made it unlikely there would be any bumping. In qualifying, the Chevrolet engines were clearly strongest, sweeping the first two rows. Cunningham eventually qualified twenty-sixth, with Conway twenty-ninth. Conway would also be fined $10,000 for using non-approved parts but was allowed to retain his starting position as a record thirteen cars were hit with infractions. Despite the struggles, Conway was still optimistic going into the race.

"I love having [A.J.] on the pit wall, on the radio. He gets pretty vocal sometimes, but he's passionate. It's his team at the end of the day and he wants the best for it."[47]

While Cunningham was dogged by electrical problems early in the race, Conway was the biggest mover through the first 125 miles, picking up nineteen spots and moving into the top ten. During a series of green-flag pit stops for all the cars beginning at about the seventy lap mark, he moved into third before entering the pits for his own stop on lap seventy-seven. That's when it started to unravel.

Forced to swing wide around another car being worked on in the pit behind his, Conway came in too fast and at too sharp an angle. The No. 14 car slid into two of the awaiting crew members, knocking both to the ground. Making matters worse, the car was too close to the wall, and the tire changers struggled to complete their work. When he finally got back on the track, Conway was ordered by IndyCar to "drive through" pit road—a penalty for hitting the crew members. He never made it.

Unnoticed during the stop was damage to the front wing. Television coverage showed the wing askew, but before the team could get Conway back in the pits, he spun in the first turn and hit the outside wall. Closing fast was Will Power, who submarined the spinning car, sending it into the air and sliding backward along the wall on its side. Both drivers walked away from the accident—a credit to the new car.

"He was the class of the field," Halliday would say of Conway. "Right at the sharp end. He was moving right up and was one of the big surprises. I think he could have won it. But then mistakes were made in pit lane. Our refueling guy bounced off the front wing and broke something there, which we didn't realize in the chaos of the moment. We probably should have been more thorough about what we were doing when we were doing it, but it was the heat of the moment, I guess."[48]

Foyt was surprisingly calm after the turn of events. "We had a hell of a run going," he told the *ABC Sports* broadcast team. "We had our game plan and everything was working good. But to win this Indy 500, everything's got to fall your way. One little thing like that goes wrong and it's bad. At least he's a competitive driver and I'm happy about that."[49]

"It really don't make me mad if he's up front or running to the front if something happens. It just makes you mad if he's at the back and something happens."[50]

In a dramatic finish, Takuma Sato drove under the leading car of Franchitti heading into Turn One of the last lap in an attempt to take the lead. With the two cars nearly side-by-side, the rear of Sato's car lost traction, and he spun, crashing hard into the wall while Franchitti went on to victory.

Conway managed a ninth-place finish the following week on the Belle Isle road course in Detroit then failed to crack the top-ten in three straight oval track races. He finished third on the streets of Toronto, the team's first podium finish since 2010, although afterward the team was fined $15,000 and docked ten points for having an enlarged fuel tank "that could have potentially given Conway an advantage in track position," according to IndyCar.

After that, Conway failed to post another top-ten finish, and prior to the final race of the year at California Speedway (another oval track), he seemed to express concern about the upcoming event.

"Anytime you're driving with hesitation or fear, you're a danger to other people on the track," he said. "With a love for speed, racers must accept the danger."[51]

After participating in a midweek test session at California, he went to Larry and said he didn't want to drive in the race.

"I've come to realize I'm not comfortable on the ovals and no longer wish to compete on them," Conway said in a statement issued by the team. "I'm truly sorry for putting the team and our sponsors in a difficult position, but this is the hardest decision I have ever made in my racing career. I want to stress that I am not finished racing and to this end, I would like to continue with Foyt Racing, but that's something we need to discuss in the future."[52]

Larry Foyt also issued a statement, saying he was "disappointed that we can't finish out the season together," and that it "took a lot of courage for Mike to come forward and we respect him highly for that and we certainly want to honor his decision."

Other drivers quickly supported Conway's move.

"There's no shame in what he did, at all, considering some of the things that happened to him," Power said. "He probably had a car that wasn't right. I understand when the car's not right it is tough around this place."[53]

Ryan Hunter-Reay said, "I look up to him for looking himself in the mirror and doing what he feels inside and not letting ego stand in the way or anything like that. I don't think anybody should be out there if they don't feel absolutely comfortable. If you have an imbalance with your car at this track, the car is evil."[54]

Cunningham was brought back to drive the No. 14 in the race. He admitted, "We're not too great on the time sheets," after qualifying twenty-third in the twenty-six-car field, then added, "but not too uncomfortable."[55]

Conway would later say, "I never liked ovals, to be honest. And then I was in the Indy crash, and [Wheldon's crash] at the end of 2011, that obviously didn't sit well with me. I just felt like it was time to call it a day, and there's no sense doing something you aren't enjoying. It was the best decision for me, and I am happy I made it because I wouldn't have been able to enjoy it."[56]

Halliday said, "I enjoyed working with Mike very much, he's an extremely good driver. Towards the end at Fontana there were all sorts of things going on about the track being dangerous and all sorts of other things. I think it got to Mike. We had to work through that and we came up with what he felt most comfortable doing, which was perfect. I thought we had a pretty damn good year, considering where we started from."

Although Conway had said he hoped to return to the Foyt team, they couldn't afford the luxury of a road racing specialist and went their separate ways after California. Conway would return to IndyCar the following year, winning at Belle Isle for Dale Coyne and in 2014 at Long Beach and Toronto for Ed Carpenter. He'd eventually become a fixture on Toyota's international sports car team, where he won multiple races and championships, including the 2021 24 Hours of Le Mans. He finished fifth in the 2025 race at Le Mans.

rena
Houston
Houston
HONDA
ABC Supply Co. inc.
AJ Foyt Racing
HONDA
IZOD INDYCAR SERIES
GAF
sparco
Supply Co. inc.
PHYTER
HOUSTON verizon P1 AWARD
sparco
T. SATO
ABC Supply Co. inc.
www.takumasato.com
14

CHAPTER 36

THE ODD COUPLE

2013–2016

Despite parting ways with Mike Conway late in 2012, A.J. and Larry Foyt had several surprisingly good choices for their next driver.

One was Ryan Briscoe, who after five seasons and eight victories was released by Roger Penske. Another was Justin Wilson, who'd driven for Dale Coyne in 2012, winning at Texas Motor Speedway. He'd also been part of the winning team in the 24 Hours of Daytona.

Instead, Larry went in a different direction, reaching out to a driver who'd been on his radar for several years and had popped up on A.J.'s screen in a big way following his desperate last-lap attempt to pass Dario Franchitti at Indianapolis—Takuma Sato. The Japanese driver had ended up in the wall and Franchitti in Victory Lane, but his avowed "No attack, no chance," motto registered with A.J.

"Dad always told me that it's easier to calm a hard-charger down than prod a guy that doesn't want to charge," Larry said. "If you keeping wrecking A.J.'s race cars, you have to tell him. It's a pretty calming effect on you."[1]

Larry had talked with Sato at the end of the 2011 season only to discover the driver was already under contract to another team. He was available now, but Larry knew the selection would be a controversial one. Sato didn't have many friends after the 500, his banzai move for the victory having upset executives at American Honda after he almost took out the popular Franchitti and cost Honda a podium sweep.

Both Foyts liked Sato's aggressiveness, and there was another plus. As Honda Japan's house driver, he brought significant financial support from the manufacturer in the form of special engine leases and Panasonic sponsorship. Estimates put the total package at about $3 million. Being Honda's house driver, however, also carried the implication that perhaps he didn't belong in IndyCar on his own merit.

◀ Sato and Foyt celebrate a pole position. *ABC Supply*

He'd started racing at the relatively late age of nineteen in 1996, driving go-karts in Japan. He showed immediate ability, winning the national karting championship the next year and attracting the attention and friendship of Hirotoshi Honda, the son of Honda founder Soichiro Honda and owner of Mugen Motorsports, an aftermarket performance parts supplier and tuner for Honda products, with close ties to his father's company.

Sato moved to England to compete in the 2000 British Formula 3 series, where Honda power dominated. He won four races his first season and finished third in the overall rankings. The next year, he won a stunning fourteen events, the British championship, and the season-ending premier F3 event—the Macau Grand Prix, which brings together champions from around the world.

Sato's F3 success earned him a promotion to the Honda-powered Jordan Formula One team for 2002, completing the jump from go-karts to F1 in just five years. At that point, however, Honda was no longer the engine of choice, with Ferrari, BMW, Mercedes, and Renault all outperforming the Japanese manufacturer. During the next several years, Sato moved from one Honda-powered team to another, sometimes serving as a reserve driver. He showed signs of brilliance, including a podium finish in the 2004 U.S. Grand Prix at Indianapolis, while building a reputation as an aggressive driver—at times too aggressive. Despite the aggression, he was well-liked and known for his spirit and professionalism off the track.

His limited success was not enough to keep Sato in F1 when Honda withdrew from the series at the start of 2009. He had tryouts with several teams and performed well but was left without a ride for the year. Instead, he attended the Indianapolis 500, where Honda was the sole engine supplier, and signed on with KV Racing Technology for 2010. He earned two pole positions and three top-five finishes over two years before moving to Bobby Rahal's team for the 2012 season.

Rahal's team had helped bring Honda into Indy car racing back in the mid-1990s but was struggling financially, missing more races than it competed in, and the company was looking to help prop up the team. Sato scored two podium finishes in addition to leading thirty-one laps in the Indianapolis 500 before the failed last-lap pass. His refusal to settle for second place also cost the team about $800,000 in prize money and a destroyed race car. At the end of the year, Rahal told Sato his son Graham was joining the team. Sato was without a ride again.

Then came the call from Larry Foyt.

"Larry was very keen to talk to me," Sato remembers. "He told me that A.J. was interested in me because of the last lap of the Indy 500. I was quite happy with that and of course very proud to be recognized by A.J. Foyt.[2]

"Back in the day, he was obviously very strong and aggressive on and off track," Sato said with a laugh when asked what he knew of A.J. at the time. "He was kind of an American dream. An unbelievable guy. Just a living legend. That's what I knew about him."

While Sato had met A.J. in passing at the track during his first three years in IndyCar, he'd never had a discussion with him. Initial negotiations were conducted with Larry, who brought A.J. in to approve the deal.

"I hardly make any decisions that I don't bounce off of A.J.," said Larry, who quickly arranged a Skype call for Sato and A.J. to say hello and finalize the contract. The pair didn't talk in depth until the Japanese driver visited Houston and the Foyt racing shop in preparation for the 2013 season. It was the first chance for Sato to talk at length with A.J. and meet "the boys," as the "boss" called his team.[3]

"A.J. said he wanted someone determined to win the race," Sato recalled. "Obviously, all the race car drivers want to win the race, but probably, for him, I showed what he really wanted, that there was no second. It was an honor to be received that way.[4]

"A.J. Foyt's team's philosophy is that they really needed a driver for that. And I really needed a team that needed a driver like me. Both philosophies were matching together."

A.J. also made it clear that while he appreciated Sato's aggression while going for the win, he didn't think such moves were warranted when battling for position further down the field and wanted a driver capable of bringing "a tenth-place car home in tenth place and a fifth-place car home in fifth."[5]

Afterward, Foyt showed Sato around the race shop and his ranches:

> He gave me a tour, explaining all the great trophies. Then he drove me around his ranch and it was very interesting. He likes to talk—*a lot*—and I was really happy to listen. I was sitting in the passenger seat while A.J. was driving, trying to explain every single detail of his ranch—the land, the trees, the house—and tell me a big part of the history. It was amazing, and I really enjoyed it.
>
> To me, A.J., what a charming guy. To the people who knew A.J. Foyt back in the '60s and '70s when he was racing hard, they really wouldn't think that word for him. But to me, he was very charming. That's how I learned who was A.J. Foyt. That was quite a day for me.

While Foyt joked that, "My Japanese ain't real good," and he struggled to call his new driver "Takuma" or his nickname, "Taku"—sticking mostly with "Sato" instead—the day of bonding touched off an unlikely relationship that blossomed during the next four years. Foyt introduced Sato to Tex-Mex food and "Texas T-bone steaks," although Sato failed to interest Foyt in sushi. Both shared a love for Italian food, and it became their go-to meal of choice.[6]

It was apparent from the first preseason practice session that the new team was clicking on the racetrack as well. Lead engineer Halliday was back for his second season, and he and Sato also connected.

"Over the winter we had a series of tests, and I knew we could be quite competitive," Sato said of the first track sessions with the team. "Don and I found—it's hard for me to explain—I just really melded into the team so quickly. It was kind of [a] chemical good effect, that understanding together, and we developed the car in a very short time over the preseason. Then bang-bang, we immediately showed good speed."

Sato continued,

> I understood that A.J. Foyt wasn't one of the competitive teams at that time, although, as a single car team, it was a great team. But we couldn't afford to do our own damper program. Penske, Ganassi, Andretti—they all had in-house damper programs, which really separates teams in today's spec series.[7]
>
> Driving the legendary No. 14 car was an absolute honor, and the boys were lovely, lovely guys. We knew there was more strength coming onboard and more strength for the engineering. We had an international engineering team. We had an Italian engineer [Raul Prados, who was actually Spanish], we got a British engineer, who was Don Halliday of course [actually from New Zealand], and then we had a Japanese driver with a typical American team. To me, it was something that was very attractive. I knew we could be very competitive.

And they were, right from the start when Sato, who'd always done well on street courses, qualified second for the opening race of the year at St. Petersburg. He'd never qualified better than eleventh in the past, and it was the team's first front-row start since 2011. He suffered minor damage to his front wing early in the race and lost more time during pit stops before finishing a disappointing eighth.

He was fast again in second-round qualifying two weeks later at Barber Motorsports Park but received penalties on his two fastest laps for blocking, although most of the drivers sided with him. The penalty dropped him to twelfth at the start and, mired back in the field, he finished fourteenth. The team strongly protested the penalty but to no avail. "Glad A.J. wasn't here," read the post on the team's Twitter page.[8]

After serving as grand marshal for the 24 Hours of Daytona and attending St. Pete, A.J. had been at home preparing to go into the hospital again. He'd taken a fall at the ranch during the winter, aggravating back issues that doctors believed dated to his 1965 stock car crash at Riverside, California. He'd also regained all his weight over the past year and perhaps even added a pound or two, which didn't help his mobility challenges. Sato convinced him to try acupuncture, and when that didn't work, Foyt opted for the surgery, which had earlier helped his wife, Lucy. Doctors said if all went well, he'd be back for Indianapolis.

At Long Beach, Sato qualified fourth and immediately moved up to challenge pole sitter Franchitti. This time Sato was not to be denied, and he led a race-high fifty of eighty laps and pulled away from Graham Rahal near the end to score his first IndyCar victory—the first by a Japanese driver and the team's first since 2002.

"It was a special feeling," Sato said of the victory. "An incredible event. And winning in the No. 14 car was just an absolute plus. I was just very happy. Happy for myself, but also happy for the 14 team."[9]

Larry was on the phone to his dad, who'd been watching on television.

"I hate it that he's not here," Larry said. "He is definitely our big leader and he is the big boss man. This is for him. He was surprisingly calm. He said, 'If my memory serves me correct, I think it's been since 2002.' He's very happy." It was also the team's first road course win since Foyt won at Silverstone, England, in 1978.[10]

Sato also talked to the boss. "A.J. couldn't express how happy he was. He was just so impressed with the speed we got. We had two or three restarts and managed them really well. The pit stops, they may not have been the fastest, but they were very consistent, and we didn't make any mistakes. We managed the fuel well. It was just a great race. Simply a great race.

"He was so happy, of course for his own team, but also he was happy for me. To win like that, after only a couple of races. He was a very happy guy."

A.J. told a reporter who reached him at home, "The last five laps were the longest of anything. We've had a lot of drivers; none of them wanted to win. This boy wants to win."[11]

It was a popular win among others in the paddock, and congratulations poured in.

"I think people like to see some of the names that have been part of the past, they're still here, still to be reckoned with," said Mario Andretti. "That's a good thing in any sport." Even Bobby Unser said, "All the guys, all the old-timers, man, we're all so happy he's back winning again. That gives us a lot of pride, too."[12]

"It was overwhelming, to be honest," Larry said. "So many teams went out of their way to give us congratulations."

Years later, with the team still looking for its next win, Larry reflected on the Long Beach victory.

"Being able to bring that trophy home to him, that was certainly a proud moment. It was like, 'Look, Dad, we did okay. The race team did okay.' And he was just really happy for us. He couldn't have been more complimentary. He enjoyed seeing his race team do well."[13]

"If I could experience that with my dad (at the track) and be standing there with him and our team, that would definitely be the highlight of my life."[14]

The back surgery relieved enough of the sciatic nerve pain for A.J. to attend the Kentucky Derby ten days later. He'd elected to forgo the long plane ride to Brazil for the next IndyCar race, however, and as a result missed one of the best street course events in series history.

After qualifying twelfth and falling outside of the top fifteen in the early going, quick pit work, good strategy, and Larry's gamble not to change tires on the final stop put Sato out front with twenty laps remaining. He fended off repeated challenges from Josef Newgarden and James Hinchcliffe until the final turn of the final lap, when he slid wide and Hinchcliffe was able to get past. Sato held on for second. It was clear AJ Foyt Racing was on the way back, and A.J. gave the credit to Larry.

"He's about 100 percent in charge now," he said. "Before it was probably 50 to 75 percent. I've put him in full charge, and, you know, the kids [team members] are closer to his age anyway. Larry works them real hard every day on pit stops. We've made changes on different positions there and it's worked out good.[15]

Larry passed on the credit to Sato.

"Takuma jelled, the team jelled and it took us to the next level," he said. "It means a lot to the guys to have a guy like Takuma, who has a good attitude, who wants to win, who's smiling when he walks into the garage every day. It's lifted up the guys."[16]

"Sato has very, very good feedback. That helps the engineers a lot. He and the engineers work very close. I think that's really been successful for us."[17]

Conor Daly, who'd been impressive while filling in for Sato during a test at Sebring International Raceway in Florida when the Japanese driver had visa problems, was added to the team for Indianapolis. Daly, twenty-one, had been friendly with Anthony Foyt and met Larry at the F1 race in Austin.

It was a dream come true for Daly. His father was Derek Daly, the successful English driver who had competed in F1 and six Indianapolis 500s. His stepfather was Doug Boles, who'd been promoted from the Speedway's public relations head to its chief operating officer. His mother also worked at the Speedway, and Conor had missed the 500 only once, the previous year when he was racing at Monaco. He'd been running in Europe, competing in several GP2 events with a full-time GP3 schedule.

"I almost can't describe what it means to have the opportunity to race in the Indianapolis 500," Daly said. "It is truly my home race since I was born and raised in the Indianapolis area. I am so thankful that A.J. and Larry have given me my first shot at the greatest race in the world. I know this will sound cheesy, but I've never been happier in my life—this race means so much to me."[18]

A.J. said Daly "ran well at Sebring. He was fast, smooth and didn't get in trouble. When we made a change on the car, he felt it. I found him to be very savvy on the chassis setups. In fact, when we made a minor change which was really nothing, he thought about it and said it felt no different. I told him that was the right answer because we didn't do anything he'd be able to feel, so that impressed me too. I've run a lot of rookies at Indy and I think Conor will do a good job."

Larry added, "I've been watching him come up through the open-wheel ranks. When we met at the F-1 race in Austin last year, we hit it off immediately."

Sato was the series points leader as the teams arrived in Indianapolis. It was his first real opportunity to work with A.J. in setting up and preparing the car. Sato said,

> Going to Indianapolis as the point leader, that was an amazing feeling. I was really proud of that, really proud of being the Foyt driver to be able to do that. It was just absolute pleasure, absolute pride.[19]
>
> The people's imagination about A.J. Foyt will be [he wanted] nothing to do with technology or computers. However, he's very determined to understand the technologies and how they work. Of course the philosophy of how a car works is the same thing, but we have a lot more sophisticated

> aerodynamics and all sorts of things that weren't available in his time in terms of analysis and data. But he tries to understand it. At the end of the day, how the car behaves, it is essentially the same.
>
> When I was driving in practice I would come back to the pit box and all the engineers would plug in their data cables. I would report on how I feel, what the car is doing, while they were downloading all the data. The engineers would be waiting until they could see what the ride height is and the yaw angle and all those things.
>
> Before that A.J. would come to the radio and he would identify the problem. He was able to see it through the TV monitors while he was sitting on the pit box. Seeing my driving, he identified the car behavior, what the car was missing or what we need. A.J. was sitting there, knowing nothing about the data, however he just identified what my main problem is before I start talking. That was very impressive. I think only A.J. could do it. I've been fortunate enough to work with a lot of great team owners, drivers, and engineers, but none of them could do what A.J. could do. Only watching the TV monitor, never having driven the current aero-determined Indy car, but then he really understands everything. That was my first experience with A.J. and I was very impressed, very happy.
>
> Fundamentally, he was very keen for the technological side and he would really listen to what you say. But also he had such a strong opinion too. Sometimes, which drived me crazy. But mostly in a funny way. I think A.J. and I, we understood what it takes to go fast, and that was a fundamental feeling. I felt special but he also seemed to be enjoying . . . to working with me.

One thing Foyt didn't do was tell Sato how to drive the track:

> He never came into that territory. That was one of the great things too. He basically, really, trusted his driver. He liked my style and he completely supported my driving. He never told me how to do it. He was always supporting. That was the biggest thing. When things didn't go well, or did go well, he'd have his own opinion, but he never [instructed] me how to drive. He just never [did] that. Street course, road course, even the Indianapolis Motor Speedway, he never said that. The level of the trust I had in that environment, it was just fantastic.

Daly missed the first two days of practice—he'd been in Spain winning a GP3 race—and when he returned, it didn't take him long to make an impact—losing control coming out of Turn One and slamming the wall, tipping the car on its side and nearly flipping over. Foyt told the young driver not to worry about it, the car could be fixed, and had him back on the track in the team's backup machine before the day was out.

Daly recalled,

> The morning of the crash, someone had given A.J. a gun—a revolver, an Indy 500 specific gun. I had taken a picture with him and the gun. Then I crashed. I thought he probably wanted to use that on me.[20]
>
> A.J. was actually really cool with it, and the reaction was much better than I expected. I think the first thing he said to me was something like, "There are those who have crashed at Indy and those that will. It's just part of being around here."
>
> He always had something to say about the conditions and what the car should feel like. What he thought would be fast and good. You always had to listen. He's got a wide range of knowledge and an incredible amount of information. Obviously, the technology had come a long way and times had changed so much, but you were always listening to him because he had so much experience.

Sato qualified a disappointing eighteenth, and after blowing an engine on his qualifying run, Daly came back on Bump Day to earn the thirty-first spot. Sato noted he had started nineteenth the year before and was challenging for the lead on the last lap—which brought up the question, would he try that move again?

"I go for it when I see if I can, and if there's a good chance, I definitely go for it because that's racing," he said. "I think the 500 last year, it makes it pretty clear for the fans, if I'm given a chance, I'll go for it for sure. I've watched it a hundred times, maybe more. I think if there's a similar chance, I'd go for it for sure."[21]

Sato went for it from the start on race day, and by lap fifty was the race's fastest mover, making a three-wide pass going into Turn One to move into sixth, the highest-placed Honda-powered car. On lap fifty-seven, however, he lost control coming out of Turn Two and spun twice, somehow avoiding the wall. He got back in the race on the same lap as the leaders and despite blistering a tire, worked his way to thirteenth at the finish. Daly lost his rear brakes early and had a flash fire in the pits but still finished twenty-second, two laps back.

After a poor showing in Detroit in which Sato crashed out of the second of two races, he led a race-high 109 laps at Milwaukee before finishing seventh, the team's best showing at the track since Foyt finished fifth in 1988.

He was still fourth in points, but from there it was all downhill as he was able to finish only one of the next ten races. Three times he was involved in accidents, and the trend was upsetting other drivers.

"What an idiot," said Ryan Hunter-Reay at Pocono after being clipped by Sato entering the pits, knocking both top-five-running drivers out. Hunter-Reay said Sato, "unplugged his brain entirely."[22]

Mercifully missing most of the races was A.J. His back and legs were acting up, and he'd fallen again at the ranch. "I can barely walk, so I've got to get that fixed," he said. "I'm in too much pain to get to the races. I hate it. But hell, I'm getting old." He attended only the Texas race after Indianapolis and would eventually require a hip replacement and more knee surgery before the year was out, but that didn't keep him from coming to the defense of Sato.[23]

"We knew he was the type of driver who wants to win," he'd say. "Before, we had drivers who were what you'd call riders. Now we've got a guy who wants to hustle, while those other guys just wanted to ride around."[24]

"He stands on the gas!"[25]

Despite the collapse in the last third of the season, Sato, Halliday, and Prados all signed on to return to the team for 2014.

"Having everyone back next year is a big plus," Foyt said. "We came out strong but then had some problems. We are making changes so we will get stronger as the season goes on, which I believe is the key to being one of the contenders in the title race."[26]

Sato had discovered a closeness not typically found on the larger Indy car teams and certainly not found in F1. He enjoyed the relationship with "the boys" to the extent he returned from Japan each year in the middle of the offseason for the team's Christmas party in Houston.

"Working with A.J., Larry, Don and all the boys is just fantastic," Sato said at the time. "This team is really special for me. I always felt that the team was behind me and it gave me the confidence to go for the win in races."

2014

The confidence was apparent in the first race of 2014 as Sato came out flying, capturing the pole position at St. Petersburg. Honda had released a new twin turbocharged engine during the offseason, and for once the Foyt squad had been able to do extensive testing. Although he was still recovering from his surgeries, Foyt was also at the track.

"A.J. said, 'Very well done,' and he was happy," Sato said. "And making him happy is a very difficult thing. So I'm pleased."[27]

Sato led early, but the team went with a different tire strategy, and he fell back, finishing in seventh place. He failed to defend his title at Long Beach two weeks later when he was caught up in an accident triggered by Hunter-Reay. The crash took out most of the front-runners and allowed Conway to pick up another victory.

At Indianapolis, the team added rookie Martin Plowman, who'd been a European sports car champion and class winner at Le Mans the year before. He'd also run a couple of seasons in Indy Lights cars with a fair amount of success but was making his first start on an oval track in an Indy car.

Sato qualified sixteenth and Plowman thirty-second. Sato dropped back in the early going, but thanks to crashes that took out several of the front-runners he was up to fifth with fifty miles remaining. Although turning laps as fast as eventual winner Hunter-Reay, he fell back on the final restarts and finished a disappointing nineteenth. Plowman struggled throughout and finished twenty-third, four laps behind the winner.

The 500 was the start of a nine-race stretch where Sato failed to finish in the top fifteen. The team had its moments—a pole position on Detroit's Belle Isle course being the highlight. Four times Sato was involved in accidents that took him out of the race, although he was seldom to blame. He led early in the first of two Houston races, before being taken out by a backmarker, then did himself in during the next race. The team turned it around, finishing the final five races with three top-ten finishes, but it was too little, too late, as Sato finished eighteenth in points.

Soon after the end of the season, Foyt announced ambitious plans for the coming year. For the first time since 2002, the team would run a second car for the entire schedule. ABC Supply had agreed to increase its sponsorship and signed a new contract through 2017, although the team would still be operating with one of the smallest budgets of any full-time organization. It wasn't getting any easier to keep up with the "Big Three," however, as Penske Racing announced it was adding another driver, joining the Andretti and Ganassi teams with four car entries in the series.

"When you take these guys running three or four cars they get three to four times the information," A.J. said. "It really hurts the one-car teams. I won't ever run more than two. I think a two-car team, that's what we want. At the end of the day, we really felt two cars was the next step for us to compete week in and week out."[28]

Asked if the team would add another car for Indianapolis as it often did, A.J. seemed adamant. "I'm not Chip Ganassi, I'm not Roger Penske. My name is A.J. Foyt. So we're not looking to run three."[29]

Jack Hawksworth, a twenty-three-year-old Englishman, was hired to drive the No. 41 car. Once again Larry Foyt, who'd been promoted to company president, took the lead role in landing the driver. Hawksworth was coming off an impressive rookie IndyCar season where he picked up five top-ten finishes and the series "Rising Star" award. A.J. had seen him drive to a third-place finish in one of the Houston races and agreed to the signing.

A.J. also announced the purchase of a 45,000-square-foot building on Main Street in the city of Speedway in the shadow of the racetrack. It was becoming increasingly difficult to find experienced Indy car engineers and mechanics willing to make the move to Texas to work for the Foyt team, and the new building would be used as a base of operations throughout the racing season.

Foyt was in the news again before the year was out but for all the wrong reasons. He'd dug a 300-foot trench and was on his hands and knees laying water and electrical lines to a new horse barn when he realized something was off: "I had a burning feeling in my chest, like you put a cigarette out on me." He went to lunch, but when the sensation continued, he drove to the nearby race shop and called his doctor, who told him to go immediately to the hospital.[30]

He argued at first, then relented and allowed daughter-in-law Nancy Foyt to drive, an indication to her it must be serious. He insisted they stop at home first so he could take a shower after working in the field all day. Lucy then took him to Baylor–St. Luke's Medical Center where doctors were waiting for him and discovered blockages in three arteries in which stents had been placed just a year earlier. Foyt was admitted and scheduled for triple bypass surgery.

While the surgery went well, complications soon developed, and Foyt's breathing became irregular. There was concern about the amount of oxygen his brain was getting, and he was put into an induced coma and on a ventilator to help his lungs fully heal.

"That was a horrible experience," Larry Foyt recalled. "I just remember going to the ICU, and he was in rough shape after the surgery. They were struggling to get his lungs functioning again. It was a pretty delicate situation just to balance all the different things. They're trying medications to help the lungs, but those medications were negatively affecting the kidneys, so they couldn't do what they wanted to there. And in the induced coma, it definitely got scarier."[31]

At one point, doctors warned the family it didn't look good. A.J. wasn't coming out of the coma like they hoped, and they were going to run a brain scan. During his racing days, A.J. had often talked with Lucy about what to do if he suffered extensive injuries in an accident. He'd been firm that he didn't want to be kept alive by a machine. Now she remained firm even when some of the children questioned the decision.

"My mom told the doctors, 'Look, if there is severe brain damage, I want to uphold A.J.'s wishes from his racing days, which was that if he was mentally incapacitated or had severe brain damage, not to just keep him alive on a ventilator. Let him pass. Do not keep him alive in a vegetative state.'

"We can laugh now because he woke up the next day, and we said he must have heard us talking. We finally got him to wake up. The doctors did a great job. It was scary times, though. Very scary."

"I was proud of my wife," Foyt would say of Lucy. He was surprised to learn he'd been out for eight days.[32]

"It's been pretty rough but I guess I slept through the roughest part," he said in a statement issued by the team. "I had some problems that most people don't have after open heart surgery, so I made my doctors work extra hard but they saved my life. We've turned a corner so everything's pretty good. I've got a long way to go but I'm feeling better every day."[33]

One of the few visitors allowed to see Foyt in the hospital was Sato, who'd come from Japan for the team's holiday party and to see "the boss."

"I went to the hospital, and we would talk for hours," Sato recalled. "I spent some great time within his private time."[34]

A.J. spent more than three weeks of "sheet time," as he called hospital stays, with ten days in intensive care. He also developed bed sores that made his first days of recovery even more uncomfortable. And when doctors spotted a mark on his arm, they biopsied it, and it turned out to be skin cancer, requiring more surgery. He was never so happy to see the New Year.

2015

A.J. Foyt was moving slow but still made it to the race shop for a couple of hours to celebrate his eightieth birthday. He'd lost nearly fifty pounds during the recent health scare but was already putting some weight back on and was determined to be recovered in time to attend the Indianapolis 500.

"I can't believe it—that I'm eighty," he'd say. "I wasn't supposed to live to over twenty-two. So I don't know if that is good or bad. Somedays I feel my age, some days I don't. I'm not as strong as I was, but that comes with illness."[35]

"There's always a challenge out there," he told a reporter. "My whole life has been a challenge. I know what it's like to be on the bottom and to be on the top, and being on top is a hell of a lot better. I'm glad to be where I am, but I've still got a lot to do." And while he'd miss the first few races, he promised to be at Indianapolis, "Come hell or high water."[36]

By March, he convinced several crew members to help him up on a bulldozer so he could go back to knocking down trees and clearing the land. He continued to ignore pleas from family and friends to hire someone else to do the work.

"I always feel like when you get too damn lazy to work, you ought to lay down and die," he said. "You're no good for nothing anyway."[37]

He gradually built up his strength to where he was able to attend the Kentucky Derby by early May and then head for Indianapolis. He still tired easily, needed to rest often, and would retreat to his motorhome in the nearby driver's/owner's lot as a place he could escape to when the garage became too hectic.

The team arrived in Indianapolis with only one top-ten finish between the two drivers. There'd been signs of potential, especially at St. Petersburg where Sato qualified fifth and Hawksworth led laps before finishing eighth. Both crashed out early on a new track in New Orleans, and neither were competitive at Long Beach or Barber Motorsports Park.

Like all the teams, AJ Foyt Racing was trying to adapt to new bodywork that had been developed by the engine manufacturers to help differentiate the cars. The Chevrolets had the early advantage on the road courses, winning three of the first four races, and Foyt was on hand when Chevy made it four of five on the Indianapolis road course in early May.

The manufacturer balance improved when practice started for the 500, the first oval track event of the year. The Chevrolets were still fast, but Sato turned in one of the ten fastest times of the month as qualifying approached, and the team was hopeful of finding even more speed. Alex Tagliani, whom Foyt had added in a third car wearing No. 48 in honor of Dan Gurney, was also showing good speed. When three Chevrolet drivers had massive crashes in which they became airborne, however, officials slowed all cars by reducing horsepower levels.

"It was a tough situation because a lot of times in racing when decisions are made, it benefits some and doesn't benefit others," said Larry Foyt, who showed more restraint than his father ever had. "I wasn't happy because our cars were working really good (in qualifying setup). I'm not an aerodynamicist, but something [with the Chevrolet's] is going on there."[38]

After the changes were made, Sato could do no better than twenty-fourth in qualifying, while Tagliani qualified twentieth and Hawksworth twenty-eighth. Chevrolets swept the top-five spots and eight of the first ten.

Through it all, A.J. watched from his perch on the team's "war wagon," the engineering stand on pit road. His constant companion was Jack Housby, a former NASCAR, USAC, and sprint car owner and sponsor. Six days older than

Foyt, the pair had been friendly for more than fifty years. The Foyt team haulers came from Housby Mack, the largest Mack truck dealership in the country.

They'd grown closer in recent years as the number of their contemporaries dwindled and they faced their own medical challenges. Housby had been diagnosed with cancer the previous July, and at first they'd joked about their challenges, bragging about who had it worse.

"You son of a bitch, it's your turn now," Foyt said when he first heard of the cancer diagnosis. "You're old as hell." When Housby turned eighty, Foyt called him. "Well I made it," Housby said. "You've got a week to go, cowboy."[39]

Larry said Housby and his father "were just super friends. A.J. had a lot of respect and good memories with Jack from their racing days. And Jack was a hoot to have around. He was part of the great group of A.J.'s buddies that would be hanging out at the garage at Indy. A lot of good times."[40]

When the race started, Sato made a bold move going into the first turn, jumping to the outside of Sage Karam, a twenty-year-old driver making his second start in the 500 for Ganassi. Hunter-Reay was on the inside, making them three wide in the turn. As Karam moved up slightly exiting the turn, he made contact with Sato and was turned into the wall. Karam was knocked out of the race. Sato's damaged car was repaired, and he rejoined the field—although three laps back.

"Kind of a bonehead move," Karam said. "He sees me and Hunter-Reay side-by-side and he's trying to make it three wide. He doesn't need to go popping outside on lap one, turn one. It just doesn't make sense. It ruins a lot of people's races."[41]

"I knew he had a run but I didn't think he would be dumb enough to go around on the outside."[42]

Eddie Cheever and Scott Goodyear, former drivers serving as commentators on the ABC television broadcast, agreed with Karam. "That's just a bad bet, to be passing a car on the outside in the first corner," Cheever said. Goodyear added, "You can't win the Indy 500 in the first corner, but you can lose it."

Sato spent the rest of the race clawing his way back onto the lead lap—thanks to good pit strategy and a couple of well-timed caution flags—and eventually finished thirteenth. Hawksworth was running near the back but still on the lead lap when he tapped the back of another car on lap 176. Tagliani finished twentieth.

After the race, Karam and several of his crew members approached the Foyt engineering stand, looking for Sato. He was intercepted by Housby, and the pair exchanged words. Foyt overheard the remarks, yelled at Karam, and seemed ready to throw the first punch when others got between the two. Arie Luyendyk had discovered you don't invade A.J.'s Victory Lane and apparently that went for the engineering stand area as well. Foyt then told Sato not to be concerned.

"A lot of these guys, when they drop the green flag, they leave their brains in their helmet bag."[43]

Foyt was on hand the following week in Detroit, and the team again showed its prowess on rough street courses. Sato qualified fourth for the first of the two races and finished eleventh. He started the second race fifteenth then charged through the field to finish second. Hawksworth finished seventh in both events.

That was the team's high point of the season, however. While Sato would lead at California Speedway before being taken out by Will Power and come close again at Pocono, he'd have only two top-ten finishes over the final eight races, Hawksworth only one. Sato would finish fourteenth in points, Hawksworth seventeenth.

Missing the final two races of the year was Foyt, who had developed another staph infection in his knee. By late August, he was back on the operating table as doctors removed the artificial knee and replaced it with an antibiotic-infused cement spacer to help clear the infection.

"This is one of the worst things I've gone through in my life," he said, "knowing I have five or six weeks dealing with this and then having to get operated on again to take the spacer out and put in a new knee.

"I don't know if I'll ever be like I used to be, but I'm sure hoping so. I'm fighting awful hard."[44]

It couldn't have come at a worse time. An aggressive regimen of chemotherapy and radiation treatments had done little to slow Housby's cancer growth. Foyt had seen it before, how his father had gone through the ordeal to no avail. They talked daily on the phone, and when A.J. became concerned about Housby sounding suicidal, he insisted on going to see his friend in early September.

"We somehow figured out how to get him on the airplane and got him up there to see Jack," Larry recalled. "That was just a real important thing for A.J. He wanted to get up there to see him, and he made it happen."[45]

Housby passed away on September 10. A.J. doesn't like to talk about it, but Larry says, "We still miss him now. We still run Housby trucks to this day."

It was tough on A.J., who admitted the surgeries and Housby's death, "Really beat me down."[46]

2016

Foyt felt strong enough in the new year to travel to Daytona, where he'd been invited to help open the "reimagined" Speedway that had undergone a complete facelift.

"I'm feeling good," he said after donating a driving suit for an exhibit:

> I kind of stagger a little bit, and I'm just now getting to where I can walk again and out of the wheelchair and the walker. I made up my mind I wasn't going to walk with no cane. Every now and then, after I've been sitting down, I kind of look like I'm drunk. You don't realize at eighty-one years old you've got to learn to walk again. I'm getting there. Every day is a better day for me. I hope to go to all of the [IndyCar races]. I'm planning on it. Now, how we're going to go? That's something nobody can figure out today.[47]

Both the drivers and engineering team were back, and at first it seemed as if things would go well. At St. Petersburg, Sato finished sixth and Hawksworth eleventh. Sato was strong as usual at Long Beach, qualifying eighth and finishing fifth. At Barber Motorsports Park, the drivers were one-two on the time sheets going into qualifying then missed badly on the setups, and both finished outside the top ten.

Tagliani was added in a third car again for the Speedway. He was driving the No. 35 in recognition of Foyt's thirty-five consecutive starts in the 500. The car was decked out in Copenhagen black and Coyote orange colors, and Tagliani wore a black Hinchman driver's uniform.

While Tagliani turned in the team's best practice speeds, Sato was the fastest when it counted, qualifying up in twelfth position. Tagliani went on a wild ride during the second qualifying round, losing control coming out of the fourth turn and sliding down the track. The nose of the car clipped the inside wall at the entrance to pit road, and he spun seven times as he slid further down the track. He'd start thirty-third. Hawksworth wasn't much better and would start thirty-first.

Tagliani was on the move from the start, passing nine cars on the first lap. He continued running just inside the top twenty near the halfway point, when most of the field pitted during a caution, and Tagliani became just the second driver to start thirty-third and lead the race, joining Tom Sneva. Another car, driven by Alexander Rossi, also stayed out, and the two swapped the lead for the next ten laps before pitting.

While Tagliani led, Sato was actually better positioned, moving into the top five with about fifty laps remaining. He got as high as second when the leaders started their pit stops but was caught on the track with a number of other drivers when a yellow came out, benefiting those who had already stopped. Sato fell to tenth as a result, and in his haste to get back to the front, he brushed the wall coming out of Turn Four, ending his race. Hawksworth, who had driven a steady race, finished sixteenth, with Tagliani seventeenth. Rossi, who had stayed with a fuel-saving plan until the end, emerged the surprise winner, running out of gas on his cooldown lap.

The rest of the year didn't get any better. Neither driver led a lap, and Hawksworth failed to post a top-ten finish. Sato matched his season-best fifth place on the streets of Toronto then followed it up with a ninth place at Mid-Ohio. He qualified third at Pocono but failed to complete a single green-flag lap, slamming the wall at Turn Three.

Sato finished seventeenth in points and Hawksworth twentieth, last among the drivers running a full schedule. Larry Foyt acknowledged there would be offseason moves.

"When you've had a year like we've had, I'm sure there will be changes," he said. "They could be drivers, they could be engineers—they could be sons."[48]

Don Halliday, who'd just turned sixty-four, indicated he would leave at the end of the year. He'd been playing a reduced role as the team increased its technology focus and Prados played a bigger part. Halliday said,

> I'm more seat of the pants. Race engineering is still a touchy-feely thing. That's why I think A.J. and I got on really well. We shouted at one another

a couple of times. Sometimes it gets frustrating when you're not going as fast as you and everyone else would like to be going. We were similar spirits. I think he had respect for me, and I know I had huge respect for him.[49]

When the new formula [the DW12] was introduced, we competed pretty well. But the more people get to understand the subtle nuances of the car, there's a tendency for the smaller teams like A.J. and his group to become a little less competitive. When there are hundredths of a second separating the cars, it's tougher on the smaller teams.

Overriding everything was the camaraderie we had together, with A.J. at the head of it all. Through all the adversity, it was a great experience. When we had successes as a small group it was a great feeling for everyone. When we got close, it was still a great feeling.

L&W SUPPLY
ABC
20
SONAX

CHAPTER 37

CHANGING TIMES

2017–2020

Toward the end of the 2016 season, Larry and A.J. Foyt had already decided to replace Jack Hawksworth when they received some surprising news that would set off a chain of events impacting the team for years to come.

Honda was looking to get Chip Ganassi Racing back in the fold. Ganassi's three-year contract with Chevrolet was coming to an end, and the Japanese company wanted him back. It meant, however, that Honda would have to cut its support of one of its existing teams. A performance review narrowed the choice down to Foyt and Dale Coyne Racing, and Honda elected to continue to support Coyne, who it felt was making headway in efforts to upgrade his team. It fell to Art St. Cyr, president of American Honda's Performance Division (HPD), to break the news to the Foyts.

St. Cyr, who led HPD from 2012 to 2019, shared Honda's reasoning:

> It was a very difficult time. I really liked A.J. and Larry. To this day I respect their passion and what they do. But our currency was engine support, and we had a limited amount of resources. We had been supporting Foyt's team at the same level for a long time even though they weren't winning. In this industry, it's all about winning. We didn't want it to happen—we just couldn't support them any longer.[1]
>
> A.J. took it better than I hoped. He was disappointed, of course. In the end I think everyone understood it was a business decision, for lack of a better term. But it wasn't *just* a business decision. We had all worked together, and we all wanted to win. So breaking up was hard. They had stuck with us when we weren't very good, and that made it even harder.

◀ Tony Kanaan leads the Indy 500. *ABC Supply*

Honda also indicated the company's longtime support of Sato was coming to an end.

"Honda America was telling us they weren't going to be able to help us or Taku anymore," Larry recalled. "We couldn't do that on our own."[2]

A.J. wanted to keep Sato and didn't mince words when asked what happened.

"Honda U.S.A. fired him," A.J. said. "I was the one who told him. He didn't even know he was fired. I felt like someone at Honda had made a big mistake. The head guy in Japan had been over here, and they went to dinner together, and they thought Sato hung the moon."[3]

Sato recalled,

> It was a hard time. I was so happy with A.J. and wish we could have gone racing longer together. There was no doubt we were going to be together for 2017. Then A.J. called me and said, "Takuma, can you drive a Chevy?" I answered him, "I can physically drive it, but I cannot go race in a Chevy, especially if it is against Honda." If it was only a single manufacturer and that was the only way to go racing, then I can probably go racing with A.J. Foyt with that Chevy package. However, while Honda is racing, it is difficult. He obviously understood my situation, and we wished we could go on together.[4]

While Larry and A.J. worked on an engine deal with Chevrolet—which was looking to replace Ganassi—Sato headed back to Japan and met with Hirotoshi Honda. Not long after, St. Cyr received a call from Japan. The message to American Honda was clear: "Put Takuma in some car, somewhere."[5]

"Sato was like a rock star in Japan," St. Cyr said. "Traveling with him in Japan was like it must have been traveling with Frank Sinatra in Las Vegas during the 'Rat Pack' days. They wanted him in a car."

Sato returned to Houston to have a final dinner with the team. He said,

> That was a sad point. It was an absolute honor to be the No. 14 driver for such a long time. I just really appreciated what an amazing time I spend with the boys. I can't thank enough both A.J. and Larry. It was a special moment, but it was a little tough.[6]
>
> But selfishly talking, while on one hand I was very sad, on the other hand, you have to move on. I was excited to join one of the best teams in Indy car history. So it was sad moment, but for me it was also a changing point in your life. I wish we won together more times, particularly the Indy 500, that would have been my dream. A.J. is such a lovely person. I really respect him, from my deep heart.

A.J. felt the same way. While he often said Kenny Bräck was the best driver his team ever had, he had drawn closer to Sato over the past four years.

"It was just one of those deals," A.J. would say later. "We got along good, and we'd still be together if it hadn't been for that deal with Honda. We're still great friends, and he knows the way I feel about him. He's good people, and I still think the world of him."[7]

The car Honda lined up for Sato was the one driven the previous four years at Indianapolis by Carlos Muñoz for Michael Andretti Autosport. Muñoz had won at Detroit and been especially strong at Indianapolis, where he had two second-place finishes and a fourth. He'd also been the fastest car on the track at the end of the 2016 race but unable to overcome the fuel economy strategy of Alexander Rossi.

ABC Supply wanted a big name, but after talks with Tony Kanaan fell through, Larry signed Muñoz, one of the few options remaining, which meant the two teams effectively traded drivers. On paper it seemed an equal deal, some even saying the Foyts got the better of the trade. And at twenty-four, Muñoz was fifteen years younger than Sato.

"Foyt gave me this seat mostly because of [the Indianapolis 500]," Muñoz acknowledged. "I will win the 500 one day. I showed over the years that I'm capable of winning, so I want to show I can do really good and bring the team a good result."[8]

Conor Daly was signed to drive the team's second car, which would be based in Indianapolis. That was good news for Daly, who was born and raised in the city. The car would be No. 4, in part to reflect Foyt's four wins in the Indianapolis 500 and partly because it was the number used by the team once owned by Daly's stepfather, Speedway President Doug Boles.

After making his Indy car debut in the 2013 500 with Foyt, Daly had returned to Europe and completed the season in GP3, moving up to GP2 in 2014—the final step before Formula One. The money had run out at that point, however, and he returned to the U.S. and ran a handful of IndyCar and sports car races. He'd run a full schedule for Dale Coyne in 2016, with five top-ten finishes.

Daly had positive things to say about the new arrangement:

> This is the American dream, right? We've got an American team, American AJ Foyt Racing; Team Chevy. ABC Supply Company. That's everything I live for. I love to show my patriotism. I love to be an American. I think it's awesome to have this combination right now. It would look even better to be in Victory Lane.[9]
>
> Driving for A.J. is very special. Obviously he's a legend in our sport. I think a lot of people are intimidated by him. It's an honor to drive for him, but also really special because it makes you want to win even more for him.

Five years later, Daly would look back and admit, "To be honest, I was making zero money with Dale Coyne Racing. Larry and I talked. They were doing a full reset and had just opened a shop in Indianapolis. They were a fully sponsored team, and Larry was going to pay me a salary to drive. It seemed like a great opportunity. As a driver, this is what puts food on our table. I wanted to race, and I needed to make money. It was the best opportunity for me. I was either going to go to A.J., or I wasn't going to have anything."[10]

There were more team changes to come. Don Halliday had already gone into semi-retirement. Raul Prados left for Penske Racing shortly thereafter. Larry put the best face he could on all the changes.

"It's been a busy off-season, which to me is a great thing," he said. "There are many moving parts as we grow and continue to strengthen our team. I can't remember a time when the series has been this competitive from top to bottom, so we know we have to work around the clock this winter to meet our goals before the season starts."[11]

Will Phillips was brought in to replace Halliday and serve as race engineer on Muñoz's car. Daniele Cucchiaroni was one of the team's few holdovers and would serve as the lead engineer on the No. 4 car. He was from Italy and had spent his formative years in the GP2 ranks before running Hawksworth's car.

Phillips had a mechanical engineering degree from Oxford Brookes University in England and started his career in F1. He'd worked with a number of drivers—including Danny Sullivan and Ryan Hunter-Reay—and had spent the last five years as vice president of technology at IndyCar, where he oversaw the development and introduction of the DW12. If anybody knew the car, Phillips did. He'd also been a close friend of former Foyt team manager John "Ando" Anderson.

"I don't know Will that well yet, but if Ando respected him, that's good enough for me," A.J. said. "I think Will can do a great job for us."[12]

With Larry continuing to take on more of the management and direction of the team, A.J. had more time to spend on his ranches and his horses. He had a new three-year-old, Colonelsdarktemper, that he had purchased for $35,000. After finishing second in the $500,000 Indiana Derby, the colt won the $750,000 West Virginia Derby, the stable's biggest victory in years.

Foyt also seemed to be warming to his position as one of the sport's elder statesmen, a role he had sometimes ducked in the past. A six-month-long special exhibit featuring significant cars, trophies, and artifacts from his career was set up in the Speedway's museum, and a number of ceremonies were being planned marking his third and fourth Indy 500 victories. At an event before the Long Beach IndyCar race celebrating the 1967 Le Mans win, he was surprised to find Dan Gurney in a wheelchair and Parnelli Jones hampered by back trouble. Foyt told them he'd just spent seven days in Mexico with Lucy, where both underwent stem-cell therapy, a treatment not available in the U.S.

"I mainly did it for her," Foyt said afterward. "She's got sugar diabetes real bad and pretty sick, but of course I did it for myself too, don't get me wrong. But she's really been suffering the last five or six years. So we just thought we'd try it. I figure if we gain something, fine, and if we don't well, I've lost before."[13]

"So far I'm hanging in there pretty good. Every day's a good day. And I guess that's good when you're getting ready to kick."

The season got off to a rough start as Muñoz was the first car out of the opening race at St. Petersburg. He bounced back with a seventh at Long Beach and tenth at Phoenix. Daly was running at the finish of all five races leading up to the 500, with a fourteenth at Phoenix his best result. Arriving at the Speedway, Muñoz was fifteenth in points, Daly nineteenth.

A third car was added at Indy for Zach Veach, a rookie hoping to make his first start in the 500. Veach, twenty-two, was graduating from the Indy Lights series where he'd won six times during the past three years. Veach was assigned car No. 40 to mark the fortieth anniversary of A.J.'s fourth Indy 500 victory.

"He's had a lot of words of wisdom to give me," Veach said of the time he was spending with A.J. "Just hearing A.J.'s stories of when he came here as a rookie. He's doing his fair share to initiate me as a rookie as well."[14]

All three cars struggled during the week of practice and were in the second half of the field as qualifying approached. Muñoz qualified twenty-fourth, Daly twenty-sixth, and Veach thirty-second—slowest of the cars posting a time. Sato, meanwhile, would start fourth.

"It was a hard day, up and down, it didn't feel good," Muñoz said after qualifying. "It's been kind of a difficult start for the season for both of us. We just couldn't get the balance right so far."[15]

Asked if A.J. had provided any advice, Muñoz pointed to his right foot. "Just put more weight on this foot."

In the race, Daly quickly worked his way into the top twenty and was trying to pass several cars on the outside going into Turn Three when he lost control and slid up into the wall. Veach would drop out with alternator problems. Muñoz was running just inside the top twenty when a crash took out many of the front-runners and, as a result, would finish tenth.

The big story was Sato, who made several dramatic passes on his way to victory.

"When I come back to the pits, of course everybody is cheering," Sato recalled. "But the No. 14 boys came over the pit wall, and I swing my car to the Foyt box and touched with them [high-fived]. That was just an amazing moment. That's how happy we were together. And how proud we were together. And even though we were separated on different teams, they came over and high-touched me in the pits. It was a very happy moment. Obviously, it's a rival team, but I feel like teammates always. I want them to be as successful as we are competitive."[16]

In a raucous Victory Lane, Sato poured milk over his head and received congratulations from others, including Dario Franchitti, whom Sato had battled with five years earlier. Then Sato was surprised to see Foyt. It was the first—and still only—time A.J. visited Victory Lane at the Indianapolis 500 when his team didn't win.

"It was amazing to see A.J. came to Victory Circle and congrats on me. That was probably my happiest moment of that day, besides going through the checkered flag. To me it was an amazing moment. He said, 'I'm just so happy for you. You drove really well.' Those simple words were just amazing to me. It was just a moment of how much we respected each other, the incredible relationship we had."

Foyt said, "I always said he was going to win the 500, and I was glad to see him win it. I just wish it had been in my car."

Afterward, Foyt felt well enough to make the trip to Le Mans where Ford was holding a special celebration to mark its return to the race and the fiftieth anniversary of A.J.'s win with Gurney in 1967. Dan was unable to make it because of health reasons, so Foyt was the center of attention. It was his first trip back to Le Mans since his victory.

"I came here as a rookie and won, so I never saw the need to come back," Foyt had often said in the past. He attended a prerace banquet and was driven around in a golf cart painted to look like his race-winning "Ferrari-Red" Mark IV. An hour or two before the race he was driven around the track by Patrick Bourdais (father of Indy car driver Sébastien Bourdais and a racer in his own right), but Foyt wasn't impressed by the many changes made to the circuit since he'd raced there.

"I was shocked at how much the track had changed," Foyt said. "It doesn't even look like the track we had run. They added two chicanes to the Mulsanne Straight (which was 3.7 miles long in 1967). Now the cars have air conditioning, and they monitor it—it can't go over 90 degrees or you have to come in and fix it! Hell, our air conditioning was a window. I'm glad Dan and I raced it when we did."

Midway through the season, little had gone right for A.J.'s race team. Making matters worse, Honda was having a bounce-back year, with a clear horsepower advantage over the Chevrolet engines. Although happy for Sato, Larry couldn't help but wonder what might have been.

"We're still definitely behind a little," he said. "It's not only learning a new package, it's learning new drivers as well. What are they like and what are they looking for. Both our engineers have been a little bit out of [that role] for a while, too. So they're kind of getting adjusted as well. But we knew this would be a rebuilding year. It's been a struggle."[17]

There were few bright spots. After testing in the spring at Gateway Raceway near St. Louis, the team came back in August, and both drivers finished in the top ten, with Daly getting a season-high fifth. But it was too little too late. Muñoz finished sixteenth in points and Daly eighteenth. It was the only full-time team in the paddock not to post a podium finish all season.

"That definitely wasn't an easy year. We were doing a lot of things different, and we had our growing pains," Larry said looking back. "We had a new engine manufacturer, and we were running a car out of Indianapolis for the first time. So, all that was new and different. Conor was running a full year for the first time, and we probably weren't set up to properly support him. It was hard for us on all fronts."[18]

TK

The Tony Kanaan rumors had started midway through the year. Forty-two and headed into his twentieth IndyCar season, Kanaan continued to run strong at

Indianapolis—where he'd led twenty-two laps—and the other ovals, but was a mid-pack racer on the road courses. He'd won only once in the past four years driving for Chip Ganassi, who was going from four cars to two cars for 2018. As a result, Kanaan was one of several drivers looking for a ride, and journalist Robin Miller, who'd been instrumental in arranging talks with Foyt a year ago, pushed the pairing again.

At first, A.J. was skeptical when approached by Kanaan. He thought they'd been ready to work something out a year earlier, and then Kanaan re-signed with Ganassi.

"He gave me a really hard time because of that," Kanaan recalled. "Our first conversation was A.J. saying to me, 'Are you going to come here to talk serious or are you just going to talk to me and leverage a deal to sign somewhere else?'"[19]

Kanaan assured A.J. he was serious and looking to recreate the small-team atmosphere he'd had at KV Racing from 2011 to 2013, where he'd won his Indy 500. The Foyts eventually signed Kanaan to a multiyear contract to drive the No. 14 car, making him the oldest full-time driver in the series. He was also realistic.

"We won't be fighting for a championship right out of the gate," Kanaan said. "We have to build, and that's going to take time. But that's why this is a multiyear deal. There are going to be some frustrations along the road, but there will be successes as well. I'm excited for the challenge."

Of A.J., Kanaan said, "He's got the same personality as I do. We're fighters; we're feisty, we get emotional. This team needs results, and I still think I can deliver, so why not. And if you think about it, it's been awhile since you put two big names like this together. I mean, I'm driving for a legend, and some people consider me sort of a legend, so it's a pretty good story if we can make it work. Sometimes you need a kick in the butt in this business. I'm the kind of guy who needs to have that motivation."

In a prepared statement, A.J. acknowledged, "We've talked to Tony for the last couple of years, and I'm just glad we were able to put something together. I know he wants to win as bad as we do. I think he still has two or three good years in him. He's always been a hard charger, and I like somebody who wants to charge hard."

The team also signed Eric Cowdin to serve as its new technical director. Cowdin had been the winning race engineer on fifteen of Kanaan's seventeen IndyCar victories, including the Indianapolis 500. As he lived in the Indianapolis area and Kanaan planned to move there, the No. 14 car would be run out of the team's Speedway shop, with the No. 4 switching to Waller.

Kanaan and Cowdin didn't come cheap, however, and Muñoz and Daly were both released. For the third straight year, the team would have two different drivers.

"It was a really hard decision," Larry said. "I hated to end it after one season, but it just wasn't clicking as a team and as a whole group. Carlos and Conor are both very good drivers, but bringing them back didn't end up fitting what we had in mind. At the end of the day it came down to, is this the combination that's going to get us where we're trying to go? I guess we couldn't answer that question with a resounding yes, so that's why we went ahead and made the changes."[20]

It was a surprise for Daly, who was popular with American racing fans and had been away, bouncing around the world as he competed in *The Amazing Race* television show with fellow driver Alexander Rossi when the decision was made. He'd finished the year strong with three top-ten finishes in the final five races and had talked with Kanaan before he left about being teammates.

Daly reflected,

> It was a tough season for us. We were just a little bit behind when it came to the technology of the aero kits and the damper programs and stuff like that. It was no fault of anyone. I don't regret my time there, but we were just a step behind.[21]
>
> I had a one-year deal, but we had initially talked about it being a three-year development program. My whole goal was to be there for a while, but that never happened. I don't know why. I talked to Tony a lot, and we were planning on being teammates, which I think would have been really strong. But there was some funding in play from another driver, and they ended up dropping me off for a lot more money. I can't fault them for that. It is what it is. I still enjoyed my time there. I have an enormous amount of respect for those guys. I really wanted to hold up some trophies for those guys and celebrate with the guys because they're a great group of people.
>
> After that, it took me years to get back to IndyCar full-time. It was kind of like a dagger. I wasn't full-time again until 2020, so it took me a long time to rebound.

To replace Daly, Larry brought in Matheus Leist, a nineteen-year-old Brazilian driver, although he'd had no connection with Kanaan. He'd started racing go-karts when he was eleven and moved to England when he was fifteen, where he won the 2016 Formula 3 championship. He'd spent the past year in Indy Lights, winning three races, including the Freedom 100 at Indianapolis.

Leist had "a little bit of funding," Larry acknowledged, "but he was actually pretty quick. He had driven for a friend of mine in Europe in the junior formulas who spoke really highly of him."

It was all a bit overwhelming for Leist. "Sometimes it is hard for me to believe that I'll be driving for the legend A.J. Foyt," he said. "Having Tony as my teammate is incredible because he's been an idol since I was a child. Tony and I are from different generations but I can't wait to be with him at the track and learn as much as I can from him."[22]

2018

The year started with bad news as Dan Gurney, who was eighty-six, died two days before A.J. Foyt's eighty-third birthday. The two drivers had not always been friendly during their early years, and Gurney was one of the first—and one of the few brave enough—to call A.J. "Cassius." That changed after they'd teamed together to win Le Mans in 1967, and Gurney had been one of the first to congratulate Foyt after his fourth Indianapolis 500 victory. While the split between the IRL and CART found them on opposite sides, they'd rekindled their friendship during the fiftieth anniversary celebration of their Le Mans victory the year before.

"I never use the word legend," Foyt said. "But in the case of Dan, he was a true legend of our sport."[23]

The Foyts gave Kanaan and Cowdin a great deal of freedom on the No. 14 car, while Larry focused on Leist and the No. 4 car. Like the rest of the teams, they were trying to figure out a new aero package for the cars.

"The team has to start looking the way I expect it to look," Kanaan said at the preseason Phoenix test. "We're rebuilding a team that struggled, so it's going to take time. I look at what we did at KV (Racing Technology), and it took us three years to get to where we wanted to be. I came in with a multiyear deal to make this work. No one told me I had to make it work in the first month, but that's what I want to do."[24]

Team Brazil, as some labeled A.J.'s group, had a mixed start to the season. Leist qualified a surprising third for the St. Petersburg opener and ran as high as second in the early going before spending ten laps in the pits with a transmission problem and then hitting the wall. Kanaan followed with a pair of top-ten finishes at Phoenix and Long Beach. With the Indianapolis 500 coming up, Kanaan felt the team was making progress.

"Damn right they're ahead of last year," he said. "Or A.J. would kill me. Listen, we all came with the purpose of changing that, and I'm glad it's worked so far. That was my promise to A.J. and I'd probably be out of the job with all the effort and the money and the people we hired if it was not going to change anything."[25]

Things had not gone as well for A.J., who'd once again tangled with a swarm of Africanized killer bees on his hunting ranch in Del Rio a couple of days after the Phoenix race. It had been thirteen years since his first bee attack, and doctors had warned him at the time his reaction to future bee stings would probably be worse. He'd bought a new bulldozer a few years earlier with an enclosed and air-conditioned cabin, and it had helped him fend off occasional contact with bees, hornets, and other insects. But that dozer was in Waller. This time he was lucky again—the ranch foreman was nearby and able to quickly get Foyt to the hospital. A.J. estimated he'd been stung 200 or 300 times.

"I thought they were honey bees at first," he said. "I'm just glad the foreman had a car down there where I was working, or I probably wouldn't be talking to you today. They had my head packed in ice at the hospital, and I started to throw up, and I got pretty sick. I never itched so bad in my life. But after a couple of hours I said, 'Let's get out of here.'"[26]

He was forced to cancel a trip the following weekend to the 12 Hours of Sebring where he was to serve as grand marshal for the race and be inducted into the track hall of fame. He was back for the next IndyCar race, however, ten days later at Long Beach. Kanaan could only shake his head when he heard from Foyt what had happened.

"He keeps scaring the hell out of us. But I guess when you're eighty-three and you're A.J. Foyt, he can do whatever the hell he wants."

At Indianapolis, Kanaan was second quickest during early testing at the Speedway and qualified tenth, with Leist alongside in eleventh. He was at the top of the speed charts during the final Carb Day runs, and afterward he was effusive in his praise of A.J. and Larry.

"They gave us everything I asked, and they stepped up. I have a brand-new car for this race and Matheus has a brand-new car. They spent every single dime to give us a good car. We're a little team, but we're having a lot of fun."[27]

"I've started first, I've started last. So I've been at both ends. If it goes right, we have a pretty good chance. I think we can get there."[28]

At first it appeared the expenditures were going to pay off. Kanaan drove around the outside at the start and was sixth after two laps, second after fifty laps, and in the lead shortly thereafter. He led nineteen laps in total before another round of pit stops started about the halfway point in the race. In the process, he broke a record held by Foyt by leading his fourteenth 500.

Kanaan's day was ruined, however, when he was forced back into the pits with a punctured tire and lost a lap. He would spend the rest of the race fighting back, getting as high as sixth late in the event before losing control coming out of the second turn and spinning into the inside wall. The rookie Leist also drove a good race, running as high as seventh at one point before losing ground in a late restart and finishing thirteenth.

"I would say we could run top-ten all year long and I think we can finish in the top-five now," Kanaan said. "To win, I think it's going to take us another year. IndyCar is such a competitive series that it's really hard to just go in and win right away."[29]

A.J. was a little more succinct, saying, "They knew we were here."[30]

Indianapolis turned out to be the team's high point of the season. Kanaan recorded two more top-ten finishes and finished sixteenth in the final point standings. But in what he would call the worse race in his career, he also finished eight laps back on the oval at Iowa, where he'd won in the past and had five podium finishes and led 500 laps. Leist finished eighteenth in points, second to last among drivers who had run all the races.[31]

In what was becoming an increasingly common experience, the year ended just the way it started—on a sad note. A.J. and Lucy's longtime friend, Mari Hulman George passed away at eighty-three. They'd often traveled together in the early years and spent holidays together, especially Christmas.

"We had a lot of wonderful times together," A.J. said. "She's going to be dearly missed, especially by me."[32]

2019

With both drivers under contract for the coming year, Larry worked to enhance team management. At the urging of Kanaan, he brought in Scott Harner as vice president of operations. He'd recently left Ganassi Racing after twenty-five years, the last nineteen as team co-manager. Running the team out of two different shops was proving to be a logistical nightmare. Harner would work from the Indianapolis facility and was charged with coordinating the activities of the two teams.

Despite the changes and high hopes based on most of the team returning for the 2019 season, the year got off to a slow start with neither driver scoring a top-ten finish leading up to Indianapolis. Leist broke through first with a fourth place on the Indy road course, the team's best result since 2017.

"It's huge for him; it's huge for the team," said Kanaan, who qualified twenty-fourth and last for the race and finished twentieth. "We've been struggling so much at the beginning of the season, so a top-four finish is very welcome and we needed it."[33]

Although qualifying for the 500 was disappointing, with Kanaan sixteenth and Leist twenty-fourth, TK repeated his Carb Day feat of the year before by topping the speed charts a tick quicker than a rookie driving for Dale Coyne named Santino Ferrucci.

"I was not happy," Kanaan said about qualifying. "I was extremely angry about it. I'm happier because I found a couple of things. It's the most competitive field I've ever seen."

Kanaan's patented run to the front never materialized, however, and problems in the pits didn't help. With fifty laps remaining, he and Leist were both running outside the top twenty and a lap back. A major crash with twenty-three laps remaining took out several of the leaders and helped them get their lap back. Kanaan never challenged and finished ninth, with Leist fifteenth.

The next weekend, Leist crashed in one of the Belle Isle races, and Kanaan in the other. Frustrations were at a new high as the teams arrived in Texas and weren't helped when Kanaan qualified last with Leist only two positions better in twentieth.

"I can't stand what we're doing," A.J. said, "and I think my son Larry feels the same way. We're just not going to tolerate it no longer."[34]

Larry acknowledged that "Everyone's frustrated. From the engineers to the drivers to the owners. We feel bad for (primary sponsor) ABC Supply and for all our associate sponsors. We really are putting everything into this. Right now, I think things are a bit up in the air. But I'm already about, 'Ok, how do we make sure this doesn't happen next year.' If it's not working, you have to make changes. (A.J.) knows that. I know that. Everyone knows that."

The team had invested heavily—both money and man hours—in a damper program that failed to produce. With Indy cars tightly regulated in most areas, the dampers—a major part of a car's handling characteristics, were one of the few areas where the teams were allowed some leeway. Well-funded teams, including Penske, Ganassi, and Andretti, developed their own dampers. Smaller teams like Foyt's purchased them and looked for ways to adapt them to their cars and drivers. Larry said the team bought "the best we can get our hands on, but for whatever reason, our group is just not getting the job done on finding the speed in the car."

Leist parked his car early at Texas, saying he couldn't drive it, and openly clashed with the engineers. Kanaan soldiered on and finished sixteenth, three laps behind the winner and last among the cars still running on the track. He blamed the team's lack of engineering depth. Larry said he didn't blame Leist and agreed to some extent: "We need to beef up our engineering staff a little bit. That's a big plan for this winter. It's amazing some of the teams and the amount of engineering power they have. I don't think we're miles away. I think it's a couple of people to help out our current group."

Don Halliday came out of retirement to consult with the team, and test sessions at Mid-Ohio and the St. Louis Gateway oval proved beneficial. Kanaan put together three top-ten finishes over the final six races of the year, all on oval tracks, including the team's first podium finish since 2015. Leist added another top ten at Portland, but it was too late—his time with the team was coming to an end.

"We've had our moments of pointing fingers, of fighting," Kanaan admitted. "We're not perfect. We're human. But coming through that stuff makes us better. Look, it was getting old. I hate to see A.J. (so frustrated) and I hate to be in the position myself.[35]

"But I know I haven't gotten any slower. The fact is we've just struggled. It's a reality, and we're fighting really hard—probably too hard sometimes. But it's easy to question myself. I shouldn't allow myself to feel this way after everything I've done in my career, all my years racing, but I'm human."

The team's improvement toward the end of the year didn't help it retain ABC Supply as its primary sponsor, however. After fifteen years with AJ Foyt Racing, ABC announced it was scaling back its sponsorship to just the Indy 500 in 2020. That left Larry looking for a primary sponsor, which he put at about $15 million for a two-car team. While Leist was released, Larry said he hoped to get Kanaan back.

"I think we all feel like there's unfinished business there," Larry said. "And that goes for him too. I want him to go out on top. He definitely doesn't want, toward the end of his career, to just be riding around. He wants to win races. We still feel like we have a chance to win the Indy 500 and other races as well. We're in this together, so I think he'll definitely be with us next year."[36]

No one felt worse about the team's situation than Larry.

> As a team principal, you work all winter to put the pieces in place that you want to be a success. It was just tough that first year with Tony and Matheus. We had some really good races, and it was looking good. Then it just seemed like we were headed in the wrong direction, and the next year was so tough. With that leading into ABC scaling back, that was very tough. It was a group you worked really hard to put together. A group

> you hoped would get you where you wanted to go. And then it just didn't happen.[37]
>
> It's tough, it was just an obvious failure. I was the one who put all that together. But it just didn't work. In this sport, if you are one of the smaller teams—in the great scheme of things—you're probably going to have more tough days than great days, so you have to try and not beat yourself up too much. You have to try and set realistic goals. But I try and set goals that move us forward.

The racing world was taken by surprise in November when Roger Penske announced he was buying the Indianapolis Motor Speedway. Prior to the announcement, Penske called A.J. to tell him about the deal.

"He didn't have to do that," Foyt said shortly after talking with Penske. He'd been unaware of Tony George's plans to sell the track and obviously moved by Penske's call. "I really respect him for that. Roger will do a good job with it. He said he might have to borrow some money, and I told him I'd do what I could."[38]

2020—COVID

It wasn't until late January of 2020 that the Foyts were able to announce a cobbled-together driver lineup and schedule. Charlie Kimball, a nine-year IndyCar veteran, would run the full season in the No. 4 car. Kanaan, now forty-five, was set for the No. 14 at Indianapolis and four other oval tracks, thanks to ABC Supply at Indy and added support from his personal sponsors.
Sébastien Bourdais, a four-time CART champion, would drive the No. 14 in the first three road course events and then again at Portland. Dalton Kellett, looking to move up from Indy Lights, would drive the car on the other road courses and a third car at Indianapolis, with support from his family's company.

"I am such a lucky man," said Bourdais, who'd been released earlier by Dale Coyne racing for lack of funding and was the only driver not bringing financial support to the team. "Starting my IndyCar career driving for Paul Newman and Carl Haas, and now I get to drive for A.J. Foyt. My teammates and I will be working very hard to deliver the results this organization deserves."[39]

While Kanaan agreed to run only the ovals, it wasn't his idea, and he wasn't happy about it. Several years later, he recalled,

> It was a very tough conversation. I did not want to do that. I wanted to race the whole year. But we were having a hard time. We created big expectations, and we didn't deliver as much as we thought. They had to shake things up.[40]
>
> Larry came to me and said, "This is the situation—what do you think we can do?" He had the opportunity to add Bourdais, and my best results with the team was on the ovals. He said, "How about you share the car with Sébastien because that way we can bring in enough sponsorship to run a full year." I said I'd try it. It wasn't like, "You're fired," or, "I don't

> want to drive for you," or anything like that. It was a very grown-up conversation, and that's how it came about.

Kimball, a type 1 diabetic, brought sponsorship dollars from longtime supporter Novo Nordisk, a health care company specializing in diabetes products. While he'd been at Ganassi Racing for seven years, won a race there back in 2013, and had typically been competitive, the last couple of years had been lean at times, and he'd been a part-time driver in 2019. Novo Nordisk said it would be primary sponsor for six races, with the team looking to patch together a number of sponsors for the rest of the season.

Looming over the team's plans—and everything else for that matter—was growing concern over a spreading coronavirus that had been dubbed COVID-19. IndyCar had gone ahead with its preseason testing, and teams were in St. Petersburg setting up for the March 15 season opener when the world began to shut down. The NBA season had already been suspended, and on March 12, the entire NCAA basketball tournament was canceled. At first, the mayor of St. Petersburg said the race would go on as scheduled with "essential personnel." The next day, IndyCar announced St. Petersburg and the first four events of the season were being put on hold for six weeks, maybe more. May 1 was set as the target date to resume the season.

While team personnel already at the track reloaded the transporter, the Foyt's Waller shop shut down completely. Two weeks later, Penske announced the Indianapolis 500 was being rescheduled for August 23, three months after its traditional May date.

"It don't make any difference when it is, I'll be there," A.J. said. "I'll always be there."[41]

"It's a shame Roger has to go through this in his first year of owning Indianapolis Motor Speedway but you couldn't have a better man in charge," A.J. said when he heard about the delay. "It will still be the Indy 500. I never thought we'd see it like this, but all of the sports have been affected. I'm just glad that we will be able to race."[42]

At eighty-five and with his extensive medical resume, Foyt was considered a high risk for the virus. Restless and with nothing else to do, he and several others went to his hunting ranch in Del Rio, Texas.

"I had to get him out of my hair—he was driving me nuts," said Lucy Foyt, who remained in Houston.[43]

Those who made the trip to Del Rio and thought they were getting a nice vacation were sorely mistaken. Craig Baranouski (who'd been with Foyt more than thirty years) shared about his time on the ranch during the shutdown:

> I came down to spend four days with him, and I'm on day thirty-six. He's having a good time. At home, he doesn't really have any more projects to do at the ranch. Here he has all kinds of things to do. Whether it's a bulldozer or a backhoe, I help him get up on them, and he does what he wants.[44]

> He's eighty-five going on sixty-five. He's never been a person of his age. He stays up at the house, and we're down at the hunting lodge. He picks me up every day at eight in the morning, and we work 'til five, sometimes six. Sometimes I don't get back here until eight. Every day. We haven't taken a day off yet. We tore down a house, dug out a pond, built a fence, mowed 2,000 acres, and took some brush down. Used a road grader to maintain a road. You name it, he did it.

AJ Foyt Racing, like all the other IndyCar teams except Penske and Ganassi, used the government's Payroll Protection Plan during the COVID shutdown to keep paying everyone's salary. While other teams were forced to make layoffs, the Foyts managed to avoid making staff cuts.

"Strange times," Larry said. "I was happy that we were able to keep everybody fully employed and at 100 percent of their salaries for that time. We worked really hard on that. And obviously we used the government programs to help. It really helped us keep everybody together through what was a really bizarre time."[45]

A PPP report also provided some insight into the size of the race teams. Foyt was listed as having thirty-four jobs retained. In contrast, Andretti Autosport listed 138 retained jobs, and Dale Coyne and Meyer Shank Racing had twenty each.[46]

ABC
Supply Co. Inc.
Racing

CHAPTER 38

LEAN YEARS

2020–2022

Auto racing was one of the first sports to return to action following the COVID-19 shutdown, with a June 6 race at Texas Motor Speedway as the start of a revamped schedule. It was a one-day affair, with practice, qualifying, and the race all held in one twenty-four-hour period—with no fans present. The new schedule allowed Tony Kanaan to extend his IndyCar consecutive start record to 318.

It was also the first race of "TK's Last Lap," marking Kanaan's farewell season. He was driving the 7-Eleven-branded No. 14 car, thanks to support from one of his longtime personal sponsors. Anxious to get the season started, he was upbeat about his prospects:

> I wouldn't announce my retirement season if I couldn't win. I'm not there just to participate. I've never been in that place—no matter what car, no matter what team, no matter who I was with—I was always good.[1]
>
> I think the advantage that I have is mentally. I'm not as nervous as those kids because I know what to do. At the same time, sometimes the unknown, what you don't know you don't worry about it. I don't want to take them for granted, but I want to believe I do have the upper hand right now.

Charlie Kimball, whose wife had given birth to a daughter the day before the COVID lockdown, was also ready to get back on the track. He'd been a teammate of Kanaan's at Ganassi Racing and was looking forward to working with him again.

"Culture starts at the top, and with A.J., he's a racer's racer," Kimball said. "When you're the first four-time winner of the Indy 500, that legacy is the core of

◀ Challenging times for A.J. and Larry. *Grindstone Media Group* the team and what the enterprise is built upon. We all want to be better, do better, want more out of our results. I've been impressed by that motivation."[2]

In an encouraging start to the abbreviated season, Kanaan qualified tenth and challenged at times before a pit-road speeding penalty dropped him back, and he finished where he started. Kimball ran in the top five but had trouble in the pits, and a crash on the last lap left him in eleventh.

It was a different story as the series shifted to road course events at Indianapolis and Road America. The pre-COVID team strategy had called for Sébastien Bourdais—winner of thirty-seven Indy car races and four Champ Car titles during the split—to run the opening road courses. There was no denying the French driver's credentials, and his ability to work with engineers to set up a car's suspension—especially the dampers—was well-known. The original plan had him setting up the No. 14 car in the opening races, then turning it over to rookie Dalton Kellett.

The new schedule changed those plans, and the role now fell to Kellett, as his contract called for him to drive at those events. Bourdais would now drive only in the final three events of the year. Adding to the challenge, Kellett had signed after the team's pre-season test, and IndyCar announced it would allow only limited testing during the year. While the team would use computer simulations and to try and re-create racing action, nothing could replace on-track testing and experience.

Not surprisingly, Kellett struggled on Indy's road course, qualifying last and finishing twenty-first. Kimball wasn't much better, qualifying and finishing eighteenth. At the Road America doubleheader, Kellett qualified last and was the last car running at the finish in both races, while Kimball posted respectable eleventh- and tenth-place finishes.

The Indianapolis 500, which had been pushed back to August 23 in hopes of admitting at least some spectators for the race, was next on the schedule. Although ultimately no fans would be allowed, the decision to go on with the race was a godsend for AJ Foyt Racing and other teams.

"If we didn't have the Indy 500, I'm not sure we would have survived," Larry said. "This has to have been such a tough decision for Roger (Penske) and IndyCar. You know the losses he's taking on this have to be unbelievably tough for him. I think he made a decision that was for the best of the series and I know it wasn't an easy one. But we can't be thankful enough as teams that Roger did that and we're still going to have this race."[3]

While other drivers from Foyt's era [many with their own personal health troubles] elected to stay away from the Speedway, A.J. ignored those who tried to talk him out of attending. When he arrived at the track, Penske picked him up in a golf cart and drove him around the facility, pointing out improvements his group had started making during the shutdown. It was probably the only time two of the biggest names in track history could ride around together without being swamped by fans. For Foyt, who'd often felt overwhelmed by the crowd in the past, the experience was unsettling.

"Well I miss all my fans," he said. "It's kind of lonely out here by yourself. I never thought I'd see something like this but the whole world has changed so much. You don't know what you're going to see or what to believe any more. It's spooky in a way."[4]

Foyt followed series protocol, wearing a mask at all times. Occasionally, it even covered his nose.

"You don't know what's going to kill you," he said. "When the man upstairs calls you, you're gone. It doesn't matter how rich you are or how famous you are, you're gone. That's how I've always lived my life."

All three of the team's cars qualified outside the top twenty, and while Kimball and Kanaan finished eighteenth and nineteenth, Kellett crashed out before the halfway point. Takuma Sato passed Dixon for the win, although the Kiwi passed Foyt in terms of laps led at the Speedway.

"That Indy 500 with no fans in the stands is still probably the most surreal thing I've ever been a part of," Larry Foyt would say. "Talk about bizarre. Very, very strange, for sure."[5]

A.J. was unable to visit Sato again in Victory Lane due to COVID safety regulations. That would have to wait until the end of the year when the two saw each other at a restaurant in St. Petersburg.

"He had a big smile and congratulated me," Sato recalled. "Then he said, 'Two more to go, two more to go,' and he winked at me. It was very much A.J. It was a lovely moment."[6]

Kanaan had two more races scheduled with Foyt, a pair of back-to-back events at World Wide Technology Raceway near St. Louis, a ninth in one being his best result. Afterward, he sounded a lot like A.J. after his first farewell tour in 1990.

"It was nothing like I had planned," Kanaan said. "I had a lot of plans to enjoy with the sponsors, the fans, everybody else. I think it's not fair that I would go out this way. It's not fair for my fans. It's not fair for me."[7]

Kanaan would get his wish, quickly signing with Chip Ganassi to run the oval tracks in 2021 in partnership with Jimmie Johnson, the NASCAR champion who wanted to try his hand at IndyCars and run the road courses.

The last race of the year at St. Petersburg provided a glimpse of what might have been and hope for what was to come. With about a million dollars on the line in guaranteed Leader Circle purses for 2021 if the No. 14 car could finish among the top twenty-two in points for the year, Bourdais was in the driver's seat and qualified seventh. While at times running a conservative pace, good strategic moves on fuel economy and a series of caution flags that benefited the team moved Bourdais into fourth at the finish and Kimball into eighth. It was the only time all year the two Foyt cars finished in the top ten. In attendance was A.J., who had skipped several of the races after Indianapolis.

"We can celebrate when we do have great days like St. Pete," Larry said. "St. Pete was good for A.J., and we're looking forward to next year. It's something we can build on."[8]

Bourdais, who'd signed to drive the full season in 2021 with a new sponsor, was also looking ahead.

"Those guys were on the cusp the whole time, and we were fighting for a million dollars today," he said. "Finishing fourth in some pretty incredible situations there at the end, with a car that was legitimately fast—I'm really happy that we could finish the season on a high like that."[9]

Thanks to St. Petersburg, thanks to Roger Penske making sure the Indianapolis 500 was run, thanks to a cobbled-together group of sponsors, and thanks to government assistance programs, AJ Foyt Racing had survived COVID.

"We know another 2020 certainly isn't sustainable for anybody," said Larry, who could still find some positives in what for many had been a dark year:[10]

> A.J. has been great. He's been very understanding when we have the bad days. He's very much still the boss. He's still here every day, and I think we've gotten so close through the whole thing. I was really scared that we would butt heads, but when we do, it's good. He treats me with respect, and I treat him with respect. And we tend to come to an agreement. We've just grown so much closer.[11]
>
> Obviously, he's still super competitive. He's definitely mellowed. There's no doubt about that. He's mellowed a ton. What I try and do is take some of the stress off of him, to the point where I can say, "Look, if you're not feeling well, or you don't want to go to this racetrack, you can stay home, and we're gonna be okay. We can handle it." It took a few years, but I think he finally trusts that we can go, and he can just sit back and enjoy it.

2021

The team was able to sign Bourdais to a full-year contract thanks to Larry landing a new sponsor—ROKiT, a global conglomerate with business interests ranging from mobile phones to beverages and movie distribution. Company co-founder Jonathan Kendrick had once worked in Goodyear's racing tire division and remained a racing enthusiast. The company was already in Formula One, and Larry had been talking with Kendrick for several years before finally sealing the deal. For Bourdais, it was a chance to settle unfinished business. The forty-two-year-old driver shared,

> Ever since I came back to IndyCar in 2012, I've had the dream or goal or crazy idea of trying to bring a bit of an underdog to the front of the scene. But for one reason or another, being it money, or lack of consistency in the effort, or things just not being right, it hasn't happened. I feel like there are a lot of elements lining up to be able to try and do that with AJ Foyt Racing. Trying to bring the name back to the forefront of the field, which it has been synonymous to for a long, long time. That's really my goal, to build it and bring it back to where it belongs.[12]
>
> You look at the grid and you've got four Penskes, four Ganassis and you've got a bunch of Andrettis or affiliates. And Rahal is very strong and McLaren is very strong, so if you just look at the number of quality

> combinations, things are extremely difficult in the current environment. But in IndyCar, if you've got a good guy in the car and the right people around him, and just enough money to operate and be sensible about it, there are opportunities.
>
> I really liked the synergy on the team. They were looking for guidance, especially on the damping side of things. They'd tried a lot of things and maybe tried a little too hard on a couple of things that worked well on the shaker but didn't necessarily correlate with the track. We didn't really optimize things until St. Pete.
>
> There's been a lot of time, money and resources spent trying to understand, optimize and make [dampers] work on the race track. It's very much what IndyCar's game has turned into. It gets very complicated very quickly in an Indy car. You have to be very careful in not just trusting numbers, but also try and understand what feels good and what doesn't. If anything, that's probably the one thing where we've done the most progress.

Also back for a full season was Kellett, whose family K-Line sponsorship would move from the No. 14 car to the No. 4. Former F1 driver Romain Grosjean was rumored for the car at one point, but Larry would say that was never really in the mix. Charlie Kimball also had enough sponsorship from Novo Nordisk and its Tresiba insulin brand to run the two Indianapolis races in May.

The team got off to a good start, Bourdais turning in the fastest time in pre-season testing at the Speedway. In the first race of the year, April 18 at Barber Motorsports Park, he came from sixteenth on the grid to lead four laps during pit stop cycles and finish fifth. He qualified fifth a week later at St. Petersburg, but several mishaps during the race dropped him to tenth at the finish. He was still seventh in points after two races, however—the best start by a Foyt driver in fifteen years.

The series moved to Texas for back-to-back races May 1 and 2. Bourdais qualified seventh for the first race and was running sixth as the first pit cycle approached when he was hit from behind by Josef Newgarden and slammed backward into the outer wall.

After the team worked well into the night to repair the car, Bourdais was starting fourteenth and approaching the green flag for race two when he was hit from behind again, this time by Pietro Fittipaldi, spinning Bourdais and triggering a seven-car melee that also took out Kellett.

"He just drilled us from behind," Bourdais said after the second race, but he could have been talking about either accident. He'd completed just fifty-five of a possible 460 laps. "Someone checks up in front of you, you should be in control of your car. That's two days in a row we got drilled and taken out of the race.[13]

"Unfortunately it's a very expensive couple of days for AJ Foyt Racing."

Larry Foyt agreed. "It was an expensive weekend for sure. I'd say half-a-million bucks, 500k to 600k. You always have to have potential accident damage built into your budgets, but it's still a lot of work, a lot of parts and pieces we need to re-stock."[14]

The two wrecked machines were actually the team's road course cars, converted for the Texas oval as the others were being prepared for the 500. Now those cars had to be completely rebuilt for the Indy GP, drawing manhours away from the 500 effort. And not only would the team be running three cars in the GP with the addition of Kimball, a fourth car for J.R. Hildebrand was being added for the 500—the first time in twenty years the team would run four cars in the race. With parts at a premium due to a series-wide shortage, it meant the team couldn't afford to lose another car, and as a result took a more conservative approach to the races. All three cars performed poorly on the road course, with Bourdais's nineteenth finish the best they could do.

Hildebrand's car for the 500 was a special one. It was sponsored by ABC Supply and carried the No. 1 and livery marking the sixtieth anniversary of A.J.'s first Indy 500 victory in 1961. Ganassi and Scott Dixon, who had rights to the No. 1, agreed to make the number available for the 500. Hildebrand had nearly won the 500 as a rookie in 2011 when he came out of Turn Four in first only to crash short of the finish line. He'd since posted four top-ten finishes in the race and provided the team with a second veteran driver to work alongside Bourdais.

Joining in the ceremonies celebrating A.J.'s 1961 victory was Tony Stewart, who drove the race-winning car around the track.

"A.J. called me after I won my first [NASCAR] Cup championship in 2002, and I remember how much it meant to have him call that night and congratulate me," Stewart said. "He has given a lot back to racing and has been one of the sport's biggest supporters. Without guys like him, guys like myself wouldn't have had a chance to succeed. Being with A.J. on the pit box this year at Indy is an honor and something I'll cherish forever."

Foyt was clearly moved when he first saw the replica livery on Hildebrand's car.

"For them to do something like that, I don't know how to put it into words, but I'm very happy about it."[15]

He also didn't hold back when asked about the current generation of drivers:

> I'd like to see half of them try to drive a roadster. I don't think today's drivers could run with us back when I raced. Maybe one or two, but very few.[16]
>
> The reason they're not drawing fans the way they used to is people watched me come up in midgets and sprints and stock cars. Who do you have today you can follow? In other sports, you see them come up in high school and college to the big leagues, well, that's what draws people. Take me, Parnelli [Jones], [Jim] Hurtubise, people like that, they had a big following coming up. I had a big following and I've still got a big following, I feel like. It's great that people still recognize me. But I think we've lost that in racing. I could be wrong. But who can you follow? You might hear about a driver this year, but next year, he might not even be around.

The team struggled through qualifying, and Kimball failed to make the race. Kellett qualified by the slimmest of margins. Hildebrand landed in twenty-second, and Bourdais could do no better than twenty-seventh. Through it all, Bourdais said A.J.'s support helped keep the team going:

> It has been a pretty tough couple of weeks since Texas. A.J. has continued to be supportive, you know, "Keep your head down, don't worry about it, keep doing what you're doing." When the car didn't feel great, he told me to trust my instincts, don't force it. If your butt is telling you it just isn't there, don't push it. Your butt is probably right.[17]
>
> He's not only a leader, he's very much a motivator and tries to keep the spirits high. He keeps things in perspective, and he's been spending a lot more time kind of analyzing the situation from about thirty thousand feet, rather than digging in and pressuring and making it harder than it already is. Sure, he says what he thinks, but he's not overloading the system with things that could be destructive. The biggest thing is how supportive he has been.

In the race, none of the team cars challenged as Hélio Castroneves won his fourth 500, joining Foyt, Al Unser, and Rick Mears as the only four-time winners of the event.

"He deserved it," Foyt said. "He worked hard to get it and he finally got it. It wasn't given to him and when someone works as hard as he did, I'm glad it happened for him. As I said, he deserved it."[18]

A season that started with such promise was suddenly looking threatening. The team never recovered from Texas. The No. 14 had slid back to eighteenth after being in the top ten early in the year. Kellett's No. 4 car was now twenty-fifth and well outside the Leader's Circle top twenty-two paying positions.

ROKiT was already pushing for the team to add Tatiana Calderón, a twenty-eight-year-old Colombian driver whom the sponsor had been supporting since 2020 in Japan and World Endurance Championship events. She'd also done well in Super Formula, a series IndyCar newcomer Álex Palou had successfully graduated from. During a July test at Mid-Ohio, she turned in times competitive with Kellett and was quick enough to impress Larry.

"She could certainly be competitive in IndyCar," Larry said. "Her first day in the car showed she could get some pretty competitive times out of it. Me and our whole team of engineers were really impressed. She's certainly someone we have to think about."[19]

The lone highlight of the second half of the year came at the St. Louis track, where the team always seemed to run well. Although Kellett qualified last, he ran in the top ten and finished a career-best twelfth, thanks in part to a high attrition rate. Bourdais qualified eighteenth then drove through the field to finish fifth, matching his best result of the year.

After missing most of the races since Indianapolis, A.J. turned out for the final two races at Laguna Seca and Long Beach, saying, "I want to see what's going on for myself. I want to be able to evaluate everything." On the drive from Monterey to Los Angeles, he stopped to visit with George Snider in Bakersfield. At Long

Beach, they were joined by ROKiT's Kendrick, who was attending his first race and sat on the team's pit row timing stand along with the two Foyts.

At times ROKiT talked about expanding its IndyCar footprint and adding sponsorship of a second car, although it was being coy about an actual commitment. Both Bourdais and the Foyts hoped to team together again in 2022. After changing its driver lineup in each of the three past seasons and five of the last six, Larry said he wanted "to get more consistency in our group."

ROKiT, however, continued to drag its feet, and with no other funding lined up, Bourdais was forced to make the first move. He signed with Ganassi to drive for the owner's sports car team, while saying he was still interested in running a part-time IndyCar schedule for the Foyts. It wouldn't happen. Long Beach was the last race of his IndyCar career.

A few days later, however, Michael Andretti's misfortune turned into a bit of good luck for the Foyts. Andretti had been in talks to purchase the F1 Sauber Alfa Romeo team and was planning to move driver Colton Herta to F1. Replacing him in IndyCar would be Indy Lights champion Kyle Kirkwood, who'd been driving in the series for Andretti. Kirkwood was coming off a record-tying ten-win race season and was the first driver to win titles in all three development series leading to IndyCar, having won thirty-one of fifty races.

When the Formula One deal fell through and Herta returned to Andretti's IndyCar team, Kirkwood—and his $1.3 million "scholarship" awarded to the Indy Lights winner—was suddenly available. It took Larry less than a week to sign him to drive the No. 14. It was a one-year deal, and some said Kirkwood was already set to move to Andretti in 2023, but it was an opportunity the Foyts couldn't pass up. Larry said,

> I was surprised that Kyle didn't have a full-time deal. It was just one of those things everyone kind of assumed he was locked up where he was. When I found out that he was available, it was kind of a no-brainer for us. The kid deserves to be in a full-time IndyCar ride, and obviously with Seb [Bourdais] doing his sports car thing, there were some conflicts there, and I think we really wanted a full-time driver in the fourteen car. It just really worked out perfectly for us.[20]
>
> We feel like we've got a great driver, and we're going to put the best around him that we can and go see what we can do. Just continue to build our resources, build our team. When you've got a guy like Kyle that not only has shown how capable he is, he's got a great attitude, people want to work with that. I think it's going to help us attract the best people we can.

Larry had often been called one of the nicest guys in racing, and Kirkwood said Larry's early kindness toward him was one reason for signing with the team. Kirkwood explained,

> I actually met Larry for the first time in 2018 at Road America when I was driving USF2000. He was the first person in the IndyCar paddock to

> show me around the car and explain the dynamics of what it takes to be an IndyCar team and driver. From that moment, I felt very comfortable with the atmosphere of the team.[21]
>
> It's hard to explain in words the excitement I have to drive for such an experienced and legendary team. I know I will be filling some very big shoes, but I think it's the perfect timing and group to be able to do so.

In another interview, Kirkwood added, "They've obviously done really well in their past, maybe not in the past couple years, but we want to bring it back up to speed and contend for wins because we're all hungry, we're all racing drivers at the end of the day. Larry was, as well. A.J. was, too."[22]

Already assured of returning to the team for a third year was Kellett. Although he'd qualified only once inside the top twenty and had only one top-fifteen finish, his family's K-Line sponsorship was critical to providing the team with some stability.

Robin Miller

The end of the season was also marked by the death of Robin Miller, the former *Indianapolis Star*, television, and *Racer* magazine reporter and commentator that Foyt had tangled with during interviews, in court, and in a physical dustup on pit road at the Speedway. They'd gone from foe to friend over the years and spent a two-hour lunch together at Foyt's racing shop in Speedway just twelve days before his death. Earlier in the day, Miller had been inducted into the track's Hall of Fame, and they had lunched on sloppy joes, chips, and pickles catered by the nearby Charlie Brown's Pancake House, a favorite of both men. "This is the best day of my life," an exhausted Miller said afterward.[23]

"We got to be really good friends over the years because we respected each other," Foyt said shortly before Miller's death. "Like a lot of people, I didn't like what Robin wrote at first. But after a while, I realized that 99 percent of what he wrote was true. I don't know where in the hell he finds out all the crap. He had a knack for figuring it out or guessing it, and when he guessed, he usually guessed right."[24]

In another article Foyt commented, "Most writers are too scared. So while most of them are bullshitting, Robin's telling the truth. He doesn't care if you're A.J. Foyt or Mario Andretti or Roger Penske. He calls a spade a spade."[25]

Miller was in the midst of his battle with leukemia when he insisted on taking time during one of his treatments to talk about Foyt several months before his death:

> He calls me every week to see how I'm feeling. When A.J. Foyt takes time out of the day to call me and ask how I'm feeling, come on—you can't put a price on that. That's just pretty damn cool.[26]
>
> A.J. knew how to play the media like nobody else. He could have them eating out of his hands, or he could have them scared to death to approach

> him. He knew how to do it. It didn't matter where we were. We were in Pocono, and all the East Coast writers were in heaven because they'd got forty-five minutes with A.J. They were so excited about his quotes. He really understood how to play that game. He also knew he could be intimidating if he looked at a guy a certain way.
>
> "When he's gone, it will leave such a hole in racing and such a hole in people like me. I revel in talking to the guy. I cherish every time I talk to him. His stories are fascinating. His life was fascinating. There's just something about Anthony Joseph Foyt Jr. that transcends everything for me. Memories, emotions, happiness, anger—he is just this walking, talking American treasure. I'm so happy I got to know him more than professionally. Becoming his friend—man, that meant a lot to me.

Foyt would attend a series-wide memorial for Miller but wouldn't speak at the event. Mario Andretti did, noting, "Even A.J. loved him, and that's saying something."[27]

2022

It wasn't until mid-January that ROKiT officially renewed its sponsorship and agreed to support a second car. It was to be driven on the road courses by Tatiana Calderón and by J.R. Hildebrand on the oval tracks.

The timing for adding a third car was challenging as IndyCar racing was facing a labor shortage. The number of full-time cars competing in the series had grown from eighteen in 2015 to twenty-five expected for 2022. NASCAR continued to siphon engineers away. And it was hard to get new workers to move to Houston when the sport was centered in Indianapolis. With bonuses often based on car performance, a pair of rookie drivers and another who had finished better than eighteenth only once in two years was not enticing. Securing the ten to twelve crew members needed per car proved to be an uphill and costly battle.

The team's potential and challenges were on display at the first race of the season at St. Petersburg. With Bourdais on hand to lend support, Kirkwood made the Fast 12 in qualifying while Kellett was fourteenth, his best starting position ever in an Indy car. Not surprisingly, Calderón, who was seeing the track for the first time since 2011, qualified twenty-fifth in the twenty-six-car field. The team committed to a three-pit-stop strategy early, and for a while it seemed like it might work—before an extended caution flag period shifted the advantage to the two-stop teams. Kirkwood finished eighteenth as a result. Kellett's car suffered a broken transmission just past the halfway point and finished twenty-fifth while Calderón was the last car running and twenty-fourth.

A pattern soon developed: Kirkwood and the team ran strong on street courses and did okay on the natural road circuits. The ovals would be a learning experience. Kellett was better but still not a contender, and Calderón was going to be a back-row starter and would need a high level of race attrition to break into the top twenty.

The team itself attempted to make up in strategy what it might lack in speed, often pursuing an alternate—and riskier—strategy than the one followed by the leaders. The "off" strategy often left them needing to hit certain fuel economy numbers and for caution flags to go their way, which wasn't happening early in the year. It was a different kind of racing, and the challenges were not lost on A.J., who clearly longed for the good old days:

> The way racing is now, it's all about fuel mileage, and you've got to be lucky on the yellows. What you've got to do is catch the yellows just right, where before you used to race all day long, flat out.[28]
>
> That's what I don't like about racing. It used to be you would race when they dropped the green and you raced to the checkered. It's not that way anymore. It's just like NASCAR with stage one, stage two and stuff like that. When I was racing in NASCAR, there was no stage one or two, you'd race till it's over with.

Three weeks after St. Petersburg, Kirkwood made his first superspeedway start on the high banks of Texas. After qualifying twenty-third, he was one of the few drivers running the high line and was in the top ten within twenty-five laps. Hildebrand, making the start in the No. 11 car, wasn't far behind, and with the team pursuing an alternate strategy, the two Foyt cars ran one-two for a time as both drivers led.

After a long stop when Kirkwood slid through the pit box, he was trying to make up ground around the outside when he bounced off the wall and out of the race. Hildebrand ended up fourteenth and Kellett seventeenth. Kirkwood qualified twelfth again at Long Beach and finished tenth, continuing the team's strong performances on street courses.

Kirkwood was only twentieth in points headed to Indianapolis when word started to leak out that he had committed to Andretti for the coming year. Although the news was coming earlier than expected, it wasn't a surprise.

Larry still had nothing but praise for the driver after an early test session on the Indy oval:

> We were realistic of where we were as a team and that we were probably going to be a stepping stone for him. Kyle's an impressive young driver, and in those first two street races, he got right in there and led us in the direction he wanted to go. His car feel is really good, even though we were pretty conservative at the test. There's no reason he shouldn't have a really good finish.[29]
>
> This has been great for the whole team. These guys work a lot putting things together, between testing and racing. There's a lot of late nights, so [what Kirkwood has done so far] has definitely been rewarding. No one wants to come here and just run laps. The guys have a little pep in their step, and it's great having a driver that hops out, usually with a smile and is excited to get in and drive the thing. He's definitely been great for the team as a whole.

Kirkwood refused to address the stories directly and said all the right things.

"It's not just me taking what everyone thinks maybe is a bad car and putting it up front," he said. "We're actually doing a pretty good job as a team and coming together well. Right now I'm not really happy unless we finish in the top-ten, because I think that's where we should be."

Back as a sponsor of the No. 11 car for the 500 was ABC Supply, which was working in conjunction with Homes For Our Troops, a nonprofit company that built and donated specially adapted custom homes for severely injured post-9/11 veterans. The red, white, and blue car resembled a waving flag and was meant to generate donations to the organization, with ABC matching the first $1 million.

"I think the fans will love it, and I think the fans will be so happy to see the American flag—especially with our team," A.J. said. "People don't realize how tough some of our vets have it. What's made America great are people like that who have given so much to protect us. Now we have a chance to help them out."[30]

Not surprisingly, Hildebrand was the quickest of the Foyt cars all month and qualified seventeenth, with Kirkwood starting twenty-eighth and Kellett twenty-ninth. When the field looked stuck at thirty-two cars and in danger of not starting a full field, Foyt stepped forward to provide a car for a group forming around driver Stefan Wilson to get him into the race.

Hildebrand got caught out early by a caution flag and spent the rest of the race catching up, for a team-best twelfth-place finish. Kirkwood finished the 500 miles in fourteenth and may have been higher if not for a problem during a late pit stop. Kellett, who had crashed during a late practice session forcing the team to rebuild the car, struggled throughout the race and came home in twenty-seventh. Homes For Our Troops turned out to be the big winner, raising more than $2 million.

Andretti and Kirkwood officially announced shortly after the 500 that the driver would be replacing Alexander Rossi, but that wasn't even the worst news facing A.J. and Larry Foyt. ROKiT was falling behind on its sponsorship payments. Some payments had been missed, and in some cases only a partial payment was made. Earlier in the year, a court had ruled that ROKiT owed the Williams F1 team $35 million in unpaid sponsorship. While the sponsor was still making sporadic payments, it wasn't enough to keep the No. 11 on the track or the ROKiT name on the side of the No. 14 car long-term.

The situation reached a critical point at the July 3 Mid-Ohio race. Calderón, who had tested for the team at the track a year earlier, was on hand driving a ROKiT-sponsored car. Kirkwood's No. 14 car, still painted black, carried Sexton Properties, a former associate sponsor, in its primary position. The race itself couldn't have been worse. After qualifying a season-best ninth, Kirkwood continued his inconsistent performance and spun off the track and out of the race to finish twenty-sixth. Calderón was twenty-fifth with a busted gearbox, and Kellett ended up twenty-second and last among the cars still running at the finish. Shortly afterward, Larry announced the No. 11 team was being shut down.

Stepping into the breach with sponsorship for the No. 14 car was Marlyne Sexton, longtime Foyt family friend and owner of Sexton Properties. Her late husband, Joe, had first met A.J. in early 1962 when the defending Indy 500 champion was looking for accommodations near the track. He had just opened the first Sexton property, the Fisher Apartments, about a dozen "garden rooms" on Tenth Street in Speedway, and A.J. became one of the first tenants. While Foyt's career flourished, so did Sexton Properties, growing to more than 12,000 units in a half dozen states.

"Joe and A.J. hit it off. They had a common love of racing," said Marlyne, who would later marry Joe, become a driving force in the company, and get to know the Foyts. "I was from Dallas, and A.J. and I could talk Texan. We were all pretty down to earth, and that helped a lot. I even forgave him for being from Houston.[31]

"A.J. is an open book, although his bark is a heck of lot worse than his bite. To know A.J. is to love him—period. If you know him, you're darn well gonna like him."

Over the years, they drifted apart. The Sextons started a car collection including a number of Foyt's race cars, and Joe would drive some of them in vintage races. While Joe was racing, Marlyne turned to philanthropy, supporting the arts and becoming a board member of the White House Historical Association. She was also a major supporter of the 500 Festival Foundation and the Alzheimer's Association. Marlyne and Mari Hulman George also became friends, and at times the Sextons provided support for various racers, including Robbie Buhl and Alex Tagliani.

In 2014, Foyt met Marylne for lunch along with Anne Fornoro, and this time they stayed in touch. In 2015, Sexton Properties became an associate team sponsor, typically occupying the front wing on the car. Unlike many of the sponsors, who would watch the Indianapolis 500 from the Foyt family suite, Sexton preferred to be in the garage or the team's pit.

"I want to be right there where the action is," she'd say. "It's a lot more fun that way. You get the feeling of what's really happening."

Through it all, their friendship continued to grow.

"If you want a friend, you want somebody like A.J.," she'd say. "Someone you can rely on and that will go to bat for you. That stand up and mean what they say. If he tells you he's going to do something, he'll do it. That's hard to find.

"With A.J. what you see is what you get. He is as honest as the day is long, and you know where you stand at all times. He's also very loyal to his friends. If someone is in need, he'll be right there."

Now it was Sexton's turn to return the favor. It wasn't a traditional commercial sponsorship with minimal benefit to Sexton Properties, and the money wasn't as much as most primary sponsorships, but it was enough to help Larry piece together the necessary funding for the No. 14 car for the rest of the year.

"She ended up being a powerful supporter for us and a huge help to keeping the team going," Larry said. "She wanted the team to be successful, and she just continued to increase her support to where she became the primary sponsor.

I wouldn't say it was a full boat thing—you know—it wasn't a full primary, but it kept the whole thing going."[32]

Larry says he aged ten years working through what the *Indianapolis Star* called, "the most debilitating, frustrating IndyCar season any team has seen in recent years." At no point, however, did A.J. question his son about the team's future and viability.[33]

Larry said,

> He's never been one to quit. Getting to work with him on the team side and how our relationship has grown, that has been nothing short of just awesome. Those were some really hard times, and they would continue to be difficult. As a small team, you're grinding out the sponsorship dollars every year trying to make it. Some years you're losing a million dollars, you know, and then trying to make that back and keep it going. It's extremely stressful.[34]
>
> This is his life's work. And yeah, the money's important, but it's not about the money for us. It's more about keeping the team going and getting it back to Victory Lane.
>
> The one thing he always loves to talk about is race cars and racing. Even when he comes in and we're talking about engineers, you see his face light up because he starts thinking about racing and winning. And that's really what his whole life has been about.

The drama behind the scenes overshadowed what was happening on the race track, which was nothing good. Kirkwood crashed three times in the final eight races, including the street race in Nashville, where he looked to be headed to a top-five finish before his accident. Kellett would post only one finish inside the top twenty. At the end of the year, AJ Foyt Racing failed to qualify a car for Leaders Circle cash in the coming year, a loss of about $2 million. Kellett soon announced he and his family sponsorship wouldn't be returning, and he was stepping away from the sport.

Once again, AJ Foyt Racing was on life support.

CHAPTER 39

DARKNESS AND LIGHT

2023–2025

By the end of the 2022 racing season and thanks in a large part to Marlyne Sexton, Larry Foyt had stabilized the funding situation at AJ Foyt Racing to the point where he was able to finalize his driver lineup well in advance of the coming year.

His first move was to sign rookie Benjamin Pedersen for the team's second car, which would carry the No. 55. The Danish-born, twenty-three-year-old Pedersen was moving up after two years in the Indy Lights feeder series, where he'd posted one victory and eleven podium finishes. Prior to that he spent six years running primarily Formula 4 and Formula 3 cars in both the United States and Europe with a limited amount of success. He'd spent the past year shadowing the team, watching races from the pit stand, and listening in on radio conversations. He also brought funding from his father, a former Microsoft executive.

With the second car secure, Santino Ferrucci was announced for the No. 14, which would again be operated out of the team's Waller, Texas, shop. He'd been a part-time IndyCar driver the past two years, while also running some NASCAR races.

Ferrucci was an interesting choice. He'd been raised on a farm in Connecticut, and by five he was driving go-karts on the property. By eleven, he'd raced karts around the world and was profiled in *GQ Magazine* as the "Great Santini." By sixteen, he had moved to Europe where he was driving full-time in F3, winning a pair of races at Brands Hatch in England. Later he also served as a reserve/test driver for the Haas Formula One team. Thanks to his strong feelings about how his car should be set up, he'd also picked up another nickname: "Pita," which stood for "pain in the ass."[1]

His career seemed to plateau, however, and in 2017 to 2018, he failed to post a top-five finish. He tangled with a teammate on and off the track, admitting

◀ A.J. Foyt. *Grindstone Media Group*

later, "I made a terrible mistake." He was disqualified in one race and suspended for four more. When expected funding didn't materialize, he was released by the team and returned to the United States, where he caught on with Dale Coyne Racing for four races in 2018 and signed full-time for the 2019 IndyCar season.

Given his road racing background, he showed a surprising knack for the ovals. In his first Indianapolis 500, he led a lap, finished seventh, and was named rookie of the year. Since then, he'd finished four straight 500s in the top ten. His aggressiveness on the track didn't always sit well with other drivers, but it was one of the things that attracted him to the Foyts. After two seasons as a part-time and replacement driver, he was anxious to get back in a seat full-time.

"To race for a legend like A.J. Foyt, it's a dream come true," he said at the announcement. "I like to think of myself as an 'old school' driver who likes loose race cars and gets behind the wheel of anything with four wheels and an engine. So driving for a guy like A.J., knowing that he drove everything throughout his career, it's going to be a chance of a lifetime for me."[2]

The drivers weren't the team's only new faces. Larry hired a new team manager and a half dozen mechanics. And signing, Ferrucci helped Larry land sixty-one-year-old Michael Cannon to serve as the team's technical director. He had worked well with Ferrucci in a similar role at Coyne Racing.

Michael was the son of John Cannon, who'd driven with A.J. in the 1964 12 Hours of Sebring, where they finished second in class. In a career spanning five decades, Michael had been with several of the top teams, including Andretti Autosport and most recently Chip Ganassi Racing, where he helped guide Scott Dixon to an IndyCar title in 2020 and Indy 500 pole positions in 2021 and 2022. Like others before him, he said he preferred the small team and "family" atmosphere of the Foyt group and hoped he could make a difference.

"This struck me as an interesting challenge," said Cannon, who'd been involved with a front-row team at Indianapolis each of the past three years. We are going to try to build something better. I'm pleasantly surprised how much talent is under the roof. I didn't have any idea. I had no inkling."[3]

The hires were made possible thanks to the continued support of Marlyne Sexton as Sexton Properties was now the primary sponsor on both cars. The relationship had turned out to be more than simply financial support, and Marlyne was proving to be a valuable business mentor for Larry.

"[We] just really bonded," Larry said. "We would talk for hours on the phone, and she just had a positive energy. She just took me under her wing and, you know, really taught me to lead from a place of strength, even though I felt like I was on my back foot funding wise. She continued to teach me and motivate me to be strong and do the things that I thought we needed to do to get the team where we wanted."[4]

The new group in place, Larry said the goal was clear: "To get our 500 programs sorted and more competitive."[5]

The opening race on the schedule at St. Petersburg couldn't have gone much worse. Pedersen qualified last in the twenty-seven-car field, Ferrucci seventeenth.

Dixon triggered a multi-car crash on the first lap that took out five cars, including both Foyt entries.

Fortunately for A.J. Foyt, he didn't have to watch. He was in Houston preparing to have a pacemaker installed two days later on March 7. As usual, he'd delayed the procedure until doctors warned he was putting his life in danger. Even then, he nearly walked out of the hospital when he became impatient with delays, only to be stopped by his wife Lucy.

A month later, he was on hand at Texas where the team showed marked improvement. Despite again deciding to save the team's speedway cars for Indianapolis, Pedersen qualified thirteenth and Ferrucci fourteenth. Pedersen finished fifteenth after some problems in the pits. Ferrucci worked his way as high as twelfth and had one of the fastest cars on the track. He fell back through the field and finished twenty-first, however, when the head pad on the right side of the cockpit, critical on the high-banked Texas track, worked its way loose. After the St. Petersburg results, however, Texas almost felt like a win.

During the race weekend, A.J. had mentioned to Larry that Lucy wasn't feeling well, and by the time he got home Sunday night, she was worse. In many respects, she was as stubborn as her husband, and it wasn't until Tuesday that A.J., along with Nancy Foyt and Dr. Gary Friedman, were able to convince her to go to the hospital. Doctors there diagnosed her with pneumonia, and her condition continued to rapidly deteriorate. She suffered a massive heart attack, and Foyt once again heard the "code blue" call.

"The nurses, they knew who I was," Foyt recalled, "and they came out and told me the treatments weren't doing nothing, and they said, 'Mr. Foyt, it's bad.'"[6]

Like A.J., Lucy was opposed to the use of life support to keep her alive, and as the family gathered, Foyt found himself in the position of doing something he never thought he'd have to—saying goodbye to his wife of nearly sixty-eight years.

"It was super sudden," recalled Larry Foyt. "Things went downhill, really, really fast. By the time I got there, she was already in a coma. I stayed at the hospital all night, and I remember in the early morning hours, a doctor—she looked me in the eye and said, 'Look, death is imminent.' I'll never forget that phrase."[7]

Lucy Foyt, "Nana" to her eight grandchildren and twenty-one great-grandchildren, died Wednesday morning, April 5. She was eighty-four. Her death was announced on the team's website:

> Lucy had a special appreciation for life, always embracing new experiences, people, and challenges. There was never a dull moment being married to the auto racing legend; for nearly 68 years, Lucy was his rock, keeping him grounded as he ascended to superstardom in motorsports. Her steadfast support and amazing grace under pressure throughout A.J.'s career and post-career, which was marked by life-threatening injuries on several occasions, made it possible for him to stage the remarkable comebacks that added to his legendary status. . . .[8]

> With a passion for culture, arts, and global travel, Lucy shared a broadened perspective and open mind about the world that motivated and inspired adventure to those around her. That legacy will live on through her family and influence more generations of Foyts to come.

"We were all in such shock," Larry said of the immediate aftermath. "I think all of us expected something would probably happen to dad first. He was always having more issues and things like that. Everyone knows Lucy was a rock for his whole career, right? And really, for our whole family. She held the family together."

The word most often used to describe Lucy was "angel." George Snider, A.J.'s closest friend among the drivers, said it best: "She was an angel. She had to be to put up with him." It had been Lucy and A.J. who brought Snider into their Houston home after he was badly injured in a sprint car crash and then cared for him during the recovery.[9]

"Lucy is a queen, a saint," said another close friend, Tim Delrose. "Putting up with him, he's a tough dude. He may give her a hard time, but behind her back, the way he talked about her—I've seen him cry many times because of things that were bothering her. He'd always take care of her. Whatever she wanted, he took care of it."[10]

Now A.J. was one of the first to emerge from the shock of Lucy's sudden death. She had wanted to keep memorial services small—just family and the closest of friends. Snider drove nonstop from Bakersfield, California, to be there. Delrose and Jim Greer were there, along with Dr. Friedman and his wife. Daughter Terry put together a musical video tribute heavy on family and Lucy's travels.

"I'm kind of glad she died," A.J would say bluntly, the only way he knew how. It had saved the family from making the decision on life support. "I hate to say it like that, but once your heart stops, your lungs, your kidneys, never recover. She couldn't live like that. I wouldn't want her to."[11]

He had his own ideas about the service and didn't want to hear from those who suggested something else. That included what dress he wanted his wife buried in.

"I'm gonna bury her the way I want her buried, not what y'all think," he told those with suggestions. In retrospect, he related, "I probably shouldn't have blowed up, but I got mad and said, 'Y'all shut your [expletive] mouths—excuse my language—I'm making the decisions, so you all get the [expletive] out of here.'

"The lady at the funeral home, she said, 'You don't put up with nothing!' And I said, 'No ma'am, not when it's my decision.'"

He had her dressed in yellow, Lucy's favorite color, and covered the casket in yellow roses. She was laid to rest in the family plot at Memorial Oaks Cemetery alongside A.J.'s parents, Tony and Evelyn, although he asked that the casket not be lowered into the ground until he left the area.

"The pain I had about my wife is more pain than I have had from anything on the rest of my body," he'd say. "You go to sleep and you don't feel the physical pain. Now I go to sleep and I think about my wife."[12]

The outpouring of support from the racing world was immediate, led by Roger Penske, who released the following statement:

> I have known A.J. and Lucy Foyt nearly as long as I have been involved in racing. So much of A.J.'s racing success was rooted in the solid foundation of the love and support that Lucy provided for him throughout his career. Racing can be a tough business, and A.J. was not immune to the dangers drivers often face.[13]
>
> It was Lucy who was always there to help A.J. navigate through the hard times and get him back to his winning ways. Most importantly, Lucy's commitment to the Foyt family is her biggest legacy. Keeping the family connected allowed A.J. to focus on being one of the greatest race car drivers of all time. I truly believe that it would have been hard for A.J. to achieve all of his on-track success without Lucy.

Everything had happened so fast and there was so much to do, A.J. decided to skip the next two races at Long Beach and Barber Motorsports Park, and then he skipped the Kentucky Derby. He said he might not attend the Indianapolis 500. The race team was turning in mixed results at best, but an eleventh at Long Beach by Ferrucci lifted the team's spirits and especially A.J.'s.

"For all things considered, that was the best-case scenario for us to move forward and get our legs to stand on," Ferrucci said after Long Beach. "It's great to lift everybody's spirits. I know A.J. was really happy; he called the team immediately after the checkered flag came out, and I wasn't even back in the pits yet. That was the first thing I was told when I got out of the car, that A.J. was really happy with the result and he watched the whole race."[14]

In a roller coaster of emotions, however, the team was quickly dealt another blow as it prepared to assemble in Indianapolis for the month of May. Drew Fornoro—the husband of team marketing and public relations vice president Anne Fornoro and the father of their daughter, Marie, who handled the team's social media activities—died on May 1 after a long battle with diabetes and chronic kidney disease. Drew had been a renowned racer himself and a member of the National Midget Auto Racing Hall of Fame.

Neither Foyt driver had much luck in the May 13 Indy GP on the track's road course. Despite showing good speed at times, they finished twenty-third and twenty-fourth as the last two cars still running.

It wasn't until practice for the 500 started that the team had something to smile about. After the successful 2022 promotion, the No. 14 car was once again decked out in the red-white-and-blue colors of the Home For Our Troops non-profit, and Cannon had the cars ready to run on day one. Ferrucci responded, posting the third-fastest time and quickest of the Chevrolet entries and noting, "The raw speed of the car out of the box was phenomenal."[15]

Watching it all was A.J., who said he came to Indianapolis because he just needed to get away.

"I wanted to be here for Larry," he said. "I wanted to be support for him. My wife raised him. He is our kid. I didn't want him to come up here and fall apart. He hasn't. He has worked very hard."[16]

One of those happiest to see A.J. was Ferrucci. In a relatively short time, he'd developed a closer relationship with Foyt than the other younger drivers the team had employed in recent years. Most had been in awe of "The Boss" and reluctant to approach him. Not Santino, who sought out A.J. to share what he was experiencing on the track. Not even Ferrucci's curly mohawk-style hair seemed to bother Foyt, who had once told Snider he had to get a haircut before he could drive a team car.

"It's good to see him," Ferrucci said. "I know for a fact he was really, really happy to see the car and see the progress, to see something he hasn't seen out of his team in a long time as far as build quality and all the work and development that has gone into this car. He's super excited. It's a huge confidence boost for the whole organization."[17]

Ferrucci and Pedersen were working well together, and the rookie had also developed a relationship with Foyt.

"At first it was like, 'Holy Cow, it's A.J. Foyt, my boss,'" Pedersen said. "Obviously I have so much respect for him. But he talks to me as just a completely regular person. He's super bright. He was spinning our hubs the other day to see how free our uprights were and everything, so he's super in tune with what's happening."[18]

It wasn't easy for Foyt as there was a constant flow through the garage of those offering condolences. Snider flew in to be with him for a few days because, "I felt like he might need a little support." Mario Andretti and Johnny Rutherford, who'd both lost their wives in recent years and had reached out to A.J. after Lucy's death, stopped by the garage to see him in person.

"I just know what he is going through," Andretti said. "That's part of life that is going to happen, but why does it have to happen to them first? Looking at my wife, there is no way in the world I would have ever thought she would go before me. You have to move on, but the loss is there every day."[19]

On occasion, Foyt would venture out onto pit road to watch a practice session, but for the most part he stayed in the team garages. At times the crush there got to be too much, and he retreated to the relative privacy of his nearby motorcoach. One of those visiting A.J. was his former driver Davey Hamilton, whom Foyt invited to the coach.

"It was just the two of us, and the true emotions of a human being came out in both of us," Hamilton recalled. "He talked about what he went through and how hard it was. I can't imagine how hard. He was a very, very different A.J. He kept saying, 'I never thought she would be first. I always thought I was gonna go before her.' And who probably didn't think that?"[20]

As qualifying approached, Foyt elected to watch from the garage. Pedersen was the first of the two cars on the track. The No. 55 was painted in what was once called poppy red when Foyt first adopted the color for his cars in 1967. Now it was known simply as Foyt Orange. Like his car, Pedersen was also outfitted in vintage attire, with a specially made retro driver's suit reminiscent of A.J.'s early years.

Pedersen's opening lap of more than 233 miles per hour set a new rookie track record and contrasted with Foyt's first-year speed in 1958 of a little more than 143 mph. Ferrucci went a tick quicker, and at the end of the first day, both had moved on to the second round of qualifying—the first time a Foyt car had accomplished the feat since the format change in 2010.

While Pedersen held station in eleventh in Sunday's Fast 12 runs, Ferrucci moved into the final as one of the six fastest cars. Each of the six made a final qualifying run, and Ferrucci ended up fourth—the best start for a team car since Robby Gordon in 2001. When Ferrucci and Larry expressed regrets at not landing the pole or a front-row starting position, A.J. was quick to point out he'd never won from the front row but had won twice starting fourth.

"We've had a lot of bad things happen the last two months," A.J. acknowledged at one point. "I lost my wife and our family has been very upset, so I'm glad to see things start to turn around because it's been very sad in our home. Everyone on the team has worked really hard. I'm glad to see it paid back a little bit today and we can enjoy life again."[21]

If anyone needed proof that AJ Foyt Racing was once again the fan favorite—or at the very least, the sentimental favorite—they found it race morning as the early crowd around the team's open garage doors stood at least five deep. For nearly forty years, the team had occupied garages A-1 through A-8 at the entrance to Gasoline Alley, and the race-day crowd had often slowed access to the area.

Those pressing against the stanchions strung outside the garages strained to catch a glimpse of A.J., and when they did, a cheer went up. Many carried die-cast race cars, photographs, and other Foyt memorabilia on the offhand chance he might agree to sign it.

Hidden away in the north corner of the garage was a workroom area with several high-top tables and chairs where the King of Indianapolis held court. Race morning always saw a constant flow of former drivers, sponsors, well-wishers, and hangers-on. This year there was a heavy military presence thanks to the Homes For Our Troops sponsorship, adding to the Memorial Day festivities.

Many were seeing Foyt for the first time since Lucy's death and expressed their condolences, which he accepted with a nod and a smile, all but numb to the experience by now. On occasion, he'd ask if there was still a crowd out front and wonder aloud why so many people were there.

"Sometimes he's like, 'What the hell? Why are all these people here?'" said Hamilton, who stopped by prior to his stint as a color commentator on the 500 radio broadcast. "But I think deep down, it's special to him. There's not a more crowded garage, and people just stand around waiting for him. And as much as he bitches about it, I think if they weren't there, he'd be pissed off. You know, he gets overwhelmed at times for sure, but he also loves it. And thirty years later, they still love him."[22]

Foyt admitted as much.

"I love my fans," he said. "Fans kept me in the game all these years. There's no doubt about it. In 1990 when I was hurt so bad, the people were all there for me. I do love them, but sometimes I get tired and you want to be by yourself."[23]

A little more than an hour before the start, the garages began to clear out. The cars had already been moved to the track, and the drivers were tending to their prerace responsibilities. That's when Larry's wife, Kelly, arrived with four-month-old Lucy and their son Larry.

Joining them was sponsor Marlyne Sexton. As always, she planned to watch the race mainly from the garage, occasionally wandering out to the pits to get a feel for the action. Now everyone turned their attention to young Lucy, and A.J. did the things grandfathers normally do with their new grandbabies. It was the most animated he'd been in some time, and those still in the garage seemed to hang back, not wanting to intrude.

As the start of the race approached, he climbed on a golf cart with Fornoro and headed for Turn One. He still had one more task: to ride around the track on the back of a pace car and wave to the fans. The best part of the lap—he was one car ahead of Mario Andretti.

At the start of the 500, Ferrucci rode easily in fourth, occasionally moving up or dropping back a spot. The first three-quarters of the race were relatively uneventful, with only a single caution flag slowing the 150 laps. But that was about to change.

Coming out of a caution with fifty laps remaining, Ferrucci wanted to see if he could lead and went from fifth to first in two laps, taking the front spot from defending champion Marcus Ericsson to the day's largest roars from the crowd. On the timing stand, Cannon wasn't sure what was happening.

"I really haven't heard anything like it," Cannon would recall. "I couldn't believe it. I was like, '*What's that sound?*' And then I realized what it was, and that was really neat—a really cool thing to be a part of. Just one of those things that I was so glad to be here to witness and be part of."[24]

Ferrucci led for ten laps before going into fuel conservation mode and being passed back by Ericsson.

"Can I just say what a pleasure it is to be talking about A.J. Foyt and him having a car in contention," said broadcaster Leigh Diffey, as NBC's cameras focused on Foyt while his car was out front. "On Memorial Day weekend in the stars and stripes, AJ Foyt Racing with Santino Ferrucci leads the Indianapolis 500!"[25]

A loose tire on his final pit stop slowed Ferrucci momentarily, but he was still running in the top ten with the leaders in sight when the first of several race-stopping accidents took place.

Going into Turn One on lap 186, Josef Newgarden passed Felix Rosenqvist, taking the downforce off the nose of Rosenqvist's car. He slid into the wall, and with the front wheel knocked askew, rolled back down into the middle of the track. Coming fast was Ferrucci, who managed to slow enough to somehow miss the sliding car. Kyle Kirkwood, driving the next car on the scene, was not so fortunate. He clipped Rosenqvist and lost his left-rear wheel, sending his car airborne and into the wall, the tire flying over the fence.

Both drivers climbed from the cars unhurt, and officials stopped the race to clear the track. It looked on the video replays that Ferrucci may have touched one or both cars, and Larry nervously asked him on the radio if he had hit anything.

"He just missed us," said an excited Ferrucci. "Holy shit! I don't know how he didn't hit me."[26]

Larry had an idea. "I remember thinking, *Mom's got a hand in this.* It just felt like everything was aligning our way."[27]

The race had barely restarted when another of the leaders, Pato O'Ward, crashed hard in the third turn, and the red flag came out again. The accident moved Ferrucci into third behind Newgarden and Ericsson. Coming down for the restart with three laps remaining, Newgarden went high around Ericsson near the start/finish line and then Ferrucci went even higher around the Penske driver going into the first turn. It appeared for a moment the No. 14 was in the lead, the crowd roaring its approval once again. But the second half of the field was already crashing behind them, and Newgarden had started to slow after spotting the yellow light. Officials made the unusual decision to stop the race with less than two laps remaining, and timing and scoring officials reset the field based on the last green light timing line. The order would be unchanged: Ericsson, Newgarden, Ferrucci.

Sitting on pit road contemplating a last lap move, Ferrucci overheard the public address announcer asking fans to cheer for the car they wanted to win.

"I could hear the announcer, and one of the things that kind of kept me sane and really part of the reason I was also so emotional, was because every time they called the 14 car to win, it was incredibly loud around this place. More so than anything else I've ever heard."[28]

It was not to be. While Newgarden was able to get around Ericsson on the backstraight of the one-lap shootout, Ferrucci was unable to mount a challenge and finished third. Pedersen, who'd been running eighteenth on the same lap as the leaders, was caught up in the final accident and finished twenty-first, earning rookie of the year honors.

Victory Lane at the Indianapolis Motor Speedway on Memorial Day rivals Disneyland as the happiest place on earth, and for the second straight year, Newgarden and Team Penske were celebrating. The most emotional place at the Speedway, however, was in front of the AJ Foyt Racing stand on pit road, where Ferrucci had parked the No. 14.

Ferrucci spoke with NBC, his voice still trembling with emotion minutes after getting out of the car and sharing tearful hugs with the team:

> It's just tough, you know? We were there all day. I mean, *all day*. I'm just so proud of our AJ Foyt Racing team.[29]
>
> You know, we had a few people riding on board with us. Obviously, Larry's mom, Lucy, Marie and Anne's father and husband who just passed away as well. I mean, I was trying not to tear up getting into the race car

> before we started. I've actually never been that emotional before this race. It was different.
>
> I just wish we had a couple more laps to finish that off. So this one stings. It's bittersweet but I'm happy for third, I'm happy for the team. I'm really proud of what we've done today.

More active during the race than he had been in years, A.J. stayed on top of the strategy plays throughout the event, nearly overwhelming Larry with questions at one point.

"That boy can drive!" he said of Ferrucci afterward. "I thought the crew did a great job and Larry called a good race. I felt like we did have a winning car but it's one of those deals. The yellows didn't help us but Santino drove a helluva race to run third. He did a great job."[30]

High hopes that the Indianapolis results were an indication of better things to come never materialized as the two drivers failed to post a top-fifteen finish until late August at St. Louis. Pedersen recorded only three top-twenty finishes during the year while being involved in four accidents. He would finish twenty-seventh in points, last among drivers running the full season and behind several who ran only partial schedules. His best finish, a sixteenth in the last race of the year at Laguna Seca, came too late to save his ride.

Ferrucci would have a string of eight straight races where a twentieth starting position on the Indianapolis road course was his only top-twenty start. He did manage four top-twenty finishes in his last five races, enough to move him into nineteenth in the final point standings and secure a Leader's Circle paycheck in the coming year for at least one of the Foyt cars.

Ferrucci's improvement was partly the result of a move by Larry some thought had been too long in coming—signing a technical alliance with another team. Talks had started the previous year between Scott Harner and Tim Cindric but ended when Harner split with the team. Larry eventually reached out to Cindric midway through 2023, and they struck a deal.

"I've known Larry and A.J. Foyt forever," said Cindric, who let the news slip during an interview. "And just before Iowa, Larry called me up and said, 'Hey, I don't know if you're open to revisiting it, but would you be interested in trying to help us in some way and maybe working together in a way that you and Scott had talked about?'"[31]

As a result of the deal, the Foyt cars had immediate access to the Penske damper program, which resolved their previous struggles with dampers that had been a drain on the team's financial and manpower resources. The dampers also came with technical assistance on chassis setup and other areas. In return, even though Penske cars were winners of the past two Indy 500s, they had struggled in qualifying, and Cindric was hoping to tap into some of the Foyt team's newfound speed at the track.

"The mutual respect shared between Roger and A.J., joined with my respect for Tim Cindric and everything they have accomplished, is a great pairing," Larry said. "I have no doubt we can help each other to always keep improving and keep pushing forward in this competitive IndyCar environment."[32]

In addition to parts and technical assistance, Foyt and Cindric also discussed the possibility of the Penske team placing crew members, engineers, and drivers with Foyt Racing to gain IndyCar experience that wasn't immediately available on the deep Penske squad.

"We're not really the team to put a rookie into one of our cars right away, but you want to have some connection to them," Cindric explained. "So if I've got two or three engineers that are ready to be race engineers, I don't want to lose them to our competitors. But they've got to grow too, so this would be an opportunity for that to happen with Foyt."

The 2023 season marked yet another turning point in the life of A.J. Foyt. His race team had survived its darkest hour. With Larry Foyt orchestrating the recovery, hiring Ferrucci, and arranging the alliance with Team Penske, he was now clearly in charge.

He replaced Pedersen, bringing in a second-year driver with one of the most appropriate names in the sport—Sting Ray Robb. Just twenty-two, Robb had made a quick run up the ladder of IndyCar's development series and also brought a good sponsorship package for the car.

With the second car secured, Ferrucci was re-signed, and Larry revamped the team, bringing in sixteen new crew members. One of those was James Schnabel, a Penske engineer who had been on the Indy 500 winning teams of Will Power and Newgarden. While remaining an employee of Team Penske, he would serve as race engineer on the No. 14 car.

Larry also set ambitious goals for the upcoming year. "If we can end the season with a car in the top-ten and both cars in the Leaders Circle, I would say it's a big success."

Ferrucci got off to a good start, with a top-ten finish at St. Petersburg. A revitalized A.J. joined the team for a series-wide test session at Indianapolis, where Ferrucci was consistently one of the ten fastest cars on the track.

"Larry's worked very hard the last three or four years so he's finally getting it together pretty good," A.J. said at the Speedway. "I think he's learned a lot. I've let him kind of hang himself and he's come a long ways and I think he's doing a very successful job this year. He's learning every day and you know, you got to crawl before you can walk."[33]

The trip also gave A.J. an opportunity to meet with Roger Penske for the first time since the new working relationship between the two teams had been announced.

"Roger and I've been friends for years and we've got a young engineer that's working with us and I think it's been very successful. We're giving information back and forth. And Roger does a lot more tests than us right now, so that's good. I'm just happy that we're operating together. We talked about it at the test and he seems real happy too."

When Penske, his team, and the IndyCar series were rocked by a cheating scandal two weeks later surrounding the team's illegal use of a car's push-to-pass feature, A.J. was one of the few to come to his defense.

"I think it was all just a big misunderstanding," he said. "I have known Roger longer than anyone in my career. He is straight up. He's not a B-plus guy, he's an A-plus guy. He doesn't need to cheat for his cars to win races and I really respect him for standing up to the owners and offering his side."[34]

While Ferrucci arrived at the Speedway tenth in points, he suffered brake problems in the early going of the Indy GP, and when more mechanical gremlins surfaced, the team parked the car. He finished twenty-seventh and last as a result, dropping him to fifteenth in points. It would also be Ferrucci's only mechanical DNF of the year.

Based on the team's performance from the year before, expectations were high when practice started for the 500. Both drivers struggled early, however, complained about the amount of practice time they were getting, and were unable to match the previous year's speed. Adding to the frustration, Team Penske was showing good qualifying form for the first time in five years, obviously benefitting from the relationship with the Foyt team and Cannon.

Despite his struggles, Ferrucci was again among the twelve fastest cars on day one of qualifying, keeping him in contention for the pole position. On day two, however, he complained about the car's handling in practice and was unable to complete a four-lap mock qualifying run. With Cannon and team making a number of last-minute changes before taking to the track for the real thing, Ferrucci was able to grab the last spot of the Fast Six, in contention for the pole. He finished sixth after nearly brushing the wall during the final run. Robb would start twenty-third as Team Penske swept the front row.

"Man, you know, we were kind of missing that little half mile an hour and it's tough, it's a tough field, a tough grid," Ferrucci said after his final run. "I came out of [Turn] One on lap three, I got into the apex and it moved and I was like 'I don't know.' Then it moved again on the exit and I was scrambling to hit my tools before Two. I was still trying to gather up the car but when I turned in, I was able to adjust it going down the backstretch and I was just hoping that my following lap it was going to stick. It was one of the moments where you don't lift, and hope and pray."

In the race it was Robb, following an alternate strategy, who led twenty-three laps—third most in the race, although he ended up eighteenth. Ferrucci was running his race, staying in the top ten, and keeping the leaders in sight, until the second-to-last pit stop, after which he struggled to maintain his pace. The team was able to right the wrong on the final stop, and Ferrucci ran his fastest lap of the race while moving from fifteenth to eighth and setting a record for his sixth straight top-ten finish.

After Indianapolis, Ferrucci went on to post eight top-ten finishes in the final twelve races and captured his first pole position at Portland. That moved him into ninth place in points for the season—the best finish by a team driver since 2002.

Ferrucci also led the series in total passes for the season and in net positions gained, earning IndyCar's "Passmaster" award and further endearing him to A.J., although Ferrucci was already looking toward the next year.

"It's a cool stat to have," he said, "but it's not something that I'm proud of, because while a lot of those passes were pretty awesome, it's just not something I'd like to see next year. I'd like to be more upfront consistently."[35]

They held a small birthday party for A.J. Foyt at his race team's Waller, Texas, shop when he turned ninety years old on January 16, 2025. The party was more for team members than A.J., who would have been happy to spend the day working on one of his properties.

"I love to get on my bulldozers and tractors," he said. "I do that almost every other day. People say you're out there by yourself. I say, it's peaceful. I don't have to listen to anybody but me."[36]

Somebody inevitably asked if there was anything he'd change in his life.

"Nope," was his answer whenever the question came up. "I come from nothing and had a wonderful life. Who'd ever think I'd be here now at ninety years old? I don't think I'm s'posed to live this long. I'm living for a reason but I don't know why!"

Asked what advice he had for someone just starting out, he had a typical A.J. Foyt answer:

"Don't take no bullshit off nobody."

There were more changes afoot for AJ Foyt Racing for 2025, including Team Penske's biggest impact yet. The first step was the signing of David Malukas, a highly rated young driver, to replace Sting Ray Robb. While it was announced as a multiyear deal, most thought Malukas was destined for Team Penske in 2026 as a replacement for Will Power, whose contract was expiring. Adding credence to the scenario, Penske engineer Schnabel was moved to the No. 4 car to work with Malukas.

The team then lost Cannon, who wasn't able to reach an agreement with Larry on the upcoming season. Ferrucci would also be without another key member of the team, crew chief Didier Francesia, who wanted to spend less time on the road and was headed to McLaren for a shop-based position, although he would work with Kyle Larson at the Speedway.

"Larry was kind enough to hand me his team, let me run with it, and never denied me the tools I needed," Cannon said. "He also forged a very fruitful alliance with the fine group at Team Penske and their generosity has been remarkable."[37]

Perhaps the year's biggest move for the team was already being put in motion as Larry started to consolidate its engineering operations in Indianapolis. The Texas shop would remain open and serve as the administration center, but the team would run out of the facilities on Main Street in Speedway.

"When I was down there driving it wasn't hard but it's so hard to get people," said A.J., who signed off on the move. "Up here you've got a lot of race people. And I felt like since I had my shop up here, I'd do all my operations up here."[38]

The team got off to a slow start as neither driver managed a top-ten finish in the five road course events opening the season and leading up to the Indianapolis 500. The team's focus on the ovals was evident from the start of practice as both Malukas and Ferrucci showed good speed, Malukas qualifying seventh and Ferrucci fifteenth.

Although he'd taken a fall at the ranch and was using a walker at times to get around at the Speedway, A.J. was on hand for the month and at his spot on the No. 14's pit stand for the race. Both cars ran in the top ten and both benefited when initial second-place finisher Ericsson was penalized to the rear of the field. Malukas was moved into second and Ferrucci to fifth.

While in past years the team often peaked at the 500, the improving strength and depth of the group was on display afterward as both Ferrucci and Malukas remained competitive. Malukas would post six top-five qualifying runs, five top-ten finishes, lead nearly one hundred laps, and finish eleventh in points. While not showing the same qualifying speed, Ferrucci posted six top-ten finishes, including a second place at Detroit. His sixteenth in points would have been higher if the team had not been docked points for being underweight by a pound at Detroit, and Ferrucci had also missed the Toronto race after injuring his hand in a practice crash.

The team suffered another loss during the year as Marlyne Sexton died on June 11 at age eighty-six. The No. 14 was wrapped in a special tribute livery for the race at Road America, and Ferrucci responded with his most dramatic run of the year, finishing third and then celebrating with a beer tossed from the crowd near Turn One where he ran out of fuel.

"All I could think about was that we were doing this for Marlyne," said an emotional Ferrucci, who credited her with making him feel welcome on the team. "This one goes to Marlyne. She was riding with us today. I'm very proud. This one tastes a little bit sweeter."

To the surprise of no one, Malukas was announced as the replacement for Power at the end of the year, taking Schnabel with him. Much of Team Penske's depth had been wiped out after Cindric and others were fired following another cheating scandal, and while the relationship between the two teams continued, it was unclear if there would be any personnel movement.

To replace Malukas, Larry brought in Caio Collet, who'd driven for David's father, Henry Malukas, in the Indy NXT series, winning three road course races, finished second at Indianapolis and second in the series standings. Collet also brought a full season of sponsorship from Combitrans Amazônia, a shipping and logistics company based in his native Brazil.

Stepping up to take over season-long sponsorship of the No. 14 car was Diane Hendricks, co-founder of ABC Supply Co., through her Hendricks Commercial Properties and Geronimo Hospitality Group. As she had done at ABC Supply, she donated the livery to the "Home For Our Troops" organization. The nonprofit had seen four years of growing donations linked to its support of the car at Indianapolis, raising more than $15 million in the month of May campaigns.

Despite the upheaval and uncertainties, Larry set high expectations for 2026.

"The goal this year is to get back to Victory Lane," he said. "I think we're ready. Obviously, we'd love to win the big one [the Indianapolis 500] in May. We've shown the pace. There's no doubt we can get there. If we don't win a race next year, I'll be really disappointed."[39]

Privately Larry would go further.

"I just want to get that win for A.J. while we still have him around," he said. "It would mean everything to us."[40]

ACKNOWLEDGMENTS

When I was first asked if I was interested in doing A.J. Foyt's biography, I said no—it was too much work. Then my wife asked, "How can you tell A.J. Foyt no?" She was right, of course—as she often reminds me. But I was right too. It's been more than six years since I first started on what became two volumes and roughly 1,200 pages. I can count on one hand the number of days during that time when I didn't work on the books, and as a result, the list of those to thank is a long one.

It begins and ends with family and friends, starting with my mom and dad, journalism graduates who gave me both a love of writing and an interest in auto racing. My brother and his wife and my sister and brother-in-law were always supportive and encouraging. We lost my mom and brother while I was writing the books, and I'll always regret they didn't get to see the final product. And, of course, my wife, who not only convinced me to write A.J.'s story—she put up with me while I did. Friends too numerous to mention individually provided the support and encouragement needed to overcome the doubts that inevitably arise during a project like this.

Like volume one, this book is very much a hybrid; part traditional biography, part narrative nonfiction, and part oral history. Once again, I relied heavily on reporting from the day to tell the story and Newspapers.com provided an unparalleled resource of nearly all the news that was fit to print. Those sources are identified extensively in the notes section of the book, but many deserve more than mere line-item mention. Those include Robin Miller, Dick Mittman, Ron Lemasters, Mike Harris, Ed Hinton, Curt Cavin, Shav Glick, William Nack, John Sturbin, Charlie Vincent, Terry Blount, Michael Knight, and I fear many others I've overlooked here.

The roughly fifty years covered in volume two has also seen a remarkable change in the news media. When Foyt won his fourth Indianapolis 500 in 1978, nearly every major newspaper in the country had a reporter on hand to cover the event, and many were also represented by a columnist. The internet has changed all that, and now many of those newspapers no longer exist or are available only online. Only a handful of reporters cover IndyCar racing full-time, and Jenna Fryer of the Associated Press, Nathan Brown of the *Indianapolis Star*, and Marshall Pruett of *Racer* magazine deserve special mention for their ongoing work.

For the oral history portion of the book, I had an opportunity to interview many of the top names in the sport, well over a hundred in all. New to volume two are folks like Al Unser Jr., Rick Mears, Kenny Bräck, Takuma Sato, Danny Sullivan, Hurley Haywood, Robby Gordon, Billy Boat, Davey Hamilton, Ed Welburn, Doug Boles, Eddie Cheever, Scott Sharp, and Marlyne Sexton. Doctors James Stiehl and Jeffrey Johnson, who helped piece Foyt back together following his Road America accident, told their stories for the first time. Dr. Terry Trammell, IndyCar's "Magician" who took over for the Milwaukee Med doctors, and Houston Oiler trainer Steve Watterson, who rebuilt the driver's strength, also shared their in-depth memories of the recovery.

Several interviews stand out, including Tony Stewart, who graciously also agreed to provide the foreword for the book. Then there was Jeff Gordon. We had agreed to talk on Tuesday, February 20, 2024, two days after the Daytona 500. Only the 500 was rained out and then ran late into the night on February 19 before William Byron drove his No. 24 car—Gordon's old car—to victory. The last thing I saw that night before going to bed was Gordon partying and spraying champagne in Victory Lane. *No way am I gonna hear from him*, I thought.

Right at 8:00 a.m. the next morning, however, Jeff was on the phone, hoarse and exhausted. "This was important to me," Gordon said, and he went on to talk about what Foyt had meant to him growing up, how excited he'd been to receive a trophy from him after winning the Foyt-Hulman 100 (and meeting Linda Vaughn!) and how A.J. had been one of those telling him to pursue a career in NASCAR because of the state of IndyCar racing in 1991.

I also want to thank several photographers who went out of their way to work with me on this project, especially Dan Boyd, John Mahoney, and David Nearpass. John Kyros at the GM Archives, Kate Sayers at the NASCAR Archives & Research Center, Walter Arce at Action Sports Photography, and Joe Skibinski at the IMS Photography Archives were also especially helpful in tracking down photography, much of which has never been seen before.

Special thanks to Octane Press publisher Lee Klancher and his team for putting out a quality book, especially project editor Faith Garcia, who balanced the right amount of patience and persistence to make this happen, copyeditor Katie Pacard, proofreader Dana Henricks, and book designer Tom Heffron.

Then there's Anne Fornoro. Her commitment to the project was unwavering, and her help and guidance cannot be overstated. Without her, there would not have been an A.J. Foyt biography. At least not by me.

SOURCES

Author Interviews

Danny Allen—Son of Hardy Allen, A.J. Foyt crew member (March 27, 2021)
Donnie Allison—Race car driver and Foyt teammate (July 7, 2020)
Kenny Anderson—Technical director at AJ Foyt Racing (March 6, 2021)
Mario Andretti—Race car driver (September 3, 2022)
Jack Arute—Reporter and Foyt friend (November 5, 2021)
Ann Hagedorn Auerbach—Author of *Wild Ride* (November 12, 2023)
Jim Aust—Vice president of motorsports at Toyota (August 26, 2025)
Craig Baranouski—Longtime Foyt crew member and friend (April 20, 2020)
Becky Baranouski—Associate at A.J. Foyt Racing (April 23, 2021)
Brian Barnhart—Employee for A.J. Foyt, Indianapolis Motor Speedway, and the IRL (November 20, 2020)
Billy Boat—Race car driver (November 18, 2020)
Doug Boles—President, Indianapolis Motor Speedway (May 18, 2024)
Bones Bourcier—Author (May 2022)
Sébastien Bourdais—Race car driver (October 26, 2025)
Kenny Bräck—Race car driver (May 2023)
Donna Dale Burt—Foyt family friend, daughter of Dale Burt (January 2020)
Ed Carpenter—Race car driver (May 24, 2022)
Pancho Carter—Race car driver (February 23, 2023)
Phil Casey—Crew chief (November 2023)
Hélio Castroneves—Race car driver (February 1, 2023)
Eddie Cheever—Race car driver (November 11, 2020)
Tim Cindric—Former president, Penske Racing (May 16, 2025)
Dale Coyne—Car owner (May 2022)
Conor Daly—Race car driver (May 24, 2022)
Donald Davidson—Retired Indianapolis Motor Speedway historian (May 26, 2021)
Tim Delrose—Race car owner and family friend (November 17, 2020)
Dominic Dobson—Race car driver (April 20, 2020)
Bobby Dorn—Foyt crew member (May 2021)
Corinne Economaki—Racing journalist, daughter of Chris Economaki (December 28, 2023)

Ray Evernham—Car owner (August 26, 2025)
Santino Ferrucci—Race car driver (May 19, 2024)
Jimmy Finger—Race car driver, family friend, and neighbor (October 4, 2022)
Anne Fornoro—Vice president of marketing and public relations, AJ Foyt Racing (November 18, 2022; September 9, 2025)
Anthony Joseph "A.J." Foyt Jr—(2012*; 2016**; November 7, 2019; April 19–24, 2021; May 11, 2021; May 22, 2021; May 28, 2021; 2022; 2023)
A.J. Foyt Jr., interview with David Goldstein, The Houston Oral History Project (2008)
Anthony Joseph "Tony" Foyt III—A.J.'s son (April 26, 2021)
Anthony Joseph "Anthony" Foyt IV—A.J.'s grandson (May 27, 2021)
Jerry Foyt—A.J.'s son (January 30, 2021)
Larry Foyt—A.J.'s grandson and adopted son (November 10, 2020; February 11, 2021; April 28, 2021)
Lucy Foyt—A.J.'s wife (2016**; April 2, 2020)
Marlene Foyt—A.J.'s sister (June 23, 2021; January 8, 2024)
Nancy Foyt—A.J.'s daughter-in-law, married to Tony (April 21 & 23, 2021)
Terry Foyt—A.J.'s daughter (April 21, 2021)
Lewis Franck—Motorsports journalist (January 19, 2021)
Dr. Gary Friedman—Foyt family doctor (2020)
Edsel Ford—Retired Ford Motor Company executive (October 8, 2021)
Chip Ganassi—Car owner (October 7, 2025)
Tony George—Former owner, Indianapolis Motor Speedway (May 2021)
Jeff Gordon—Race car driver (February 20, 2024)
Robby Gordon—Race car driver (March 12, 2021)
Charlie Gray—Ford racing executive (October 2022)
Jim Greer—Family friend, car sponsor, and entrant (2021)
Dan Gurney—Race car driver (2012*)
Evi Gurney—Wife of Dan Gurney (January 29, 2020)
Don Halliday—Auto racing engineer (February 11, 2021)
Davey Hamilton—Race car driver (May 27, 2023)
Mike Harris—Associated Press motorsports reporter (April 2021)
Don Hayward—Engineer at Ford and numerous race teams (January 7, 2023)
Hurley Haywood—Race car driver (June 16, 2025)
Bryan Herta—Race car driver (May 22, 2025)
Ryan Hunter-Reay—Race car driver (May 25, 2023)
Jonathan Ingram—Motorsports writer (February 8, 2021)
Bob Jenkins—Motorsports reporter and broadcaster (June 11, 2020)
Dr. Jeffrey Johnson—Milwaukee Medical Center (March 22, 2020)
Davy Jones—Race car driver (October 2, 2023)
Steve Jordan—Foyt crew member (April 28, 2021)
Ed Justice Jr.—Racing sponsor (March 10, 2021)
Tony Kanaan—Race car driver (April 28, 2021)
Godwin Kelly—Sports reporter (November 12, 2023)
Dave Kindred—General sports reporter and columnist (December 11, 2020)

Michael Knight—Motorsports reporter (May 28, 2021)
Frank Lance—Foyt crew member (April 2022)
Dan Layton—Honda public relations (February 10, 2021)
Bill Luchow—CART official (March 26, 2020)
David Luck—ABC Supply executive (September 6, 2025)
Peter Manso—Author (January 18, 2020)
Mark Martin—Race car driver (February 3, 2023)
Bruce Matthews—Houston Oiler (January 23, 2025)
T.E. McHale—Honda motorsports (February, 2021)
Rick Mears—Race car driver (December 1, 2020)
John Mecom—1960s car owner and sponsor (November 18, 2020)
Robin Miller—Motorsports reporter (December 1, 2020; October 2, 2021)
Chocolate Myers—Dale Earnhardt crew member (November 27, 2021)
Mose Nowland—Ford engineer (December 2019)
Paul Page—Radio and television announcer (September 28, 2020)
Roger Penske—Race car driver (provided written response to a list of questions submitted to his public relations representatives) (2023)
Richard Petty—Race car driver (March 11, 2021)
Bill Porterfield—Aerotech project manager (October 4, 2023)
Tex Powell—NASCAR chief mechanic, car owner (August 8, 2020)
Bobby Rahal—Driver, car owner (May 23, 2025)
Bob Riley—Coyote designer (February 18, 2021)
Johnny Rutherford—Race car driver (June 17, 2020)
Takuma Sato—Race car driver (February 3, 2021)
Kenny Schrader—Race car driver (November 13, 2020)
Marlyne Sexton—Sponsor (June 24, 2021)
Scott Sharp—Race car driver (April 14, 2021)
Carroll Shelby—Race car driver, team owner, and founder of Shelby American (2012*)
George Snider—Race car driver and friend (December 12, 2020)
Art St. Cyr—President, Honda Performance Development (April 6, 2021)
Jack Starne—Longtime Foyt crewmember, crew chief, and friend (January 13, 2021)
Jackie Stewart—Formula One World Champion (April 28, 2022)
Tony Stewart—IndyCar and NASCAR champion (December 16, 2020)
Dr. James Stiehl—Milwaukee Medical Center (April 17, 2020)
Danny Sullivan—Race car driver (October 22, 2020)
Mike Teske—Automotive restorer (April 3, 2020)
Dr. Terry Trammell—Orthopedic surgeon (2020)
Kevin Triplett—Racing historian (October 14, 2020)
Al Unser Jr.—Race car driver (November 5, 2020)
Al Unser Sr.—Race car driver (December 16, 2020)
Bobby Unser—Race car driver (2012*)
Bobby Waltrip—Business associate and family friend (April 27, 2021)
Darrell Waltrip—NASCAR driver (November 6, 2020)

Steve Watterson—Houston Oiler trainer (November 23, 2020)
Ed Welburn—Aerotech designer (September 17, 2023)
Leonard Wood—NASCAR team co-owner (April 15, 2020)
Billy Woodruff—Foyt crewmember and family friend (January 20, 2021; January 3, 2024)
Cale Yarborough—Race car driver (2021)

*Author interviews originally conducted for *Black Noon: The Year They Stopped the Indy 500,* St. Martin's Press, New York, 2014.
**Author interviews originally conducted for *Indy 500 Memories: An Oral History of "The Greatest Spectacle in Racing,"* CreateSpace, 2016.

Books

Alexander, Tyler. *Tyler Alexander: A Life and Times with McLaren.* David Bull Publishing, 2015.

Andretti, John, and Jade Gurss. *Racer.* Octane Press: 2020.

Andretti, Mario, with Bob Collins. *What's It Like Out There?* NTC/Contemporary Publishing, 1970.

Andretti, Mario, with Gordon Kirby. *Mario Andretti: A Driving Passion.* David Bull Publishing, 2001.

Argetsinger, Michael. *Mark Donohue: Technical Excellence at Speed.* David Bull Publishing, 2009.

Bechtel, Mark. *He Crashed Me So I Crashed Him Back.* Little, Brown and Company, 2010.

Bourcier, Bones. *Foyt, Andretti, Petty: America's Racing Trinity.* Coastal 181, 2015.

Brawner, Clint, with Joe Scalzo. *Indy 500 Mechanic: The Inside Story of Big Time Auto Racing.* Chilton Books, 1975.

Buss, Ted. *Lloyd Ruby: The Greatest Driver Never to Win the Indy 500.* Midwestern State University Press, 2000.

Clark, Jim. *Jim Clark at the Wheel.* Pocket Books, 1966.

Considine, Tim. *American Grand Prix Racing: A Century of Drivers & Cars.* Motorbooks International, 1997.

Cotter, Tom, and Al Pearce. *Holman-Moody: The Legendary Race Team.* Motorbooks International, 2003.

Daley, Robert. *The Cruel Sport: Grand Prix Racing 1959–1967.* Prentice-Hall, 1963.

Daly, Derek. *Race to Win: How to Become a Complete Champion Driver.* Motorbooks International, 2008.

Davidson, Donald, and Rick Shaffer. *AutoCourse Official History of the Indianapolis 500.* Crash Media Group, 2006.

Dewitt, Norm. *Making It Faster II: The Indianapolis and Grand Prix Cars.* Faster Publishing, 2018.

Dilamarter, Jimmy, and Ren Wicks Jr. *The Cars of Vel Miletich and Parnelli Jones.* Dalton Watson Books, 2013.

Dorson, Ron. *The Indy 500: An American Institution Under Fire.* Bond/Parkhurst Books, 1974.

Economaki, Chris, and Dave Argabright. *Let 'Em All Go!* Books by Dave Argabright, 2006.

Engel, Lyle Kenyon. *The Incredible A.J. Foyt.* Arco Publishing Company, 1977.

Ferguson, Andrew. *Team Lotus: The Indianapolis Years.* Haynes Publishing, 1996.

Fox, Jack C. *Mighty Midgets: The Illustrated History of Midget Auto Racing.* Carl Hungness Publishing, 2004.

Foyt, A.J., with William Neely. *A.J.: My Life as America's Greatest Race Car Driver.* Times Books, 1983.

Garner, Art. *Black Noon: The Year They Stopped the Indy 500.* St. Martin's Griffin, 2014.

Garner, Art, and Marc B. Spiegel. *Indy 500 Memories: An Oral History of "The Greatest Spectacle in Racing."* CreateSpace Publishing, 2016.

Gates, Bob. *Hurtubise.* Witness Productions, 1995.

Gauld, Graham. *Jim Clark: Racing Hero.* McKlein Media, 2014.

Golenbock, Peter. *Miracle: Bobby Allison and the Saga of the Alabama Gang.* St. Martin's Griffin, 2006.

Granatelli, Anthony. *They Call Me Mister 500.* Henry Regnery Company, 1969.

Guthrie, Janet. *Janet Guthrie: A Life at Full Throttle.* Sportclassic Books, 2005.

Hallberry, Andy, and Jeff Olson. *Lionheart: Remembering Dan Wheldon.* Lionheart Books LLC, 2016.

Henry, Charlie. *Kar-Kraft: Race Cars, Prototypes, and Muscle Cars of Ford's Specialty Vehicle Program.* Forest Lake. Car Tech Books, 2017.

Hill, Bill. *One Tough Circuit: Midget Racing in America's Heartland.* Bill Hill Productions, 1998.

Kenyon, Mel. *Burned to Life.* New Leaf Press, 1976.

Kirby, Gordon. *Jim McGee: Crew Chief of Champions.* Racemaker Press, 2014.

Kirby, Gordon. *Penske's Maestro: Karl Kainhofer and the History of Penske Racing.* Racemaker Press, 2016.

Kirk, Connie Ann. *Taken by Speed: Fallen Heroes of Motor Sport and Their Legacies.* Rowman & Littlefield, 2017.

Lerner, Preston, and Dave Friedman. *Ford GT: How Ford Silenced the Critics, Humbled Ferrari, and Conquered Le Mans.* Motorbooks, 2015.

Levine, Leo. *Ford: The Dust and the Glory, A Racing History.* McMillan Company, 1968.

LeVrier, Philip. *Texas Legacy: Tales from the Golden Days of Midget Auto Racing in Texas.* Georgetown Lounge Productions, 1987.

Libby, Bill. *Foyt.* Hawthorn Books, 1974.

Libby, Bill. *Parnelli: A Story of Auto Racing.* E. P. Dutton & Co. 1969.

Ludvigsen, Karl. *Indy Cars of the 1960s.* Iconografix, 2001.

Manso, Peter. *Vrooom!: Conversations with the Grand Prix Champions.* Funk & Wagnalls, 1969.

McGinnis, Joe. *They Call Him Cale: The Life and Career of NASCAR Legend Cale Yarborough.* Triumph Books, 2008.

Moss, Stirling. *A Turn at the Wheel.* Putnam Books, 1961.
Neely, William. *The Jim Gilmore Story: Alone in the Crowd.* Aztex Corporation, 1988.
Neely, William. *Tire Wars: Racing with Goodyear.* Aztex Corporation, 1993.
Nye, Doug. *The Story of Lotus 1961–1971: Growth of a Legend.* Motor Racing Publications, 1972.
O'Leary, Mike. *Rodger Ward: Superstar of American Racing's Golden Age.* Motorbooks, 2006.
Olvey, Dr. Stephen. *Rapid Response.* Haynes Publishing, 2011.
Riley, Bob, with Jonathan Ingram. *The Art of Race Car Design.* Icon Publishing, 2015.
Rutherford, Johnny, and David Craft. *Lone Star J.R.: The Autobiography of Racing Legend Johnny Rutherford.* Triumph Books, 2000.
Scalzo, Joe. *The American Dirt Track Racer.* Motorbooks International, 2001.
Scalzo, Joe. *City of Speed: Los Angeles and the Rise of American Racing.* Motorbooks International, 2007.
Scalzo, Joe. *Indianapolis Roadsters: 1952–1964.* Motorbooks International, 1988.
Scalzo, Joe. *Stand on the Gas! Sprint Car Racing in America.* Prentice-Hall, 1974.
Sutton, Len. *My Road to Indy.* Walsworth Publishing, 2002.
Sutton, Stan. *The Curse of the Indy 500: 1958's Tragic Legacy.* Red Lightning Books, 2017.
Tremayne, David. *Jim Clark: The Best of the Best.* Evro Publishing Limited, 2018.
Tulloch, Andrew. *Jim Clark: Grand Prix Legend.* Weidenfeld & Nicolson, 2009.
Wallen, Dick. *United States Auto Club: Fifty Years of Speed and Glory.* Dick Wallen Productions, 2006.
Waltrip, Robert L., with James Chandler Harbour II. *A Boy from the Heights.* LifeStories Company, 2020.
Whitaker, Sigur E. *Tony Hulman: The Man Who Saved the Indianapolis Motor Speedway.* McFarland & Company, 2014.
Young, Eoin S. *Bruce McLaren: The Man and His Racing Team.* Haynes Publishing, 1995.

Additional Reference Sources

Benson Ford Research Center, The Henry Ford Museum
The Dave Kindred Papers, Tate Archives, & Special Collections, The Ames Library, Illinois Wesleyan University, Bloomington, Illinois, https://iwu.libraryhost.com/repositories/3/resources/11
Indiana State Library
Indy 500 and USAC racing 1971–1978, OldRacingCars.com
Indianapolis Motor Speedway Archives
International Motor Racing Research Center, Watkins Glen, New York
Ultimate Racing History, https://www.racingsportscars.com/driver/results/A.%20J._-Foyt-USA.html

ENDNOTES

INTRODUCTION: ONE TOUGH DUDE

1. Dr. James Stiehl, April 17, 2020, interview with the author.
2. Dr. Jeffrey Johnson, April 22, 2020, interview with the author.

CHAPTER ONE: CROSSROADS

1. Pat Putnam, "Ali's Desperate Hour," *Sports Illustrated*, Oct. 10, 1977.
2. Johathan Eig, *Ali: A Life* (Houghton Mifflin Harcourt: 2017).
3. Gary Kale, "A.J. Foyt Thinks He Understands Ali," United Press International, *Muncie* (Indiana) *Star Press*, February 18, 1978.
4. Jim Murray, "As Night Follows Day . . .," *Los Angeles Times*, May 30, 1977.
5. "Notes," *Fort Worth Star-Telegram*, June 6, 1962.
6. Kale, "A.J. Foyt Thinks He Understands Ali."
7. George Cunningham, "Petty 'Iffy' for 500 After Crash," *Atlanta Journal-Constitution*, February 18, 1978.
8. Jesse Outlar, "Foyt Enigma Among Racing Good Ol' Boys," *Atlanta Constitution*, February 18, 1978.
9. Bill Skutt, "Drivers Tire Quickly of Blowout Problems," *Orlando Sentinel*, February 20, 1978.
10. Ron Lemasters, "Will '78 Be A.J.'s Final Fling?" *Muncie Star Press,* March 26, 1978.
11. "Q&A with Jack Starne," AJ Foyt Racing, March 13, 2020, https://www.foytracing.com/single-post/2020/04/13/qa-with-jack-starne.
12. Jackie Stewart, "Daytona 500 Coverage," *ABC Wide World of Sports*, February 19, 1978.
13. Gary Kale, "A.J. Foyt Needs No Reminder of Fear," United Press International, *Galveston Daily News*, April 13, 1978.
14. George Moore, "A.J. Made It with Own Car, Engine," *Indianapolis Star*, May 30, 1977.
15. Michael Knight, "Johncock Scores at Trenton," *Philadelphia Daily News*, April 24, 1978.
16. Bob Adair, "Tony Foyt Makes A.J. Smile by Saddling Winner at Downs," *Louisville Courier-Journal*, May 9, 1978.
17. Gary Kale, "'I've Done Everything I Wanted to Do'–Foyt," United Press International, *Muncie Star Press*, June 25, 1978.
18. Dick Mittmann, "A.J. Had a Way of Being There," *Indianapolis News*, May 26, 1978.
19. "Foyt Unaffected by Indy Washout," Associated Press, *Owensboro* (Kentucky) *Messenger-Inquirer*, May 15, 1978.
20. "'My Fault, as Usual,' Foyt Declares," *Louisville Courier-Journal*, May 21, 1978.
21. Steve Herman, "Foyt's Unmatched Feats Fulfill Prophecy of 1958," Associated Press, *Richmond* (Indiana) *Palladium-Item*, May 28, 1978.
22. "A.J. Will Be Racing 'Real Conservative,'" Associated Press, *Owensboro* (Kentucky) *Messenger-Inquirer*, May 22, 1978.
23. Dick Mittmann, "Car Was All Over the Track, Says A.J.," *Indianapolis News*, May 29, 1978.
24. "Janet Guthrie Still Battling Chauvinism," Associated Press, *Laredo* (Texas) *Times*, December 9, 1978.
25. Rick Mears, December 1, 2020, interview with the author.
26. Kale, "I've Done Everything I Wanted to Do."
27. Bob Clanton, "Foyt Holds off Rutherford in Texas Grand Prix," *Fort Worth Star-Telegram*, August 7, 1978.
28. Bob Clanton, "Slow-Down Boycott Gets No Sympathy from Foyt," *Fort Worth Star-Telegram*, August 7, 1978.
29. Clanton, "Foyt Holds off Rutherford."
30. Ken Squier, Dan Gurney, and Paul Page, "Texas World 200," *ABC Sports*, August 6, 1978.
31. Gary Taylor, "A.J. Foyt Slugs Way to Texas Grand Prix Victory," United Press International, *Galveston Daily News*, August 7, 1978.

32. "A.J. Tours Texas Grand Prix for 60th Career Win," Associated Press, *Taylor* (Texas) *Daily Press*, August 7, 1978.
33. Clanton, "Foyt Holds off Rutherford."
34. George Moore, "Ongais Quick—Bickering Think," *Indianapolis Star*, August 20, 1978.
35. J.D. Lewis, "A.J. Foyt Denies Report of Indy Speedway Purchase," *Columbus* (Indiana) *Republic*, August 30, 1978.
36. Shav Glick, "Foyt and Parnelli Jones Hook Up for Cal 500," *Los Angeles Times*, September 1, 1978.
37. Robin Miller, "500 Miles of an Unfunny Folly," *Indianapolis Star*, September 7, 1978.
38. Kale, "A.J. Foyt Needs No Reminder of Fear."
39. "Foyt Gains Finals with MIS Victory," Associated Press, (Michigan) *Herald-Palladium*, September 18, 1978.
40. Bob Collins, "A.J. Has Corner at Silverstone," *Indianapolis Star*, October 2, 1978.
41. Bob Collins, "It's a Show the Englishmen Love," *Indianapolis Star,* October 6, 1978.
42. A.J. Foyt, April 19–24, 2021, interviews with the author.
43. Mears, December 1, 2020, interview.
44. Mike Morrow, "Mario Wins IROC; Angry A.J. Leaves," *San Pedro* (California) *News-Pilot*, October 16, 1978.
45. Norm Frauenheim, "Andretti Hero to Rutherford, but Villain to Foyt," *Arizona Republic*, October 29, 1978.
46. "Stock Car King Foyt 'Tired of Racing,'" United Press International, *Columbus* (Indiana) *Republic*, November 13, 1978.
47. Tyler Alexander, *Tyler Alexander: A Life and Times with McLaren* (David Bull Publishing: 2015).
48. Dick Mittman, "Racing on a Crash Course," *Indianapolis News*, September 18, 1978.
49. Robin Miller, "USAC's Life Threatened by CART," *Indianapolis Star*, November 19, 1978.
50. Ron Lemasters, "USAC Dead at Age 22, Leaves Few Survivors," *Muncie Times Star*, December 17, 1978.
51. Robin Miller, "CART, SCCA Sign Racing Pact," *Indianapolis Star*, December 14, 1978.

CHAPTER TWO: A.J. AND THE SEVEN DWARFS

1. Robin Miller, "Foyt Quits CART; Rejoins USAC," *Indianapolis Star*, February 1, 1979.
2. Dick Mittman, "CART Budget Set: Penske," *Indianapolis News*, January 23, 1979.
3. "A.J. Changes His Tune on CART's Benefits," Associated Press, *Kokomo* (Indiana) *Tribune*, February 1, 1979.
4. Dick Mittman, "Others May Jump CART, Says Foyt," *Indianapolis News*, February 1, 1979.
5. Miller, "Foyt Quits CART."
6. Gary Kale, "CART's Doing Snow Job—Foyt," United Press International, *Muncie Star Press*, February 14, 1979.
7. Bob Myers, "God or Devil? There May Never Be Another Foyt," *Charlotte News*, February 16, 1979.
8. Ray Holliman, "Waltrip Drives His 'Women' Very Fast," *St. Petersburg Times*, February 16, 1979.
9. "Baker, Waltrip Take Qualifying Races for Stock Daytona 500," Associated Press, *Vincennes* (Indiana) *Sun-Commercial*, February 16, 1979.
10. George Cunningham, "Same Olds Story: Baker, Waltrip Best," *Atlanta Constitution*, February 16, 1979.
11. Joe Menzer, "A.J. Foyt Recounts on 'Race Hub' How He Blew a Daytona 500," *Fox Sports*, February 2, 2017.
12. Jim Mathews, "A.J. Dwarfs Meager USAC Field for Twin 200s at OMS," *San Bernadino County Sun*, March 23, 1979.
13. Shav Glick, "USAC Defectors Blasted by Foyt," *Los Angeles Times*, March 25, 1979.
14. Paul Oberjuerge, "Nobody to Gain from War," *San Bernardino County Sun*, March 26, 1979.
15. Robin Miller, "The Speedway Belongs to A.J.—Today," *Indianapolis Star*, April 1, 1979.
16. Bob Clanton, "Leaking Tire Causes Foyt to Slow at the End," *Fort Worth Star-Telegram*, April 9, 1979.
17. Jerry Garrett, "A.J. Not Too Popular with Foes," Associated Press, *Kokomo* (Indiana) *Tribune*, April 11, 1979.
18. "CART Vows to Not Enter Indy 500 Race," Associated Press, *Vincennes Sun-Commercial* (Indiana), April 11, 1979.
19. "Drivers Level Blast at Foyt, Speedway," Associated Press, *Tipton County* (Indiana) *Tribune*, April 14, 1979.
20. Roger Jaynes, "Checkered Flag Won't End Speedway Feud," *Milwaukee Journal*, June 16, 1979.
21. Dick Mittman, "500 Concrete Chaos," *Indianapolis News*, April 20, 1979.
22. David Rohn, "USAC, CART So Close, Then Phfft," *Indianapolis News*, June 7, 1979.
23. Steve Herman, "CART Termed a 'Definite Threat,'" Associated Press, *Kokomo* (Indiana) *Tribune*, May 5, 1979.
24. Dick Mittman and David Rohn, "Foyt Started 'Ban CART' Move, Federal Court Told," *Indianapolis News*, May 3, 1979.
25. Robin Miller, "Judge Gives CART 'Go Sign,'" *Indianapolis Star*, May 6, 1979.
26. Dick Mittman, "Everybody Is a Winner in CART-USAC-500 Suit," *Indianapolis News*, May 7, 1979.
27. Dick Mittman, "A.J.'s Back and He's A-Rarin,'" *Indianapolis News*, May 8, 1979.

28. Steve Herman, "Foyt Denies He Tried to Keep Rivals Out," Associated Press, *Kokomo* (Indiana) *Tribune*, May 8, 1979.
29. Zach Dunkin, "A.J. Fuels 'Boost Debate,'" *Indianapolis News*, May 10, 1979.
30. Jerry Garrett, "CART Drivers Dominate Indy," Associated Press, *Lafayette* (Indiana) *Journal and Courier*, May 14, 1979.
31. William Anderson, "Roar of Speedway from Drivers Saying No to Court Summonses," *Indianapolis Star*, May 25, 1979.
32. David Israel, "It's Divorce Court, Alas, for Indy Feuds," *Chicago Tribune*, May 28, 1979.
33. Roger Jaynes, "Cheating at Indy '500,'" *Milwaukee Journal*, June 15, 1979.
34. Dave Beener, "Foyt Celebrates 2d-Place Finish," *Indianapolis Star*, May 28, 1979.
35. "Young Mears Wins Indy," *Munster* (Indiana) *Times*, May 28, 1979.
36. Beener, "Foyt Celebrates 2d-Place Finish."
37. "A.J. Gracious and Lucky," Associated Press, *South Bend Tribune*, May 28, 1979.
38. Dick Mittman, "Don't Count Ol' Fox Foyt out of 500," *Indianapolis News,* May 24, 1980.
39. Michael Knight, "Trenton Won't Compete with Pocono," *Philadelphia Daily News*, June 12, 1979.
40. Michael Knight, "Scoreboard: Foyt 64, Others 20," *Indianapolis News*, June 21, 1979.
41. Robin Miller, "Racing Rumors? Take Your Pick!," *Indianapolis Star*, June 7, 1979.
42. Michael Knight, "CART-USAC Picture Isn't Pretty to Andretti," *Philadelphia Daily News*, June 19, 1979.
43. "Foyt Reflects: It's Great to Be Alive," United Press International, *Scranton Tribune*, June 23, 1979.
44. Michael Knight, "Issues and Answers with A.J. Foyt," *Philadelphia Daily News*, June 22, 1979.
45. Wayne Fuson, "Foyt Won't Race at Ontario," *Indianapolis News*, July 5, 1969.
46. "Foyt Withdraws Indy Race Support," United Press International, *Muncie Star Press*, July 14, 1979.
47. Dick Kaegel, "Wallace Takes Advice and Du Quoin 100," *St. Louis Post-Dispatch*, August 26, 1979.
48. Kenny Schrader, November 13, 2020, interview with the author.
49. "Wallace Challenges Foyt at Texas 250," United Press International, *Galveston Daily News*, November 9, 1979.
50. Carter Cromwell, "Top Rookie Aims at National Title in Texan 250," *Austin American-Statesman*, November 10, 1979.
51. "Allison Happy; Foyt Fuming," *Waco Citizen*, November 16, 1979.
52. "Speaking of Sports," *Alexandria* (Indiana) *Times-Tribune*, January 16, 1980.
53. A.J. Foyt, April 19–24, 2021, interviews with the author.
54. Terry Lynn Foyt, April 21, 2021, interview with the author.
55. Larry Foyt, November 10, 2020, interview with the author.

CHAPTER THREE: DEATH AT DAYTONA

1. "Racing Factions May End Feud," Associated Press, *South Bend Tribune*, December 21, 1979.
2. William Neely, *The Jim Gilmore Story: Alone in the Crowd* (Aztex Corporation: 1988).
3. Dick Mittman, "Foyt Carts Away Big USAC Bucks," *Indianapolis News,* January 28, 1980.
4. "Angry Foyt Hands USAC Resignation," Associated Press, *South Bend Tribune*, February 5, 1980.
5. Robin Miller, "Foyt Surprised USAC," *Indianapolis Star*, February 6, 1980.
6. Tom Ford, "Pressure Off, A.J. Foyt's Just Having Fun," *Tampa Tribune*, February 16, 1980.
7. Sandra McKee, "At 45, A.J. Foyt Can Look Beyond Weekly Races," *Baltimore Evening Sun*, February 15, 1980.
8. Mike Hembree, "Driver Dies in Daytona Crash," *Greenville* (South Carolina) *News*, February 15, 1980.
9. George Smith, "Race Claims Knotts' Life," *Anniston* (Alabama) *Star*, February 15, 1980.
10. "Could Knotts' Tragedy Have Been Prevented?," *Orlando Sentinel*, February 15, 1980.
11. John Sonderegger, "How Did It Happen? Rookie Race Driver Dies in Crash," *St. Louis Post-Dispatch*, February 19, 1980.
12. Godwin Kelly, "It's Been a Fun 44 Years of Motorsports Journalism in Daytona Beach Area," *Daytona Beach News-Journal,* December 1, 2020.
13. Dave Kindred, December 11, 2020, interview with the author.
14. Dave Kindred, "They're Alive While Baiting Death," *Washington Post*, February 16, 1980.
15. Larry Guest, "What's This? Foyt Actually Soft-Hearted," *Orlando Sentinel*, February 16, 1980.
16. A.J. Foyt, 2008 interview with David Goldstein for the Houston Project.
17. George Cunningham, "Waltrip, Whittington Still Going at It," *Atlanta Constitution*, March 14, 1980.
18. Tex Powell, August 8, 2020, interview with the author.
19. Ron Lemasters, "And You Thought USAC and CART Were Getting Together," *Muncie Star Press*, March 9, 1980.
20. Robin Miller, "Hall's 'Effect' Was Felt at Ontario," *Indianapolis Star*, April 15, 1980.
21. Dick Mittman, "At 45, A.J. Foyt Still as Fiery as a Colt .45," *Indianapolis News*, May 12, 1980.
22. "A.J. Foyt Passing Another Milestone," Associated Press, *Danville* (Kentucky) *Advocate-Messenger*, May 23, 1980.
23. Dick Mittman, "Don't Count Ol' Fox Foyt out of 500," *Indianapolis News*, May 24, 1980.
24. Bruce Lowitt, "Slower Indy 500 Really Safer?," Associated Press, *Lafayette* (Indiana) *Journal and Courier*, May 24, 1980.

25. D.G. FitzMaurice, "A.J. Rivals J.R. with Post-Indy Comments," *Lexington* (Kentucky) *Herald*, May 26, 1980.
26. Bill Verigan, "Angry A.J. Lashes Out at Turtle-Like Indy 500; Says Race Was a Bore," *New York Daily News,* May 27, 1980.
27. Robin Miller, "A.J. Too Far Back, Perhaps," *Indianapolis Star*, May 29, 1980.
28. Robin Miller, "Foyt the Quickest; Was He Legal?" *Indianapolis Star*, June 19, 1980.
29. Michael Knight, "Retirement Rumors Have Foyt Chuckling," *Philadelphia Daily News*, June 21, 1980.
30. Ted Meixell, "Foyt Smiling . . . That WASN'T Understandable," *Allentown* (Pennsylvania) *Morning Call*, June 23, 1980.
31. "No Way A.J. Was Cheating Say Mech," *Indianapolis News*, June 23, 1980.
32. Ted Meixell, "A.J. Foyt: A Case Study in Contradiction," *Allentown* (Pennsylvania) *Morning Call*, June 22, 1980.
33. "Speedway Opens Door to Outside for 500 Sanction," *Indianapolis Star*, June 24, 1980.
34. Robin Miller, "Cooper Declares Independence," *Indianapolis Star*, June 25, 1980.
35. Dick Mittman, "USAC 'Hanging' While Waiting," *Indianapolis News*, July 10, 1980.
36. Tim Delrose, November 17, 2020, interview with the author.
37. Dick Mittman, "Gary B Having Best Year Ever," *Indianapolis News*, September 8, 1980.
38. Kenny Schrader, November 13, 2020, interview with the author.
39. Tim Delrose, November 17, 2020, interview with the author.

CHAPTER FOUR: MILLERGATE

1. Wayne Fuson, "Racing War Lingers On," *Indianapolis News*, February 2, 1981.
2. Teddy Heffner, "Foyt on New Cars: Biggest Pile of Junk," *Columbia* (South Carolina) *State*, February 15, 1981.
3. Ray Holliman, "Foyt's Listed as Longshot, But . . .," *Tampa Bay Times*, February 15, 1981.
4. "Daytona Notes," *Indianapolis News*, February 17, 1981.
5. Bob Riley, February 18, 2021, interview with the author.
6. A.J. Foyt, April 19–24, 2021, interviews with the author.
7. Riley, February 18, 2021, interview.
8. Robin Miller, "500 Drivers Set for Hot Laps," *Indianapolis Star*, May 9, 1981.
9. Robin Miller, "Andretti Quickest on Windy Track," *Indianapolis Star*, May 8, 1981.
10. A.J. Foyt, April 19–24, 2021, interviews.
11. "Foyt Lashes Out at Star Scribe," *Indianapolis Star*, May 9, 1981.
12. Zak Keefer, "The Preposterous Sports Writing Life of Robin Miller, Racing's Legendary Hellion," *The Athletic*, August 17, 2020.
13. Robin Miller, October 2, 2021, interview with the author.
14. John McGill, "Foyt Survives Scare to Lead Qualifiers," *Louisville Courier-Journal*, May 10, 1981.
15. Riley, February 18, 2021, interview.
16. David Barnes, "Foyt Sitting Pretty on Rainy Day," *Kokomo* (Indiana) *Tribune*, May 10, 1981.
17. Riley, February 18, 2021, interview.
18. Dick Mittman, "Speedway Gambler Knew When to Run," *Indianapolis News*, May 11, 1981.
19. A.J. Foyt, April 19, 2021, interview.
20. "Foyt's Mother Dead at 65," United Press International, *Greenfield* (Indiana) *Daily Reporter*, May 11, 1981.
21. Robin Miller, "A.J.'s Nasty Side Hidden by Legend," *Indianapolis Star*, May 10, 1981.
22. Jim Murray, "A.J. and the Volcano," *Los Angeles Times*, March 10, 1974.
23. J.D. Lewis, "Racing Group Asks Foyt to Apologize," *Columbus* (Indiana) *Republic*, May 12, 1981.
24. "Foyt Sues Newspaper for Slanderous Column," United Press International, *Muncie Star Press*, May 23, 1981.
25. "A.J. Foyt Sues *Indianapolis Star*," *Richmond* (Indiana) *Palladium-Item*, May 22, 1981.
26. "Foyt Suit Dismissed," *Indianapolis Star*, November 1, 1981.
27. "Foyt, Paper Settle Libel Suit," *South Bend Tribune*, December 2, 1981.
28. Keefer, "The Preposterous Sports Writing Life of Robin Miller."
29. A.J. Foyt, April 19, 2021, interview.
30. David Heuschkel, "For Foyt, It's an Old Story," *Hartford* (Connecticut) *Courant*, June 13, 1997.
31. Miller, interview with the author.
32. Jack Starne, January 13, 2021, interview with the author.
33. A.J. Foyt with William Neely. *A.J.: My Life as America's Greatest Race Car Driver* (Times Books: 1983).
34. Zach Dunkin, "'Old George' Makes Qualifying Look Easy," *Indianapolis News*, May 18, 1981.
35. Dick Mittman, "Top Drivers Object to Buying Rides," *Indianapolis News*, May 22, 1981.
36. Dick Mittman, "Pit It in the Bank, Buy George," *Indianapolis News*, May 21, 1981.
37. Zach Dunkin, "Tim Richmond Replaces Snider in Foyt's 2nd Car," *Indianapolis News*, May 21, 1981.
38. Bob Ottum, "Get Out of the Way, Here Comes A.J.," *Sports Illustrated*, May 25, 1981.
39. Tim Povtak, "Haywood Itching to Drive Despite Cast on Left Foot," *Orlando Sentinel*, February 1, 1984.
40. Kurt Freudenthal, "Fuming Foyt Blames Crew, Faulty Radio for Race Failure," *Indianapolis Star*, May 25, 1981.

41. Kurt Freudenthal, "Foyt Confirms Wave for Andretti to Pass," *Indianapolis Star*, June 11, 1981.
42. Dick Mittman, "'Heavies' Scrap in 500 Appeal Battle," *Indianapolis News*, June 11, 1981.
43. "Unser: A.J. Didn't Want Me to Win Third Indy," Associated Press, *South Bend Tribune*, June 12, 1981.
44. Jim Hawkins, "Bobby Unser Still Fuming over the 'Indygate' Fiasco," *Detroit Free Press*, July 19, 1981.
45. "A.J. to Stick with Stocks," *Indianapolis News*, July 3, 1981.
46. Jack Jordan, "A.J. Foyt Learns Lessons," *Scranton Time-Tribune*, June 22, 1981.
47. Ted Meixell, "Foyt Wins Shortened Pocono Race," *Allentown Morning Call*, June 22, 1981.
48. Ray Saul, "Speaking of Sports," *Hazleton* (Pennsylvania) *Standard-Speaker*, June 22, 1981.
49. Charlie Vincent, "A.J. Would Rather Race than Fight," *Detroit Free Press*, July 16, 1981.
50. Mike Harris, "A.J. Foyt Just Wants to Race," Associated Press, *Indianapolis News*, July 16, 1981.
51. Mike Harris, "Foyt Concerned About Steep Banks on Track," Associated Press, (Michigan) *Herald-Palladium*, July 19, 1981.
52. Riley, February 18, 2021, interview.
53. A.J. Foyt, April 19, 2021, interview.
54. Mike Harris, "Foyt 'Fair' After Arm Surgery," Associated Press, *Richmond* (Indiana) *Palladium-Item*, July 26, 1981.
55. "Foyt List 'Good' After Surgery," *Detroit Free Press*, July 27, 1981.
56. "Q&A with Jack Starne," AJ Foyt Racing, March 13, 2020, https://www.foytracing.com/single-post/2020/04/13/qa-with-jack-starne.
57. Gary Long, "Is the End Near for A.J. Foyt's Track Escapades?," *Muncie* (Indiana) *Evening News*, February 5, 1982.
58. Mike Harris, April 2021, interview with the author.
59. "Foyt Says Injuries Won't Retire Him," United Press International, *Indianapolis Star*, August 1, 1981.
60. Dave Overpeck, "After Scars and Scares, A.J. Back," *Indianapolis Star*, February 13, 1982.
61. Foyt and Neely, *A.J.: My Life as America's Greatest Race Car Driver*.
62. Bob Riley with Jonathan Ingram, *The Art of Race Car Design* (Icon Publishing: 2015).

CHAPTER FIVE: COOGIN!

1. Bob Barnet, "That's Enough A.J.!," *Muncie* (Indiana) *Star Press*, July 28, 1981.
2. Shav Glick, "25 Years at the Brickyard," *Los Angeles Times*, May 23, 1982.
3. "Foyt Anxious to Return," Associated Press, *Passaic* (New Jersey) *Herald-News*, January 14,1982.
4. Tracy Dodds, "The Indy Class of 1958," *Los Angeles Times*, May 30, 1982.
5. Dick Mittman, "Profile: Driver A.J. Foyt," *Indianapolis News*, May 11, 1982.
6. Jeff Rude, "Legendary Texan Sees Comeback at Daytona," *Florida Today*, January 14, 1982.
7. "Foyt Returning," *Indianapolis News*, January 13, 1982.
8. Brian Schmitz, "For A.J., Light Is Green Again," *Orlando Sentinel*, January 19, 1982.
9. Brian Schmitz, "Under A.J.'s Wing," *Orlando Sentinel*, February 8, 1982.
10. Gary Long, "Is the End Near for A.J. Foyt's Track Escapades?," *Muncie* (Indiana) *Evening News*, February 5, 1982.
11. Dave Kindred, "A.J. Foyt's Back Where He Belongs—Racing in 200 mph Traffic and Lovin' It," *Washington Post*, February 13, 1982.
12. Dave Overpeck, "Cale, Buddy Daytona Winners," *Indianapolis Star*, February 12, 1982.
13. "Foyt: 'I'm Not Talking,'" *Orlando Sentinel*, February 15, 1982.
14. Dick Denny, "Foyt: I Can Win This Race If . . .," *Indianapolis News*, May 27,1982.
15. A.J. Foyt, April 19, 2021, interview with the author.
16. Kindred, "A.J. Foyt's Back Where He Belongs."
17. Dick Mittman, "A.J. to Challenge 'Good Ol' Boys,'" *Indianapolis News*, February 13, 1982.
18. J.D. Lewis, "Gentlemen, Foyt Is Back: Now Start Your Engines," *Columbus* (Indiana) *Republic*, May 8, 1982.
19. Robin Miller, "200 Club Filling up Fast," *Indianapolis Star*, May 14, 1982.
20. Robin Miller, "It's Mears vs. Cogan for Pole," *Indianapolis Star*, May 15, 1982.
21. Dave Overpeck, "Getting Front Row Spot Still a Challenge: Foyt," *Indianapolis Star*, May 16, 1982.
22. "Mears Grad Indy Pole; Smiley Killed," Associated Press, *Vincennes* (Indiana) *Sun-Commercial*, May 16, 1982.
23. Mittman, "Profile: Driver A.J. Foyt."
24. Long, "Is the End Near?"
25. Overpeck, "Getting Front Row Spot Still a Challenge."
26. Mike Harris, "Ground Effects Give off False Security, Says Foyt," Associated Press, *Indianapolis Star*, May 29, 1982.
27. Kurt Freudenthal, "4 Drivers Test Out at 200," *Indianapolis Star*, May 28, 1982.
28. "1982 Indianapolis 500," same-day tape-delayed broadcast, *ABC Sports*, May 30, 1982.
29. Dick Mittman, "A Day of Ups, Downs," *Indianapolis News*, May 31, 1982.
30. "1982 Indianapolis 500," *ABC Sports*.
31. Bill Verigan, "Foyt's 25th Unhappy One Due to Crash," *New York Daily News*, May 31, 1982.
32. D.B., "Crash Spoils A.J.'s Anniversary," *Indianapolis Star*, May 31, 1982.

33. "New Driver's Suit," *Indianapolis Star*, May 20, 1982.
34. Verigan, "Foyt's 25th Unhappy."
35. D.B., "Crash Spoils A.J.'s Anniversary."
36. Verigan, "Foyt's 25th Unhappy."
37. Mittman, "A Day of Ups, Downs."
38. Billy Woodruff, January 20, 2021, interview with the author.
39. Curt Cavin, "'82 Crash Turned Promising Young Driver into 500 Pariah," *Indianapolis Star*, May 20, 2015.
40. A.J. Foyt with William Neely, *A.J.: My Life as America's Greatest Race Car Driver* (Times Books: 1983).
41. Rick Mears, December 1, 2020, interview with the author.
42. "A.J. Means Sellout," Associated Press, *Columbus* (Indiana) *Republic*, June 9, 1982.
43. Cliff Guilliams, "Amazing Love Victorious by Two in Downs' Stakes," *Evansville Press* (Indiana), June 6, 1982.
44. "A.J. Takes Aim at Derby Title," Associated Press, *Indianapolis News*, May 20, 1982.
45. Dick Mittman, "Gordy Fills It Up, Wins Milwaukee," *Indianapolis News*, June 14, 1982.
46. *Terre Haute Tribune*, May 26, 1968.
47. "Gordy's 'Sudden Success' Is Really Not So Sudden," United Press International, *Columbus* (Indiana) *Republic*, August 13, 1982.
48. Foyt and Neely, *A.J.: My Life as America's Greatest Race Car Driver*.
49. Jerry Bonkowski, "1973 Indy 500 Winner Gordon Johncock 'Always Tried to Do the Right Thing,'" *AutoWeek*, May 22, 2023.
50. Foyt and Neely, *A.J.: My Life as America's Greatest Race Car Driver*.
51. "A.J. Back to 'Going After Em,'" Associated Press, *Elwood* (Indiana) *Call-Leader*, July 17, 1982.
52. Mike Downey, "Another MIS-Fortunate Puts Foyt out of the Running," *Detroit Free Press*, July 19, 1982.
53. Dick Mittman, "A.J.: Some Can't Drive," *Indianapolis News*, July 19,1982.
54. "Pit Notes," *Philadelphia Daily News*, August, 16, 1982.
55. Dick Mittman, "Guess Who Ran into Foyt Again?" *Indianapolis News*, September 27, 1982.
56. Mittman, "Guess Who Ran into Foyt Again?"
57. Robin Miller, "Rahal Michigan Victor," *Indianapolis Star*, September 27, 1982.
58. Robin Miller, "Cogan's Dream Crashes amid Horrible Season," *Indianapolis Star*, September 30, 1982.
59. Leal Beattie, "Mears Compares Favorably to A.J.'s Beginning Years," *Daytona Daily News*, December 19, 1982.
60. Mike Harris, "Bobby Unser Will Quit Racing," Associated Press, *Muscatine* (Iowa) *Journal*, December 21, 1982.
61. Dave Matthews, "Unser's Decision Wise," *Lansing State Journal*, December 22, 1982.

CHAPTER SIX: ONE MORE FOR TONY

1. Jerry Garrett, "The Man," *On Track Magazine*, April 7, 1983.
2. Mike Harris, "Aging A.J. Rarin' to Go," Associated Press, *Indianapolis News*, January 7, 1983.
3. Dr. Gary Friedman, 2020 interview with the author.
4. Darrell Waltrip, November 6, 2020, interview with the author.
5. A.J. Foyt, 2008 interview with David Goldstein for the Houston Project.
6. Waltrip, November 6, 2020, interview.
7. Jack Arute, November 5, 2021, interview with the author.
8. Garrett, "The Man."
9. Arute, November 5, 2021, interview.
10. Brian Schmitz, "A.J. Makes 24 Hours His Day," *Orlando Sentinel,* February 7, 1983.
11. Bob Wollek, "Bob Wollek Interviewed at the 1983 Daytona 24 Hours," Interview by David Hobbs. HRN, *YouTube*, posted November 8, 2017, https://www.youtube.com/watch?v=GC7fCMzLdfA.
12. Tom Archdeacon, "A Racing Family Making History," *Miami News*, February 11, 1983.
13. Hurley Haywood, January 16, 2025, interview with the author.
14. Schmitz, "A.J. Makes 24 Hours His Day."
15. "Foyt's Team Overcomes 12-Lap Deficit to win Daytona," Associated Press, *Bradenton* (Florida) *Herald*, February 7,1983.
16. Mike Harris, "Race Cars Alike to Foyt," Associated Press, *Billings Gazette,* February 9, 1983.
17. Haywood, January 16, 2025, interview.
18. Gary Long, "Picking Foyt Was a Gamble, Henn Admits," *Miami Herald*, February 8, 1983.
19. Harris, "Race Cars Alike to Foyt."
20. A.J. Foyt, April 19–24, 2021, interviews with the author.
21. Brian Schmitz, "A.J. Makes 24 Hours His Day," *Orlando Sentinel*, February 7, 1983.
22. Jerry Garrett, "The Man," *On Track Magazine*, April 7, 1983.
23. Mike Harris, April 2021, interview with the author.
24. Darrell Waltrip, November 6, 2020, interview with the author.
25. Tom Archdeacon, "Winning Is the Cure-All for Tough Guy A.J. Foyt," *Miami News*, February 4, 1984.
26. Cale Yarborough, 2021 interview with the author.
27. Ed Hinton, "Old Tony: A.J. Foyt Wants to Win One More Race Before Dad Dies of Cancer," *Atlanta Constitution,* February 17, 1983.

28. A.J. Foyt, April 19–24, 2021, interviews.
29. Jerry Garrett, "The Man," *On Track Magazine*, April 7, 1983.
30. Cooper Rollow, "Having His Say," *Chicago Tribune*, February 17, 1983.
31. A.J. Foyt, April 19–24, 2021, interviews.
32. Jack Starne, January 13, 2021, interview with the author.
33. George Snider, December 12, 2020, interview with the author.
34. A.J. Foyt, April 19–24, 2021, interviews.

CHAPTER SEVEN: CALUMET FARM

1. S.L. Burpo, "Look for A.J. Foyt to Give Extra Effort," *Martinsville* (Indiana) *Reporter-Times*, May 7, 1983.
2. Maryjean Wall, "Foyt Increases 'Horsepower,'" *Lexington Herald*, September 11, 1974.
3. Harry King, "Auto Racer Foyt's Son Works to Restore Calumet Farm's Greatness," Associated Press, *Baxter* (Arkansas) *Bulletin*, February 6, 1984.
4. Eddie Donnally, "This Foyt Fools Around with Horses," *Dallas Morning News*, March 13, 1983.
5. Ann Hagedorn Auerbach, *Wild Ride* (Henry Holt and Company: 1994).
6. Skip Hollandsworth, "The Killing of Alydar," *Texas Monthly*, June 2001.
7. Auerbach, *Wild Ride*.
8. Will Grimsley, "A Horse Connection," Associated Press, May 27, 1983.
9. J.D. Lewis, "Horsepower Plus Horsepower," *The Columbus* (Indiana) *Republic*, May 5, 1983.
10. Leal Beattle, "Gravely Ill Father Will Miss A.J.'s 26th Indy Run," *Daytona Journal Herald*, May 5, 1983.
11. Lewis, "Horsepower Plus Horsepower."
12. Beattle, "Gravely Ill Father."
13. Mark Purdy, "A.J. Mingles with the Horsy Set," *Cincinnati Enquirer*, May 6, 1983.
14. Dave Overpeck, "A.J. Foyt, Racing's Legend Larger than Life," *Indianapolis Star*, May 19, 1983.
15. "Trying Time for A.J.," *Indianapolis News*, May 23, 1983.
16. Marlene Foyt, June 23, 2021, interview with the author.
17. Lemasters, "Foyt Threatens to Put Records Out of Reach."
18. A.J. Foyt, April 19–24, 2021, interviews with the author.
19. William Nack, "Twilight of a Titan," *Sports Illustrated*, September 30, 1991.
20. A.J. Foyt with William Neely, *A.J.: My Life as America's Greatest Race Car Driver* (Times Books: 1983).
21. Jack Starne, January 13, 2021, interview with the author.
22. Anthony Joseph "Tony" Foyt III, April 26, 2021, interview with the author.
23. Tim Delrose, November 17, 2020, interview with the author.
24. David Casstevens, "Foyt's Crew Missing One Important Man," *Dallas Morning News*, May 27, 1983.
25. Bob Barnet, "Matchless Skill—And Inspiration," *Muncie* (Indiana) *Star Press*, May 26, 1983.
26. "Emotions Encircling A.J. Foyt," Associated Press, *Marion* (Ohio) *Star*, May 29, 1983.
27. Bill Verigan, "Foyt's Agony, Fabi's Ecstasy Both Short Stories in Race," *New York Daily News*, May 30, 1983.
28. Jack Arute with Jenna Fryer, *Tales from the Indy 500* (Sports Publishing: 2004).
29. Brian Schmitz, "Foyt Wipes Out Firecracker 400," *Orlando Sentinel*, July 4, 1983.
30. Tom Archdeacon, "A.J. Foyt Makes the Pain Go Away," *Miami News*, July 4, 1983.
31. Hurley Haywood, January 16, 2024, interview with the author.
32. Jon Saraceno, "Foyt, Haywood Triumph in Paul Revere 250," *Florida Today*, July 4, 1983.
33. Tom Archdeacon, "A.J. Foyt Makes the Pain Go Away," *Miami News*, July 4, 1983.
34. Hurley Haywood, January 16, 2024, interview with the author.
35. "Foyt Takes Control," Associated Press, *Philadelphia Inquirer*, September 21, 1983.
36. Shav Glick, "Foyt Fans Legion, but A.J. Is No. 1," *Los Angeles Times*, December 1, 1983.

CHAPTER EIGHT: A LITTLE HELP FOR HIS FRIENDS

1. Tom Archdeacon, "Winning Is the Cure-All for Tough Guy A.J. Foyt," *Miami News*, February 4, 1984.
2. Sandra McKee, "Wollek Mouthed Off, but Foyt Had Him Eating His Words," *Baltimore Evening Sun*, February 3, 1984.
3. Jenny Kellner, "Racing Driver Thinks Miami's 'Different,'" *Miami News*, February 7, 1984.
4. Gary Silvers, "South African Beat Daytona Odds," *Orlando Sentinel*, February 6, 1984.
5. Paul Heidelberg, "Porsche Turbo Races to Victory in 12 Hours of Sebring," *Fort Lauderdale News*, March 25, 1984.
6. Tom McEwen, "Just Like Sebring, A.J. Foyt Endures," *Tampa Tribune*, March 24, 1984.
7. Charlie Vincent, "It's the Pits for Allison, Petty, Foyt," *Detroit Free Press*, February 20, 1984.
8. Tom Keating, "Foyts Win in Slower Contests, Low Power," *Indianapolis Star*, May 25, 1984.
9. Robin Miller, "An Interview with Super Tex," *Indianapolis Star*, May 26, 1984.
10. "Foyt Becoming Amiable with Age," Associated Press, *Vincennes* (Indiana) *Sun-Commercial*, May 16, 1984.
11. Dick Mittman, "Big Money Pays Off in 500 Qualifying," *Indianapolis News*, May 21, 1984.
12. Dave Overpeck, "J.R. Joins the Field with Help of Foyt," *Indianapolis Star*, May 20, 1984.

13. "Fastest Indy field Has Seven Former Winners," Associated Press, *Muncie* (Indiana) *Evening Press*, May 21, 1984.
14. "Foyt Leaves Future in Doubt After Race," Associated Press, *Indianapolis News*, May 28, 1984.
15. Bill Verigan, "Farewell for Foyt May Be Start of New Era for Mears," *New York Daily News*, July 1, 1984.
16. Hurley Haywood, January 16, 2025, interview with the author.
17. Bill Verigan, "Foyt Geared up to Give Jersey Roads a Ride," *New York Daily News*, June 27, 1984.
18. Gary Ronberg, "CART Hopes New Meadowlands Race Will Be a Winner," *Philadelphia Inquirer*, June 24, 1984.
19. Wendy Grubow, "Foyt Just Watches Time Trials," *Asbury Park* (New Jersey) *Press*, June 29, 1984.
20. Barry Gramlish, "Foyt: 'If I Can't Go Fast Enough, the Hell with It," *Passaic* (New Jersey) *Herald-News*, June 30, 1984.
21. Bill Huneke, "Meadowlands Grand Prix First-Rate," *Central New Jersey Home News*, June 30, 1984.
22. Bill Bilinski, "Rutherford Gets a Lift from Gilmore and A.J. Foyt," *South Bend Tribune*, July 18, 1984.
23. Steve Morse, "Rutherford Aims for Michigan 500," *Battle Creek* (Michigan) *Enquirer*, July 18, 1984.
24. Paul Bailey, "Disqualification Hurts Foyt's Pride," *Akron Beacon Journal*, July 20, 1984.
25. Dick Mittman, "Foyt Banned at Michigan," *Indianapolis News*, July 20, 1984.
26. Robin Miller, "Foyt Ready to Run in Michigan 500," *Indianapolis Star*, July 21, 1984.
27. Malcolm Moran, "Defying the Odds at Indy," *New York Times*, May 25, 1986.
28. Steve Morse, "It's Quite a Day for the Races," *Battle Creek* (Michigan) *Enquirer*, July 23, 1984.
29. Mike Harris, "Foyt Issues Challenge for Michigan 500 Race," Associated Press, *Vincennes* (Indiana) *Sun-Commercial*, July 22, 1984.
30. Tom Archdeacon, "A.J. Wants to Race Again," *Miami News*, January 31, 1985.
31. Phillip Marshall, "Foyt Not Back off in Talladega 500," *Montgomery* (Alabama) *Advertiser*, July 28, 1984.
32. Johnny Rutherford, June 17, 2020, interview with the author.
33. Tom Archdeacon, "The Twinkle Is Back on Lone Star J.R.," *Miami News*, November 6, 1986.
34. "Fined Foyt Fumes, Then Flees," *Indianapolis Star*, September 23, 1984.
35. Al Palmeri, "World's Fastest Racer: Rutherford Hits 215," *Battle Creek* (Michigan) *Enquirer*, September 23, 1984.
36. "Foyt Rankled by CART Rules," Associated Press, *South Bend Tribune*, October 13, 1984.
37. Mike Harris, "Foyt in Phoenix with Big Chip on His Shoulder," Associated Press, *Muncie Evening Press*, October 13, 1984.
38. Shav Glick, "He's 44, but Champion Andretti Is Having Too Much Fun to Quit," *Los Angeles Times*, November 29, 1983.
39. Harris, "Foyt in Phoenix."
40. Moran, "Defying the Odds at Indy."
41. Verigan, "Foyt Geared Up."
42. Moran, "Defying the Odds at Indy."
43. Jan Shaffer, "A.J. Foyt Interview," *Indy Car Racing Magazine*, November 1985.
44. Jerry Foyt, January 31, 2021, interview with the author.
45. Dick Mittman, "A.J. Foyt Surprised by Son's Initiative to Race," *Indianapolis News*, September 24, 1987.
46. Robin Miller, "With or Without Dad's Blessing, Jerry Foyt Is Off and Running," *Indianapolis Star*, April 5, 1992.
47. Jerry Foyt, January 31, 2021, interview with the author.

CHAPTER NINE: HERO OR AN ASS

1. Mike Harris, "Foyt, Bouchard Lead Atlanta Qualifiers," Associated Press, *Owensboro* (Kentucky) *Messenger-Inquirer*, November 3, 1984.
2. Leo Mehl, "Book by Foyt Omits More than It Tells," *Akron Beacon Journal*, January 28, 1985.
3. Bob Larkin, "Al Unser Can Win Title Today," *Albuquerque Journal*, October 23, 1983.
4. "Sullivan to Replace Unser on Penske Racing Team in '85," *Albuquerque Journal*, December 8, 1984.
5. Mark Armijo, "Angry Foyt Launches Verbal War on CART," *Arizona Republic*, October 13, 1984.
6. Ron Lemasters, "R.J. Reynolds Pours More Money into New NASCAR Events," *Muncie Star Press*, December 21, 1984.
7. Tom Archdeacon, "An Old Dog Learns New Tricks," *Miami News*, February 4, 1985.
8. Dick Mittman, "Unsers Sr. and Jr. Get Racing Rides," *Indianapolis News*, January 23, 1985.
9. "CART Season Looking Brighter for Unser," *Albuquerque Journal*, January 25, 1985.
10. Tom Archdeacon, "A.J. Wants to Race Again," *Miami News*, January 31, 1985.
11. Mike Harris, "Record Field Set at Daytona for 24-Hour Endurance Race, Associated Press, *Palm Beach Post*, February 2, 1985.
12. Ray Halliman, "Versatile Foyt Adds Sebring to Crowns," *Tampa Bay Times*, March 25, 1985.
13. Archdeacon, "An Old Dog."
14. Tom Archdeacon, "Old-Fashioned Racing Fits Style of David Pearson to T," *Palm Beach Post*, February 17, 1985.
15. "Sneva-Gurney Combo Will Hit Indy Circuit," United Press International, *Carlisle* (Pennsylvania) *Sentinel*, April 6, 1985.

16. Jonathan Ingram, February 8, 2021, interview with the author.
17. Tom Ford, "Foyt, Wollek Pilot Porsche 962 to Win," *Tampa Tribune*, March 24, 1985.
18. Halliman, "Versatile Foyt Adds Sebring."
19. Malcolm Moran, "Defying the Odds at Indy," *New York Times*, May 25, 1986.
20. Bucky Albers, "Bleep! Foyt Tells of Qualification Frustration," *Dayton Journal Herald*, May 13, 1985.
21. John Fineran, "Fire Burns Bright Inside A.J. Foyt," *South Bend Tribune*, May 12, 1985.
22. Zach Dunkin, "A.J. Takes Blame for Poor Qualifying," *Indianapolis News*, May 13, 1985.
23. Bill Benner, "Nish Jumps at Chance Foyt Gives Him," *Indianapolis Star*, May 16, 1985.
24. Benner, "Nish Jumps at Chance Foyt Gives Him."
25. Dick Mittman, "Ganassi Just Happy to Be Back at Track," *Indianapolis News*, May 16, 1985.
26. Chip Ganassi, October 7, 2015, interview with the author.
27. Bob Walters, "Everything Falls Fast into Place for Chip Ganassi," *Indianapolis Star*, May 19, 1985.
28. David Fink, "Ganassi Returns to Indy for Qualifying," *Pittsburgh Post-Gazette*, May 16, 1985.
29. Chip Ganassi, October 7, 2015, interview with the author.
30. Fink, "Ganassi Returns to Indy."
31. Ganassi, October 7, 2015, interview.
32. Dick Mittman, "Snider Slips into 500 Field Again, *Indianapolis News*, May 20, 1985.
33. "Foyt Again Gives Ride to Snider," Associated Press, *Muncie Evening Press*, May 24, 1985.
34. Rex Kirts, "Indy Field Fill Up; 3 cars Bumped Out," *Bedford* (Indiana) *Times-Mail*, May 19, 1985.
35. Mike Harris, "Foyt Says He'll Quit After 30," Associated Press, *Indianapolis Star*, May 21, 1985.
36. Jerry Garau, "Foyt's Burning Desire Bursts into Flames," *Indianapolis Star*, May 27, 1985.
37. Ganassi, October 7, 2015, interview.
38. Dick Mittman, "Gilmore, Foyt Not Parting Yet," *Indianapolis News*, June 14, 1985.
39. Jan Shaffer, "Interview A.J. Foyt," *Indy Car Racing Magazine*, November, 1985.
40. Ganassi, October 7, 2015, interview.
41. Sandra McKee, "Sneva, Rahal Put Dent in Foyt's Image," *Baltimore Evening Sun*, August 15, 1985.
42. Sandra McKee, "Foyt Strikes Back at Rahal, Sneva, Says His Racing Record Speaks for Itself," *Baltimore Evening Sun*, August 19, 1985.
43. Mike Harris, "A.J. Foyt's a Darlington Rookie," Associated Press, *Rock Hill* (South Carolina) *Herald*, August 29, 1985.
44. Wayne Fuson, "A.J. Foyt a Rookie in Darlington," *Indianapolis News*, August 6, 1985.
45. Brian Biggane, "Foyt Earns His NASCAR Stripes at Darlington," *Palm Beach Post*, August 31, 1985.
46. "Foyt Gets His First Look at Darlington Raceway," *Columbia* (South Carolina) *State*, August 21, 1985.

CHAPTER TEN: STILL THE MASTER

1. Mike Harris, "Foyt a 'Serious Race Again," Associated Press, *Muncie Star Press*, February 12, 1986.
2. Don Coble, "A.J. Foyt: Urge for Victory Burns Like a Raging Fire," *Florida Today*, February 1, 1986.
3. Danny Sullivan, October 22, 2020, interview with the author.
4. Tom Ford, "Marathon Man Holbert Wins SunBank 24," *Tampa Tribune*, February 3, 1986.
5. Don Coble, "Holbert, Bell, Unser Take It," *Florida Today*, February 3, 1986.
6. Ira Winderman, "Holbert Team Flashes to Victory," *Orlando Sentinel*, February 3, 1986.
7. Shav Glick, "He's the Talented Toast of Tinseltown," *Los Angeles Times*, June 22, 1986.
8. Danny Sullivan, October 22, 2020, interview with author.
9. Brian Biggane, "Foyt Earns His NASCAR Stripes at Darlington," *Palm Beach Post*, August 31, 1985.
10. "Foyt, Sullivan Might Skip Miami Grand Prix," United Press International, *York* (Pennsylvania) *Dispatch*, March 1, 1986.
11. Brian Biggane, "Dispute May Keep Foyt, Sullivan Out of Miami Grand Prix," *Palm Beach Post*, February 6, 1986.
12. Tom Archdeacon, "In A.J.'s Words, Miami Prix Idea Is Mickey Mouse," *Miami News*, February 12, 1986.
13. "Dispute Settled, Foyt to Drive," United Press International, *Indianapolis Star*, March 2, 1986.
14. Sullivan, October 22, 2020, interview.
15. Marty Klinkenberg, "Foyt Gets a Kick Out of Race Controversy," *Miami News*, March 3, 1986.
16. Craig Doich, "Foyt Enjoying Auto Racing's Life of Luxury, and He's Proved He's Worth a Hefty Price," June 21, 1986.
17. Marty Klinkenberg, "Bickering Continues; Foyt, Sullivan May Not Race," *Miami News*, February 26, 1986.
18. Brian Biggane, "Foyt Says He's Tired of Being Henn's Pawn," *Palm Beach Post*, March 21, 1986.
19. Herb Branham, "Foyt, Sullivan a Lock, Finally," *Tampa Tribune*, March 21, 1986.
20. Ira Winderman, "Foyt, Wollek Have Reunion of Sorts," *South Florida Sun Sentinel*, March 21, 1986.
21. Gary Long, "Still A.J. After All These Years," *Miami Herald*, February 27, 1987.
22. Brian Biggane, "Henn to Leave Racing; Foyt May Form Own Porsche Team," *Palm Beach Post*, November 11, 1986.
23. Hurley Haywood, January 16, 2024, interview with the author.
24. Harry King, "Auto Racer Foyt's Son Works to Restore Calumet Farm's Greatness," Associated Press, *Baxter* (Arkansas) *Bulletin*, February 6, 1984.

25. Jim Lassiter, "This Foyt Prefers Whinnies," *Daily Oklahoman*, February 9, 1985.
26. Tim Povtak, "Foyt's Philosophy: Go the Distance, Remain Distant," *Orlando Sentinel*, February 14, 1985.
27. Eddie Donnally, "Foyt's New Machine Runs on . . . Oats," *Dallas Morning News*, April 13, 1986.
28. "Rare Brick (7 for 7) Survives in Rebel," Associated Press, *Louisville Courier-Journal*, March 30, 1986.
29. Gary West, "Rare Brick Has Just Enough in Rebel," *Shreveport (Louisiana) Journal*, March 31, 1986.
30. Pohla Smith, "Rare Brick, A.J. Foyt's Undefeated Kentucky Derby Prospect Shows Heart," *United Press International Archives*, March 30, 1986.
31. Harry King, "Arkansas Derby Favorite Faces Surgery for Bone Chip in Ankle," Associated Press, *Baxter* (Arkansas) *Bulletin*, April 9, 1986.
32. Lassiter, "This Foyt Prefers Whinnies."
33. Mike Harris, "A.J. Still Stirs Excitement," Associated Press, *Muncie Evening Press*, May 21, 1986.
34. Anthony Joseph "Tony" Foyt III, April 26, 2021, interview with the author.
35. Bob Ottum, "Get Out of the Way, Here Comes A.J.," *Sports Illustrated*, May 25, 1981.
36. Bill Verigan, "At Age 51, A.J. Trying for A-Ok," *New York Daily News*, May 25, 1986.
37. Malcolm Moran, "Defying the Odds at Indy," *New York Times*, May 25, 1986.
38. Dick Mittman, "Foyt Says He Is No 'Has-Been,'" *Indianapolis News*, May 8,1986.
39. "A.J. Foyt Gets Faster with Age," Associated Press, *South Bend Tribune*, May 12, 1986.
40. Mittman, "Foyt Says He Is No 'Has-Been.'"
41. Susan Hanafee, "Gen Yeager Throttles Back for '500,'" *Indianapolis Star*, May 21, 1986.
42. "Rain Turns Brickyard into a Mud Puddle," Associated Press, *Palm Springs Desert Sun*, May 26, 1986.
43. Ira Winderman, "Don't Ask A.J. to Win for Old-Timers," *South Florida Sun Sentinel*, May 22, 1986.
44. Brian Schmitz, "Foyt Wants to Prove at Indy He's Still King of the Hill, Not over It," *Orlando Sentinel*, May 25, 1986.
45. Moran, "Defying the Odds."
46. Robin Miller, "Provimi Reducing Operation," *Indianapolis Star*, June 12, 1986.
47. Charlie Vincent, "He's Balder, Broader, but Fire Is Back in Foyt," *Detroit Free Press*, August 2, 1986.
48. Miller, "Provimi Reducing Operation."
49. Ed Welburn, September 17, 2023, interview with the author.
50. Dick Mittman, "A.J. of Old Makes Serious 500 Bid," *Indianapolis News*, February 17, 1986.
51. "Elliott Wins Pole, Snaps Mark," United Press International, *Kingsport* (Tennessee) *Times-News*, November 1, 1986.
52. Bill Simons, "Foyt Is Also Fast to Five Opinions," *Philadelphia Inquirer*, December 21, 1975.
53. Welburn, September 17, 2023, interview.
54. "Setting Records," Oldsmobile promotional video, narrated by Sam Posey, 1986.
55. Evan McCausland, "Ed Welburn Drives the Oldsmobile Aerotech," *Motor Trend*, December 30, 2010.
56. Welburn, September 17, 2023, interview.
57. David Mannweiler, "Nothing but the Truth," *Indianapolis News*, December 29, 1986.

CHAPTER ELEVEN: HAVING FUN AGAIN

1. Hurley Haywood, January 16, 2024, interview with the author.
2. Jack Starne, January 13, 2021, interview with the author.
3. Chris Sherman, "Upscale Racing Sponsors Run in the Best Circles," *Orlando Sentinel*, January 31, 1987.
4. Danny Sullivan, October 22, 2020, interview with the author.
5. Al Unser, December 16, 2020, interview with the author.
6. Don Coble, "Foyt's Nature Surprises Crew at Daytona," *Florida Today*, February 3, 1987.
7. Unser, December 16, 2020, interview.
8. Sullivan, October 22, 2020, interview.
9. Haywood, January 16, 2024, interview.
10. Sullivan, October 22, 2020, interview.
11. Starne, January 13, 2021, interview.
12. Beth Rhodes "Foyt Gets Quick Ride from Wilson," *Orlando Sentinel*, February 13, 1987.
13. Jeff Snook, "Bodine Leads Final 20 Laps, Wins First 1987 IROC Race," *Palm Beach Post*, February 14, 1987.
14. "Daytona Notes," *Tampa Tribune*, February 15, 1987.
15. Tom Archdeacon, "Dancing with a Chainsaw," *Miami News*, February 2, 1987.
16. "Try A Hanky," *Tampa Tribune*, February 16, 1987.
17. Gary Long, "Still A.J. After All These Years," *Miami Herald*, February 27, 1987.
18. Dick Mittman, "'Coach' Foyt a Success," *Indianapolis News*, May 18, 1987.
19. Davy Jones, October 2, 2023, interview with the author.
20. Shav Glick, "A.J. Foyt a Winner as a Teacher, Too: Four-Time Champion Has Coached Two Rookie Drivers into the Field," *Los Angeles Times*, May 22, 1987.
21. Bill Fleischman, "A.J. and Mario Remain as Link to Another Era," *Muncie Evening Press*, May 20, 1987.
22. Dave Koerner, "Foyt, Still Going Strong at 52, Qualifies for 30th 500," *Louisville Courier-Journal*, May 10, 1987.
23. Jones, October 2, 2023, interview.
24. "Despite Position, Cogan Optimistic About Race," *Indianapolis Star*, May 17, 1987.

25. Mittman, "'Coach' Foyt a success."
26. Jones, October 2, 2023, interview.
27. Randy Huggler, "Foyt Team Grabs 4 Spots in Indy 500 Field," *Muncie Evening Press*, May 18, 1987.
28. Zach Dunkin, "'Sophomores' Shut out of Race," *Indianapolis News*, May 18, 1987.
29. Sarajane Freligh, "Indy Drivers Feel the Heat," *Knight-Ridder Newspapers*, May 24, 1987.
30. Bill Verigan, "All Hell Broke Loose—A.J. Foyt," *New York Daily News*, May 22, 1987.
31. Zach Dunkin, "Foyt Still Wants Fifth Victory," *Indianapolis News*, May 25, 1987.
32. Jones, October 2, 2023, interview.
33. Dave Garlick, "Fox Gets Big Kiss After Fine Showing," *Indianapolis Star*, May 25, 1987.
34. Suzanne Halliburton, "A.J., An American Folk Hero," *Austin American-Statesman*, February 17, 1991.
35. "Big Al Gets Big Check," United Press International, *Franklin* (Indiana) *Journal*, May 26, 1987.
36. Dunkin, "Foyt Still Wants Fifth Victory."
37. Jones, October 2, 2023, interview.
38. Mike Harris, "Michael Andretti Outruns Foyt to Earn Pole for Marlboro 500," Associated Press, *Muncie Star Press*, August 1, 1987.
39. Anne Fornoro, November 18, 2020, interview with the author.
40. Dick Mittman, "All's Not Fine with Foyt," *Indianapolis News*, September 21, 1987.
41. A.J. Foyt, April 19–24, 2021, interviews with the author.
42. Joseph Foyt, April 2021, interview with the author.
43. Bill Porterfield, October 4, 2023, interview with the author.
44. A.J. Foyt, April 19–24, 2021, interviews.
45. Ed Welburn, January 16, 2021, interview with the author.
46. Porterfield, October 4, 2023, interview.
47. A.J. Foyt, April 19–24, 2021, interviews.
48. Chris Perkins "Watch A.J. Foyt Set a Closed-Course Record in the 1987 Oldsmobile Aerotech," *Road & Track*, April 7, 2016.
49. David Kasey, "Delco Has a Hand in Foyt's Aerotech Tests," *Kokomo* (Indiana) *Tribune*, October 23, 1987.
50. Ron Lemasters, "Super Tex Goes High Tech, for Racing and Passenger Cars," *Muncie Star Press*, October 23, 1987.
51. Rick Shaffer, "Mechanical Woes Slow Foyt in Speedway Record Quest," *Indianapolis Star*, October 23, 1987.
52. Dick Mittman, "Foyt Chases 200 in High Winds," *Indianapolis News*, October 22, 1987.
53. Jimmy Finger, October 4, 2022, interview with the author.
54. "Race Notes," *Miami News*, November 2, 1987.
55. Jones, October 2, 2023, interview.

CHAPTER TWELVE: MOST IMPROVED

1. Dick Mittman, "Foyt Preparing to Make Final Grand Circuit Tour," *Indianapolis News*, January 16, 1988.
2. Robin Miller, "Fun Is Gone in Indy Cars for This Guy," *Indianapolis Star*, July 25, 1988.
3. Bill Center, "Foyt Still Making Points," *San Pedro News-Pilot*, April 12, 1988.
4. Bill Neely, "A.J. Foyt, the Man Who Won't Quit," *AutoWeek,* October 3, 1988.
5. Al Unser Jr., November 5, 2020, interview with the author.
6. Gary Long, "Jaguar Wins at Daytona," *Miami Herald*, February 1, 1988.
7. Bruce Lowitt, "Jaguar Takes Easy Victory," *Tampa Bay Times*, February 1, 1988.
8. "Legends from Legends," *1991 A.J. Foyt Racing Media Guide*.
9. Tex Powell, August 8, 2020, interview with the author.
10. Dave Despain, *ABC Wide World of Sports*, February 14, 1988.
11. Shav Glick, "He's Still King," *Los Angeles Times*, February 14, 1988.
12. "NASCAR Drivers Put Work Before Pain," Associated Press, March 25, 1988.
13. Shav Glick, "A.J. Foyt Will Join the Men in the Street at Long Beach for First Time," *Los Angeles Times*, April 14, 1988.
14. "Foyt Jockeying Between Two Races," Associated Press, *Fort Myers News-Press*, March 20, 1988.
15. Tex Powell, August 8, 2020, interview with the author.
16. Dick Mittman, "Hollywood Comeback Spoiled by Andretti," *Indianapolis News*, April 11, 1988.
17. Glick, "A.J. Foyt Will Join the Men in the Street."
18. Dave George, "Foyt Exacts Frontier Justice," *Palm Beach Post*, April 25, 1988.
19. Craig Davis, "How Sweat It Is—Action, Tempers Boil," *South Florida Sun Sentinel*, April 25, 1988.
20. Hurley Haywood, January 16, 2024, interview with the author.
21. George, "Foyt Exacts Frontier Justice."
22. Gary Long, "Foyt Attempts to Get Revenge After Crash," *Miami Herald*, April 26, 1988.
23. Haywood, January 16, 2024, interview.
24. Bill Robinson, "Foyt Suspended After Forcing NASCAR Men to Dive over Wall," *Atlanta Constitution*, May 2, 1988.
25. Powell, August 8, 2020, interview.
26. Charles Goldberg, "As Usual, A.J. Does It His Way," *Anniston* (Alabama) *Star*, July 29, 1988.

27. Tom Higgins, "Suspension of Foyt Lifted," *Charlotte Observer*, May 10, 1988.
28. *1991 A.J. Foyt Racing Media Guide*.
29. Dick Mittman, "A.J. Says Bad Luck a Good Omen," *Indianapolis News*, May 17, 1988.
30. "Foyt in Unfamiliar Situation," United Press International, *Noblesville* (Indiana) *Ledger*, May 19, 1988.
31. Mike Harris, "Foyt Help Benefits Drivers," Associated Press, *Odessa* (Texas) *American*, May 24, 1988.
32. John Bansch, "Foyt Qualifies with 209-Plus," *Indianapolis Star*, May 22, 1988.
33. "Snider Denies Rift with Foyt," *Indianapolis News*, May 24, 1988.
34. Dick Mittman, "Foyt Stands Test of Time," *Indianapolis News*, May 23, 1988.
35. A.J. Foyt, April 19–24, 2021, interviews with the author.
36. Harold Lowe, "Indy's Epilogue: That Wasn't Good Racing," *South Bend Tribune News*, May 31, 1988.
37. Mike Bianchi, "Tardy Foyt Angry About NASCAR Penalty," *Florida Today*, July 4, 1988.
38. "Foyt in Hospital," Associated Press, *Franklin* (Indiana) *Daily Journal*, August 5, 1988.
39. Powell, August 8, 2020, interview.
40. Robin Miller, "Foyt Earns Another Prestigious (?) Award," *Indianapolis Star*, November 13, 1988.
41. Mike Bianchi, "Racers Rule 1: Don't Cross Foyt," *Florida Today*, July 1, 1988.
42. Mark Armijo, "'Improved' Foyt Back on Track, Looks for Fun at Copper World." *Arizona Republic*, January 24, 1989.
43. Joe Scalzo, "Sumbitch on Wheels," *Circle Track Magazine*, May 1993.
44. Miller, "Foyt Earns Another Prestigious (?) Award."

CHAPTER THIRTEEN: AN OUTRIGHT EMBARRASSMENT

1. Mark Armijo, "'Improved' Foyt Back on Track, Looks for Fun at Copper World." *Arizona Republic*, January 24, 1989.
2. Tex Powell, August 8, 2020, interview with the author.
3. William Neely, *Tire Wars: Racing with Goodyear* (AZTEX Corporation: 1993).
4. Bruce Lowitt, "Draft Gone with Wind," *Tampa Bay Times*, February 18, 1989.
5. Mike Kupper, "A.J. Has the Drive," *Los Angeles Times*, April 16, 1989.
6. Robin Miller, "IMS About to Make a Stupid Move," *Indianapolis Star*, May 8, 1989.
7. Kupper, "A.J. Has the Drive."
8. David Benner, "A.J. Eyes 5th Win, 5th Decade, After Strong Qualifying Dash," *Indianapolis Star*, May 15, 1989.
9. Wayne Fuson, "Foyt Thinks He Can Win," *Indianapolis News*, May 15, 1989.
10. Wayne Fuson, "Age Is No Barrier in the 500," *Indianapolis News*, May 16, 1989.
11. George Snider, December 12, 2020, interview with the author.
12. Johnny Rutherford, June 17, 2020, interview with the author.
13. Ron Lemasters, "Vogler Knocks Rutherford from 500," *Muncie Star Press*, May 22, 1989.
14. A.J. Foyt, April 19–20, 2021, interviews with the author.
15. Thomas Wyman, "Foyt, Mario Outlast Former Champions," Associated Press, *Indianapolis News*, May 29, 1989.
16. Dick Mittman, "Mechanical Woes Costing Michael Andretti Money," *Indianapolis News*, June 20, 1989.
17. "Foyt Pulls Out," *Indianapolis News*, June 26, 1989.
18. Tom Archdeacon, "Reputation Follows Foyt to Columbus," *Dayton* (Ohio) *Daily News*, July 7, 1989.
19. "A.J. Dealt Assault Charge," Associated Press, *Binghamton* (New York) *Press and Sun Bulletin*, July 15, 1989.
20. Rich Libero, "Fittipaldi Uses Lucky Backup Car to Earn Top Position," *Mamaroneck* (New York) *Daily Times*, July 19, 1989.
21. Charlie Vincent, "Pain and Gain: MIS Is Spiced by Surprises," *Detroit Free Press*, August 7, 1989.
22. "Michigan 500," broadcast, *ABC Sports*, August 6, 1989.
23. Dick Mittman, "Foyt Should Hang It Up After '90 Race," *Indianapolis News*, July 21, 1989.
24. Kupper, "A.J. Has the Drive."
25. "Foyt Update," *Indianapolis News*, October 13, 1989.
26. Tom Higgins, "Foyt Had a Feeling Something Bad Was Going to Happen, *Charlotte Observer*, October 6, 1989.
27. "Foyt Released from Hospital, Goes to Texas," Associated Press, *Rocky Mount Telegram*, October 7, 1989.
28. Robin Miller, "Foyt Losing Races, Touch with Reality," *Indianapolis Star*, August 21, 1989.
29. Malcolm Moran, "Defying the Odds at Indy," *New York Times*, May 25, 1986.
30. Paul Reinhard, "A.J. Foyt Sounds Off for Racing's Little Guys," *Allentown Morning Call*, September 17, 1989.
31. Robin Miller, "CART Post Easy to Fill; IMS Spot Not," *Indianapolis Star*, December 14, 1989.

CHAPTER FOURTEEN: THE ROAD TO ELKHART LAKE

1. John Sturbin, "A.J. Foyt Could Get Chevrolet," *South Bend Tribune*, December 5, 1989.
2. Mike Harris, "Foyt Back with Top Engine," Associated Press, *Franklin* (Indiana) *Daily Journal*, February 3, 1990.

3. Dick Mittman, "Foyt Might Pull Out," *Indianapolis News*, February 15, 1990.
4. Jim Litke, "Records Are Never Enough for A.J. Foyt," Associated Press, *Hanover Evening Sun*, May 26, 1990.
5. Bryant-Jon Anteola, "Indy Mechanic to the Stars, Fresno Native Phil Casey Entering Hall of Fame," *Fresno Bee*, May 20, 2015.
6. Phil Casey, October 20, 2023, interview with the author.
7. Mark Armijo, "Foyt Gets Jump Start on Season," *Arizona Republic*, February 2, 1990.
8. Mike Bianchi and Don Coble, "Glue in New Helmet Makes Foyt 'Drunk,'" *Florida Today*, February 19, 1990.
9. Robin Miller, "A.J. Puts Pedal to His Mettle for Run That Rolled Back Years," *Indianapolis Star*, May 20, 1990.
10. Tom Hayes, "Legendary Foyt Is Just A.J.," *Franklin* (Indiana) *Daily Journal*, May 23, 1990.
11. Hayes, "Legendary Foyt."
12. Dave Koerner, "Unser Jr., Luyendyk Can't Deny Fittipaldi Indy Pole," *Louisville Courier-Journal*, May 20, 1990.
13. "A.J. Rolls Dice, Qualifies," Associated Press, *South Bend Tribune*, May 20, 1990.
14. Miller, "A.J. Puts Pedal to His Mettle."
15. Jim Murray, "Smell of the Grease, Roar of Engines Endures in Him," *Los Angeles Times*, May 23, 1990.
16. Casey, October 20, 2023, interview.
17. John Fineran, "Foyt Enjoys Racing," *South Bend Tribune*, May 16, 1990.
18. Mark Armijo, "Veteran Foyt Takes Backseat to No One," *Arizona Republic,* May 26, 1990.
19. Hayes, "Legendary Foyt."
20. Tom Hayes, "Foyt Favors Senior Racing Circuit," *Franklin* (Indiana) *Daily Journal*, May 23, 1990.
21. Norm Frauenheim, "True Grit: A.J., Racing Are One and the Same," *Arizona Republic*, February 4, 1990.
22. Brian Schmitz, "Foyt's Road to Success Paved with Victories," *Orlando Sentinel*, May 27, 1990.
23. Jim Russell, "A.J. Returns to Top 10," *Indianapolis News*, May 28, 1990.
24. Steve Crowe and Scott Walton, "Crash Course," *Detroit Free Press*, June 18, 1990.
25. "Foyt a Driver for the Ages," Bruce Lowitt, *St. Petersburg Times*, May 25, 1990.
26. "Best Finish," *Hanover* (Pennsylvania) *Evening Sun*, July 22, 1990.
27. Casey, October 20, 2023, interview.
28. Dick Mittman, "A.J. Foyt Hot over CART Treatment," *Indianapolis News*, September 18, 1990.

CHAPTER FIFTEEN: ROAD AMERICA

1. Danny Sullivan, October 22, 2020, interview with the author.
2. Dominic Dobson, April 20, 2020, interview by author.
3. Dave Kallmann, "A.J. Foyt Returns to Road America, Reminisces About Worst Crash of His Career," *USA Today,* June 25, 2016.
4. The Turn One gravel pit at Road America would be expanded and improved following Foyt's crash. In 1992, this improvement would be credited with helping prevent serious injuries to David Brabham in a similar crash.
5. Derek Daly, "Road America 500," broadcast, *ABC Sports*, September 23, 1990.
6. Rick Shaffer, "Michael's Win Tightens Race for CART Title," *Indianapolis Star*, September 24, 1990.
7. Kallmann, "A.J. Foyt Returns."
8. Rick Shaffer, "Unsinkable A.J. Recovering Faster than Anticipated," *Indianapolis Star,* October 10, 1990.
9. A.J. Foyt, April 19–24, 2021, interviews by author.
10. Gary Long, "Foyt Learns Patience After Brutal Accident," *Miami Herald*, May 24, 1991.
11. Dr. Terry Trammell. October 28, 2023, interview with the author.
12. Dr. Stephen Olvey, *Rapid Response* (Haynes Publishing: 2011).
13. Bill Luchow, March 26, 2020, interview with author.
14. Phil Casey, October 20, 2023, interview with author.
15. Bill Luchow, March 26, 2020, interview with author.
16. Sullivan, October 22, 2020, interview.
17. Trammell, October 28, 2023, interview.
18. "Larry Foyt: Moving AJ Foyt Enterprises into the Future," MotorSport, June 19, 2009, https://au.motorsport.com/indycar/news/larry-foyt-moving-aj-foyt-enterprises-into-the-future/2923804/.
19. Lucy Foyt, April 2, 2020, interview with the author.
20. "Charles 'Doc' Aprahamian M.D.," *Milwaukee Journal Sentinel,* June 29, 2010.
21. Dr. James Stiehl, April 17, 2020, interview with the doctor.
22. Years later reporters would quote Foyt as saying, "Don't cut off my legs—just fix 'em up so I can push down on my right foot." As no one involved at the time remembers him saying that, it seems more likely to be part of Foyt mythology.
23. *LA Times* staff and wire reports, "Foyt Hurt in Crash in Wisconsin," *Los Angeles Times,* September 24, 1990.
24. Dr. Jeffrey Johnson, April 22, 2020, interview with the author.
25. Ed Hinton, "The Last Ride of A.J. Foyt," *The National,* May 7, 1991.

CHAPTER SIXTEEN: I'LL BE BACK

1. Dr. James Stiehl, April 17, 2020, interview with the author. Several years later, Stiehl's father knocked on the door of Foyt's trailer and introduced himself. Foyt invited him in, and they spent more than an hour talking. "I think it was maybe one of the greatest things that ever happened to my dad," Stiehl said.
2. Dr. Jeffrey Johnson, April 22, 2020, interview with the author. Prior to doing an interview, Johnson—who was still practicing—said he needed a HIPPA (Health Insurance Privacy and Portability Act) release form before discussing Foyt's injuries and procedures. Foyt called him and thanked Johnson for his work nearly thirty years earlier. That was good enough for the doctor.
3. Anne Fornoro, November 18, 2020, interview with the author.
4. Mike Harris, "Doctor: Foyt Could Return in Four Months," Associated Press, *Salina* (Kansas) *Journal*, September 25, 1990.
5. Rick Shaffer, "Foyt Can Race Again in 4 to 6 Months," *Indianapolis Star*, September 25, 1990.
6. Robert Markus, "Elkhart Lake Crash Perils Foyt's Career," *Chicago Tribune*, September 24, 1990.
7. Harold Lowe, "Foyt Hurt Himself for Nothing," *South Bend Tribune*, September 25, 1990.
8. Robin Miller, "Retirement Good Idea Even if A.J. Doesn't Agree," *Indianapolis Star*, September 28, 1990.
9. Rick Mears, December 1, 2020, interview with the author.
10. Craig Baranouski, May 2021, interview with the author.
11. "General Information About the Ilizarov Method," Ilizarov.com, accessed December 18, 2025, https://ilizarov.com/genel-bilgiler.html.
12. Wolfgang Saxon, "Dr. Gavriil A. Ilizarov Dies at 71; Pioneer Bone Surgeon in Russia," *New York Times*, July 25, 1992.
13. Dr. Terry Trammell, October 28, 2020, interview with the author.
14. "Richmond: He Was the Life of the Party," *Daytona Beach News-Journal*, August 13, 2006.
15. Trammell, October 28, 2020, interview.
16. Anthony Joseph Foyt IV, May 27, 2021, interview with the author.
17. Trammell, October 28, 2020, interview.
18. Lucy Foyt, April 2, 2020, interview with the author.
19. Trammell, October 28, 2020, interview.
20. Robin Miller, December 1, 2020, interview with the author.
21. Rick Shaffer, "Unsinkable A.J. Recovering Faster than Anticipated," *Indianapolis Star*, October 10, 1990.
22. Robin Miller, "Surprisingly, Foyt Able to Walk Already," *Indianapolis Star*, January 27, 1991.
23. Dick Mittman, "Foyt Nearly Lost Leg in Crash," *Indianapolis News*, October 9, 1990.
24. Dick Mittman, "Foyt Hurting, His Attitude Isn't," *Indianapolis News*, October 10, 1990.
25. Ron Lemasters, "Foyt Says He'll Retire After 1991 Season," *Muncie Star Press*, October 12, 1990.
26. Joan Niesen, "Director's Cut: 'The Last Ride of A.J. Foyt,' by Ed Hinton," *Grantland*, September 13, 2003, https://grantland.com/features/director-cut-ed-hinton-aj-foyt/#fn-35.

CHAPTER SEVENTEEN: REHAB

1. Lucy Foyt, April 2, 2020, interview with the author.
2. Suzanne Halliburton, "A.J., An American Folk Hero," *Austin American-Statesman*, February 17, 1991.
3. Anthony Joseph "Tony" Foyt III, April 26, 2021, interview with the author.
4. Nancy Foyt, April 25, 2021, interview with the author.
5. Ann Hagedorn Auerbach, *Wild Ride* (Henry Holt and Company: 1994).
6. Dr. Gary Friedman, 2020, interview with the author.
7. A.J. Foyt, April 19, 2021, interview with the author.
8. Larry Foyt, November 10, 2020, interview with the author.
9. Halliburton, "A.J., An American Folk Hero."
10. Lucy Foyt, April 2, 2020, interview.
11. Steve Wilstein, "A.J. Buckles up for Final Run in Indianapolis 500," Associated Press, *North County Times*, May 24, 1991.
12. "Ailing Foyt Says 1991 Indy 500 to Be His Last," Associated Press, *Daily Oklahoman*, November 21, 1990.
13. Unless otherwise noted, all Steve Watterson quotes are from a November 23, 2020, interview with the author.
14. John Sturbin, "The Slow Road to Recovery," *Fort Worth Star-Telegram*, January 27, 1991.
15. Dave Caldwell, "The Long, Hard Road to a Last Indy Drive," *Philadelphia Inquirer*, May 26, 1991.
16. "Foyt Trying for Speedy Recovery," Associated Press, *Arizona Daily Star*, December 8, 1990.
17. Ken Delinger, "Career Down to the Last Lap for Mending Foyt," *Washington Post*, December 2, 1990.
18. Sturbin, "The Slow Road to Recovery."
19. Halliburton, "A.J., An American Folk Hero."
20. Joseph Siano, "Foyt Fights His Way Back with Therapy, Will Race," *New York Times News Service*, February 25, 1991.
21. Bruce Matthews, January 23, 2025, interview with the author.
22. Steve Watterson, November 23, 2020, interview with the author.
23. Dr. Terry Trammell, October 28, 2020, interview with the author.

CHAPTER EIGHTEEN: COMEBACK

1. "Foyt Will Drive Pace Car at Phoenix Race Sunday," *Arizona Daily Star*, February 1, 1991.
2. Joseph Siano, "Foyt Starts Indy Engines for Last Time," *New York Times*, May 26, 1991.
3. Mark Armijo, "Foyt Bouncing Back Sooner than Expected," *Arizona Republic*, February 3, 1991.
4. Mike Harris, "A.J. Foyt at Daytona 500: 'I Had to Be There,'" Associated Press, *Muncie Star Press*, February 20, 1991.
5. Shav Glick, "Foyt Is Hedging on Retirement," *Los Angeles Times*, February 16, 1991.
6. Steve Watterson, November 23, 2020, interview with the author.
7. Dr. Terry Trammell, October 28, 2020, interview with the author.
8. Leal Beattie, "Recovery Foils Foyt's Starting Streak at Daytona," *Daytona Daily News*, February 15, 1991.
9. Dr. Terry Trammell, October 28, 2020, interview with the author.
10. Suzanne Halliburton, "A.J., An American Folk Hero," *Austin American-Statesman,* February 17,1991.
11. Jerry Foyt quote. Interview or previous story.
12. Phil Casey, October 20, 2023, interview with the author.
13. Dick Mittman, "Foyt Has One Footnote Left," *Indianapolis News,* March 15, 1991.
14. "What They're Saying About A.J." *South Bend Tribune,* May 25, 1991.
15. Bill Livingston, "Foyt Rates as Legend Already," *Cleveland Plain Dealer*, July 10, 1991.
16. Curt Cavin, "A.J. Foyt Ready to Step Back into Race Car Today," *Indianapolis Star,* April 4, 1991.
17. Beth Harris, "Foyt Gets Behind the Wheel for First Time Since Accident," Associated Press, *Pittsburgh Post-Gazette*, April 4, 1991.
18. Mike Harris, "Foyt to Pass Up Race at Phoenix," Associated Press, *Muncie Star Press*, April 17, 1991.
19. Robin Miller, "Foyt's Speed on Track Exceeded Only by Quickness of Recovery," *Indianapolis Star*, April 7, 1991.
20. Pete Stavros, "Foyt Confident He'll be Ready for Indy 500," Associated Press, *South Bend Tribune*, April 7, 1991.
21. Anne Fornoro, November 18, 2020, interview with the author.
22. Curt Cavin, "Riley Back with A.J. for May," *Indianapolis Star*, May 8, 1991.
23. Dick Mittman, "Jourdain Looks Ahead in Foyt Stable," *Indianapolis News,* May 4, 1991.
24. Mike Harris, "Foyt to Pass Up Race at Phoenix," Associated Press, *Muncie Star Press*, April 17, 1991.
25. Robin Miller, "Substituting for Foyt Lets Unser Return Favor," *Indianapolis Star*, April 20, 1991.
26. Bob Hurt, "Foyt Nailed to the Wall at Roast in His Honor," *Arizona Republic*, April 21, 1991.
27. Steve Herman, "One More Time: Foyt Must Pass Physical to Race at Indy," Associated Press, *Muncie Evening Press*, May 6, 1991.
28. Al Unser Sr., December 16, 2020, interview with the author.
29. Dick Mittman, "Physical for Race Complete," *Indianapolis News*, May 19, 1991.
30. Zach Dunkin, "A.J. Makes Comeback's First Stops," *Indianapolis Star*, May 7, 1991.
31. John Dempsey, "A.J. Factor Rings True in Foyt's Rehab," *Kokomo Tribune*, May 26, 1991.
32. Jim Litke, "Making Indy Field 'Agettin' to Foyt," Associated Press, *Fort Myers News-Press*, May 12, 1991.
33. Rick Bozich, "A.J. Put Pedal to Metal; Therein's the Story," *Louisville Courier-Journal*, May 12, 1991.
34. Tim Sullivan, "Foyt: Racing's Feistiest Fossil," *Cincinnati Enquirer*, May 12, 1991.
35. "It Was Some Ride for 'Tough' A.J.," *Muncie Star Press,* May 12, 1991.
36. Steve Crowe, "Four-Time Winner Fights Pain for One Last Run at Indy Glory," *Detroit Free Press*, May 11, 1991.
37. Danny Sullivan, October 22, 2020, interview with the author.
38. Bob Riley, February 18, 2021, interview with the author.
39. Dominic Dobson, April 20, 2020, interview with the author.
40. Bob Zeller, "Richard Petty's Career as Driver Spinning to End," *Roanoke Times*, June 23, 1991.
41. John McGauley, "Indianapolis Fans Soon Will Have to Seek Another Hero," *Muncie Evening Press*, May 13, 1991.
42. Jeff Gordon, February 20, 2024, interview with the author.
43. Steve Wilstein, "A.J. Buckles up for Final Run in Indianapolis 500," Associated Press, *North County Times*, May 24, 1991.
44. David Pryce, "Foyt Plans Indy Return, but Not as Driver," *Dallas Morning News*, May 26, 1991.
45. A.J. Foyt, "Foyt Won't Dwell on Possible Last Indy 500," Associated Press, *Franklin* (Indiana) *Daily Journal*, May 25, 1991.
46. Pryce, "Foyt Plans Indy Return."
47. "Indianapolis 500," *ABC Wide World of Sports*, May 26, 1991.
48. Watterson, November 23, 2020, interview.
49. Steve Herman, "A.J. Leaves the Indy Door Open," Associated Press, *Great Falls* (Montana) *Tribune*, May 27, 1991.
50. William Nack, "A Hero Survives Life on the Edge," *London* (UK) *Observer*, June 2, 1991.
51. Dustin Long, "Foyt's Sly Smile," *Lafayette* (Indiana) *Journal Courier*, May 27, 1991.
52. Herman, "A.J. Leaves the Indy Door Open."
53. Nack, "A Hero Survives."

CHAPTER NINETEEN: NO FEET, NO HEART

1. John McGauley, "Will A.J. Return to Indy as Car Owner in 1992," *Muncie Evening Press*, May 13, 1991.
2. Rick Shaffer, "Mears Literally on the Edge with Record-Setting Run," *Indianapolis Star*, Jûne 2, 1991.
3. Charlie Vincent, "Foyt Pushes Pain Aside for Love of Racing," *Detroit Free Press*, June 15, 1991.
4. Charlie Vincent, "A.J. Misses Indy," *Detroit Free Press*, June 15, 1991.
5. Vincent, "Foyt Pushes Pain Aside."
6. Tommy Cameron, "Gearbox Problem Forces Frustrated Foyt to Make Early Exit," *Grand Rapids Press*, June 17,1991.
7. Jeff Gordon, February 20, 2024, interview with the author.
8. "Horseheads Fan Boosts Tom Kendall," *Elmira* (New York) *Star-Gazette*, July 3, 1991.
9. Robin Miller, "Mears Keeps CART Pole; Foyt Seeking Replacement," *Indianapolis Star*, July 14, 1991.
10. Mike Weber, "Painful Old Injuries Prevent Foyt from Challenging in Grand Prix," *Newark Star-Ledger*, July 15, 1991.
11. Mike Harris, "Foyt Says He Might be Back in 1992," Associated Press, *Indianapolis Star*, July 20, 1991.
12. Robert Markus, "Pain Forces Foyt to Pass Torch to Grateful Groff," *Chicago Tribune*, July 20, 1991.
13. Associated Press, "Foyt Still Plans to Drive," *Matton* (Illinois) *Journal Gazette and Times-Courier*, July 20, 1991.
14. Markus, "Pain Forces Foyt to Pass Torch."
15. "Hot Foyt to Race, But Not for CART," Dick Mittman, *Indianapolis News*, August 3, 1991.
16. "Hoosier Hundred Once Again a Headline Attraction," Curt Cavin, *Indianapolis Star*, August 9, 1991.
17. "Feral Foyt," *Sydney* (Australia) *Morning Herald*, August 10, 1991.
18. Robin Miller, "CART May Ask George to Revamp Indy-Car Racing," *Indianapolis Star*, September 6, 1991.
19. Robin Miller, "A.J. Berates CART After Latest Run-In," *Indianapolis Star*, August 25, 1991.
20. Miller, "CART May Ask George to Revamp."
21. Robin Miller, "CART Has Much to Gain in Deal with Indy," *Indianapolis Star*, September 6, 1991.
22. Jack Arute and Paul Page, "Bosch Spark Plug Grand Prix," television broadcast, *ABC Sports*, Nazareth, Pennsylvania, October 6, 1991.
23. Bill Fleischman, "Foyt's Finale?," *Philadelphia Daily News*, October 7, 1991.
24. "Foyt in '92 Still a Possibility," *Indianapolis News*, October 7, 1991.
25. Robin Miller, "New Buick V-8 In, But Will Buick V-6 Be Frozen Out?" *Indianapolis Star*, September 8, 1991.
26. Richard Dean, "Motor Sports," *Houston Chronicle*, November 6, 1991.
27. "Notes," *Indianapolis News*, December 20, 1991.
28. Mike Harris, "A.J. Says He May Not Be at Road's End," Associated Press, *Vineland* (New Jersey) *Daily Journal*, November 23, 1991.
29. "Even Gilmore was surprised," *Kalamazoo Gazette*, December 5, 1991.

CHAPTER TWENTY: WILL HE OR WON'T HE?

1. Leal Beattie, "Foyt Says Chances Are Good He'll Enter Indy 500 Again," *Daytona Daily News*, January 25, 1992.
2. Dick Mittman, "Foyt Set to Return," *Indianapolis News*, January 25, 1992.
3. Ron Somers, "When Talk Turns to Retirement, A.J. Foyt Isn't listening," *Arizona Daily Star*, February 3, 1992.
4. Mike Harris, "Petty Begins the End of an Era," Associated Press, *Bradenton* (Florida) *Herald*, February 15, 1992.
5. Mark Armijo, "Foyt Hurt in Crash, Out of Race," *Arizona Republic*, April 4, 1992.
6. Dick Mittman, "Crash Jeopardizes Foyt's Indy Plans," *Indianapolis News*, April 4, 1992.
7. Steve Herman, "Foyt on Himself: 'You Never Know What A.J. Will Do,'" Associated Press, *Muncie Evening Press*, April 25, 1992.
8. Herman, "Foyt on Himself."
9. A.J. Foyt, April 19–24, 2021, interviews with the author.
10. Steve Herman, "Piquet Says Hello to Old A.J.," Associated Press, *South Bend Tribune*, May 2, 1992.
11. Rick Shaffer, "Bubble Doesn't Pop as Jeff Andretti Makes Second Race," *Indianapolis Star*, May 19, 1992.
12. "Foyt Lends Hand to Jeff Andretti," Associated Press, *Logansport* (Indiana) *Pharos-Tribune*, May 4, 1992.
13. Robin Miller, "Off the Wall or into It. A Month of Moments," *Indianapolis Star*, May 11, 1992.
14. John Gilbert, "He Changed His Mind," *Minneapolis–St. Paul Tribune*, May 20, 1992.
15. John Sonderegger, "Foyt's Back for 35th Indy 500," *St. Louis Post-Dispatch*, May 17, 1992.
16. Shaffer, "Bubble Doesn't Pop."
17. Sandra McKee, "Driving with Fear," *Baltimore Sun*, May 24, 1992.
18. Gilbert, "He Changed His Mind," *Minneapolis–St. Paul Tribune*, May 20, 1992.
19. "Foyt Dodges Bullets," Associated Press, *Racine* (Wisconsin) *Journal Times*, May 25, 1992.
20. Wayne Fuson, "Old A.J. Keeps Us Guessing," *Indianapolis News*, May 27, 1992.

21. John Hill, "Victory Banquet," *Syracuse Post-Standard*, August, 12, 1992.
22. Robert Markus, "A.J. Foyt Still Hoping to Find Worthy Successor," *Chicago Tribune*, June 29, 1992.
23. Michael Vega, "Bonner Still Riding High After Indy," *Boston Globe*, June 7, 1992.
24. Robert Markus, "Not Even Fabi Is Impressed with Pole in Detroit," *Chicago Tribune*, June 6, 1992.
25. Michael Vega, "Bonner Taken for a Ride," *Boston Globe*, June 21, 1992.
26. Paul Buker, "Cheever to the Rescue," *Portland Oregonian*, June 18, 1992.
27. Danny "Chocolate" Myers, November 27, 2021, interview with the author.
28. "Speedway Notebook," *Indianapolis News*, June 23, 1992.
29. Jerry Bonkowski, "NASCAR Ready to Discuss Indy Race Deal," *USA Today*, June 24, 1992.
30. Robin Miller, "NASCAR Race Irks Indy pilots," *Indianapolis Star*, June 28, 1992.
31. Larry Woody, "Foyt Sees NASCAR Revving up at Indy," *Nashville Tennessean*, July 16, 1992.
32. Pancho Carter, April 2023, interview with the author.
33. Robin Miller, "This Is a Garage Sale That Can't Be Beat," *Indianapolis Star*, August 12, 1992.
34. Dave Koerner, "Auctioning A.J.," *Louisville Courier-Journal*, August 14, 1992.
35. Jerry Bonkowski, "Foyt Cleans Garage for Public Auction," *USA Today*, August 12, 1992.
36. Steve Herman, "Heavy Hitters out for Foyt's Auction," Associated Press, *Franklin* (Indiana) *Daily Journal*, August 14, 1992.
37. "Foyt's Rarest Indy Items," *Fort Worth Star-Telegram*, August 17, 1992.
38. Miller, "This Is a Garage Sale."
39. Darrell Fry, "Foyt Becomes a Wheeler Dealer," *Tampa Bay Times*, August 13, 1992.
40. "A.J. Is Having a Garage Sale," *Vincennes* (Indiana) *Sun*, August 12, 1992.
41. Smokey Yunick, "Selling the Dream," *Circle Track Magazine*, January 1993.
42. Beth Harris, "For Once, Foyt Turns Back on Victory Lane at Indianapolis," Associated Press, *Park City* (Kentucky) *Daily News*, August 16, 1991.
43. Harris, "For Once, Foyt Turns Back."
44. Larry Woody, "Foyt Sees NASCAR Revving up at Indy," *Nashville Tennessean*, July 16, 1992.
45. Robin Miller, "Americans Are Foreign to Indy-Car Owners," *Indianapolis Star*, October 5, 1992.
46. "Surfer's Paradise Australian Grand Prix," post-race interview, television broadcast, *ABC Sports*, March 21, 1963.
47. Robin Miller, "Foyt Hires Gordon as Replacement," *Indianapolis Star*, November 24, 1992.
48. Miller, "Foyt Hires Gordon."
49. John Sturbin, "Foyt Protégé Gordon Kicks up Dust at Indy," *Fort Worth Star-Telegram*, May 25, 1993.
50. John Sturbin, "A Hair-Raising Pair," *Fort Worth Star-Telegram*, November 10, 1992.
51. Tom Higgins, "Andretti Top Driver of Past 25 Years," *Charlotte Observer*, October 7, 1992.
52. Robin Miller, "Burnout Main Factor for Mears," *Indianapolis Star*, December 16, 1992.
53. "Two Indy-Car Drivers Surprised," Associated Press, *Easton* (Maryland) *Star-Democrat*, December 14, 1992.
54. Miller, "Burnout Main Factor for Mears."
55. Rick Mears, December 1, 2020, interview with the author.

CHAPTER TWENTY-ONE: IT'S TIME

1. John Sturbin, "A.J. Foyt Puts Gordon in His Own Driver's Seat," *Fort Worth Star-Telegram*, November 24, 1992.
2. Dick Mittman, "Gordon Mirrors New Boss Foyt," *Indianapolis News*, November 24, 1992.
3. Tom Archdeacon, "Robby and A.J. Just 2 Peas in Pod," *Dayton Daily News*, May 30, 1993.
4. Kenny Anderson, March 6, 2021, interview with the author.
5. Dick Mittman, "Foyt Should Call It a Career," *Indianapolis News*, February 12, 1993.
6. Robert Markus, "Unser Takes Stock of His Career," *Chicago Tribune*, February 7, 1993.
7. Anderson, March 6, 2021, interview.
8. Robin Miller, "Gordon Fears Nobody on the Track Once He Puts on Helmet," *Indianapolis Star*, April 16, 1993.
9. Anderson, March 6, 2021, interview.
10. Robin Miller, "Mansell Cautious About His First Go-Around on Oval Track," *Indianapolis Star*, April 3, 1993.
11. Bobby Unser, "Valvoline 200," broadcast, *ABC Sports*, April 4, 1993.
12. Anderson, March 6, 2021, interview.
13. Mark Armijo and Larry Ward, "Mansell Will Race Again in 2 Weeks," *Arizona Republic*, April 5, 1993.
14. "Valvoline 200," broadcast, *ABC Sports*, April 4, 1993.
15. Armijo and Ward, "Mansell Will Race Again."
16. Miller, "Gordon Fears Nobody."
17. Anderson, March 6, 2021, interview.
18. Leah Reiter, "Crashes Highlight Day at Long Beach Grand Prix," *San Bernardino County Sun*, April 19, 1993.
19. Shav Glick, "Canadian Paul Tracy Gets His First Indy Car Victory in Record-Setting Time," *Los Angeles Times*, April 19, 1993.
20. John Sturbin, "Foyt Protégé Gordon Kicks up Dust at Indy," *Fort Worth Star-Telegram*, May 25, 1993.

21. Robby Gordon, March 12, 2021, interview with the author.
22. Jack Moss, "Gilmore and Foyt Reunite as Indy Team," *Kalamazoo Gazette*, March 24, 1998.
23. "Rookie Driver Takes a Few Tips from the Master," Associated Press, *Twin Falls* (Idaho) *Times-News*, May 2, 1993.
24. Anne Fornoro, "A.J.'s Retirement," unpublished article, May 15, 1993.
25. Steve Herman, "Foyt May Come Back for Indy," Associated Press, *Ithaca* (New York) *Journal*, May 13, 1993.
26. Dick Mittman, "Will A.J. Race or Won't He," *Indianapolis News*, May 12, 1993.
27. Mark Robinson, "Gordon Awaits Return of Foyt to Get Back to Qualifying Basics," *Indianapolis Star*, May 17, 1993.
28. "Patient A.J.," *Valparaiso Vidette Messenger*, May 15, 1993.
29. Gordon, March 12, 2021, interview.
30. Anderson, March 6, 2021, interview.
31. Craig Baranouski, April 20, 2020, interview with the author.
32. Anne Fornoro, interview with the author.
33. Anne Fornoro, "A.J.'s Retirement," May 15, 1993.
34. Bill Brenner, "Foyt Straps in to Race and Instead Retires," *Indianapolis Star*, May 16, 1993.
35. Mike Harris, "Gordon Getting Adjusted to Driving for Foyt at Indy," Associated Press, *Fort Myers News-Press*, May 18, 1993.
36. Ron Lemasters, "A.J. Says He's Done," *Muncie Star Press*, May 16, 1993.
37. Brenner, "Foyt Straps In."
38. John Sonderegger, "Foyt Love Affair with Indy Ends," *St. Louis Post-Dispatch*, May 16, 1993.
39. Lemasters, "A.J. Says He's Done."
40. "Reaction to Foyt Retirement," *Indianapolis Star*, May 16, 1993.
41. Larry Foyt, interview with the author.
42. Steve Herman, "Foyt Hangs up Career," Associated Press, *Greenfield Daily Reporter*, May 17, 1993.
43. "Reaction to Foyt Retirement," *Indianapolis Star*.
44. John Fineran, "Mears Salutes Foyt," *South Bend Tribune*, May 16, 1993.
45. George Snider, December 12, 2020, interview with the author.
46. "Reaction to Foyt Retirement," *Indianapolis Star*.
47. Robin Miller, "The Style was Solely A.J.'s But the Pleasure Was All Mine," *Indianapolis Star*, May 16, 1996.
48. Tom Archdeacon, "Robby and A.J. Just 2 Peas in Pod," *Dayton Daily News*, May 30, 1993.
49. "A.J. Foyt Took to Heart Advice from Ray Harroun," Associated Press, May 28, 1993.
50. Anderson, March 6, 2021, interview.
51. Dick Mittman, "Thanks for the Memories, A.J.," *Indianapolis News*, May 17, 1993.
52. Lucy Foyt, April 2, 2020, interview with the author.
53. Terry Foyt, April 21, 2021, interview with the author.
54. Gary Friedman, 2020 interview with the author.

CHAPTER TWENTY-TWO: TEAM OWNER

1. Dick Mittman, "Veteran, Rookie Bide Their Time," *Indianapolis News*, May 18, 1993.
2. Mike Harris, "Gordon Getting Adjusted to Driving for Foyt at Indy," Associated Press, *Fort Myers News-Press*, May 18, 1993.
3. Mark Robinson, "Gordon Awaits Return of Foyt to Get Back to Qualifying Basics," *Indianapolis Star*, May 17, 1993.
4. Harris, "Gordon Getting Adjusted."
5. "A.J. Foyt Took to Heart Advice from Ray Harroun," Associated Press, May 28, 1993.
6. Bones Bourcier, *Foyt, Andretti, Petty: America's Racing Trinity* (Coastal 181: 2015).
7. Gary Long, "J. Andretti Seeks Ride in Indy 500," *Miami Herald*, May 22, 1993.
8. Bill Benner, "Andretti Flies into Field After Accepting Godfather's Offer," *Indianapolis Star*, May 23, 1993.
9. Robin Miller, "John Andretti and Robby Gordon Charge into '500' with Strong Qualifying Runs," *Indianapolis Star*, May 23, 1993.
10. Steve Crowe, "Veteran Racer Drives Rookie Replacement," *Detroit Free Press*, May 29, 1993.
11. Miller, "John Andretti and Robby Gordon Charge into '500.'"
12. "The Jigger Is Up," *Racine* (Wisconsin) *Journal Times*, May 30, 1993.
13. John O'Neill, "Broadcast Sports," *Indianapolis Star*, June 5, 1993.
14. "Safe Harbor," *Racine* (Wisconsin) *Journal Times*, May 30, 1993.
15. "Indy 500 Notes," *Baltimore Sun*, May 31, 1993.
16. John Bansch, "This Time, Foyt Learns How Other Half Lives," *Indianapolis Star*, May 31, 1993.
17. Tom Rietmann, "Owner Foyt Satisfied," *Indianapolis News*, May 31, 1993.
18. "Detroit Notebook," *Indianapolis News*, June 14, 1993.
19. Charlie Vincent, "Gordon Challenge Thwarted by Ben Hur Squeeze Play," *Detroit Free Press*, June 14, 1993.
20. Robin Miller, "Foyt and Protégé Gordon Share Blame in Late Mishap," *Indianapolis Star*, June 7, 1993.

21. Vincent, "Gordon Challenge Thwarted."
22. Robin Miller, "Ford's Racing Chief Creating Team," *Indianapolis Star*, August 1, 1993.
23. Jack Weber, "IndyCar's System for Parts Irks Foyt," *The* (Bridgewater, New Jersey) *Courier-News*, August 28, 1993.
24. "Gordon to Remain with Foyt in '94," Associated Press, *The* (Wilkes-Barre, Pennsylvania) *Times Leader*, August 15, 1993.
25. A.J. Foyt, April 22, 2021, interview with the author.
26. Dennis Latta, "Vancouver Victory Lightens Load," *Albuquerque Journal*, September 2, 1993.
27. Kenny Anderson, March 6, 2021, interview with the author.
28. Robby Gordon, March 12, 2021, interview with the author.
29. "Indy Notes," *Indianapolis Star*, May 14, 1994.
30. Robby Gordon, March 12, 2021, interview with the author.
31. John Sturbin, "As an Owner, Foyt Shows Drivers It's His Way or the Highway," *Fort-Wort Star-Telegram*, November 29, 1993.
32. Steve Herman, "Davy Jones Joins Foyt Racing Team," *Greenfield* (Indiana) *Daily Reporter*, November 23, 1993.
33. Ron Lemasters, "Davy Jones Will Drive Indy Car for Foyt in 1994," *Muncie Star Press*, November 23, 1993.
34. Herman, "Davy Jones Joins Foyt Racing Team."
35. Anderson, March 6, 2021, interview.

CHAPTER TWENTY-THREE: HELP WANTED

1. Robin Miller, "Racers Hoping to Avoid Taking a Bath in Old Tub," *Indianapolis Star*, February 6, 1994.
2. Davy Jones, October 2, 2023, interview with the author.
3. Robert Markus, "A.J. Foyt Drives His Hired Help," *Chicago Tribune,* May 10, 1994.
4. "Davy Jones Leaves Foyt Team," *Bedford* (Indiana) *Times-Mail*, April 29, 1994.
5. Jones, October 2, 2023, interview.
6. Robin Miller, "Gary B. Joins Tony; Jones Out," *Indianapolis Star*, April 27, 1994.
7. Dick Mittman, "Two-Race Day Can't Be Easy," *Indianapolis News*, January 20, 1994.
8. Miller, "Gary B. Joins Tony."
9. Bryan Herta, May 22, 2025, interview with the author.
10. "Driver Lives Dream in Foyt's Race Car," Associated Press, *Carlisle* (Pennsylvania) *Sentinel*, April 30, 1994.
11. Robin Miller, "Herta Hopes Lights Title Yields More than Lightweight Indy Race," *Indianapolis Star*, May 1, 1994.
12. Scott Horner, "Herta the Latest Driver Trying to Do It A.J.'s Way," *Franklin* (Indiana) *Daily Journal*, May 25, 1994.
13. Herta, May 22, 2025, interview.
14. John Andretti and Jade Gurss, *Racer* (Octane Press: 2020).
15. "Made Other Plans," *Atlanta Journal*, May 15, 1994.
16. Horner, "Herta the Latest Driver."
17. Herta, May 22, 2025, interview.
18. Robert Markus, "Herta Rides Bubble Through 4 Bump Tries," *Chicago Tribune*, May 23, 1994.
19. Brian Schmitz, "Rookie Herta Slow But in Indy 500 Field," *Orlando Sentinel*, May 23, 1994.
20. Tom Kubat, "Bubble Day Far from Bubbly," *Richmond* (Indiana) *Palladium-Item*, May 23, 1994.
21. Horner, "Herta the Latest Driver."
22. Johnny Rutherford, June 17, 2020, interview with the author.
23. Herta, May 22, 2025, interview.
24. Ken Fox, "Emotional Rutherford Retires," *South Bend Tribune*, May 22, 1994.
25. Terence Moore, "End of an Andretti Era," *Atlanta Journal*, May 27, 1994.
26. Brian Schmitz, "Arrivederci, Mario: Andretti Revved up for Final Start at Indy," *Orlando Sentinel*, May 27, 1994.
27. Robin Miller, "A.J., Big Al, J.R., Mario Mark Changing of the Guard," *Indianapolis Star*, May 29, 1994.
28. Robin Miller, "Here's Hoping NASCAR Debut Is More Exciting," *Indianapolis Star*, May 30, 1994.
29. "Mercedes Engine Latest Indy Star," Associated Press, *Rock Hill* (South Carolina) *Herald*, May 30, 1994.
30. Mark Ambrogi, "Foyt Happy with Herta's Rookie Run," *Indianapolis Star*, May 30, 1994.
31. "Pat on the Back," *Hammond* (Indiana) *Times*, May 30, 1994.
32. "Andretti Completes 820 Miles," Associated Press, *Muncie Star Press*, May 30, 1994.
33. Bones Bourcier, *Foyt, Andretti, Petty: America's Racing Trinity* (Coastal 181: 2015).
34. Herta, May 22, 2025, interview.
35. Wayne Fuson, "Foyt: Stocks Feel Like '60s Indy Car," *Indianapolis News*, August 6, 1994.
36. "Indy Drivers Wonder if NASCAR Can Hold Fans' Interest at the Brickyard," Associated Press, *Winston-Salem Journal*, May 28, 1994.
37. Dick Mittman, "Wallace Names Car After Penske," *Indianapolis News*, May 28, 1994.

38. John O'Neill, "It's Historic (But We Can't See It on TV)," *Indianapolis Star*, August 6, 1994.
39. Darrell Waltrip, November 6, 2020, interview with the author.
40. David Benner, "Was Foyt Ready and Willing to Step In?," *Indianapolis Star*, May 23, 1994.
41. Dick Mittman, "A Foyt Just May Race Brickyard," *Indianapolis News*, November 26, 1993.
42. Dick Mittman, "Herta Loving Foyt Ride, Spurned Jones Is Looking," *Indianapolis News*, July 9, 1994.
43. Herta, May 22, 2025, interview.
44. Robin Miller, "Foyt Busy in IndyCar, NASCAR," *Indianapolis Star*, July 27, 1994.
45. "Foyt's Back," *Greensboro* (North Carolina) *News and Record*, August 2, 1994.
46. Mike Harris, "Veteran A.J. Foyt Eager to Run at Brickyard Again," Associated Press, *Thomasville* (North Carolina) *Times*, August 3, 1994.
47. Charean Williams, "Foyt Putting Stock in Brickyard 400," *Orlando Sentinel*, August 4, 1994.
48. "Foyt Thrills Crowd in Fitting Historical Run," Associated Press, *Richmond* (Indiana) *Palladium-Item*, August 6, 1994.
49. Dan Korb, "When A.J. Talks, Mast Listens," *Evansville* (Indiana) *Courier and Press*, August 5, 1994.
50. "Foyt Fails to Recapture Old Glory," Associated Press, *Marion* (Indiana) *Chronicle Tribune*, August 7, 1994.
51. Mark Robinson, "Foyt Short on Speed at Brickyard Quals," *Indianapolis Star*, August 5, 1994.
52. "Foyt Fails to Recapture Old Glory," AP.
53. Eddie Cheever, November 11, 2020, interview with the author.
54. Steve Crowe, "NASCAR, IndyCar Drivers Make Off-Season Moves," *Detroit Free Press*, December 9, 1994.
55. "Noteworthy," *Indianapolis News*, September 10, 1994.
56. "Cheever, Foyt Join Forces Again in '95," *Indianapolis Star*, October 5, 1994.
57. Brent Engh, "Herta Gets Thrill Driving for Legends," *Madison* (Wisconsin) *Capital Times*, May 8, 1995.
58. Herta, May 22, 2025, interview.
59. "Following in His Father's Footsteps," *Louisville Courier-Journal*, October 13, 1994.

CHAPTER TWENTY-FOUR: A GATHERING STORM

1. Tim McKinney, "Foyt on Indy," *Columbus* (Indiana) *Republic*, January 27, 1994.
2. Dick Mittman, "Foyt Leaning to Speedway," *Indianapolis News*, April 12, 1994.
3. Dick Mittman, "Circuit Leaving Some Confused," *Indianapolis News*, July 9, 1994.
4. David A. Kasey, "A Nostalgic Year for Indianapolis 500," March 29, 1995.
5. John Sonderegger, "Indy Racing League Forges Alliance with Walt Disney," *St. Louis Post-Dispatch*, January 28, 1995.
6. Dick Mittman, "Ex-Foyt Protégés Rule Phoenix," *Indianapolis News*, April 3, 1995.
7. Eddie Cheever, November 11, 2020, interview with the author.
8. Curt Cavin, "Cheever's Career Frustrations Mount," *Indianapolis Star*, April 24, 1995.
9. Robin Miller, "Cheever-A.J. Combo Is Working," *Indianapolis Star*, May 7, 1995.
10. John Gilbert, "Cheever, Foyt Making Good Driver-Owner Team," *Minneapolis Star Tribune*, May 12, 1995.
11. Mark Armijo, "Indy's Odd Couple," *Arizona Republic*, May 26, 1995.
12. Cheever, November 11, 2020, interview.
13. Scott Sharp, April 14, 2021, interview with the author.
14. Jeff Snook, "Foyt Show up Penske," *Palm Beach Post*, May 22, 1995.
15. Ed Hinton, "Singular Foyt Presence Still Looms Large," *NASCAR*, May 27, 2011.
16. Cheever, November 11, 2020, interview.
17. Michael Vega, "Sharp Had Just Enough Time to Qualify for Indy 500," *Boston Globe*, May 27, 1995.
18. Leal Beattle and Chick Ludwig, "The Wrecks: Race Was Marred from the Start," *Daytona News*, May 29, 1995.
19. Phil Richards, "Foyt's '500' Hopes Reduced to Wreckage," *Indianapolis Star*, May 29, 1995.
20. Cheever, November 11, 2020, interview.
21. Scott Sharp, April 14, 2021, interview with the author.
22. "Indy 500 Notebook," Associated Press, *Odessa American*, May 27, 1995.
23. Elton Alexander, "Foyt Rides Uut Rough Start," *Cleveland Plain Dealer*, July 22, 1995.
24. Cheever, November 11, 2020, interview.
25. Chrisopher Broussard, "Sixteen Years, and Cheever Still Is Looking for That First Victory," *Akron Beacon Journal*, July 22, 1995.
26. A.J. Foyt, April 22, 2021, interview with the author.
27. Cheever, November 11, 2020, interview.
28. Jeff Madsen, "Foyt Itching to Stand on the Gas Again," *Franklin* (Indiana) *Daily Journal*, August 2, 1995.
29. Mike Harris, "Foyt: There's No Fun Like Racing at Brickyard," Associated Press, *Bowling Green* (Kentucky) *Park City Daily News*, August 2, 1995.
30. Tom Rietmann, "Defiant A.J. Dismisses Talk about Retirement," *Indianapolis Star*, August 5, 1995.
31. Bill Bothwell, "Foyt Struggles to Keep Track of His Drivers," *Marion* (Indiana) *Chronicle Tribune*, September 11, 1995.

32. John Bansch, "Cheever, Foyt Part," *Indianapolis Star*, August 30, 1995.
33. Cheever, November 11, 2020, interview.
34. A.J. Foyt, April 22, 2021, interview with the author.
35. Tony Stewart, 2021, interview with the author.
36. Mark Armijo, "Foyt Has a Stock Answer: 'Racing Is My Life,'" *Arizona Republic*, October 11, 1995.
37. Tony Stewart, 2021, interview with the author.
38. Ron Lemasters, "Ol' Tex Lets Foyt-Menard Rivalry Crash and Burn," *Muncie Star Press*, May 17, 1998.
39. Craig Baranouski, May 2021, interview with the author.
40. Tony Stewart, December 20, 2019, interview on *Around the Track with Jeff Gordon*.
41. Tony Stewart, 2021, interview with the author.
42. Bill Bothwell, "Another Foyt Goes Racing," *Marion* (Indiana) *Chronicle Tribune*, July 8, 1995.
43. Mark Armijo, "Foyt's Got His Motor Racing Again," *Arizona Republic*, October 13, 1995.
44. Shav Glick, "Car Wars: Could New Race Slowly Supplant the Indy 500?" *Los Angeles Times*, December 23, 1995.
45. Glick, "Car Wars."
46. Jeff Madsen, "Neutral A.J. Set to Race IRL Ovals," *Franklin* (Indiana) *Daily Journal*, August 2, 1995.
47. "Foyt Rediscovers Competitive Flame," Associated Press, October 12, 1995.

CHAPTER TWENTY-FIVE: THE SPLIT

1. Dick O'Brien, "Hamilton Takes a Shot at the Big Time," *Syracuse Herald-Journal*, December 14, 1995.
2. Mark Armijo, "Driver Can Add Name to Copper Record," *Arizona Republic*, February 2, 1996.
3. Jim Conway, "Kinser Is a Top Gun in World of Outlaws," *Kansas City Star*, June 22, 1996.
4. Michael Graczyk, "A.J. Foyt Suing CART," Associated Press, *Marion* (Indiana) *Chronicle Tribune*, January 11, 1996.
5. Davey Hamilton, May 27, 2023, interview with the author.
6. Mark Woods, "Hamilton Hoping New Career Gets Green Flag," *Florida Today*, January 26, 1996.
7. "Foyt Sounds off for IRL," Scripps Howard News Service, *Oshkosh* (Wisconsin) *Northwestern*, January 27, 1996.
8. Scott Sharp, April 14, 2021, interview with the author.
9. Sharp, April 14, 2021, interview.
10. Robin Miller, "Luyendyk Gets the Best of the Kids at Phoenix," *Indianapolis Star*, March 25, 1996.
11. Shav Glick, "Driving Home a Point," *Los Angeles Times*, May 21, 1996.
12. Dan Proudfoot, "Volatile Foyt Rips Indy 500 Deserters," *Toronto Sun*, May 15, 1996.
13. Mike Harris, "Foyt Says Indy Is Still the Place to Drive," Associated Press, *Casper* (Wyoming) *Star-Tribune*, May 12, 1996.
14. Robin Miller, "IMS in May," *Indianapolis Star*, May 8, 1996.
15. Davey Hamilton, May 27, 2023, interview with the author.
16. Ken Fox, "Rookie Richie Hearn a Hot Item," *South Bend Tribune*, May 6, 1996.
17. Harris, "Foyt Says Indy Is Still the Place to Drive."
18. Hamilton, May 27, 2023, interview.
19. Proudfoot, "Volatile Foyt Rips Indy 500 Deserters."
20. Dick Mittman, "Speedway Is Solemn as the Race Goes On," *Indianapolis News*, May 18, 1996.
21. Jim Litke, "Like Pitching, There's Not Enough Drivers to Go Around," *Morganton* (North Carolina) *News Herald*, May 29, 1996.
22. Glick, "Driving Home a Point."
23. Dick Mittman, "Snider Crosses Line First but Win Disallowed," *Indianapolis News*, May 26, 1996.
24. Hamilton, May 27, 2023, interview.
25. Phillip B. Wilson, "Sharp's Smooth Sunday Ended Against the IMS Wall," *Indianapolis News*, May 27, 1996.
26. Ken Fox, "Indianapolis 500 Notebook," *Indianapolis Star*, May 27, 1996.
27. "500 Promoters Promise More Races," Associated Press, *La Grande* (Oregon) *Observer*, May 28, 1996.
28. "A.J. Takes a Shot," *Indianapolis Star*, May 27, 1996.
29. Steve Crowe, "Feud Has Some Pointing Fingers at Owner Walker," *Detroit Free Press*, June 6, 1996.
30. Crowe, "Feud Has Some Pointing Fingers."
31. A.J. Foyt, April 2021, interview with the author.
32. Robin Miller, "Hoosier Hundred Is History," *Indianapolis Star*, July 23, 1996.
33. Dan Korb, "Foyt Fails to Qualify His Car, but He'll Try Again Next Year," *Evansville* (Indiana) *Courier and Press*, August 3, 1996.
34. Dick Mittman, "Faithful Want Foyt to Come Back," *Indianapolis News*, August 3, 1996.
35. Korb, "Foyt Fails to Qualify."
36. Mike Recht, "First IRL Win Slips Away," Associated Press, *Rushville* (Indiana) *Republican*, August 19, 1996.
37. Dick Mittman, "Sharp Turn of Fate in IRL Opener," *Indianapolis Star*, August 19, 1996.
38. Mittman, "Sharp Turn of Fate."
39. Jeff Novotny and Yuri Pride, "Sharp's Win Brings Owner Foyt to Victory Lane," *Concord* (New Hampshire) *Monitor*, August 19, 1966.

40. Ben Blake, "Dura Lube 500 Trails Were Gone with the Wind," *Richmond* (Virginia) *Times-Dispatch*, October 26, 1996.
41. Sharp, April 14, 2021, interview.

CHAPTER TWENTY-SIX: TEXAS SHOWDOWN

1. Steve Kaminski, "Racing Legend Foyt Makes Pit Stop in GR," *Grand Rapids* (Michigan) *Press*, April 24, 1997.
2. Mike Harris, "Sharp Wants IRL Title to Himself," Associated Press, *Stuart* (Florida) *News*, September 13, 1996.
3. Gary Long, "Sophomore Jinx? IRL Engines Untested," *Miami Herald*, January 25, 1997.
4. Robin Miller, "IRL Bows to One Storm, Weathers Another," *Indianapolis Star*, January 27, 1997.
5. "IRL Notebook," *Daytona Beach News-Journal*, January 25, 1997.
6. Mel Reisner, "Foyt's Strategy: He'll Take One of Each," Associated Press, *Syracuse Post-Standard*, March 21, 1997.
7. Mark Armijo, "Sharp Driver," *Arizona Republic*, February 26, 1997.
8. Billy Boat, November 18, 2020, interview with the author.
9. Phil Richards, "Sharp Out, Andretti In for Foyt," *Indianapolis News*, May 12, 1997.
10. Curt Cavin, "Sharp Will Sit This One Out," *Indianapolis News*, June 4, 1997.
11. Steve Herman, "Foyt Considered a Driving Comeback After Injury to Sharp," Associated Press, *Noblesville* (Indiana) *Ledger*, May 14, 1997.
12. "Drivers Run Wild at the Winston," Associated Press, *Marion* (Indiana) *Chronicle Tribune*, May 16, 1997.
13. Robin Miller, "Foyt Hopes to Get Andretti as Sub," *Indianapolis News*, May 13, 1997.
14. Dan Korb, "Changing the Bad Luck," *Evansville* (Indiana) *Press*, May 18, 1997.
15. "One Mean Foyt Machine," *Fort Worth Star-Telegram*, May 28, 1997.
16. Curt Cavin, "Durant Makes Qualifying Look Easy," *Indianapolis Star*, May 19, 1997.
17. Robin Miller, "IRL Flew over the Cuckoo's Nest Sunday at Speedway," *Indianapolis News*, May 19, 1997.
18. Ron Lemasters, "Make Room for 35, not 33," *Muncie Star Press*, May 19, 1997.
19. Eric Crawford, "Indy 500 Critics Get No Support from A.J. Foyt," May 23, 1997.
20. "Hamilton Finishes Sixth After His Car Runs Out of Fuel Twice," *Idaho Statesman*, May 28, 1997.
21. Mike Harris, April 2021, interview with the author.
22. John Sturbin, "Drive of a Lifetime," *Fort Worth Star-Telegram*, June 1, 1997.
23. Cavin, "Sharp Will Sit This One Out."
24. Mark Armijo, "Foyt Finds Spot for Glendale Driver," *Arizona Republic*, June 4, 1997.
25. Davey Hamilton, May 27, 2023, interview with the author.
26. Dave Ivey, "Luyendyk Tangles with Foyt," *Fort Worth Star-Telegram*, June 8, 1997.
27. "Contested '97 Finish Ignited Foyt's Fire," *Fort Worth Star-Telegram*, November 4, 2006.
28. Steve Crowe, "Names Will Never Hurt Him: Foyt's Still on Fire at Indy," *Detroit Free Press*, May 14, 1998.
29. Boat, November 18, 2020, interview.
30. Hamilton, May 27, 2023, interview.
31. Ivey, "Luyendyk Tangles with Foyt."
32. "Contested '97 Finish Ignited Foyt's Fire."
33. Jamie Aron, "Sorry Arie," Associated Press, *Franklin* (Indiana) *Daily Journal*, June 9, 1997.
34. John Sturbin, "Two Trophies, No Hard Feelings," *Fort Worth Star-Telegram*, June 4, 1998.
35. Robin Miller, "Foyt Phones Luyendyk to Apologize for Scuffle," *Indianapolis News*, June 11, 1997.
36. Michael Graczyk, "Foyt Apologizes to Luyendyk: I Blowed Up," Associated Press, *Detroit Free Press*, June 11, 1997.
37. "IRL Hands Out $34,000 in Fines to Foyt, Luyendyk for Scuffle," *Vincennes* (Indiana) *Sun-Commercial*, July 11, 1997.
38. "IRL Dumps USAC, Will Sanction Own Events," *Muncie Star Press*, June 17, 1997.
39. Drew Davison, "Foyt, Luyendyk Scuffle Helped Put TMS on the Map," *Fort Worth Star-Telegram*, June 5, 2016.
40. "Stewart, Hamilton Renew Battle for IRL Series Lead," Associated Press, *Kokomo* (Indiana) *Tribune*, August 17, 1997.
41. Ed Nathman June 18, 2025, interview with the author.
42. Tim Dahlberg, "Stewart, Menard Capture IRL Title," Associated Press, *South Bend Tribune*, October 12, 1997.
43. Shav Glick, "Stewart Looking for Even More Fun in Valley of Sun," *Los Angeles Times*, March 21, 1998.
44. Dick Mittman, "Stewart Makes Run for Crown of IRL," *Indianapolis Star*, October 9, 1997.
45. Steve Herman, "Indy Never Second-Rate to Foyt," Associated Press, *Hammond* (Indiana) *Times*, May 23, 1997.
46. Mark Armijo, "Boat, Sweden's Bräck Foyt's Likely IRL Drivers," *Arizona Republic*, November 29, 1997.
47. Scott Sharp, April 14, 2021, interview with the author.

48. Hamilton, May 27, 2023, interview.
49. "Another Foyt," *Ventura County* (California) *Star*, December 7, 1996.

CHAPTER TWENTY-SEVEN: CHAMPIONS AGAIN

1. Mark Armijo, "Boat, Sweden's Bräck Foyt's Likely IRL Drivers," *Arizona Republic*, November 29, 1997.
2. Robin Miller, "Boat Earns Full-Time Ride When Foyt Replaces Drivers," *Indianapolis Star*, November 23, 1997.
3. Kenny Bräck, May 2023, interview with the author.
4. Bräck, May 2023, interview.
5. Miller, "Boat Earns Full-Time Ride When Foyt Replaces Drivers."
6. Bräck, May 2023, interview.
7. "Bräck Says He Gets Enough Horsepower on Racetrack," *Newark Star-Ledger*, September 10, 1998.
8. Steve Herman, "Foyt Drivers Making Bid for Front-Row Positions for this Year's Indianapolis 500," Associated Press, *Richmond* (Indiana) *Palladium-Item*, May 13, 1998.
9. Robin Miller, "Boat, Bräck Keeping Cantankerous Boss Happy," *Indianapolis Star*, May 14, 1998.
10. Robin Miller, "Speeds Heat up at Track," *Indianapolis Star*, May 12, 1998.
11. Miller, "Boat, Bräck Keeping Cantankerous Boss Happy."
12. Bräck, May 2023, interview.
13. Ron Lemasters, "Rivalry Brewing at Indy," *Muncie Star Press*, May 16, 1998.
14. Lemasters, "Rivalry Brewing at Indy."
15. Dan Korb, "Indy's Elder Stateman-to-Be Sometimes Feels Like Rookie," *Evansville* (Indiana) *Courier and Press*, May 22, 1999.
16. John Fineran, "Foyt Still Gets Cheers at the Speedway," *South Bend Tribune*, May 17, 1998.
17. Ken Fox, "Driver Loses Sponsor, Wins Front Row Spot," *South Bend Tribune*, May 17, 1998.
18. Steve Herman, "Boat Gives A.J. Foyt Thrill Ride," Associated Press, *Muncie Star Press*, May 17, 1998.
19. Tom Kubat, "Foyt Lands Two Drivers on the Front Row," *Lafayette* (Indiana) *Journal and Courier*, May 17, 1998.
20. Robin Miller, "IRL Notebook," *Indianapolis Star*, March 22, 1998.
21. "Indy 500 Front Row a Nameless Bunch," Associated Press, *Springfield* (Missouri) *News-Leader*, May 23, 1998.
22. Steve Crowe, "Names Will Never Hurt Him: Foyt's Still on Fire at Indy," *Detroit Free Press*, May 14, 1998.
23. Jack Moss, "Gilmore and Foyt Reunite as Indy Team," *Kalamazoo Gazette*, March 24, 1998.
24. Jack Moss, "Together Again at the Brickyard," *Kalamazoo Gazette*, May, 10, 1998.
25. Danny "Chocolate" Myers, November 27, 2021, interview with the author.
26. Curt Cavin, "A.J.'s Nephew Keeps Him on Track," *Indianapolis Star*, May 20, 1998.
27. Frank Benson, "Sodus Crew Chief Hopes to Become King of Indy," (Michigan) *Herald-Palladium*, May 23, 1998.
28. Shav Glick, "Same Ol' A.J.," *Los Angeles Times*, October 9, 1998.
29. Robin Miller, "Boat Steals the Show," *Indianapolis Star*, May 17, 1988.
30. Glick, "Same Ol' A.J."
31. Jerry Miller, "A.J. Foyt, Bräck Indy Odd Couple," *Franklin* (Indiana) *Daily Journal*, May 21, 1998.
32. "Foyt Hungry for Victory at Indianapolis," Associated Press, *Bedford* (Indiana) *Times-Mail*, May 19, 1998.
33. Glick, "Same Ol' A.J."
34. Charlie Vincent, "Boat Finds Calm Waters in His Relationship with Still-Fiery Foyt," *Detroit Free Press*, May 23, 1998.
35. John Sturbin, "Driving Mr. A.J.," *Fort Worth Star-Telegram*, May 24, 1998.
36. Shav Glick, "Age 82 or 2, Indy 500 Is Wiser, Faster," *Los Angeles Times*, May 24, 1998.
37. Phillip B. Wilson, "Gearbox Failure Sinks Boat's Run," *Indianapolis News*, May 25, 1998.
38. Bräck, May 2023, interview.
39. Terry Blount, "Car Sabotaged on Eve of Indy 500, Foyt Says," *Houston Chronicle*, May 30, 1998.
40. Robin Miller, "Foyt's Theory of Sabotage Doesn't Pass the Road Test," *Indianapolis Star*, June 3, 1998.
41. Mark Armijo, "Boat Leaves No Doubt About Texas Win," *Arizona Republic*, June 8, 1998.
42. Curt Cavin, "Boat's True Value 500K Win Erases Last Year's Nightmare," *Indianapolis Star*, June 7, 1998.
43. Dr. Gary Friedman, 2020, interview with the author.
44. A.J. Foyt, April 19–24, 2021, interviews with the author.
45. Armijo, "Boat Leaves No Doubt."
46. Bräck, May 2023, interview.
47. "Boat on a Roll After Winning Pole," Associated Press, *Jackson* (Michigan) *Citizen-Patriot*, June 28, 1998.
48. Billy Boat, November 18, 2020, interview with the author.
49. Curt Cavin, "Menard Says He'll Boycott to Protest Alleged Cheating," *Indianapolis Star*, June 29, 1998.
50. Robin Miller, "Family Feud Replacing Good Times for the IRL," *Indianapolis Star*, July 15, 1998.

51. Cavin, "Menard Says He'll Boycott."
52. Dick Brinster, "A.J. Gets a New 'Boat,'" Associated Press, (Newark) *Star-Ledger,* July 16, 1998.
53. Mel Reisner, "Fledging IRL Circuit Struggles to Rid Itself of Anonymity," Associated Press, *Wausau* (Wisconsin) *Daily Herald*, April 4, 1999.
54. David Poole, "Menard's Two-Race Protest Costs Buhl, Targets Foyt Team," *Charlotte Observer*, July 29, 1998.
55. "Bräck Overcomes Pit Mixup," Associated Press, *Vincennes* (Indiana) *Sun-Commercial*, July 26, 1998.
56. Curt Cavin, "Bräck Peaks on Fumes," *Indianapolis News*, August 17, 1998.
57. Boat, November 18, 2020, interview.
58. John Sturbin, "Bräck 'Threatening' to Wreck IRL's Balance of Power," *Fort Worth Star-Telegram*, September 10, 1998.
59. Steve Herman, "Bräck Credits Foyt for Success," Associated Press, *Kalamazoo Gazette*, September 3, 1998.
60. Paul Newberry, "Bräck, Foyt Are an Unbeatable Team," *Kalamazoo Gazette*, August 31, 1998.
61. Herman, "Bräck Credits Foyt for Success."
62. John Sturbin, "Boat Seizes Lone Star Pole," *Fort Worth Star-Telegram*, September 19, 1998.
63. Steve Ballard, "Legend of A.J. Is IRL's Biggest Ally," *USA Today*, October 8, 1998.
64. Glick, "Some Ol' A.J."
65. Curt Cavin, "Bräck Survives for IRL Crown," *Indianapolis Star*, October 12, 1998.
66. Mike Harris, "Fearsome Foyt Having Fun," Associated Press, *Kalamazoo Gazette*, October 8, 1998.
67. Glick, "Same Ol' A.J."
68. Shav Glick, "Bräck Struggles, But Still Ends up as Leader of Pack," *Los Angeles Times*, October 12, 1998.
69. Mark Armijo, "One More Time," *Arizona Republic*, September 5, 1998.
70. Curt Cavin, "Reports That Time Is Right to Make Deal with CART Are Termed Exaggerated," *Indianapolis Star*, August 16, 1998.
71. Steve Ballard, "Legend of A.J. Is IRL's Biggest Ally," *USA Today*, October 8, 1998.
72. Cavin, "Reports That Time Is Right Exaggerated."
73. Glick, "Same Ol' A.J."

CHAPTER TWENTY-EIGHT: THE KING OF TEXAS

1. Dick Brinster, "Ray, Bräck Figure to Battle for IRL Title," Associated Press, *Bennington* (Vermont) *Banner*, January 15, 1999.
2. John Sturbin, "Bräck-Foyt Team Provides IRL with Marketing Opportunity," *Fort Worth Star-Telegram*, October 15, 1999.
3. Mike Harris, "Bräck Set to Defend IRL Title," Associated Press, *Kokomo* (Indiana) *Tribune*, January 22, 1999.
4. Robin Miller, "Drivers Expect Wide-Open Competition," *Indianapolis Star*, January 17, 1999.
5. Mark Armijo, "Boat Wants to Finish What He Starts," *Arizona Republic*, January 23, 1999.
6. Kenny Bräck, May 2023, interview with the author.
7. Richard Huff, "Champ Gearing up for Back-to-Bräck," *New York Daily News*, January 20, 1999.
8. Mike Harris, "Fearsome Foyt Having Fun," Associated Press, *Kalamazoo Gazette*, October 8, 1998.
9. Mike Harris, "Bräck Begins Defense of His 1998 IRL Title," Associated Press, *Bradenton* (Florida) *Herald*, January 22, 1999.
10. Curt Cavin, "Officials Cancel Race After Debris Enters Stands," *Indianapolis Star*, May 2, 1999.
11. Robin Miller, "3 Drivers Hit Walls in Winds," *Indianapolis News*, May 18, 1999.
12. Dave Lance, "Foyt Not Flustered," *Daytona Daily News*, May 20, 1999.
13. "Notes," *Indianapolis News*, May 19, 1999.
14. Steve Herman, "Boat in Front Row, Despite Crashes," Associated Press, *Saginaw* (Michigan) *News*, May 24, 1999.
15. Mark Ambrogl, "Boat Overcomes Crash to Qualify for Front Row," *Indianapolis Star*, May 23, 1999.
16. Mark Armijo, "Foyt's Poise Boosts Boat's Confidence," *Arizona Republic*, May 27, 1999.
17. David Leon Moore, "Bräck Seeks Break After Rough Start," *USA Today*, May 28, 1999.
18. Ron Ware, "Buhl Receives a Hand from Foyt, Weather," *Springfield* (Ohio) *News-Sun*, May 24, 1999.
19. Dave Koerner, "Boat Vows to Set Sail in 500 with Patience," *Louisville Courier-Journal*, May 27, 1999.
20. Moore, "Bräck Seeks Break."
21. Mike Harris, "What a Gas!" Associated Press, *Modesto Bee*, May 31, 1999.
22. Bräck, May 2023, interview.
23. Angelique Chengelis, "No Secrets for Buhl's Indy Success," *Detroit Free Press*, May 31, 1999.
24. Mike Harris, "Bräck Rides Gordon's Bad Luck to Indy Win," Associated Press, *Marion* (Indiana) *Chronicle Tribune*, May 31, 1999.
25. Bräck, May 2023, interview.
26. Mike Harris, "Indy 500 Champ Earns Most Money in Racing History," Associated Press, *Scottsbluff* (Nebraska) *Star-Herald*, June 1, 1999.
27. Phillip B. Wilson, "Foyt Delights in His Winning Turn," *Indianapolis News*, May 31, 1999.
28. Phillip B. Wilson, "Finishing Second Was Not an Option," *Indianapolis News*, May 31, 1999.
29. Dan Korb, "Kenny Bräck Wins with a Patient Ride," *Evansville* (Indiana) *Courier*, May 31, 1999.

30. Bräck, May 2023, interview.
31. Mike Harris, "The Odd Couple," Associated Press, *Wichita* (Kansas) *Eagle*, June 3, 1999.
32. Robin Miller, "Speedway, IRL Will Benefit from Bräck's Stirring Victory," *Indianapolis News*, June 1, 1999.
33. Shav Glick, "Bräck's Victory a Real Gas," *Los Angeles Times*, May 31, 1999.
34. John Sturbin, "Rival Indy-Car Circuits Discuss Reconciliation," *Fort Worth Star-Telegram*, May 27, 1999.
35. "Drivers Like Merger Idea," Associated Press, *Springfield* (Ohio) *News-Sun*, May 28, 1999.
36. John Sturbin, "New Sponsor Provides Boost to Foyt Racing," *Fort Worth Star-Telegram*, June 11, 1999.
37. Bill Koenig, "Conseco Could Rev up Brand with NASCAR," *Indianapolis News*, September 11, 1999.
38. Robin Miller, "Conseco Helps Foyt Return to NASCAR," *Indianapolis News*, September 4, 1999.
39. "Foyt Decides to Enter NASCAR Circuit in 2000," Associated Press, *Evansville* (Indiana) *Courier and Press*, September 4, 1999.
40. Curt Cavin, "Foyt's Team Tries to Put Setbacks in Perspective," *Indianapolis News*, September 25, 1999.
41. John Sturbin, "Boat's Status on Hold," *Fort Worth Star-Telegram*, October 17 1999.
42. Curt Cavin, "Bräck's Fast Lap Offers Confidence," *Indianapolis News*, June 26, 1999.
43. "Bräck Considering Offers from Other Race Teams," *Columbus Indiana Republic*, August 28, 1999.
44. Cavin, "Foyt's Team Tries to Put Setbacks in Perspective,"
45. Billy Boat, November 18, 2020, interview with the author.
46. Len Hayward, "Broken Bearing Ruins Bräck's Plan for Winning Race, Title," *Fort Worth Star-Telegram*, October 18, 1999.
47. Mike Harris, "Foyt Team Will Run Pontiacs in 2000," Associated Press, *Statesville* (North Carolina) *Record and Landmark*, October 10, 1999.
48. Patrick Zier, "Foyt Putting Together Winston Cup Team," *New York Times* News Service, *Austin American-Statesman*, November 27, 1999.
49. Terry Blount, "Rolling On," *Houston Chronicle*, February 20, 2000.
50. Harris, "Foyt Team Will Run Pontiacs in 2000."
51. Barry Svrluga, "Foyt's Team Slowly Coming Together," *Raleigh News and Observer*, October 10, 1999.
52. Mike Harris, "Irwin, Bliss Get New Rides for Next Season," *Kalamazoo Gazette*, November 20, 1999.
53. John Sturbin, "Foyt Selects Bliss to Drive Winston Cup Car in 2000," *Fort Worth Star-Telegram*, November 20, 1999.
54. Steve Crowe, "Foyt's 65, But Daytona Comes Before Medicare," *Detroit Free Press*, February 17, 2000.
55. Lee Spencer, "With a New I-77 Exit 33 Site, Foyt Sets Sights on NASCAR," *Charlotte Observer*, September 12, 1999.
56. Kenny Bräck, May 2023, interview with the author.
57. A.J. Foyt, April 19–24, 2021, interviews with the author.
58. Steve Ballard, "Bräck Moves to Rahal Team with One Eye Still on Indy 500," *USA Today*, November 11, 1999.
59. Skip Myslenski, "Indy 500 Champion Bräck's Jump to CART Is No Small Step," *Chicago Tribune*, November 12, 1999.
60. Bräck, May 2023, interview with the author.
61. Boat, November 18, 2020, interview.
62. A.J. Foyt, interview with the author.
63. Mike Harris, April 2021, interview with the author.
64. Mike Harris, "Foes Andretti, Foyt See Yardstick in Sport," Associated Press, *Victoria* (Texas) *Advocate*, December 19, 1999.
65. Harris, April 2021, interview.
66. Harris, "Foes Andretti, Foyt."
67. Harris, April 2021, interview.
68. "Andretti, Foyt Drivers of Century: They're Racing Legends Who Tied for the Title and Whose Rivalry Has Roots in Allentown," *Allentown* (Pennsylvania) *Morning Call*, December 11, 1999.

CHAPTER TWENTY-NINE: GRUMPY OLD MEN

1. John Sturbin, "A.J. Foyt's Son, Larry, Takes His Lumps Chasing Dream," *Fort Worth Star-Telegraph*, March 30, 2001.
2. Terry Blount, "Foyt Hoping Trickle Can Jumpstart Team," *Houston Chronicle*, March 18, 2000.
3. Blount, "Foyt Hoping Trickle Can Jumpstart Team."
4. Larry Foyt, November 10, 2020, interview with the author.
5. Terry Blount, "Rolling On," *Houston Chronicle*, February 20, 2000.
6. Monte Dutton, "Foyt's NASCAR Team Is on Track," *Anderson* (South Carolina) *Independent-Mail*, January 1, 2000.
7. Godwin Kelly, "Foyt's Team Full of Bliss over Faster Testing Time," *Daytona Beach News-Journal*, January 12, 2000.
8. Ken Willis, "Is Foyt Still the Someone That We Used to Know?" *Daytona Beach News-Journal*, January 16, 2000.
9. Joe Schad, "Foyt Still Racy Off Track," *Orlando Sentinel*, January 28, 2000.

10. Dick Brinster, "Ray Newest Champion to Be Tempted," *Associated Press*, *Ventura* (California) *County Star*, January 21, 2000.
11. H.A. Branham, "Cantankerous A.J. Foyt Still a Dominant Figure on the Track," *Tampa Tribune*, January 28, 2000.
12. "Foyt Will Be Hobbling Around Daytona Pits," *Richmond* (Indiana) *Palladium-Item*, February 11, 2000.
13. Schad, "Foyt Still Racy Off Track."
14. Bob Pockrass, "Injuries Fail to Soften, Slow Foyt," *Daytona Beach News-Journal*, February 15, 2000.
15. Sandra McKee, "Still Mending, Foyt Has That Same Old Drive," *Baltimore Sun*, February 17, 2000.
16. Bob Pockrass, "Open to Invasion Stock Cars See Influx," *Daytona Beach News-Journal*, February 24, 2000.
17. Clyde Bolton, "Foyt Was Action Hero as Driver," *Birmingham* (Alabama) *News*, April 14, 2000.
18. "Darlington's Turns Challenge Even the Best in NASCAR," Associated Press, *Fort Myers* (Florida) *News-Pilot*, March 16, 2000.
19. "Taking A Back Seat," Associated Press, *Greensboro* (North Carolina) *News and Record*, March 18, 2000.
20. Shav Glick, "Motor Racing," *Los Angeles Times*, March 31, 2000.
21. Jimmy Moore, "'Old Dogs' Getting Good at New Tricks," *Kingsport* (Tennessee) *Times-News*, March 28, 2000.
22. Charean Williams, "A Slow Start for Foyt," *Fort Worth Star-Telegram*, March 24, 2000.
23. Steve Crowe, "Foyt Still Looking for Perfect Fit," *Detroit Free Press*, March 31, 2000.
24. John Sturbin, "Bliss Defends Himself in Wake of Dismissal from Foyt Team," *Fort Worth Star-Telegram*, April 2, 2000.
25. Robin Miller, "Foyt Fights Through Bad Start to Improve His Team's Results," *Indianapolis Star*, August 3, 2000.
26. Ken Willis, "Bliss Happy to Be Back Riding the Busch Circuit," *Daytona Beach News Journal*, February 14, 2001.
27. Dustin Long, "Foyt Team Sways Mast from Hedrick," *Roanoke Times*, March 29, 2000.
28. Skip Wood, "Loyalty Costs Mast in Past but Endears Him to New Boss Foyt," *USA Today*, April 12, 2000.
29. "Foyt Team Gets New GM," Associated Press, *Fargo Forum*, April 27, 2000.
30. Curt Cavin, "Where A.J. Is at His Best," *Indianapolis Star*, May 23, 2000.
31. Mike Harris, "Mast Still Optimistic About Future of Foyt Team," Associated Press, *Goldsboro* (North Carolina) *News-Argus*, June 25, 2000.
32. Miller, "Foyt Fights Through Bad Start."
33. Andrew Booth, "Foyt Busy Making Changes, A.J. Shakes up First-Year Team," *Daytona Beach News-Journal*, April 30, 2000.
34. Sandra McKee, "For Andretti, Induction Cheers Come from Heart," *Baltimore Sun*, April 16, 2000.
35. Terry Blount, "As Usual, Foyt Goes into Motorsports Hall His Way," *Houston Chronicle*, April 15, 2000.
36. Kenny Bräck, May 2023, interview with the author.
37. "Pit Notes," *USA Today*, March 7, 2000.
38. Terry Blount, "Bräck Gears up for Transition to CART," *Houston Chronicle*, March 25, 2000.
39. "Local Hero," *Detroit Free Press*, May 19, 2000.
40. Curt Cavin, "Where A.J. Is at His Best," *Indianapolis Star*, May 23, 2000.
41. Curt Cavin, "Banking on a Level Play Field," *Indianapolis Star*, May 19, 2000.
42. Terry Blount, "CART Racers Wear Target at Indy 500," *Houston Chronicle*, May 20, 2000.
43. "Pole," *South Bend Tribune*, May 21, 2000.
44. Terry Blount, "Guerrero Gets Foyt Team Spot," *Houston Chronicle*, May 20, 2000.
45. Terry Hutchens, "Ward Nails 6th Place, Even with Slow Gear," *Indianapolis Star*, May 21, 2000.
46. Terry Hutchens, "Salazar's Slight Slip up Slows Him on Final Lap," *Indianapolis Star*, May 21, 2000.
47. Billy Boat, November 18, 2020, interview with the author.
48. Robin Miller, "IRL's Rules Enforcer Answers Questions About Foyt, Stewart," *Indianapolis Star*, May 24, 2000.
49. Mike Harris, "Boat Qualifies in Final Minute at Indy," *Winston-Salem Journal*, May 22, 2000.
50. John Sturbin, "Boat Ekes into Indy Field," *Fort Worth Star-Telegram*, May 22, 2000.
51. Mike Harris, "Foyt Talks and Owns as Well as He Drove," Associated Press, *Noblesville* (Indiana) *Ledger*, May 27, 2000.
52. Mark Armijo, "Salazar's Dream Comes True," *Arizona Republic*, March 18, 2000.
53. Hutchens, "Salazar's Slight Slip Up."
54. Terry Hutchens, "Ward Comes Close 1 More Time," *Indianapolis Star*, May 29, 2000.
55. Ed Hinton, "It's an Easy Sunday Ride for Montoya," *Los Angeles Times*, May 29, 2000.
56. Shav Glick, "Early Accident Takes Women Out of the Race," *Los Angeles Times*, May 29, 2000.
57. Paul Newsberry, "Montoya Breezes to Victory at Indy," Associated Press, *Goldsboro News-Argus*, May 29, 2000.
58. Cavin, "Where A.J. Is at His Best."
59. David Poole, "Mast Can't Mask Hopes for Future," *Charlotte Observer*, August 20, 2000.

60. Jim Utter, "Foyt Takes Momentum to Brickyard," *Charlotte Observer*, July 24, 2000.
61. Robin Miller, "Heart Surgery Can't Keep Foyt off the Track," *Indianapolis Star*, September 22, 2000.
62. Larry Woody, "Larry Foyt Can Handle Pressure of Racing Name," *Nashville Tennessean*, May 19, 2000.
63. Larry Foyt, November 10, 2020, interview with the author.
64. Mike Harris, "Younger Foyt to Give Busch Series a Go," Associated Press, *Vincennes* (Indiana) *Sun-Commercial*, January 18, 2001.
65. Larry Foyt, November 10, 2020, interview.
66. Lee Spencer, "Larry Foyt, Son of Legendary Racer, Takes His Turn at Wheel," *Charlotte Observer*, November 12, 2000.

CHAPTER THIRTY: SURPRISE, SURPRISE

1. Mark A. Peinado, "Palmdale's Hornaday Glad to Have a Ride," *Barstow* (California) *Desert Dispatch*, March 3, 2001.
2. David Poole and Jim Utter, "Foyt Tabs Hornaday for 2001," *Charlotte Observer*, November 4, 2000.
3. Al Stilley, "Foyt, Earnhardt Will Never Change Their Ways," *Martinsville* (Indiana) *Reporter-Times*, February 8, 2001.
4. "Hornaday Has Trouble," *Houston Chronicle*, February 16, 2001.
5. "Another Foyt," Associated Press, *Bradenton* (Florida) *Herald*, February 18, 2001.
6. "Young Foyt Enrolls in New Classroom," Associated Press, *Corpus Christi Caller-Times*, February 17, 2001.
7. Terry Blount, "Disgruntled Drivers Drop Boycott Hints," *Houston Chronicle*, March 31, 2001.
8. Blount, "Disgruntled Drivers Drop Boycott Hints."
9. Chris Jenkins, "Daytona Plans Low-Key Tribute to Earnhardt," *USA Today*, July 7, 2001.
10. "Salazar in Foyt No. 14," *Houston Chronicle*, February 3, 2001.
11. Terry Blount, "Around the Circuits," *Houston Chronicle*, April 14, 2001.
12. Jorge Milian, "Indy League's Young Guns Dominate Homestead," *Palm Beach Post*, April 9 2001.
13. Curt Cavin, "Boat Declines Foyt's 2nd Car," *Indianapolis Star*, April 11, 2001.
14. Terry Blount, "Odd Couple of Indy," *Houston Chronicle*, April 21, 2001.
15. "Speedway Notes," *Indianapolis Star*, May 9, 2001.
16. Shav Glick, "Sharp Takes Pole for Indy 500," *Los Angeles Times*, May 13, 2001.
17. Marot, "Foyt Finds Niche as Great Teacher."
18. "Indy Notes," *Miami Herald*, May 12, 2001.
19. "2001 Indy Racing League Casino Magic 500," television broadcast, ESPN, June 9, 2001.
20. Jeff Wilson, "Foyt's Help Keeps Driver in IRL Series," *Fort Worth Star-Telegram*, June 9, 2001.
21. Curt Cavin, "Beechler Has a Lot Riding on 4 Tires," *Indianapolis Star*, June 9, 2001.
22. Richard Biebrich, "Win, Don't Coast, Foyt Tells Salazar," *South Floria Sun Sentinel*, February 28, 2002.
23. John Sturbin, "IRL Driver Ray Back on Track, *Fort Worth Star-Telegram*, November 2, 2001.
24. Gary Long, "Hornish, Salazar Among Favorites," *Miami Herald*, February 28, 2002.
25. Steve Ballard, "Provisionals Help Strong Teams," *Indianapolis Star*, August 4, 2001.
26. Al Stilley, "Foyt Hopes to Turn His Team's NASCAR Season Around," *Martinsville* (Indiana) *Reporter-Times*, August 1, 2001.
27. Richard Biebrich, "Out of the Show," *South Florida Sun Sentinel*, November 11, 2001.
28. Quotes of the Year, "That's Why You Make the Big Bucks," *Seymour* (Indiana) *Tribune*. January 2, 2002.
29. John Sturbin, "A.J. Foyt's Son, Larry, Takes His Lumps Chasing Dream," *Fort Worth Star-Telegraph*, March 30, 2001.
30. "No. 14 Conseco Pontiac," *Raleigh News and Observer*, February 10, 2002.
31. "Foyt Chooses Compton," *Franklin Daily Journal* (Indiana), January 11, 2002.
32. "Race Notes," *Charlotte Observer*, January 18, 2002.
33. Len Hayward, "Compton's Main Job Is Reviving Team Foyt," *Fort Worth Star-Telegram*, April 3, 2002.
34. Stephen Hawkins, "Foyt Still Showing Patience," *Grass Valley* (California) *Union*, April 4, 2002.
35. Juan C. Rodriguez, "Daré Makes the Most of His Chance to Shine," *Miami Herald*, March 3, 2002.
36. Gary Long, "Salazar Can't Stay Away from Indianapolis," *Miami Herald*, May 17, 2000.
37. "Eliseo Salazar," *Evansville* (Indiana) *Courier and Press*, April 21, 2002.
38. "Auto Racing," *Bryan-College Station* (Texas) *Eagle*, April 19, 2002.
39. John Clayton, "Ray to Drive for Foyt," *Rushville* (Indiana) *Republican*, May 16, 2002.
40. "Ray Back with Foyt," Associated Press, *Lafayette* (Indiana) *Journal and Courier*, May 24, 2002.
41. John Sturbin, "Ray Could Use A.J.'s Magic Touch," *Fort Worth Star-Telegram*, May 2, 2002.
42. Bobby Rahal, May 23, 2025, interview with the author.
43. John Sturbin, "Foyt Fumes After His Teams Fail to Qualify," *Fort Worth Star-Telegram*, May 13, 2002.
44. Kenny Bräck, May 2023, interview with the author.
45. "Ray Back with Foyt," AP.
46. Curt Cavin, "Beechler Swallows Pride to Accept Ride from Foyt," *Indianapolis Star*, May 15, 2002.
47. "Racing Is about Speed, Not Limits Says Team Owner A.J. Foyt," *Indianapolis Star*, May 25, 2002.

48. Curt Cavin, "IRL, CART Will Cooperate but Demand Independence," *Indianapolis Star*, May 21, 2002.
49. Stephen Hawkins, "Foyt Sees Better Results from Ray," Associated Press, *Abilene* (Texas) *Reporter-News*, June 13, 2002.
50. John Sturbin, "Foyt IV Gets a Ride," *Fort Worth Star-Telegram*, May 26, 2002.
51. John Milburn, "Familiar Name Will Lead Field in First Race of New Series," Associated Press, *Lafayette* (Indiana) *Journal Courier*, July 7, 2002.
52. Curt Cavin, "Foyt Team Scores Double Victory," *Indianapolis Star*, July 8, 2002.
53. D.C. Williams, "Compton Set for Title Run: After Foyt Split, Team Is Focused," *Daytona Beach News-Journal*, January 24, 2003.
54. Curt Cavin, "Foyt Regrets Opening Shop in N.C.," *Indianapolis Star*, August 2, 2002.
55. John Sturbin, "Foyt Team's Fortunes Take Turn for Better," *Fort Worth Star-Telegram*, August 12, 2002.
56. Len Hayward, "Ray Ends Racing with Foyt," *Fort Worth Star-Telegram*, August 28, 2002.
57. Len Hayward, "This Foyt Ready to Build on Family's Racing Legend," *Fort Worth Star-Telegram*, September 12, 2002.
58. "Foyt IV Has Tough Sell," *Indianapolis Star*, September 20, 2002.

CHAPTER THIRTY-ONE: ALL IN THE FAMILY

1. Bob Pockrass, "Foyt Builds Stronger Foundation," *Daytona Beach News-Journal*, February 10, 2003.
2. "Foyt's Shuffle," *Rocky Mount* (North Carolina) *Telegram*, January 15, 2003.
3. Pockrass, "Foyt Builds Stronger Foundation."
4. John Sturbin, "Foyt Steps up to Cup," *Fort Worth Star-Telegram*, January 24, 2003.
5. Larry Foyt, November 10, 2020, interview with the author.
6. Davey Hamilton, May 27, 2023, interview with the author.
7. Curt Cavin, "Foyt Likely Heading to IRL," *Indianapolis Star*, October 11, 2002.
8. Cammy Clark, "Foyt IV Must Prove He's Not Just a Legacy," *Miami Herald*, February 28, 2003.
9. John Sturbin, "Another Foyt on Move," *Fort Worth Star-Telegram*, November 1, 2002.
10. "Foyt Changing Engines," Associated Press, *El Paso* (Texas) *Times*, January 28, 2003.
11. Curt Cavin, "IRL to Start Testing with Many Contenders," *Indianapolis Star*, February 4, 2003.
12. Curt Cavin and Steve Ballard, "Foyt Has Conseco, Hattori on IRL Team," *Indianapolis Star*, February 7, 2003.
13. Bob Pockrass, "Foyt builds stronger foundation," Daytona Beach News-Journal, February 10, 2003.
14. Curt Cavin, "Castroneves Sends Foyt to Wall," *Indianapolis Star*, March 1, 2003.
15. Clarissa Aljentera, "Relieved Foyt Sneaks into Field," *Fort Worth Star-Telegram*, March 29, 2003.
16. Mike Mulhern, "A.J. Foyt Calls NASCAR 'Crooked,'" *Morganton* (North Carolina) *News-Herald*, April 14, 2003.
17. Clark, "Foyt IV Must Prove He's Not Just a Legacy."
18. "A.J. Foyt IV Youngest to Pass Indy Rookie Test," *Herald News Service*, April 22, 2003.
19. "'Spider-Man' Goes for Sequel," *Franklin* (Indiana) *Daily Journal*, May 3, 2003.
20. Art Garner and Mark B. Spiegel, *Indy 500 Memories* (CreateSpace Publishing: 2016).
21. Megan Manfull, "A.J. Foyt IV Keeps Family Tradition Rolling," *Houston Chronicle*, May 25, 2003.
22. Steve Ballard, "Notes," *Indianapolis Star*, May 12, 2003.
23. "A.J. Foyt IV Isn't Trying to Match His Grandfather," Scripps Howard News Service, *Muncie Star Press*, May 16, 2003.
24. Ed Hinton, "Crash Course: Bobby Unser Says 18-Year-Old A.J. Foyt IV Not Ready for Indy," *Orlando Sentinel*, May 19, 2003.
25. Manfull, "A.J. Foyt IV Keeps Family Tradition Rolling."
26. Michael Marot, "Foyt Defends Rookie Grandson," Associated Press, *Vincennes* (Indiana) *Sun-Commercial*, May 19, 2003.
27. Hinton, "Crash Course."
28. Phillip Wilson, "Carpenter Wins Freedom 100 Pole," *Indianapolis Star*, May 17, 2003.
29. Ed Carpenter, May 24, 2022, interview with the author.
30. Mike Kupper, "Grand Legacy Has Some Burdens Too," *Los Angeles Times*, May 24, 2003.
31. Terry Hutchens, "Pit Stop Typifies Foyt's Odd Day," *Indianapolis Star*, May 26,2003.
32. "2003 Indianapolis 500," television broadcast, ABC, May 25, 2003.
33. Michael Marot, "Foyt IV Hoping for Smoother Ride," *San Angelo* (Texas) *Standard-Times*, May 28, 2004.
34. Hutchens, "Pit Stop Typifies Foyt's Odd Day."
35. "2003 Indianapolis 500," ABC.
36. Eddie Pells, "Spiderman's Run Lost in Tangled Web," Associated Press, *Stuart* (Florida) *News*, May 26, 2003.
37. Hutchens, "Pit Stop Typifies Foyt's Odd Day."
38. Ken de la Bastide, "Larry Foyt Out to Make His Mark," *Rushville* (Indiana) *Republican*, August 1, 2003.
39. "Another Foyt Taking on Fabled Track," Associated Press, *Merced* (California) *Sun-Star*, August 2, 2003.
40. NASCAR Notebook, "Accepting Blame," *Arizona* (Tucson) *Daily Star*, August 3, 2003.
41. Larry Foyt, interview with the author.

42. David Poole, "Frustrating Year Has Foyt Unsure of Future," *Charlotte Observer*, November 13, 2003.
43. John Sturbin, "Foyt Team's Future Uncertain After Today," *Fort Worth Star-Telegram*, February 15, 2004.

CHAPTER THIRTY-TWO: ABC FINDS ITS MATCH

1. John Sturbin, "Foyt Team's Future Uncertain After Today," *Fort Worth Star-Telegram*, February 15, 2004.
2. Larry Foyt, April 28, 2021, interview with the author.
3. John Sturbin, "Another Foyt Chases His Indy 500 Dream," *Fort Worth Star-Telegram,* April 28, 2004.
4. Foyt IV Ready to Put Rough Rookie Season Behind Him," Associated Press, *Richmond* (Indiana) *Palladium-Item*, February 20, 2004.
5. Richard Biebrich, "Hornish Takes Pole for Toyota Indy 300," Knight-Ridder, *Greenville* (South Carolina) *News*, March 26, 2006.
6. Jim Aust, August 26, 2025, interview with the author.
7. Steve Herman, "Larry Foyt Tests Speedway with Other Rookie," Associated Press, *Columbus* (Indiana) *Republic*, April 27, 2004.
8. Steve Herman, "Another Foyt," Associated Press, *Allentown* (Pennsylvania) *Morning Call*, May 16, 2004.
9. "They Said It," *Indianapolis Star*, May 16, 2004.
10. Terry Hutchens, "Toyota-Powered Cars Qualify at Back of Field," *Indianapolis Star*, May 16, 2004.
11. "They Said It," *Indianapolis Star*, May 16, 2004.
12. Mike Brudenell, "Foyts Feel Pressure of Family Name," *Detroit Free Press*, May 21, 2005.
13. Mickey Herskowitz, "Foyts Continue Family Tradition at the Brickyard," *Houston Chronicle*, May 22, 2004.
14. Mike Brudenell, "Stewart to Try for '05 Indy," *Detroit Free Press*, May 24, 2004.
15. Steve Ballard and Curt Cavin, "Stewart Adds Drama to Track's Bump Day," *Indianapolis Star*, May 24, 2004.
16. Tony Stewart, December 16, 2020, interview with the author.
17. Brant James, "Outspoken Foyt Unflinching in Views of Sport," *Tampa Bay Times*, April 1, 2006.
18. John Sturbin, "We Are family," *Fort Worth Star-Telegram*, May 29, 2004.
19. "2004 Indianapolis 500," television broadcast, ABC, May 30, 2004.
20. Ed Hinton, "Crashes Ruin Day for Foyts," *Orlando Sentinel*, May 31, 2004.
21. "2004 Indianapolis 500," television broadcast, ABC, May 30, 2004.
22. Michael Pointer, "Crashes Mar Day for Foyts," *Binghamton* (New York) *Press and Sun-Bulletin*, May 31, 2004.
23. Lucy Foyt, April 2, 2020, interview with the author.
24. Larry Foyt, interview with the author.
25. Dave Kallmann, "A.J. Foyt Still in Business to Win," *Milwaukee Journal*, July 22, 2004.
26. Terry Blount, "Foyts Speeding Toward 2005," *Greensboro* (North Carolina) *News and Record*, October 17, 2004.
27. Jeff Davis, "Testing His Limits," *Fresno Bee*, August 26, 2004.
28. Steve Ballard and Curt Cavin, "Foyt Program Optimistic Despite Tough Season," *Indianapolis Star*, August 20, 2004.
29. Blount, "Foyts Speeding Toward 2005."
30. Kallmann, "A.J. Foyt Still in Business to Win."
31. Herman, "Larry Foyt Tests Speedway with Other Rookie."
32. Sturbin, "Another Foyt Chases His Indy 500 Dream."
33. Alan Tays, "BAM Racing Crosses Fingers," *Palm Beach Post*, November 18, 2004.
34. Mickey Herskowitz, "As Boss, Super Tex Still as Tough as His Indy Days." *Houston Chronicle*, April 23, 2005.
35. Brant James, "Road Warrier," *Tampa Bay Times*, March 5, 2005.
36. "Castroneves's High Hopes End on Disappointing Note," *Tampa Tribune*, April 4, 2005.
37. "Race Notes," *Tampa Bay Times*, April 4, 2005.
38. Mike Brudenell, "Foyt Still a Crowd Pleaser at Indy," *Detroit Free Press*, May 20, 2004.
39. David Luck, September 6, 2025, interview with the author.
40. Ed Hinton, "Gentlemen (and Danica) Start Your Engines," *Orlando Sentinel*, May 25, 2005.
41. Ed Hinton, "Old Softie," *Orlando Sentinel*, May 19, 2005.
42. Phillip B. Wilson, "Foyt Cars Struggle to Get Up to Speed," *Indianapolis Star*, May 22, 2005.
43. Michael Marot, "Foyt's Temper Smolders After More Team Woes," Associated Press, *Lafayette* (Indiana) *Journal and Courier*, May 22, 2005.
44. Mike Harris, "Bräck's Performance Impresses Indy Veteran A.J. Foyt," Associated Press, *Saginaw* (Michigan) *News*, May 22, 2005.
45. Mike Brudenell, "Giaffone Gets Last Indy Spot—After Shopping," *Detroit Free Press*, May 23, 2005.
46. Steven Herman, "No Feud Between Foyt, Luyendyk," *Marion* (Indiana) *Chronicle Tribune*, May 23, 2005.
47. Jamie Little, "2005 Indianapolis 500," television broadcast, ABC, May 29, 2005.
48. Neil Hohlfeld, "Times Are Tough, But Foyt Not About to Quit," *Houston Chronicle*, June 8, 2005.

49. "Foyt to NASCAR," *Charlotte News and Observer*, July 1, 2005.
50. "Foyt Brushes Off Bee Attack," *Orlando Sentinel*, August 11, 2005.
51. Curt Cavin, "Foyt Has Reminder for Stewart," *Indianapolis Star*, August 10, 2005.
52. Curt Cavin, "Foyt IV Locates Some Power," *Indianapolis Star*, August 14, 2025.
53. "Younger Foyt Returning to NASCAR," *Houston Chronicle*, October 8, 2005.
54. Curt Cavin, "Foyt Breaks Family Ties," *Indianapolis Star*, October 8, 2005.
55. Neil Hohlfeld, "Seeking a Road of His Own," *Houston Chronicle*, January 26, 2026.

CHAPTER THIRTY-THREE: ANTHONY MOVES ON AND LARRY MOVES HOME

1. "Foyt Hires Giaffone as New Full-Time Driver," Associated Press, *Naples* (Florida) *Daily News*, December 16, 2005.
2. "A.J. as Outspoken as Ever," *Houston Chronicle*, March 25, 2006.
3. "Foyt Hires Giaffone," AP.
4. Notes, "Foyt to Bring Back Old Number for Indy 500," *Bay City* (Michigan) *Times*, March 24, 2006.
5. "Life Goes on in IRL After Fatal Crash," *New York Times*, March 28, 2006.
6. Neil Hohlfeld, "Cars Get Safer, but Death's Always Knocking," *Houston Chronicle*, March 30, 2006.
7. Anthony Andro, "Foyt Hoping to Get Team up to Speed," *Fort Worth Star-Telegram*, April 7, 2006.
8. Neil Hohlfeld, "A.J. Plans 3 Indy Entries," *Houston Chronicle*, April 8, 2006.
9. "At Indy, A.J. Foyt's Profile Remains Larger than Life," *Fort Worth Star-Telegram*, May 11, 2005.
10. Holly Cain, "Foyt Downplays Talk of Potential Merger," *Tampa Tribune*, April 2, 2006.
11. Brant James, "Outspoken Foyt Unflinching in Views of Sport," *Tampa Bay Times*, April 1, 2006.
12. Tim Ethridge, "Foyt Remains as Feisty as Ever," *Evansville* (Indiana) *Courier and Press*, May 25, 2006.
13. Debbie Arrington, "Money Raises Risks on Track," *Sacramento Bee*, May 12, 2006.
14. "Foyt's Follies," Associated Press, *Lafayette* (Indiana) *Journal and Courier*, May 29, 2006.
15. "Foyt Struggles," *Columbus* (Indiana) *Republic*, May 29, 2006.
16. Neil Hohlfeld, "Foyt Hires Bucknum for No. 14," *Houston Chronicle*, July 13, 2006.
17. Larry Foyt, November 10, 2020, interview with the author.
18. Mike Brudenell, "Foyt Wants Sting Back in Team," *Detroit Free Press*, August 1, 2006.
19. Anthony Andro, "Larry Foyt Hasn't Retired; He's Driven by a Challenge," *Fort Worth Star-Telegram*, August 24, 2006.
20. Brudenell, "Foyt Wants Sting Back in Team."
21. Russ Goodall, "Meira, Foyt, Ready," Houston Chronicle, April 3, 2009.
22. Neil Hohlfeld, "Foyt Makes Promised Changes," *Houston Chronicle*, November 15, 2006.
23. Larry Foyt, November 10, 2020, interview.
24. Neil Hohlfeld, "Foyt May Finally Be Slowing Down," *Houston Chronicle*, November 18, 2006.
25. Larry Foyt, November 10, 2020, interview.
26. Mike Brudenell, "50 Years and Counting," *Detroit Free Press*, March 16, 2007.
27. Mike Brudenell, "Unification Needed to Save Open Wheel Racing," *Detroit Free Press*, May 21, 2006.
28. Brant James, "The Rugged One," *St. Petersburg Times*, March 27, 2007.
29. Joanne Korth, "A So-So Finish Isn't Too Bad," *Tampa Bay Times*, April 2, 2007.
30. "A.J. A-OK," *Tampa Bay Times*, April 1, 2007.
31. Korth, "A So-So Finish Isn't Too Bad."
32. Mike Harris, "New Driver, New Attitude Giving Foyt Team a Boost," Associated Press, *Vincennes* (Indiana) *Sun-Commercial*, April 8, 2007.
33. Al Unser, December 16, 2020, interview with the author.
34. Mike Harris, "Unser Jr. Finding Challenges Both On, Off the Track," Associated Press, May 19, 2007.
35. Al Unser Jr. November 5, 2020, interview with the author.
36. Al Unser, December 16, 2020, interview with the author.
37. A.J. Foyt Jr., April 19–24, 2021, interviews with the author.
38. Steve Herman, "A.J. Foyt Celebrates Milestone," Associated Press, *Muskegon* (Michigan) *Chronicle*, May 19, 2007.
39. John Sturbin, "Indy 500 Is Family Business," *Fort Worth Star-Telegram*, May 14, 2007.
40. Al Unser Jr., November 5, 2020, interview with the author.
41. Mike Brudenell, "A.J. Foyt Comes to MIS After Nearly Drowning," *Detroit Free Press*, August 4, 2007.
42. A.J. Foyt, *Wind Tunnel* interview with Robin Miller, Speed Channel, October 4, 2009.
43. Larry Foyt, November 10, 2020, interview with the author.

CHAPTER THIRTY-FOUR: REUNITED

1. John Sturbin, "Open-Wheel Racing's Future Can't Arrive Quickly Enough," *Fort Worth Star-Telegram*, February 28, 2008.
2. Brant James, "Penske Defends Moving Points," *Tampa Bay Times*, February 16, 2008.
3. Bob Goodall, "Houston Grand Prix Lost in Translation," *Houston Chronicle*, February 23, 2008.
4. Godwin Kelly, "We've Got the Goods," *Daytona Beach News-Journal*, February 3, 2008.
5. "Foyt Ranked No. 1," *Indianapolis Star*, May 24, 2008.
6. Steve Ballard, "Foyt Says Son Won't Drive," *Indianapolis Star*, May 8, 2008.
7. "Larry Foyt: Moving AJ Foyt Enterprises into the Future," Motorsport, June 1, 2009, https://au.motorsport.com/indycar/news/larry-foyt-moving-aj-foyt-enterprises-into-the-future/2923804/.

8. Steve Herman, "Simmons to Pull Indy Double," Associated Press, *Corpus Christi Caller-Times*, May 21, 2008.
9. "Stop, Stop, Stop," *Houston Chronicle*, May 25, 2008.
10. "AJ Foyt Racing Signs Vitor Meira," Motorsport, September 28, 2008, https://au.motorsport.com/indycar/news/aj-foyt-racing-signs-vitor-meira/2805690/.
11. Curt Cavin, "Making Contract," *Indianapolis Star*, May 22, 2009.
12. "AJ Foyt Racing Signs Vitor Meira," Motorsport.
13. "Larry Foyt: Moving AJ Foyt Enterprises." Motorsport.
14. David Luck, September 6, 2025, interview with the author.
15. Jenna Fryer, "All A.J. All the Time," Associated Press, *Evansville* (Indiana) *Courier and Press*, July 26, 2008.
16. Fryer, "All A.J. All the Time."
17. Sean Kernan, "Don't Mess with 'Super Tex,'" *Daytona Beach News-Journal*, February 14, 2009.
18. Sarah Rothschild, "Stewart, Foyt Share Bond," *Miami Herald*, February 14, 2009.
19. "Breakdown," Associated Press, *Columbus* (Indiana) *Republic*, February 13, 2009.
20. Mark DeCotis, "Tony Stewart, A.J. Foyt Exchange Compliments, and a Few Jibes Too," *Tallahassee Democrat*, February 14, 2009.
21. Mark DeCotis, "Tony Stewart, A.J. Foyt Exchange Compliments, and a Few Jibes Too."
22. Eddie Cheever, "2009 Indianapolis 500," television broadcast, ABC, May 24, 2009.
23. Phillip B. Wilson, "Cars Have Trouble Getting Through IMS' Turn One Side-By-Side," *Indianapolis Star*, May 25, 2009.
24. Dave Kallmann, "Foyt's Legacy Is Indy," *Milwaukee Journal*, May 29, 2011.
25. "Tracy Bounced from Foyt Racing," *Windsor Star*, June 4, 2009.
26. Ryan Hunter-Reay, May 25, 2023, interview with the author.
27. Curt Cavin, "Heartbreak Hits Cockpit," *Indianapolis Star*, August 20, 2009.
28. Hunter-Reay, May 25, 2023, interview.
29. Ryan McGee, "Meet Vitor Meira: Indy Car Cult Hero," ESPN, May 19, 2010.
30. A.J. Foyt, *Wind Tunnel* interview with Robin Miller, Speed Channel, October 4, 2009.
31. Russ Goodall, "Meira Looking for More," *Houston Chronicle*, March 26, 2010.
32. "Foyt IV Awaits Indy," *Houston Chronicle*, April 23, 2010.
33. Anthony Foyt IV, May 27, 2021, interview with the author.
34. Davey Hamilton, May 27, 2023, interview with the author.
35. Larry Foyt, April 28, 2021, interview with the author.
36. Anthony Foyt IV, interview with Derek Daly, *Channel 8 News*, Indianapolis, May 26, 2010.
37. Curt Cavin, "Foyt Says Bump Day Dispute 'Was No Big Deal,'" *Indianapolis Star*, May 25, 2010.
38. Anthony Foyt IV, May 27, 2021, interview.
39. Nancy Foyt, April 23, 2021, interview with the author.
40. Curt Cavin, "Grade: B AJ Foyt Racing," *Indianapolis Star*, July 3, 2010.
41. Curt Cavin, "IndyCar's Oval Award to Be Named After Foyt," *Indianapolis Star*, June 6, 2010.

CHAPTER THIRTY-FIVE: LIFE AND DEATH

1. "Foyt Undergoes Stent Insertion," *Houston Chronicle*, March 27, 2011.
2. Curt Cavin, "Foyt Has Procedure to Put Stent in Heart," *Indianapolis Star*, March 27, 2011.
3. Tony Fabrizio, "IndyCar Leader Proving Popular," *Tampa Tribune*, March 25, 2011.
4. Curt Cavin, "Pace Car Invitation an Honor," *Indianapolis Star*, May 7, 2011.
5. Cliff Brunt, "Indy Car Great Back on Track," Associated Press, *Columbia Missourian*, May 13, 2011.
6. Ed Hinton, "Singular Foyt Presence Still Looms Large," ESPN, May 27, 2011.
7. Steve Ballard, "Meira Likes His Chances," *Indianapolis Star*, May 20, 2011.
8. Hinton, "Singular Foyt Presence."
9. Dean McNulty, "Tagliani Win Has Big Boys Scared," *St. Catharines* (Canada) *Standard*, May 26, 2011.
10. Gary Graves, "Andretti, Foyt Swing Driver Deal for Indy 500," *USA Today*, May 24, 2011.
11. "Hunter-Reay's New Ride," *Raleigh News and Observer*, May 27, 2011.
12. Will Graves, "Andretti Autosports Buys Ride for Hunter-Reay," Associated Press, *Fort Smith* (Arkansas) *Times-Record*, May 27, 2011.
13. McNulty, "Tagliani Win."
14. Hinton, "Singular Foyt Presence."
15. "Hunter-Reay," *Indianapolis Star*, May 30, 2011.
16. "Meira Done at Foyt," *Indianapolis Star*, October 15, 2011.
17. Larry Foyt, April 28, 2021, interview with the author.
18. Michael Marot, "A.J. Foyt's Team Picks Honda for 2012," *Evansville* (Indiana) *Courier and Press*, July 20, 2011.
19. "AJ Foyt Sticks with Honda Engine in 2012," Associated Press, (Michigan) *Herald-Palladium*, July 20, 2011.
20. Nathan Brown, "IndyCar Remembers Dan Wheldon," *Indianapolis Star*, October 16, 2021.
21. Andy Hallberry and Jeff Olson, *Lionheart: Remembering Dan Wheldon* (Lionheart Books LLC: 2016).

22. "2011 Las Vegas Accident Investigation," IndyCar, December 15, 2011.
23. A.J. Foyt, 2019, interview with the author.
24. A.J. Foyt, April 28, 2021, interview with the author.
25. Larry Foyt, October 22, 2025, interview with the author.
26. Jenna Fryer, "Indy Car 'In Crisis,'" Associated Press, *South Bend Tribune*, October 26, 2011.
27. Davey Hamilton, May 27, 2023, interview with the author.
28. Associated Press, "NASCAR's Johnson Clarifies Call for Oval Bans," *Reno Gazette-Journal*, October 20, 2011.
29. Nate Ryan, "IndyCar Legends Defend Oval Racing," *USA Today*, October 19, 2011.
30. Nate Ryan, "Money, Not Safety, Drives Reduction in IndyCar Ovals," *USA Today*, October 19, 2011.
31. Tim McKinney, "Tony to Lead Team Full of Champions," *Columbus* (Indiana) *Republic*, December 30, 2011.
32. Jenna Fryer, "War of Words," Associated Press, *Saginaw* (Michigan) *News*, November 18, 2011.
33. Jenna Fryer, "A Title up in Smoke," Associated Press, *Santa Barbara News-Press*, November 21, 2011.
34. Jenna Fryer, "Edwards Shows Class in Losing Title," Associated Press, *Brownsville* (Texas) *Herald*, November 22, 2011.
35. Fryer, "A Title up in Smoke."
36. "Presidential Praise for Stewart," Associated Press, *Wilmington* (Delaware) *News Journal*, April 19, 2012.
37. Andrew Lewin, "Meira Bids Farewell to US Racing," *Crash*, March 30, 2012, https://www.crash.net/indycar/news/176692/1/vitor-meira-bids-farewell-to-us-racing.
38. Marot, "A.J. Foyt's Team Picks Honda for 2012."
39. Sandra McKee, "A.J. Foyt, One on One," *Baltimore Sun*, August 12, 2012.
40. Don Halliday, February 11, 2021, interview with the author.
41. "Don Halliday Joins AJ Foyt Racing as Chief Engineer," Motorsport, January 27, 2012, https://au.motorsport.com/indycar/news/don-halliday-joins-aj-foyt-racing-as-chief-engineer/2604665/.
42. Tim Tuttle, "It's All in the Family at A.J. Foyt Racing," *Road & Track*, May 14, 2012.
43. McKee, "A.J. Foyt, One on One."
44. Halliday, February 11, 2021, interview.
45. Michael Marot, "Hildebrand Eyes Redemption," Associated Press, *South Bend Tribune*, May 13, 2012.
46. Greg Billing, "Foyt Drivers Conway, Cunningham Excited for Indy," *Dayton Journal News*, May 23, 2012.
47. "Drivers Love the Anthem, but Not Milk," *Hamilton* (Ohio) *Journal News*, May 23, 2012.
48. Halliday, February 11, 2021, interview.
49. "2012 Indianapolis 500," television broadcast, ABC, May 27, 2012.
50. "Loving Life Trackside," Mike Brudenell, *Detroit Free Press*, June 3, 2012.
51. "With a Love for Speed, Racers Must Accept the Danger" Kevin Cowerd, *Baltimore Sun*, September 2, 2012.
52. Jim Peltz, "IndyCar Driver Mike Conway Drops out of Fontana Season Finale," *Los Angeles Times*, September 13, 2012.
53. Jim Peltz, "Mike Conway Reaction," *Los Angeles Times*, September 15, 2012.
54. "Conway Call Supported," *Indianapolis Star*, September 15, 2012.
55. Peltz, "Mike Conway Reaction."
56. "Conway Signs 1-Race Deal with Rahal," Associated Press, *Daytona Beach News-Journal*, January 28, 2013.

CHAPTER THIRTY-SIX: THE ODD COUPLE

1. Dave Skretta, "A.J. Foyt Back at Track with Chance to Win Indy 500," Associated Press, *Independent-Record*, May 26, 2013.
2. Takuma Sato, February 3, 2021, interview with the author.
3. Curt Cavin, "Odd Couple Gets Long-Awaited Win," *Indianapolis Star*, April 22, 2013.
4. Sato, February 3, 2021, interview.
5. Skretta, "A.J. Foyt Back at Track."
6. Jenna Fryer, "Open-Wheel Fans Ready for IndyCar season," Associated Press, (Michigan) *Herald-Palladium*, March 21, 2013.
7. Sato, February 3, 2021, interview.
8. Curt Cavin, "Foyt Racing Fumes About Sato's Penalty," *Indianapolis Star*, April 7, 2013.
9. Jim Peltz, "Sato Has Historic Run in Long Beach," *Los Angeles Times*, April 22, 2013.
10. "Sato First Japanese Driver to Win on IndyCar Circuit," Associated Press, *Elwood* (Indiana) *Call Leader*, April 22, 2013.
11. Cavin, "Odd Couple Gets Long-Awaited Win."
12. Phil Richards, "Foyt's Body Ravaged by Racing, but His Team Thrives," *Indianapolis Star*, May 23, 2013.
13. Larry Foyt, November 10, 2020, interview with the author.
14. Jim Peltz, "Foyt's Aim: Own Like He Drove," *Los Angeles Times*, May 26, 2013.
15. "Foyt Team Surges Forward Before Indy Race," Associated Press, *Decatur* (Illinois) *Herald and Review*, May 12, 2013.

16. Richards, "Foyt's Body Ravaged by Racing, but His Team Thrives."
17. Tim Tuttle, "Indy 500 Crash Proved Valuable for Takuma Sato," *Sports Illustrated*, May 24, 2013.
18. Jenna Fryer, "Daly to Run 500 for Foyt," Associated Press, *Somerset* (Pennsylvania) *Daily Item*, April 3, 2013.
19. Sato, February 3, 2021, interview.
20. Conor Daly, May 24, 2022, interview with the author.
21. Skretta, "A.J. Foyt Back at Track."
22. Bill Fleischman, "Easy as 1-2-3 for Ganassi at Pocono," *Philadelphia Daily News*, July 8, 2013.
23. Jeff Olson, "Foyt Has Painful Winning Season," *Des Moines Register*, June 21, 2013.
24. Rod Evans, "Sato, Foyt an Unlikely Pairing but a Good Match," *Houston Chronicle*, May 25, 2013.
25. "New Deal Next for Sato?" *Indianapolis Star*, October 6, 2013.
26. "Takuma Sato and A.J. Foyt Continue Partnership for 2014," Speedwaymedia.com, December 20, 2013, https://speedwaymedia.com/2013/12/20/takuma-sato-and-a-j-foyt-continue-partnership-for-2014/.
27. Jenna Fryer, "Sato Wins Pole for IndyCar Opener," *Anderson* (South Carolina) *Independent-Mail*, March 30, 2014.
28. Genaro C. Armas, "Hawksworth Heads into Second IndyCar Season," Associated Press, *Wichita Falls Times-Record-News*, March 5, 2015.
29. Michael Marot, "Foyt Adding 2nd Full-Time Car to Team," Associated Press, *Vincennes* (Indiana) *Sun-Commercial*, October 30, 2014.
30. A.J. Foyt, April 19, 2021, interview with the author.
31. Larry Foyt, October 22, 2025, interview with the author.
32. Mike Brudenell, "Foyt Still Winning Race Against Time," *Detroit Free Press*, May 31, 2015.
33. "IndyCar Legend A.J. Foyt Released from Hospital," Associated Press, December 4, 2014.
34. Sato, February 3, 2021, interview.
35. Brudenell, "Foyt Still Winning Race Against Time."
36. David Barron, "Even at 80 Foyt Still Has His Foot on the Gas," *Houston Chronicle*, January 16, 2015.
37. Allison Copenbarger Vance, "Back Home Again in Indiana: A.J. Foyt Returns to the 500," *SB Nation*, June 19, 2015.
38. Michael Marot, "IndyCar's Walker Has Safety in Mind," Associated Press, *Waco Tribune-Herald*, May 23, 2015.
39. Copenbarger Vance, "Back Home Again."
40. Larry Foyt, October 22, 2025, interview.
41. Greg Billing, "Sato Collision Ends Karam's Race Early," *Austin American-Statesman*, May 25, 2015.
42. "2015 Indianapolis 500," television broadcast, ABC, May 25, 2015.
43. Copenbarger Vance, "Back Home Again."
44. Surgeries Mean Season Over for Foyt," Associated Press, *Lafayette* (Indiana) *Journal and Courier*, August 20, 2015.
45. Larry Foyt, October 22, 2025, interview.
46. "Foyt to Miss Final Two Races," *Indianapolis Star*, August 20, 2015.
47. "Foyt Revved up and Raring to Go to IndyCar Races," Associated Press, *Houston Chronicle*, January 30, 2016.
48. "Hawksworth's Knee 'Fine' After His Crash at Texas," *Indianapolis Star*, August 30, 2016.
49. Don Halliday, February 11, 2021, interview with the author.

CHAPTER THIRTY-SEVEN: CHANGING TIMES

1. Art St. Cyr, April 6, 2021, interview with the author.
2. Larry Foyt, April 28, 2021, interview with the author.
3. A.J. Foyt, April 22, 2021, interview with the author.
4. Takuma Sato, February 3, 2021, interview with the author.
5. St. Cyr, April 6, 2021, interview.
6. Sato, February 3, 2021, interview.
7. A.J. Foyt, April 22, 2021, interview.
8. Jim Ayello, "Muñoz Puts the Hardest Heartbreak Behind Him," *Indianapolis Star*, April 2, 2017.
9. George Sipple, "Conor Daly Is Driving Toward American Dream," *Detroit Free Press*, May 28, 2017.
10. Conor Daly, May 24, 2022, interview with the author.
11. Heather Tucker and Brant James, "Daly, Muñoz to Drive for A.J. Foyt Racing," *USA Today*, November 16, 2016.
12. Tony DiZinno, "Foyt Confirms Hire of Will Phillips as Technical Director," *NBC Sports*, January 23, 2017, https://www.nbcsports.com/motor-sports/news/foyt-confirms-hire-of-will-phillips-as-technical-director.
13. Jim Ayello, "Foyt Talks About Fear, Facing Death and More," *Indianapolis Star*, May 11, 2017.
14. Brody Miller, "Rookie Trying to Elbow in on Alonso," *Indianapolis Star*, May 16, 2017.
15. George Sipple, "Muñoz, Daly Are Foyt's Yin and Yang, *USA Today*, May 25, 2017.
16. Sato, February 3, 2021, interview.
17. Jim Ayello, "Daly Weathers Unrelenting Setbacks," *Indianapolis Star*, July 2, 2017.
18. Larry Foyt, October 22, 2025, interview with the author.

19. Jim Ayello, "Kanaan Joins Foyt Racing," *Indianapolis Star*, October 6, 2017.
20. Jim Ayello, "Leist Joins Kanaan to Form Team Brazil at Foyt," *Indianapolis Star*, November 17, 2017.
21. Conor Daly, May 24, 2022, interview with the author.
22. Ayello, "Leist Joins Kanaan."
23. Jim Ayello, "Racing Legend Gurney Dies at 86," *Indianapolis Star*, January 18, 2018.
24. Jim Ayello, "Offseason Brings Overhauls at Foyt, SPM," *Indianapolis Star*, February 28, 2018.
25. Jim Ayello, "A.J. Foyt Racing Breaks Through for Its First Top-10 of the Season," *Indianapolis Star*, April 6, 2018.
26. "Foyt Racing Legend Still a Huge Impact on the Auto Racing World," *Odessa* (Texas) *American*, May 25, 2018.
27. Jim Ayello, "Carpenter Surprising Indy Pole Winner," *Indianapolis Star*, May 21, 2018.
28. "Foyt Driver Kanaan Tops Final Indy Practice," *Houston Chronicle*, May 26, 2018.
29. Drew Davison, "At 43, Tony Kanaan Still Feels the Need for Speed," *Fort Worth Star-Telegram*, June 5, 2018.
30. "The Resurgent A.J. Foyt Racing," *Indianapolis Star*, June 15, 2018.
31. Jim Ayello, "Distress Mounting for Foyt Racing," *Indianapolis Star*, June 15, 2019.
32. Dana Hunsinger Benbow, "Matriarch of Indy Speedway Dies at Home Saturday at 83," *Indianapolis Star*, November 4, 2018.
33. Robby General, "Leist's Finish Gives Foyt Racing Boost," *Indianapolis Star*, May 12, 2019.
34. Ayello, "Distress Mounting."
35. Jim Ayello, "Kanaan, Foyt Find Hope, Progress," *Indianapolis Star*, July 20, 2019.
36. Nathan Brown, "Kanaan Confident of Return to IndyCar with A.J. Foyt Racing," *Indianapolis Star*, December 11, 2019.
37. Larry Foyt, November 10, 2020, interview with the author.
38. A.J. Foyt, November 3, 2019, interview with the author.
39. Nathan Brown, "Bourdais Lands Part-Time Ride with A.J. Foyt Racing," *Indianapolis Star*, February 5, 2020.
40. Tony Kanaan, April 28, 2021, interview with the author.
41. Michael Marot, "Speedway Awaits Return of Racing," Associated Press, *Abilene Reporter-News*, April 27, 2020.
42. Jenna Fryer, "Indy 500 Moved to August," Associated Press, *Hammond* (Indiana) *Times*, March 27, 2020.
43. Lucy Foyt, April 2, 2020, interview with the author.
44. Craig Baranouski, April 20, 2020, interview with the author.
45. Larry Foyt, October 22, 2025, interview.
46. Nathan Brown, "8 IndyCar Teams Approved for Federal PPP Loans," *Indianapolis Star*, July 8, 2020.

CHAPTER THIRTY-EIGHT: LEAN YEARS

1. Drew Davison, "IndyCar Veteran Tony Kanaan Still Driven to Win at Texas," *Fort Worth Star-Telegram*, June 3, 2020.
2. Nathan Brown, "Kimball Joins Foyt Full-time in 2020," *Indianapolis Star*, January 23, 2020.
3. Nathan Brown, "Without Indy, Some Teams Would Fold," *Indianapolis Star*, August 9, 2020.
4. Michael Marot, "Foyt Doing His Part to Bring Fans Back to Indianapolis 500," Associated Press, *The Republic*, August 20, 2020.
5. Larry Foyt, October 22, 2025, interview with the author.
6. Takuma Sato, February 3, 2021, interview with the author.
7. Nathan Brown, "Kanaan Uncertain If 2020 Signals End of His IndyCar Career," *Indianapolis Star*, September 1, 2020.
8. Larry Foyt, April 4, 2021, interview with the author.
9. "Sébastien Bourdais," AJ Foyt Racing website, October 25, 2020.
10. Nathan Brown, "IndyCar Bracing for Unknowns," *Indianapolis Star*, October 2, 2020.
11. Larry Foyt, April 4, 2021, interview.
12. "Sébastien Bourdais," April 18, 2021, *Wind Tunnel* interview with Jack Arute.
13. Xpel 375 Texas race broadcast, May 2, 2021.
14. David Malsher-Lopez, "Foyt Counts the Cost of Disastrously Unlucky Texas Weekend," Motorsport.com, May 3, 2021.
15. "A.J. Foyt," AJ Foyt Racing website, May 28, 2021.
16. Bob Kravitz, "I'm Still A.J.," *The Athletic*, May 30, 2021.
17. Sébastien Bourdais, May 27, 2021, interview with the author.
18. "Race Report: Indianapolis 500," AJ Foyt Racing, May 30, 2021, https://www.foytracing.com/single-post/race-report-indianapolis-500.
19. Nathan Brown, "Calderón Impresses in IndyCar Test," *Indianapolis Star*, July 10, 2021.
20. Jerry Bonkowski, "A.J. Foyt Racing Plans Future IndyCar Hopes on Lights Champ Kyle Kirkwood," *Autoweek*, November 10, 2021.
21. Nathan Brown, "Kirkwood to Run Full-Time with A.J. Foyt Racing in 2022," *Indianapolis Star*, November 12, 2021.
22. Bonkowski, "A.J. Foyt Racing Plans Future."

23. "Robin Miller (1949–2021)," AJ Foyt Racing, August 25, 2021, https://www.foytracing.com/single-post/robin-miller-1949-2021.
24. Preston Lerner, "Robin Miller, the Gutsy Motor Sport Writer Who's Better-Known than Most Drivers," *MotorSport*, August 5, 2021.
25. Zak Keefer, "The Preposterous Sportswriting Life of Robin Miller, Racing's Legendary Hellion," *The Athletic*, October 26, 2021.
26. Robin Miller, December 1, 2020, interview with the author.
27. Mario Andretti, "Robin Miller Celebration of Life, *YouTube*, October 2, 2021, https://www.youtube.com/watch?v=FaSIHcdQYps.
28. "Notes and Quotes: Indianapolis 500," AJ Foyt Racing, May 2022, https://www.foytracing.com/single-post/notes-quotes-indianapolis-500-1.
29. Nathan Brown, "Kirkwood off to Andretti After Rookie Year with Foyt," *Indianapolis Star*, May 6, 2022.
30. "ABC Supply Unveils Homes For Our Troops–Themed Indy 500 Car and $1 Million Donation Match," AJ Foyt Racing, May 9, 2022, https://www.foytracing.com/single-post/abc-supply-unveils-homes-for-our-troops-themed-indy-500-car-and-1-million-donation-match-to-the.
31. Marlyne Sexton, June 24, 2021, interview with the author.
32. Larry Foyt, October 22, 2025, interview.
33. Nathan Brown, "After Dreadful Season, Foyt Has Reason for Hope for '23," *Indianapolis Star*, October 11, 2022.
34. Larry Foyt, October 22, 2025, interview.

CHAPTER THIRTY-NINE: DARKNESS AND LIGHT

1. Gregg Doyel, "Fast and Charming Ferrucci May Just Win 500," *Indianapolis Star*, May 25, 2023.
2. Nathan Brown, "Ferrucci Lands 2023 Full-time Ride with AJ Foyt Racing Team," *Indianapolis Star*, October 9, 2022.
3. Bruce Martin, "As Foyt Seeks Past Glory, Team Retools with Cannon's Engineering Expertise, Title Record," NBC.com.
4. Larry Foyt, October 22, 2025, interview with the author.
5. Dave Skretta, "Finding Speed," Associated Press, *McAllen* (Texas) *Monitor*, May 25, 2023.
6. Jenna Fryer, "A.J. Foyt Returns to the Indy 500, His Legacy Long Secured and Grief Fresh from His Wife's Death," Associated Press, May 24, 2023.
7. Larry Foyt, October 22, 2025, interview.
8. "Lucy Foyt (1938–2023)," AJ Foyt Racing, April 5, 2023, https://www.foytracing.com/single-post/lucy-foyt-1938-2023.
9. George Snider, December 12, 2020, interview with the author.
10. Tim Delrose, November 17, 2020, interview with the author.
11. Fryer, "A.J. Foyt Returns to the Indy 500."
12. Bruce Martin, "After Loss of Wife, Foyt Finds Indy 500 Refuge: 'It's More Pain Than Anything On My Body,'" *NBC Sports*, May 25, 2023.
13. Jenna Fryer, "Lucy Foyt, Wife of Indy 500 Winner A.J. Foyt, Dies at 84," Associated Press, April 5, 2023.
14. Marshall Pruett, "Ferrucci on Long Beach: 'It's Great to Lift Everybody's Spirits.'" *Racer*, April 19, 2023.
15. "Opening Day of Practice Bodes Well," AJ Foyt Racing, May 17, 2022, https://www.foytracing.com/single-post/opening-day-of-practice-bodes-well.
16. Martin, "After Loss of Wife."
17. Fryer, "A.J. Foyt Returns to the Indy 500."
18. Skretta, "Finding Speed."
19. Martin, "After Loss of Wife."
20. Davey Hamilton, May 27, 2023, interview with the author.
21. "Indianapolis 500 Qualifying Report: Round 1," AJ Foyt Racing, May 20, 2023, https://www.foytracing.com/single-post/indianapolis-500-qualifying-report-round-1.
22. Hamilton, May 27, 2023, interview.
23. Sandra McKee, "A.J. Foyt, One-On-One," *Baltimore Sun*, August 31, 2012.
24. Nathan Brown, "'Nothing Like' Michael Cannon Reflects on Returning Foyt to Front of the Indy 500 Grid," *Indianapolis Star*, May 24, 2024.
25. 2023 Indianapolis 500, *NBC Sports*, May 28, 2023.
26. 2023 Indianapolis 500.
27. Larry Foyt, October 22, 2025, interview.
28. Chloe Peterson, "Ferrucci 3rd, Gives Hope for AJ Foyt Racing," *USA Today*, May 29, 2023.
29. 2023 Indianapolis 500.
30. "Race Report: Indianapolis 500," AJ Foyt Racing, May 28, 2023, https://www.foytracing.com/single-post/race-report-indianapolis-500-1.
31. Marshall Pruett, "Team Penske, A.J. Foyt Racing Form Technical Alliance," *Racer*, August 22, 2023.
32. "Notes & Quotes: Bommarito Automotive Group 500," AJ Foyt Racing, August 25, 2023, https://www.foytracing.com/single-post/notes-quotes-bommarito-automotive-group-500-4.
33. "Notes & Quotes: Acura Grand Prix of Long Beach," AJ Foyt Racing, March 2024, https://www.foytracing.com/single-post/notes-quotes-acura-grand-prix-of-long-beach-4.

34. Jenna Fryer, "Legacy at Stake," Associated Press, *Brownsville* (Texas) *Herald*, May 1, 2024.
35. Marshall Pruett, "An Exceptional Amount of Passing Took Place Throughout the 2024 NTT IndyCar Series Season," *Racer*, December 25, 2024.
36. "A.J. Foyt Turns 90!," AJ Foyt Racing, January 16, 2025, https://www.foytracing.com/single-post/a-j-foyt-turns-90.
37. Marshall Pruett, "A.J. Foyt Racing Parts Ways with Technical Director Cannon," *Racer*, November 12, 2024.
38. Chloe Peterson, "A.J. Foyt Racing Sees Moving to Indianapolis as Next Step," *Indianapolis Star*, October 12, 2024.
39. Curt Cavin, "Foyt Team Hopes Upward Trajectory Drives Return to Victory Lane," IndyCar Series, November 17, 2025, https://www.indycar.com/news/2025/11/11-17-foyt-climb.
40. Larry Foyt, October 22, 2025, interview.

INDEX

Page references in italics indicate images. Photo section pages are indicated with a "P–" before the page number.

14